ANCIEN

WA

Ancient and Medieval

Warfare

Oliver Lyman Spaulding
and
Hoffman Nickerson

CONSTABLE · LONDON

Published in Great Britain 1994
by Constable and Company Limited
3 The Lanchesters, 162 Fulham Palace Road
London W6 9ER
ISBN 0 09 473190 X
Printed in the United States of America

A CIP catalogue record for this book
is available from the British Library

CONTENTS

CONTENTS

LIST OF PLATES

PART I

ANCIENT WARFARE: TO THE DEATH OF
JULIUS CÆSAR

CHAPTER I

INTRODUCTION

WAR is war. Its outward forms change, just as the outward forms of peace change. But from the stylus to the typewriter is just as far as from the club to the machine-gun—a weapon also known, affectionately or otherwise, as a "typewriter." And the development of tactics is neither more nor less remarkable than the development of office methods.

Strip any military operation of external identifying details, and one will find it hard to put a place and a date to the story.

"Once upon a time" there was a small kingdom, with a powerful empire for a neighbour. The small kingdom was not without warlike traditions, and in fact, its capital was in territory conquered within the last few centuries. But it was not at the time a military power, nor was its policy aggressive. The empire was, on the contrary, both military and aggressive.

The military systems of the two powers were not greatly dissimilar. Both were strongly centralized governments, and the sovereign was the field commander. The smaller state at the time of the conquest had a simple military system, somewhat imperfectly developed, but based upon the militia idea and universal service. Its tactics were based upon light armament and free manœuvre. But during the more quiet period its organization and tactics had been affected by those of its neighbours; they had become conventionalized, and approached very closely to those of the enemy. Their characteristics were heavy armament and strong defensive positions, with frequent raids and demonstrations by the stronger party to tempt the weaker into the open. In actual combat, fire power was imperfectly understood, and distinctly subordinated to shock; and the two were not well combined.

The imperial army finally invaded the weaker state in force, and the lines soon became stabilized. The imperial forces began their raids and demonstrations, one general especially being very

3

active in this work. The king refused to be drawn into a general engagement, and so avoided defeat; but his troops soon acquired a feeling of inferiority, and their morale was seriously impaired.

At this critical moment, a young man came forward with a suggestion for a new method of meeting the enemy's attacks, consisting in a return to earlier national manœuvre methods, and a more perfect co-ordination of fire and shock. It involved combat in the open, and hence the assumption of a considerable risk; but the king had become convinced of the necessity of positive action, and approved the plan. Apparently this decision was against the advice of the conservatives on the staff, for propositions were made for a modification of the plans, so as to depart less from the conventional mass and shock tactics. Evidently the king was impressed by the arguments advanced, for he urged acceptance of some of the modifications. But he wisely did not insist, standing by his approval, and refusing to force the adoption of half measures.

Troops were trained in the new tactics, and the position reorganized accordingly. The changes appealed to the national spirit of the troops, and their morale improved.

Then one day the particularly dreaded general led a strong force forward, and advanced across No Man's Land in dense masses, trusting in the known weakness of the defence in fire. Everything went as usual until they had come to close range; then, without warning, a vigorous and well directed fire was opened from the trenches. The losses were heavy; the general himself was seriously wounded, and the attack was checked but not repulsed.

At the same moment, before the enemy could recover himself and reorganize, a counter attack was launched. The royal troops, although light armed and inferior to the imperialists in pure shock action, struck them at the critical moment, when the heavier masses were out of hand and immobilized. The result was a complete success for the defence. More than this, the advantage was swiftly and skilfully utilized to penetrate the main position, and the invader was forced to abandon his whole campaign.

This battle was fought about 1000 B. C. The king was named Saul; the imperial general was Goliath, and the young innovator in tactics was David.[1]

---

[1] Wise, 12.

Here, in allegorical form, are illustrated the first and most important questions that we must ask and answer in studying any army, of whatever period, viz:—

1. The general situation and policy of the state.
2. Relation of the army to the government.
3. Its military theories, and their origin.
4. Its tactical organization and method of fighting.

To these must be added two more, not illustrated above because our allegory began on a stabilized line, and because our reports are incomplete, viz:—

5. The information system.
6. The supply system.

Now, to get a point of departure, we must ask and answer these questions for the earliest and most primitive peoples. We never saw any prehistoric men, and they could not write; but we, or our immediate predecessors, have seen and fought primitive peoples, who were in or not far from the Stone Age—American Indians, Sudanese, Zulus—and we have records of ancient peoples who had developed a little beyond this stage, and had moreover learned to write about it. Let us first try to estimate what primitive warfare was, and then follow the development, asking ourselves the same questions at every step.

Is it worth while? That we must find out by trial; but not infrequently we hear of an incident which stimulates the imagination and encourages us to make the experiment. One such incident bridges the gap between Saul and ourselves. An officer of the British 60th Division, serving in Palestine in 1918, tells the story.[2]

February 13th we took over the Deir Ibu Obeid—Ras es Suffa—Hizmeh line from the 53rd Division, and on the fourteenth of the same month operation orders were issued for an attack on Jericho with the object of driving the enemy across the River Jordan.

Before the main attack could take place it was necessary to strengthen the line by the capture of a small village, directly to our front, known as Mukhmas or Mickmash.

Mickmash was on a high rocky hill. The brigade outpost line was on a chain of hills, too, and between us and the enemy ran a deep valley.

A frontal attack was decided upon; that is, supported by artillery and

[2] Gilbert, 183.

machine guns, the brigade was to advance down into the valley just before dawn, and take Mickmash from the front.

All orders were given out and the troops were getting what rest was possible before zero hour.

In his bivouac, by the light of a candle, the brigade major was reading his Bible. When the raid was first discussed the name Mickmash had seemed vaguely familiar, although he could not quite place it. Just as he was about to turn in for the night, however, he recollected and thought he would look it up. He found what he was searching for in Samuel I, Chapters 13 and 14:

"And Saul and Jonathan his son, and the people that were present with them, abode in Gibeah of Benjamin: but the Philistines encamped in Michmash. . . .

"Now it came to pass upon a day that Jonathan, the son of Saul, said unto the young man that bare his armour, 'Come and let us go over to the Philistines' garrison, that is on the other side.' But he told not his father. . . . And the people knew not that Jonathan was gone.

"And between the passages, by which Jonathan sought to go over unto the Philistines' garrison, there was a sharp rock on the one side, and a sharp rock on the other side: and the name of the one was Bozez, and the name of the other Seneh.

"The forefront of the one was situate northward over against Michmash, and the other southward over against Gibeah.

"And Jonathan said to the young man that bare his armour, 'Come, and let us go over unto the garrison. . . It may be that the Lord will work for us: for there is no restraint to the Lord to save by many or by few.'"

And the major read on how Jonathan went through the pass, or passage, of Michmash, between Bozez and Seneh, and climbed the hill dragging his armour-bearer with him until they came to a place high up, about "an half acre of land, which a yoke of oxen might plow"; and the Philistines who were sleeping awoke, thought they were surrounded by the armies of Saul, and fled in disorder, and "the multitude melted away." Saul then attacked with his whole army. It was a great victory for him; his first against the Philistines, and "so the Lord saved Israel that day, and the battle passed over unto Beth-aven."

The brigade major thought to himself: "This pass, these two rocky headlands and flat piece of ground are probably still here; very little has changed in Palestine throughout the centuries," and he woke the brigadier. Together they read the story over again. Then the general sent out scouts, who came back and reported finding the pass, thinly held by Turks, with rocky crags on either side, obviously Bozez and Seneh; whilst in the distance, high up in Mickmash the moonlight was shining on a flat piece of ground just about big enough for a team to plough.

The general decided then and there to change the plan of attack, and instead of the whole brigade, one infantry company alone advanced at dead of night along the pass of Mickmash. A few Turks met were silently dealt with. We passed between Bozez and Seneh, climbed the hillside, and just before dawn, found ourselves on the flat piece of ground. The Turks who were sleeping awoke, thought they were surrounded by the armies of Allenby and fled in disorder.

We killed or captured every Turk that night in Mickmash; so that, after thousands of years, the tactics of Saul and Jonathan were repeated with success by a British force.

The earliest weapons were undoubtedly the stone and the club—fire and shock. We have little practical experience in historic times of anything quite as primitive as this, but it is readily deducible *a priori*, and the quarrels of children are not a bad indication of the fighting of the infant race. Every development in tactics comes through organization, improvement and combination of these elements—fire and shock. Assuming this, and reasoning from conditions found in the earliest historic times, we may, through our six questions, form a reasonably safe conception of war at the dawn of history.

1. Government was merely an association of individuals, generally more or less related by blood, for mutual aid. It must have been loose and informal; a tribal council system as long as the individuals were about equal in physical and mental strength, tending toward control by an individual surpassing the rest in one or both of these characteristics.

2. The relations of the government to the army were simple, for the two were identical—the whole body of the tribe, physically and mentally qualified, considered from the alternative points of view of peace and war.

3. The primitive elements of warfare seem to be two only —surprise, and individual strength and skill—their relative importance varying with the comparative mental and physical development of the opposing parties.

4. The simplest conceivable organization is the group composed of the champion and his followers. The defeat of the champion was necessarily followed by the slaughter or enslavement of the followers, who themselves had but little influence upon the battle. This organization, in a high development, we find in the battles of the Iliad, Homer's kings being glorified tribal chieftains. Here, however, we do find a certain recognition of the fighting power of the common people, and can also trace the beginnings of

an aristocracy, in that the public opinion of the minor champions and the sages—not yet of the masses—acts as a certain check upon arbitrary rule. Thus Nestor, in the ninth book of the Iliad, speaks very respectfully, but very independently, to Agamemnon, giving unpalatable advice, and plainly pointing out that power is given him as a responsibility, not as a privilege.

5. A certain amount of organization of an intelligence service must have originated very early. The skill of primitive races, notably the American Indians, in minor scouting, is familiar. This small scouting develops very rapidly into reconnaissance expeditions covering considerable times and long distances, as witness the expeditions sent out by Moses "to spy out the land." Also very early comes the differentiation between military scouting and reconnaissance on the one hand, and secret intelligence work or espionage on the other, as will appear in the chapter on Egypt.

6. A supply service is of slower development, since it necessarily implies much organization to handle details. A small party could subsist on the country as it passed, but not so a large one. Early large expeditions, therefore, are only such as can dispense with elaborate supply arrangements. If by land, they are tribal migrations, like the Hebrew Exodus, moving slowly, robbing the natives, perhaps, of what they possess, but depending for the most part upon long stops and the maintenance of agriculture and herding. If by sea, as in the case of the Trojan War, they depend upon the ships' stores, supplemented by piracy, until the foreign advanced base can be established; after which they are tied to that base at least until one crop can be raised to permit moving to another, and can never get far inland. This is illustrated in Egyptian history by Necho's expedition to circumnavigate Africa, and in later times by the 15th Century explorers, as, for example, Henry the Navigator's African expeditions, which landed on the coast to raise crops.

We cannot, of course, expect to be able to trace developments in detail for the earliest civilizations. Our knowledge of the facts is fragmentary, and the answer to our questions must therefore be incomplete. Our information may naturally be expected to improve in proportion as we approach more recent times; and this is generally, but not always the case. It is necessary for us to start without preconceived ideas as to what we are to find, to collect the solid and proven facts, to superpose upon them the fragmentary and doubtful statements, and then to see how far we can reconstruct the system that we seek—remembering always that fact, probability and pure inference must be distinguished and earmarked as such, that the reader may not be misled or deceived.

CHAPTER II

THE EARLY ORIENTAL MONARCHIES

1. EGYPT (3000–525 B. C.)

By 3000 B. C. Egypt was well advanced in civilization. There was a centralized royal authority, sometimes spoken of as the Old Empire; this was the period of the pyramid builders. The country appears to have been fully occupied with its own internal development, for there is little indication of military activity. What there was came from the necessity of defence against incursions, for the fertile country, bordered everywhere by deserts, was well worth robbing.

In the 6th Dynasty, say about 2500 B. C., one such incursion seems to have been serious—at least in the mind of the commander of the army of defence, for an elaborate description of it is found in inscriptions by him. The system of the time was local militia in each *nome*, or province. To meet an incursion of marauders from the direction of Syria, the king assembled these contingents into an army, grandly and vaguely described as composed of "tens of thousands" of men. The details of the tactical dispositions do not appear, but we find a little about the supply system. It was simple; to quote the commander, "each one carried as much with him as another; some of them stole the dough and the sandals from the traveler; some of them took the bread from each village; some of them took the goats from everybody." [1]

This Old Empire seems to have become split up toward 2000 B. C., and again consolidated into a sort of feudal state known as the Middle Empire. The country prospered greatly, and began to acquire knowledge of the outside world. Its maritime commerce was large and important; a canal was actually dug from the Red Sea to a branch of the Nile, so that shipping could pass from the Mediterranean into the Red Sea.

During this period, military operations in the field were few

[1] Erman, 522.

10

and unimportant, but the art of fortification became highly developed; the country was isolated by nature, and sought to maintain its isolation. There was a great fortress on the southern frontier, at Assouan, and another at Pelusium covering the isthmus, as well as numerous minor works. These were comparable in size to the feudal fortresses of the European Middle Ages, although simpler in plan. Some of them have been completely excavated, and these remains, taken together with the inscriptions picturing or describing them, permit fairly safe reconstruction of them. Some of the inscriptions show also the methods of attack and defence, with rudimentary forms of battering rams, scaling ladders, and even machicoulis galleries for the defence.

About 1500 B. C., a New Empire began with the 18th Dynasty. This was a centralized military power, very different from either of the governments that had preceded it. It immediately began to extend its interests abroad, to come in contact with foreign civilizations more intimately than they had done in the earlier trading voyages, and to take a position in world affairs.

Thothmes I conquered Palestine and Syria, and penetrated as far as the Euphrates. His immediate successors failed to maintain his conquests, but Thothmes III again invaded Syria, and decisively defeated the allied forces of that region in a great battle at Megiddo, better known as Armageddon. From here he pushed his conquests again to the Euphrates, and established alliances, if not protectorates, in Mesopotamia.[2] Among the peoples subdued by him are mentioned the Hittites, who later became so powerful, and turned the tables on Egypt.

We have very good accounts of the Armageddon campaign. Thothmes assembled his army at Zalu, on the frontier, just east of the present Suez Canal. Marching rapidly to get across the desert, he reached Gaza, 160 miles, in twelve days, and then moved to Carmel, 90 miles, in ten days more.[3]

At Yemma, sixteen miles southwest of Megiddo, the army entered the mountains, and found three roads available; two of them good but circuitous, one bad but direct. Crossing the mountains so close to the enemy was recognized as a delicate undertaking, and some care was taken to secure information. The

[2] Breasted, 42–45; Erman, 41, 44, 526. See Plate 1.
[3] Petrie, II, 101.

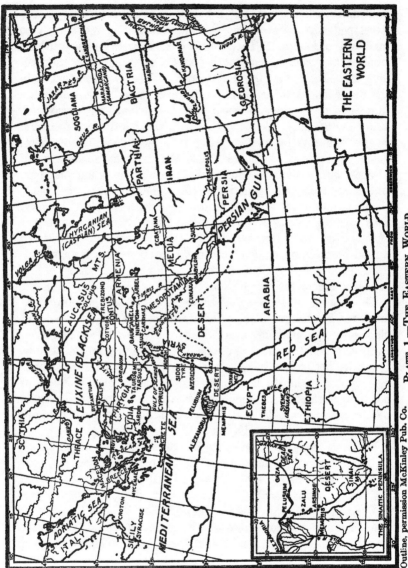

PLATE 1.—THE EASTERN WORLD.

summary of intelligence, with the staff recommendations, runs as follows:

"What is it like that we should march on this road, which becomes a narrow pass? Men have come saying that the enemy are waiting to attack where there is no passage for a numerous host; does not one chariot have to follow behind another, and man behind man? Ought our vanguard to be engaged while our rearguard is waiting at Aaruna" (seven miles southwest of Megiddo) "without fighting? Now there are two roads, one to Taanaka" (five miles south of Megiddo), "the other to the north side of Zefta, and we should come out at the north of Megiddo. Let then our mighty lord march on one of these two ways, but let us not go on that difficult road."

But Thothmes rejected the proposals of his staff, for moral effect upon the enemy. "As I live, I will go on this road of Aaruna; for the enemy consider this; 'Has his Majesty gone on another road? Then he fears us.'"

Realizing the danger of the operation, Thothmes took personal command of the advance guard. "Not a man shall go forth before my Majesty; . . . he shall go forth . . . horse walking after horse, while his Majesty protects them of the best of his army."

The enemy tried to block the pass, but failed. "His Majesty cried out at them and gave battle." But it seemed that he might venture too far in pursuit; for "the rear guard of the valiant troops of his Majesty were yet in Aaruna, while the van was going forth to the valley, and occupied the head of that valley." The staff therefore urged caution. "They spake before his Majesty, saying, 'Let our lord keep for us the rear of his army; then when the rear comes out to us behind, they will fight against these foreigners, and we need not give thought to the rear.' His Majesty halted, guarding the rear of his valiant troops." By one o'clock in the afternoon the crossing, if not entirely completed, was regarded as secure; for "behold, when the van had come forth on this road the shadow turned, and when his Majesty came to the south of Megiddo, on the edge of the waters of Qina, it was the seventh hour of the day. Then his Majesty's tent was pitched and command was given saying, 'Prepare ye, . . . for we move to fight with the vile enemy tomorrow.' The baggage of the chiefs was prepared, and the pro-

visions of the followers, and the sentinels were spread abroad.
. . . Came one to report to his Majesty, the country is safe and
the army south and north likewise." So we see that neither outpost duty nor reconnaissance was neglected.

We have enough to form some rough idea of Thothmes' force;
for his column through the mountains was something like seven
miles long. We can not tell how much of a concentration there was
at Aaruna, but probably not much, for that place itself is in the
mountains. Even granting that the mention of marching in single
file is an exaggeration of the difficulties, and that some force stood
fast at Aaruna while the column moved forward, ten thousand
men will remain a very high estimate of the army.

"Early in the morning command was given to the entire army
to spread abroad. . . The south horn of the army was on a hill at
the south of the waters of Qina, the north horn at the north of
Megiddo. . . . Then his Majesty prevailed over them at the head
of his army . . . ; they fled headlong toward Megiddo . . . ;
they left their horses and their chariots of silver and gold, and were
drawn up by hauling them by their clothes into the city, for the
men shut the gates of the city upon them." But the same thing
happened that happened to the Germans when they made their
counter-attack south of Cambrai on November 30th, 1917; they
stopped to plunder.[4] "Had but the troops of his Majesty not given
their hearts to spoiling the things of the enemy, they would have
taken Megiddo at that moment." However, Thothmes besieged
the city, which was compelled to surrender.

Internal dissensions, mostly religious, now arose, and the eastern
provinces were overrun by the Hittites. In the 19th Dynasty
attempts were made to regain them and Rameses II (Sesostris)
reconquered Palestine.

A fairly complete story of this campaign has been preserved.[5]
As written, its primary purpose was to glorify Rameses; but
without too much guess work we may perhaps piece together a
description. Some of the geographical points are partly conjectural, but there is little doubt on essentials.

The two powers had assembled their whole forces, and advanced
slowly to meet each other. The Hittites apparently counted on

---

[4] Ludendorff, "Kriegserinnerungen," 396.
[5] Erman, 528.

subsisting largely from the country; at least, their king "had left no silver and gold behind him in his country, he had despoiled everything in order to take all with him." The Egyptians, whose force has been estimated at some 15,000 men, had to cross 100 miles of desert, and it seems probable on general principles that they depended largely upon sea communications; for their route lay near the coast, and Egypt was strong at sea. As for water, this road was familiar to them, and the tanks and wells had been repaired in preparation for the campaign. The Egyptian march was in four corps; this seems to have been for logistical, not tactical, reasons, for later it will appear that the distances were so great that the leading body came very near being defeated before the next could come to its support.

In this order, the advance guard reached the upper Orontes, having marched 400 miles in about a month. The Hittites had not yet been located, but the intelligence service was active, and reported them still some distance to the north. At the last camp south of the town of Kadesh this was confirmed by two spies, ostensibly deserters, who came into the Egyptian camp, and reported that some of the Hittite auxiliaries were disaffected, and wished to come over to the Egyptians.

The Egyptians therefore continued the march with the same long distances between corps. But as they approached Kadesh, a patrol brought in two Hittite prisoners, members of a reconnoitring party. These, being questioned—and in no gentle manner—said that the Hittites had come up in force, with both infantry and chariots, and were at that moment concealed "in fighting order behind the town of Kadesh, more numerous than the sands of the sea."

Rameses immediately assembled his generals and gave them the new information. He also expressed, publicly and emphatically, his opinion of his own intelligence service, and it is not too much to guess that he took suitable action with its chiefs, whatever that suitable action may have been. He then sent orders to collect his troops; but before they could be concentrated the Hittites attacked and surrounded the king and his Guard. It would appear that the chariots bore the brunt of the fighting, although this may be merely a part of the glorification of the king, who himself fought in one. But evidently the Egyptians made a gallant stand, and held off the enemy until the corps in rear came up and relieved the situation.

The inscriptions and sculptures give some indication of trains and camps in this same campaign. A fortified camp is clearly shown, rectangular in shape, with parks and picket lines carefully laid out and separated from the tents. Both pack animals and ox-carts appear among the trains.

But Rameses had to stop here, and make peace with the Hittites, for new dangers were arising on the western borders, where the Libyans, together with peoples of European stock from the Mediterranean islands and perhaps even from the northern coast began incursions. These were effectively checked by Rameses' son, Merenptah. It appears that the invaders advanced in a very scattered formation, or lack of formation, as might have been expected from a heterogeneous marauding expedition. The Egyptians made no effort to prevent their concentration, which took two days after the first contact, but counted upon destroying them at one blow. The Libyans finally got together and attacked with chariots and infantry; considering their origin, and their probable degree of civilization, it may be assumed that the attack was a dash, in loose order. The Egyptians received them with archers, very much as the English infantry received the charges of the Sudanese, and prevented them from coming to close quarters. When the attack was thoroughly broken up, the Egyptians charged in turn, and gained a complete victory.

In Syria the Hittites succumbed to Europeans, who pushed down the coast from Asia Minor, not as armies, but as migrating nations. Rameses III had to fight a defensive war with these both by land and by sea, and succeeded in checking them in Palestine.[6] For several centuries after this Egypt was in the hands of weak kings, under whom the ancient priesthood and the Libyan mercenaries in the army struggled for supremacy.

About 650 B. C., the internal struggles were brought to a close by foreign conquest, Assyria holding the control for a short time. Egypt again gained independence under the 26th Dynasty, with which we are acquainted through Herodotus. Psammetichus, Necho and Amasis are the great names of this time. They established relations with the Greeks, favored their immigration, and

⁶ Erman, 47–48; Breasted, 50–51; Petrie, III, 75, 150.

used them freely as mercenaries in the army. Psammetichus, it seems, was told by an oracle that "men of brass" would come to assist him. The Greeks proved in truth to be such both literally and figuratively—in nerve and discipline as well as in equipment; Maspero says, "The charge of the Spanish soldiery among the lightly clad foot-soldiers of Mexico and Peru could not have caused more dismay than that of the hoplites from beyond the sea among the half naked archers and pikemen of Egypt and Libya." [7] But in 525 another foreign power, this time the Persians under Cambyses, subdued the land and it became a Persian province; the names Darius, Xerxes, etc., in Egyptianized forms, appear in the inscriptions as Egyptian kings. It never regained its power and was finally overrun by Alexander, passed to Ptolemy on his death, and became a Roman province in 30 B. C.

We are unable to reconstruct completely the Egyptian organization and tactics, but may collect certain suggestive fragments. Both the Old and Middle Empires had organized companies of archers, other companies of heavy infantry equipped with spears and shields, still others of light infantry, with smaller shields or none at all, and with battleaxes. The shield of the heavy infantry is sometimes represented as very large and in this form it continued in use long after the fall of the empire; for Xenophon mentions in Artaxerxes' army a body of "heavy infantry with wooden shields covering them from head to foot," adding, "It was said they were Egyptians." Representations of slingers are also found, and often rudimentary armour. But the Egyptian seems never to have been warlike by nature, and the use of mercenaries, Libyans largely, begins very early. The New Empire depended chiefly upon mercenaries; the tribal contingents were kept separate, under their own chiefs, and separate companies had uniform armament.[8]

The horse was a foreign importation; no representation of one is found in the sculptures of the Old and Middle Empires. But the New Empire very promptly discovered him in Syria and used him, never for riding, but always in chariots. The chariots formed a corps d'élite, the king himself always fighting with them; we have a picture of Rameses II in his chariot at the battle of Kadesh.

[7] Herodotus, II, 152; Erman, 50–51; Maspero, 495.
[8] Xenophon, Anabasis, I, 35; Erman, 521–524.

The Egyptians manned their chariots with two men, a driver and an archer; the Hittite chariots are represented with three, the third a shield-bearer. This gives us all the elements of Homeric warfare—the champions in their chariots; the heavy armed foot, in close and regular formation, fighting behind them; and the light armed troops, archers, slingers, and skirmishers. And in fact Homeric warfare is not so remote from Egyptian after all; through the Hittites they are more or less connected, for these were neighbors in Asia Minor, and the Dardani or Trojans appear in the Hittite inscriptions.

The chariots are interesting; we seem to see in the Egyptian and Hittite types the germs of the distinction between the light and heavy tanks—one swift but vulnerable, the other protected but slower. But probably we must class all these chariots as heavy cavalry rather than as tanks; they were the principal arm, bearing the brunt of the fighting independently and merely supported by the infantry. It is only later on that we shall find the chariots adopting tank tactics and fighting for the infantry, not on their own account and against other chariots.

No details of the administrative system of the army can be given with certainty, but evidently there was a definitely established organization, for "scribes of the army" are referred to as high officers. Some of these were attached to particular bodies of troops and others to headquarters. Their duties were not merely those of a "scribe" or clerk, but extended to supply, transport, etc.; sometimes they were given actual commands.[9] The documents on the Armageddon campaign show, too, that the intelligence service mentioned was not haphazard, but permanently and regularly organized.

2. ASSYRIA (1500–600 B. C.)

Egypt is based upon the fertile strip of the Nile, bordered by desert. Passing this desert to the northeast, we reach fertile country again in Syria, the scene of the great Egyptian wars. Exploring this fertile region farther we find it to be another narrow strip, crescent-shaped, with mountains to the north and desert to the south. It runs up the eastern coast of the Mediterranean, swings eastward, then south again to the head of the Persian Gulf.

[9] Erman, 547–550.

Toward this strip of country there tended naturally the mountaineers of the north and the nomads of the desert.

The eastern horn of the crescent is Mesopotamia—the Tigris and Euphrates valleys. At the mouths of these rivers there grew up a civilization parallel to, and contemporary with, the Egyptian Old Empire, with Babylon as its capital; but this had little connection with the outside world, and began to decay as early as 2000 B. C. Only two great names stand out—Sargon of Akkad, an up-river Semitic state of desert origin, who conquered the Sumerian towns in the delta and consolidated the whole region into one kingdom at about the time of the building of the Great Pyramids; and Hammurabi, of a later desert-born conquering race, who lived toward the end of the period in question and who collected the laws of the land into the earliest known code.

Evidently there was fighting here, and plenty of it, for we have seen that there were at least two great conquests, and perhaps still an earlier one when the Sumerians came from the mountains into the plain. We can form little idea of this fighting, but it was far from primitive. Sumerian sculpture a century or two before Sargon shows heavy infantry, with spears, shields and helmets, in a solid phalanx formation; although perhaps we should not deduce too much from this, for the sculptor's technique was not of the best by modern standards, and doubtless the easiest way to represent many warriors was to make them all alike and in a line. The earliest known Semitic work of art is a figure of one of Sargon's immediate successors, in action, armed with bow and spear.

But all this time there was developing another kingdom at Assur, well up in the Tigris valley—a pleasant and fertile country, close under the mountains, and temperate in climate. The people were Semitic, akin to the Babylonians, and may actually have come from Babylonia—at least it is tempting to adopt that hypothesis, for there is much to support the Biblical version, that "out of that land Nimrod went forth to Assyria." Nimrod, we are told, was a "mighty hunter"; and the Assyrians maintained his reputation. Their country was full of "big game"; lions and other dangerous animals abounded.[10] Constantly compelled to defend

[10] Genesis, X, 9–11; Breasted, 64–65; Rawlinson, I, 221.

their lands against their mountain and desert neighbors, and their herds and crops against wild beasts, they grew strong and warlike.

By the time of Tiglath-Pileser I, about 1100 B. C., Assyria had expanded greatly. We hear of expeditions into the northern mountains; eastward into Media; down to Babylon; up the Euphrates to its very head, to the kingdom of the Hittites; and even to the Mediterranean, "the upper ocean of the setting sun." Herodotus credits them at this time with sovereignty over all upper Asia; that is, everything beyond Asia Minor.[11] The fortunes of the empire were varying, and its boundaries constantly changing; its whole history is a continuous succession of campaigns. Each one appears in the inscriptions as a great victory; but it is noticeable that the victories are against the same peoples over and over again, so that it is evident that the reverses were also there, but were simply ignored—a process not entirely unfamiliar in our own day.

Now follows the period during which the growing Assyrian power came into contact with the waning Egyptian, and followed it down the coast. This is reflected in the Biblical accounts of the Assyrian conquests—mostly minor affairs for Assyria but of absorbing importance for the Jews. Between the decay of the Egyptian power in Syria and the advance of Assyria came the brief period of the power and glory of the Jewish state. But about the middle of the eighth century, probably in the reign of Tiglath-Pileser II, Palestine began to feel the pressure from the north. The Jewish power declined, and Assyrian influence predominated down to the desert. Similar progress was made on the other frontiers of the empire.

Under Shalmaneser IV, about 725 B. C., friction with Egypt had become pronounced. This king spent most of his reign in Syria, personally conducting his wars; this was the time when the essentially inland empire first conducted a naval campaign—apparently against Tyre, using Phoenician ships and crews, with a very slight admixture of Assyrians.[12]

In 722 the throne was seized by a usurper, who adopted the name of Sargon II. He at once restored and extended the Assyrian

[11] Herodotus, I, 95; Breasted, 70; Rawlinson, II, 58–80.
[12] 2 Kings, XV, XVI; Isaiah, IX; Rawlinson, II, 123, 137.

dominion in Babylonia, Media and Persia, and at the same time pushed south through Syria and against Egypt.

His son and great successor was Sennacherib, who further extended his empire in all directions. His campaign against Egypt, however, was a failure. Herodotus accounts for this by the Egyptian priests' tale of swarms of field mice, which came in the night and "devoured their quivers and their bows and the handles of their shields." This checks with the Biblical account of the mysterious destruction of his army, both being taken to refer to a disastrous epidemic, of which the mouse is a not uncommon symbol. This, being a serious reverse, naturally is not mentioned in Sennacherib's inscriptions, which deal only with victories in other directions. In one campaign to the southeast he actually brought Phœnician ship-builders to Mesopotamia and constructed a fleet, which he used against the eastern coast of the Persian Gulf. Another expedition took him into Cilicia, in southeastern Asia Minor; this is notable in that it brought Assyria into direct contact with Greeks.[13]

Sennacherib's son and successor resumed the Egyptian wars, and it was under him that the conquest was completed. Under the next king, Assurbanipal, probably the Sardanapalus of the Greeks, the Egyptian conquest was held, and contact with the Greeks in Asia Minor extended.

But the great military state was over-extended. Maintenance of her armies was too much for her; and Assyria now collapsed under pressure from the Medes and the Chaldæans from the east.

So much for the general history. This summary pretends to no critical profundity, but may serve as a foundation for discussion of the military system of the empire, whose great glory was under the Sargon dynasty.

And first, the nature of the state itself.

Assyria proper was an absolute monarchy, not unlike that of Egypt. The king considered himself, and his subjects considered him, as ruling by divine right—the direct representative of the gods, whose greatest duty was to spread abroad the worship of the gods. At the same time he was never to be regarded as himself partaking of the divine nature; he was a man, and the shepherd

[13] 2 Kings, XIX; Herodotus, II, 141; Delitzsch, 5; Rawlinson, II, 175.

of his people. The meanest of his subjects could address him direct on his personal affairs, sure of sympathetic consideration.

The empire, on the contrary, was something new—a loose body of tributary states. Each conquered country in succession was added to the string, but retained its own government untouched, except for occasional attempts to introduce the worship of the Assyrian gods—rough missionary work, for that was a rough time, but perhaps no more so than some of the extensions of the Mohammedan or even the Christian faith. The subject state had to acknowledge the sovereignty of the king, and to pay him tribute; sometimes a royal governor was appointed, often the native king was left on his throne. The dominant power on its part owed the subject state protection; this was given in part by local levies, but largely by Assyrian regular armies.[14]

Such a loose organization evidently was unstable. It gave the impression of wonderful wealth and splendor, but it might at any moment crumble and have to be reconstructed. This accounts for the constantly recurring wars against the same peoples, and also for the swift and sudden extinction of the empire when control was once lost.

The relation of the army to the state was therefore simple. The king was necessarily the military leader, and habitually led his main army in person. Sennacherib's inscriptions tell of mountain campaigns, when he left his chariot and marched on foot with the troops, sharing all the hardships of his men. As we have seen, the state had to fight for its life from the very beginning. Its army was then the people, and the whole people. As its territory grew, so also grew the need for military force to keep the new acquisitions in subjection, and to protect them. The earlier and nearer acquisitions gradually became assimilated with the old kingdom; the later and more distant retained the full characteristics of tributaries. As extreme instances, Cyprus and Lydia may be mentioned.

An embassy came to Sargon from the Phœnician chiefs of Cyprus, "a country of which none of the kings of Assyria or Babylonia had ever heard the name," lying "in the sea of the setting sun," bringing gifts in token of submission. In token of acceptance, Sargon returned his own image, in the form usually

[14] Delitzsch, 10, 32–33; Rawlinson, II, 235.

used when taking possession of a conquered country; this image has been found in modern times on the island. But this was the extent of his assertion of authority. And after Assurbanipal's expedition into Asia Minor, when he went farther than any Assyrian had ever gone before, Gyges of Lydia, in the extreme west on the Ægean Coast—another "remote place," of which Assyria "had never heard the name," sent presents; but the king in this case did not even hint at assuming authority, and Lydia remained an ally rather than a dominion.[15]

The character of the people—bold, vigorous, and trained to big game hunting—inclined them to the offensive, both strategic and tactical. This, and the procedure natural to hunters, manœuvre and envelopment, dictated their tactical methods. Sennacherib mentions in an inscription, "attack in front and flank." We have, however, no adequate evidence from which to reconstruct the dispositions for any particular battle.

Assyrian armies from the earliest times consisted of both horse and foot. The horse, while not native to Mesopotamia, had been introduced there about the time of Hammurabi, coming from the eastern hills. At first he was used only in chariots; the warfare was somewhat of the Homeric type, the nobility fighting in chariots and their peasantry supporting them on foot, but with something more of organization than Homer shows.

The chariot was manned by a charioteer, an archer, who was sometimes armoured, and usually a shield bearer or even two. The archer is sometimes represented as dismounted to fight on foot, in which case his shield bearer accompanies him. The infantry included archers and spearmen; in the equipment of the latter appears the characteristic long wicker shield. The two classes appear to have been organized in separate companies, but they are often represented as working together in pairs, both men kneeling behind the long shield, the archer firing, and his companion standing guard with drawn sword.[16]

By the time of Sargon the use of the chariot had somewhat declined, and cavalry had made its appearance. At first these were archers, mounted infantry; later, lancers, but equipped for skirmishing rather than for the charge boot to boot; still later,

[15] Delitzsch, 15; Hunger, 4; Rawlinson, II, 149, 203.
[16] Delitzsch, 13; Breasted, 68; Hunger, 5; Rawlinson, I, 421, 429.

and rarely, dragoons, lancers carrying a bow. The marksmanship and horsemanship must both have been excellent, for the riders are constantly shown as firing at a gallop, the reins on the horse's neck—and this without stirrups, which, strangely enough, were never invented by any ancient people.

The foot archers had become differentiated into light and heavy armed. The light archer is a skirmisher; he is represented in front of the other troops. He has no shield, nor is he accompanied by a shield bearer, so he cannot have been infantry "of the line." The heavy archer varies in equipment, but has always helmet and armour, and is accompanied by an attendant with a shield—usually the characteristic long one of wicker, now grown to enormous proportions, curving back at the sides and even overhead.

There is still no heavy phalanx of lances. The foot spearman is only partially armoured; he wears a helmet, and carries a round shield and a short spear. He is found in all battle scenes, but is especially conspicuous in the storming parties at sieges.

Sennacherib's army included also slingers. Unlike the corresponding troops in other armies, these wore armour, and were able to take their place with infantry of the line. Such use of them conformed to the spirit of the Assyrian tactics, which depended so largely upon fire; it was impracticable in an army based upon the phalanx and shock tactics. A heavier armed spearman makes his appearance at this time, but still does not form a phalanx; these troops are usually represented as few in number, and near the king, and may perhaps have constituted his bodyguard.[17]

Reference has been made above to sieges. The art of fortification was well developed throughout the civilized world known to the Assyrians; cities were habitually walled, and representations are found of very elaborate castles. The type of castle would have been perfectly familiar to a mediæval European—walls 30 or 40 feet high, with battlements and loop-holes, faces flanked by frequent battlemented and machicolated towers, generally moated, and often with an outer and an inner court. An army defeated in the field generally took refuge in its walled cities, in which case the Assyrians opened a formal and a very active siege. A line of countervallation was established, and the walls were attacked with battering rams, and by mining operations against the foot, the

[17] Hunger, 11, 14; Rawlinson, I, 423–439.

workers protected by the great wicker shields. To cover these operations a fire was kept up by the archers and slingers; there are even some slight indications that siege artillery, in the form of rude ballistæ, was occasionally used. The siege engines were worked not only from the ground, but often from artificial mounds. Storming parties with scaling ladders went forward under cover of the fire; these were mixed parties of archers and spearmen, each archer availing himself of the protection of the spearman's shield in the characteristic Assyrian fashion.

Such siege work implies technical troops. To what extent these were developed is uncertain, but there are indications that a pioneer corps did exist; either this, or the line troops were remarkably trained in pioneer duties, for a vast amount of engineer work was done, both at sieges and in the open field.[18]

Training and equipment were the strong points of the army. Drill was certainly careful and thorough; for the cavalry, at least, there was a technical school giving instruction in riding and driving. There were royal arsenals, storehouses containing all manner of equipment—not only weapons, but even wagon parks, harness, and stables with at least a part of the necessary animals. It is worthy of note that the earlier weapons were of bronze, but by the time of Sargon iron had been substituted, coming probably from the Hittites.[19] To all this care for training and equipment the Assyrian armies undoubtedly owed their success.

The elaborate establishments of arsenals clearly imply a service of supply and transportation, but the details are lost. We see, however, from camp scenes, that the service was efficient. Camps of any permanence were regularly laid out, fortified with a circular wall, tents pitched, picket lines and parks established. Granting the maximum use of local supplies for subsistence, all this could not have been done without well organized trains.

The system was strong enough to permit great flexibility. The Assyrian campaigns were of every possible description—across mountains, into the deserts, overland a thousand miles from home, overseas across the Persian Gulf. Granting that there were reverses of which we hear nothing, besides the success of which we get exaggerated reports, the expansion of the empire speaks for

[18] Hunger, 17, 21; Rawlinson, I, 438, 468.
[19] Delitzsch, 13; Hunger, 21; Breasted, 72.

itself. There was a good and a well thought out military organization, of which we can still form a clear, though incomplete, picture.

The strength of these conquering armies is uncertain. Statements are generally vague and presumably exaggerated—"multitudes not to be counted"—but some may be accepted as at least credible. Shalmaneser II, a century before Sargon, gives the strength of a Syrian coalition that defeated or at least checked him, as 77,900, with 3940 chariots and 1000 camels. When he next went out against this coalition he says that he crossed the Euphrates with 102,000 men. The regular army under the Sargon Dynasty has been estimated at from 50,000 to 100,000 fighting men; the whole force, with auxiliary contingents, at 150,000 combatants.[20] How many of these were actually present on the battle field at any one time is unknown.

3. PERSIA (6TH CENTURY B. C.)

We have seen Assyria give place to a coalition of the Medes and Chaldæans. This happened somewhat in this wise.

The Chaldæans were Semites, akin to the earlier rulers of the land. The Medes were a new people, Aryans, coming from the plateau of Iran. They had long been under Assyrian rule, but about the middle of the seventh century B. C. they became strong enough to raise the standard of rebellion.

Their first invasion of Assyria was decisively repulsed. But Cyaxares, the Median king, was no ordinary barbarian; he was a soldier, able to see the reasons for his defeat, and to learn from the enemy. "It was he who first divided the troops of Asia according to arms, and organized them into separate companies, spearmen and archers and horsemen; until then they had been mixed together." That is, he passed at one step from Homeric warfare, where each chief led his own men very much as he pleased, to an organized army, presumably on the Assyrian model. From the fact that the horse was native to their country, and from later developments, it is safe to say that cavalry was their principal arm, in the form of the mounted archer, not the lancer or the chariot warrior. Having made this reorganization, Cyaxares attacked Assyria again, and penetrated to the gates of Nineveh; but here he had to

[20] Delitzsch, 14; Hunger, 6; Rawlinson, I, 103–104.

turn back to meet an invasion by the Scythians, a tribe from southern Russia.[21]

The invaders made no effort to establish a settled government, but contented themselves with tribute and plunder. Monumental evidence shows them as horsemen, and (alone in all antiquity) using a long, straight, heavy cavalry sabre. They overran all Mesopotamia and Syria, and even threatened Egypt, but everywhere as marauders. Finally, exhausted by wars and by their own excesses in the conquered countries, their power waned, and by the end of the century they were gone.

As they grew weaker in Media and Assyria, Cyaxares returned to the attack, cleared his own territories, and renewed the siege of Nineveh, this time with success, allying himself for the purpose with the Chaldæans and with other disaffected Assyrian provinces. The division of the spoils was on the natural basis; the Chaldæans took the southern provinces, the Euphrates valley and Syria, and the Medes the Tigris country and the region toward the Black Sea.[22] The Median power now rapidly spread westward, and in a few years they controlled all Asia "above the Halys"—that is, to the frontiers of Lydia. This state was an important power. Its traditions showed relations, commercial if not political, east to Mesopotamia and west to Italy. Its actual history shows a rich state controlling all western Asia Minor, until, threatened by the barbarian invasion mentioned above, it had sought alliance with Assyria (675 B. C.). The barbarians having been driven out, and Assyria having fallen, Lydia and Media stood face to face.

The resulting war, the Medians and Chaldæans against a coalition of the powers of Asia Minor headed by Lydia, continued for several years, but was finally terminated by receiving Lydia into a new triple alliance (585 B. C.). The dual alliance itself, meanwhile, had become further cemented by a combined campaign in southern Syria, resulting in preservation of those provinces to Chaldæa, against Egyptian aggression under Necho. It was in this campaign that there was fought another battle, the Biblical one, at Armageddon, (608 B. C.), the Jews, then tributaries of Babylon, seeking to block the Egyptian advance.[23]

[21] Herodotus, I, 103–104; Rawlinson, II, 312, 384.
[22] Herodotus, I, 106; Rawlinson, II, 392–395.
[23] 2 Chron., XXXV; 2 Kings, XXIII; Rawlinson, II, 409–414.

But this alliance, and the Median power, were short lived. Cyaxares' successor, Astyages, was not the man to hold it together.

There was a little kingdom on the eastern shore of the Persian Gulf, held by the Persians, a people closely related to the Medes. This was apparently under the nominal sovereignty of Media, and its crown prince, Cyrus, resided at the Median court. Here he learned the Median art of war, and also observed the growing luxury and degeneracy of the king and court; and decided that the time was ripe for rebellion. After some initial reverses, he decisively defeated the Medes, and captured Astyages about 560 B. C. Nebuchadnezzar of Chaldæa was dead, and the reigning king was not on the best terms with Media; the other ally, Lydia, was too distant to help. The whole Median dominion speedily submitted to Cyrus.

Crœsus, king of Lydia, was greatly alarmed at the sudden appearance of this new power, and made an alliance against it with Babylon, Egypt, and the republic of Sparta. But Cyrus defeated Crœsus before his allies could come to his aid, and took Sardis, the Lydian capital, by assault, after a short siege (546 B. C.). This exploit resembles that of Wolfe at Quebec, for it was accomplished by scaling a steep cliff, carelessly guarded because it was supposed to be inaccessible.[24]

The Assyrian tactics, as indicated above, depended upon fire power, open order, and free manœuvre. The Medes, naturally a race of mounted archers, grafted the Assyrian infantry system upon their own, and adopted their wicker shields and short spears. Being horsemen they continued to emphasize the cavalry, and being mountaineers they neglected the chariot. The Persians copied the Medes, their native institutions being presumably very similar. They made the bow their principal weapon, and their infantry armament and equipment were not well adapted to the phalanx and shock tactics. The spear was short; the shield either small and rounded, or else copied from the Assyrian type and used primarily to cover an archer while firing. The sword was very short, little more than a dagger. Pictures show a thong, tying the tip of the scabbard to the leg, precisely as we do our pistol holsters, whether for comfort on the march or to facilitate drawing

[24] Herodotus, I, 84; Rawlinson, II, 369.

is conjectural. Armour appears to have been exceptional in the time of Cyrus.[25]

In the battle of Thymbra, which resulted in shutting Crœsus up in Sardis, the mounted archer encountered the mounted lancer—for this arm was the main reliance of the Lydians. Having nothing in his own force which he trusted to meet its charge, Cyrus improvised a camel corps, taking mounts from his trains. This he put in the front line, supporting it with infantry and holding back his cavalry. The enemy's horses were frightened by this novel attack, and the Lydian cavalry lost its formation, giving the Persian infantry its chance. The Lydian troopers dismounted to fight on foot, but were at a disadvantage in armament and equipment for this work; the whole army was driven from the field.[26]

Cyrus now turned his attention eastward, leaving a force to complete the subjugation of Asia Minor. This western campaign had far-reaching consequences, bringing the Persians in contact with the Greek settlements on the Asiatic coast and on the neighboring islands, and sowing the seeds for the Great War later.

The eastern campaign resulted in the capture of Babylon, and in the extension of the empire to the Indus. In one of these campaigns Cyrus was killed, and his son Cambyses succeeded him. It was this Cambyses who conquered Egypt, as mentioned above.

The Egyptian expedition was a serious matter, by reason of the distance to be covered, and the desert separating the two countries. But Cambyses made careful preparation, providing water supply by means of agreements with the Arabs and by considerable engineering works; other supply was assured by an alliance with Phœnicia, then independent, securing him the use of the Phœnician fleets. Thus the situation at the time of Rameses' conquests was directly reversed, control of the sea being used against Egypt instead of for her. An effort to extend the conquest to Carthage failed, since the Phœnicians would not co-operate against their own people; and an expedition into Ethiopia had to return with heavy loss, for lack of that forethought for water and supplies which Cambyses had previously used.[27]

[25] Rawlinson, II, 312; III, 172.   [26] Herodotus, I, 79-80.
[27] Herodotus, III, 1-25.

During Cambyses' absence his throne was seized by a usurper; but the legitimate line was soon restored through the influence of a group of powerful Persian nobles, who placed Darius, a close relation of Cambyses, upon the throne.

The immediate result was a long series of revolts. But these were soon put down, and a new type of empire gradually established.

The power of the king was somewhat limited, but at the same time his throne supported, by a strong aristocracy, the six great families headed by the nobles who had helped Darius to the throne. The loose system of tributary kingdoms characteristic of the earlier empires grew into a stronger organization. Each tributary state or group of states was constituted a crown province; its local usages were not materially changed, but upon them was superimposed a Persian control system. A royal governor, or satrap, was appointed, who was the direct personal representative of the king, clothed with the full royal authority in civil affairs, personally responsible to the king but to no one else. Instead of a variable and uncertain tribute, the satrap was charged with the collection of a fixed and definite assessment.[28]

The military system was centralized, even more than that of Assyria. Local levies were called for only in great wars, and then as auxiliary forces. Median and Persian regular troops were the main reliance, and of these a strong garrison was maintained in each province. The provincial commander was responsible, not to the satrap, but to the king, so that the civil and military officers acted as checks upon each other. There was also a system of inspection, a representative of the king coming occasionally to the province and overhauling the whole administration.

This plan, of course, never worked with entire uniformity over the whole empire. Local exceptions were always to be found, and in the later days of the empire it was not uncommon for the satrap to combine military and civil power.

Toward the end of the sixth century B. C. Darius had this organization working more or less completely, and was ready to use it.

North and south his empire was bounded by seas, deserts, or difficult and barren regions. East and west he was not so confined.

[28] Herodotus, III, 89–96; Rawlinson, III, 417.

To the eastward, across the Indus, was the Punjab, and westward, beyond the Bosporus, was Thrace, both rich prizes. Persia, and every empire known to the Persians, had gained power by conquest; nothing was more inevitable than that the Great King should look forward to more conquests. So much for the political situation; as for the military, Persia had had contact with all the peoples concerned, knew them to be warlike, but also felt herself, from experience, to be stronger.

But Darius did not rush heedlessly into wars; he carefully sought information beforehand.

The eastern expedition was undertaken first. As a preliminary step an expedition was fitted out on the upper Indus, which explored the river thoroughly down to its mouth. It then worked back along the coast, around Arabia and up to Egypt. Over two years were devoted to this work, so that Darius had detailed information of the territory into which he was going, and of all the water communications. In the expedition which followed, he used the sea as well as the river lines.

This expedition resulted in the annexation of parts of the Punjab, Rajputana and Scinde; no details, however, have come to us either of the tactics or of the supply system. The Persians learned from the Indians the use of elephants in battle, but it remained with them a military curiosity, and was not seriously applied.[29]

Equally careful reconnaissance was made for the western expedition. A small squadron sailed from Sidon, under the guidance of Democedes of Croton, the king's physician. This squadron explored the coast of Greece, and pushed as far as their guide's native town in Italy.[30]

Since an expedition against Greece would have an enormously long line of communications, vulnerable from the north, it was necessary to overawe the Scythian tribes beyond the Black Sea. A naval raid upon the north coast brought back prisoners and the necessary information; then followed a grand demonstration, which illustrates the logistical skill of the Persians.

Darius assembled a combined land and sea force, utilizing contingents from the whole empire, the Greeks of Asia Minor providing the maritime force. The fleet patrolled the west coast

[29] Herodotus, IV, 44; Rawlinson, III, 182.
[30] Herodotus, III, 136–139.

of the Black Sea, and constructed a floating bridge over the Bosporus. Darius crossed, marched up to the Danube, crossed that on another floating bridge, left a strong guard there, and maintained himself in Scythia for a month or two, living on the country. He is said to have gone even as far as the Don or the Volga, but we can hardly follow our ancient authorities so far as that; he clearly suffered some serious reverses, but in any event, he made a lasting impression upon the natives. When he returned, he left a force in Thrace, which established a firm footing on the northern coast of the Ægean.[31]

The way was now clear for an attack upon Greece. The circumstances of this, and its military lessons, may be more advantageously discussed later, from the Greek point of view; but it will be convenient at this time to examine the Persian military system at that period.

The armament and tactics have already been briefly touched upon; no great changes had taken place between Cyrus and Darius. A comparison of accounts of both earlier and later dates[32] would indicate a steady increase in the weight of cavalry armour, a gradual substitution of the javelin for the bow in the mounted service, and an increase in the use of slingers. But these modifications did not alter the essential character of the army. It still made cavalry its principal arm, and fire its principal mode of action. The heavy infantry formed the centre of the line; having come to bowshot, it halted and opened fire from behind its wicker shields. The slingers and light infantry undoubtedly acted as skirmishers, retiring behind the line when they were "squeezed out," and possibly using overhead fire—although the opportunity for this must have been very scant, for the heavy troops themselves were formed with considerable depth. The infantry made no effort to close with the enemy; the fire must have been in the nature of a holding attack. The decisive charge was delivered by the cavalry on the wings.

This plan has its merits, especially against an enemy not well armed and disciplined, or against a commander unfamiliar with it or lacking resource and quick decision. Against first-class heavy infantry, well led, its deficiencies are obvious. It assumes that

---

[31] Herodotus, IV, 83–144; Grundy, 50–55.
[32] Rawlinson, III, 172.

the fire will actually immobilize the enemy, and that the cavalry charge can be driven home. But the bow is not a long-range weapon, and the Persian tactics were such that preparation to use it was clearly observable; a well-timed and determined charge in close order stood a good chance of breaking through. And the typical Persian cavalry charge was not boot to boot with the lance; it was in loose order, "as foragers," with the bow and javelin, although each man did carry a second javelin to use in the mêlée. Light infantry or obstacles on the flanks might break its cohesion.

By drawing in contingents from the provinces, a Persian army might readily be made of enormous size, of course, at the expense of heterogeneous armament ranging from the typical Persian archer to the Greek heavy-armed pikeman in his phalanx formation. But the Greek estimates, although accepted by many modern writers, are clearly out of all reason. Herodotus talks of four million men, and gives a most elaborate description of a Persian army on the march. This is too much to ask us to believe. Delbrück calculates that the tail of such an army would still be in Susa, beyond the Tigris, when the head was engaged at Thermopylæ[33]—extending, say, from New York to Denver. Of course, one may say that the march would not be in a single column on a single road; but this comparison will serve to bring out the absurdity of supposing that such a mass could be handled and used, even if brought together. The Greek writers tell us in one breath that the Persians were good fighters, and in the next that they were in overwhelming number. Palpably, there is something wrong with the figures; they cannot be accepted, even with discounts, for there is no way to calculate discounts on purely imaginative estimates.

Infantry organization is said to have been in divisions of ten thousand men, with decimal subdivisions all the way down to the squad. This sounds a little artificial for an army made up of local contingents, and we cannot tell how nearly practice approached to theory. The division of the Guards, the famous "immortals," was always kept up to full strength—hence its name; but the very fact that this was emphasized indicates that it was exceptional. Doubtless this division had a "waiting list" of old soldiers.

To judge from reports of a slightly later period, a day's march

[33] Herodotus, VII, 40; Delbrück, I, 10.

for seasoned troops was about twenty miles, but large armies were encumbered with numerous camp followers and large baggage trains, so must have moved very slowly. Camps were well laid out, and often fortified.

The supply train, carrying chiefly grain, consisted of both carts and pack animals. When campaigns were near the seacoast, water transport was used; several examples of this have been given above, and it seems to have been standard practice. The service was well organized; we read not only of supply ships, but of transports for both men and horses. Supplies were always obtained locally if practicable; within the empire this was by an orderly and well-regulated requisition system. Chains of advance bases were established, ahead of the army in a friendly country.[34]

The navy being made up entirely from provincial contingents, a corps of marines, Medes and Persians, was formed, and a small detachment placed on each ship,[35] where they performed much the same function as the Persian regular troops in the mixed army.

Siege work was uncongenial to the Persians, who were all for manœuvre in the open field. At least, no mention is found of heavy siege engines, except in Xenophon's Cyropædia; and this, while very valuable for some purposes, has to be used with caution, for it is a novel rather than a history, and reflects the writer's military experience and theories rather than those of an earlier time. When compelled to lay siege to a fortress, they employed means not demanding heavy siege equipment, such as countervallation and subterranean mining.[36]

[34] Xenophon, Anabasis, I; Rawlinson, III, 187–193.
[35] Herodotus, VII, 184.
[36] Herodotus, I, 162; IV, 200.

CHAPTER III

GREECE: THE TROJAN AND PERSIAN WARS

(1200–479 B. C.)

THE FREEDOM OF THE DARDANELLES

THE earliest civilization in the Ægean region was contemporary with and related to the Egyptian. Crete, in particular, had close commercial relations with the Egyptian Old Empire, and by 2000 B. C. was a highly developed and wealthy maritime power. By 1500 B. C., this civilization, still developing, had spread to the mainland in the region of Mycenæ.

During the same period trading communities had grown up at the Ægean entrance of the Dardanelles, the chief town being Troy. These communities were in close relations with the Hittites, and through them with other oriental peoples and with Egypt.

North of this fringe of cities and villages were the semicivilized tribes of the Balkans. Between 2000 and 1500 B. C. some of these mountaineers, calling themselves Hellenes, pressed down into Greece by wave after wave of tribal migrations, and submerged and absorbed the Mycenæan and Cretan civilizations.[1]

The new rulers of the land formed themselves into little independent communities, doubtless representing the smaller groups of the invading tribes, and constituting, all together, three larger distinct groups, Dorians, Ionians and Æolians. A curious parallel is found in the Philippine Islands, where we can seem to trace three waves of invasion, by races closely akin but distinct, driving out the aborigines and warring among themselves, and the more civilized of them having as the unit of self-government the *barangay*, or ship's crew.

Among the Hellenes, these little communities rapidly grew strong, and the head men easily developed into the Homeric "kings." The new people acquired the maritime knowledge of

[1] Breasted, 110–125. See Plate 2.

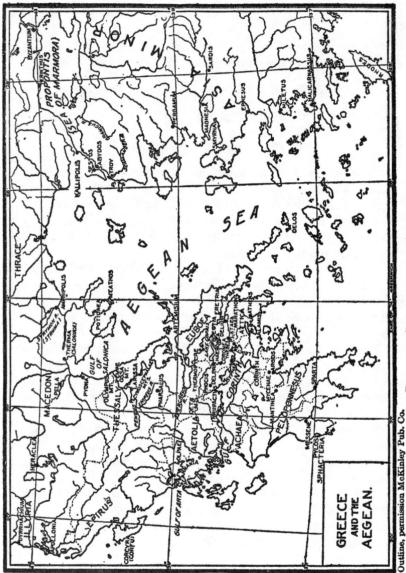

Outline, permission McKinley Pub. Co.   PLATE 2.—GREECE AND THE AEGEAN.

Crete, and began trading voyages, typified by the legends of the Argonauts. Through these voyages they became familiar with the coasts far and wide, even to the remote ends of the Black Sea, and picked up marvelous Arabian Nights stories of the mysterious back country. In their voyages in this direction they necessarily came in conflict with the Trojans, the guardians of the Black Sea gates, and this led in about the twelfth century B. C. to the Trojan War. And here we begin to get impressions of the state of the art of war. For this war is historically a fact even though our records of it are not in historical form.

The Greeks appear in the Iliad as the loosest kind of association. Agamemnon is merely *primus inter pares*, and can only request or threaten, not command—rather a Joffre than a Foch. Each chief heads his own men, himself in a chariot, the rest on foot. This chariot must have been a relic of nomadic days, for in the settled life of Greece it disappeared, and was never heard of in later times. It was merely a means of transportation, not a weapon—a mount, not a tank—and was given up when the Greeks learned to ride. The chief is always described as fully armoured and carrying a large shield; he fights with every kind of weapon, missile preferred—bow, javelin, sword, and in emergency even heavy rocks. Both heavy and light infantry are found among his followers; the heavy armed formed a genuine phalanx, but there were also skirmishers with bow or sling. The phalanx was unwieldy in attack, and hesitated to close, but was very powerful in defence, and could check even the best of the champions. It did, however, advance on occasion to the charge and fight hand to hand.

The single combats of the champions, being more lively and picturesque than the collision of lines, have undue prominence in Homer's descriptions; but with it all he does not forget the fundamental importance of the phalanx, and probably knew that his audience—"the market-girls and fishermen, the shepherds and the sailors too"—would not misunderstand him. The chiefs all pride themselves upon their skill in forming the line of battle. On at least one occasion Nestor, recognizing the great variations among his men in skill and courage, selects the best, the "rampart of battle," for the rear ranks, putting the less trustworthy where they will have to fight whether or no—a device sometimes employed in the 'phalangial formations of later days, and exemplified by the formations of Morgan at the Cowpens and Greene at Guilford Courthouse, where the reliable troops were all in the third line.

The troops had a certain degree of discipline. Although it was the practice to charge home with a shout, still it was expected that silence would be preserved during the advance, as a mark of respect to the chiefs, and to permit commands to be heard—for the voice was chiefly relied upon to communicate orders, and a good tone of command was highly esteemed and is frequently referred to.[2]

The Greek army was representative of all Hellas—that is, of the western wing of this northern line of civilization. Homer gives a detailed catalogue of ships, fanciful of course, but reflecting the notion of Panhellenism. Thucydides discusses this passage very much in the style of a modern critic in an effort to estimate the strength of the expedition;[3] his line of reasoning would give it about 100,000 men, but naturally numerical calculations based upon this material cannot lead to reliable results.

Troy was the head of another alliance, this time of Asia Minor, the eastern wing. It was not confined strictly to Asia Minor, however, for among the allies enumerated in the Iliad and elsewhere there appear names from other regions. This is doubtless to be interpreted merely as meaning that the Greeks felt this to be a World War, in which they encountered peoples before unknown. This is pertinent to the present discussion, in that it suggests contact of the Greeks with the military systems of earlier great empires.

Thus there is the legend of Memnon, king of Ethiopia, who brought a force to Troy. This may reflect stories of Egypt, heard secondhand through the Hittites; or it may mean interior Asia, for the Ethiopians, "the most remote of peoples," were "divided into two parts, one toward the setting and one toward the rising sun," and the Greeks were long in doubt, whether or not a land connection existed. Herodotus speaks of the Asiatic Ethiopians, and considers Memnon as having come from Susa.[4] The name Memnonion was currently given to the citadel of that

---

[2] Iliad, IV, 299, 425–436; XIII, 130–145; Leaf, Ch. VI.
[3] Iliad, II; Thucydides, I, 10–11.
[4] Odyssey, I, 23; Herodotus, III, 94; V, 54.

place. In any event, all this indicates a broadening of the Greek view through the military associations of this war.

The operations are commonly referred to as a siege, but they were not so, technically. The Greeks simply forced a landing and established a fortified camp. Troy was at no time blockaded, and always had free communications with the back country. The war was one of position on stabilized lines. Each party had its defensive works, which neither could take by direct assault, and neither side used siege engines. The combats were all in the open, in No Man's Land.

Thucydides, in the passage cited above, gives a very thoughtful analysis of this situation; and it may not be amiss to recall that he himself had some experience of overseas expeditions, having had command of a small Athenian squadron operating independently at the mouth of the Struma River, east of Salonika, in 424 B. C. He attributes the indecisive character of the operations to difficulties of supply.

This matter has been mentioned above, in the introductory chapter. The Greeks had command of the sea, and did use it for supply, but unsystematically and without any central control. Thucydides points out that the strength of the expedition was limited, in the first place, to that which could maintain itself upon the country; further, that a large part of its energy and attention was constantly diverted from operations against the enemy, to keep up supply by the only two means available—agriculture and piracy, in both of which they were perfectly at home, and both of which apparently were equally honorable. The overseas supply, to judge from such casual references as those just cited from the Iliad, was chiefly in the way of trade, not in the way of direct shipments from home. In fact, Greece was not a productive country, and was more likely to depend upon imports herself than to send large quantities abroad. An indication of the commercial bearing of the Trojan War is found in the fact that in later times Greece, and especially Athens, depended largely for her ordinary supplies upon the Black Sea trade,[5] so that the freedom of the Dardanelles was vital.

But leaving Troy and its legends, we may reach firmer ground in the Persian Wars. We now come to a period where the reliable

[5] Iliad, VII, 454–475; IX, 60–78; Strabo, VII.

material for narrative history is so abundant that serious entrance
into that field would serve but to confuse the military discussion.
Only a few characteristic and critical points will be touched upon
to illustrate the military development.

The nature of the Persian state and its military system have
been discussed above. It is necessary next to say a word on the
Greek political and military systems at the moment when the
conflict with Persia began.

As already noted, there was no Greek empire. There were
countless little city states, each jealously independent, showing
great variety in governmental forms and an equally great variety
in local interests and customs. All were Hellenes, and all felt
intensely the Panhellenic spirit; but this did not in the least prevent
fierce wars among themselves, and even appeals by one Greek
state for "barbarian" assistance against another. And the Greeks,
the "Swiss of the ancient world," were always ready to serve as
mercenaries in foreign armies, even at the risk of being called upon
to serve against Greeks. A very close parallel is found in mediæval
Italy.

Three types of Greek political organization, existing at the
period under consideration, may be noted as the most important
for present purposes.

First are the Ionian colonies in Asia Minor and on the Ægean
islands. They were in general city or island principalities, each
under its own "tyrant," and at the end of the sixth century B. C.
were under Persian domination. One of these tyrants in particular, Miltiades of the Thracian Chersonese or Gallipoli Peninsula,
should here be mentioned; he was at this time acquiring his knowledge of the Persians. As early as the Scythian expedition of
Darius, in which he commanded his local contingent, he was
already displaying that impatience under Persian rule that later
brought him into disfavour with Darius and drove him back to
his native city and to an Athenian military command.[6] These
Ionians not only furnished land troops, but were one of the main-
stays of the Persian navy—bold mariners, second only to the
Phœnicians if to any.

[6] Herodotus, IV, 137.

The next type is Athens, which in the Trojan War had been of minor consideration, but had now become the leading power north of the Isthmus of Corinth. Her earlier monarchy had passed into an aristocracy, this had merged again into autocratic rule, and the tyrants had not been finally driven out until the very end of the sixth century. The system that took their place is commonly spoken of as a democracy, but for the time it remained largely aristocratic. The council of the Areopagus and the Senate had aristocratic tendencies, the elected archons and the general assembly democratic. Classes remained among the citizens, and the citizens themselves were sharply set off from the disfranchised classes and the slaves. But the power of the hereditary nobility as such had been destroyed, through the breaking up of the four old clans based upon blood relationship, and the substitution of ten new ones based upon locality.

Athens, politically, included all Attica. She was a commercial and maritime state.

Sparta, the dominant power of the Peloponnesus, is the third type. This region was held, at the time of the Trojan War, by the Achæans under Menelaus, but shortly after was occupied by the Dorians in their great southward migration. Gradually gaining in power, Sparta was selected as the greatest Greek state when Crœsus of Lydia sought a Greek ally against Persia.

She was a purely military state. Full citizenship could be gained only by Spartiate birth and by completion of a rigid course of military training and service extending from boyhood to the thirtieth year. The Spartiate devoted himself exclusively to his military duties. He was debarred from trade and manufacture, which were in the hands of non-citizens, and supported by agriculture on an allotment of state land tilled by Helots, the descendants of conquered natives reduced to serfdom by the Dorians. The government was an oligarchy. A peculiar feature was the hereditary kingship—not one king, but two, each representing a separate royal family, and equal in authority, so that each could exercise a sort of veto on the acts of the other. Their functions were not political, but religious, judicial and military—chiefly military, in which field they were supreme at the time of the Persian wars, although later their powers were somewhat re-

stricted. Political power lay in the Senate and in the elected
ephors.

The Greek military system everywhere was based upon universal
service. Every citizen had his military duties in war, precisely
as he had his political duties in peace. Very clearly was exemplified the principle, formulated for us in later days, that war is
merely a continuation of political activity by other means.[7] The
citizen was expected to present himself when called, armed and
equipped. Similar, but less severe, demands were made upon
non-citizen inhabitants.

Organization and tactics were based upon heavy infantry and
shock. The chariot had long since disappeared; the typical Greek
warrior was the *hoplite*, or armoured pikeman. As auxiliary arms,
there were cavalry and light infantry, including archers, slingers
and *peltasts* or javelin men protected chiefly by the small shield
which gave them their name.

In Athens, and the states similarly organized, citizens were
classed according to property, and obligations as to equipment
apportioned accordingly.. The richest served in the cavalry,
providing their own mounts; by custom, if not by law, the exceptionally rich were called upon for special money contributions—
for example, a wealthy citizen would undertake the equipment
of a ship of war, as a private citizen did with our own Astor Bat-
tery in the Philippines. The average well-to-do citizens served as
hoplites, the poorer as auxiliaries or as attendants to the hoplites.
Archers formed a special arm; the bow was a traditional Greek
weapon, but needed much practice to maintain skill. The arm
was probably made up of citizens unable to maintain a horse,
but rich enough to spare time for practice. Slingers were another
special arm, auxiliary contingents from allied cities, such as
Rhodes, where the weapon was native.

In Sparta, where theoretically the citizen had no private property, each Spartiate served where assigned. He was characteristically a hoplite, other service being depreciated.

Non-citizens were called upon according to their means. Slaves
and Helots were used freely as attendants to the hoplites and
sparingly as auxiliary troops. Hoplite equipment was entrusted
to them only in great emergencies, and with many misgivings.

[7] Clausewitz, I, 1, 24.

The universal formation was the phalanx—a heavy line of armoured pikemen. Its details varied greatly according to the tactical situation, depth being required to give weight to its shock, extension to outflank and avoid outflanking. Eight ranks was a very common depth, but instances are found of as many as twenty-five.[8] Of course only the front ranks could actually engage, the others replaced losses and kept up the forward pressure. Individual fencing probably counted for little; it demands space, and this formation seems to have been shield to shield. The phalanx itself was the battle-axe, the pikes merely its cutting edge. The quality, then, had to be fairly homogeneous within the phalanx. It would not do to put inferior men in front and give the enemy an initial advantage, nor yet in rear, for the energetic forward push was vital. Since there were necessarily inequalities in courage, strength, skill and equipment, a subordinate commander who knew his men might post them according to their qualifications, but they were of no use in the phalanx if not up to a fairly high standard.

That standard as to physical strength and skill was doubtless higher than in most other countries and times, for the Greeks had a passion for athletics; but it is unquestionably a mistake to assume, as is sometimes done, that all or even a majority were trained athletes. As for courage, that standard also may be taken as high, but skulking was common enough to invite the satire of Aristophanes in his comedies, notably in his "Peace," which would hardly have been the case if it had been a rare phenomenon.

The fire power of the phalanx was zero. Its auxiliaries remedied this defect only in part, for if used in front as skirmishers they had to be drawn off to the flanks some time before contact, and, their weapons being of short range, overhead fire could not be very effective. Its charge, however, was almost irresistible, its defence almost unbreakable. In either case its weakness was the flank, for its manœuvring ability was very small, and it was difficult to change front or refuse a flank. Here was where it most needed its auxiliary arms. But these auxiliaries dared not attack decisively, even in flank; they might annoy the phalanx, check the momentum of its charge or weaken its defence, but only another phalanx could break it.

[8] Delbrück, I, 25–93.

With this preface, we may turn to the Persian Wars—highly interesting as direct conflict between East and West, horse and foot, fire and shock—and select a few incidents for discussion.

MARATHON (490 B. C.)

The first hostilities were in an Ionian revolt against Persia, about 500 B. C. This was put down, but the Great King seems to have recognized the justice of some of the complaints, for he reorganized his provinces here, reforming the tribute system and allowing the Greek cities to replace their tyrants by democratic institutions.

The European provinces—Gallipoli, Thrace, Macedonia—had shown signs of unrest during this revolt. Besides this, continental Greece had assisted the rebels, and Darius doubtless meditated punishment or at least intimidation. A great expedition under Mardonius, by land and water, while suffering some reverses, still somewhat restored Persian prestige along the northern coast.[9] The logical next step was to punish those Greek states, notably Athens, which had helped the rebels.

The Thracian expedition had shown clearly the difficulty of managing a combined land and sea force following the coast— bad roads, stress of weather, poor means of communication. This new one (490 B. C.) was made an overseas expedition pure and simple, crossing the Ægean by easy stages, from island to island, and establishing a base at Eretria in Eubœa, in sight of the Attic coast and almost of Athens herself. With this expedition was Hippias, the recently deposed tyrant of Athens.

The strength of the expedition has been much exaggerated in popular legend. Herodotus gives the number of ships, exclusive of horse transports, as 600. He was probably guessing, but may be supposed to have guessed high enough. This gives about 60,000 fighting men as the probable maximum, and 40,000 as a conservative estimate.[10] Contrary to Persian practice in Asia, and probably owing to the difficulty of sea transport, the cavalry seems to have been weak—at any rate, it played no part in the decisive fighting.

Athens prepared in great haste for defence, and sought assistance

[9] Herodotus, V, 28; VI, 40; Grundy, 149.
[10] Herodotus, VI, 94–95; Grundy, 160–163. See Plate 3.

from Sparta. This was granted, but before it could arrive news was received of a Persian landing at Marathon, about twenty-five miles by road from Athens.

The landing place was doubtless selected on the advice of Hippias. It is a plain four or five miles long and about two miles wide, with hills inshore and a marsh at each end. The beach is clear and the anchorage sheltered. The plain is cut in halves by a small stream. The main road to Athens here follows the coast; there is another, somewhat difficult, through the hills, and several links connect the two at this point. The intention was clearly to draw the Athenian forces northward, contain them with a part of the force, then move by sea around to the city and take it by the aid of those factions opposed to the new government just established there. The plan worked in part. The Athenians were drawn, but it was the Persians that were contained.

Acting with great promptness and decision, the Athenians moved with what few allies they could get, and established themselves just back of Marathon, holding the hill roads and threatening the flank of any force moving upon Athens by the coast. Herodotus gives their force as 10,000; modern criticism, while unable to fix a definite figure, finds this not an unreasonable estimate.

The commander was Callimachus, the polemarch, i. e., that one of the nine archons or magistrates who was charged with military affairs. Among the ten "generals," or leaders of the ten district contingents, was Miltiades, who had been compelled to leave his principality by the Thracian expedition. Probably by virtue of his intimate knowledge of the Persians, as well as by his strength of character, he dominated the council of war and dictated the plan of action.

The delicate point in the Persian plan had been reached. They had drawn out the Athenians; now to take the city. Time was working with them, in that the absence of the Athenian troops gave an opportunity for treachery at home; and against them, for they must have known that the Spartans would soon be there. So after waiting as long as they dared—about three days—they offered battle, but with a detachment only, to hold the enemy while the rest moved by sea. This force was chiefly infantry, and was little if any superior to the Greeks, certainly not as much as two to one.

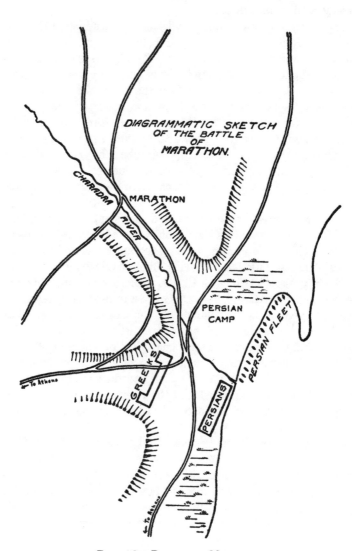

PLATE 3.—BATTLE OF MARATHON.

The Athenian position was well chosen—in the mouth of a little valley running out into the plain, where the flanks of the phalanx, essentially weak, could both be rested upon hills, and these in turn defended by light troops. The position was long for the force, and the line had to be thinned, but only the centre was weakened, the flanks being kept strong. The Persians crossed to the south bank of the stream which bisected the plain and formed facing the hills, about a mile away.

Herodotus will have it that the Athenians opened the attack. It may have been so; the movements of the Persians may have forced their hand. Certainly they would have preferred a defensive battle, for a long advance would have exposed their flanks and sacrificed the advantage of the carefully chosen position. Herodotus' notion of a rapid charge for such a distance is palpably out of the question. Even if we could accept the theory, sometimes advanced, that the phalanx used an open order and counted upon some individual fencing in the front rank, "double time" for a mile would be a heavy demand upon the best of athletes, burdened with arms and armour and required to maintain alignment. And, as explained above, the formation was probably dense, and the demands upon individual strength and upon perfection of drill even greater. The movement would have had to be slow up to the last hundred yards or so, to preserve the close phalanx formation, and the Persian light troops would have had plenty of time to worry them in flank. Unquestionably the proper tactics for the Persians was to hold back, as long as the enemy made no move, since all they wanted was to keep the Athenians away from Athens. But without accepting in its entirety Delbrück's account of the battle,[11] one is strongly inclined to conclude, with him, that the Persians did yield to the temptation to attack.

As we know, they depended upon the combination of their archers in front and their cavalry on the flanks. But here the cavalry was weak and the enemy's flanks protected, at least so long as they stood fast. As soon, then, as the fire began to be effective, but before it had caused serious loss, the Athenians charged; either they increased the pace of their long advance, according to the ordinary theory, or made a counter-attack from their original position, according to Delbrück's. In either case,

[11] Herodotus, VI, 103–111; Delbrück, I, 35–49; Grundy, 174–185.

the distance to be covered at the increased gait would be short—a hundred yards, or at most two hundred.

The weak Athenian centre was broken, but the strong wings converged upon the Persians and routed them. So, if the war plans of Germany in 1914 showed us the influence of Cannæ (see Chapter VI) coming down even to our day, Marathon shows us its forerunner—but Marathon has had no Schlieffen.

Thus happily freed from its awkward situation, facing two equally urgent and utterly irreconcilable tasks, the Athenian force pursued the enemy to his ships, then made all haste to avail itself of its interior lines to Athens, and reached there before the Persian fleet. The expedition had failed.

During the next few years the wealth of Athens increased greatly, partly owing to the rapid development of the silver mines owned by the state. Under the guidance of Themistocles, the new revenue from this source was devoted to the building of a navy.[12] And she needed it; troubles in Egypt occupied Darius and his successor Xerxes for a few years, but in 480 B. C., ten years after Marathon, Persia came to Greece again. This time it was no mere punitive expedition, but a definite effort at conquest, with all the power of Persia and commanded by the king in person.

THERMOPYLÆ (480 B. C.)

The plan was again that of a combined land and sea force moving by the north coast of the Ægean. In spite of the difficulties encountered by Mardonius in 492, it had become evident that nothing less would do. The difficulties were recognized and faced, the preliminary work occupying some three years. A canal was dug across the isthmus behind the stormy promontory of Mount Athos, in rounding which Mardonius' fleet had been badly shattered. A bridge was built across the Struma River, and material assembled for others at the Dardanelles. Supplies were collected, and at least five great depots established along the intended line of march, in Thrace and Macedonia.

The land and naval forces were assembled at the Dardanelles. Herodotus gives a detailed account of this concentration, with the force of each contingent on land and sea—apparently a list of all the races and states that the legend makers had ever heard of.

[12] Grundy, 203.

The numbers are wholly unreliable, as remarked in the preceding chapter, but it is undoubtedly true that the whole empire, including the Ionian Greek colonies, was drawn upon for men and ships. Modern estimates by careful writers give the land force from 500,000 down to less than 100,000.[13] The smaller estimate depends largely upon discussion of purely military considerations as to marching and supply, and probably gives modern ideas too much weight. The larger rests upon comparison and criticism of ancient sources, and perhaps takes military difficulties too little into account. But both writers put forward their figures modestly, and both agree that no one really knows.

The Dardanelles were bridged at Abydos, where the strait is less than a mile wide, the roadways being borne upon large sea-going ships. The swift current made this no light task—the first bridges went out, and the engineers were beheaded *pour encourager les autres*. Their successors were more careful or more fortunate. The army crossed, and marched along the coast, in touch with the fleet, as far as Therma, the modern Salonika. Here a halt was made while the navy explored the coast as far as the pass of Tempe, just below Mount Olympus. The Greeks made some show of an intention to hold this pass, but reconnaissance showed that a position here could readily be turned through other passes, and the idea was given up. Thessaly and all the north submitted to the Persians.

The next favourable defensive line was the Œta mountain barrier, the southern rampart of the Spercheus River valley. A strong sentiment, chiefly Peloponnesian of course, favoured withdrawing to the Isthmus of Corinth. The priests of Delphi—most sagacious political observers, undoubtedly possessing a highly organized international intelligence service—had at first inclined to the belief that the Persians could not be stopped short of there, and caused their oracle to suggest that Athens must be abandoned. Later, however, remembering the Persian fleet, they hinted in the same manner at dependence upon the Athenian sea power, which suggestion led naturally to further consideration of the Œta position, covering Athens.

The decision was to send troops to Œta, and the fleet to Artemisium, the north end of the island of Eubœa, where it was in close touch with them, almost in sight. It must have been realized

[13] Herodotus, VII; Delbrück, I, 10; Grundy, 211–212.

that the Persian army could not be definitely stopped, but it might be possible to delay it long enough for the navies to try conclusions. The fleet was made as powerful as possible; a Spartan was in command, but much the largest contingent, over a third of the whole, was Athenian.[14] The land force was also under a Spartan, Leonidas; its composition seems to confirm the idea that only delay was sought, for it was small, and made up of a dozen little contingents, 5000 to 7000 men in all. The Spartan hoplite contingent was only 300; Athens sent none at all.

Œta is steep and rugged, almost pathless. The main road swung east along its foot, following the south coast of the Gulf of Lamia by the narrow defile known as Thermopylæ. There was another road, but very obscure and difficult; this was left unguarded by the Greeks, although very likely it was observed. If the Persians knew of it at all, they considered it too difficult for a large force, or felt that it led them too far inland away from the fleet.

Thermopylæ, now a broad plain formed by deposits of river silt, was then a defile eight or ten miles long, broadening out decidedly in places, but with three narrow "gates." Leonidas took position at the middle one, Thermopylæ proper, the "gate of the hot springs," where the free space between mountain and sea was only fifty feet. Knowing that there was a mountain trail leading to his rear, he sent a thousand men to hold it. The Persians reconnoitred the main position, but hesitated to attack, doubtless hoping for a naval victory which would render it unnecessary. Operations at sea were delayed by violent storms, and were not at best energetically pushed, so after four days' delay Xerxes attacked, and the fighting continued two days. But in a position like this he could not bring his numbers to bear, and man for man at close quarters the Persians were no match for the Greeks. The defence was not passive, but active, sharp counterattacks being made which forced the Persians back and compelled them to begin new approaches.

But meanwhile Xerxes had learned from the local inhabitants of the mountain trail, and had sent a detachment into it by night. The defenders had grown careless, and were completely surprised; the road was open. It was a Cerro Gordo, but with a Leonidas instead of a Santa Anna.

[14] Herodotus, VIII, 1; Grundy, 234–238.

"The critics say, Leonidas should now have fallen back; this much is certain—the critics would have done so." He knew of the approach of the turning column in time. The Spartan version, given by Herodotus, is that he sent away most of his force and deliberately sacrificed himself with the rest. This is not entirely inconsistent with what we know of the Greek character, but it smacks of propaganda. One explanation is that he remained to cover the retreat. But if this was the idea he needed not only his own rear guard at Thermopylæ, but another at the exit of the mountain trail; and for a rear guard Leonidas' detachment, nearly half the force he had left after the loss of the flank guard, is excessive. Another interpretation does more credit to Leonidas' skill, and no less to his courage. He may still have seen a fighting chance to save the day. Holding the post of greatest danger himself with a part of his force, he may have sent the rest to dispute the exit of the trail. If both Persian columns could be delayed another day or two, the fleet might win the victory. And if the contingents thus sent weakened in the face of the desperate under-taking—Herodotus hints that they were not anxious to fight it out—neither they nor the authorities at home would care to ad-vertise the facts.

The fleets were actually engaged in a general action off Artemi-sium on this final third day at Thermopylæ.[15] The battle was not decisive, but the Persians had rather the better of it, and news of the disaster on land found the Greeks very ready to re-tire. The Persians were in no haste to follow, either by land or by sea, but took their time in overrunning the country.

The next good defensive line is the defile of Chæronea, with Helicon and Parnassus on one side and a lake on the other; the Peloponnesians, however, reverted to their plan of holding the Isthmus of Corinth. Bœotia being thus given over to the enemy, the Athenians had no choice but to lend their aid at the Isthmus, abandoning all Attica and even the city. But the sweeping naval victory at Salamis soon put an end to the Persian advance, and forced them to look to their own communications—not only that, but to look to Asia Minor, where an Ionian revolt was now prob-able. What was left of the fleet went back to protect the Dar-danelles, and the army withdrew to Thessaly. Xerxes returned

[15] Herodotus, VIII, 16; Delbrück, I, 65; Grundy, 277–308.

to Asia with part of the force, Mardonius remained with the bulk of it to save what provinces he could from the wreck. Deprived of control of the sea for supply, the Persian forces suffered extreme hardships in the retreat, and their losses were enormous.[16]

PLATÆA (479 B. C.)

The next spring Mardonius, having reorganized his supply system as best he might, moved down into Bœotia. As before, most of the people of Attica abandoned their homes, and sought help from the Peloponnesus. Mardonius occupied Athens, but burned it and retired to Thebes upon the advance of Greek troops to the Isthmus. The Greeks followed, and took position at Platæa, at the northern base of Mount Cithæron, covering their own communications to the Isthmus and threatening the flank of any Persian advance toward Attica. Some partial engagements resulted favourably to the Greeks, strengthening their confidence. Herodotus gives them a little over 100,000 men, the Persians three times as many. Delbrück discounts the Greek force over a half, and gives Mardonius less than two to one.

After some manœuvring and skirmishing, the two armies faced each other across the Asopus River, a small stream, readily fordable, but a serious obstacle if a crossing is opposed. Then came a pause; neither wanted to attack.

Pausanias the Spartan king, commanding the Greek forces, was having his troubles with his many little contingents. They could not understand a waiting game, and wanted to fight or go home. Skilfully using his agencies for morale, he secured a prophecy that he would win if he did not cross the Asopus. Mardonius had prophets too, and they announced the same thing; so the *status quo* was maintained.

Experience had not yet taught the Greeks the true value of the Persian cavalry, and so their position had been taken well in front of Mount Cithæron, their flanks more or less exposed, and the passes in rear not fully covered. After a number of days Mardonius' priests let him undertake minor operations, and his cavalry cut up a supply train. Encouraged by this it began harassing the main position, and found that it could do so with impunity. After several days of this, the omens presumably growing more

[16] Herodotus, VIII, 115.

and more favourable, the cavalry came on in force, and, while it could not even try to break the phalanx by a charge, it did force it to give ground. What was worse, the water supply in the new position taken up by the Greeks was very precarious, and the mountain passes were more than ever at the mercy of raiding parties. A position was therefore selected a mile farther back; orders were issued for the left and centre to retire to it in the night, while the right, Spartans under Pausanias himself, was to open the passes for the supply trains.

This move was necessary, but it was also risky for a loosely knit and ill-disciplined force, which might easily fall to pieces. Even in the Spartan contingent one subordinate commander felt his honour touched by orders to fall back, and refused obedience. Pausanias had no power to enforce his order, and had to bring the question before the council of war. The whole night was thus wasted, and finally at dawn Pausanias had to move without the obstinate officer. Finding his command isolated, he unwillingly followed, and more time was lost in waiting for him.

Meanwhile the centre had missed the way in the dark, and found itself in the morning close to the town of Plataea, some distance too far back. The Athenians of the left moved in the direction ordered, but became engaged with Mardonius' Greek contingents and never reached the new position. The Persian cavalry overtook Pausanias' column, and brought him to a halt; the Persian infantry followed rapidly to deal the deciding blow.

Pausanias chose his ground and waited. Hoplites could do nothing with the Persian light cavalry and skirmishers, and they on the other hand could not break the phalanx. To hold his troops steady under fire, Pausanias again used his invaluable corps of priests, who found the omens unfavourable to attack. But when the Persian infantry had come to bowshot, planted their shields and opened fire, he called upon Demeter of Eleusis, whose temple stood close by, the omens became favourable, and the hoplite phalanx advanced to its irresistible charge. It was Marathon over again. The Persian infantry broke, Mardonius himself was killed, and the battle was over. There was no pursuit, and Herodotus forgets to tell us what became of the defeated Persians; we only know that they disappeared from Greece, never to return.[17]

[17] Herodotus, IX; Delbrück, I, 82; Grundy, 461.

CHAPTER IV

GREECE: THE PELOPONNESIAN WAR AND AFTER

(460–369 B. C.)

THE ATHENIAN EMPIRE

THE Persian wars were Spartan wars. Wherever there was a combined Greek force, large or small, by land or sea, there was a Spartan commander, even though the Spartan contingent were negligible.

But Athens, although she had borne the brunt of the wars, although her territory had been ravaged and her city burned, had come out of the war stronger than ever. On land, she could turn out a force as large as Sparta, and at sea she was easily supreme. Besides, where allied forces were concerned, pure efficiency was not the only thing to consider; and the Spartan was not a comfortable person to deal with. In the overseas operations contemporary with and subsequent to Platæa, assisting the Ionian colonies in their revolt against Persia, Spartan prestige rapidly declined, and the command finally passed into Athenian hands.

Thus there grew up the Delian League, a loose but effective association of the free Ionian cities, led by Athens, and managed by a council sitting at Delos. Its purpose was protection of the Ægean against Persia.[1] But gradually the power passed from the board of directors to the president—from the council to Athens. The allied states came more and more to commute their contributions of men and ships to a money payment, and even the treasury was transferred from Delos to Athens. Athens then began to use this power for her own purposes, and against Greeks; it developed into an Athenian empire, which came into conflict with the Peloponnesian confederacy headed by Sparta.

Hostile contact began about 460 B. C., and continued intermittently until the end of the century; the period from 431 to 404,

[1] Thucydides, I, 96.

however, is looked upon as *the* Peloponnesian War. The earlier operations are of no great importance, at least for our present purposes, but contributed much to the military education of the leaders; notably Pericles, who held the Athenian command in several of these campaigns.

The Athenian empire is one of the paradoxical manifestations of the paradoxical Greek mind. Athens herself, during the whole century, was growing more and more democratic, with a most turbulent and fickle democracy. At the same time, she was introducing an imperialistic idea into her league, most of the members of which were themselves democracies. Sparta held to the oligarchy, and this was as a rule the tendency of the states of her league; hence, perhaps, a part of the antagonism between the two leagues. But what was more important, the Spartan league stood for autonomy of the members, in spite of the Spartan leadership; in modern terms, it was a Confederation, not a Federal Union. And paradoxically again, the destruction of the imperialistic state by the confederation led immediately to a new Spartan empire.

The Delian League was made up chiefly of insular and maritime states; it was supreme at sea. The members of the Peloponnesian League (not all of them Peloponnesian states, by the way—one of its most powerful members was Bœotia) were chiefly land powers, with just enough of them trading peoples to bring in the element of commercial rivalry; it was superior on land.

The Persian wars had caused no material alteration in Greek organization and tactics. Two different systems had met on the battlefield, the Greeks had found their own superior to the Persian and had learned how to make that superiority effective. One development in the Athenian system of command may be noted. During the Persian wars, the method of choosing the archons had been changed, election being superseded by the drawing of lots. The polemarch at once ceased to be a qualified man, and became a mere figurehead; control of military affairs rested, constitutionally, in the council of the ten "generals," constituting a sort of war office. Any statesman desiring influence in public affairs sought election as one of these generals. In campaign, they were assigned to specific commands as required, their functions sometimes overlapping and conflicting in a way somewhat puzzling to a modern; or sometimes one was designated by the assembly as commander-in-chief.[2]

A peculiarity of this war was the indecisive character of most of its operations. The land power could raid the continental territory of its adversary almost at will, which meant that while the islands suffered little, Attica was devastated year after year, and the people driven to refuge in the city. Hence great suffering among both refugees and city dwellers, lack of food, light and fuel, and hence also a terrible epidemic—manifestations familiar in the Europe of recent years.[3] The maritime power, on the other hand, could blockade the enemy's entire coast, raid it at will, and paralyze his commerce—also familiar manifestations. Tactical decisions could not be the aim of the war plans, and a wearing down policy seemed indicated.

The mercenary system, already familiar for foreign service, grew rapidly at home during these years, at the expense of the old universal service; and this for several reasons. The purely citizen soldier could not leave home for an indefinite period, maintaining himself at his own expense. More and more the state was driven to providing supplies and equipment, and pay to maintain his family. It was an easy step then to the professional soldier. Athens in particular was able to do this, through the cash commutation of service paid in by her allies; first her fleet, then her land army, became professional.

It was not quite the same with Sparta, but she reached much the same result. Her Spartiates had no civil occupation, and were already professional soldiers; but she could not turn them all out and let them bear the whole burden of the war, when it extended itself so greatly in time and space. It had always been the custom to reinforce the Spartiate hoplites with non-citizen inhabitants, and to support them by using Helots as light troops and attendants. It was natural and inevitable that, under this pressure, Helots came more and more to be equipped and trained as hoplites, developing quickly and readily into professional soldiers.

While the hoplite remained the chief reliance, even Sparta was forced to give more attention to the auxiliary arms. Until after

[2] Grundy, 432.   [3] Murray, 17.

the fall of the Athenian empire, "peltasts" or lightly armed javelin men were hardly recognized as constituting a separate arm, except among the Thessalians, Macedonians and other northerners, whose Hellenism was felt to be a little doubtful at best; but cavalry and archers were in good standing, although distinctly subordinated. Sparta found that heavy infantry alone could not effectively meet the Athenian raids from overseas, and cavalry and archers had to be organized even by that highly conservative power.

Discipline grew stronger under the mercenary system. In the older citizen army it could hardly be said to have existed, its absence being partly counterbalanced by a strong cohesion and public spirit natural to these small, intensely proud and patriotic states. Thus Demosthenes (the general, not to be confused with the later orator), being in command of an Athenian expedition on the Peloponnesian coast, wished to seize and fortify the promontory of Pylos, the modern Navarino, a measure which later events proved to have been judicious. But Thucydides says, in a very matter-of-fact manner, that he "could not persuade either the generals, or the soldiers, or the subordinate officers," [4] and so he had to wait until they changed their minds. A commander had little actual power to enforce his orders; about all he could do was to prefer charges in the assembly at home, after the campaign. Even the Spartan discipline was only fair; an instance of disobedience at Platæa has been mentioned in the preceding chapter, and a similar case occurred at Mantinea, in the war now under consideration.

A peculiarity of phalangial tactics, doubtless not unrecognized before, became strongly apparent now—that is, an uncontrollable tendency to drift to the right. [5] The shield being on the left arm, single combatants always worked to the right, and the whole phalanx felt the same impulse during the charge. The usual result was that each right wing outflanked and defeated the hostile left, and the battle was decided by the relative positions and conditions of the two victorious rights. It seems not improbable that recognition of the right as the post of honour was in some degree due to this; thus, Callimachus as polemarch took the right of the

---

[4] Thucydides, IV, 4, 55; Delbrück, I, 109, 250.
[5] Delbrück, I, 91.

line at Marathon. But while this condition became fully realized during the Peloponnesian Wars, it remained for the next century to base a tactical system upon it.

We think of the phalanx as an unbroken mass, and so it was in the tactical sense. Actually there must have been slight intervals, or it could not have had even the limited manœuvring power which it did show. There was no tactical subdivision of it, but it did possess subordinate elements. The Spartan organization was the most complete. [6] The fundamental unit was the *mora*, or perhaps we might say battalion, of 400 or more hoplites under a polemarch—a different officer, it will be noted, from the Athenian polemarch. This included four *lochoi* or companies, each under a *lochagos*—which name, it is interesting to note, is still used in the Greek army in the sense of *captain*, as *strategos* is in the sense of *general*. Each company was further divided into what roughly correspond to platoons and sections. None of these was a tactical unit in the sense of having a combat function as such, but each had its use in camp, on the march and in manœuvre. The drill was based upon the section; it was habitually formed in column and trained simply to follow its chief. The breadth of the section column was varied at will, and this regulated the depth of the phalanx, for the line of battle was a line of sections.

One important special form of war had heretofore attracted little attention in Greece—the siege. Long continued and complicated operations were unusual. Even the Trojan War, as we have seen, showed no siege work. Earlier empires had conducted sieges, but Persia, the only one of which the Greeks had intimate personal knowledge, did not favour them. The Peloponnesian War furnishes examples of occasional half-hearted efforts, but real siege work did not come in until the Carthaginian inroads into the Greek colonies of Sicily, toward the end of the period. The Carthaginians, being Phœnicians, had learned the art of war from Assyrian and Egyptian sources, and understood the siege. Dionysius of Syracuse seized eagerly upon the new engines and the new tactics, and developed them. From Syracuse they spread through all Greece. [7]

The supply system was rudimentary. There is no indication of any officer charged with full and systematic supervision of

[6] Smith, art. "Exercitus." [7] Delbrück, I, 118.

it. Originally the Greek never thought of a long campaign; the citizen soldier took a few days' supply with him, and the state did what it could, in a sketchy fashion, to keep it up. By force of circumstances some degree of system had to be introduced, and we have already seen the tactics of Platæa influenced by consideration for the supply trains. In this new war distant expeditions grew more frequent, and supply was more considered, but this remained the weakest point. [8]

A few campaigns may now be taken up to illustrate the military development of the period.

The operations in the middle of the fifth century, referred to above, terminated (445 B. C.) in a truce which was stipulated to last for thirty years. Athens also concluded, at this late date, a formal peace with Persia. But the commercial rivalry continued, especially between Athens and Corinth. A sort of aggravated Agadir incident took place in 434 at Corfu; and a direct conflict came a little later in the region of Salonika. There was a city in that region, Potidæa, technically a Corinthian colony, but a tributary ally of Athens. The relations of the two powers being now strained almost to the breaking point, Athens wished to end this anomalous condition, and demanded that Potidæa break the ties that still bound her to Corinth. Again there were hostile demonstrations, complicated by the defection of Macedon, formerly an Athenian ally but now siding with Corinth; and finally a pitched battle was fought. The two cavalry forces were detached, and neutralized each other. In the main action, each side was victorious on its own right. The battle remained without tactical decision, the two intact wings not daring to engage each other, but the Corinthians and Potidæans withdrew into the city, where they were blockaded.

Then followed negotiations, more and more heated, between Athens and Sparta. Pericles proposed arbitration, and it is barely possible that war might have been averted; but in 431 B. C. hotheaded subordinates destroyed even the faintest hope. Platæa, although in Bœotia, was in closer relations with Athens than with Thebes. Local Spartan sympathizers tried to get control, and called in the help of Thebes; Athens supported her local partisans, and the war was on.

[8] Gauldrée-Boilleau, 201, 212.

Pericles, then one of the ten "generals," was the guiding mind in Athens. His war plan, which was accepted, abandoned rural Attica to the enemy, and concentrated upon the navy. Athens was well provided with ready money, for she had a war reserve of 6000 talents in coin, upwards of eight million dollars, besides her annual cash revenue of a thousand talents, or nearly a million and a half. But, as noted above, she could more readily make her financial strength felt at sea than on land.

This first phase of the war continued for ten years, when a truce, nominally for fifty years, was patched up on the basis of the *status quo ante bellum*, both sides being quite ready for a rest. [9] But while the political results were slight, certain operations have a military interest.

In the summer of 429 Athens had a small expedition operating north of Potidæa, under one Xenophon—not the military writer, who was but a child at this time. [10] In an encounter with local troops, the Athenian hoplites defeated the opposing phalanx, but their cavalry and light troops were beaten. In the typical Greek battle this would not have been a serious matter, but these were northerners, who, as suggested above, were accustomed to make up for their deficiencies in heavy infantry by the use of peltasts. A reinforcement of this arm came up just when most needed, and with the cavalry began to harass the Athenian phalanx, now deprived of its auxiliaries. Avoiding close combat but never giving the enemy any rest, they finally forced the Athenians back into Potidæa, whence they returned to Athens, abandoning the whole expedition, with a loss of over 400 men killed including Xenophon and the two other generals.

The same thing happened in Ætolia in 426. Demosthenes, already mentioned, was raiding the west coast of the Peloponnesus. In consultation with some of his local allies, he conceived an idea akin to that which led Lee into Maryland and Pennsylvania— to take Bœotia in rear, joining forces with Phocis, the state on her northwest border, which was traditionally an ally of Athens and might be expected to help her. Landing on the north coast of the Gulf of Corinth with a few Athenians and a large allied force, he marched northeast, expecting to round Parnassus and move

[9] Thucydides, I, 56–65; II, 2–13; V, 18; Breasted, 185.
[10] Thucydides, II, 79.

then southeast through Phocis, a detour of perhaps a hundred miles. But the Ætolians, a wild hill people, resented his invasion and gathered to prevent it. Having only light troops they avoided a pitched battle, but harassed the camp and column. The expedition had a considerable proportion of archers, and defended itself well enough at first; but the attacks continued, the leaders of the archers were killed, and their ammunition became exhausted. Demosthenes took up the retreat, but his guide was killed and his men soon became dispersed. Only a remnant reached the base. Neither his total force nor his total loss is known, but out of 300 Athenian hoplites he lost 120 killed. The expedition returned by sea to Athens, but Demosthenes was afraid to go home while memory of his disaster was fresh, and remained at Naupactus on the Gulf of Corinth. General Braddock might have done well to study this campaign before starting for Fort Duquesne.

A strong force of Peloponnesian hoplites under the Spartiate Eurylochus was at once sent to the region of Delphi, and collected Ætolian and other local auxiliaries for a counter stroke against Naupactus and the other Athenian posts on the gulf and west coasts. Demosthenes on his part collected all available forces and the two armies met near Olpæ, a fortified town on the Gulf of Arta. Demosthenes, in spite of all efforts, was inferior in numbers. The resulting battle shows interesting tactical peculiarities on both sides.[11]

Eurylochus, with his own proper command, took post on the left. Demosthenes, with the best of his troops, was as usual on the right. The Ambracian troops of the Peloponnesian right drove back the Acarnanians opposed to them, and even Demosthenes and his Messenians, outnumbered, gave ground before Eurylochus and his Mantineans. But Demosthenes, foreseeing some such result, had detached a party of 400 men, both light and heavy troops, and posted them under cover in rear of his line. These now charged, struck the Mantineans in flank and rear, and drove them from the field. The whole army was routed and Eurylochus himself was killed. His successor seems to have been a man of little courage and no ability, and the campaign ended somewhat discreditably to Sparta.

The purpose of Eurylochus in putting his best troops on the

[11] Thucydides, III, 95–109.

left is not clear. If it was expressly for the purpose of breaking the Athenian right, the formation is a forerunner of the Theban tactics of the next century. And the disposition of counterattack troops by Demosthenes was distinctly a novelty.

Two years later, in 424, the Athenians themselves tried light troops against heavy. Reference has been made to the seizure and fortification of Pylos by Demosthenes. As a result of the naval operations there, something over 400 Spartiate hoplites with about as many Helots were cut off on the neighbouring island of Sphacteria.[12] Demosthenes held back his heavy infantry, surrounded the Spartans with a cloud of light troops, wore them out, and finally compelled them to surrender. This unheard of event, the surrender of a formed body of Spartiate hoplites, was a terrible blow to Spartan prestige.

In Thrace, things went better for the Spartans, through the ability of their commander Brasidas and the incapacity of Cleon, who, after gaining some credit at Sphacteria, had taken over the Athenian command in the north. Both these commanders were killed at Amphipolis in 422.[13] Only one other campaign of this period need be noted, that of Delium in 424.

This was a part of an ambitious effort by Athens to secure control of Bœotia, the hostile state on her northwestern boundary, by giving military support to the democratic factions there. The main attack was to be at Delium, on the east coast near the Attic border. Uprisings were planned for the same day at Chæronea on the northern frontier, to be assisted by the Athenian sympathizers of Phocis, and at Syphæ on the Gulf of Corinth, where an Athenian fleet was to arrive at the proper moment. But the plan was too complicated. In the first place, too many people had to know of it, and the Bœotians got warnings; in the second place, the Athenian expeditions were not accurately timed. Demosthenes, at Syphæ, arrived first, and found the place occupied in force. Chæronea also had been warned, troops had been sent there, and the uprising did not take place.

An Athenian fleet under Hippocrates appeared off Delium a little later, landed a force of Athenians and allies, and fortified. The Bœotians, also with allies, advanced to dislodge them; command

---

[12] Thucydides, IV, 8, 31.
[13] Thucydides, IV, 78; V, 6–11.

of the force was in the hands of a council of war of eleven members. Finding that the bulk of the Athenian force had moved off a short distance in the direction of Attica, leaving a garrison in the works, ten of the members were for waiting, to see if the enemy would not abandon the project, but like Miltiades before Marathon, the eleventh, Pagondas, advocated aggressive action and carried his point.[14]

Each side had some 7000 hoplites. The Bœotians had 10,000 light troops also; the Athenians had brought even more than this, but poorly armed and equipped, and after completion of the fortifications most of them had been dismissed. Thebes had always been known as a cavalry country, and the Bœotians were greatly superior in this arm, having 1000 against 300 or 400.

Pagondas formed just behind a hill, which concealed his dispositions and which gave him the opportunity of quickly taking the upper ground and advancing down hill to the attack. The available space being narrow, the right wing, formed of Theban infantry, was made very heavy, 25 ranks deep; the rest of the phalanx was much thinner. Both flanks were protected by ravines, and also by light troops and cavalry farther out. The practicable ground broadened farther down hill, and the Athenians formed a normal phalanx, eight deep. They had no light troops, as noted above; most of the cavalry, instead of remaining on the flanks, was detached and left near the fortifications as a manœuvring force, but Pagondas noted this and neutralized them entirely by a detachment of his own horse.

Both lines advanced, and met midway. The Athenian line being too long for the narrow ground, its flanks were crowded out, but the Bœotian left was crushed in and enveloped, while the heavy Theban phalanx was successful on the other flank. The Bœotian light infantry was hampered by the ground, and apparently indifferently led; at any rate it did nothing. But just at the proper moment Pagondas sent the cavalry from the right, where it was no longer needed, around behind the hill to his left, where it charged the victorious Athenian right. The Athenian army was broken, and suffered heavy loss in the pursuit by cavalry and light infantry. A garrison was left in Delium, but the main force returned home by sea.

[14] Thucydides, IV, 76–96.

The truce of Nicias in 421 brought no real peace, but some vestiges of it remained for eight years. The whole period was one of small fighting and manœuvring for advantage, alliances being constantly rearranged.

THE SICILIAN EXPEDITION

The only operation calling for detailed description is the great Sicilian expedition, into which Athens was led by the rash counsel of Alcibiades, and against the judgment of Nicias, who was associated with him in the command. Athens had long coveted this rich island, which sent so much grain to the Peloponnesus, and now pretexts were found in some of the local disturbances for intervention, and for an attack upon the great Dorian city of Syracuse, founded as a colony of Corinth.

There had already been some effort to reach out in that direction —Athenian colonies planted in Italy, and small expeditions dispatched. The great one sailed in 415, the largest and best equipped ever fitted out in Greece. It counted at first over 5000 hoplites, with a great number of light troops, not to mention the crews of its 136 war vessels and numerous auxiliary ships. On account of difficulties of transport, the original cavalry force was negligible, but was increased later. In all, before the end of the operation, something like 50,000 men were sent over.[15]

The weakest point was supply. Only thirty supply ships, properly speaking, accompanied the troops, although a great number of merchant vessels went along on private account, seeking the army trade. Even before reaching Sicily, difficulties were encountered, for dependence was placed upon local purchases, and the Italian cities refused to open their markets.

Lamachus, the third in the council of command, urged immediate attack; but Nicias, always half-hearted in this undertaking, delayed, and lost any opportunity he might have had of taking Syracuse unprepared. Alcibiades meanwhile was recalled under charges preferred at home, and promptly went over to Sparta; on his advice an able Spartan general, Gylippus, was sent a little later to direct the Syracusan operations.

When the Athenians finally did approach Syracuse, they established an intrenched camp and enticed the defenders out to

[15] Thucydides, VI, 43; Breasted, 206–207; Gauldrée-Boilleau, 66.

fight in the open. A point of some tactical interest may be noted; the Athenians adopted a novel formation, using two lines. The second line phalanx was charged not only with protecting the trains, but also with the duties of a reserve, to be used when and where needed. The Syracusans formed a phalanx of double depth, sixteen deep; but the formation was hardly complete when the Athenians attacked, and they had to move, half in disorder, to meet them. The Athenians were successful all along the line; but the strong Syracusan cavalry accomplished an unusual feat—checked an infantry pursuit and enabled the army to make good its retreat. The approach of winter, and the difficulties of supply, prevented the Athenians from pressing their advantage; they drew off, and went into winter quarters.[16]

The operations then passed into a siege, which was little better than a blockade. The Athenians were strongly reinforced, but the arrival of Gylippus gave more energy to the defence. At last the Athenian fleet, venturing into narrow waters where its superior seamanship and manœuvring ability could not be made to count, was decisively defeated. In spite of the energy of Demosthenes, who commanded the Athenian reinforcements, fortune on land also favoured Syracuse. Demosthenes and others of the council now urged the necessity of raising the siege and withdrawing—if not to Athens, at least to some distance, where time and space would be available for collecting supplies. But Nicias was undecided, hoped vaguely that things would improve, and delayed. The Syracusans finally succeeded in shutting up the Athenian fleet in its harbour. The land army had no longer a choice—it had to retire; and the fleet, its chief reliance for transport and supply, was gone.

The dead, wounded and sick were abandoned. Trains hardly existed, and servants and auxiliaries deserted. Nothing could be taken except what each man could carry for himself. Demosthenes commanded the rear guard; constantly harassed, he still tried to maintain order and cover the march, but finally was brought to bay and forced to surrender. The main body was cut to pieces, scattered in every direction. Nicias and Demosthenes were assassinated, after surrendering. The prisoners were treated with great severity, and most of them soon died of wounds and disease.[17]

[16] Thucydides, VI, 64–71.   [17] Thucydides, VII, 75–87.

Sparta, meanwhile, seeing things going so badly for Athens, and being advised by Alcibiades, had seized and fortified Decelea, almost within sight of Athens, keeping her in a' state of siege. Agriculture ceased, and the city was absolutely dependent upon imported grain. Sparta recognized Persian sovereignty over the cities of Asia Minor and the islands belonging to the Delian League, and made an alliance with the Persian satraps of Asia Minor.

Alcibiades, whatever his character, had ability, and Athens now dropped all her charges against him, recalled him, and elected him general. He won some successes at sea, and re-established control of the Ægean, but lost favour again after slight reverses, and had to go into exile. The main battle fleet was surprised and captured by the Spartan Lysander at Ægospotami, in the Dardanelles, and the Athenian empire was annihilated (404 B. C.).

One battle of the earlier confused fighting should be mentioned for its tactical interest, as an unusual case of manœuvre on the battlefield—the first battle of Mantinea, in 418, Spartans and several allied groups under the Spartan king Agis, against a mixed force of Argives and Mantineans with a few Athenians.[18]

The Spartans were taken somewhat by surprise, but thanks to their thorough organization got quickly into order, each captain forming his own company on his own judgment, the king simply directing the whole. As Thucydides says, in a Spartan army every officer was a "commander of commanders." Both lines advanced, the Argives rapidly and impetuously, the Spartans, according to their custom, slowly and to the sound of field music. Each phalanx drifted to the right, and Agis, seeing his left about to be enveloped, sent orders for it to extend. This it succeeded in doing, but a gap opened in the centre. This result Agis had foreseen, and had ordered two companies from the extreme right to fill it. The captains refused to leave their post of honour there, saying that they would be charged with cowardice at home if they did so. The enemy penetrated the gap, and routed the left wing. In the meantime, however, the Spartan right was victorious. Agis had attempted a manœuvre which was ahead of his times; but fortune favoured him, and he held the field at the end of the day.

[18] Thucydides, V, 66–73; Breasted, 207–209.

THE SPARTAN EMPIRE

A Spartan empire now grew up on the ruins of the Athenian. Sparta ruled with a heavy hand, establishing oligarchies backed by Spartan military force in all the dependent cities. It was not many years before serious rebellions began; but meanwhile, in the short period of Spartan peace, the numberless professional officers and soldiers created by the Peloponnesian War sought employment abroad, in Egypt, Asia Minor, Persia—wherever mercenaries were wanted. They thus gained greater and more varied military experience, perfected their organization, and began to make a serious study of the art of war.

XENOPHON

Xenophon is the highest type of these soldiers of fortune, a man of broad and liberal education, distinguished alike as a field commander and as a military student and writer. His own account of the experience of the Greek mercenaries, of whom he was one, who served under the younger Cyrus in his revolt against his brother the Persian king Artaxerxes in 401 B. C., indicates well the military development of the time.[19]

The long march up illustrates the supply system. While Cyrus took a train of reserve supplies, for emergency only, he depended upon local purchases. Markets were sought everywhere, in which the troops could purchase their own supplies. Mention is often made in the narrative of the *agoranome*, or commissary of markets, an administrative officer of the army who was responsible for the organization and operation of these markets. The matter was simpler than it would be nowadays, for grain was the staple of the ration, meat and wine if they could be had. The normal allowance was about a quart of grain per man per day.[20]

The great battle that decided the fate of the revolt was at Cunaxa, a little town in Babylonia, on the Euphrates. We know little of the battle at large, but Xenophon gives enough description of the Greek part in it to show us that they had developed considerable skill in manœuvre.

The Greeks held the right of the line, with their flank on the river. Their charge was successful, but the Persians on their

[19] Xenophon, Anabasis, *passim*.　　　　[20] Gauldrée-Boilleau, 201.

left were beaten, and Cyrus was killed. The royalist cavalry charged the Greek peltasts, who covered the left of the phalanx, but these light troops opened out, let them through, and closed again, showing a skill that draws a word of praise from Xenophon. The king had chariots, armed with scythes, which he used as tanks, not as cavalry, sending them forward with wide intervals ahead of his infantry to break the enemy's line. They were entirely ineffective; the charioteers were killed and the horses ran away. Some reached the Greek line, which opened and let them pass. Only one man was struck by a chariot, and he was not materially injured.

Popular legend has much to say of the "Persian chariots," and we shall meet them again, but we have seen in Chapter II that they were not a characteristic of the Persian system. Xenophon himself may be responsible for some of the legends, for he often mentions them in his Cyropædia, but that work is not, and was not intended to be, history.

The threatening position of the enemy, on flank and rear of the phalanx, led the Greeks to undertake a change of front to the rear, on the right as a pivot, so as to bring their backs to the river. The Persians did not venture an attack, and the manœuvre was not carried out, but merely to undertake it in the face of the enemy implies a high degree of discipline and perfection of drill.

After the battle, the five leaders of the "free companies" among the Greeks organized themselves into the familiar council of command, under the presidency of the Spartan Clearchus. Xenophon's pen picture of this *condottiere* is most interesting.

Fifty years old at this time, he had spent his life in war, serving Sparta as long as he could, then turning to Cyrus for employment. He preferred war to peace, and spent his money upon it as others upon pleasures. Bold and self-reliant, he always sought independent command, and was hard to handle as a subordinate. Loving danger, he led his troops in attack, night or day; he was prudent, and fertile in expedients; possessed in high degree the art of command; watched carefully over supply; tolerated not the slightest sign of insubordination, and punished severely, often so severely that he repented afterward, but on the principle that an undisciplined man is no man and that a soldier should fear his commander more than the enemy. With it all, he was recognized as just. Soldiers sought his command in active operations, but avoided it in peace.

Under the leadership of this man, negotiations were opened for safe conduct of the Greeks back home. The five leaders were treacherously taken and assassinated. Xenophon had heretofore been a free lance, without specific assignment, but serving apparently as a sort of aide to Proxenus, one of the five. He now came to the front with judicious suggestions, was chosen as successor to his former chief, and by common consent was accorded the leadership that Clearchus had held.

The Ten Thousand were apparently at the mercy of the king; but he realized that their destruction was a serious undertaking, and preferred to leave it to the inhabitants of the wild regions through which they would have to pass. The conduct of their march—122 marching days and over 1700 miles to Cotyora on the Black Sea, eight months on the road—is told very modestly and in matter-of-fact language, but reads like a romance. To lighten the column, they burned all the wagons and all the tents, cut all communications, and lived on the country. The route chosen was up the Tigris and into the mountains of the Carduchi, or Kurds, who harassed the column by incessant skirmishing after it had shaken off the Persians.

A curious modern reminiscence of this fighting is found in our own history. European tactics of the 18th Century were rigid; like the phalanx, the heavy infantry line of battle was better suited to pitched battle in the open than to minor tactical operations. The need for light infantry was felt, especially in the American colonial wars, and experiments were made in its organization. One such light infantry force was set up by Wolfe at Louisburg in 1758. An acquaintance remarking one day that its manœuvre reminded him of Xenophon's description of the Carduchi, Wolfe replied: "You are right; I had it thence, but our friends are astonished at what I have shown them because they have read nothing." [21]

Under this daily pressure the marching formations of the Greeks became more flexible, and they grew expert in flank and rear guard tactics, using counter-attacks with peltasts and archers supported

[21] Wright, Life of Wolfe, 442.

by heavy infantry. Presumably they were already more or less familiar with such work—Brasidas, for example, had shown skill in it in Illyria and Macedon—but this was the first expedition demanding it on such a scale. The roads were unknown, and guides had to be secured by capture and held by intimidation. Maintenance of discipline and cohesion in the force itself required the most skilful mingling of diplomacy and decision, for all authority rested upon the consent of the governed. Crossing Armenia, they reached the divide, between the headwaters of the Euphrates and the Black Sea; and here it was that Xenophon, marching with the rear guard, heard shouting and confusion from the front, increasing so greatly that he feared something serious had occurred. But hastening forward, he found that the shouts were cries of rejoicing—"The sea, the sea!"

They still encountered resistance, but in a few days reached Trebizond; then Cotyora, where they secured ships; then moved westward along the coast, both by land and by water, and finally Xenophon and most of the rest took service with a Spartan force operating against the local Persian satraps.

Even on the march along the coast they often had to fight their way. In an engagement at Calpe, near the Bosporus, they had to deal not only with the local inhabitants but with the troops sent by the Persian satrap Pharnabazus. In this battle Xenophon used a true reserve, somewhat as Demosthenes had done at Olpæ, posting three parties of 200 hoplites each, thirty or forty yards in rear of his flanks and centre.

In the mountains of Colchis, just above Trebizond, Xenophon devised an even more striking innovation in the tactics of heavy infantry. The natives held the crest of a ridge; the phalanx in its close formation could not cross the broken ground to reach them. He therefore formed a line of companies—eighty of them, each about a hundred men—each in column, and at intervals so as to extend both his flanks beyond those of the enemy. Each company was ordered to advance by the most practicable route, disregarding exact interval and keeping only approximate line. A battalion of light infantry, 600 strong, covered each flank, and another battalion moved in front of the centre to act as skirmishers. This formation would not have worked against a Greek army in open country, but fitted perfectly the conditions for which it was devised. Perhaps some of our highly modern attack formations are not so highly modern after all.

When Xenophon finally returned to Greece he found himself more in sympathy with Sparta than with his native Athens, and served at Coronea and elsewhere under the Spartan king Agesilaus, who became one of his heroes. In the intervals of his military service, and after his retirement, he devoted himself to literature—sometimes philosophical, following in the footsteps of his old teacher Socrates; sometimes political, but above all military. He is perhaps the first, certainly the first conspicuous, writer of military history and of strictly military text-books, whose work has come down to us.

THE RISE AND FALL OF THEBES

In 394 a formidable rebellion against Sparta broke out, and Agesilaus was recalled from his wars with the Persian satraps to put it down. Before his arrival a battle was fought at Corinth, a typical phalanx battle, in which both left wings were defeated, but the Spartan right kept its cohesion, refused to become involved in pursuit, and cut up the enemy's right, disordered by its own success. At Coronea in Bœotia the Thebans and their allies blocked Agesilaus' way, and the same kind of battle ensued; but this time both victorious right wings kept their cohesion and turned against each other. Agesilaus finally held the field, but the Thebans fought their way through and retreated in good order. Xenophon characterizes this battle as the hardest fought in his experience.[22]

This period shows us the development of the peltast, from a semi-barbarian or irregular force into a well-organized arm. The great representative of this development is Iphicrates the Athenian. He gave his peltasts light protective armour and a larger shield, longer javelins and swords, and perfected their discipline and drill, preserving their mobility and fire power with the javelin, at the same time giving them enough cohesion and defensive power so that they no longer feared to encounter hoplites. This development was possible only under a mercenary system, with professional soldiers; the old citizen soldier could fight in phalanx, but the new peltast required long and careful training. In this

[22] Xenophon, Hellenica, IV, 2; Plutarch, Agesilaus; Delbrück, I, 121–122.

work, the commander acquired the rare distinction of seeing his name become a common noun; for the soldiers gave the name "iphicratides" to the stout leggings that he introduced into their equipment, and perhaps came to use the word with as little thought of its origin as our mountain artillerymen feel when they speak of the "Rice frames" on their aparejos.

With this force he cut up a detached *mora* of Spartan hoplites under the walls of Corinth. He gained other similar successes against heavy infantry when he could take them at any kind of disadvantage; but Agesilaus demonstrated, in a later engagement, that peltasts were not yet hoplites, and could not stand against them in equal battle.[23]

This development of the peltast as a distinct arm intermediate between the hoplite and the irregular light troops is strikingly similar to that of modern light infantry in the latter part of the 18th Century—a movement which was so strongly influenced by the American wars. Iphicrates, then, may stand as a prototype of Wolfe, the Howes, and their great successor Sir John Moore.

Sparta held her own through the next few years, but was unable to keep up two wars at once, and had to make peace with Persia in 387, on very disadvantageous terms, yielding all the Greek cities of Asia Minor. But Thebes was not satisfied, and continued the war, under the leadership of Epaminondas.

The genius of this leader profoundly changed the nature of phalangial tactics, substituting an oblique for the parallel order of battle, and deliberately utilizing the natural drift of the lines to the right. A forerunner of this plan we have noted at Olpæ. The idea was to concentrate heavily on the left, and push this flank ahead so as to beat the enemy's formidable right; then, when this fight was well developed, to advance one's own right against the enemy's left.

The decisive battle was in 371, at Leuctra, not far from Platæa in southern Bœotia. Epaminondas put his best Theban troops on the left, not on the right, and formed them, not in a heavy line, but in a very deep column of attack, fifty ranks. His centre and right, in ordinary formation, were held back. The two forces being somewhere near equal, between 6000 and 10,000 hoplites—

[23] Plutarch, Agesilaus; Delbrück, I, 117, 119.

the Spartans the stronger, probably—the Theban line was much shorter, but the flank was covered by cavalry, and probably also by difficult ground. The Spartan right was broken by the Theban charge, and the king Cleombrotus killed. The rest of the Spartan line gave way on the mere approach of the Theban centre and right. The army was entirely routed, with terrific loss. The prestige of Sparta vanished almost at a breath, and Thebes succeeded her as the leading power of Greece.

For nearly ten years she held this position, growing in power, and ravaging Spartan territory at will. Sparta herself was saved chiefly by the skill and prudence of Agesilaus. Thebes also constructed a navy, and challenged Athens at sea. But again her domination roused opposition, and in 369 several strong Peloponnesian states joined Sparta. Each side put a great force in the field, probably between 20,000 and 30,000. The second battle of Mantinea was another Leuctra, the heavy Theban column cutting through the Spartan line "like a trireme," as Xenophon says. The Bœotian cavalry was reinforced for its duty of covering the flank by light infantry, mounting with the troopers or holding to their horses for rapid movements ; this combination would have been impossible for a charge boot to boot, but might serve "as foragers," and no ancient cavalry could charge with full weight as in later times, for lack of stirrups. Another new feature at Mantinea was protection of the refused right by small detached echelons.[24]

Epaminondas was killed in this battle, and Thebes had no one to take his place. Her power declined, but Sparta was too much weakened to resume the leadership. Greece was open for a new conqueror; and Macedon produced him.

But before turning to him, it will be interesting to see what Xenophon thinks of the qualities necessary for a general.[25] The tactics of the phalanx were simple; knowledge of them might be taken for granted. Administrative ability and care for supply were of greater importance. Coupled with this, there were demanded the qualities of leadership—simplicity and uprightness of life, calmness, good temper, justice, paternal firmness, intimate knowledge of subordinates. The general must always study the military situation and foresee the next move; "during the night

[24] Delbrück, I, 130–135. [25] Gauldrée-Boilleau, 433–440.

he must meditate what is to be done in the morning; during the day, what is to be done at night." He must be "hard-working, painstaking, patient, cool-headed; he must be at once indulgent and severe, frank and reserved, quick to act and cautious, liberal and avaricious."

CHAPTER V

MACEDON

(370–180 B. C.)

MACEDON, while not strictly Greek, was closely related. We have seen in Chapter IV how she had been a Persian tributary, but a dissatisfied one, with Greek tendencies. Later, the Persian power receding, we have seen how Macedon allied herself, first with one and then with another of the warring Greek states.

The government was a simple monarchy, but the authority of the king apparently did not reach far or stand firm. About the time of the battle of Leuctra, when Thebes was establishing her leadership in Greece, the situation was especially chaotic. The king Amyntas died in 370 B. C., and the succession was disputed. Thessaly became involved; and Pelopidas, the Theban general, intervened in an attempt to quiet matters. As one of his steps to that end, he took hostages for good conduct, and sent them to Thebes; among these was Philip, a younger son of Amyntas.[1]

Philip resided at Thebes for several years, where he received a Greek education and had an opportunity to study the Theban military system. Shortly after his return to Macedon, taking advantage of more local disturbances, he seized the throne, being then between 20 and 25 years old.

His kingdom was an agricultural country, with few towns and little wealth, but with wealthy neighbours. Most of the people could not afford expensive military equipment, and the sparse population did not lend itself well to the highly centralized phalanx organization. The business of war, therefore, fell chiefly to the nobility, who served as cavalry. Reference is occasionally found to Macedonian hoplites, but the infantry was generally an auxiliary arm only, equipped at best as peltasts, with little organization or training. This primitive system Philip now set himself to perfect

[1] Plutarch, Pelopidas; Breasted, 225.

75

and to use in consolidating his power and extending it to the richer surrounding country.[2]

Employing Greek mercenaries, and using them both as combat troops and as models, he began his wars and the organization of his new army at the same time. His first battles were with his western and southern neighbours in Illyria and Thessaly, and were won chiefly through his superior cavalry. The combination of the national cavalry spirit with the principles, if not the precise form, of Theban infantry tactics, led to an improved system of combined tactics.

The cavalry remained, if not the principal arm, at least the equal partner of the heavy infantry. It had nothing to learn from the Greeks, being already superior, but Philip developed it by perfecting its organization and training, giving it better cohesion and discipline than any previous mounted force had had. Paintings and mosaics, as well as written descriptions, give us a good idea of its equipment and method of fighting. The men were armoured, and carried small shields; the armament consisted of spears and short swords. The spear was a long javelin, fit either for throwing or for personal combat in the mêlée; it was light enough to hold free in the hand, and did not have to be held in rest or under the arm, like a lance.

The heavy infantry was organized on the Greek model, but was not an imitation. The formation was similar to the Theban—a very deep and very dense phalanx. The lance or sarissa was much longer than anything heretofore used—some accounts say as much as 24 feet; at any rate, the lances of the fifth rank reached beyond the men in the first. Armour was much the same as that of the Greek hoplite, but since the long lance required both hands, the shield was smaller and designed to be fastened to the upper left arm. With armament and formation like this, the phalanx was slower and more cumbersome than the Theban column of attack. The usual proportion of peltasts and archers was maintained as auxiliary to it.

The improvement in the cavalry made it possible to apply the ideas of Epaminondas in a freer form. The Theban cavalry could not deliver the decisive blow; the Macedonian could. Philip was

<hr />

[2] Thucydides, IV, 124; Delbrück, I, 139–148; Breasted, 228; Smith, art. "Exercitus."

not forced to use a rigid "sealed pattern" of battle, making the main attack with his left. He could now revert—unconsciously, without doubt—to the old Persian practice of an attack with infantry in front and cavalry on the flank, but now his infantry attack was as strong as the Theban, seeking an actual decision by shock. It was a secondary attack, but in the modern sense— an attack that sought to become principal, and went as far as its strength would carry it. If the cavalry attack was generally the decisive one, it was only because it was stronger and quicker. The infantry never stopped and admitted itself to be a mere holding force.

Philip gained his results largely through close attention to details. Having now a truly regular army, he had a stronger discipline than was possible to the Greeks, and was able to demand more of his troops. He cut down the noncombatant force greatly, dispensing with the personal attendants and *cargadores* to whom the Greek horseman or hoplite was accustomed, and requiring the soldier to carry all his own equipment and rations. In this heavy equipment he practised long marches—thirty miles and over.[3] While our ancient authority does not say so, we must of course take this to mean only an occasional special effort, but even so it shows that the troops were kept hard, and that there was assiduous drill and good road discipline.

Philip eagerly seized also upon the new art of siege warfare, recently introduced in Greece through Syracuse as noted in Chapter IV, and conducted two important sieges, at Perinthus and Byzantium, using heavy siege engines.

The rise of Philip's power, extending itself rapidly into both Thrace and Thessaly, on the one hand brought him into conflict with Persia, and on the other caused great concern in Greece. In Athens especially it became the great political issue. One party, led by Demosthenes, looked upon him as a semi-barbarian and a menace to the liberties of Greece. The other, led by Isocrates, welcomed him as a strong leader of a kindred race, who could broaden the provincialism of the Greek cities, realize the ideals of Panhellenism, and destroy Persia. The war party won, and the issue with Philip was fought out in 338 at Chæronea, in northern Bœotia, by a league of Athens, Thebes and some minor powers.

[3] Frontinus, IV, 1–6; Polyænus, IV, 2–10.

Of this battle we have no entirely satisfactory accounts. It seems, however, that the king held back one wing, drawing the Athenians on too far for safety; meanwhile the other wing, under his young son Alexander, defeated the Bœotians. The refused wing then came into action against the Athenians, disordered by their advance, and completed the victory.[4]

Philip was now recognized as a Greek, and as general-in-chief of the Greeks against Persia. Only Sparta held aloof. He began preliminary operations in Asia Minor, but was assassinated in the year 336, Alexander succeeding him. But, if he could not complete his ambitious plans, he could at least, like a greater Frederick William of Prussia, turn over to a greater Frederick a perfected military machine with which to do it.

Alexander's alterations in his army were made gradually, as his experience in war broadened. One of his earliest was the introduction of a new class of infantry, intermediate between Philip's heavy troops, with their long lances and deep, dense formation, and the light infantry. These were the *hypaspists*— "big shield" men, perhaps one might say, as distinguished from the *peltasts*, or "little shield" men. They formed a phalanx, and were used in the line of battle; in fact they were much the same as the regular Greek hoplites.[5] They seem, however, to have been freer in manœuvre, and are sometimes classed as peltasts; perhaps they may be regarded as the legitimate development of the peltasts of Iphicrates. This corps served well as a connecting link between the infantry and cavalry attacks.

A very peculiar formation is mentioned, as having been introduced after the conquest of Persia. The text of the passage is not quite clear, but has been taken to mean that the phalanx was formed sixteen deep, twelve interior ranks being made up of Persian archers and javelin men, with a thin fringe front and rear of Macedonian heavy spearmen. The theory of this must have been to combine in one unit the power of both fire and shock, but in this form it could hardly have been successful. Probably we must look upon this as a theoretical proposition, like others of the same nature in the Cyropædia. It is not unlikely that experiments may have been made, but there is no record anywhere of

[4] Polyænus, IV, 2, 2-7; Delbrück, I, 147; Breasted, 225.
[5] Smith, art. "Exercitus"; Delbrück, I, 144.

the appearance of this phalanx on the battlefield, either under Alexander or under any of his successors.

Similarly, there came to be a distinction between Philip's old original heavy cavalry force, and a new corps, the lancers. These were apparently less heavily armed, and were used in reconnaissance and similar work; but the fact that they were given, not a javelin, but a shorter form of the infantry *sarissa*, longer than Philip's cavalry pike, indicates that they were trained for shock action. Mounted archers and javelin men are found among the auxiliary troops, perhaps adopted from the Persians.

Siege warfare came to be a matter of course under Alexander, who constantly had to deal with fortified cities. He could not stop for the slow process of blockade, so used every variety of engineering works and heavy siege engines. His use of artillery was not limited to sieges—he employed missile engines even in the field, in situations where mobility was of minor importance, as at the crossing of rivers. Instances of this are found in his Illyrian campaign of 335, and at the crossing of the Jaxartes, north of Samarcand, in 328.

Alexander had been immediately recognized by Greece as the successor of Philip, not only as king of Macedon but as commander-in-chief of the Greeks. No sooner, then, had he returned from the Illyrian campaign mentioned above, than he placed a regent in charge of the government of Macedon and Greece, and organized an expeditionary force for Asia. Macedon alone could furnish few troops, but the king now had at his disposal numerous auxiliaries from Thrace and the Balkans, and hoplite contingents from Greece. These latter troops, so closely resembling his own, were readily incorporated in his army and placed under Macedonian officers. We no longer hear, as in the Greek wars, of the contingent of Athens, of Thebes, etc., but of the phalanx of Perdiccas, of Amyntas, or of other Macedonian chiefs, and all the battle descriptions mention independent movements by them. Each such phalanx, that is to say, was treated as a separate tactical unit, giving the army at once stability and flexibility. These corps gradually came to be marked by a difference in uniform, each having its distinctive shield. Thus, we read of corps known as the silver shields, the white shields, the bronze shields.

Having provided such troops as he considered necessary to his regent as home guards, he crossed the Hellespont by ships in 334, with some 30,000 infantry and 5000 cavalry. He himself visited Troy, dramatically offered sacrifices to the Trojan Pallas, hung up his arms in her temple, and assumed those fabled to be of Achilles. Rejoining the army, he moved forward, covering his front with a screen of cavalry, both light and heavy.[6]

THE GRANICUS (334 B. C.)

The Persian satraps of the region concentrated what troops they could, but remained inferior in infantry, although probably superior in cavalry. As usual, the Greek writers differ widely on Persian numbers, and their estimates are rarely of much value.[7] The infantry of the satraps seems to have been made up entirely of Greek mercenaries, for they are expressly named, while no mention is anywhere made of the Persian foot archers. The representative of these troops in the council, evidently trusting little in the Persian cavalry, advocated a retirement, devastating the country in passing so as to prevent or at least delay pursuit; but the satrap of Phrygia announced angrily that he "would not permit the burning of a single house in the country where he commanded," so the decision was to give battle.

The feeling of inferiority seems, however, to have pervaded the army, and so a purely defensive position was selected, behind a natural obstacle, the Granicus River—a small stream flowing into the Sea of Marmora, apparently fordable everywhere, but with high slippery banks. This was a most unusual attitude for an ancient army. All the dispositions that we have studied hitherto have been planned with the idea of an offensive sooner or later, and no position has been seen which would hamper such an offensive. An army won or lost in the open field; the loser abandoned the theatre, or sought refuge in a fortress.

According to the Greek accounts of the battle, the Persian cavalry held the river bank, and all the Greek mercenary infantry was put in a second line. Why this strange formation was adopted is not known, and probably was not known to the writers themselves. It may be that the loyalty of these troops was suspected and that they were not trusted to fight against Greeks.

[6] Arrian, I, Ch. 1, 3, 4; IV, Ch. 1; VII, Ch. 6. See Plate 1.
[7] Arrian, I, Ch. 4; Delbrück, I, 151.

Alexander's cavalry seems to have given him timely information, for as he approached the Granicus he formed "double" line of battle—that is, forming each phalanx sixteen ranks deep. His independent cavalry now became a local reconnoitring force, and 500 lancers and light infantry were sent up to it as a support, taking the place of the heavy cavalry that had hitherto acted as such. The heavy infantry line was covered on the right by all the regular cavalry, with the archers and light infantry; on the left, by the Thessalian, Thracian and other auxiliary cavalry.

Alexander himself took post on the right, and designated an officer to command the left. This officer strongly advised against attack, pointing out the difficulties of the crossing, and the probability that the enemy would withdraw during the night. But Alexander overruled him, saying that he would be ashamed to let a rivulet stop him, after crossing the Hellespont.

The attack was led by the light cavalry of the advance, doubtless acting as ground scouts, followed by a squadron of heavy cavalry supported by infantry. Behind this, Alexander moved his line up by echelon from the right. The leading infantry phalanx was unable to force its way up out of the stream bed under archery and javelin fire from the Persian cavalry, and suffered considerable loss, but the heavy cavalry of the right wing gained the higher ground of the bank, and a hand-to-hand fight began, in which the Macedonians had the advantage through their armament and training. The Persian centre was pierced, and both flanks pushed aside.

The Macedonian infantry now made good its crossing, and both cavalry and infantry moved against the Greek mercenaries. The reports seem to imply that these were too much frightened either to fight or to run, and that they were cut down at will; but this does not at all agree with what we know of Greeks, even of Ionian colonial Greeks, who were always held in a certain contempt by their kinsmen in Europe. Their position was hopeless at best, with a phalanx in front and good cavalry on both flanks. In any case, they did nothing and were either killed or captured.

ISSUS (333 B. C.)

Alexander then overran western Asia Minor, meeting but little resistance except at Halicarnassus, where he had to conduct a long and difficult siege. He then concentrated at Gordium, in Phrygia, for a campaign against Syria; for the Persian fleet was constantly threatening his communications across the Dardanelles, he could not meet it at sea, and so proposed to control the coasts. The famous incident of the "Gordian knot" occurred here, a prophecy having promised the sovereignty of Asia to him who could unlash the yoke from the pole of the ancient royal chariot.

Leaving here in 333, he crossed the Taurus Mountains by the pass known as the Cilician Gates, reached the sea at Tarsus, moved around the head of the Gulf of Issus, and started down along the narrow strip of its eastern coast, between the mountains and the sea. His force is not accurately known, but probably it was about the same as at the Granicus. While he had suffered losses there, and had had to leave detachments behind, still, according to Callisthenes, the King's old schoolmate, who was with him, he had received about 6000 reinforcements from home.[8] Callisthenes is very careless with his figures, but we may accept the general fact of the arrival.

Darius, thoroughly alarmed by now, had collected a large force, and was in the plain to the east, just beyond the mountains. Amyntas, a renegade Macedonian general, urged him to stay there, pointing out that Alexander could not disregard him, but would have to fight to maintain his communications, and that numbers would count for more in the open plain than on the narrow coast strip. Darius, however, became impatient, and moved across the mountains. He very probably expected to get in front of Alexander, but actually did come out ten or twelve miles behind him at Issus. Had he not moved, Amyntas' prediction would probably have been fulfilled, for Alexander was then at the entrance of the Beilan Pass, by which he apparently intended to enter the Syrian plain. It is of course possible that Darius actually intended to strike in behind Alexander, but such a plan would imply very accurate knowledge of positions, close calculation, and swift decision and movement. The details of reconnaissance activity on either side are not known. Alexander certainly did send infantry as well as cavalry to the passes leading into Syria, before attempting his march along the coast; but we have no report of their operations, nor of any counter-measures taken by Darius. The

[8] Arrian, I, Ch. 5; Polybius, XII, 19. See Plate 4.

march must have been screened to some extent at least; on the other hand, Darius' movement was a surprise, and the news was not believed until a reconnaissance by water had confirmed it.

But, whether by accident or design, Darius was in Alexander's rear and had cut his line of retreat, while keeping open his own, back through the mountains. This was not as serious as it would be now, for there were no "communications," properly speaking, but it was serious enough. Alexander put the best face upon it that he could, and played up strongly, for his own troops, the idea that Darius had made a bad mistake in leaving the plain. He realized, nevertheless, that he had to fight at once, and at a disadvantage, so went about it carefully and methodically.[9] Just behind him was a defile, the Syrian Gates, and it would have been awkward to be cut off there. Sending cavalry to reconnoitre, he moved his whole army back to the defile without delay, and occupied it about midnight.

The eyewitnesses of the ensuing operations, who left written accounts, were Ptolemy, the general, afterward king of Egypt; Aristobulus, the historian; and Callisthenes, above mentioned. Of these, only Ptolemy was a soldier, and the other two, as civilians, were probably not on the battlefield and got their descriptions of the fighting second-hand. None of their writings have come to us except in fragments; but Arrian, himself a soldier, used Ptolemy and Aristobulus, while Polybius, another soldier, used Callisthenes. Both treat their authorities in a highly intelligent and modern fashion. Arrian says in his preface that he has accepted statements on which his two authorities agree, and suspected those where they differ. Polybius' critical analysis of Callisthenes' account is quite in the modern vein, and is well worth reading even now as an excellent example of internal criticism.[10]

Darius had made no effort to seize the Syrian Gates, but had remained at Issus. Learning that Alexander had turned back, he took position behind a little stream, the Pinarus—another purely defensive position with a natural obstacle in front. There was little room to deploy, for the space between mountains and sea was only about 3000 yards. The contemporary accounts exaggerate the Persian numbers so enormously that their own

[9] Arrian, II, Ch. 3–5; Delbrück, I, 154.   [10] Polybius, XII, 17–22.

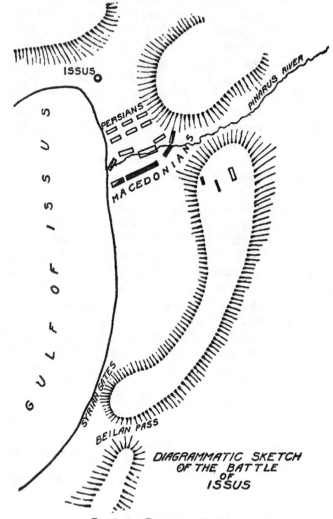

PLATE 4.—BATTLE OF ISSUS.

details of formations become impossible, but disregarding their figures we get a fair agreement on the rest.

Darius sent his cavalry and light infantry forward across the Pinarus to cover his deployment, and posted his infantry, putting his Greek mercenary hoplites in front and supporting them with Persian troops in Greek hoplite equipment. At some points he palisaded the banks of the stream. On the heights to his left he posted infantry, presumably light, well in front, to threaten the flank of an approaching army. These dispositions completed, he recalled the cavalry and posted most of it on the right of the infantry, on the seashore, where the ground was flat, sending a smaller part to cover the left. The formation was extraordinarily deep, and many troops were present who could not be used.

Alexander deployed as soon as he passed the Gates, and advanced in a line of columns, covering the whole coast strip. As he approached, he formed line of battle, his heavy infantry in six or seven distinct commands. The cavalry followed, and as soon as space would permit came up on the flanks, most of it on the right. The whole front was covered by light infantry as skirmishers, with a few light cavalry patrols. The depth of the phalanx is variously given, from eight to thirty-two, but a little calculation will show that if the strength was anything like that at the Granicus it must have been very deep.

A detachment of light troops drove Darius' flanking force up into the hills, and a small party of cavalry was left to keep them there. Alexander's own light troops then extended into the hills, and worked around the left of the hostile phalanx. His line of battle advanced very slowly, preserving its alignment, until within bowshot, say a hundred yards or a little more; then Alexander, with the heavy cavalry of the right, forced a crossing, and with the help of the light troops on the flank drove back the weak Persian cavalry there. The right of the heavy infantry tried to keep touch with the cavalry, but in crossing the stream a gap opened in the phalanx. Darius' Greek mercenaries penetrated it, and came near breaking through, but the right swung in, closed the gap again, and began to roll up the Persian line.

The Persian cavalry on the seashore tried to do the corresponding thing; but Alexander's left had been refused, and by the time the Persians had crossed the stream and begun their attack their left flank had already been defeated. They lost their confidence, and fell back. The Persian line crumbled, and the fragments made for the mountain passes, pursued by cavalry.

Darius himself escaped, and assembled the remnant of his force again behind the Euphrates. His family was captured; and the contemporary writers tell, apparently with some surprise, of the distinguished consideration shown them by the victor.[11] Alexander now took possession, quite at his leisure, of Syria. This he had to do before advancing farther, to deprive the Persian fleet of its bases. At only two places did he meet serious opposition—at Tyre and Gaza, where he had to open formal and elaborate sieges. Darius sought peace, offering to give up all territory west of the Euphrates. This proposition being considered in council, Parmenio, one of Philip's old officers and Alexander's most trusted general, said, "If I were Alexander, I should accept." "And so should I, if I were Parmenio," replied Alexander, and rejected the overtures.

The siege of Tyre is one of the most famous in ancient history. The Tyrians abandoned the old city on the mainland, and concentrated their defence in the new city, on an island half a mile from shore. Alexander constructed a mole giving access to the island, collected ships from newly captured Asiatic cities to blockade the Tyrian fleet, and brought siege engines to bear upon the walls, both from the mole and from floating platforms. The defence was no less active than the attack; the Tyrians set fire to the siege works, not only using fireboats but throwing firepots from their ballistæ, made sorties with their ships, and opposed counterworks to every new construction. But at last the Macedonians opened a breach on the sea front, gained a footing on the walls, and captured the citadel. The city fell, after holding out for seven months.

Evidently feeling that there would be no danger from Darius for the coming year, and his force being too small to divide, Alexander continued on to Egypt, which readily yielded to him. The enemy no longer had a seaport and there could be no hostile fleet in his rear. Returning to Syria, and collecting the reinforcements that had come out from home in the meantime, he moved again against Persia in 331.

[11] Arrian, II, Ch. 6.

ARBELA [12] (B. C. 331)

Crossing the Euphrates in the early summer, he moved through Mesopotamia at leisure, meeting only small reconnoitring parties. No hostile army having yet been located, he kept well to the north to get out of the plains and into cooler weather, and selected his route so as to find supplies. His force is given as 40,000 infantry and 7000 cavalry. Prisoners having reported that Darius was on the Tigris, and meant to hold that line, he moved to meet him, but crossed the river without opposition and turned down the left bank. The coincidence of an eclipse of the moon has made it possible to date the crossing with certainty, as September 20, 331.

Larger parties of the enemy began to appear, and finally the main army was located on the plain of Gaugamela, near the ruins of Nineveh and seventy miles northwest of the town of Arbela. Prisoners told the most fantastic stories of its numbers—contingents from all Asia, a million infantry, forty thousand cavalry, two hundred chariots, fifteen elephants. What Alexander thought he has not told us—certainly he did not hesitate to attack; but evidently these stories found credence in the army.

According to Aristobulus, the whole Persian order of battle was found later. It shows an infantry line of many provincial contingents, backed by a second, covered by cavalry on each flank. The centre was composed of what little Greek infantry still remained to Darius, and here he himself, with the cavalry of his guard, took post according to the Persian custom. The whole front was covered by a line of chariots at wide intervals; the elephants are not mentioned except in a summary of "captured material."

There are strong indications that Darius had tried to replace his losses in Greek mercenaries by arming and training Persians as hoplites. If so, it was with little success, for the Greeks are mentioned as the only troops that were fit to meet the Macedonian phalanx. All the rest of the infantry, then, must have been archers and light troops. Their line would naturally have been thin and long, which would have contributed to the tendency to exaggerate their numbers. Perhaps calculating that this would be the case,

[12] Arrian, III, Ch. 4–5; Delbrück, I, 172, 177.

Alexander made no effort to extend his front correspondingly, but rather contracted it. As usual, he himself took the right, Parmenio the left. On the right was the heavy cavalry, then the heavy infantry, finally the lighter cavalry. Light infantry covered the front. Now appear the novel features of the formation; envelopment had been foreseen and prepared for.

A second line of heavy infantry followed as a true reserve, with orders to be ready either to face about to meet an attack in rear, or to extend the line in either direction. More than this, troops in several columns were placed in echelon outside and behind both flanks of the front line, infantry closer in, cavalry farther out, to meet an envelopment offensively.

Darius stood fast, and Alexander moved to the attack, his right directed upon the enemy's centre. He made some movement toward the right, but just how is not quite clear. Possibly only the natural drift of the phalanx is meant; possibly an actual extension of the line. A change of direction of the whole phalanx seems out of the question. The cavalry of the Persian left swung in to envelop, but was met by the troops placed in echelon for that purpose, and repulsed after a hard fight.

The chariots now advanced, but were met by the skirmishers, the charioteers killed, and the horses stampeded. They were almost as ineffective as those of Artaxerxes had been at Cunaxa.

The Persian line advancing, Alexander charged with his cavalry and the right of his infantry, and broke the centre, Darius and his guard taking flight. In this movement, a gap opened in the centre of the phalanx, and Persian cavalry broke through, passing even beyond the second line. But they now forgot the battle in the excitement of plundering Alexander's camp; the second line changed front by a counter-march, and drove them out with heavy loss.

Meanwhile a movement to envelop the Macedonian left had been more successful. The flank guard had not been able to check it entirely, and it reached the main line. Parmenio held his ground and sent for support. It was this check to the left that opened the gap in the line, through which the Persian cavalry penetrated·

We find here an illustration of the flexibility given to the whole army through the solidity and independence of each subordinate unit—a quality foreign to earlier armies, and thoroughly developed only under Alexander. For Simias, commanding the left unit of Alexander's own wing, saw Parmenio's difficulties, or perhaps learned of them through his messenger. This gave him a genuine tactical decision to make; should he carry out his existing orders, continue the advance and leave Parmenio's wing to take care of itself, or should he join Parmenio? The gap was bound to open in any case; should he take it on his left or on his right? Acting on his own estimate of the situation and his own independent judgment, he joined that wing which seemed to need him most. Evidently his judgment was correct, for the right was successful without him. With him, Parmenio held out; whether he could have done so without him we cannot tell. But there is no hint anywhere that Simias was ever called to account for acting on his own initiative, and stopping his advance.

When Parmenio's message reached Alexander, he was about to take up the pursuit of the beaten troops in his own front, but at once abandoned it, and turned his cavalry to the left. His arrival was delayed, however, for on the way he cut the path of the Persian and Indian cavalry driven out from his camp. This party, although in disorder, fought desperately to cut its way through, but very few succeeded.

When he finally was free to go on, he found that Parmenio had repulsed the flank attack without his assistance, so returned at once to the pursuit and continued it until dark. After a short rest, he started again at midnight, and pushed as far as Arbela. By this time the Persians were utterly dispersed. Darius himself had passed through the town on horseback, without stopping, abandoning his war chest, his chariot, and even his armour.

This pursuit is notable, as perhaps the first instance of relentless pressure of a defeated enemy to the limit of the endurance of man and horse, hopelessly scattering his army in its own home country. Alexander lost more horses from exhaustion in the pursuit than he did in the battle itself.

Darius fled into Media, with a small force under his cousin Bessus. Alexander marched first to Babylon, which opened its gates to him, and before winter set in had occupied Susa and Persepolis. In the spring he started in pursuit of Darius; but Bessus and his associates turned against the king, and, toward midsummer, when the pursuit became too close, they murdered him, somewhere in the region of Teheran. Bessus proclaimed himself king, and tried to organize new resistance in Bactria, his own satrapy, but was finally betrayed to Alexander by his own followers.

The three or four years following Arbela make an intensely fascinating story—ceaseless activity, civil and military, consolidation of the whole Persian empire under the new rule, expeditions into the limitless regions of the trans-Caspian, establishment of a luxurious semi-Oriental court, conspiracies and their ruthless repression. It was this period chiefly that turned Alexander into a mythological character hundreds of years later, both in Europe and Asia, and placed his name everywhere on the map of the eastern world, from Alexandria in Egypt to Alexandreschata in Turkestan, from Scanderoon in Syria to Kandahar in Afghanistan. The many campaigns and sieges are full of incidents of military interest, such as the use of field artillery to cover the crossing of the Jaxartes, above noted. New problems must have arisen almost daily, and were solved with great energy and skill. But material for their technical discussion is scanty, and only one other campaign will be touched upon, the invasion of India.

INDIA (327–324 B. C.)

Starting from Bactria in the spring of 327 B. c.,[13] he seems to have made a detour southward, and to have come around by way of Kandahar to Kabul. During this march he sent a deputation to the Indian princes beyond the Indus, demanding submission. The nearer ones, those between the Indus and the Jhelum, complied, but not those beyond the latter river, then known to the Greeks as the Hydaspes.

In the region of Kabul, Alexander divided his forces. Most of the heavy infantry and half the heavy cavalry, under Hephæstion and Perdiccas, moved straight down the Kabul valley to the Indus; the Indian princes accompanied this column, which met but little opposition. Alexander himself, with the rest of the army, took a longer route through the rough hill country north of the Kabul River, and had to fight his way through. In a part of this expedition he moved ahead with the cavalry, leaving the infantry to follow as best it could; as a support for the cavalry

[13] Arrian, IV, Ch. 8–10; V, Ch. 2–6; Plutarch, Alexander; Delbrück, I, 184.

he took only a battalion, eight hundred men, of infantry, mounting them behind troopers. The episode most strongly "played up" was the capture of Aornus, a fortress situated on a high precipitous rock, which, legend said, Hercules had tried in vain to take. The army was again concentrated in the spring of 326, near the mouth of the Kabul River, where Hephæstion, with the assistance of the subjugated Indian princes, had built a floating bridge over the Indus.

Crossing into the Punjab, he moved across the territory of the friendly princes, and reached the principal town of the section, Taxila, in the vicinity of the present Rawal Pindi. Here he learned that an army was assembling to oppose the crossing of the Hydaspes, under Porus, the principal chieftain of that region. He therefore sent back for the boats that he had used on the Indus. These were separated into two or three sections each, and brought overland, a hundred miles, to the camp which he established on the Hydaspes.

Porus was in fact found on the other bank of the Hydaspes. He placed the bulk of his force opposite Alexander, but did not neglect to place detachments in observation elsewhere. Alexander at once began a series of manœuvres calculated to mystify the enemy. He spread his force out widely, reconnoitring the line of the river for crossing places, but at the same time establishing his various camps with the appearance of permanence, and collecting large quantities of supplies. He sought thus to give the impression that he meant to wait for the winter season, which is the time of low water for the rivers of the Punjab.

At the same time, however, he habituated the enemy to the sight of constant activity in his camps. Preparations were made, more or less unconcealed, for crossing, and parties often started out, day or night, with that apparent intention. These feints were directed upon various points; some were carried almost to the point of embarkation, others ended in nothing but noise. Finally Porus came to pay little attention to anything that Alexander did.

When this effect appeared to have been gained, the serious work began. A place was selected, fifteen or twenty miles above the main camp, where a high point commanded the opposite bank, and a wooded island lay in midstream. Alexander left Craterus with a strong force in the main camp; his orders were not to force a crossing, but to move only if Porus withdrew the bulk of his force.   Other detachments were placed along the river bank, up toward the selected crossing, to make demonstrations and actually to cross after a footing had been gained on the opposite bank.

Alexander himself led the troops assigned for the first crossing. Selecting a dark and stormy night, he moved by a route well back from the river, got into position and had the boats and rafts ready by daylight.   The storm ceased at about the same time.

The surprise was complete, and the whole force, 5000 cavalry and 6000 infantry, reached the island undetected.   Indian mounted scouts discovered the movement only when the boats began to push off from the island for the opposite shore.   Ptolemy, by the way, who was one of Arrian's two principal authorities for his narrative, embarked in Alexander's own party, possibly even in the same boat.

But Alexander had made one mistake.   Instead of one island, there were two, and after effecting his second landing he found himself still cut off from the shore by a channel, narrow but deep. Some time was lost in finding a ford, and at the best place to be discovered the water was shoulder-deep.   This gave Porus time to send troops to the spot and a force estimated by Ptolemy at 2000 cavalry and 120 chariots was met on the bank.

The chariots proved useless, for the ground was soft from the night's heavy rain; and the superior Macedonian cavalry quickly succeeded in forcing the crossing.   The whole force then moved down the left bank of the river, the cavalry pushing rapidly ahead and the infantry following more slowly.

Porus had left a strong detachment opposite the Macedonian camp, and marched to meet Alexander with a force estimated by Arrian (liberally, no doubt) at 30,000 infantry, 4000 cavalry, 300 chariots and 200 elephants.   Other Greek estimates vary widely, and all are apparently little better than guesses.   It seems safe only to assert that Alexander was much the weaker, numerically, in infantry, but distinctly superior in cavalry; that in quality his troops were very decidedly the better; and that Porus had a hundred or more elephants, and at least as many chariots.   The chariots would seem to have carried archers, and to have been used somewhat as cavalry. The elephants, tactically, were "tanks"—carrying several archers each, fighting with the infantry, and intended to break the hostile lines.

Upon establishing contact, Porus assumed a defensive attitude. The framework of his formation was a line of elephants at 100-feet intervals, backed by a line of infantry so close up that it actually pushed forward into the intervals. The infantry armament is not known; it formed a sort of a phalanx, but was evidently looked upon as inferior in quality, fit only to protect the intervals in the line of elephants and exploit any success that they might have. The cavalry covered the flanks, and chariots were disposed in front.

Alexander's cavalry skirmished along the whole front, and drew off to the flanks as the infantry began to arrive. The plan of attack was for Alexander, with the cavalry of the right, to move first, envelop the flank, and draw the Indian cavalry upon himself; next for Cœnus, with the cavalry of the left, to strike for the enemy's rear; and finally for the infantry to charge in front. This plan was carried out, and was successful. The chariots gave no trouble; the Indian cavalry, outnumbered, fought hard but was ridden down.

The elephants proved the most serious problem. Even though the Macedonians had been in contact with the Indians for nearly a year, and had become more or less familiar with elephants, it was still hard to get horses to face them. To penetrate the intervals was hazardous, on account of the close support of the Indian infantry. The fight, then, was long and hard, but finally most of the "crews" of the elephants were picked off by archers; and the uncontrolled animals, in the press of the close fighting, became nervous and broke into the ranks of the Indian infantry. The Macedonians gradually gained the upper hand; and the detachments that had been left on the right bank of the river now began to come into action and completed the victory.

Porus, fighting on an elephant, kept up the resistance until it was beyond all hope; then dismounted and surrendered to Alexander in person. Alexander received him graciously, and asked him how he expected to be treated, to which he replied, "as a king." Alexander accepted his submission, and established him as governor, not only of his own former kingdom but of all the adjacent territory beyond the Hydaspes.

Plutarch quotes a letter, apparently by Alexander himself, which checks in a general way with the account of Ptolemy and Aristobulus, used by Arrian. It implies, however, that everything happened just as Alexander had intended, even in the crossing of the river. Critics have shown themselves a trifle suspicious, and tend to regard this letter as a Napoleonic bulletin or a headquarters communiqué, in which, as we know, things always happen *planmässig*.

The conquest was pushed a little farther, but the army was growing weary. At the Hyphasis River—the modern Beas, the next stream northwest of the Sutlej—the discontent came so near mutiny that Alexander was forced to yield, and consent to return westward.

A flotilla was built on the Hydaspes, and the army moved, both by land and by water, to explore the lower Indus. Craterus, with part of the army, was detached to return by way of Kandahar and the Helmund valley. Then, the Indus delta having been explored, a new fleet was built and sent, under command of Nearchus, around through the Arabian Sea and the Persian Gulf to the mouth of the Tigris. Alexander, with the main body, started overland in the autumn of 325. It was his intention to follow the coast and keep more or less in touch with Nearchus; but the nature of the country compelled him to turn inland, and march for some 150 miles through the deserts of Gedrosia, or Mekran. While he had been warned what to expect here, no ancient supply system, not even that of an Alexander, was equal to the task of providing rations, and above all water, for the army and its many camp followers. The sufferings were intense, and the losses heavy. Finally a more hospitable country was reached, communication with the fleet reopened, and the march proceeded with less hardships. Near the entrance of the Persian Gulf a junction with Craterus was effected, and the army went on to Babylon, reaching there early in 324.

Here Alexander planned new and ambitious voyages of exploration; but in the summer of 323 he died, at the age of 33 years, and his empire was divided.

His conquests mark the highest point ever attained, perhaps the highest attainable, by an army of the truly ancient type—that type in which the general combines in himself the functions of all grades. Alexander himself conceived his plans of campaign; himself directed his intelligence service, and himself dictated the organization and the war plan. There being no established supply system, with a responsible head, decisions in this field also had to be his. He was the tactical leader of his own army, laying out the marches and planning the battles. He was his own siege engineer. Finally, in action, he placed himself at the head of the leading column, and fought hand to hand.

In strategy and logistics he accomplished more than any general who had preceded him. It is little to say that he surpassed all the Greeks; for the Greek wars were strictly limited in space and time. Their greatest foreign expedition was that of Nicias to Sicily, and that broke down. Their longest overland march was that of Xenophon and the Ten Thousand, an unencumbered force, seeking no conquest but only its own safety. But Alexander's campaigns far surpassed in extent and duration those of the earlier Asiatic military monarchies, even those of Persia. Nevertheless, on the battlefield, he remained the dashing colonel of cavalry.

Such a combination of functions is inconceivable now, even for a Napoleon. The explanation doubtless lies, not alone in Alexander's superior genius and wonderful energy, but also in the "state of the art" in his time. Commercial and political relations, the foundations of strategy, were simple. So also were organization and tactics, even after all Alexander's improvements. The demands upon a supply system were small, from our point of view. Marches were planned largely with reference to the local supply situation, as appears in his march across Mesopotamia to the battlefield of Gaugamela; the rudimentary organization sufficed in good country, and in bad country like Gedrosia it broke down. On the battlefield, the use of reserves was not yet understood, although suggestions of it are found, as at Gaugamela. The general's work was ended at the first shock; he could no longer influence the course of the action, and was free to fight in the ranks. Alexander's battles show better and quicker use of troops to meet emergencies than earlier ones, but this seems to have been due to better internal organization, giving facility of manœuvre, and to the training of subordinate leaders to independent decision—the indirect rather than the direct influence of the general.

This last mentioned development, freedom of manœuvre by minor units, was a great forward step in tactics, although only a first step on the road to be travelled. Progress had been slight in the combination of fire and shock, but, as has been noted, the need seems to have been felt.

Great changes were becoming inevitable—the co-ordination of fire and shock; the development of an organization permitting freedom of manœuvre by subordinate units; the continuous control of the course of battle, which this would make possible to a general; his consequent withdrawal from the front line to headquarters; the organization of these headquarters, with tactical and administrative staffs, relieving the general of details. But conditions were not now favourable for these forward steps in the Greek world; how Rome took them we shall see in the next chapter.

THE "SUCCESSORS"

The military history of the next century and a half is the history of wars among the states which took their rise in the division of the empire—particularly Macedon, under the dynasty of Antigonus; Egypt, under that of Ptolemy; and Syria and the East, under that of Seleucus. These wars are too complicated to follow here, although numerous interesting battles and campaigns are to be found.

In a general way it may be said that the period was characterized by a refinement, coupled with a gradual degeneracy, of Alexander's system.[14] All sorts of heterogeneous elements became incorporated into the armies, especially in the Asiatic kingdoms, but the nucleus remained the Macedonian phalanx. Influenced by political centralization, this nucleus became purely professional, and increased according to the ability of the kings to maintain it, sometimes approaching or even exceeding a hundred thousand men. In the regular establishments, heavy infantry was favoured rather than the more expensive cavalry, so that the proportion of the latter arm diminished. The theory and practice as to combined

[14] Delbrück, I, 200.

tactics, however, did not essentially change. Siegecraft, already highly esteemed by Alexander, grew more technical and refined; Demetrius II of Macedon took his surname of Poliorcetes, "the taker of cities," from his skill in the art. Elephants were much in fashion, but success with them was precarious; sometimes they won a sweeping victory, sometimes caused a disaster. Theoretical study of the military art was carried to an extent before unknown. But the centre of the military world was about to shift westward again. A new power had arisen; it was challenging Carthage, the western outpost of the old Asiatic civilization, and the Greek cities of the western Mediterranean.. This new power was about to come in conflict with the Alexandrian military system, whose ultimate form can best be illustrated in the discussion, from the Roman side, of the battles of the Epirote invasion of Italy. Meanwhile, this chapter may well close with a brief mention of Philopœmen, the great general of the Achæan League, known as the "last of the Greeks." [15]

Born at Megalopolis in Arcadia, he early showed military tastes. His first war experience was in the conflicts between Macedon and Sparta, about 220 B. C. He next served in Crete, which was torn by minor civil wars, apparently for the sole purpose of acquiring military experience. Returning home in 210, he was appointed to the command of the Achæan cavalry, and soon after became, general of the Achæan League, a federation including most of the states of the northern Peloponnesus.

His first battle as general was at Mantinea, in 207, against Machanidas, tyrant of Sparta. An account of this battle is given by Polybius, who enjoyed the personal acquaintance of Philopœmen, being the son of his friend and successor Lycortas, and nephew and namesake of one of his chief lieutenants. Comparison of this account with that of Plutarch enables us to make out at least the striking and novel features, if not to be certain of all the details. [16]

Philopœmen was at Mantinea in Arcadia, Machanidas at Tegea, ten or twelve miles to the south. Expecting an attack, Philopœmen moved out in three columns—on the right his Achæan heavy cavalry, in the centre his regular infantry, and on the left his

---

[15] Plutarch, Philopœmen.
[16] Polybius, XI, 11; Delbrück, I, 213. See Plate 5.

allied and mercenary troops, horse and foot, mostly light armed. About a mile south of the town he deployed behind a ravine, small and dry, but constituting a slight tactical obstacle. The noticeable feature of the formation was in the heavy infantry of the centre; it was in two lines of small phalanxes with intervals,

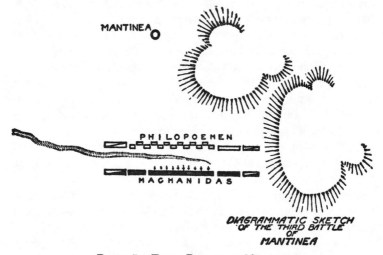

PLATE 5.—THIRD BATTLE OF MANTINEA.

the second line covering the intervals of the first—an excellent formation for manœuvre, and one characteristic of the Roman rather than the Greek system.

Machanidas also showed skill and originality in the handling of his troops. Advancing in three columns, his heavy infantry in the centre, light troops and cavalry on the flanks, he directed his centre upon the Achæan right; but at the last moment, presumably when just out of bowshot, each column changed direction to the right, marched its own length, and formed line of battle to the left. This in itself was a good showing; but now came the real innovation in tactics. As the infantry executed this manœuvre, numbers of carts swung clear of the tails of the columns, pushed forward through the closing intervals, and as the infantry deployed dropped a line of small catapults along its front, each with a store of heavy arrows. Alexander, it is true, had used small siege engines as batteries of position to cover river crossings, but here for the first time we see real field artillery, actually manœuvring on the battlefield, and taking position precisely in the manner familiar in the modern world down to the introduction of rifled cannon. If the scheme did not work out very successfully in this, its first application, the fault was in the matériel, not in the idea.

The artillery opened fire, which, if not very effective, at least compelled Philopœmen to take the initiative. He opened the attack with his left, on the level ground at the head of the ravine. This attack presumably had a certain effect in disconcerting the gunners, who must at best have been more or less nervous in their novel position; but if it was intended as the first move in a general advance it failed, for after a hot fight the Spartan light troops completely routed the Achæans of the left and drove them in disorder to the very gates of the city.

But now Machanidas forgot the duties of a general in the more exciting employment of a colonel of cavalry. Instead of swinging forward the right of his phalanx to roll up the enemy, like Alexander at Issus, he went on in the pursuit, and Philopœmen had time to re-form his lines. Skilfully using the manœuvring ability of his open phalanx, he moved his front line rapidly to the left—dangerously thinning his formation, it is true, but extending his left again to and even beyond the Spartan right. At the same time he directed Polybius, uncle of the historian, to collect such light troops as remained on the field, and hold Machanidas in check in case of his return from the pursuit. The Achæans, with their long line, now succeeded in passing the head of the ravine and enveloping the right of the Spartan phalanx, before the Spartans could cross the deeper part of the ravine and break the centre. The part played by the heavy cavalry of the Achæan right does not appear; it seems to have been inactive, a strange thing considering that Philopœmen had just relinquished command of that arm to take up the duties of general. Neither the actual nor the relative strengths of the armies are anywhere given. In the end the Spartans were entirely defeated; Machanidas, returning too late from the pursuit, was cut off and killed in single combat by Philopœmen himself.

This great general never met the Romans in battle. Rome recognized the independence of the Achæan League, and he contented himself with protecting its liberties as best he might by peaceful means. He continued the leader of the Achæans until his death, about 180 B. C. His campaigns will not be described further, since this one battle has well shown the state of the military art in his time. It remains only to say that he was, to the end of his life, distinguished for theoretical study of tactics as much as for their practice in the field. He constantly studied such treatises on tactics as then existed, and devoted himself assiduously to the reading of military history, especially that of Alexander's campaigns.

He may be said to have been the father of the modern applicatory system of tactical instruction; for it was his custom to conduct parties of his friends for a study of the ground in view of an assumed tactical situation, and discuss proposed solutions of problems in marching or combat.[17] These interesting details rest upon the authority of Livy, later copied by Plutarch, both of whom are careless in such points of fact; but whether or not such exercises were invented in the 2d Century B. C., it is at least evident that they had been thought of by the 1st Century, when Livy wrote, and the point as to the antiquity of this method of instruction stands the same.

[17] Livy, XXXV, 28.

CHAPTER VI

ROME: THE KINGDOM AND THE EARLY REPUBLIC

(750–216 B. C.)

THE rise of civilization in the western Mediterranean was as complicated an evolution as that in the eastern, and the two cases are not dissimilar.[1]

We have already seen the westward extension of Semitic civilization to Carthage, whence it spread along the African coast and up into Sicily. The next element is supplied by a migration not unlike the coming of the Hellenes—nomadic Indo-European tribes drifting down from the north into Italy, and there becoming settled as a group of city states which may properly be called Italic.

Legends of all kinds point to another element coming from Asia Minor. It has been noted above (Chapter II) that Lydia claimed connexion with Italy; and the legends upon which the Æneid is founded claim the same thing for Troy. Archæological study in Italy suggests the arrival, about the time of the Trojan War or shortly after, of a seafaring race known to us as the Etruscans. Whence they came is not surely known; but the centre of their power was in Etruria, extending north and east to the Apennines, and ultimately down the west coast even as far as Naples.

Finally there were the Greek colonies, planted in Sicily and southern Italy as early as the 8th Century B. C.—warring among themselves, like the cities of their mother country, but nevertheless bringing Greek civilization into Italy. Here, then, are the elements from which grew the next world empire.

There was a little Italic state occupying a district called Latium, just south of the Tiber River. This was an important region commercially, for the lower river was navigable, an unusual thing for Italy. It attracted both the exploring Greeks and the neighbouring Etruscans, and about the middle of the 8th Century the

[1] Breasted, 256.

101

Etruscans overran the district. The Latin village of Alba Longa sank into insignificance and disappeared; the seat of the new state was at the head of navigation of the Tiber, ten or fifteen miles up, where there was an island in the river, a good ford, and a group of low hills. On one of these, later known as the Palatine, stood a little fortress, which was the nucleus of the new town. The population seems to have been much mixed, as would be natural at such a point. The bulk of it was doubtless the subdued Latin tribe, but other Italic groups were represented also, the whole under Etruscan domination. Students of the Roman constitution point out the influence of the mixture of population upon the governmental institutions of the new state.

THE ROYAL MILITARY SYSTEM

The early history of Rome is legendary, and we are unable to affirm positively anything as to its original military organization. The traditions are so definite, however, and were so firmly believed in later Rome, that the general outline of them is accepted by modern students, and may be sketched briefly as a foundation for discussion.

The old three tribes were apparently three racial stocks. The earliest division of these was into thirty *curiæ;* for military purposes, each curia furnished ten horsemen, presumably the richest men, and one hundred footmen. The three "centuries" of horse and the thirty "centuries" of foot constituted the *legio,* or "gathering" of the clans.[2]

The infantry used a phalanx formation, but was secondary in importance to the cavalry, at whose head the king or general fought. The single combat of the opposing leaders is often spoken of as deciding the battle. The old Latin word for commander was "prætor"—"he who marches at the head."

With the growth of the city, the number of centuries was doubled, making six of horse and sixty of foot. The *curia* still remained, however, as the primary unit of both civil and military administration.

Among the many reforms attributed to Servius Tullius was one very similar to that of Cleisthenes in Athens, when he substituted

[2] Livy, I, 13, 42–44; Plutarch, Romulus; Smith, arts. "Curia," "Tribus," "Exercitus."

a territorial division for the old one based upon descent (Chapter III). Servius created four tribes in place of the old three, giving them local names. To him is attributed also an increase of the military force, and a more thorough organization of it, reflecting an increased importance of the infantry.

His organization did not depend upon the curia, but upon the century. The classification did not consider the tribe primarily, if at all, but was based upon property as determined by a periodical census. The richest served as cavalry, and twelve new equestrian centuries were added to the old six; they were not, however, called upon to bear the entire expense of mounted service, but received an allowance from the public treasury—"mounted pay," so to speak.

THE PHALANX LEGION

The infantry was divided into junior and senior—active and reserve—centuries, according to age. The first property class provided forty active centuries, with full armour, spear and sword; the second and third, each ten centuries, with inferior armour but a larger shield, and otherwise similarly armed; the fourth, ten centuries of unarmoured javelin men; the fifth, fifteen centuries of slingers, field musicians, etc. There were also two centuries of engineers. All other citizens were grouped, nominally, into a single century, not normally to be called upon for military service. The reserve force, made up of older men, was in principle the same in organization and strength, and was intended as a home guard. The formation was still a phalanx, consisting probably of the first three classes, with the best armed in front, the fourth and fifth classes providing the light troops.

This scheme sounds artificial and rigid, and can hardly be accepted as statistically accurate in detail, but doubtless it is correct in general outline. Delbrück, after a study of population densities, concludes that the probable number of citizens capable of bearing arms agrees very closely with the number which it demands.

The century became also the primary civil governmental unit, if not at first, at least under the republic. The *comitia centuriata* was the great popular assembly, voting by centuries according to a somewhat complicated plan which gave the greater influence to the centuries of the higher classes—that is, to those upon whom the greater demand was made in war.

The legion was still one body—the levy of citizens. It began to assume the character of a tactical unit, very probably, at the beginning of the republic. When the last king was expelled, the highest executive power was entrusted, not to one magistrate, but to two, co-ordinate in station. This institution may have been a relic of the plan introduced at the time of the absorption of the Sabines, when the two kings are said to have reigned conjointly; or perhaps it originated simply from a revolutionary reaction against undivided power, and the Sabine legend grew up later. These magistrates were called consuls, or prætors; the latter title was afterward conferred upon a separate magistrate, but traces of its older use remain, as in the word *prætorium* in the sense of a commander's headquarters.

The army of Servius Tullius had, as we have seen, sixty centuries of heavy infantry, with twenty-five centuries of light troops, which included musicians, and as Delbrück deduces from a study of numerous authorities, perhaps also clerks and other similar "special duty" men. If each consul took half, it gave him thirty centuries of legionaries proper, with a share of other troops, theoretically five centuries of javelin men of the fourth property class, and say seven of slingers, etc., of the fifth.[3]

EARLY WARS OF THE REPUBLIC

The traditional date of the establishment of the republic is 509 B. C. The revolution naturally weakened Rome, and for a hundred years or more she was on the defensive. About 400 B. C. she seized Fidenæ, which controlled the next good crossing of the Tiber above her, pushed northward, and took Veii, a strong Etruscan town about twelve miles from the river. This expedition is a sort of military landmark; for the war continued for a number of years, and in order to keep troops continually in the field regular pay had to be given them, as happened in Greece at the time of the Peloponnesian Wars. Meanwhile, Gallic tribes had crossed the Alps, driven the Etruscans out of the Po valley, and gained control of the country down to the Rubicon, the region later known as Cisalpine Gaul. Continuing their incursions, they took

[3] Livy, I, 13; Delbrück, I, 224–231.

VERCELLAE
TURIN
LIGURIA
CIS-ALPINE GAUL
PLACENTIA
APENNINES
RAVENNA
ARIMINUM
ILLYRICUM
METAURUS
ARRETIUM
SENAGALLICA
ANCONA
CORTONA
LAKE TRASIMENE
ETRURIA
PICENUM
CORSICA
TIBER
CORFINIUM
ROME
PRAENESTE
LATIUM
SAMNIUM
NAPLES
CAPUA
APULIA
CANNAE
BRUNDISIUM
CALABRIA
VESUVIUS MT.
TARENTUM
CAMPANIA
GRUMENTUM
METAPONTUM
LUCANIA
HERACLEA
GULF
TARENTUM
SARDINIA
THURII
BRUTTIUM
MESSINA
RHEGIUM
SICILY
NUMIDIA
UTICA
CARTHAGE
AGRIGENTUM
SYRACUSE
TUNIS
MALTA
NARAGGARA
ZAMA
HADRUMETUM
RUSPINA
LEPTIS
THAPSUS

ITALY
AND
CARTHAGE.

PLATE 6.—ITALY AND CARTHAGE.

and burned Rome in 387 B. C., withdrawing only upon payment of heavy tribute; and for fifty years more they continued a menace to central Italy. But, recovering herself, Rome began anew to expand. The Latin cities were again subdued, and finally the Samnites and Etruscans. By the beginning of the 3d century B. C., Rome was in full control from the Rubicon to the Greek sphere of influence in the extreme south.[4]

THE MANIPULAR LEGION

In all these wars we find no accounts of battles clear and reliable enough to be used as illustrations of tactical methods. Certain very material changes in organization, however, can be traced.[5]

The solid phalanx gave place to more flexible formations, perhaps in order to meet the needs of mountain warfare against the Samnites. The class distinctions disappeared, if indeed they ever existed in as complete a form as tradition says. The classification was now according to age, or length of service. Very young men, and perhaps those who were unable to make any contribution whatever to their own equipment, served as light troops, for skirmishing and other secondary purposes. Those fit for the line of battle fell into three categories. The youngest were known as *hastati*, literally "spearmen"; the next, a little older and presumably fully developed and trained soldiers, as *principes* or "leaders"; and the oldest as *triarii* or "third line men."

The normal strength of the legion in fully armed men was still 3000, and it still had its thirty companies; but these were now known as *maniples*, the word referring back to the old custom of using a *handful* or bundle of straw on a pole, as a guidon. The name *century* was still suggested in the titles of the officers, each maniple having a senior and a junior centurion; and a half maniple was often called a century, although no longer containing a hundred men. Each class furnished ten maniples, normally 120 men for the *hastati* and *principes*, sixty for the *triarii*.

The earlier legion was probably formed six deep; this gave a front of 500, and such a mass was hard to manœuvre, as the Greeks well knew. Rome had now solved this problem better

---

[4] Livy, IV, 59; Boak, 33–39. See Plate 6.
[5] Livy, VIII, 8; Polybius, VI, 19; Delbrück, I, 235.

than Greece; for she formed each maniple separately, and arranged them with intervals and distances. The normal depth
seems to have remained for the time six men.

The hastati formed a first line armed with javelin and sword.
The name was now a misnomer, for the *hasta* was a long pike,
not a javelin, and had formerly been the weapon of all legionaries.
How the term came to be applied to one specific class is obscure.
Disregarding this question of name, perhaps we may venture the
conjecture that this youngest class had been skirmishers, and had
only recently become full-fledged legionaries, through a development on the lines of the peltasts of Iphicrates and the hypaspists
of Alexander; for Livy says that at the time of the Latin wars
twenty men in each maniple of hastati were still unarmoured, and
armed with javelins only. Later, all were fully equipped. The
pilum, or javelin, was a very cleverly contrived weapon. It was
so constructed that, upon striking, the long slender iron head bent
or partly broke loose from the wooden shaft. Thus it became
useless to the enemy; at the same time it hung in the shields, and
rendered them also useless.

Close behind this line, and covering the intervals, were the
maniples of principes, whose name becomes comprehensible on
the theory just suggested. These were all fully armoured, armed
with javelin and sword, and evidently constituted the élite of the
legion. Behind them again were the maniples of triarii—steady
veterans, but no longer in full vigour of youth.

The tactics of this legion are nowhere satisfactorily described.
Livy's account comes nearest to doing so, but, as Delbrück points
out, the evolutions there mentioned sound much more like drill
than like actual battle tactics. But it would appear that the battle
was opened by the *velites*, or light infantry, and by the cavalry.
As the heavy infantry neared the enemy, the hastati began the decisive action, throwing their javelins at close range; their armoured
men then instantly closed with the sword, the unarmoured presumably keeping up an overhead fire. The principes followed very
closely, and pushed in by maniples or centuries to close gaps;
this evidently presupposes strong discipline, good drill, and quick
judgment and decision on the part of the centurions.

The triarii constituted a reserve, not in the sense of a force
for independent manœuvre, but rather to give stability to the

line. They became actually engaged only in a close and hard-fought fight. Their arms, therefore, were not the heavy javelins of the forward maniples, but the old long pikes, and each maniple was a little phalanx. Apparently their use was a matter for the general only, and the modern maxim, that he will win who has the last formed reserve, was already in honour. Thus, the legend is [6] that in the decisive battle with the Latins, at the foot of Vesuvius, the Romans were hard pressed. The consul Decius was killed, heading a desperate charge on the left, which partially restored the situation; but on the right the armies were almost at a deadlock, the Latins a trifle the stronger. Both forces had the same organization, and neither had yet put in the triarii. Finally the remaining consul, Manlius Torquatus, who commanded here, collected all available light troops and pushed them into the front line. Their attack in itself can hardly have accomplished much, but doubtless it encouraged the heavy troops already engaged, and increased the activity enough to lead the Latins to send in their last reserve. After these had become thoroughly engaged, but not before, Manlius sent in his triarii and won.

The tactics, then, still somewhat resembled those of a phalanx, but an improved and flexible phalanx with some fire power of its own. The formation was not in successive lines, tactically speaking, but the single line was well organized in depth. Such a formation was made workable only by strong discipline. The Roman appreciated, better than the Greek, the strength of union; he was willing to yield his individual will to the collective good. The Greek was capable of devotion, but the Roman of subordination. The Greek would fight, but he would not work. Demosthenes, we have seen, had the greatest of difficulty to get his force to undertake even so important a task as the fortification of Pylos; a Roman army entrenched every camp, even for a one-night stop. A Roman officer, even a centurion, had actual power to enforce his orders on the spot, which, we have seen, the Greek did not possess. Hence the certainty, uniformity and order of the Roman troop leading, which led Pyrrhus to say, after his first reconnaissance, "these barbarians have nothing barbarous in their dispositions"; and hence also the complete confidence with

[6] Livy, VIII, 9–10.

which the Romans later spoke of the superiority of their own
generals to Alexander.[7]

For this was the legion that first met the Greeks. We are reaching slightly firmer ground historically, and may venture upon
some little description of the operations.

PYRRHUS (280 B. C.)

In southern Italy the Greek colonies, led by Tarentum, were
continually at war with the neighbouring Italic peoples, on the
outer fringe of the Roman sphere of influence. Whenever Tarentum was unable to handle the situation she called for help from
Greece, or from Syracuse, the great Greek power of the west.
Continental Greeks frequently came over, in the latter part of
the 4th century—notably Alexander of Epirus, uncle of Alexander the Great, who fought much in Italy, and was killed there in
331 B. C. The remark is attributed to him, that his nephew had
fought only women, but he had fought men.

Rome was not involved in these wars until 282, when the city
of Thurii, being attacked by Italic neighbours, appealed to her for
help. She promptly responded, with both land and sea forces.
Roman ships having thus entered the Gulf of Tarentum, the
Tarentines felt aggrieved, claiming breach of an agreement; they
sank the Roman ships and drove out the troops. In the ensuing
war, Tarentum needed help, and appealed to Pyrrhus, nephew
of Alexander of Epirus, who now occupied his throne.[8]

Hannibal is said to have ranked Pyrrhus as the first general
of his age and as second only to Alexander the Great. Certainly
he was one of the first, although, as he was perhaps a better soldier
than statesman, his kingdom did not profit permanently by his
wars. He was at this time between thirty and forty years old,
and had been familiar with war from childhood, having been deposed, restored and again deposed by force of arms before he was
eighteen. He had then served his military apprenticeship under
the best of masters, his brother-in-law, Demetrius Poliorcetes of
Macedon. Later, having married a princess of Egypt, he returned
to Epirus with the backing of Ptolemy, and regained his throne,
this time permanently. Still later, he broke with Demetrius,

---

[7] Plutarch, Pyrrhus; Livy, IX, 16–19; Delbrück, I, 247.
[8] Livy, VIII, 3–24 ; Plutarch, Pyrrhus; Delbrück, I, 262; Boak, 39–40.

attacked Macedon, and for a time controlled most of her territory. He was a dashing, generous and very popular prince, and an ardent admirer of Alexander the Great; his army was modelled on the most improved Alexandrian lines. He was also a military writer of high reputation, although none of his works have been preserved.

Having been compelled to relinquish his Macedonian conquests in 286, he was ready for other expeditions, and eagerly assented to the appeals of the Tarentines, which opened to him visions of the conquest of Italy, Sicily, and even Carthage and all the west. He sailed for Italy in 280, with something over 20,000 foot, 3000 horse and 20 elephants. Reaching Tarentum, he very promptly showed that he meant to command, not to reinforce, and by his energy forced the Tarentines to take the war more seriously, and to help themselves as the price of his help.

Rome, although at the same time engaged in other wars, realized the seriousness of this situation, and promptly dispatched an army into Lucania, under the consul Valerius Lævinus. The first contact was at the Siris River, near the town of Heraclea on the Gulf of Tarentum. Plutarch's narrative of this battle is not entirely satisfactory, but is evidently written with care, and after study of earlier accounts, some of which, including the commentaries of Pyrrhus, he names.

It appears that Pyrrhus took a defensive position behind the Siris—a small stream, readily fordable in many places—not making it his line of resistance, but rather using it to hamper the Roman deployment. Of the Italian allies that he counted upon, only the Tarentine contingent was present, and he apparently calculated that his strength would increase more rapidly than that of the Romans. The actual strengths are unknown.

Watching the river bank with cavalry only, he formed his infantry some little distance back. The Roman cavalry made a long turning movement, crossed the river at an unexpected point, and closed rapidly in again. Under cover of the general cavalry action which ensued, the Roman infantry crossed, and moved against the hostile main body. Pyrrhus himself was fighting with the cavalry, and at the same time exercising command over the whole army, which may have been the reason why his infantry did not advance more promptly, before the Romans could rectify their formation. Plutarch takes great pains to explain that owing to his superior genius Pyrrhus could perform both functions at once, which sounds as if his authority, perhaps Pyrrhus himself, felt that there was something to be explained. However that may have been, the crossing was effected, and a hot fight followed, the advantage, if any, being somewhat on the Roman side. The battle was finally decided by the advance of the elephants, which threw the Romans into such confusion that they were readily dispersed by a cavalry charge. This use of elephants is novel; they engaged, not with the infantry, as tanks, but independently, as heavy cavalry.

This account has been questioned, largely because of the lack of co-ordination in Pyrrhus' movements. It certainly does not accord with that general's great reputation, to fight three successive battles—cavalry, infantry, elephants—instead of one battle with all his forces. But the three phases may not have been as separate and distinct as the narratives make them; they may have been planned as parts of one operation, the closing of the trap. If Pyrrhus was misled by the Roman turning movement into accompanying his cavalry too far, a certain lack of co-ordination is readily accounted for; he paid heavily for his error, for while statements of losses differ widely, they agree that the victor suffered almost as heavily as the vanquished. The Roman accounts represent him as expressing the utmost admiration for the Roman soldier; and attribute to him the famous expression, that if he won another such victory he would return to Epirus alone.

In Rome, the accepted view was that while Pyrrhus might have defeated Lævinus, the Epirotes had not defeated the Romans. But while their confidence in the consul was badly shaken, they left him in command, and reinforced him. Pyrrhus marched upon Rome, Lævinus avoiding battle but harassing the columns, and reached Præneste, only twenty miles from the city. Meanwhile the other consul, having successfully finished his campaign in Etruria, had brought his army back to Rome, and Lævinus, stronger than ever, was in rear. Pyrrhus therefore set his priests to work and found that the omens did not favour immediate battle, so returned to Tarentum.

Pyrrhus remained in the west for six years, and had some success against the Carthaginians in Sicily, so that at one time he actually contemplated an expedition into Africa. He met the Romans in at least two more pitched battles, but the accounts of these are even less clear and certain than those of Heraclea. They also seem to have been "Pyrrhic victories"; but in any event they show us nothing new in organization or tactics. He finally returned to Epirus, his expedition a loss both materially and in reputation. One more saying, attributed to him on leaving Sicily, deserves mention here—"O my friends, what a fine field of battle do we leave here for the Romans and Carthaginians!"

THE FIRST PUNIC WAR (265 B. C.)

He was a true prophet, for in ten years more these two peoples were at war. This First Punic War caused little change in the Roman military system, but it greatly broadened her horizon, causing her to develop her sea power and to undertake her first overseas expeditions. And, on the other hand, the Carthaginian land forces were extensively reorganized and improved.

Carthage was a republic, but strongly aristocratic; the dominating group was that of the great commercial families, much like those of mediæval Venice. She controlled the western sea; her military establishment was treated as secondary, and was made up of mercenary troops from all quarters of the Mediterranean, armed and trained in the post-Alexandrian fashion, but inferior in cohesion and discipline.

But Carthage was far from negligible on land, nor was Rome without experience at sea. We have seen the part played by Roman ships in the events leading up to the Pyrrhic wars; and a whole series of treaties, dating from the very beginning of the Roman republic, shows that Carthage, while remaining in close friendship with Rome, had felt it necessary to use all peaceful means to hamper Roman maritime commerce.[9]

Syracuse and Carthage, being close neighbours in Sicily, were always at war or on the verge of it. Shortly before the Pyrrhic wars a band of Italic mercenaries, in the pay of Syracuse, had revolted and seized the city of Messina, on the strait separating the island from Italy, and made it a base for wholesale brigandage. In 265 Hiero of Syracuse undertook to subdue these Mamertines, or Sons of Mars, as they called themselves, and so nearly succeeded that they began to look for help. One faction of them appealed

[9] Polybius, III, 22–29; Boak, 70–72.

to Carthage; seeing a chance to extend her power, she placed a
garrison in the town. Another faction sent to Rome; although
hesitating to give aid to organized robbery, she feared to have
Carthage for so close a neighbour, so sent an expedition of her
own. The Carthaginian garrison withdrew, and the Roman entered; Syracuse and Carthage now joined against Rome.

But Rome strengthened her expeditionary force and soon
frightened Syracuse into coming over to her. In 262 the new allies
attacked and captured Agrigentum, the chief Carthaginian stronghold on the island, which was held by Hannibal, son of Gisco; the
siege operations were long continued, but ended in a decisive battle
in the open against a relieving force commanded by Hanno, which
had gained possession of the Roman base of supplies, the neighbouring town of Erbessus. The chief point of interest in this battle
is the complete success gained by the Romans against elephants.

As usual, these were posted as tanks close in front of the phalanx,
protected by a cloud of skirmishers. The Romans, apparently
with their light troops, attacked the skirmishers so vigorously
that they were driven in confusion among the elephants. These
becoming unruly, in turn brought disorder into the phalanx, which
was then easily defeated. Hannibal, however, profited by the
confusion to effect the escape of his army.[10]

The Romans meanwhile had constructed a battle fleet. Fleet
tactics were unfamiliar to them, but they had enough nautical
experience to be quick learners, and two naval battles cleared the
sea enough to permit them in 256 to send an expedition to Africa
under the consul Regulus.

At first he was completely successful, and Carthage sued for
peace; but the conditions proposed were so severe that in desperation she set to work to reorganize her armies for further resistance.
Command was entrusted to Xanthippus, a Spartan soldier of
fortune. He is sometimes given credit for a complete reorganization of the army, but this is an exaggeration. It is more accurate
to say that he improved the discipline of the troops, inspired them
with confidence in himself, and showed better tactical judgment
and skill than the native commanders who had preceded him.[11]

Polybius here probably follows Philinus, who was a Greek,

---

[10] Polybius, I, 16–19; Boak, 72.
[11] Polybius, I, 14–15, 32–35; Delbrück, I, 267.

writing from a Carthaginian point of view, and who may himself
have taken part in these operations. It may be well to note that
Polybius depends for this period chiefly upon Fabius Pictor for the
Roman side and upon Philinus for the Carthaginian. Fabius was
a mere child at the close of this war, but doubtless got most of
his material at first hand from participants. Both writers are
prejudiced. But Polybius, in his analysis of their writings, shows
that he had formed a very definite estimate of their value; and we
have seen before (Chapter V) how intelligently he uses varying
authorities.

Xanthippus wisely refused to allow himself to become involved
in difficult country, but manœuvred in such a manner as to compel
Regulus to meet him in the plain, where his superior cavalry and
his elephants could be used with full effect. The Romans, having
great respect for the elephants, but having also some experience
in meeting them, used a very deep formation—retaining their
small manipular units, but posting them apparently in more than
the regulation three lines. They also covered their front with
strong skirmish lines. But the superior Carthaginian cavalry made
its way around the flanks, and forced the rear maniples to change
front to meet its attack. Then when the front lines were broken
by the elephants and heavy infantry, nothing was available to
back them up, and the army was cut to pieces, Regulus himself
being captured. The discretion of Xanthippus seems to have
equalled his valour and skill; for he resigned his command and
returned home while his credit was still at its height.

The Roman operations were now restricted to Sicily, where the
Carthaginians were pushed into the extreme western end of the
island. Even then, Hamilcar Barca, who took command in 247,
not only maintained himself, but even harassed the coast of Italy.
At last Rome established an effective blockade on the Sicilian
coast, and Carthage was forced to conclude a most disadvantageous peace in 241.

The Carthaginian mercenaries now mutinied, and seriously
threatened the city until subdued by Hamilcar in 238. Rome took
advantage of this situation to seize Sardinia and Corsica, the remaining fragments of the Carthaginian island empire, and to extort
further indemnities, thus sowing more seed for a new war.[12]

[12] Polybius, I, 32–35; Boak, 74–75.

Rome, having established control over the Greek cities of southern Italy, had inherited their quarrels. The Illyrian tribes of Albania, professional pirates, became so serious an annoyance to them that in 229 Rome had to send out another overseas expedition, this time to the east. It met no serious difficulties, but this move had far-reaching consequences, for it brought Rome into hostility with Macedon, the great power with which the Illyrians claimed alliance. The Illyrian troubles continued intermittently for ten years; at the same time, Rome had to deal with new Gallic incursions. But none of these operations show any noteworthy developments in the art of war.[13]

THE SECOND PUNIC WAR (219 B. C.)

A new war, then, was brewing in the east; but a more dangerous one in the west. For Hamilcar Barca, after putting an end to the mercenary war, had gone into Spain, and laid the foundations of a new Carthaginian empire to replace the lost islands. When he was killed in battle in 229, his son-in-law Hasdrubal succeeded to his command and carried on his work. Under these two great men Spain became almost a separate state, controlled by an army personally devoted to its chiefs, but firmly bound to Carthage through the personal loyalty of these chiefs.

The wealth and strength of this new power alarmed Marseilles and the other Greek cities of that region; and to protect them Rome, their great ally, concluded a treaty with Hasdrubal which established the Ebro as a boundary. But south of the Ebro lay the free city of Saguntum, now Murviedro, or the "ancient walls," which concluded an alliance with Rome; so the nominal boundary did not long suffice to keep the peace.

Hasdrubal was assassinated in 221, and Hannibal, son of Hamilcar, was placed in command. And now it became clear that the whole purpose of the Barca dynasty had been to renew the war with Rome. For Hannibal immediately began to overstep treaty limits; and finally, in 219, took Saguntum by siege, using some local disturbances as a pretext. Rome demanded that these acts be disavowed, and that Hannibal be surrendered to her; Carthage refused, and Rome declared war.

The normal consular army at this time was two Roman legions,

[13] Polybius, II; Delbrück, I, 271–273; Boak, 75–78.

with contingents from the Italian allies equal or superior in numbers. For this year, however, three such armies were raised instead of two. The consul Tiberius Sempronius was to assemble one of them in Sicily, together with the principal battle fleet, and attack Carthage; his force, Roman and allied, was 30,000 infantry, 4000 cavalry and 160 battle-ships. The other consul, Publius Scipio, with an army slightly weaker in its allied contingents, and with 60 battle-ships, was sent to Spain against Hannibal. The third army, about as strong as Scipio's, was assigned to the prætor Manlius for the protection of Cisalpine Gaul, which was still turbulent, and where it was to be expected that Carthaginian agents might attempt to stir up trouble.[14]

Hannibal, fully realizing that Rome, not Carthage, now held command of the sea, planned to reach Italy by land. Expecting, or at least suspecting this, Rome made the operations of Sempronius contingent upon the success of Scipio's.

HANNIBAL'S INVASION OF ITALY (218 B. C.)

Hannibal's troops were greatly superior in quality to those which had fought under Xanthippus, or even under Hamilcar in Africa, although their armament and training seems to have been on the same lines. They were both African and Spanish—the Africans either Carthaginians or close allies, the Spanish formed on the strong nucleus of the regular army of Hamilcar and Hasdrubal. Sending strong garrisons back into Africa, and leaving his brother Hasdrubal in command of large land and naval forces in Spain, Hannibal crossed the Ebro in the spring of 218 B. C., with about 100,000 men and 37 elephants. The country between the Ebro and the Pyrenees was subdued by midsummer, and a garrison of 10,000 men left there. Finding that some of his Spanish troops were showing signs of nervousness at the campaign in prospect, and were beginning to desert in mass, he dismissed 10,000 more. His ineffectives also were left behind; and with 50,000 foot and 9000 horse, all veteran troops, he entered Gaul.

Scipio's departure to meet him was delayed, for the anticipated revolts in Cisalpine Gaul came more quickly and were more serious than had been expected. Manlius, marching to relieve a threatened town, and neglecting ordinary precautions, was attacked

[14] Polybius, III, 9, 40; VI, 26; Livy, XXI, 1, 17; Boak, 78–79.

while involved in mountain passes and badly defeated. One of
Scipio's legions had to be sent to him, and another raised to replace
it. When Scipio finally reached Marseilles he found to his surprise,
that the Carthaginians were already on the Rhone, four days'
march from the coast. For long before he crossed the Ebro,
Hannibal had sent numerous officers and secret agents all along
the Gallic coast, had secured detailed information as to the country and the roads, had gained the friendship of many tribal chiefs,
and had arranged for supplies. Hence his march had been without
serious delay or hardship.

After giving his men a few days' rest, and sending cavalry to
reconnoitre, Scipio moved to attack with his whole force. But
Hannibal, not to be diverted from his main purpose even by the
prospect of a victory over a Roman detachment, had effected
his crossing of the Rhone in spite of opposition by the Gauls,
and had marched on up the left bank. His strength was now
38,000 foot and 8000 horse.

Near the mouth of the Isère he halted, established friendly
relations with the local chiefs, and rested and•refitted his army;
then advanced again, and entered the Alps, by what pass it is
uncertain. The actual crossing took fifteen days; it was opposed
by the Gauls, and rendered difficult by snow—for autumn was now
well advanced, and the weather was cold. It was a serious undertaking; but, as Polybius (who says that he studied the operation
on the ground, with the assistance of eyewitnesses) points out,
it was neither a superhuman effort nor a rash exploit. It was
a triumph simply of skill, good judgment, careful collection of
information, thorough preparation, and energetic execution.
The army reached the Po valley with 20,000 infantry and 6000
cavalry, not including a somewhat indefinite number of Gallic
allies.

The numbers thus far given rest upon the authority of Polybius; Livy agrees, but doubtless he copied them. The losses from
point to point seem extraordinarily heavy, and tend to throw doubt
upon the whole estimate; but Polybius quotes as his authority no
less a personage than Hannibal himself, who, before leaving Italy,
set up bronze tablets containing a summary of his operations.
These tablets Polybius personally studied. Delbrück analyzes
the figures very thoroughly; his not unreasonable conjecture

is that the tablets did not give the strength on the Ebro, but only on the Po, and that Polybius filled in the gaps from other sources.

After a very short rest, Hannibal took Turin, and by fear or favour won over the Turini and most of the other tribes in the upper Po valley.

Scipio's orders had been to assume command in Spain, and to hold Hannibal in check. Hannibal having gotten past him, he could not do both, and he decided that Hannibal's army was his real objective, Spain a secondary consideration. He therefore sent his brother Gnæus on to Spain with most of the force, and himself marched along the coast with a small detachment, collected Manlius' troops, quelled the revolts south of the Po, crossed that river and moved against Hannibal. Each general seems to have been surprised at the rapidity of the movements of the other.[15]

In a cavalry skirmish on the Ticinus, the Romans were badly beaten, and Scipio, himself severely wounded, withdrew to Placentia, on the south bank of the Po. Hannibal followed slowly and cautiously; when he found the bridge destroyed he retraced his steps, crossed on a pontoon bridge two days' march upstream, and came down the south bank. Scipio took position on the Trebia, and waited for reinforcements. Sempronius joined here, having brought his army in forty days, by sea from the western end of Sicily up the Adriatic to Ariminum, thence overland; and he now assumed the active command. The force on each side was about 40,000, Hannibal superior in cavalry and inferior in infantry.

Scipio advised a defensive attitude; but Sempronius had just come from a series of victories. Eager for action when he first arrived, he was made more so by some small successes, and by Hannibal's apparent inaction. Hannibal's intelligence service kept him advised of this situation, and he planned to take advantage of it.

BATTLE OF THE TREBIA (218 B. C.)

One morning in December, before daylight, he sent his light cavalry across the river and began to harass the Roman camp. Sempronius turned out first his cavalry, then his light infantry, and finally his whole force, and pursued the Numidians across

[15] Polybius, III, 33–61; Livy, XXI, 21–38; Delbrück, I, 326–328.

the deep fords, although it was cold and snowing. Hannibal, meanwhile, had prepared for battle at his leisure. His men were warm, dry and well-fed, the Romans cold, wet and hungry.

Although inferior in infantry, Hannibal gave his front an extension equal to the Roman, by placing his elephants on the flanks instead of in front, probably by forming his phalanx with intervals, and partly, perhaps, by thinning his line. Both sides covered their fronts with skirmishers and their flanks with cavalry, and Hannibal posted a small mixed detachment under cover, well out to his front and flank.

As the lines of battle came together the skirmishers withdrew—the Romans, it would seem, back through the intervals, the Carthaginians to the flanks. The heavy infantry became closely engaged, the Roman front line at least holding its own. But the strong Carthaginian cavalry readily pushed aside the Roman, and then, with the light infantry, enveloped both flanks. The elephants were soon stopped, but they assisted in throwing the flanks into confusion. The detachment posted in ambush fell upon the Roman rear, and compelled the triarii to turn against them.

The Roman army was soon completely surrounded and almost destroyed. Only the legionaries of the front line in the centre, a scant ten thousand, cut their way through the weak Carthaginian centre and made their way to Placentia, where the camp guards and many stragglers joined them. Hannibal's loss was small in comparison, but still considerable. It included nearly all his elephants, which suffered more from exposure to the wintry weather than from the fighting.

Hannibal spent the rest of the winter in the Po valley. Scipio retired across the Rubicon into Umbria, Sempronius across the Apennines into Etruria. Their successors as consuls for the next year were Gnæus Servilius and Gaius Flaminius. The outlook was hopeless enough—two consular armies wrecked; but there were some gleams of hope. Things had gone very well on the sea; Malta had been taken, and the friendship of Syracuse confirmed; and Gnæus Scipio, with the remaining army, had pushed the frontier to the Ebro again. Finally, as Polybius says, Rome was never so much to be feared as when she had most reason to fear. The consuls-elect went about reorganization with energy.

At this period, the consuls entered upon their office on March

15th. Servilius relieved Scipio at Ariminum; Flaminius took over the other army at Arretium in Etruria.

Hannibal had had great difficulty during the winter to keep his Gallic allies in hand. The army was quartered among them, and they felt that they were bearing more than their share of the burden. This situation, together with his own natural energy, led him to start at the earliest practicable moment in the spring. Meanwhile, as was his practice, he collected detailed information of the country and the roads, and also as to the characters of his new opponents. His intelligence service was excellent and widespread; later in this year, one of his spies is said to have been discovered in Rome, where he had lived for two years.

Everything considered, it seemed best to strike at Flaminius. This general was naturally rash and impetuous, and these faults just now were doubtless accentuated by exasperation, for he was in high disfavour with the Senate. Furthermore, he had all the passes of the Apennines to watch, and, since he had but recently arrived and the winter was barely over, his dispositions were very incomplete.

Hannibal found that the usually travelled roads led by circuitous lines through the eastern passes of the Apennines; that those through the western passes, although providing a more direct route into Etruria, ran from the mountains into a marshy country, extremely difficult for troops. The eastern roads led directly to Arretium; the western route offered an opportunity to turn that position, and Hannibal selected it, fully realizing what he would have to meet.[16]

TRASIMENE (217 B. C.)

The mountains were crossed without difficulty, but the marsh country meant four days and three nights in mud and water, almost without sleep. The columns were lightened to the utmost; each body of troops had trains to carry its own supplies, but provision was made only for the march itself. The general reasoned that if he got through and won, he could take supplies at will; if he lost, he would need none. The hardships of the march were extreme; Hannibal himself, being unable to give prompt attention to a slight infection of the eyes, lost the sight of one of

[16] Polybius, III, 65–79; Livy, XXI, 54–56; XXII, 2, 33.

them. But the army got through, and surprised Flaminius by its sudden appearance in the Etrurian plain.

The army now moved slowly eastward and southward, collecting such supplies as it needed and destroying everything else. Flaminius wished to strike at once, but his advisers all urged caution. They pointed out that Rome was in no danger for the present, and that it would be taking unnecessary risks to fight before Servilius could join. But when Hannibal had reached Cortona, actually cutting the direct road to Rome, Flaminius could no longer be restrained, and moved out with his whole army.

Hannibal marched on southward, drawing Flaminius after him. At Lake Trasimene there is a narrow defile, between the lake and the mountains, and here Hannibal awaited the enemy. Flaminius having entered the defile without reconnaissance and without suitable dispositions for security, his army was surrounded and annihilated, and himself killed.[17]

Servilius, on learning that Hannibal had crossed the mountains, started to join his colleague. But a force of 4000 cavalry, which he sent ahead, was captured by Carthaginian cavalry, and Servilius, learning of the Trasimene disaster, came no farther. Hannibal did not feel strong enough to attack Rome, but moved over to the Adriatic side and down the east coast, hoping to shake the loyalty of the Italian allies and so break up the Roman power.

FABIUS CUNCTATOR

At Rome, Quintus Fabius was made dictator. Taking over the army of Servilius, and raising additional levies, he adopted the delaying policy that won him the name of Cunctator. Realizing that his raw troops stood little chance against a veteran army with such a leader, he contented himself with harassing the enemy and affording such protection as he could to the country.

This conservative method dissatisfied many of the Romans, both at home and in the field. One of the hottest malcontents was Marcus Minucius, the Master of the Horse, or second in command to the dictator. This title, be it said parenthetically, is interesting for its similarity to the mediæval title of Lieutenant-General of the Cavalry, meaning the second ranking officer of an army. The word *cavalry* disappeared from this latter title

[17] Polybius, III, 84; Livy, XXII, 4-7.

when that arm ceased to be principal; in Rome the word remained after its significance had disappeared.

This Minucius carried his opposition to or even beyond the verge of insubordination. Having gained some considerable, though indecisive, successes, he was appointed a second dictator, with power equal to that of Fabius. With his half of the army—which was now four Roman legions in all, with allied troops about equal in number—he got himself into such serious difficulties that Fabius had to come to his relief; after which he loyally acknowledged his fault and placed himself again under Fabius' command.[18]

But the radical party at Rome was not so easily satisfied. One of the consuls-elect for the year 216 was Æmilius Paulus, an experienced and conservative man; but his colleague, or more properly opponent, as Livy happily puts it, was Terentius Varro, a politician of no birth, breeding or military skill, who was one of the leaders of the opposition to Fabius.

The six months' term of office of the dictator having expired, Servilius and the successor of Flaminius resumed command, and for the time being continued the Fabian policy. The consuls-elect raised new legions and strengthened the old; when they took office in the spring, their combined armies consisted of eight Roman legions, each 5000 strong, with an equal number of allied troops.

CANNÆ (216 B. C.)

Hannibal, thoroughly informed of the dissensions between the consuls, and knowing that two-thirds of the Roman troops were green, tried in every way to entice them into battle. His troops were beginning to chafe under their inaction; supplies were hard to get, and he feared desertions. Varro was more than willing to fight, but Æmilius succeeded in restraining him. Finally Hannibal moved by night down to the region of Cannæ, and gained possession of the Roman depot at that place, as well as of the grain country of southern Apulia, where the harvest was fast approaching.[19]

The consuls followed, and established themselves some six miles from the enemy, who kept carefully in an open plain, where

[18] Polybius, III, 87–104; Livy, XXII, 8–30.
[19] Polybius, III, 106–107; Livy, XXII, 35–43. See Plate 7.

his strong cavalry could be used to the best effect. Æmilius, fully realizing the necessity of battle, wished to manœuvre, and try to draw the fight into more broken country; but since when the two armies were united the two consuls alternated daily in command, Varro took advantage of his day to move closer, and a partial action was fought, amounting to a draw, but claimed by Varro as a victory. The armies were now in too close contact to be withdrawn, and established themselves in entrenched camps, on the Aufidus River.

Absurd as this system of rotation in command may seem to us, it was perfectly natural to a Roman or to a Greek. And when the extent and limitations of the system are fully understood, perhaps it is not quite so absurd after all. Even as late as the 18th Century we find traces of it. At Blenheim, for example, Marlborough and Eugene each held his own command, and they alternated daily in command of the whole force, in camp and on the march. In battle, each had his own wing, but so also did the Roman consuls. Varro, it is true, could use his day of authority to force the hand of his colleague; but in all times, even a subordinate may sometimes be in a position to force the hand of his superior.

Accounts are not definite enough to locate the field with certainty; apparently it was on the right bank of the river, but even this has been doubted. But disregarding these questions, the formations and tactics are clear enough.

Hannibal, although now a little better off for supplies, still felt the need for immediate action, and after a few days began again to seek it. Æmilius, probably feeling that time was now working with him, would not be drawn out, but the next day Varro took the initiative.

Varro adopted a very deep and narrow formation; his maniples seen to have been placed according to regulation, but each one in column rather than in line, and at reduced intervals. This may have been due to the character of his troops—unusually large numbers and inferior training, causing him to revert more or less to the mass tactics of the phalanx, much as Napoleon did with large bodies of recruit soldiers. Both flanks were covered by cavalry. The consuls were all in the line—Æmilius on the right, Varro on the left, those of the previous year in the centre. As usual, there was no thought of manœuvre, simply of the strongest

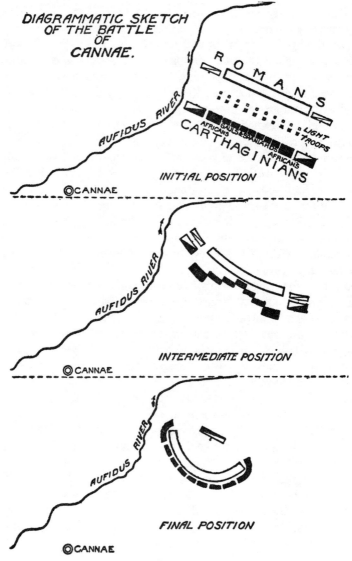

DIAGRAMMATIC SKETCH
OF THE BATTLE
OF
CANNAE.

ROMANS

AUFIDUS RIVER

LIGHT TROOPS

AFRICANS
GAULS & SPANIARDS
AFRICANS
CARTHAGINIANS

INITIAL POSITION

CANNAE

AUFIDUS RIVER

INTERMEDIATE POSITION

CANNAE

AUFIDUS RIVER

FINAL POSITION

CANNAE

PLATE 7.—BATTLE OF CANNÆ

possible push, straight to the front.   Ten thousand men were left in the camps; those engaged were about 70,000 infantry and 6000 cavalry.

Hannibal's dispositions showed the same characteristics as at the Trebia, but now perfected in detail.   As before, he was weak in infantry—40,000 men—and strong in cavalry—10,000.   He used a single line, long and comparatively thin.   His centre was made up of alternate companies of Spanish and Gallic heavy infantry, whose defensive armour was inferior to the Roman; the African infantry, fully armoured, was on both sides, and the cavalry out on the flanks.   Hannibal himself took post in the centre; apparently, like Alexander, he planned the principal moves of the battle beforehand, and after it had once fairly opened was himself free to take part in the fight.   His officers could evidently be trusted to act independently in the spirit of his general plan, and the Romans, as he well knew, were not trained to manoeuvre.

The formation here, in fact, bears great similarity to Alexander's at Arbela; for by the time the combat was well begun the African infantry must have been echeloned well back, ready for either defensive or offensive use.   Whether Hannibal himself gave these echelons the signal to advance, or their commanders acted on their own judgment, does not appear.

The Roman right rested on the river.   The wind blew strongly from the Carthaginian side, throwing dense clouds of dust in the Romans' eyes.

The fronts being screened by the preliminary combats of the light infantry, and doubtless also by the dust, Hannibal held back his Africans, so that his infantry line took the form of a wedge, or crescent convex toward the enemy.   Thus the cavalry became hotly engaged on both flanks, and at the same time the Roman centre struck the Spaniards and Gauls; in front of the Africans, there was quiet.   The Carthaginian cavalry was successful, so the Roman infantry was unable to extend and envelop the enemy.   On the contrary, it crowded inward, making the Roman formation also tend to the wedge shape.

This Roman wedge penetrated irresistibly.   The African infantry closed upon its flanks, while Hannibal's centre was pressed almost to the breaking point.   But now the Carthaginian heavy cavalry closed in behind, forced the triarii to turn, and as at the

Trebia brought the "steam roller" to a stand. The Numidian light cavalry pursued the defeated Roman horse, and prevented it from interfering; and the African infantry, pressing in more formidably than the elephants at the Trebia, prevented even the centre of the legionary front from cutting its way through.

The ancient accounts say that all but 3000 of the Roman infantry were killed. Even if this is taken as an exaggeration, certainly the army was destroyed as such. Æmilius was killed; Varro escaped to report his own disaster.[20]

This astounding success—an inferior army enveloping both flanks of the enemy and winning—has been a favourite study of military men ever since. It is still fresh in our memories how profoundly Schlieffen's studies based upon it influenced German military thought at the beginning of the recent war, and how his disciplines applied his doctrines, as at Tannenberg. It was superb audacity, justifiable only by the character of the two armies and of their commanders. The Romans had had their warning at the Trebia, and had not profited by it. It has been said that for a Cannæ two things are necessary—a Hannibal and a Varro.

[20] Polybius, III, 113–118; Livy, XXII, 44–49; Delbrück, I, 291.

CHAPTER VII

ROME: THE LATER REPUBLIC

(215–60 B. C.)

To both sides, the battle of Cannæ seemed a crushing blow to Rome. Hannibal's officers urged him to march at once upon the city, where the populace seemed given up to mourning and despair. One blow followed upon another. The southern allies began to go over to the Carthaginians; Capua, the second city of Italy, followed; Syracuse finally joined the enemy; Philip of Macedon sent an embassy to Hannibal to discuss an alliance; two legions and a large allied force were destroyed by the Gauls; the commanders in Sicily and Sardinia appealed for assistance.[1] But Hannibal did not let triumph get the better of his judgment. Realizing that he was not yet in a condition to undertake the siege of Rome, he sent detachments among his new allies of the south to consolidate their friendship, placed the bulk of his forces in winter quarters at Capua, and sent his brother Mago to Carthage to ask support.

The popular legend reported by Livy is that the luxury of this winter in Capua ruined Hannibal's men as field soldiers. Considering what they accomplished in the next few years, this may be taken as rhetorical exaggeration. But if he maintained the force he had without serious injury, he got little support from home; the peace party was too strong. Livy puts in the mouth of Hanno, the leader of this party, a most brilliant speech showing their point of view. "'I have cut to pieces the army of the enemy,' says Hannibal; 'send me troops.' What else would he ask if he had been defeated? 'I have taken two camps of the enemy, filled with plunder; send me grain and money.' What else would he ask if his own camp had been taken?" The Carthaginian Senate indeed voted to support Hannibal, and ordered some reinforcements; most of these, however, were to come from Spain, and never were actually sent.

---

[1] Livy, XXIII; Boak, 82–84.

The Roman Senate kept its poise throughout the whole series of disasters, and addressed itself with the utmost energy to restoring the situation. Varro seems to have been sobered by his defeat, collected some 10,000 men from the wreck and reconstituted something resembling an army; the Senate accepted the responsibility, publicly thanked him "for not having despaired of the Republic," and retained him in his command. In Spain the two Scipios—for Publius had joined Gnæus there after recovering from the wounds he had received at the Ticinus—retained the initiative, and made progress south of the Ebro. New armies were raised to face Hannibal. When recruits could not be obtained in sufficient numbers, slaves were armed, as had been done in Greece in the Peloponnesian Wars. Command of the sea was retained, and a fleet was dispatched to Greek waters which prevented Philip from sending troops to Italy. He raided the Roman possessions in Illyria, but Rome concluded alliances with his enemies in Greece, and held him in check.

For the next three or four years Rome avoided decisive battles. Her numerous fortified towns hampered Hannibal, and her field force, skilfully and cautiously led, harassed his detachments, prevented him from taking the towns, and interfered with his supply. Support from Africa was scanty, on account of the war in Spain and local troubles at home; and the Romans in spite of some serious defeats, were constantly growing stronger. The great body of her Italian allies, perhaps from some half unconscious racial instinct, would have nothing to do with the aliens whose religion and whose whole culture were so fundamentally different from their own; and their loyalty saved Rome and Europe.

In 212 the proconsul Marcellus took Syracuse after a long siege, in which the mathematician Archimedes distinguished himself as an engineer of the defence. In the same year the Romans laid siege to Capua; Hannibal made a great raid even to the gates of Rome in an effort to raise the siege, but failed, and the city fell.

This success gave Rome a little relief, but very little. For now Hasdrubal, Hannibal's brother, strongly reinforced, took the offensive in Spain and pushed the Romans back north of the Ebro; both the Scipios were killed in battle. The war in Spain being looked upon as an integral part of that in Italy, a new army was sent thither under Publius Scipio, son of the elder Publius, later known as the great Africanus. Although only twenty-four years old, he had already seen service, having been with his father in the campaign of 218. As he was too young to have held the higher magistracies, a special law was passed giving him the command with the rank of proconsul—the first instance in Roman history of such command having been conferred upon a citizen without official status.

SCIPIO IN SPAIN (209 B. C.)

Scipio, like Hannibal, was most painstaking in his ·collection of information as to the enemy's country, his troops, and the character of his commanders. At the time of his arrival, the principal forces of the Carthaginians had been withdrawn from the Ebro front, and were engaged in several local operations in different parts of the peninsula. New Carthage, now Cartagena, was their principal port and base; it was well garrisoned and fortified, but the nearest field force was in the region of Toledo, two hundred miles away—almost as far away as Scipio's own headquarters at Tarragona. He therefore decided to strike at once for that city. The rest of the winter he devoted to preparations for a campaign both by land and by sea, and to collection of the most minute information, especially as to New Carthage; but he gave no intimation of his plans, except to Gaius Lælius, who was to command his fleet.

This Lælius, by the way, was a very intimate friend, whò served with Scipio through most of his campaigns. Polybius was later acquainted with him, and quotes him as authority for many of his statements. That writer refers also to letters of Scipio's on certain points, especially on the collection of information.

In the spring of 209 Scipio crossed the Ebro with 25,000 foot and 2500 horse, suddenly appeared before New Carthage by seven rapid marches, and completely invested it by land. These marches must have averaged 35 miles a day at least, and perhaps we may take it that only his leading troops made this speed. His fleet at the same time assembled in the harbour, and the city was attacked on all sides and taken by assault. With it were captured vast quantities of military stores, large sums in gold and silver coin and bullion, and, perhaps even more important, the hostages held by the Carthaginians as security for the loyalty of their Spanish allies.[2]

Scipio's success continued, and his strength steadily increased through defections of Spanish leaders to him. He also placed out of commission most of his fleet, which he no longer needed, equipped the crews from the captured arsenals, and added them to his land force. In 208 he marched against Hasdrubal, who, being badly defeated in the region of Cordova, gave up hope of regaining Spain, crossed the Pyrenees, and marched with his remaining force to join his brother in Italy. Scipio did not pursue, but remained in Spain, for the detachments that Hasdrubal had had in Portugal and elsewhere had assembled, and his army was kept busy to control the peninsula.

During all this time Scipio had been giving much attention to the training and reorganization of his army. He laid out regular schedules of instruction, emphazing care of equipment, individual skill in arms, and, above all, freedom in manœuvre and regularity and rapidity in marching. The training in manœuvre had already begun to bear fruit when he met Hasdrubal near Cordova, for that battle was won by good co-ordination of a frontal holding attack with turning movements to both flanks, commanded by himself and Lælius.[3]

NERO IN ITALY (207 B. C.)

But if Spain was well on the way to becoming a Roman province, Hasdrubal had now to be reckoned with in Italy. Rome had a great army on foot, but it was scattered. Four legions were in Spain, two each in Sicily and Sardinia, three in garrison at Rome and Capua; even with all this, twelve remained for a field force in Italy. Apparently these legions were weak, for the troops on foreign service were called upon for drafts to strengthen them, and slaves were again armed and incorporated in two of them. It is very probable also that the allied force, normally equal to the Roman, was deficient.

The consul Claudius Nero, apparently with six legions estimated at 40,000 foot and 2500 horse, including allied contingents, faced Hannibal in the south. His colleague Livius, with the

[2] Polybius, X, 3–16; Livy, XXVI, 42–49.
[3] Polybius, X, 20–40; Livy, XXVI, 51; XXVII, 17–20.

other six, moved to intercept Hasdrubal, who, judging from Livy, must have had well over 50,000 men, mostly Gauls. At any rate, he was strong enough to cause serious anxiety as to Livius' ability to hold him.

Nero met the enemy first. Hannibal had found the Romans pressing upon him with increasing strength, had met some minor reverses, and had fallen back in the spring of 207 into Bruttium, the toe of the Italian boot. Moving up again into Lucania to attempt to regain lost ground, he met Nero at the town of Grumentum, and was beaten with heavy loss in a battle in the open plain. Hannibal seems to have been less careful in reconnaissance than usual, and Nero showed skill and ability in manœuvre, for the battle was won in part by the use of a small turning column moving through a group of hills to the enemy's left rear. Hannibal extricated himself, however, fell back to the coast at Metapontum, and finally moved up again and established himself in the region of Cannæ, where he was closely watched by Nero.

Hasdrubal meanwhile had crossed the Alps with much less difficulty than his brother had met ten years before, and reached Placentia on the Po. From here he sent messengers to Hannibal, to arrange a junction of forces in Umbria. These messengers made their way in safety the whole length of Italy; but Hannibal being just then engaged in the manœuvres described above, they missed his camp and fell into the hands of the Romans. Nero promptly sent the dispatches to Rome, recommending that the city garrison be moved out to support Livius, and saying that he himself was starting with a detachment to join him.

This bold decision, going entirely outside of his orders, caused great anxiety in the Senate, but Nero had already started. His march was conducted with extraordinary secrecy and celerity. He sent forward officers with mounted escorts, to arrange for quarters and subsistence along his route, and to collect wagons at suitable points to carry such men as could not keep up with his column. Taking 6000 infantry and 1000 cavalry, all picked men and carrying nothing but their arms, he gave them to understand that he was undertaking a surprise attack upon a neighbouring town. Getting away by night, without causing special excitement in the camp, he joined Livius at Sena, near Ancona, and slipped unobserved into his camp under cover of darkness.

In the morning the consuls moved out to offer battle. Hasdrubal
at once noticed the increased force, and also observed the companies
of travel-stained men, with rusty arms and thin horses, evidently
just off the road from a long march. He was at a loss to understand
how these reinforcements had arrived, and decided that his brother
must have met a serious defeat—for he could not conceive that
Hannibal had been outwitted by a Roman. He therefore retired
that night, meaning to get behind the Metaurus River; but missing the proper fords, he moved up the right bank looking for others.
Finding none, for the banks grew higher and higher, he was brought
to bay in the morning.

Hasdrubal placed his Spanish regular troops on his right, in
a very narrow and deep formation, occupying the whole width of
a piece of open ground, flanked by hill country. His left, Gallic
allies, extended into the hills. His few elephants were in front
of the Spaniards. Fighting desperately, his right held its own
against Livius, and even ventured upon a counter-attack. The
Gauls, by irregular fighting in the hills, held Nero also, but did not
come out against him. It seemed a deadlock, with the advantage
if any on Hasdrubal's side. But Nero again showed originality
and manoeuvring ability. He drew back the troops of his extreme
right, marched across Livius' rear, and struck the right flank of
Hasdrubal's Spaniards, already heavily engaged in front. The
line was promptly rolled up, and complete disaster ensued. Hasdrubal himself was killed.

In considering this astonishing march and battle, one is led to
wonder if it was in Jackson's mind when he made his famous move
from the Valley of Virginia to the Chickahominy to aid Lee against
McClellan. The two operations resemble each other, almost
from point to point. But striking as is the modern instance, it
must be admitted that it does not equal its prototype.

His energy not even yet exhausted, Nero started back the same
night, and reached his camp, 250 miles away, in six days. This
was a little better time, we are told, then he had made on the
march up, but we have no direct report as to what that time was.
He had been gone fifteen or sixteen days; he had marched for say
thirteen of them at the rate of nearly forty miles a day; and his
two or three days' stop on the Metaurus had been constant manoeuvring and fighting. His second in command, who remained

behind, had also shown skill in concealing his absence; for Hannibal's first news of the expedition was when Hasdrubal's head was thrown over his ramparts, and prisoners were exhibited in chains. Giving up all hope of further victories, he withdrew into Bruttium, seeking only to maintain a foothold in Italy.[4]

SCIPIO IN AFRICA (204 B. C.)

During 207 and 206, Scipio, not without hard fighting, cleared Spain of the Carthaginian forces. Being showered with congratulations upon his victories, he answered that the Punic War was now only about to begin; that Rome had thus far been on the defensive, but was ready to take the offensive.

His first move was to seek allies in Africa, and to this end he opened negotiations with Massinissa and Syphax, the Numidian chiefs. Neither would treat with an envoy, and Scipio had to visit them in person. To meet Syphax he crossed over into Africa. Hasdrubal, son of Gisco, who had succeeded Hasdrubal Barca in the command in Spain, and who had just been defeated by Scipio, was there also in the interest of Carthage, and the two generals met on terms of personal cordiality. Some sort of alliance was concluded with Syphax, but he later married Hasdrubal's daughter Sophonisba, and returned to his Carthaginian allegiance. An effective and permanent alliance was made with Massinissa, at a meeting near Cadiz.

In this same year, peace, or at least a sort of truce, was concluded with Philip of Macedon. Rome was at last free from anxiety for her flanks, and could take up the plan for invading Africa, which had been in abeyance ever since Hannibal had crossed the Alps. Scipio returned to Rome, was elected consul for the year 205, and given the province of Sicily with instructions to prepare for this expedition.[5]

As soon as he reached his province he set to work with his training schedules again, much as he had done in Spain. This continued throughout his year as consul, and into the next, when he was continued in his command as proconsul. Just what he did does not appear, but evidently he made great innovations, both in his military administration and in his tactical methods. Apparently,

[4] Polybius, XI, 1–3; Livy, XXVII, 36–51.
[5] Polybius, XI, 24a; Livy, XXVIII, 17–18, 35; Boak, 85.

too, he was so much engrossed in his preparations that he failed to go personally into the civil affairs of his province, for the citizens of one of his towns made complaint to the Senate of the tyranny of their military governor, saying that they could get no redress from Scipio. Other complaints came in from dissatisfied officers and soldiers, representing that he was departing from established military methods and impairing the discipline and efficiency of the army.

Fabius, always conservative, had from the first opposed trusting Scipio so far. He now demanded his recall, saying that he was conducting his command "like a king," not like a Roman magistrate. The Senate finally sent a commission of ten senators, with the prætor Pomponius and several subordinate magistrates, to investigate, authorizing them to relieve Scipio if they thought best, and replace him by Pomponius.

Scipio received the commissioners with the highest honours, and showed them in detail everything that he was doing. He turned out his troops and his fleet, held manœuvres to show the state of discipline and tactical instruction, and took the commissioners on tours of inspection through all his arsenals and storehouses. They returned to Rome highly enthusiastic over what they had seen; the delinquent city governor was punished, but Scipio was cleared of responsibility for his acts, and given even greater authority and independence than before.[6]

In 204 he went to Africa. In selecting the troops to go, he used as his nucleus the two legions made up of survivors of Cannæ, who had been under a cloud ever since. But they were old solid legions, not newly raised levies; the men were professional soldiers, tried in war and trained in peace, and their enthusiasm was great at being thus treated, not as men in disgrace, but as the élite of the army. Recruits were assigned to raise these legions to a strength of 6500 each, thus utilizing to the maximum the old substantial framework, and avoiding the creation of too many new units. The allied force was made up with a nucleus of men of the Latin allies who had served at Cannæ. This being an overseas expedition, the strength had to be limited; the highest estimate mentioned by Livy is 35,000, and he intimates that he considers this excessive.

[6] Livy, XXIX, 16–22.

Landing in the Gulf of Tunis, north of Carthage, Scipio established himself near Utica, laid siege to that city, intending to use it as his base, and entered into relations with his ally Massinissa. Carthage was greatly alarmed, having but few troops at hand for defence; but Hasdrubal and his son-in-law Syphax arrived before Utica could be taken, and the two armies remained observing each other, without undertaking any decisive operations, throughout the winter. The siege of Utica continued. Scipio's term as proconsul was extended, and quite contrary to precedent was made "for the duration of the war."

By a bold night march, Scipio surprised the enemy, destroyed his camps and dispersed his army. Hasdrubal and Syphax got together the remnant, reinforced it to about 30,000 with new troops, and met Scipio in the open field, in a battle which gives us our first insight into Scipio's tactical innovations.

He opened the battle much in the usual form; but as it progressed his principes did not push straight forward into the line of the hastati. Instead, the hastati alone made a holding attack, while the principes and triarii executed an independent movement and enveloped the flanks. The Carthaginians, inferior troops hastily organized, were decisively defeated. Scipio sent Lælius westward into Numidia, where he dethroned Syphax, and established Massinissa as king of all Numidia.[7]

Scipio meanwhile overran all the country about Carthage, and established himself at Tunis, only ten miles from the city. The Carthaginians sought an armistice, recalled Hannibal from Italy and sued for peace. Hannibal abandoned Italy, where he had ruled almost as a king for fifteen years, and where even now he remained a terror to the Romans, returning home as reluctantly "as if going into banishment."

Landing at Hadrumetum, south of Carthage, he assembled all available troops and reorganized an army. Unduly encouraged by his return, the Carthaginians violated the truce by seizing some Roman ships. Hannibal moved out early in 202, and reached Zama, some fifty miles southwest of Carthage. Scipio marched westward, effected a junction with Massinissa, and awaited Hannibal at Naraggara, on the Bagradas River.[8]

---

[7] Polybius, XIV, 1–9; Livy, XXIX, 24–34; XXX, 1–15.
[8] Livy, XXX, 20, 29; Polybius, XV, 1–5. See Plate 8.

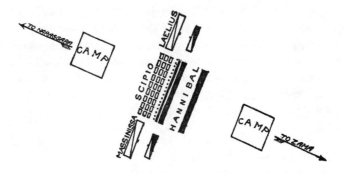

INITIAL POSITION

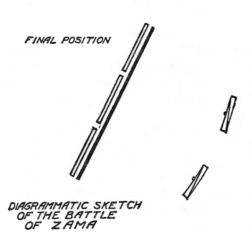

FINAL POSITION

*DIAGRAMMATIC SKETCH
OF THE BATTLE
OF ZAMA*

PLATE 8.—BATTLE OF ZAMA

ZAMA (202 B. C.)

Hitherto the Romans had usually been superior in infantry, inferior in cavalry. This time the Numidians were with them, and they were superior in cavalry; it is probable that they were distinctly inferior in infantry.

Scipio's dispositions were calculated primarily for manœuvre, very much as in the battle with Hasdrubal and Syphax the year before. Other Romans, notably Nero, had begun to show an inclination to manœuvre; Scipio, with his long command, his veteran troops, his strict discipline and his careful training, had developed a system based upon it.

His lines were formed much as usual. Polybius says that' the second-line maniples covered those of the first, instead of the intervals, but the reasons given—leaving gaps through which the elephants could be allowed to pass—does not fully explain. Taken in connexion with what follows, this passage indicates that the arrangement was for the convenience of his own light troops in dealing with the elephants, as will appear below.

THE THREE-LINE LEGION

The noteworthy feature was not this disposition, but the fact that the rear lines did not close on the hastati. They were posted at an increased distance in the first place, and were not involved in the earlier stages of the action.[9]

A simple increase in distances may seem at first sight a small matter, but really it represents a distinct tactical advance. Rome had suffered defeats through opposing mass tactics to a manœuvring enemy. Scipio had now taught the legion to manœuvre. With a conservatism truly Roman, and with the simplicity of genius, he had done it without copying the enemy, and without revolutionary changes in armament or organization, but by cleverly utilizing and developing what he had. What he had done was to teach the hastati to carry on a holding attack, without expecting support, thus establishing the Napoleonic "fixed point" for the manœuvre of the rest. "First one must see; then one engages all along the line."

Hannibal also formed for manœuvre. He did not adapt his Cannæ plan, but adopted a new one. His Cannæ manœuvre had been cut and dried; all was arranged beforehand. He must unquestionably have known what his opponent had done in training and in battle; known, too, that he had no Varro to deal with, but a Scipio who had profited by the mistakes of a Varro and the successes of a Hannibal, as well as by his own experience. The cut and dried manœuvre would not work against him.

[9] Polybius, XV, 9; Livy, XXX, 33; Delbrück, I, 334.

Hannibal, then, formed his heavy infantry in two lines—the newly raised African troops in front, his veterans from Italy behind. Like Scipio, he had distance enough between lines to permit free manœuvre—something over two hundred yards. Moreover, his veterans were ordered to stand fast when the rest advanced. According to traditional military ideas, they were almost off the battlefield.

Both armies covered their flanks with cavalry. Hannibal pushed forward his light infantry as usual, and sent his elephants ahead with them, instead of keeping them with his heavy infantry. Scipio held his light infantry back, close to the line of battle.

After some preliminary cavalry skirmishing, the light infantry engaged. The elephants advanced, but the Roman light infantry manœuvred so as to herd them into the lanes through the lines, and keep them away from the maniples. During this confused fighting the superior Roman cavalry was successful on both flanks, drove the Carthaginians off the field and themselves disappeared in the pursuit.

Hannibal's light troops, retiring in some confusion, nearly broke the line of battle; but the heavy infantry, lowering their pikes as against an enemy, kept them off; and they also disappeared from the field. The battle was now for the heavy infantry alone, and in this Hannibal probably had the superior force. So far, the advantage was on his side.

The Africans and the Roman hastati became fully engaged, and fought for some time without support on either side, the superior training and steadiness of the Romans gaining them some ground. The mechanism of the next movement is obscure, but Hannibal appears to have used his reserve to prolong the line— the Cannæ manœuvre in improved form. Scipio drew back his hastati a little, presumably to avoid envelopment—which in itself was a triumph in troop leading, for they obeyed the sound of the trumpets in the heat of action; then sent his reserve forward on both flanks, extended in his turn, and restored the situation. Everything was now in action, one single long heavy line. Again there was a deadlock, and who would win was uncertain.

But now Lælius, who commanded the Roman regular cavalry, and Massinissa with the Numidians, succeeded in rallying their troops. Leaving the pursuit of the Carthaginian horse, they returned and struck Hannibal in rear. This was too much; the Carthaginians broke. Most of them—Polybius says 40,000—were captured or killed. Hannibal succeeded in rallying a small force, and made good his retreat to Hadrumetum.

Hannibal's last fight, although a defeat, was worthy of him. Polybius analyzes it as a military man and finds no fault on his part. As at Waterloo, the defeated commander remained the greatest general of his times. He went before the Carthaginian Senate, admitted defeat, and advised peace. This was made, at a heavy cost; the settlement shows curious similarities to the Treaty of Versailles of 1919. Carthage lost all her territory except the immediate region of the city, paid a crushing indemnity, surrendered her navy and most of her war material, and was placed under obligation not to engage in war without the consent of Rome. Numidia was consolidated under Massinissa, and set up as a buffer state between Carthage and the Roman dominion in Spain.[10]

Scipio returned to Rome, was accorded an entry in triumph, and received the name of Africanus. Hannibal went into exile in Asia, where he lived for twenty years more. The story is familiar, how Scipio once went as an envoy to the court where his great opponent was residing. In conversation, he asked Hannibal what generals he considered greatest. Hannibal answered, Alexander first, Pyrrhus second, himself third. "But what," asked Scipio, "if you had beaten me?" "Ah, then," said Hannibal, "I should have ranked myself above Alexander."

But while Rome was fighting for supremacy in the western world, Macedon and Syria were arranging to divide all the eastern between themselves. Such an expansion of these powers meant destruction to many smaller states which had friendly relations with Rome. More than this, it seemed dangerous to Rome herself. In 200 B. C., two years after Zama, Rome for the first time sent a powerful land army to Greece, joined forces with the Achæan League, and opened hostilities with Philip of Macedon.

PHILIP OF MACEDON

When Greece and Rome had met before, at the time of Pyrrhus, the legion was not a manœuvring unit. Moreover, the Greek system did not appear in its normal form, for Pyrrhus used Italian

[10] Polybius, XV, 11–16; Livy, XXX, 33–35; Boak, 86–90.

allies and to some extent at least modified his own Greek armament and tactics. He was of course familiar with what Alexander of Epirus and other Greeks had done in Italy, and he went so far as to incorporate Epirotes and Italians by alternate units in the same line of battle.

The Macedonian phalanx as it now appeared in Philip's army was not materially different from that of Alexander the Great. It is not reasonable to suppose that so alert and warlike a king as Philip did not know what the Romans had been doing to improve their army, but if he did know he did not imitate. Either he did not appreciate the value of the innovations, or he did not feel that it would be possible to remake the Macedonian soldier from an exponent of pure shock action into a spear-throwing, sword-fighting, all-around man. At any rate, he had accepted the pure shock theory, and made his phalanx into the heaviest hammer that he could. The normal formation was sixteen deep. In fighting order each man had one yard front and one yard depth; possibly, to permit more freedom of movement, each man may have been placed to cover the interval of the men in the rank ahead. The sarissa was now twenty-one feet long, and was held in both hands, six feet from the butt. Thus five ranks of spearheads stood in front of the phalanx. Opposed to this was the flexible legion, which could open ranks when it engaged so that each man might have as much as six feet front, giving free use of his weapons. These two orders of battle have been analyzed in detail and compared by Polybius, a practical soldier who saw them both in action. Evidently, in a purely frontal fight in an open plain, the legion stood no chance—each sword had ten sarissas to meet. The strength of the legion lay in its manœuvring power and in its combination of fire and shock. There was a moral difference, too, no less marked. This is analyzed in masterly style by Colonel du Picq:

It is a strange error to believe that the last ranks will go to meet that which made the first ones fall back. On the contrary, the contagion of recoil is so strong that the stopping of the head means the falling back of the rear!

The Greeks, also, certainly had reserves and supports in the second half of their dense ranks. But the idea of mass dominated. They placed these supports and reserves too near, forgetting the essential, man.

The Romans believed in the power of mass, but from the moral point of view only. They did not multiply the files in order to add to the mass, but to give to the combatants the confidence of being aided and relieved. The number of ranks was calculated according to the moral pressure that the last ranks could sustain.

There is a point beyond which man cannot bear the anxiety of combat in the front lines without being engaged. The Romans did not so increase the number of ranks as to bring about this condition. The Greeks did not observe and calculate so well. They sometimes brought the number of files up to thirty-two and their last files, which in their minds, were doubtless their reserves, found themselves forcibly dragged into the material disorder of the first ones.

In the order by maniples in the Roman legion, the best soldiers, those whose courage had been proved by experience in battle, waited stoically, kept in the second and third lines. They were far enough away not to suffer wounds and not to be drawn in by the front line retiring into their intervals. Yet they were near enough to give support when necessary or to finish the job by advancing.[11]

It would be interesting to know if the novel tactics employed by Philopœmen at Mantinea (Chapter V) were a result of Roman influence; superficially at least the similiarities are striking. Hostile contact between Philopœmen and a Roman general might have shown startling developments, but as noted above this never occurred.

CYNOSCEPHALÆ (197 B. C.)

The decisive battle of this war was fought in 197 B. C., at Cynoscephalæ in Thessaly. The two armies were separated by a range of hills, and neither expected an immediate engagement; but contact was established by reconnoitring detachments in the hills, each side sent support, and Philip was finally led by apparent success to move up his whole force into ground unfavourable to it.

The head of this column reached the crest, and formed in ground that seems to have been satisfactory. The Romans met him, and their left was pushed back by a frontal attack. But the rest of Philip's troops came up slowly, and found the space inadequate to form their phalanx; the Roman right struck them while trying to deploy, and shattered them. The battle was now decided in favour of the Romans by the independent action of a subordinate. For a tribune of the right legion, seeing from a hilltop that the fight of his own wing was won but that the left was losing, moved with twenty maniples against the rear of Philip's right. This is the first

[11] Polybius, XVIII, 28; Du Picq, 53; Delbrück, I, 361.

great battle in which we find the Romans using elephants—either those of their Greek allies, or those surrendered by Carthage. In this attack upon a march column they proved very successful, but they never found great favour in Rome.

Philip had to make peace, paying heavy indemnity and admitting the "principle of self-determination" and autonomy for all his subject peoples. Only Macedon proper was left to him, and this only because Rome wanted it as a buffer against the tribes of the lower Danube.[12]

ANTIOCHUS OF SYRIA

Syria's turn came next. Antiochus the Great had extended his dominion again over most of the Asiatic empire of Alexander the Great, entered Thrace in 195 B. C., and sent an expedition to Greece in 192. He was becoming as serious a menace to Rome as Macedon had been. Incidentally, Hannibal was at the court of Antiochus, and urged him to invade Italy. This was altogether too bold for Antiochus, and might have proved too heavy a task for Hannibal himself; but even in other things his advice was disregarded. And what, asks Delbrück, can be expected of a king "who has a Hannibal and does not know how to use him"? Antiochus was beaten at Thermopylæ and his small expeditionary force driven out of Greece. Scipio Africanus and his brother Lucius went into Asia Minor in 190, and overwhelmingly beat him at Magnesia.

The accounts of this battle are vague and unreliable but they give the impression of a very deep phalanx—Livy says thirty-two ranks—and a large and heterogeneous mass of allied contingents, with chariots, elephants, and every variety of armament, perhaps not unlike the army of Darius at Gaugamela. Antiochus was badly beaten, and the usual form of peace was made—reduction of territory, surrender of the navy and heavy war matériel, indemnity, and the setting up of numerous small powers with conflicting interests to keep them apart.[13]

PERSEUS OF MACEDON

Other minor troubles occurred in Greece, where there was always some fighting going on, but for the most part things were reason-

[12] Polybius, XVIII, 24–27; Boak, 91. See Plate 9.
[13] Livy, XXXVII, 50; Delbrück, I, 368; Boak, 92–94.

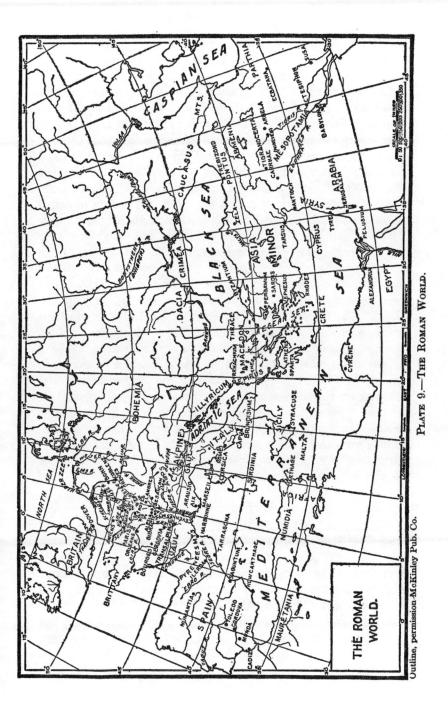

Outline, permission-McKinley Pub. Co.

PLATE 9.—THE ROMAN WORLD.

THE ROMAN WORLD.

ably quiet there, so far as Rome was concerned, for some twenty years. But gradually the Greek states began to chafe under the restrictions that Rome placed upon their freedom of action; Philip encouraged them in their discontent, and there was danger of a Greek confederation against Rome headed by Macedon. To prevent this, Rome endeavoured still further to bind the hands of Perseus, Philip's successor, and when he refused her demands declared war. Roman armies were sent against him in 171; the war dragged for a time, but was finally brought to a close in 168 by Æmilius Paulus Macedonicus, son of the consul who was killed at Cannæ.

Æmilius showed something of the spirit and energy of Scipio Africanus. He found the discipline and training of his army unsatisfactory, and took these matters firmly in hand. To him are attributed important reforms in the system of outpost duty. He cut down the length of the tour on post of sentries and vedettes, and took other measures to increase their vigilance. Thus, it had been the custom for a sentinel to wear his armour and carry his long shield. The flash of metal frequently revealed his post; furthermore, cases were not unknown in which a sentinel, standing motionless, leaning on his spear, was found to be sleeping, his head supported upon his shield. Æmilius had all this equipment left in camp. He also suppressed unnecessary shouting of orders, substituting simple methods of passing the word. He paid especial attention to instruction in reconnaissance, often leading parties in person. By his forethought in matters of supply, and by his skill in field expedients, he greatly improved the comfort and health of his troops, and forced even old soldiers to admit themselves but recruits in comparison with their general.[14]

PYDNA (168 B. C.)

The decisive battle was at Pydna, on the west coast of the gulf of Salonika. It is unfortunate that Polybius' account of this battle has been lost, for he was then master of the horse, or second in command, to his father Lycortas, general of the Achæan League, and as representative of the League accompanied Æmilius. We have only secondary accounts.

Livy's account quotes Polybius and other eyewitnesses, but it is long and involved, and is a collection of stories concerning

[14] Livy, XLIV, 33-34.

various incidents rather than a military picture of the battle. It appears, however, that Æmilius very cleverly manœuvred Perseus out of his position between Mount Olympus and the sea, and into that of Pydna, twenty miles back. He then re-established contact, and for some days tantalized Perseus by appearing to offer battle, until he enticed him into moving out to the attack; and finally won by manœuvre against the superior but unwieldy enemy. An interesting touch is that his men were anxious to attack, but that he restrained them by the old but always new device of getting his priests to declare the omens favourable only to defensive battle. Another is that an eclipse of the moon occurred during the wait at Pydna; Æmilius had an officer learned in such matters, who predicted and explained it to the troops, so that they were not surprised by it, while the Macedonians took it as an evil omen and were accordingly dispirited.

The Macedonian kingdom was cut up into four separate little republics, which were allowed to have no mutual trade or other relations which might tend to bring them together; and a heavy annual tribute was exacted from them.[15]

Very definite settlements were now imposed upon the other Greek states, to keep down their power. To hold the Achæan League in line a thousand of their leading men were taken to Rome as hostages. Among them was Polybius, who for nearly twenty years lived at Rome on the most intimate terms with Æmilius and all his aristocratic circle. So highly was he regarded that he was charged with the education of Æmilius' son, who, having been adopted by the son of Scipio Africanus, assumed the name of Scipio Æmilianus, and by destroying Carthage won for himself that of Africanus Minor. Polybius accompanied him on his campaigns, so that what little remains of his accounts of these is by a highly competent eyewitness at headquarters. These remains are very slight indeed, but the historian's long association with such families gave him a wonderful opportunity for collecting information from the principal actors in all events, civil and military, of recent Roman history, just as his family standing at home had given him contact with those of Greece.

[15] Livy, XLIV, 37; Boak, 96.

During the period of eastern wars Rome had extended and consolidated her power westward also. By the middle of the 2nd Century B. C., she was supreme in the Mediterranean world. But her supremacy was by no means unchallenged, and she fought many campaigns to maintain it, in Africa, Spain and Greece.

Numidia took advantage of her favoured position to harass Carthage, until, driven beyond endurance, Carthage made war without permission. Rome sent an expedition to Africa, and demanded unconditional surrender. This being accomplished, she further demanded abandonment of the city and transfer to an inland site. In desperation Carthage closed her gates and improvised means of defence; a two years' siege followed. At last, in 146, Scipio Æmilianus took and destroyed the city.

Revolts in Spain were frequent and dangerous until 133, when the same general took Numantia and pacified the peninsula. About the time of the sack of Carthage an attempt was made to restore the monarchy in Macedon. This led to further wars, resulting in the reduction of that country to the status of a Roman province, and shortly after to campaigns in southern Greece, as a result of which the confederacies there were broken up and the cities placed under the supervision of the governor of Macedon. In 129 Asia Minor also was finally reduced to a province.

DEVELOPMENT OF THE ROMAN MILITARY SYSTEM

These wars brought about no notable changes in tactics or in organization, but they did cause a steady trend toward a professional army, and bring about the full development of the system of military government and administration. Rome herself was being transformed from a city-state into an empire, and her military system, too, had to change.

The transition from a militia to a professional army had long been in progress, although it was not fully and officially recognized until the end of the 2nd Century. But such a transition was inevitable when wars were so continuous. Armies continued to be raised for each campaign and disbanded at its close, but old soldiers were more and more sought, and were embodied year after year in the new legions. Along with the professional soldier class there grew up the professional officer class, for the centurion began to object to starting a new campaign in the ranks.

This came prominently to the front in 171, at the beginning of the war with Perseus. At the outset, the regulation four legions were raised, and on the rolls there were found the names of twenty-three men who had served as senior centurion of a legion—as *primus pilus prior*, the senior centurion of the pilani of the first cohort, commonly called primipilus. These appealed to the tribunes of the people, saying that they were anxious to serve, but thought it unjust that they should be placed under men of less rank and service. Their spokesman, Spurius Ligustinus, outlined his service, long and honourable, but apparently not exceptional.

He had entered the service in the year 200, and had served two years as a private, against Philip. In his third year he had been promoted, and had served as *decimus hastatus posterior*, or junior centurion of the hastati of the tenth cohort, the lowest ranking officer of his legion. This war being over and the army disbanded, he had volunteered for service in Spain, had been again promoted, and had attained the rank of *primus hastatus prior*, the senior centurion of the hastati of the first cohort, one-third of the way up the list of centurions of the legion. Discharged with that rank he had volunteered for the war against Antiochus, and advanced to *primus princeps prior*, or senior centurion of the principes of the first cohort, another third of the way up the list. After this war he remained in service for two years, then went again to Spain, and reached the grade of *primipilus*, which he had held four years. His age at this time was over fifty; he had served in twenty-two campaigns, had been selected to accompany his commander in a triumph, had received thirty-four rewards from his generals, and held six civic crowns as decorations.

On this occasion the centurions withdrew their appeal, feeling apparently that its purpose had been accomplished in inviting attention to the situation, and consented to serve wherever they might be placed. Ligustinus was made primipilus of his legion.[16] But as the number of men with records like his increased, the militia character of the legions must have disappeared entirely.

The centurions, two to each maniple, were all promoted from the ranks; their position was somewhat analogous to that of our

[16] Livy, XLII, 32–35.

company officers. Each centurion had an assistant, selected by himself, and each maniple had its own standard-bearer. References are found to various special duty men—orderlies, musicians, etc.—but there was nothing at this time that corresponded to our non-commissioned grades, for the formations and the methods of fighting rendered them unnecessary. Old and trusted soldiers doubtless exercised authority over their juniors, as file-leaders, drill-masters, etc., but they held no actual rank.

The field officers of the legion were the military tribunes, six in number. They organized, commanded and administered the legion, and appointed the centurions, subject to the approval of the commander-in-chief. They were elected by the people or appointed by the consul; originally certain qualifying service in the ranks was required, but this requirement gradually became obsolete. In the later republic a soldier could rarely advance beyond the grade of centurion, and that of tribune was reserved for men of wealth or birth—sometimes men of experience, and even of senatorial or consular rank, but more often young men. Scipio Africanus, for example, was a tribune when only twenty years old.

Delbrück compares the situation to that of the English army in the 18th Century, when the higher grades were chiefly filled by young aristocrats. Wellington was a lieutenant colonel at twenty-four. The English battalions, like the legions, were highly disciplined, and contained a large number of old soldiers. Foreigners were as a rule not incorporated into English battalions, but formed separate units. The parallel fails when we come to the English company officers, for few of them rose from the ranks; the old professional sergeant corresponded in some degree to the centurion.[17]

As we have already seen, it was not the original Greek or Roman practice to have a single command for any force. There was rather a governing council, and a rotation in office for executive control, something like our system of rosters for officer of the day. Actual personal command was a slow development, even for an independent force. The monarchical system of Macedon introduced it into Greece, but Rome had her own separate development of it. The legion was not at first a tactical unit, but rather an administrative device. It acquired its tactical character slowly,

[17] Polybius, VI, 24; Delbrück, I, 394.

and naturally its administrative machinery changed even more slowly. Hence we find that the six tribunes constituted a sort of board of directors. Command and administrative functions were performed by the members of this board, singly or in pairs, as agents or committees of the board. No one of them commanded the legion, or any part of it, permanently. Direct control of a subdivision or detachment was exercised by the senior centurion present, unless a tribune was specifically assigned.

The system of personal command of an army, and that of provincial military government, grew up together, inseparably linked. Very early, as has been shown above, the need was felt for more commanders than there were consuls or other magistrates available. The practice grew up of assigning someone, usually of senatorial or consular rank, to command as procounsul or proprætor. Later, the same expedient was adopted in order to confer a command upon someone legally ineligible for it. Thus, when Hasdrubal pushed the Roman armies out of Spain in 211, no one cared to accept the command there. Scipio offered himself, but he was too young, and too low on the list of magistrates, to receive such a command in the ordinary way. Hence he was sent out as proconsul, by virtue of a special law.

Since there were generally several wars at once, each with its own theatre of operations, each such theatre was given to a commander as a province. Command in the province for war very naturally passed into governorship for peace, if by any chance peace happened to reign for a time. Finally it came to be accepted that a consul, or prætor, on leaving office at home, should normally go to some province as proconsul or proprætor. There could be only two consuls at a time, and their term was limited; but there was no limit, except the pleasure of the Senate, to the possible number of proconsuls or their tenure of office.

Command and civil magistracy, then, were almost synonymous. Similarly, military administration was indistinguishable from civil. In Rome there were magistrates called quæstors, a sort of deputies of the consuls for handling administrative details. When the consul took the field, a quæstor went along. The quæstor gradually acquired almost the position of a chief of staff; but operative affairs were generally handled by the general in person, and hence the quæstor's duties were chiefly in the field of supply. He might at times exercise command—Lælius, when he led the cavalry at Zama, was Scipio's quæstor—but it was by virtue of a specific assignment, just as any modern commander may send a member of his staff to command troops. The quæstor was the second ranking officer of the force, and in the absence of his chief assumed temporary command.

The most important point to note here is, that Rome never experienced the difficulties in supply that the Greeks did. Her civil system of handling money and property automatically went along with her armies, and there was always someone on hand, with proper authority, organization and equipment, to handle the problems arising in the field. And the magnitude of the problems increased so gradually that the system had time to expand.

The quæstor was expected, as a matter of course, to handle everything relating to supply. In overseas expeditions, he was charged with organization of the whole line of communications, and to this end had both merchantmen and ships of war under his direct command.

Complete accounts of funds and property were kept. Thus, after the battle of Zama, one of the terms of the treaty of peace was restitution of the ships and cargoes seized by the Carthaginians in violation of the truce. The ships themselves were located, for restoration in kind, but in the confusion of the times the cargoes had disappeared, apparently into unauthorized private hands. Scipio had a complete statement prepared by his quæstors, which was used as a basis of settlement.

The quæstor paid the troops, and had charge of finance in general. Space was reserved in every camp for his offices and stores, and detailed regulations existed for guard and other service there.[18]

In the course of time the clerical force of the quæstors in Rome assumed a permanent character—became an organized civil service. Cato the Younger, when quæstor about the middle of the 1st Century B. c., found that these employés, through their long service and perfect knowledge of precedent and routine, practically controlled the quæstors, with their short term of office.[19]

[18] Polybius, I, 52; VI, 31–35; X, 19; Livy, XVIII, 29; XXX, 37–38; Smith, art. "Quæstor."
[19] Plutarch, Cato.

How far this condition prevailed in the army quæstorium we cannot tell; probably to a less extent than at home.

When war was imminent, stocks of equipment and supplies were accumulated by the Senate, and when the theatre of operations was not distant shipments were made direct. For more distant operations, the country was exploited with system and care, and neighbouring provinces drawn upon.[20] If these resources failed, it became necessary to fall back upon shipments from home, and these were sometimes precarious.

The solution of one such problem is interesting. It will be remembered that the two Scipios had very considerable successes in Spain just after Hannibal came into Italy; but they were unable to support their army indefinitely on local supplies, and sent requisitions to Rome. Rome had armies on foot in so many places at once that neither money nor supplies were available; some credit arrangement had to be devised.

Public notice was given, calling for offers to supply Spain by commercial methods. Three associations were formed, which undertook the service, on condition that the contractors were to be exempt from military duty, and that the state should bear any loss by "act of God or the public enemy," as we should put it. This system gave excellent results.[21]

But the profiteer and the dishonest contractor are not modern inventions. It was not long before some of the shippers began to take fraudulent advantage of the last-mentioned clause in the contract—to falsify their bills of lading and wreck their own unseaworthy ships, carrying paper cargoes. In 212 B. C., one of these contractors was brought to trial, and many persons implicated had to go into exile.[22]

When necessary, land lines of communication were established; roads built, advance depots organized, and complete arrangements made for guarding them and the convoys; as, for example, in the war with Perseus, when the Romans pushed up into the rough country north and east of Mount Olympus, and had to bring up their supplies from Thessaly.[23]

[20] Polybius, II, 22–23; Livy, III, 23; V, 7; XXIX, 25, 36; XLII, 27, 64.
[21] Livy, XXIII, 48–49.   [22] Livy, XXV, 3–4.   [23] Livy, XLIV, 9.

MARIUS

The next great developments in organization and tactics are connected with the name of Gaius Marius. Born of a well-to-do plebeian family in 155 B. C., this great leader and organizer served first in the cavalry at Numantia, where he attracted the favourable notice of Scipio Æmilianus. He left the army, however, and returned to Rome, where he was chosen tribune of the people; but the opposition of the aristocratic party kept him out of the higher magistracies until he was forty years old, when through his marriage with Julia, aunt of Julius Cæsar, he added a semi-patrician status to his plebeian popularity, and was elected prætor.

This was the period of Gallic and Numidian wars, in which Rome both gained victories and suffered reverses. She pushed forward through Transalpine Gaul, and gained control of the land route to Spain. As proprætor Marius fought with much success in that province, and later served under Metellus against Jugurtha, king of Numidia. Having gained some successes here too, and having opposed Metellus to or beyond the verge of insubordination, he returned to Rome, and secured election as consul. He then went back to Africa, superseded Metellus and completely subdued the province.

Meanwhile Germanic and Celtic tribes, headed by the Cimbri and Teutones, had made serious inroads in Roman Gaul. Several Roman consuls were defeated, and finally, in 105, the combined armies of the consul Mallius and the proconsul Cæpio were annihilated at Arausio, now Orange, on the lower Rhone—a disaster comparable only to that of Cannæ. Italy was open to invasion, but fortunately the tribes turned toward Spain instead.[24]

Marius was again elected consul, and continued in that office—unconstitutionally—for several years. The tribes attempted nothing against Italy, and he had time to organize an army.

The disaster at Arausio destroyed even the last vestiges of the old militia system, which, as we have seen, had long been decaying. An entirely new army had to be raised, and all resources had to be used. The effort was so strenuous that distinctions of class or age disappeared—a man was a man. He was enlisted, not for a year, but for a term of sixteen years, and of course became a professional

[24] Plutarch, Marius; Boak, 135.

in spirit when he took the oath—which oath, be it noted, bound
him to his general, not to the state.   This opened the way for a
new tactical step.

THE COHORT LEGION

While the legion of Scipio could manœuvre with its lines separately, it had no proper tactical subdivision.   A single maniple was
too small for independent action, and the maniples of the different
classes were not interchangeable.   But now the men were interchangeable, and the maniples could be made so, in armament,
equipment, strength and character; hence several maniples might
be grouped into a permanent body which could undertake a serious
tactical mission.

This body already existed, in rudimentary form, for we often
find mention of a *cohort*, first as a unit of allied troops, then as a
detachment of a legion, and sometimes, specifically, as a group of
three maniples, one of each class.   This term now became stand-
ardized in the last-mentioned sense.

The Marian legion was composed of ten interchangeable cohorts,
designated by number.   Each cohort consisted of three maniples;
in place of numbers for these, the old designations triarii (or pilani)
principes, hastati, still remained, but no longer implying any difference in class or equipment.   The maniple was still divided into
two centuries or ordines.   No change was made in the system of
command; each cohort was commanded by its senior centurion
unless a tribune was attached.   Since the legions were now permanently on foot, they received permanent numbers.

Full freedom of manœuvre was thus attained.   The formation
was no longer necessarily in three lines, but in one or more as desired.   Three lines, then as now, seemed best to answer the average
tactical requirements, and a chequerboard formation of four cohorts in front line, three in second and three in third may be considered typical.

With such an organization, and with long service, drill regulations began to take on a higher development.   Within the next
generation or two they had become very complete, and movements
of all units became as simple as those of ours to-day.

The combat tactics may be reconstructed with reasonable certainty.   They were the logical development of those described in

Chapter VI, and allowing for the difference in range of weapons closely resemble those now in use. The formation was completed beyond the range of the hostile fire, and the legion then habitually advanced, maintaining intervals and distances at least approximately. Exceptionally, it awaited the enemy at a halt; but in either case it was customary to advance at a run just before collision, to get both the moral and physical effect of momentum. At close range, perhaps fifteen or twenty yards, the front ranks threw their javelins, and at once opened out, closing the intervals between cohorts and forming a continuous line of swordsmen at some two yards' interval. The rear ranks kept up the javelin fire, and filled gaps in this line. The second-line cohorts supported the first, reinforcing it as required. The third line was a reserve, for manœuvre.

Of course we are not to suppose that all this came about by the single genius or the simple order of Marius. He made his organization out of existing material, and we cannot now tell precisely to what degree he perfected it. But the change took place, and Marius marks this transition point as clearly as Scipio marks the preceding one, from straight mass pressure to a manœuvring reserve.

The Roman cavalry had been gradually giving place to allied. This change also was definitely accepted by Marius, though himself of an equestrian family, and Roman cavalry proper is rarely heard of after this time. It should be noted here, too, that Roman citizenship was extended early in the 1st Century B. C., to all Italy, and even beyond, so that "allied" no longer meant "Italian," but "foreign."

Marius' reforms did not stop with the larger organization matters, but went into detail on equipment and internal economy of units. To him is attributed, for example, the introduction of the forked sticks used by the later legionaries to carry their heavy packs—some forty pounds besides arms and armour, varying according to the amount of rations carried—and affectionately called by them "Marius' mules." He made improvements also in the design of the *pilum*, or javelin.[25]

During 104 and 103 Marius' new army organized itself, in Italy and on the lower Rhone. In addition to training, he took great pains in organizing his supply system, digging a new channel at

[25] Plutarch, Marius; Smith, art. "Exercitus"; Delbrück, I, 375.

the mouth of the river to facilitate handling his ships. His colleague Catulus remained in Cisalpine Gaul to guard the northern passes.

In 102 the tribes, reunited in Gaul, moved to invade Italy. The Cimbri went north, to cross the Carnic Alps; the Teutones along the coast, through Marius' country. The terror of their name still had its effect and he remained for the most part in his entrenchments, taking every occasion, however, to familiarize his troops with the enemy's appearance and mode of fighting, and gradually stimulating the confidence of the men. This having been accomplished, he still delayed action by the old expedient of prophecies and oracles, until the enemy lost patience, marched contemptuously past his works, and started east again.

Marius followed cautiously. At Aquæ Sextiæ, now Aix, twenty miles north of Marseilles, a partial engagement, apparently accidental but very likely intentionally caused by Marius, brought the enemy to a stand; the armies remained in close contact for a day or two, then joined battle.

Marius took position on a hill, and sent out a turning column of 3000 men. Pushing forward cavalry and skirmishers, he induced the enemy to attack. This attack he received at a halt, with volleys of javelins; then moved his legions slowly down the slope, pushing the disordered enemy back to the plain. Before they could re-form on the level ground, they were struck in rear by the turning force and routed. The tribe was entirely broken up; legend puts the number of killed and captured at a hundred thousand.

Marius then moved quickly into Cisapline Gaul and joined Catulus, who had been pushed back by the Cimbri into the Po valley. The united Roman armies now turned against them, and won at Vercellæ, near Turin, a victory as complete as that at Aix. The accounts of this, however, are so vague that no tactical description is possible. Other wars followed, with the Italian allies and in Greece and Asia; the greatest was with Mithridates of Pontus and Tigranes of Armenia, early in the 1st Century B. C. The Italian allies won their Roman citizenship; among the Roman commanders we find Marius, his former quæstor and present rival Sulla, and Pompeius, father of Pompey the Great. The war in the east was fought first by Sulla, later by Lucullus. Pompey the Great quelled a serious insurrection in Spain, led by Quintus Sertorius, later going to Asia and completing the work of Lucullus there.

But, although the Roman power in western Asia was firmly established, the boundary was never pushed much farther east; the advance was checked by the Parthians. This people, originating in the country southeast of the Caspian Sea, had established a considerable empire on the ruins of Alexander's Asiatic dominions, and extended it west to the Euphrates. Here they came in conflict with Mithridates and Tigranes, and finally with the Romans as successors to their power in Asia Minor. In 54 B. C., Marcus Crassus, one of Sulla's old officers, who had gained high reputation through crushing the dangerous insurrection of gladiators and slaves led by Spartacus, undertook an expedition against them, but was defeated at Carrhæ, his army destroyed, and himelf and his son Publius killed. The Parthians, like the early Medes and Persians, were characteristically horsemen and archers; unable to stand against a Roman legion in shock, they did not try, but used their skill in horsemanship to keep out of the way of the regular troops and their marksmanship to destroy them. Other subsequent expeditions, including an important one led by Mark Antony in 36 B. C., while resulting in no such disaster as that of Crassus, failed to inflict a definite defeat. The Parthians, however, were unable to advance farther against Rome; their military system was well adapted to the defence of a country such as theirs, but not to a sustained offensive. Under Augustus, a *modus vivendi* was arranged, the Euphrates being accepted as a boundary, the standards taken from Crassus being returned, and Armenia becoming a buffer state. Political manœuvring continued, and Armenia was controlled sometimes by Roman, sometimes by Parthian influence.

Antony, after his Asiatic expedition, evolved ambitious plans for a new series of conquests like Alexander's. But there was no new Alexander. Even granting that Antony or another might have possessed the ability, the conditions did not permit. The Parthians had proved too dangerous to be rushed; to subdue them meant no mere expedition, but a systematic and long-continued extension, with military occupation of each captured district. No one could do that but an emperor, controlling the resources of his state and certain of his throne. Rome had no emperor in this sense, and never was in a position to undertake the task. She had no need of further conquest, only of a defensive frontier.[36]

During all the earlier part of the 1st century B. C., constant and bloody civil war went on among the partisans of Marius, Sulla, Pompey and the other ambitious politicians. But there is little of military importance to be learned from these wars. We must rather pass on to consider the career of a young man now coming into prominence—Gaius Julius Cæsar.

[36] Delbrück, II, 150; Boak, 172, 192. See Plate 9.

CHAPTER VIII

CÆSAR

Cæsar marks the highest development of the Roman art of war; and yet we shall find in his campaigns little that is new in organization, tactics or military administration. His fighting machine was the Marian legion, and the Marian legion it remained at his death. Instead, we shall find the full development of the art of handling the perfected instrument; we shall see with what boldness he planned, with what energy and skill he executed, and with what ease and flexibility the Roman military system accommodated itself to the most varied conditions and satisfied the most varied requirements.

Cæsar was born about 100 B. C., of a patrician family, perhaps the most illustrious in Rome, but his political relations were from the first with the popular or Marian party; his aunt was the wife of Marius, and he himself married Cornelia, daughter of Cinna, the great leader of that party. Great as he was as a soldier, he was primarily a politician. He was a Roman, and fought the battles of Rome, but he never for a moment forgot that in fighting the battles of Rome he was maintaining in his service an army devoted to himself, which would give him strength and prestige in fighting his own political battles; and the time came when he needed it and used it. His Commentaries are inevitably coloured, to a certain extent, by politics and personal interest, but for a study of his military system they are accurate and reliable.

His first military service was purely incidental to political manœuvring; for when Sulla returned in 82 B. C., from his victories in the east and overthrew the Marian government, Cæsar found it convenient to disappear from the city, so served in minor wars in the Ægean regions until Sulla's death in 78. He then re-entered political life at Rome, and held most of the usual magistracies; he also saw further military service in western Spain, in 69 as quæstor and in 61 as proprætor and governor.

In Rome or abroad, he was in close touch with all the political intrigues. Even his debts, which were enormous, he made into political assets, securing through them the favour of Crassus, the richest man in Rome and his chief creditor, who preferred to advance his fortunes and collect rather than to throw him into bankruptcy and lose.

THE GALLIC WAR

In B. c. 59, he was consul, having succeeded in reconciling Pompey and Crassus, old rivals, and getting them to join with him. The Senate at first arranged to assign him as proconsul in 58 to internal improvement work in Italy, but a vacancy occurred in Cisalpine Gaul through the death of the proconsul there, and Cæsar obtained the province, to which Pompey's influence added Transalpine Gaul. His term of office was fixed at five years, and his force at four legions.

The Roman province of Transalpine Gaul, as we have seen in Chapter VII, consisted of the coast strip from the Alps to the Pyrenees—in a general way, what was later known as Provence. Beyond this was a vast and vaguely known region, filled with numerous small states, very warlike, but of inferior civilization and without more than a vague national sentiment to bind them together.

A Germanic chief, Ariovistus, had come over into Alsace some ten years before this, and subdued the Gallic tribes on the upper Saône. During Cæsar's consulship his government had been recognized by Rome, but strong factions of the Gauls still opposed his rule. The Swiss tribes also were giving some concern to the Roman province. Feeling themselves cramped for room, they looked for an outlet westward such as Ariovistus had found, and with this in view they established relations with neighbouring Gallic states, particularly with the discontented elements among the Æduans, in the Côte d'Or, who were nominally subject to Ariovistus.[1]

CAMPAIGN OF 58 B. C.—THE HELVETIANS AND ARIOVISTUS

Early in 58 the Helvetians assembled on Lake Geneva, prepared not for a mere campaign, but for a tribal migration. Cæsar hastened to Geneva, and by diplomacy, together with a skilful use

[1] Cæsar, B. G., I, 2–3; Boak, 161–167.

of the one legion that was at hand and such auxiliaries as he could raise, prevented their making a serious effort to cross the Rhone. Instead, they negotiated with their friends among the Æduans for a right of way farther north. The negotiations and the movement were of course slow; and Cæsar had time to return to Cisalpine Gaul, bring back his other three old legions and two newly raised ones, and intercept the Helvetians at the Saône a little above its junction with the Rhone. After a partial defeat they turned northward, Cæsar following and keeping touch.

For supplies, he was depending largely upon the promises of the Æduans, especially when the Helvetians left the river valley and led him away from his water transportation. To secure grain, he broke contact and moved toward Bibracte, now Autun, the chief town of the region; whereupon the Helvetians ventured to attack him. He stood on the defensive on a hill, very much as Marius had done at Aix. The Helvetians attacked in a dense phalanx formation, and the Roman pilum proved very effective, a single javelin often piercing two overlapping shields, locking them together and hampering or exposing both men. The enemy was pushed back, but reinforcements came up on their flank; Cæsar used his third line to meet them. The battle lasted from midday to dark but ended in defeat for the Helvetians, who fell back to the Langres plateau, and when Cæsar followed begged for peace and consented to return home.[2]

Certain of the Æduans now appealed to Cæsar for protection against Ariovistus, who not only oppressed them but was bringing more Germans into Gaul. He took a very independent tone, refused Cæsar's demands, and moved upon Vesontio (Besançon), evidently intending to defend himself in that strong position until his new allies, then encamped on the Rhine, could arrive. By rapid marching Cæsar seized Besançon, garrisoned it, and made it a base of supplies. From this point he moved against Ariovistus in Upper Alsace, and found him between Mulhouse and Thann, or perhaps farther north near Colmar. Ariovistus does not seem to have been superior in force to Cæsar, perhaps inferior, but he had a strong cavalry, some 6000, and a corps of light infantry equal in number, trained to manœuvre with cavalry, holding on to the horses' manes. Although Cæsar himself had

[2] Cæsar, B. G., I, 21–28; Holmes, 26.

a strong force of Gallic cavalry, it was not equal to this mixed force, and legionary infantry could not force the Germans to accept battle. Screened by this mobile force, Ariovistus moved around Cæsar's flank and posted himself so as to cut off his supplies. Cæsar promptly countered by placing two legions in a smaller camp, in sight of his main one but interposed between the Germans and his line of supply. This new camp he entrenched under the eyes of the enemy, setting his whole army in battle order and doing the work with his third line. Ariovistus attacked the new camp, but not energetically; Cæsar found by inquiry from prisoners that for reasons of superstition he did not want a general engagement before the new moon.

Cæsar's own men were more than a little afraid of the Germans, about whom the Gauls had told all manner of frightful stories. There had even been danger of a mutiny at Besançon. Here was his opportunity to restore their morale; he offered battle daily, and Ariovistus refused to come out from the shelter of his wagons, which he used as a fortification. After a few days of this, Cæsar left small garrisons in his camps, put all the allies, who were still afraid, out in plain sight where they would have at least a moral effect, and pushed his legions so close up that the Germans were at last induced to fight. They came out in seven closely formed columns of attack, so suddenly and violently that some of the Romans did not even have time to throw their javelins.

Cæsar had taken personal command of his right, and directed his main effort against the enemy's left, which, as usual in a phalangial formation, was the weak spot, and which soon gave way. Meanwhile the German right, again as usual, began to push back the Roman left; but the Romans formed no mere phalanx. The third-line cohorts promptly came up, and the line held; Publius Crassus, son of Cæsar's political ally, who was in command of the cavalry, saw the need and took the responsibility of ordering the movement, thus winning a word of praise from Cæsar. The Germans broke for the Rhine, and were badly cut up by the pursuing cavalry.[3]

This action of Crassus illustrates an old Roman institution, which developed strongly under Cæsar. It had always been the practice for a commander to have with him *legati*, or assistants,

[3] Cæsar, B. G., I, 51–53; Holmes, 37; Delbrück, I, 449.

assigned by the senate or selected by himself. In this battle Cæsar had a *legatus* with each legion, and one with the cavalry; they were as yet hardly in command, but represented the central authority with the unit. By the end of his Gallic campaigns they had acquired almost the status of actual commanders, and they received that status in full under the Empire, their title being finally changed to prefect of the legion. As the legion came to be more and more an independent manœuvring unit, the tribune system demonstrated its inadequacy to the new requirements, and a personal commander was introduced into the scheme in this manner.

Cæsar now had to return to Cisalpine Gaul to look after the civil affairs of his province, but he left his troops in winter quarters in the region of his base at Besançon. Having pushed his conquest so far, he could not go back, but had to go on. All Gaul was deeply stirred by his campaign, and if he now shrank from the task of subduing the whole country he might look for a return of the Germans and a coalition of Gaul, which would not only crush those states that had supported him but threaten his own province.

This year's campaign has shown us what to expect in his conduct of war—boldness in conception, rapidity and energy in execution. His troops had shown the qualities to be expected—discipline, training, marching power, and tactical flexibility. His supply system depended upon exploitation of local resources, use of waterways as lines of communications, and advanced bases where needed, all under the direction of a quæstor. All this is confirmed in the later campaigns.

CAMPAIGN OF 57 B. C.—THE BELGIC STATES

During the winter the unrest in Gaul began to take definite shape among the warlike Belgic states north of the Marne. On his own responsibility Cæsar raised two new legions, and sent them to join his old army. He himself followed, made his arrangements for supplies, and took the field as soon as the grass had grown enough for grazing—not waiting to be attacked, but taking the initiative. On the Marne he was met by envoys from the Remans, the nearest Belgic state, who allied themselves with him. Every other Belgic state was in arms, they told him, and several Germanic tribes with them; the total of fighting men they estimated as nearly 300,000. Galba, king of Soissons, was their leader.

How many men had actually been assembled the Remans could not say. Cæsar induced his Æduan allies to organize raids across the lower Marne and Oise, to keep as many of the enemy at home as possible; he himself advanced to the Aisne to protect his new allies, whose chief town was Durocortorum, now Reims. He established his fortified camp on the north bank, at Berry-au-Bac, on the little peninsula between the Aisne and the Miette; the bridge in his rear by which the Remans brought him his supplies, was fortified and held by six cohorts.

The Belgæ came down in large force from the direction of Laon, and encamped north of the Miette. Cæsar was protected by the streams everywhere except on his right flank, and here by the fortified camp, connected by trenches with both rivers. He therefore remained quiet, waiting for the Æduan raids to have their effect— a tactically defensive phase of his strategic offensive. The Belgæ could not make a direct attack, but finally tried to turn the position by a ford of the Aisne a few miles below. Cæsar broke up this attempt by a rapid movement with cavalry and light infantry; discouraged by their ill success and heavy loss, and their rudimentary supply system failing, the confederation fell to pieces, its dissolution hastened by the Æduan raids.

The states as far north and west as Amiens soon submitted, and were received as allies, but farther northeast the Nervians and their related tribes were not yet ready to give up. Cæsar moved into their country, between the Sambre and the Scheldt, picking up country people as guides. Near Maubeuge he was informed that the enemy was in force only a few miles away, south of the Sambre. He decided to halt for the night, and sent a party of centurions and scouts ahead to select a camp. They chose a place on the north bank of the river, and marked out the usual camp streets and walls; the cavalry crossed the river, only three feet deep, and made a perfunctory reconnaissance, covering only the open ground near the river, and not entering the woods a few hundred yards back. This developed only hostile cavalry patrols.

Some of Cæsar's guides, it afterwards appeared, had escaped and informed the enemy of his habitual order of march, which placed each legion's own train with it; for a train of five or six hundred pack animals, carrying tents and other camp equipage, was an integral part of the legion. But on this day, knowing that the enemy was near, he had changed this, consolidating the trains in rear, under guard of the two new legions. Thus the six old legions reached camp earlier than usual, and began the customary entrenching—very carelessly, for nothing was done to check up the report of the cavalry, and no troops were sent forward to cover the working parties. The Nervians seized the opportunity, and made a sudden dash from the woods, across the river.

Only good discipline now saved the Romans. Every man fell in with those nearest him; no cohort was intact. There was no time to form a regular line of battle; it was every group for itself. The 9th and 10th Legions, on the left, succeeded in getting into formation, and pushed the enemy, who were out of breath from the dash, back across the river. The 8th and 11th Legions, in the centre, held their ground or a little better; but the 7th and 12th, on the right, were in extreme peril. Separated from each other and from the rest of the force, they were enveloped on both flanks, and would soon be surrounded. The men of the 12th were so crowded that they could not use their swords; most of the centurions were killed or wounded; the primipilus was almost fainting from loss of blood; a standard had been lost. A troop of the Gallic horse took flight, and spread the report that the Romans were cut to pieces.

Cæsar caught up a legionary's shield and dashed into the front lines, calling upon the centurions by name, and by sheer energy of leadership brought the men forward a little so as to get elbow room. Then he gradually brought the two endangered legions together and formed square.

By this time the train guard legions were in sight, and the 10th Legion was on its way back from the pursuit. The tables were turned; but the Nervians, with a desperation and gallantry that brings hearty praise even from Cæsar, fought almost to annihilation. The whole battle was over before dark—so swiftly did the Romans lose, recover themselves again and win. It may not be out of place to remark here that most ancient battles were very swift and violent, like a modern cavalry charge. Massacre was the normal result of defeat, and the casualties of the loser were out of all proportion to those of the winner. Fire power was poorly developed, and there was nothing to slow down the development of the action or to cover a retreat.

The tribes had had enough, and begged for peace, which Cæsar granted on easy terms. There was still some resistance farther east, and Cæsar went on to the junction of the Sambre and Meuse, and thence down the Meuse, half way to Liége. But it was not long before everything was quiet, the states from Brittany to the Rhine and even beyond sending in their submission. The troops went into winter quarters along the line of the Loire and Cæsar went back to Cisalpine Gaul.[4]

CAMPAIGN OF 56 B. C.—BRITTANY

During the winter of 57–56 Cæsar renewed his alliance with Pompey and Crassus, secured an extension of his term as proconsul, which was now half over, and obtained ratification of his action in raising the four new legions, with authority to raise two more if necessary. The year 56 was one of military occupation rather than war—plenty of fighting, but by widely scattered detachments, from the Spanish border almost to the North Sea. The most important campaign was the naval one against the Veneti of Brittany, which ended in their complete overthrow.[5]

CAMPAIGN OF 55 B. C.—INVASION OF GERMANY AND BRITAIN

In 55 a new German migration came across the lower Rhine. Cæsar started in the early spring and marched to the region of Coblenz, where he practically annihilated the invading tribes; on his own statement, his course here is hard to justify against the charges of inhumanity and treachery, which were made at Rome. He ended this campaign by a punitive expedition across the Rhine, for the purpose of which he constructed his famous pile bridge, somewhere between Coblenz and Bonn—a notable engineering feat, all done within ten days, including the assembling of material. The plans were presumably those of Mamurra, the *præfectus fabrorum* or chief engineer; but Cæsar seems to have taken great interest in construction and siege work, and to have been something of an engineer himself.

After all this there still remained time to take two legions into Britain, partly a punitive expedition and partly a reconnaissance. Here Cæsar had the novel experience of landing a force on an open beach against opposition. The transports were given rendez-

[4] Cæsar, B. G., II, 1–35; Holmes, 53–56, 824.　　　[5] Cæsar, B. G., III.

vous somewhere in the region of Dover; when all were assembled, they moved in a body to the selected landing place and anchored close to the shore. It was necessary to land troops by wading; to make this possible, the war vessels took position on the flank of the line of transports, and opened fire with their artillery and with slingers. At the same time all available small boats were filled with troops, and sent in to support the wading men wherever it seemed that they had good prospects of gaining a foothold on shore. This operation suggests Alexander's use of artillery at river crossings. Cæsar often mentions his *tormenta*, or artillery weapons. He used them in sieges and in his camps, and sometimes in the defence of a field position, but in active operations their effect did not seem to justify transportation. Later they became an integral part of the legion, for Vegetius, in the 4th Century A. D., mentioned them as such.

A camp was finally established, and the natives seemed inclined to make peace. But a storm, together with a high tide—a thing unfamiliar to Mediterranean sailors, against which no provision had been made—damaged many ships; supplies were scarce; and the natives returned to the attack. Cæsar defeated them in a defensive battle; then, having "saved his face," he hastened his return to Gaul before the equinoctial storms.[6]

The troops were quartered for this winter north of the Marne.

CAMPAIGN OF 54 B. C.—SECOND INVASION OF BRITAIN

The principal operation planned for the year 54 was a second expedition to Britain, on a much larger scale. The landing was in the same place as before, but the Romans moved inland beyond the Thames, and established a nominal supremacy in that region.

Arrangements for winter quarters were more difficult than usual. Gaul was full of unrest, and needed watching; and crops had been short, so that supplies were scanty. Hence the field force, now numbering eight and a half legions, was widely distributed in eight camps, from the borders of Brittany to the region of Liége.

SABINUS AND COTTA

The camp near Liége had a legion and a half, under the legates Sabinus and Cotta. The tribes here revolted, and attacked the

[6] Cæsar, B. G., IV; Holmes, 70, 76.

camp; then promised free passage if the Romans would withdraw. A stormy council of war was held, in which Cotta and most of the officers favoured holding the camp and standing siege. Sabinus, almost alone, wished to accept the terms. As the senior, he carried his point, and the troops started out the next morning. Trusting in the word of the Gallic chief, Sabinus formed his column as for a march in friendly country, the trains with the troops. As soon as they were well clear of the camp, the Gauls fell upon them and destroyed the whole command. The few survivors made their way to the camp of Labienus, in Belgian Luxemburg.

QUINTUS CICERO

Encouraged by this, more tribes, including the Nervians, joined the rebellion, and made an attack upon the camp of Quintus Cicero, on the lower Sambre. Cicero, with better judgment than Sabinus, held his camp, and sent messengers to Cæsar for relief. Most of these were captured, but one, a Gaul, got through to Amiens.

The message arrived late in the afternoon. Cæsar at once sent for Marcus Crassus, his quæstor, who was near Montdidier with one legion, to bring it up to hold Amiens. At nine the next morning the legion was arriving, and Cæsar started himself with one weak legion and a little cavalry, picking up *en route* another weak legion, which gave him some 7000 men in all. Messengers from Labienus met him, with news of Sabinus' disaster.

Nearing Cicero's camp he sent a native messenger to announce his approach and urge the garrison to hold out, writing in Greek so that his letter, if captured, would probably be unintelligible. The messenger delivered it by securing it to a javelin and throwing it over the wall.

The Gauls raised the siege and moved to meet Cæsar, in greatly superior force. Again combining the tactical defensive with his offensive purpose, Cæsar entrenched and induced the Gauls to attack, then dispersed them by a sudden counter-attack and entered Cicero's camp. The news of this relief spread rapidly; on the same day it reached the camp of Labienus, sixty miles away, and prevented a threatened attack there. Later, when an attempt was actually made upon him, he repulsed it by a skilfully planned counter-attack, and killed the chief of the rebellious tribes.[7]

[7] Cæsar, B. G., V, 4–58.

CAMPAIGN OF 53 B. C.—PUNITIVE EXPEDITIONS

Nevertheless the destruction of Sabinus had badly shaken Roman prestige. Cæsar himself remained in Gaul for the winter, devoting himself to military and civil intelligence work and to diplomatic negotiations with the tribes. By his own agents at home, and by the assistance of Pompey, he brought his force up to the authorized ten legions. The campaign opened early, its purpose being to complete the subjugation of the Belgic country.

The first expedition was by Cæsar himself with five legions, to the lower Meuse. Meanwhile Labienus, in Luxemburg, defeated the Treviri, who had collected forces to attack his camp. Joining forces with him, Cæsar led another expedition across the Rhine, building a new bridge a little above his old one, but he was unable to bring the Germanic tribes to a decisive battle.

Returning from Germany, he left all his heavy impedimenta, and all men unfit for hard field service, at Sabinus' old camp, under guard of his newest recruit legion, the 14th, with Quintus Cicero in command. The rest of his force he divided into three columns of three legions each, under Labienus, Trebonius and himself, which spent a week or ten days marching rapidly through the country, north, east and west, scattering hostile parties and hunting down their chiefs. Cicero grew careless, and allowed his foraging parties to stray; his camp was attacked while weakly held, and was saved only by personal efforts of the old centurions.

Of the foraging parties, one, made up of convalescent veterans, formed up promptly and cut its way back to camp. The recruits lost their heads altogether, huddled together on top of a hill, and then made hasty and disordered attempts to break through. Their centurions were mostly old soldiers, promoted from the junior grades in old legions to the senior grades here; they showed energy and determination in trying to re-establish order. But the new companies lacked cohesion, and a few veterans could not give it to them. Most of the centurions fell fighting; groups of men made their way back, but many were killed; the loss was equal to about two cohorts.

Activity in the field continued until late in the fall, but Ambiorix, the chief insurgent, was not taken. Two legions were stationed for the winter in the northeast, two on the Langres plateau, the rest on the lower Yonne.[8]

CAMPAIGN OF 52 B. C.—VERCINGETORIX

The great insurrection began in the next year, 52, and involved almost all southern Gaul, from the Garonne to the Seine. The first break was about the end of winter, at Orleans, where natives massacred the Roman merchants and the commissary officer in charge of Cæsar's depot. Vercingetorix, a powerful Arvernian chieftain, raised the standard of rebellion, and gradually drew the whole country to his support.

Cæsar, in Italy, heard the news, but found himself cut off from his troops, for Vercingetorix was on the upper Loire; and Lucterius, one of his lieutenants, on the upper Garonne, was threatening the land route from Italy to Spain. Cæsar went to Narbonne and arranged for the defence of the threatened region; then entered the Rhone valley and, with a few of the local militia and the parties of recruits that he had brought from Italy, struck across the Cevennes Mountains against Lucterius' rear—to the utter surprise and consternation of the Gauls, who never dreamed that anyone would come that way before the deep snows were off. This drew Vercingetorix south again. Leaving Decimus Brutus to keep up active demonstrations, Cæsar returned to the Rhone; with a small cavalry force he marched quickly to Langres, and assembled his army on the Yonne.

Moving rapidly, he took and destroyed Orleans, relieved a friendly town, besieged by the insurgents, and then laid siege to their principal town, Avaricum, now known as Bourges. Vercingetorix, realizing—as the Gauls hitherto had not realized—that he was no match for the Romans in the open, acted as Fabius might have done under similar circumstances. He remained some miles away, and with his numerous light cavalry cut off supplies and otherwise annoyed the besiegers.

Cæsar constructed very elaborate siege works; the defence was active, and on one occasion succeeded in firing and nearly wrecking the terrace and towers built to command the walls. At last, under cover of a violent storm, the Romans gained a footing within the defences, and seized the city.

[8] Cæsar, B. G., VI, 1–10, 36–42.

Having thus gained breathing space, and replenished his supplies, Cæsar took steps to strengthen the wavering allegiance of the Æduans. He then sent Labienus, his most trusted legate, with four legions, to re-establish control in the Seine valley, and himself moved against Gergovia, the home town of Vercingetorix, in the region of Clermont Ferrand.

Vercingetorix met him on the Allier River, and for some time prevented a crossing. Finally Cæsar encamped one night under cover of a large wood close to the river; in the morning four legions only continued the march, with the entire train, the column formed in such a manner as to give the impression, from a distance, of six legions. Vercingetorix being thus induced to follow, along his own bank of the river, Cæsar effected the crossing with the two remaining legions.

Vercingetorix now placed his force in Gergovia, and Cæsar established his fortified camp in close touch. Having reconnoitred the position, which he had not the force to invest all around, his first step was to seize a hill commanding the best route by which supplies could enter, and to connect the two camps by trenches.

A large body of Æduan auxiliary infantry, *en route* to join him, was won over by insurgent agents. Cæsar, learning of this, instantly moved to meet them with four legions and all his cavalry, leaving only two legions to hold both camps. Finding the Æduans about twenty miles away, he overawed them by show of force, and persuaded them to drive out the ringleaders of mutiny and return to him. Without further delay he marched back, and arrived just in time to save his detachment from destruction. The whole march of over forty miles, and the entire negotiation, had been accomplished in less than twenty-four hours.

Cæsar next attempted an assault, which failed largely through overzeal and haste of one of the columns. Fighting for the next few days, while somewhat to the advantage of the Romans, was small and indecisive, and Cæsar abandoned the siege. This decided the Æduans, who definitely went over to the insurrection and seized the Roman depots in their territory. Cæsar and Labienus were now both in extreme peril, and the Province itself was open to attack.

Labienus was on the right bank of the Seine, at Paris; his depot was on the Yonne. A strong Gallic force was just across the Seine from him. By clever night movements he misled the enemy, effected a crossing and gained a victory, enabling him to get back to his depot. Cæsar marched up to meet him, and concentrated near Troyes, where the people were still friendly to Rome. Almost all Gaul was now in rebellion under Vercingetorix.

The Lingones and Remans being still friendly, Cæsar moved in the direction of Langres; somewhere in this region he could protect his friends, supply his troops, and at the same time be within striking distance if any serious attack should be made upon the Province. The provincial local guards were strong enough to deal with raids. In this march, Cæsar again made the mistake, which had once cost him dear on the Sambre, of marching as in peace through a friendly country, without adequate measures for security. Vercingetorix moved quickly in front of him, barred the way with infantry, and attacked the column in front and both flanks with his powerful cavalry.

Although surprised, the legions formed in good order, covering the trains, and held their ground. Cæsar's cavalry, backed by the infantry in position, engaged the superior enemy all along the line. A body of German horse, which had recently joined him, was held in reserve for a time, well out to the flank, and then by a vigorous and well-timed charge broke up the Gallic attack. Vercingetorix retired to Alesia, near Dijon, where Cæsar besieged him.[9]

Both sides clearly saw that this siege would be the decisive operation. Cæsar completely invested the place, and constructed strong lines of contravallation, ten miles in perimeter, which he elaborated with the utmost pains and labour. They were no mere hasty entrenchments, but serious engineering works. His ditches at some points were twenty feet in width and depth; where possible, a stream was turned into them. Some of his walls were as much as twelve feet high, with parapets and numerous towers; and abattis, *trous de loup* and other obstacles were provided in infinite variety. Vercingetorix, before the works were complete, sent out all his cavalry and reduced his garrison to a minimum to save supplies. Cæsar intimates, but does not affirm, that there remained 80,000 men, with supplies for one month. This seems excessive; Napoleon I estimates that 20,000 would have been an ample garrison,

[9] Cæsar, B. G., VII, 1–68.

assuming that Cæsar's ten legions, with auxiliaries, were about 80,000.

Those who were thus dismissed had instructions to raise relief forces, each in his own country. This army was soon in the field; Napoleon I, after a study of its operations, inclines to the belief that its strength, estimated at 240,000, was in reality nearer 100,000.

However this may be—and Delbrück clearly points out the difficulties involved in handling a large force with as little organization as the Gauls seem to have possessed—Cæsar maintained his blockade, and built elaborate lines of circumvallation to protect himself. The fighting was constant and at times desperate, but all efforts to break either out or in failed. Finally the relieving army, loosely organized and possessing no unity of command, was definitely broken up and driven away. Vercingetorix was forced to surrender.

The states separately submitted, and the legions were widely dispersed for the winter to hold them in subjection. Cæsar himself remained in Gaul for the winter. The next year, 51 B. C., saw many local disturbances, some of them serious enough to employ several legions, but none demanding a campaign by the whole force. The conquest, for all practical purposes, was complete by the end of the year.[10]

THE CIVIL WAR—THE RUBICON (49 B. C.)

And none too soon, for Cæsar's position at Rome was growing more and more insecure. Crassus was dead. Pompey was supreme there, emperor in all but name; "he would tolerate no equal, nor Cæsar a superior."[11] Cæsar's term as proconsul was approaching an end, and he found it necessary, in order to maintain an official status and an army, to stand for the consulate for the year 48. But a law was passed concerning tenures of office, general in its terms, whose effect in this particular case would have been to terminate Cæsar's command on March 1st, B. C. 49, and leave him to stand for the consulate as a private citizen. Cæsar refused to accept the situation. In January, 49, with the 13th

[10] Cæsar, B. G., VII, 69-90; VIII, passim; Napoleon I, Précis; Delbrück, I, 472.
[11] Florus, 2, 13.

Legion, the only one that he had south of the Alps, he crossed the Rubicon, the boundary of his province, and entered Italy. This constituted open rebellion. Heretofore he had fought barbarians, or semi-civilized states; now legion was to meet legion.

Pompey's troops were mostly in Spain. In Italy, for use against Cæsar's single legion, he had two, and active recruiting was in progress for new units. But the new troops actually under arms were largely in garrison in towns whose possession had political importance, and the two old legions had been a part of Cæsar's army, recently withdrawn from him for service in Asia, so that they were hardly to be trusted against him. Cæsar had eight more legions in Transalpine Gaul; two of them, the 8th and 12th, were *en route* to join him, three were on the Saône, and three in the coast region west of the Rhone.

Popular sympathy was with Cæsar. He gained control without difficulty of northeastern Italy, where the 12th Legion joined him. The Senate abandoned Rome and moved the seat of government to Capua, while Pompey concentrated his troops in the southeast. Cæsar shut up a large part of the Pompeian force in Corfinium, and forced its surrrender; but Pompey, who still had control of the sea, decided to abandon Italy temporarily, to return after getting an army together. The consuls and many senators joined him at Brundisium. Cæsar, reinforced by his 8th Legion and by three new ones formed from local levies, tried to cut him off here, but he succeeded in withdrawing to Epirus. In February, less than two months after crossing the Rubicon, Cæsar returned to Rome, master of all Italy.[12]

ILERDA (49 B. C.)

Spain was held by the Pompeian faction, with three separate forces aggregating seven legions. Pompey himself controlled Greece and the East, but his immediately effective force was small. Cæsar decided first to fight the "army without a general," then turn against the "general without an army," so started for Spain. Marseilles stood out against him, so he organized a siege, left the legate Trebonius to continue it, and went on.

Meanwhile the legate Fabius had been sent ahead with the three legions that had wintered in southwestern Gaul, and three more,

[12] Stoffel, I, 1–35, 203–211; Boak, 174–175.

with Gallic auxiliaries, horse and foot, had followed. No resistance of any consequence was met in the passes of the Pyrenees, but two of the Pompeian commands, five legions with a large auxiliary force, had assembled at Ilerda, some hundred miles south of the border.

This town, now called Lérida, lies on the right bank of the Segre River, and was an important road centre flanking the main route into Spain. It was strong by nature, and it possessed a bridge, so that whoever held the town could manœuvre on either bank. Afranius and Petreius, Pompey's legates, proposed to utilize these advantages to delay Cæsar, who suspected that during the long wait at Marseilles Pompey might have crossed into Africa, thence to march northward through Spain, raising troops as he came. To insure the loyalty of his own troops, Cæsar employed an interesting expedient, of which he himself naïvely tells us; he borrowed money from all his officers and used it to pay the troops. Thus he secured a contented army, with officers pecuniarily interested in his success.

Fabius had established himself on the right bank, well above the city, and had built bridges, but the floods of the river rendered communication precarious. Cæsar moved the whole force down, and entrenched close to the enemy's position. There was some fighting, but indecisive, and Cæsar's position grew critical, the floods not only taking out his bridges and cutting off his convoys, but preventing any considerable amount of foraging. At last he began work on a canal, to divert the waters of the river and render it fordable. A number of tribes having meanwhile been won over, Afranius gave up Ilerda and fell back upon the Ebro line.

Cæsar's ford was not yet ready, but he got his cavalry across and stopped the enemy. Then with much difficulty his infantry crossed, and blocked the line of retreat. After making every effort to extricate themselves, the Pompeian leaders surrendered.

The remaining small force in Spain now promptly submitted, and Cæsar went back to Marseilles, where the siege had been progressing with great energy. The city being finally taken, he returned to Rome as dictator.

These operations had included no decisive battle, but much manœuvre and some hard, even though incidental, fighting. The forces, although organized alike, were not the same in quality.

Cæsar's troops bore the stamp of the Gallic wars, in which they had met enemies assembled in force and ready to fight to a finish. Afranius and Petreius had legions whose recent experience had been in the minor actions incident to a military occupation. They had picked up irregular tactics, and were quite prepared to fight in small independent detachments, using loose formations.[13]

This gave them a certain temporary advantage over Cæsar's men, whose instinct was for regularity. If they had had this individual self-reliance in addition to their legionary stability, they would have been the better troops; but to all appearances they had it as a partial substitute, and hence were the poorer. Cæsar instantly saw the situation, and the dash of the Spanish troops caused him no uneasiness after the first engagement. The moral superiority thereafter tended to his side, where the numerical superiority had been almost from the first.

DYRRHACHIUM (48 B. C.)

In December, B. C. 49 he assembled twelve legions at Brundisium (Brindisi) and prepared to seek out Pompey. Having regularized his legal position by securing election as consul, he resigned his dictatorship and rejoined the army. Ships were scarce, and he could not collect enough for his whole force; besides, Pompey's fleets controlled the sea and made transport hazardous. Nevertheless he accepted the risks and sailed with seven legions, probably about 3000 men each,[14] and 600 cavalry. It was midwinter, but he chose his time and his weather, and he rightly calculated that the hostile fleet would be less vigilant than if he waited until spring. Avoiding Dyrrhachium (Durazzo) and the other large ports, which he assumed would be held for Pompey, and eluding the hostile fleet which lay at Corfu, he effected his landing at Palæste, a little town north of that island. His ships went back for the rest of the army, but were attacked *en route* and many lost.

Pompey had collected nine legions with many Greek and Asiatic auxiliaries, and two more legions were on the way from Syria to join him under Scipio Nasica, his father-in-law. On learning of Cæsar's landing he concentrated at Dyrrhachium, and the two armies established contact on the line of the Apsus River, just south of that town. Pompey was superior in force, but his troops

---

[13] Cæsar, B. C., I, 36–44; II, 20.   [14] Stoffel, I, 128, 334.

were inferior in quality; a serious mutiny was barely averted, largely through the influence of Labienus, Cæsar's old legate, who had taken Pompey's side. Neither leader wished to take the offensive; Cæsar preferred to wait for Antony and the rest of his troops, Pompey hoped that his fleet could prevent their sailing and that Cæsar would ultimately have to yield.

Antony succeeded in crossing, however, and landed north of Dyrrhachium with four legions and eight hundred horse. Pompey moved against him, but instead of attacking prepared an ambush. Antony learned of this from the natives, and remained in camp; the next day Cæsar effected a junction, having started just after Pompey but having had to make a detour to reach a ford of the Apsus. Pompey fell back again to the vicinity of Dyrrhachium; Cæsar followed, and managed to interpose between Pompey and his depots there.

This caused Pompey nothing more than inconvenience, for his water communication with Dyrrhachium, and in fact with the whole world, was still open. He might even have tried a counterstroke at Rome, but Cæsar had troops in Italy and elsewhere, and perhaps it might have been possible for him to march his own force home by way of the coast. At any rate, Pompey did not try this.

But Pompey would not risk a decisive battle, for his troops were inferior both in number and in quality. Cæsar therefore decided to contain him with the bulk of his force, but to send flying columns into the interior, to win alliances among the Greeks and to keep the two Syrian legions away. Three such columns went out, aggregating three and a half legions.

With the rest, Cæsar attempted the ambitious project of blockading a superior enemy. He drew lines about Pompey fifteen miles in length, fortifying them with redoubts on all the commanding hills. He could not and did not expect to establish a complete blockade. His purpose was to facilitate supply for himself and hamper it for the enemy, and above all to gain a moral advantage by making it appear to the world at large that Pompey dared not fight.

Pompey built a line of redoubts of his own, and the lines remained stabilized for a time. Finally Pompey, using his interior lines and his control of the sea, concentrated a superior force at the point where Cæsar's left touched the shore, and at the same time landed a party in rear. Both Pompeian parties knew precisely what to do, for two Gallic officers, reprimanded by Cæsar for misconduct, had gone over to Pompey and given him minute information. Cæsar suffered a serious defeat, losing a thousand men and thirty-two standards. He abandoned his works, lest a worse thing befall him, and withdrew to Apollonia, forty miles south on the coast. His escape from ruin had been narrow; he is quoted as saying that "to-day the victory had been the enemy's, had there been anyone among them to gain it." [15] The retreat itself is remarkable—three days' march through difficult country, with a victorious enemy at his heels; it succeeded through superior energy and discipline, and skilful playing upon the enemy's known weaknesses.

PHARSALUS (48 B. C.)

But Cæsar, having been pushed so far south, was anxious for his detachments in the interior, especially the principal one, two legions under Domitius Calvinus, which was near Heraclea (Monastir), between Pompey and Scipio. He established a depot at Apollonia, and started inland with seven legions less three cohorts, probably about 18,000 men.[16] He gives us his own estimate of the situation. Pompey might follow him, cross into Italy, or attack his depot. In the first case, he would have to cut loose from the seacoast and his fleet, and the two could fight on equal terms in the interior; in the second Cæsar would march home by land to the relief of Rome; in the third, he would join Domitius, crush Scipio, and return to raise the siege. Pompey issued bulletins broadcast, exaggerating Cæsar's defeat and painting his retreat as a rout; this had much effect in the country, and Cæsar's messengers were intercepted, so that Domitius learned of the situation only through indiscretion of some of Pompey's scouts, and moved to meet Cæsar with only four hours' start on the main hostile army. For Pompey could not make up his mind to go to Italy, as some of his officers urged; and had moved to crush Domitius and join Scipio, then attack Cæsar. His camp was full of senators and high-ranking officials who were now wildly jubilant over his success; they were indulging in heated disputes as to who should succeed to Cæsar's offices and honours, and how they might divide

[15] Cæsar, B. C., III, 1–76; Plutarch, Pompey.   [16] Stoffel, II, 5.

the spoil among themselves, excluding all claimants who had not accompanied the army.

Both junctions being effected, the armies established contact near Pharsalus in Thessaly. It was to Pompey's interest to fight, for he was in superior force, he expected no reinforcements, and Cæsar did—two detachments in Greece, and a column on the way from Italy by land, some three and a half legions in all. But Pompey wanted to fight on his own terms, so entrenched his camp on a hill, overlooking Cæsar's in the plain, and invited attack. Cæsar tried by manœuvre to draw him down into the plain, and succeeded, Pompey's hand being forced by his supporters, who wanted to finish the war and go home to enjoy the fruits of victory. Cæsar then joined battle without waiting for his reinforcements.

Cæsar gives Pompey's strength as 110 cohorts, 45,000 men; his own as 80 cohorts, 22,000 men.

These numbers do not quite check with all his previous statements, nor with other accounts. Each had eleven legions in the theatre of operations, and Cæsar seems to have deducted all his own detachments but forgotten to deduct Pompey's; there are other minor discrepancies, too, which need not trouble us. It is sufficient to say that Pompey was considerably stronger, both in the number and in the strength of his cohorts. As for cavalry, Cæsar says Pompey had 7000 to his own 1000. This also is exaggerated, but Pompey's certainly outnumbered his at least two or three to one. In quality, the advantage was decidedly with Cæsar. The number of auxiliary troops does not appear; it was probably small, and these troops had little influence on the battle.

Pompey's right and Cæsar's left rested on the river Enipeus. Pompey massed his strong cavalry, with a few slingers, on his left, under Labienus; Cæsar's weaker cavalry, strengthened by picked footmen trained to work with them—a trick learned in Gaul—seem to have been opposite them.

Pompey held back his infantry and sought to envelop Cæsar's right with his cavalry. Cæsar attacked with his first two lines, holding his third in reserve; at the last moment, noting the heavy concentration of hostile cavalry, he drew six cohorts from the third line and placed them behind his right. Pompey's cavalry, completely successful at first, was beaten back by a determined charge

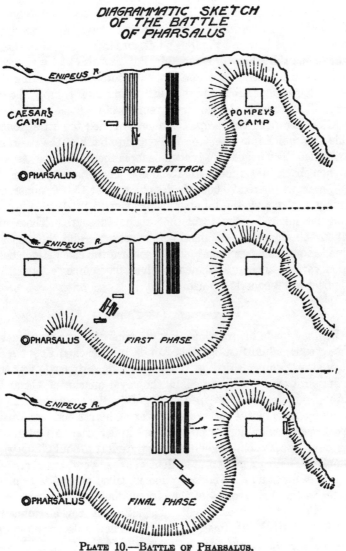

DIAGRAMMATIC SKETCH
OF THE BATTLE
OF PHARSALUS

ENIPEUS R.

CAESAR'S
CAMP

POMPEY'S
CAMP

○ PHARSALUS   BEFORE THE ATTACK

ENIPEUS R.

○ PHARSALUS   FIRST PHASE

ENIPEUS R.

○ PHARSALUS   FINAL PHASE

PLATE 10.—BATTLE OF PHARSALUS.

of these six cohorts, using their javelins as pikes, for their swords were too short to fight cavalry.

The infantry was by now engaged all along the line, and fully employed with the frontal fight. The six cohorts—and doubtless the cavalry also, which does not appear to have been completely routed—lapped around Pompey's left, and at the same time Cæsar sent in his third line. Presumably Pompey also had his reserve, but if so his fighting line was broken before he could bring it to bear. His legions broke for the hills behind their camp, "the officers still leading," as Cæsar dryly remarks.

After occupying the camp, Cæsar surrounded the little group of hills by a quick movement on the opposite bank of the river, and compelled the surrender of the whole force there. Pompey escaped on horseback and almost unattended. The prisoners, according to Cæsar, numbered 29,000; the loss he puts at 15,000, apparently simply subtracting the number of prisoners, actual or estimated, from his inflated estimate of the original strength. There were taken 180 standards—of maniples or cohorts—and the eagles of nine legions; this last item tends to confirm the calculations based upon various ancient statements, which fix Pompey's strength in the field at 88 cohorts instead of 110.[17]

ALEXANDRIA (48–47 B. C.)

Pompey made his way into Egypt, where he was assassinated. Cæsar sought him first in Asia Minor, and reached Egypt a few days after Pompey's death. Taking sides in a dynastic war then going on, Cæsar was besieged in the royal quarter of Alexandria throughout the winter of 48–47. The Egyptians invested him entirely by land; but he succeeded in keeping his sea communications open, and was finally relieved by troops from Syria. An interesting episode, showing some ingenuity, was the effort to shut off his water supply. The regular conduit system was easily cut, but there were still wells and tanks. The Egyptians installed pumps, to bring sea water to the higher parts of the city, and allowed it to run down; the wells gradually became salt. The situation grew alarming, but a sufficient supply was finally secured from new wells on the shore.[18]

[17] Cæsar, B. C., III, 78–90; Frontinus, II, 3; Stoffel, II, 20–29, 245; Delbrück, I, 500, 507. See Plate 10.

[18] Hirtius, Alexandria, 6; Stoffel, II, 43–69.

Settling the affairs of Egypt involved other military operations, interesting enough in themselves, but of no particular importance in the development of the art of war. The same may be said of all the later operations of the Civil War; it had reached its climax at Pharsalus, and everything later comes in a way as anticlimax. Besides, the historical material is less substantial. Cæsar's own Commentaries end in Egypt, and, while they are of course political tracts, and essentially one-sided, it is not difficult to allow for and eliminate this influence. Other contemporary, or nearly contemporary, writings serve well enough as checks and sidelights on Cæsar, but without Cæsar they give only an obscure picture. For every reason, then, a brief mention of the later campaign will suffice.[19]

ZELA (47 B. C.)

From Egypt Cæsar was called to Asia, where Pharnaces, son of Mithridates, taking advantage of Rome's internal troubles, had regained and extended the old kingdom of Pontus. This uprising was put down at the battle of Zela, with such rapidity as to inspire Cæsar's famous letter, "Veni, vidi, vici." His comment on the field was, "Lucky Pompey, to win the title of Great by victory over enemies like these."

RUSPINA AND THAPSUS (47–46 B. C.)

During all Cæsar's absence in the East, republican forces had been gathering in Numidia, under Scipio and King Juba, and were now strong enough to threaten Italy. Disorder prevailed in Rome, and Antony, Cæsar's representative there, could not check it. Cæsar returned in 47, was made dictator again, and went over into Africa. But first he had to deal with a general mutiny of his soldiers, who chose to consider that the old war was over and a new one beginning, and that they should receive their promised rewards on the spot. By remarkable boldness and diplomacy he regained their allegiance; his last delicate touch, when he had played upon their feelings so that their purpose was wavering, was to address them as "Quirites"—the word used from time immemorial to characterize the Roman citizen in his purely civil capacity. Their military instincts shocked by this explicit repudiation of military

[19] Hirtius, Africa and Spain; Stoffel, II, 70; Napoleon I, Précis; Boak, 177.

ties, which they themselves had been about to make, they returned to duty.

Cæsar landed his first troops on the beach near Hadrumetum, which was held by the enemy. To secure a base on the coast, he at once occupied Ruspina and Leptis, fifteen or twenty miles to the southeast. The minor fighting here was mostly to his disadvantage, for his troops arrived slowly. One action near Ruspina well illustrates the flexibility of his tactics.

With thirty cohorts and a few hundred cavalry and archers, he encountered Labienus, with a superior force of cavalry and light infantry, in a broad open plain. Having no fears of a frontal attack, but being apprehensive for his flanks, he formed his cohorts in a single line. The enemy surrounded him with a cloud of skirmishers, driving his weak cavalry into the intervals between the cohorts, and harassing him from every side. Seeing that his men were being crowded into a helpless mass, he faced each alternate cohort to the rear, formed two lines back to back, pushed these lines in both directions, and extended them more and more to the flanks. His cavalry guarded the intervals, and made dashes out through them. In this manner he cleared both flanks, and then scattered the enemy enough to permit him to make his way back to Ruspina.

His position continued precarious, for he controlled only the immediate vicinity of his camps, and was dependent almost entirely upon the sea for supply. As soon as he felt strong enough he laid siege to Thapsus, an important seaport some thirty miles southeast of Hadrumetum. Meanwhile he had been studying the enemy's organization and tactics. In particular, he noted their numerous cavalry, and their elephants. As an answer to the first, he trained three hundred men from each legion to fight in the ranks of his cavalry, an expedient used by the enemy, and not unknown to him. As for the elephants, he saw that they were formidable only when unfamiliar, so he obtained some himself and trained his men in manœuvre against them. His force was by now twelve legions; exclusive of garrison troops, Scipio had ten, and Juba four. An attempt to raise the siege led to the decisive battle of the campaign.

Scipio apparently had nearly all his field force in line, with the cavalry and elephants on the flanks. Cæsar had ten legions,

two having been left in the camps at Thapsus. He put nine of
them in his line; the 5th Legion, trained in "anti-tank" tactics,
placed five cohorts on each flank to engage the elephants. These
animals were stampeded, and in turn stampeded the Numidian
cavalry; Cæsar's legions then defeated their opponents in a straight
legionary fight. In distributing rewards and honours after the
battle, Cæsar authorized the 5th Legion to bear the image of an
elephant on its standards.

MUNDA (45 B. C.)

This practically ended the Civil War, and Cæsar returned home
the undisputed monarch of the Roman world. Only once more
did he take the field. Pompey's sons, with Cæsar's old legate
Labienus and a few other "unreconstructed" leaders, raised a revolt in Spain, and got together a force of thirteen legions. Cæsar,
perhaps rashly, attacked them with only eight, at Munda (probably Montilla, twenty-five miles south of Cordova). The troops
on both sides were good, and superiority in numbers soon began
to count. Cæsar's line was pushed back, and stiffened again
only when he seized a legionary's shield and personally led a charge,
as he had once done in Gaul. But his utmost efforts could only
restore the balance, not incline it to his side; and for Cæsar a
drawn battle here was a decisive defeat. The battle was finally
won almost by accident. A party of Cæsar's cavalry, on its own
initiative, made a dash for the enemy's camp. Labienus took
five cohorts out of the line to protect it. The reduction of force
would have made little difference; but the movement of so many
men to the rear, when the nervous strain was heavy everywhere,
caused a certain hesitation and uncertainty in the Pompeian
lines, and a corresponding increase of energy in Cæsar's. This
little sufficed to turn the scale, and the enemy gave way. Cæsar's
cavalry saw its chance, and completed the victory. After this,
all Spain was speedily pacified again.

The battle of Munda was in March, 45 B. C. Cæsar was back in
Rome in September, and celebrated his last triumph. To secure
a satisfactory eastern frontier for his empire, he planned a campaign
against the Parthians; an army was assembled in Greece, and he
was about to start to take command, when he was assassinated,
on the Ides of March (March 15th), B. C. 44.

CÆSAR'S LEADERSHIP

We have said that Cæsar was first a politician, secondly a soldier. But, soldier or politician, he was a leader of men. He had a deep understanding of and sympathy with soldiers; to them he was at once master and comrade. He seemed to divine infallibly, not only what they were thinking, but what they were about to think, and could unerringly apportion severity and indulgence. His devotion to his men was repaid manifold by theirs to him; and yet his conduct cannot have been actuated solely by cold calculation. Soldiers generally manage to form a fairly correct estimate of their commanders, and the most consummate actor could hardly have maintained an unreal pose for so many years of varied action.

But highly as he appreciated and much as he loved his old soldiers, he never tried to fight his battles with individuals. He saw that his weapon was the legion, not the legionary. He counted for his results upon regimental spirit, slowly and carefully cultivated; and his whole career justified him. A new legion never meant the same thing to him as an old one. Experiences like Cicero's in 53 B. C. showed him that even veteran officers could not make the legion veteran, and battles like Pharsalus showed what old legions could do against new. His standard for a veteran legion was high; in one of the minor closing operations of his campaign of 51 B. C., we find him drawing a distinction between certain "old" legions and a new one, very promising young troops indeed but with only eight years' war service.

Perhaps his most striking characteristic, apart from his judgment and leadership of men, was his resourcefulness. Although he made little change in the fighting machine that he found ready to his hand, he was continually inventing new ways to use it. It has been said [20] that an enemy might, with a little study, work out what to expect of Alexander, but no one could guess what Cæsar would do next.

It is difficult, in a paragraph or two, to characterize Cæsar's place in military history or his contribution to the art of war. Instead, it will be best to pass on at once to later times, keeping him in mind and noting his influence, active through the ages.

[20] Hirtius, Gaul, 8; "Cæsar's Art of War."

BIBLIOGRAPHY

PART I

ANONYMOUS, "Cæsar's Art of War and of Writing." In *Atlantic Monthly*, Vol. xliv (Sept., 1879).

A remarkably keen and striking study of Cæsar's generalship, discussing the character of his troops, and concluding with an analysis of the composition and style of the *Commentaries*.

ARRIAN, *Anabasis of Alexander*.

The Bible.

BOAK, A. E. R., *A History of Rome to 565 A. D.* New York, 1921.

A very convenient brief outline.

BREASTED, JAMES H., *Survey of the Ancient World*. Boston and New York, 1919.

A short school history, convenient as an outline to connect different countries. By the same writer are other more extended and very valuable works, among which may be mentioned a monograph on the *Battle of Kadesh*.

CÆSAR, *Commentaries* (*Bellum Gallicum* and *Bellum Civile*).

DELBRÜCK, HANS, *Geschichte der Kriegskunst*. 4 vol., Berlin, 1900–1920.

Very valuable; well arranged and with copious citations and discussions of authorities. The writer is very independent in his views, and departs often from accepted notions, but usually gives an able argument for his contentions. Citations are to Vol. I.

DELITZSCH, FRIEDRICH, "Assurbanipal und die assyrische Kultur seiner Zeit."—In *Der alte Orient*, Leipzig, 1909, No. 1.

A brief but clear and interesting review of the civilization of Assyria at the height of her power.

DUPICQ, ARDANT, *Battle Studies* (transl. Greely and Cotton). New York, 1921.

A brilliant and fascinating study of the psychology and the mechanism of battle, by a soldier of great experience.

ERMAN, ADOLPH, *Life in Ancient Egypt* (transl. H. M. Tward). London and New York, 1894.

The discussion of military institutions is brief but good.

FLORUS, *Epitome*.

FRONTINUS, *Strategematica*.

GAULDRÉE-BOILLEAU, A. F. M., *L'Administration militaire dans l'antiquité*. Paris, 1871.

Very good; interesting and critical discussion, with long quotations and numerous citations of authority.

GILBERT, MAJOR VIVIAN, *The Romance of the Last Crusade.* New York, 1923.

An interesting little personal narrative of the campaign of 1917–18 in Palestine.

GRUNDY, GEORGE B., *The Great Persian War and Its Preliminaries.* London, 1901.

An excellent analysis and study of the period, primarily from the military point of view, with the proper political and social comment. It is based upon the best of both ancient and modern authorities, supplemented by careful personal study of the ground.

HERODOTUS, *Histories.*

HOLMES, T. R. E., *Cæsar's Conquest of Gaul.* London, 1911.

A critical study of all the Gallic campaigns, based not only upon the *Commentaries,* but upon all available literature and upon personal visits to most of the important places. The narrative itself is brief, but it is supplemented by very elaborate notes, three or four times as voluminous, collecting information needed for understanding and judging the narrative and forming one's own views.

HOMER, *Iliad, Odyssey.*

HUNGER, JOHANNES, "Heerwesen und Kriegführung des Assyrier." In *Der alte Orient,* Leipzig, 1911, No. 4.

An essay on the military art of the empire of Sargon, with quotations from the inscriptions and references to modern authorities.

LEAF, WALTER, *Troy: a Study in Homeric Geography.* London, 1912.

A striking study of the theatre of the Trojan War, with comments upon the commercial aspects of the operation.

LIVY, *Histories.*

MASPERO, G. C. C., *The Passing of the Empires* (transl. M. L. McClure). New York, 1900.

One only of the important books of this recognized authority.

MURRAY, GILBERT, *Our Great War, and the Great War of the Ancient Greeks.* New York, 1920.

A small and non-technical essay, bringing out similarities between the Peloponnesian War and the recent war with Germany, illustrated by numerous quotations from Greek comedy.

NAPOLEON I., "Précis des guerres de Jules-César." In Napoleon's *Correspondence;* also separately published, Paris, 1836.

Napoleon's thoughts on Cæsar, dictated at St. Helena.

PETRIE, W. M. FLINDERS, *A History of Egypt.* 6 vol., London, 1898–1905.

A conveniently arranged work, with much valuable geographical discussion and numerous extended quotations from papyri and inscriptions.

PLUTARCH, *Lives* of Agesilaus, Pelopidas, Alexander, Philopœmen, Romulus, Cato, Marius.

POLYÆNUS, *Strategica.*

POLYBIUS, *General History.*

RAWLINSON, GEORGE, *The Five Great Monarchies of the Ancient Eastern World*. 3 vol., New York, 1881.
A mine of information on antiquities, very compact and conveniently arranged. Being an old book, it has not the advantages of the more recent discoveries or the more recent criticism, and is to be used with caution for chronology and history.

SMITH, WILLIAM, *A Dictionary of Greek and Roman Antiquities*. 2 vol., London, 1890–91.
The standard book of reference on the subject.

STOFFEL, COLONEL, *Histoire de Jules-César, Guerre Civile*. 2 vol. and atlas, Paris, 1887.
The classic modern study on the Civil War; a companion piece to NAPOLEON III, *Histoire de Jules-César, Guerre des Gaules*, 2 vol. and atlas, Paris, 1865–6.

STRABO, *Geography*.

THUCYDIDES, *History of the Peloponnesian War*.

WISE, LIEUTENANT COLONEL JENNINGS C., *Hegemonics, or Thoughts on Leadership and Training*. Washington, 1922.
An interesting study on the fundamentals of military training, presenting some novel points of view and some well worked-out illustrations.

XENOPHON, *Anabasis, Hellenica*.

For maps, any good classical atlas should be sufficient. Parallel use of modern maps is recommended. For closer study, on Greece and Rome, there is recommended—

KROMEYER, JOHANNES AND VEITH, GEORG, *Schlachtenatlas zur antiken Kriegsgeschichte*. Leipzig, 1922.

This is a remarkable collection of maps and battle plans, with condensed bibliographies, short narratives, and notes and sketches showing varying opinions and interpretations.

In the maps and plans inserted in the text, no effort has been made at strict consistency in the rendering of names. Ancient and modern forms have been used indiscriminately as seemed most suitable in each particular case.

PART II

WARFARE IN THE ROMAN EMPIRE, THE DARK AND
MIDDLE AGES: TO 1494 A. D.

CHAPTER I

THE IMPERIAL ROMAN ARMY

(FROM AUGUSTUS TO HADRIAN—29 B. C. TO 117 A. D.)

CÆSAR was assassinated (March 15, B. c. 44) almost exactly a year after Munda, and his death was followed by fifteen years of renewed civil war. Not until 29 B. c. was Cæsar's nephew Augustus the sole master of the Roman state.

That state was in imperative need of repose. After seventy years of foreign conquest and internal strife, no man alive in 29 B. c. could remember an era of political stability or of peace.

Augustus was himself a statesman rather than a soldier. In military affairs he depended upon advisers, particularly upon Tiberius who afterward succeeded him as Emperor. However, since Augustus was head of the state when the army reforms were put in operation, and since the army reforms themselves were a part of his general scheme of consolidation, it is fitting that they should bear his name. For the sake of brevity and convenience they can be treated as a single programme—if we remember that different items of this programme were conceived and applied at different times throughout Augustus' forty-three years of ascendancy.

First of all, what was the nature of the Roman state, and what was its general policy? From immemorial time the shores all around the Mediterranean had been covered with city-states each enjoying high civilization but without lasting political union between one city-state and another. Now one city—Rome—had conquered all the others and had carried the frontiers of civilization to the Atlantic and the Rhine. In this achievement the Roman governing class had been, and still was, sustained by the sense of a great mission. On the other hand the Roman temper was severely practical. The Roman had no silly love of conquest for its own sake. Hence he was utterly unwilling to invade territories whose subjugation would be of no material benefit to the state. He would, of course, occupy small districts of barren land when their pacification was necessary for the sake of public order in rich agricultural territories near by.

With the purely political side of Augustus' arrangements this book is little concerned. It is enough to note that his problem was to replace the institutions normal to a city-state with others fitted to administer so vast an empire, and that he solved it by creating a centralized, bureaucratic, civil service taking its orders from the commander-in-chief of the army. This commander-in-chief or "Imperator," from which title our word emperor is derived, was appointed for life by the Senate, and once appointed became the lawful head of the government.

Only on one tiny fraction of its circumference did the Empire border upon another civilized state. That was in northern Syria where the Euphrates marked the boundary with Parthia. South and southeast were deserts inhabited by a few nomads; north were forests thinly peopled with shifting tribes whose small numbers, lack of organization, and total lack of national or racial solidarity made them contemptible antagonists. Still a certain slight pressure was always to be expected from these outer barbarians in the way of raiding parties intent upon enjoying the fruits of civilization, without the discipline which civilization must necessarily impose.

Since Mesopotamia (defended as it was by the far from contemptible Parthian army) was distant from the centre of Roman power, and since there was practically nothing worth conquering anywhere else, Augustus decided, in general, upon a defensive policy. The war weariness of the community made such a policy inevitable for the time being. Circumstances were to make it permanent.

On the other hand, Augustus' policy, defensive though it was in its general purpose, was by no means purely defensive. Indeed, through its contrast with the strict strategic defensive begun by Hadrian in 117, the period from Augustus to the death of Trajan may be called the offensive phase of imperial strategy. In order that the frontiers might be defended with a minimum of force they must be established upon obstacles. Accordingly, the entire southern basin of the Danube was conquered so that the river itself, from its source to its mouth, was the frontier. A methodical attempt was made to advance the frontier from the Rhine to the Elbe—although the attempt was abandoned after the defeat of Varus in 9 A. D. That disaster (though it was rightly considered shocking and disgraceful) in no way threatened the existence or even the general well-being of the state. Rome thought of it somewhat as America thought of the Custer massacre, or as England thought of the fall of Khartoum and the death of Gordon.

So much for the general military policy of Augustus. Let us now consider the army which was its instrument.

By 29 B. C. the Roman army had already become professional. Indeed Marius had taken the decisive step in this direction nearly eighty years before. Theoretically the old universal obligation to serve still remained, but it had become a dead letter. Ever since Marius' time the soldier had taken an oath to his general (i. e., "Imperator") as well as to the state, and had served for pay, booty, and a bonus or "donative" which he expected to get when discharged. The huge force of forty-five legions (from 162,000 to 270,000 men plus an equal or even greater number of auxiliaries) on foot at Augustus' accession had been recruited and paid in haphazard fashion. There was no definite term of enlistment or rate of donative (i. e., bonus) upon discharge.[1] In matters of organization all was chaos.

Augustus continued the professional army, but he greatly reduced its numbers and put the chaos in order.

Modern historians have shed so much ink in trying to prove that Augustus should have introduced conscription, universal service, and what not, that it may be well for us to consider the point. In general the situation was much like that of France after Napoleon or that of the United States after the Civil War and again in 1919: a large army in being, military problems of no great difficulty, and a thorough weariness of war. In the first place, Augustus was not an innovator except where innovation was absolutely necessary. The crying need of the time was consolidation and stabilization. In the second place, the thing would have been politically impossible. The whole force of public opinion would have been against it, for the community was sick and tired of the whole idea of military service, and a government much more strongly established than that of

[1] Dion Cassius: Bk. 55, sec. 23.

Augustus and the Senate would have had trouble in enforcing it. Finally conscription would have been both unnecessary and inexpedient; unnecessary because no formidable internal or external enemy threatened the Roman state (and no civilized community in all history has ever shouldered such a burden without the spur of evident necessity); inexpedient because the task of the imperial army was hardly more than constabulary work. For internal policing, and for campaigns in remote and thinly peopled theatres of war an army of short-term conscripts is an inefficient and enormously expensive instrument.

To-day the colonial troops of both England and France are professionals.

The one real military danger which menaced Rome—that of a general insurrection in some province—would have been all the greater if she herself had trained the mass of the provincials in arms. There was nothing she dreaded so much as internal disorder. In a third-century author, Dion Cassius (150–235), this factor of the problem is dwelt upon in the course of a discussion of the military policy put in the mouth of Maecenas, an Augustan statesman.[2] Altogether then, Augustus' decision to go on with a professional army is perhaps as nearly inevitable as anything in human affairs can be. So much for the pedants.

Augustus' most important step was the reduction of the numbers of the army. All slaves, freedmen and criminals were discharged. Of those with good records who were anxious to leave the service, great numbers were settled in "colonies" upon public land given them by the state. One account says there were as many as 120,000 so favoured. Only 25 of the 45 existing legionary organizations were continued.

The strength of the 25 legions which remained seems to have been fixed at 6000; plus a detachment of mounted men serving (in our own military phraseology) as "divisional cavalry." If we assume, as it seems we should, that this meant an increase in numbers per legion then that increase was provided for by raising the strength of the first and fifth cohorts to 1000 men each. At all events, the later distinction between quingenary ("quingenaria") cohorts 500 strong, and miliary ("miliaria") cohorts 1000 strong seems to date from this time. The possible

[2] Dion Cassius: Bk. 53, sec. 27.

change of formation involved in this change of organization will be discussed later.

I repeat that Augustus thought of himself as a consolidator, not an inventor. There seem to have been no changes in tactics or equipment. On the other hand, a regular training schedule was laid down and strictly adhered to, including strenuous practice marches three times a month in full field equipment. Sometimes the weight carried by the soldiers on these marches would be doubled—to increase their endurance.[3] Modern soldiers bitterly resent "dummy packs" and since the Roman soldier equally resented them [4] there is some question whether the practice was judicious. At any rate it indicates a high standard of training and discipline. Furthermore, Roman discipline was more brutal than ours.

Good order and discipline were particularly promoted by Augustus through reform of military finance. Rates of pay had varied scandalously and the worst sort of abuses had grown up in connection with the "donative," the bonus expected upon discharge. The Senate had played the fool by refusing to concede this bonus in principle, and then granting it over and over again when frightened by threats. Not to mention recent burning issues, our own Continental Congress had a similar experience with our Revolutionary army—and did about the same thing as the Roman Senate. Augustus now fixed a sum which the discharged soldier might lawfully claim. In the face of stubborn political opposition he created a fund, under control of the emperor alone and nourished by special taxes, from which all army expenses, pay, supply and bonuses, were met.[5]

The legions were usually stationed near the frontier. To serve as the Imperial body-guard and supplement the municipal police of Rome, ten miliary "prætorian" cohorts were raised.

Assuming 25 legions at 6000 per legion and 10 prætorian cohorts at 1000 per cohort, the total number of heavy infantry amounted to about 160,000 men. These troops were recruited from Roman citizens, who comprised the Italians plus the enfranchised com-

---

[3] Dodge, Cæsar, 775.

[4] Tacitus, Annals, Bk. 1, Sec. 20, for mutineers' resentment at heavy (probably dummy) packs.

[5] Dion Cassius: Bk. 55, sec. 23.

munities outside Italy, i. e., the descendants of veterans' colonies and the cities or tribes to whom citizenship had been granted as a favour. Whether enlistment was purely voluntary we do not know. There may have been legal machinery for drafting men if enough did not come forward. If so the draft must have borne very lightly on the communities involved.

The soldier was expected to spend his entire life in the army, which meant to leave him only "a little repose before old age comes on."[6] Exactly how long the term of service was is uncertain. The figure of twenty-five years given by some authorities is inconsistent with the information that replacements were sought every three years, unless we assume a one-year training period before being assigned to a unit, the training period not counted toward the enlistment. We know that there had been training units (tirocinia) ever since Marius' time,[7] but a one-year training period seems long. Maurice tells us in the "Strategicon"[8] that in the sixth century A. D., recruits were called in the spring, trained in the summer, furloughed home for the winter and assigned to units in the following spring.

Besides the legions, the Roman army at Augustus' accession comprised non-citizen forces at least equal and probably superior to them in numbers. These troops, the auxiliaries, were recruited from the more warlike of the unenfranchised inhabitants of the Empire. Their units were incorporated in the Roman army and served as cavalry and light infantry under Roman officers. Although they were considered less important than the legions, nevertheless an auxiliary contingent about equal in number to that of the legionary troops formed a part of all armies. Without auxiliaries and especially without cavalry the legions would have been at a grave disadvantage.

Under Augustus the auxiliaries were supplemented by allied units from the little states theoretically independent of but practically dependent upon the Empire. As time went on, however, and these states in Morocco, Thrace, Northeastern Asia Minor, and elsewhere in the East were one by one painlessly absorbed by the Imperial system, their contingents were assimilated to the other auxiliaries. For our purpose, therefore, we may treat them as such from the first.

[6] Dion Cassius: Bk. 53, sec. 27.   [7] Boutaric, 20.   [8] Aussaresses.

The pay in the auxiliaries was less than in the legions. Never-theless, since their recruiting ground was so much larger than that for legionary troops, and since the average level of culture in the populations from which they came was often lower than that of Roman citizens, their enlistment seems to have been entirely voluntary. One of the inducements to serve as an auxiliary was that such service carried with it the grant of full Roman citizen-ship to soldiers honourably discharged. The term of service, like that of the legionaries, was long, apparently twenty-five years.

There was no permanent auxiliary unit higher than the infantry cohort and the cavalry "ala" (literally "wing" as we should say "squadron"). In general such troops served with the equipment best suited to their capacity and local habits. Thus the Gauls were famous as cavalry, the Cretans and most of the Orientals were archers, etc. A sentence in Hadrian's speech to the army of Africa indicates that all auxiliaries were trained to use the sling.[9] Most had helmets although some had not. Some are represented with chain-mail or scale-mail shirts, which must have been lighter than the legionary cuirass of strap-metal, some with no armour at all. The greater number seem to have worn short leather tunics. Instead of the heavy legionary pilum they carried a light thrusting lance, to which the cavalry seem to have added a couple of javelins carried in a quiver slung on the back. On the other hand, in contradiction to the lightness of most of their equipment, the long broadsword, or "spatha" characteristic of all auxiliaries, was bulkier and must have been heavier than the short legionary thrusting sword or "gladius."

The tactics of the Imperial Roman army are known only in a general way. In battle, the legionaries were the chief arm and were used to deal the decisive blow. The auxiliaries, or-ganized as cavalry and light infantry, were usually posted on the flanks. They might be used to begin an attack, for instance in working over difficult ground to which light infantry were partic-ularly suited. The mobility of the auxiliaries, especially of the cavalry, made them useful in pursuit.

The legions were officered partly by young men of the upper classes, partly by promotion from the ranks. For the auxiliaries, officers were sometimes found among their own tribal chiefs.

[9] Cheesman, 132.

Sometimes an old legionary centurion would be promoted to command an auxiliary cohort or ala—we may reasonably guess that this was done when the troops in question proved hard to discipline. Usually the auxiliaries, like the legions, were officered by upper-class young men from civil life. What training these last received to fit them to hold a commission, we do not know.

Obviously, in the service of a world-state like Rome, no strong patriotism such as that inspired by the ancient free cities and (more fitfully perhaps) by our modern nations, could be expected of the rank and file. Morale was assured through *esprit de corps* and an elaborate system of rewards and punishments. *Esprit de corps* could easily be fostered, thanks to the permanence of the organized units, and rewards could be generously distributed, since, as in most professional armies, there was a large proportion of noncommissioned officers and extra-pay men.

Siege works were elaborate and skilful, and the number of catapults used in sieges was large; at the siege of Jerusalem in 70 A. D., the besieged had 340, which would be a high proportion of guns for a considerable force to-day.[10]

To what extent, if at all, catapult-artillery was used in mobile warfare we do not know. Indeed we know almost no details of the tactical method and the campaigns of the Roman Imperial army for over four centuries. On minor tactics we get only scraps, such as Josephus' statement that the legions marched in columns of sixes.[11] It so happens that from Cæsar's African campaign, culminating at Thapsus in 46 B. C., to Julian the Apostate's victory near Strassburg in 357 A. D., not one single account of a campaign in the field, written by a good military historian, has survived. We might be morally certain that a technical literature existed, even had its existence not been referred to by one of the historians of the time,[12] but the books which have come down to us (including that of the great Tacitus) do not pretend to interest themselves in the art of war as such. Even Cæsar's last campaign, in Spain in 45 B. C., has many obscure points: for instance, the site of the battle of Munda has been endlessly disputed in vain. From Munda to Strassburg we must content ourselves with outlining our subject

---

[10] Josephus: Bk. 5, Chap. 9.   [11] Josephus: Bk. 5, Chap. 2.
[12] Dion Cassius, II, 15, 6, and Lucian, De Hist. Conscrib., cited by Cheesman, 102, footnote.

and filling in the details within that outline only faintly and timidly because of our insufficient equipment in facts.

The first question to be asked of any military policy is, did it succeed? That is, did it avoid disaster at an expense in men and money which was reasonable in view of the problem to be solved?

Even if we take the entire Roman period, the Roman army succeeded. Leaving so general a statement for later discussion, let us (for the moment) confine ourselves to the period from 29 B. C. to 380 A. D. Throughout these four centuries, the Imperial armies suffered no general disaster at the hands of foes from without. Naturally through the chances of war over so long a period, there were severe local disasters, but they were surprisingly few, and in every case the general military position was soon re-established. These results were obtained at a minimum expenditure in men, and (as far as we can judge) at a cost in money not out of proportion to the budget as a whole. Unquestionably, therefore, the Roman Imperial army of the first four centuries succeeded.

While always willing to fight, the Romans were intensely practical. Accordingly, their strategy was that typical of a long-service professional army, that is of a highly trained force whose replacements can arrive only slowly and in small numbers, since those replacements take a long time to train and are expensive to hire. Such an army is a most keen and easily managed weapon. On the other hand, when opposed to great numbers it is, as it were, brittle like other highly tempered weapons; for its commander cannot undertake violent action which necessarily implies a high rate of wastage unless he can hope to get a decision at once. If he accept battle in the open field (or have it forced upon him) and then fail to finish off his campaign then and there, he may find himself impotent through the reduction of his numbers. It is true that under the ancient and mediæval conditions of short-range weapons the losses of the victor were usually small, whereas for want of artillery to cover a retreat the loser was usually wiped out unless he could take refuge in a near-by fortress. It is also true that the total population of the empire was much larger than that of its opponents. On the other hand, the numbers of the Roman army (as distinguished from population as a whole) were deliberately kept low to save expense, and because a comparatively small force possessed of civilized organization and traditions of war can usually defeat a horde of semi-savages.

Incidentally, all Rome's enemies were of this sort except the Parthians and the Persians, the successors of the Parthians, in the East.

The army as reorganized by Augustus had two main weaknesses, the lack of a central reserve and the encouragement given to revolt through the military training furnished to those of the newly conquered peoples who enlisted in the Roman auxiliaries.

The prætorians could not act as an efficient reserve. Only 10,-000 strong, they were too few in numbers, and their duty as parade troops and metropolitan police was not calculated to make them efficient field soldiers. Indeed, prætorianism has come to be a name for the abominable tendency of unprincipled troops to bully the very government they should obey.

The danger arising from the want of a central reserve was recognized, and an attempt was made to meet it by improving the lateral communications inside the frontier. In particular, great roads were built over the Alps between Lyons and Turin and between, say, Verona and the newly founded city of Augsburg near the Danube, thus shortening the time required to transport an army between Gaul and the Danubian theatre of operations. Northern Switzerland seems then to have been too poor and barbarous to be a good lateral highway for armies. That more was not done was probably because the pressure on the frontiers was normally that of Roman upon barbarian rather than vice versa.

The other danger, that of revolts in newly conquered territories, was responsible for most of the serious military work of the offensive phase. The leaders would usually be men trained in arms as Roman auxiliary soldiers. On the other hand, such revolts were not inspired by anything like modern national patriotism. They were mere explosions of resentment against administration in an alien tongue, economic penetration, and the individual rogueries and villainies so frequent in modern colonial experience, plus personal ambition on the part of a few leading spirits. That these revolts were not more frequent and more serious, shows how large a part persuasion played in the building up of the Empire. Rome's political genius and power of assimilation have never been equalled in history.

Even so, revolt was a far more dangerous thing than the original occupation of a country. Thus the greatest peril Cæsar had had to meet in Gaul had been the revolt led by Vercingetorix in 52 B. C. six years after his first campaign.

Except Trajan's conquest of Dacia, all the chief military incidents of the first, that is the offensive, phase of imperial strategy were revolts. Let us take them in their chronological order.

First of all come the operations on the northern frontier during the reigns of Augustus and Tiberius. Before achieving supreme power, Augustus had already (in 35 B. C.) conquered Pannonia, the country between the Save and the Danube. In the following year he had put down a revolt in Dalmatia, between the Save and the Adriatic Sea. The operations had been economically profitable in themselves as they had brought in quantities of slaves, money and ships. In the first decade after his accession he occupied what is now Switzerland, together with southern Germany and upper Austria to the line of the Danube. By the year 13 B. C., although these regions still required military occupation and occasional punitive expeditions, nevertheless they seemed quiet enough to warrant attempting another enterprise. It was therefore decided to conquer Germany from the Rhine to the Elbe, partly because hope of German aid might encourage sedition in Gaul—the richest and most populous province of the West. The operation was methodically prepared. Since communications and supply were difficult in the savage densely wooded country, it was decided to have the fleet support the army by sailing up the rivers, and since the Romans feared open tidal water, a canal was dug from the Rhine to the lagoon which later became the Zuyder Zee. The occupation was a military success, but an economic failure, for the booty was small. No tribute could be had from the wild and undeveloped country, and the profits of its trade were a bagatelle compared with the cost of the army of occupation.

Nevertheless, the government of Augustus persisted, and in 6 A. D., eighteen years after the beginning of the operation, Augustus' general Tiberius was in what is now Bohemia stamping out the last embers of resistance, when he was recalled with many of his troops to meet a new danger. Angered at the heavy demands upon them for supplies and recruits for the auxiliaries, the Dalmatians and Pannonians revolted. The Roman garrisons and the traders were massacred, and the rebels increased their numbers until they were estimated at 200,000. Only Sirmium, the modern Mitrovitza on the Save, held out.

In Rome itself, the news produced a panic. The men whose ancestors two centuries before had shown such magnificent courage against Hannibal, whose grandfathers had kept a stiff upper lip in the face of Spartacus' slave insurrection, imagined the Pannonians to be marching on the city. Cohorts of freedmen were raised, and even slaves (freed by law for the purpose) were enlisted as so-called "volunteers." Grave risks were run in exacting tribute even from the poverty-stricken tribes of newly conquered Germany. It was proposed to recall Tiberius at once.

While sending for Tiberius, Augustus began preparations for moving against the rebels from all sides. The hodge-podge of newly raised troops from Italy were hurriedly pushed forward to Siscia, the modern Sisek on the Save, to cover Venetia. Meanwhile there were three legions on the lower Danube, in what is now Bulgaria. Augustus ordered two legions stationed in Syria to join them, and called upon the "allied" (i. e., dependent) king of Thrace for his contingent. The five legions and the Thracians, when concentrated, were to march up the Danube.

Meanwhile Tiberius had kept his head. He knew the revolted districts well, having often campaigned in them; and he correctly estimated the situation, judging that Italy was in no immediate danger. On the other hand, he knew that the revolt was dangerous because of the military training its leaders and many of their followers had enjoyed while serving as Roman auxiliary soldiers. He therefore began negotiations with the Bohemian chiefs and left for Pannonia only when he had come to a satisfactory understanding with them. On reaching Siscia early in the autumn, he was joined by the forces from the lower Danube who had just relieved Sirmium after hard fighting.

At Siscia he finally concentrated ten legions, seventy cohorts of auxiliary foot, ten "alæ" (i. e., squadrons) of auxiliary cavalry, the Thracian allied cavalry, ten thousand re-enlisted veterans and the scratch troops recently raised in Italy—all told his force was almost certainly well over 100,000 effective, possibly nearer 150,-000. Pannonia was a barbarous and barren country whose topography was little known in detail. Accordingly, supply was difficult and there was great danger of being ambushed upon the march. The troops from the lower Danube had already lost heavily in several ambushes. Tiberius' decision was worthy of the severely practical Roman temper at its best. We are reminded of Marius' operations against the Cimbri and Teutones. Instead of hunting for glory by trying for a pitched battle, he determined to distribute his troops in fortified posts, for like all barbarians the rebels were not good at sieges—they had not the necessary method and persistence. The Roman posts were therefore in little danger. Thus distributed, the Romans would be able to devastate the country systematically, and could, in the long run, starve out the rebels by making agriculture impossible. The commander-in-chief took upon himself the hard and tedious work of superintending the supply department.

Such measures did not suit public opinion in Rome, which had chopped around from panic to hopeful and excited demands that the war be ended at once by a great victory. In city populations of unmilitary temper such exhibitions are common, for instance "On to Richmond" in 1861, "À Berlin" in Paris in 1870, and the Londoners' delight in "killing Kruger with their mouths" in 1900. But in Romans such conduct is pathetic.

Tiberius, unmoved, stuck to his decision. In 7 A. D. resentment in Rome ran so high that a new commander, Germanicus, was sent out as his first lieutenant, or even his equal, so determined was the capital upon a striking victory. Opinion concerning Tiberius soon changed for the better, for Germanicus was ambushed and his command nearly cut to pieces on reaching the theatre of war. In the course of the year 8 A. D., the rebellion completely collapsed in Pannonia. The year 9 A. D. saw it stamped out in Dalmatia after a victory won by Tiberius there.

At the same time hostile feeling in Germany had been steadily rising. Only five days after the news of Tiberius' Dalmatian victory, word reached Rome that all Germany from the Rhine to the Elbe had revolted, that Varus, the Roman commander there, had been killed and his force of three legions wiped out.

Varus, who had previously shown ability in Palestine, had been completely taken in. Whether the fault lay chiefly with his intelligence service or in his own failure to estimate correctly the reports sent in, is not clear. We know that reports or at least rumors of coming trouble had reached him but that he utterly failed to estimate the situation. When he learned that his outposts to the northeast were being attacked, he moved forward with three legions, plus a proper proportion of auxiliaries, no doubt, to their relief. Mistakenly believing himself still in friendly country, he encumbered his column not only with masses of baggage but also with the wives and children of the army of occupation. Thus hampered, he was ambushed in passing through a dense forest, and his entire command was cut to pieces.

Tiberius, who was put in command, judged that the game was not worth the candle. War against poverty-stricken northern savages could not be made to pay as the conquest of Carthage, Gaul, and the populous and wealthy East had paid. Opinion in Rome had been disgusted even at his own recent Pannonian victories because they had emptied rather than filled the treasury. Accordingly, the greatest soldier of his time decided to withdraw the surviving garrisons. Five years later, when he himself had become Emperor, he authorized invasions of Germany in the three successive years, 14, 15 and 16 A. D. These operations, however, were little more than military promenades intended to put the fear of Rome into the hostile tribes. No further occupation was attempted, and the Rhine and Danube remained the frontier of civilization.

Two years after the last German campaign in 18 A. D., one Tacfarinus who had been trained in the Roman auxiliaries rebelled in Africa. The neighbouring allied king of Morocco remained loyal, like the king of Thrace during the Pannonian revolt, and furnished a contingent to the army which suppressed the revolt.[13]

Next in the order of time comes the conquest of Britain, but inasmuch as we know it in greater detail than any other operation of the offensive period of the Empire, let us postpone its discussion until the close of the period. Its crisis came in the revolt of Boadicea in 61 A. D.

In 69–70 A. D. occurred the Gallic revolt under Civilis. The Batavians, a poor but warlike tribe living around the mouth of the Rhine, had been exempted from Roman taxation on condition of finding a considerable number of recruits for the auxiliaries.

[13] Tacitus: Annals, Bks. 2, 3 and 4.

One of their chiefs, Civilis, had shown ability as an auxiliary officer but was a marked man because of repeated insubordination. In 69 A. D., Civilis saw his chance in the confusion and civil war which followed the death of Nero. He revolted, and was followed first by the eight Batavian auxiliary cohorts, and then by most of the Gallic and German auxiliaries serving on the Rhine frontier. With these forces, plus hordes of wild tribesmen, he defeated the two near-by legions and shut them up in Castra Vetera, the modern Xanten on the left bank of the Rhine opposite the mouth of the Lippe. The result of this action was a revolt which, for a moment, swept all Atlantic Gaul and was joined by the Roman troops stationed there. However, it collapsed as suddenly as it had sprung up, when Vespasian, having settled the civil war, moved vigorously against it. Civilis was defeated near Treves and disappears from history.[14]

While the revolt of Civilis was going on, the Roman troops in the East were also seeing active service in suppressing the rebellion of the Jews. These last were almost the only people in the Empire inspired by strong national patriotism in the modern sense. They resisted the Romans desperately, with the intense determination familiar to modern students of the Jewish character. On the other hand, their strategy was stupid, for after correctly deciding that they could not face the Roman army in a pitched battle in the open, they shut themselves up in cities and allowed themselves to be besieged without harassing the rear of the besieging troops by continuous guerrilla operations. Accordingly, their fierce resistance only made their agony longer and more bitter—while leaving the modern student without any account of first-century Roman methods in open warfare from the able pen of Josephus.

In the various sieges, especially of Jerusalem, pre-gunpowder position warfare may be said to have reached its climax. The army of Titus was composed of four legions, with a due proportion of auxiliaries, and possessed 340 catapults. Jerusalem resisted for about six months, the besieged suffering greatly from shortage of provisions toward the end. Titus threw up four huge banks or terraces to overtop the defences. One of Vespasian's battering rams weighed 100 tons, so that 1500 men were needed to swing

[14] Tacitus: History, Bks. 4 and 5.

it in striking against the wall. For transport it required 150 yoke of oxen or 300 pair of mules.[15]

The change in military policy necessitated by the western revolts will be discussed presently in connexion with the other changes during the offensive phase. Meanwhile let us consider briefly the operations of Trajan with which that phase ends.

In connection with the campaigns of Tiberius, I have already noted the poverty of the Danubian basin when first conquered by Rome. This poverty, however, was due not to the natural barrenness of the country but only to its lack of development. After a century, its natural fertility was apparent, and the Romans had found out that to the north of the river lay another highly fertile region extending to the Carpathians and comprising the plains of Hungary and the present territories of Rumania, including Bessarabia to the Dniester.

After six years' campaigning (101–107 A. D.), in which the Moroccan auxiliary cavalry particularly distinguished itself, Trajan conquered Dacia. The Carpathians and the Dniester made a defensible frontier, and the country was soon thoroughly Romanized.

Subsequently, in four years' campaigning (113–117 A. D.) against the Parthians in Armenia and Mesopotamia, Trajan advanced to the Caspian and the Persian Gulf. However, since the countries invaded were far from the centre of Roman power and possessed no good military frontier, most of them were promptly abandoned. Only certain districts on the left or east bank of the upper Euphrates were retained.

Insurrections among the Jewish colonies throughout the Roman East, particularly in Cyprus and Cyrenaica, probably helped to bring about the decision to withdraw. After over a million provincials and vast numbers of Jews had been massacred the insurrections were crushed. Nevertheless they must have added considerably to the military liabilities of the moment.

I have put off considering the conquest of Britain from a wish to end this summary of the chief military episodes of the Imperial offensive period with an account of one of those episodes at greater length. For this purpose, the conquest of Britain is well suited, for it is known in some detail and includes all the characteristic features of Roman occupations—especially the attraction of

[15] Dodge: Cæsar, 776.

rich agricultural districts, and the constant search for defensible frontiers.

The decision to invade Britain was made in 43 A. D., and its motive, we may reasonably guess, was a knowledge of the possibilities of agricultural wealth in England.

The force assigned to the operation included four legions, the II, IX, XIV, and XX, plus an equal or greater number of auxiliary light infantry and cavalry (including some Batavian horse) making a total of about 48,000 effective. It should be noted as an example of the extraordinary permanence of units under the Empire that two of these legions remained in Britain at least 364 years, until 410 A. D., the year of Alaric's mutiny! For the moment, however, the expeditionary force was most unwilling to move. The troops said that Britain was outside the known world, and probably (like most inhabitants of the Empire) they disliked and feared the sea, especially the Atlantic with its tides.

At this point the reader should fix in his mind that the chief Roman landing places in England were always on the coast of Kent. Later a secondary group of ports of entry was set up around Southampton Water. North of the Thames the length of the sea voyage seems to have prevented organized communication for large bodies of men.

Finally, Aulus Plautius, the commander of the expeditionary force, got his troops embarked (probably at Boulogne) and landed them in Kent. The Britons took up a defensive position behind the Medway, protected by forests and marshes. The Batavian cavalry, born and bred in exactly this sort of country, turned the position by swimming the river. The Britons then stood behind the Thames, but the Batavians swam its lower reaches and turned the British left. The Britons now retreated to the marshes of Essex, which held up the Romans, whereat Aulus Plautius asked for reinforcements and for the Emperor Claudius in person. The operations in Essex may have been a check, and Plautius' request a confession of weakness; or (more probably) the Emperor was asked to take the credit of a campaign already virtually won, and the reinforcements were needed only to replace the wastage incidental to active service.

Claudius concentrated the replacements for the British expeditionary force at Ostia. Among his contingent were some war-elephants. The private comments of his transport officers when directed to move such huge beasts from Italy to Gaul must have been worth hearing.

Pyrrhus had moved elephants across the Straits of Otranto and Hannibal had done the like along the highly civilized Mediterranean shores and over the Alps as well. Even so, to get the great beasts across Gaul and then across the Channel must have been a business.

Starting in 44 A. D., the troops went from Ostia to Marseilles by sea, made their way across Gaul, crossed the channel and joined Aulus Plautius, who was holding the general line of the Thames. The Britons had concentrated at Colchester. They were defeated somewhere in the neighbourhood of that place, and with the minor operations which reduced what is now Norfolk and Suffolk, the first stage of the conquest was completed.

The territory in Roman hands was bounded from northeast to southwest by the Welland, the Avon, the lower Severn, Exmoor and the lower Exe. Of course, near their headwaters the Welland and the Avon were not serious military obstacles, but it is probable that at that time the gap between the points at which each stream began to have military value was not much more than 30 miles wide, from near Coventry on the Avon to near Ashley on the Welland. About thirty miles in rear of the centre of that gap, a permanent fortified station was established at Towcester. From this the garrison, in a single day's march, could strike any force which had passed the gap and was moving south or east. The first-class engineered road known as the Watling Street which started at Canterbury (the road-centre for the Kentish harbours) and went on through Rochester to London, was continued northwest to Towcester. Three cities, London, Colchester, and St. Albans, were colonized with veterans and established as fully organized Roman municipalities. The choice of the three points shows clearly the systematic way the conquest was organized; London the lowest crossing of the Thames, the most important road centre in the island and its natural capital, Colchester the centre of resistance to Claudius in 44 A. D., and St. Albans, 25 miles—a long day's forced march—northwest from London on the Watling Street leading to Towcester, the advanced G. H. Q. of the army of occupation. The whole southeast, the most fertile and most densely inhabited part of the island was thus rounded off and secured to the Empire.

The four legions of the original expeditionary force remained

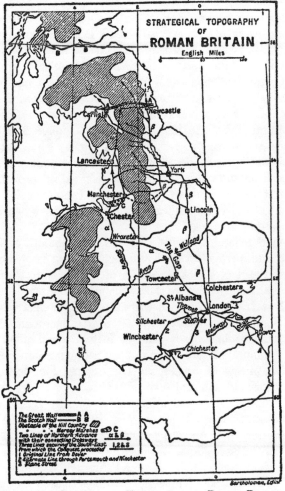

PLATE 11.—STRATEGICAL TOPOGRAPHY OF ROMAN BRITAIN.

in the island. The IX legion, based upon Colchester, held the right. The XIV and XX composed the centre, whose axis was the Watling Street from London through St. Albans to Towcester and the gap. On the left stood the II, based perhaps upon Cirencester.[16] The auxiliaries were stationed in advance of the legions and were usually brigaded in groups of three or four cohorts or alæ.[17]

Rome was not long content to stand still. Her authorities in the island were tempted by the fertility of the unoccupied Midlands northwest of the Avon-Welland line, and annoyed in a military sense by raids based upon the Welsh hills to the west and the Pennines to the north of the Midlands. The occupation of the northwest Midlands was begun in 49 or 50 A. D. and garrisons were pushed forward to Wroxeter and Lincoln. From thence the Romans found themselves compelled to move against Wales and the southern Pennines, just as every conquerer finds himself compelled to coerce " . . . . districts which, while exterior to those it is worth his while to occupy, furnish reservoirs of discontent and opposition; hill-places to which the defeated rulers of the fertile plain can retire and fastnesses of little value to commercial development, but of indefinite military value as a reserve whence attack can proceed." [18]

A Roman general, Ostorius, marched to the mouth of the Dee, broke an attack from the north and then (turning east) subjugated the greater part of Wales.[19] Master of Wales, the Roman provincial government saw before it the island of Anglesea, the centre of the British religion, which was naturally the chief inspiration of the islanders' resistance. In 60 A. D., Suetonius Paulinus, then Roman commander-in-chief in Britain, determined for the sake of the moral effect to wipe out the population, and especially the Druid priests of Anglesea. The original four legions were still in the island and had maintained their respective positions, but by this time they had all moved forward. In the east the headquarters of the IX legion was Lincoln. The XX, based upon Chester, was operating northward. The II was in the Severn valley; its headquarters may have been already as far forward as Caerleon-on-Usk. The XIV legion was based either upon Chester or upon Wroxeter, two days' march to the south; at any rate it was operating westward against North Wales, and

[16] Haverfield, E. B., Vol. IV, 583.
[17] Cheesman, 105–107. See Plate 11.
[18] Hilaire Belloc: Warfare in England, 70.
[19] Tacitus: Annals, Bk. 12.

was chosen as the legionary component of the force which was to advance upon Anglesea.

In itself the operation against Anglesea was a complete success, but under the political conditions of the moment the decision to undertake so distant a march proved a most serious politico-military error. Eastern and central Britain was angry at the overbearing attitude of the Roman colonists. Various cruelties and outrages on the part of individual Roman officials (especially the scourging of Boadicea, the queen of the Norfolk tribes, and the ravishing of her two daughters), had aroused resentment. Seizing her chance while Suetonius was far away in Anglesea, Boadicea revolted and carried the whole country with her. She began by attacking Colchester. When the IX legion advanced to relieve the place, she defeated and almost destroyed it, its commander being killed in the action. Colchester then fell, and after it St. Albans and London. Tacitus tells us that they had been better provided with handsome public buildings than with defences. Boadicea massacied their inhabitants and the entire Roman and non-British population, about 70,000 in all.

Upon hearing of these disasters, Suetonius moved eastward from Anglesea to Chester, where he was joined by a considerable detachment of the XX legion. Why, in the face of this awful peril he did not take the whole XX with him is hard to say, for if his small force had failed to crush the rebellion, the troops left behind at Chester would almost certainly have been cut off and massacred. However, it is justifiable in a military sense to detach troops if their presence in a subsidiary theatre of war serves to keep a greater number of the enemy out of the principal theatre, and it may be that the units of the XX near Chester were keeping northern hostiles at bay while Suetonius was dealing with Boadicea.

From Chester the Roman general moved on London which he reoccupied. He had sent an order to the II legion in the southwest, but that order (which was probably to concentrate on Suetonius himself) was not obeyed. The commander of the II may have been panic-stricken and considering escape by sea, or his disobedience may have been only excessive caution and slowness in joining—we do not know. At all events, Suetonius could not for the moment count upon the II. If there was anything left of the IX, the remnant must have been far to the northeast around Lincoln, separated from the commander-in-chief by the whole strength of the rebellion. The forces under his hand, therefore, were only the XIV legion and the detachment he had taken from the XX, plus certain units of auxiliary cavalry and light infantry, about 10,000 effective in all. Nevertheless he took counsel of his courage and determined to meet Boadicea in the field.

In some unknown locality, probably in the neighbourhood of London, Suetonius found a defensive position with cover of some sort for his flanks, a wood in rear, and an open field of battle in front—in which he could not be ambushed should he advance. He formed his troops with the legionaries in the centre (as usual) and in close formation, and the auxiliaries on the wings, the auxiliary cavalry in front of the foot and concentrated on either wing. The Britons came on in enormous numbers, so confident that they ringed in their own flanks and rear with wagons from which their wives and children were to see the battle as if in a theatre. At the beginning of the action the Romans stood fast. Then, when the British supply of missiles was exhausted, the legionary troops counter-attacked in "wedge" formation, the auxiliaries conforming to the movement. The Britons were broken. Ringed in by their own wagons, nearly 80,000 of them were massacred, the Romans losing only about 400.

The back of the revolt was completely broken, as might well have been expected after such a smash. Boadicea took poison, and the disobedient commander of the II legion, in his envy and chagrin, stabbed himself with his own sword.[20]

In connexion with this campaign there are a number of points worth noting. First there is the large extent of country which the Romans were not only invading but also (a much harder task) attempting to hold with forces probably less rather than more than 50,000 strong. Second, the high professional standard throughout the army of occupation (even the suicide of the delinquent commander of the II testifies to this). Third, the willingness of the commander of the IX and afterwards of Suetonius to accept battle with a contempt for numbers like that of Clive and Wellesley in India. Fourth, the neglect of fortification.

[20] Tacitus: Annals, Bk. 14.

Finally, an interesting and difficult tactical point is raised by
Tacitus' description of the formation in which the legionaries
delivered the decisive attack as a "wedge" (cuneus). The word
itself suggests a triangular figure, but in practice it is hard to see
how a triangle with a true apex could have brought good results.
If we assume that it means a dense deep column, the objection
at once appears that neither the short sword nor the pilum (which
last could hardly have been worth much as a pike) would have been
effective in such a formation. The difficulty therefore remains.

After Boadicea, Britain never again required any considerable
military effort on the part of Rome. The garrison was at first
kept up to the same strength in legionary troops (i. e., four legions)
by the arrival of the VI in the eastern sector of the island to
replace the annihilated IX. In 67 A. D. it was even possible
to withdraw to Pannonia the XIV legion, which had been stationed either at Wroxeter or at Chester. However, the same
causes which had formerly made for expansion were still active,
represented by the desire to control near-by fertile lands (in this
case Lancashire and the Carlisle district on the west of the island,
together with the great plain of York on the east) and the corresponding necessity of cleaning out hill brigands (i. e., those of the
Pennine hills). Accordingly, some time in 70 A. D. or soon after,
the legionary garrison was again brought up to four legions by
the arrival of another legion bearing the number II, plus the title
"Adiutrix" to distinguish it from the old II legion known as
"II Augusta." With these forces, undoubtedly accompanied by
their due complement of auxiliaries, a new decade (70–80 A. D.)
of advance began. First the permanent headquarters of the VI
were moved forward to York. Then the fertile Scotch lowlands
south of a line drawn across the narrowest part of the island from
the Clyde to the Firth of Forth were occupied and held. This
occupation, in the inevitable sequence of Roman imperialism,
led to a punitive expedition against the Scotch highlanders in 85
A. D., and a victory over them somewhere north of the Forth at an
unknown place called Mons Graupius. Agricola, the commander
in this last advance, talked of invading Ireland, which he said could
be conquered and held by a single legion plus auxiliaries; but he
was recalled by Domitian's government at Rome.[21] At the same

[21] Tacitus: Agricola.

time Legio II Adiutrix was ordered away from Britain to Pannonia—the same province to which the XIV had been sent in 67 A. D.[22]

The recall of this legion, together with that of Agricola, ended Roman expansion in Britain. The permanent defensive organization of the province is best considered in connexion with the defensive phase of imperial strategy—more especially since Hadrian, whose accession in 117 A. D. marks the beginning of that phase, gave his name to the Great British Wall. Meanwhile I shall end my account of the offensive phase with a few words on the obscure subject of Roman minor tactics during the first century and on the changes in the recruitment of the army which had taken place by the end of the phase.

It is possible, but by no means certain, that the legions were usually formed for battle in two lines of five cohorts, instead of in three lines as ordinarily in Cæsar's time. The chief argument for the two-line idea is that the 1st and 5th cohorts (which would stand upon the flanks of a front line of five cohorts), were the two cohorts to be raised to 1000 men each.[23] Still the question is not worth the ink spilt over it, for any army kept supple by frequent field operations on a large scale is able to vary its formations to suit the requirements of each particular case. Cæsar's lieutenant, Crassus, being short of troops, had formed in two lines against the Aquitanians in 56 B. C. Cæsar himself had used four lines at Pharsalia and one at Ruspina during the African campaign.

There are indications that the men were sometimes placed closer in ranks than formerly. Tacitus expressly says that this was done against Boadicea, and the "wedge" with which that action was won strongly suggests a close order formation. On the other hand, pilum and gladius could scarcely have been wielded freely in anything but a skirmishing order, and we know beyond question that they were continued as the weapons of the legionary.

During the entire offensive phase, both legions and auxiliaries were ready to take the field at a moment's notice. The garrison of Britain, for instance, was not only on a war footing but actually in the field almost every summer from 43 to 85 A. D. The legions would often lie in pairs, as the XIV and XX were doing in 60 A. D. and in the same way, two, three or four auxiliary cohorts

[22] Dion Cassius: Bk. 55, sec. 24.   [23] Dodge: Cæsar, 772.

or alæ were usually grouped, or "brigaded," as we should say, under a single commander. A cohort of 500 infantry was supposed to require a camp of five acres, and the winter camps of the period which have been excavated run from ten, thirteen or fourteen acres up to thirty-five. Winter camps were fortified, but only with a stockade and ditch not much more elaborate than those of the nightly camps when in the field. When an army went into winter quarters it threw out towards the enemy a line of observation composed of single auxiliary cohorts in separate little camps each about one and one-half acres in area.

Each legion may or may not have had certain auxiliary units more or less permanently assigned to its support. The weight of evidence seems a little against it.

Tactically, the legions were still the chief arm, the core of a defensive action, in attack used to deal the decisive blow.

We hear of no major action decided by a cavalry charge as under Alexander or by the fire power of archery as at Crécy and Poitiers.

On the other hand, cavalry (while still subordinate) was growing in relative importance. In part this growth resulted naturally from the regular organization of the army as a whole, in contrast with the haphazard system of the later republic, for the chief weakness of republican armies had been inferior cavalry. Hannibal had consistently profited by this weakness until Zama. That action was the first in which the cavalry of the Roman side had not been driven from the field by the great Carthaginian's mounted troops. The great smash of Carrhæ had been directly due to cavalry inferiority. One of Cæsar's narrowest shaves had been at the Ruspina. Any intelligent war department might be expected to take steps towards ending such a situation. It is true that we have no direct evidence of the existence of an Imperial War Department but inasmuch as the Roman Empire never had less than 300,000 men under arms, spread out all around the Mediterranean basin, it is impossible to believe that such a force could have been used intelligently without some well-staffed central agency.

To return to the matter of cavalry, the problems set before the imperial armies were such as to give cavalry a chance to shine and thereby strengthen itself still more by attracting energetic and ambitious officers and men. The distinguished service of the

Batavian horse in the original invasion of Britain and that of the Moors in the invasion of Dacia, are examples. Obviously in frontier defences against raids (which was after all the chief task of the Imperial armies even during the offensive phase) mounted troops are of more use than foot.

Still, the growth in importance of cavalry was as yet only beginning. Far more significant were the changes during the first century in recruiting.

Under Augustus, the higher officers of the whole army and the enlisted men of the legions were still mainly Italians, while the auxiliaries were tribally recruited bodies, serving in the general neighbourhood of their homes, fighting more or less in their own traditional manner, and partly officered either by their own chieftains or by legionary centurions promoted to field rank as a reward for distinguished service. By the time of Trajan, the repeated revolts of the first century led the government to remove the auxiliary units from the neighbourhood of their homes, and to destroy their tribal character by keeping them up to strength by means of recruits from the provinces in which they happened to be stationed. Naturally, after this change we hear no more of tribal chiefs as field officers—or indeed in any capacity in the regular auxiliaries. It is not so clear why the practice of promoting centurions to field rank was stopped, but toward the end of the offensive phases such promotions had become exceedingly rare. On the other hand, the increasing Romanization of the provinces was depriving the officers' corps of the entire army and the enlisted personnel of the legions of their distinctly Italian character. A few years as a field officer of a legion, or in command of an auxiliary cohort or ala, was becoming the customary introduction to a career in the imperial civil service. Finally, the very success of the imperial policy in assuring internal peace and civic order was beginning to contract the recruiting ground of legions and auxiliaries alike to the frontier provinces. There the level of civilization was a trifle less high, and the presence of the army kept the soldierly spirit alive.

The second-century change in status of the auxiliaries from tribal bodies to mere units in the cosmopolitan Imperial army resulted in the raising of a new category of troops, the Numeri. The reader will remember that among the reasons why the Imperial government of the first century valued the auxiliaries were first that their tribal patriotism helped to build up *esprit de corps* in their units, second that the lower level of wealth and culture among the peoples from which they were recruited made them easier and cheaper to raise than troops from more highly civilized districts. Of these two advantages the first was now completely destroyed by the new practice of filling the gaps in the original auxiliary cohorts and alæ by replacements from any neighbourhood in which they happened to be stationed. The second was in a fair way to disappear through the Romanization of the provinces, a process which was to culminate in Caracalla's grant of citizenship to all inhabitants of the Empire (212 A. D.). The second-century Empire was now in touch with new tribes especially among the Moors, the Germans of Dacia, and the Orientals. Accordingly units were recruited from them, and these units were not incorporated as auxiliaries but were known as "numeri" and placed on a separate footing in order that they might serve the special purposes for which the original auxiliaries had been raised. Instead of being subjected to the uniform imperial training they were encouraged to keep their tribal methods of fighting and even their dialects and outlandish war-cries. The fact that the commanders of numeri ranked below those of auxiliary units together with the small camp space allotted to each numerus in the German forts, may indicate that numeri were only two or three hundred strong. Smaller than that they can hardly have been as we find them divided into "centuries" and the cavalry into troops (turmæ).[24]

It would be interesting to know what training the officers of the entire army received and what was the organization of the higher command and of the War Department. The practice of appointing only men of the "equestrian order," i. e., men of some wealth, to field rank, and still more that of appointing none but men of "senatorial" rank, i. e., millionaires, to serve as general officers, suggest careful staff training for such appointees as well as for their chief assistants. Unfortunately the supposition is mere inference—like that of the existence of a War Department. Nevertheless—given an army over 300,000 strong and so widely distributed in space—it is hard to see how operations could have been carried on without some sort of staff training. The fact that Claudius, in

[24] Cheesman, 88.

44 A. D., concentrated at Rome the reinforcements intended for Britain, seems to imply that Rome was the centre at least of transport and supply department. But all that we can certainly say is that there was a centralized pay department located there, and that the "Prætorian Prefect," the supreme commander under the Emperor of the whole army, spent most of his time in the capital.[25]

[25] Haverfield, E. B., Vol. 23, 474.

CHAPTER II

THE IMPERIAL ROMAN ARMY

(FROM HADRIAN TO THE DEATH OF CONSTANTINE—117–337 A. D.)

THE accession of Hadrian in 117 A. D., marks the adoption of a new military policy for the Empire, that of a strict strategical defensive. In this chapter I shall first consider the phase of successful, rigid, frontier defence beginning with 117 and ending with the assassination of Alexander Severus in 235 A. D. In order to understand the phase of confusion which begins in 235 and ends with the pacification of the Roman world by Diocletian in 297 A. D., a brief discussion of the causes of the decline of ancient civilization will then be necessary. After this, the military events will appear symptoms rather than causes of the decline. There will then follow a description of the Roman army as reorganized by Diocletian and Constantine, who abandoned the policy of rigid frontier defence and substituted for it one of elastic defence, supporting the frontier troops by means of field armies composed of the crack units of the service. The chapter will end with a word on Roman tactics about the time of Constantine's death in 337.

What then were the reasons for Hadrian's decision to adopt a defensive on all frontiers? First of all, it was emphatically not a case of severe military pressure from without, for there was no such pressure. Unless the reader thoroughly grasps that fact he will utterly fail to understand the military position of the Empire.

The reasons undoubtedly were: first, that the Romans were no longer tempted forward by districts at the same time fertile and easily defensible, lying just outside their frontiers; second, that they were beginning to feel the difficulty of administering so vast an empire without the aid of modern mechanical means of rapid transport and communication.

Let us consider this second point for a moment. From Lisbon to the Euphrates is nearer three than two thousand miles as the crow flies. From Carlisle to Wadi Halfa in upper Egypt is even more.

What this meant in terms of time is shown by the extraordinary effort made to convey to Galba in Spain, the news of Nero's death in Rome. From Rome overland to Clunia, somewhere in the district of Burgos, south of that city and east of Valladolid, is about 1100 miles as the crow flies—in actual road distance not less than 1400 miles. Nero's death was announced to Galba by mounted post in seven days, which must have been about 200 miles a day, and the feat was considered almost a miracle.[1] To get a legion over the same space and bring them in fresh enough for action without a long rest would certainly have taken three nearer than two months. From Durazzo to Constantinople by the great Egnatian road was nearly 500 miles, Allowing 15 miles a day as a high average for infantry, would mean over 27 marching days for the distance. From Belgrade to Constantinople would be about the same, and from Constantinople to Antioch rather more. Therefore we must allow over 2 months as the minimum time required to get a legion from Belgrade or Durazzo to Antioch, a little less time between Belgrade and Treves, and a month between Treves and York. In the unheard of event of a legionary march from York to Antioch, six months would be breakneck speed. The reader must remember that these time estimates are absolute minima, for the average length of a day's march was not 15 miles but somewhere between 11 and 12, as we shall see, for instance, by the spacing of the camps or "mansiones" on the Stane Street;[2] and furthermore, not every day of a long march is a marching day. Obviously such distances were a standing temptation to ambitious local commanders to mutiny and make a throw for empire. In themselves they explain well enough Hadrian's decision to advance the frontiers no further.

This decision boiled down the problem of the Roman army to policing the frontiers. Leaving out of account, for the moment, the changes produced in that army in adapting itself to its new and restricted mission, let us consider the enormous engineering works undertaken to facilitate its work. There were, first of all, the erection of artificial obstacles to supplement the natural obstacles, i. e., unfordable first-class rivers, upon which the frontier reposed throughout most of its length, and, secondly, the improvement of the road system over which the troops must move.

[1] Young, Vol. 1, 172.   [2] Belloc: The Stane Street, 114–139.

The problem of defending a frontier covered by continuous obstacles reposes upon permanent military principles. Allowing for the differences in weapons and communication, what the Romans did is what modern armies would do to-day. First of all they maintained an intelligence service with agents in the near-by unoccupied territory, so as to be warned against threatening attacks. Wherever they could—for instance on the lower Rhine—they obtained the firm friendship and co-operation of the tribes just outside the frontier. Where they could not—for instance on the middle and upper Rhine and in Britain—they devastated the country, making a No Man's Land a day's march wide in front of the frontier obstacle to prevent surprise. Where that obstacle was a river, its course was patrolled by flotillas of guardboats. The legions were stationed on the near bank in great fortified camps from 50 to 60 acres in area, and the auxiliaries strung out between them in smaller fortified posts.

When the frontier rested on the desert, as in Africa and in Syria south of the Euphrates, chains of permanent works were arranged in depth along the natural lines of approach to Roman territory. Many of these desert outposts are astonishingly careful and solid in construction. Naturally, the more advanced works were garrisoned chiefly by cavalry.[3]

Where there was neither river nor desert, continuous walls were set up. Two such walls were permanently held, the German "limes," between 250 and 300 miles long from the Rhine near Neuwied to the Danube near Ratisbon, and Hadrian's wall in Britain, 73 miles long from the Solway Firth to a point on the North Sea coast just north of Newcastle-upon-Tyne. In Germany the obstacle was an earthen mound for half its length crowned by a solid oaken palisade and by a rough stone wall for the other half. In Britain it was originally of earth but was afterwards (in Septimius Severus' time, 193–211) strengthened by a wall of good masonry 8 feet thick and 16 feet high.

Noting the elaborate nature of these walls and their ditches, unmilitary scholars have assumed that they were meant to be defended, and have puzzled over the fact that their earthen banks are generally more steeply scarped on the Roman side. Naturally, in pre-gunpowder fortification it was of the utmost

[3] Cagnat: Frontière Tripolitaine.

importance to have a steep escarpment which the assailant must climb. The fact is, of course, that the Roman walls were completely indefensible because they were never manned by anything remotely like the number of troops necessary to defend them, as I shall presently show. They served as screens behind which patrols could march in comparative safety, thus keeping the whole line under constant surveillance, and especially as obstacles not only against the advance of a raiding party, but also (which was perhaps even more important) against its retreat. The raiders, as they clambered over the obstacle, would have to leave their horses behind. To stay and break it down would take time which they could not afford to waste since their approach would have already been announced far and wide by smoke signals, and the nearest Roman detachments would be coming up. Many if not most of these detachments would be mounted and therefore far more mobile than the dismounted raiders. Furthermore, if they succeeded in driving off cattle, or in retreating with any heavy plunder, they would again find themselves in difficulties as they recrossed the obstacle. Indeed, this would be the most critical stage of the operation, from the point of view of the raiders. Byzantine military writers, treating of very similar conditions on the Saracen border in Asia Minor, recommend that the defenders should then make their main effort.[4]

This system is familiar to us now, having been applied in almost exactly the same form though on a smaller scale, by the Spanish in Cuba. Their "trochas" were largely of barbed wire, and their No Man's Land much narrower. The same general idea appeared in the British blockhouse system in South Africa.

The garrison of the wall itself was composed of auxiliaries; in Britain they were stationed in fortified permanent camps upon the wall itself, and in Germany usually close behind it although sometimes as far back as three or four miles. Each camp held a single ala or cohort. In Britain the auxiliary garrison has been estimated at 6000 cavalry, 2125 mounted infantry (a branch of the service to which I shall return in the summary at the end of this chapter) and 20,875 infantry, a total of 29,000. Since the front to be defended was 73 miles long, if all these troops were concentrated upon it they would give just under 400 men per mile,

[4] Oman, Vol. 1, 211, 214, quoting Nicephorus Phocas: "Border Warfare."

or nearly 4½ yards per man! Even if we take these figures as minima, especially in cavalry, they dispose absolutely of the theory of a formal defence of the entire wall. Between the camps, small camps about 50 feet square were dotted along the wall at intervals of about a mile, to serve as guard-houses and observation posts, and between these "mile castles" there were watch-towers about every 100 yards.

The auxiliaries were well able to deal with any ordinary raiders. For raids in great force the provincial commander would call upon his legionary troops. These lay concentrated in permanent fortified camps covering from 50 to 60 acres, not in pairs, as in the offensive phase, but singly.

Turning from obstacles and camps to the troops which manned them, let us first consider the question of numbers. From about 117 to 161 A. D. it is possible to establish a fairly complete list as follows:

Britain. Legions: II. Augusta (Isca Silurum, now Caerleon)
     VI. Victrix (Eburacum, York)
     XX. Valeria Victrix (Deva, Chester)
  Auxiliaries: 6,000 cavalry, 2,125 mounted infantry, 20,875 infantry, total 29,000.

Lower Germany. Legions: I. Minervia (Bonna, Bonn)
(Lower Rhine)   XXX. Ulpia Victrix (Vetera, Xanten)
  Auxiliaries: 1,500 cavalry, 250 mounted infantry, 1,750 infantry, total 3,500.

Upper Germany. Legions: XXII. Primigenia (Moguntiacum, Mainz)
     VIII. Augusta (Argentorate, Strassburg)
  Auxiliaries: 1,500 cavalry, 1,125 mounted infantry, 9,275 infantry, total 11,900.

Rhætia. No legion in the province before Marcus Aurelius (161–180) raised III Italica and stationed it there.
  Auxiliaries: 3,500 cavalry, 500 mounted infantry, 8,500 infantry, total 12,500.

Noricum. No legion in the province before Marcus Aurelius (161–180) raised II Italica and stationed it there.
  Auxiliaries: 1,000 cavalry, 3,000 infantry, total 4,000.

Upper Pannonia. Legions: X. Gemina (Vindobona, Vienna)
(Danube to Semlin)   XIV. Gemina (Carnuntum, Petronell)
     I. Adiutrix (Brigetio, near Komorn)
  Auxiliaries: 3,500 cavalry, 875 mounted infantry, 4,125 infantry, total 8,500.

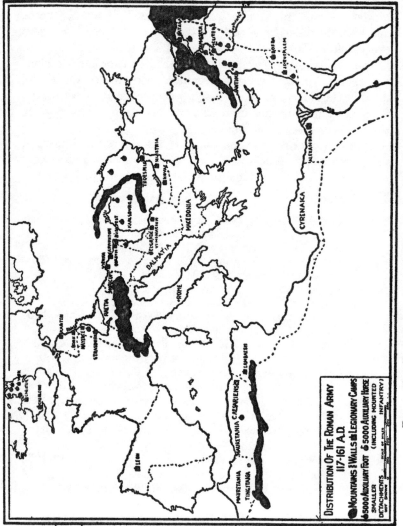

PLATE 12.— DISTRIBUTION OF THE ROMAN ARMY, 117–161 A. D.

Lower Pannonia. Legions: II. Adiutrix (Aquincum, near Budapest)
>Auxiliaries: 3,500 cavalry, 1,875 mounted infantry, 9,125 infantry, total 14,500.

Dalmatia. Auxiliaries: 250 mounted infantry, 1,250 infantry, total, 1,500.

Upper Mœsia. Legions: IV. Flavia (Singidunum, Belgrade)
(Middle Danube)   VII. Claudia (Viminacium, Kostolac)
>Auxiliaries: 500 cavalry, 250 mounted infantry, 3,250 infantry, total 4,000.

Lower Mœsia. Legions: I. Italica (Novæ, Sistov)
(Lower Danube)   XI. Claudia (Durostorum, Silistria)
>V. Macedonica (Trœsmis, Iglitza)
>Auxiliaries: 2,500 cavalry, 250 mounted infantry, 4,250 infantry, total 7,000.

Dacia (now Transylvania). Legions: XIII. Gemina (Apulum, Karlsburg)
>Auxiliaries: 6,000 cavalry, 1,125 mounted infantry, 18,175 infantry, total 25,300.

Macedonia. Auxiliaries: 500 infantry.

Asia Minor (Cappadocia). Legions: XV. Apollinaris (Satala, Armenian frontier)
>XII. Fulminata (Melitene, on upper Euphrates)
>Auxiliaries: 2,000 cavalry, 1,875 mounted infantry, 7,125 infantry, total 11,000.

Syria. Legions: XVI. Flavia (Samosata, upper Euphrates)
>IV. Scythica }
>VI. Ferrata } (near Antioch?)
>III. Gallica }
>Auxiliaries: 4,500 cavalry, 2,375 mounted infantry, 9,625 infantry, total 16,500.

Judea. Legions: X. Fretensis (Jerusalem)
>Auxiliaries: 1,500 cavalry, 125 mounted infantry, 6,875 infantry, total 8,500.

Arabia. Legions: III. Cyrenaica (Bostra)
>Auxiliaries: Unknown.

Egypt. Legions: II. Trajana (near Alexandria, a disorderly city)
>Auxiliaries: 2,500 cavalry, 750 mounted infantry, 5,950 infantry, total 9,200.

Cyrenaica. Garrison unknown.

Africa. Legions: III. Augusta (Lambæsis)
>Auxiliaries: 1,000 cavalry, 500 mounted infantry, 2,700 infantry, total 4,200.

Mauretania. Auxiliaries: 4,000 cavalry, 250 mounted infantry, 5,950
(Cæsariensis)   infantry, total 10,200.

Mauretania. Auxiliaries: 500 cavalry, 125 mounted infantry, 1,375 infan-
(Tingitana)   try, total 2,000.

Spain. Legions: VII. Gemina (Legio, Leon, in N. W. Spain)
        Auxiliaries: 1,000 cavalry, 250 mounted infantry, 2,250 infantry,
                total 3,500.
Unlocated Auxiliary Units. 1,000 cavalry, 375 mounted infantry, 5,125
                infantry, total 6,500.

In the adjoining map, interior provinces whose garrisons are not mentioned in the text are left blank. Frontier provinces with legions stationed within their borders may be identified by the legionary camps. For the sake of clearness, only the names of those provinces mentioned in the text as garrisoned solely by auxiliaries are shown on the map.

The above list establishes the following totals:

Prætorian Guard... 10,000
Legionaries...168,000
Auxiliary Cavalry.............................. 47,500
Auxiliary Mounted Infantry..................... 15,250
Auxiliary Infantry............................131,050

    Total Auxiliaries......................................193,800

      Grand Total....................................371,800

Cheesman, from whom most of these figures are taken, considers that a complete list of the auxiliaries would show about 80,000 for the cavalry plus mounted infantry, and 140,000 for the infantry. This would give a grand total of 398,000, almost 400,-000 men. To this again must be added the numeri, the personnel of the navy (including the crews of the sea-going fleets and those of the river flotillas so important in the scheme of frontier defence), the cavalry of the Imperial Guard, and the six "Urban Cohorts" which helped police some of the larger cities.

But even after making generous allowance for all possible omissions, still the striking thing about the list is that the grand total is so small considering the territory administered. We should remember that in 1914 one small poor province, Serbia, could mobilize 225,000 trained men.

On the other hand, we note that the Augustan military establishment of 300,000 has been increased by more than a third. This undoubtedly indicates an increase in the difficulty of the military problem which the Empire had to meet. In this connexion it is reasonable to suppose that the wild tribes of northern Europe would gradually become more formidable due to increasing military knowledge and improved armament derived from intercourse with Rome, that is with civilization. But when we remember that the Empire now included not only the territories ruled by Augustus but also England and the Scotch lowlands, Morocco, the Hungarian plain and Rumania, Thrace, Northeastern Asia Minor and Armenia, and also the Sinai Peninsula, it is plain that the numerical increase is not quite as formidable in comparison with the increased territory to be administered as it at first appears.

The heaviest concentration was just where we should expect it, that is on the narrow frontier between the impassable mountains of Armenia and the equally impassable Palmyrene desert, since here alone the organized forces of a civilized state were to be confronted.

It should also be noted that sometimes the legionary camps were upon the frontier itself, i. e., on the Danube and the Rhine, sometimes in the interior near unusually turbulent communities such as northwestern Spain, Palestine with its Jews, and the cosmopolitan city of Alexandria.

It would be interesting to know why new legions were designated with the numbers of legions already on foot plus the suffix "Adiutrix" (assistant) or "Gemina" (twin) but there seems to be no evidence on which to base a judgment.

The distribution of legionary troops in Britain is a little out of the ordinary for the VI at York was over 80 miles south of the east end of the wall, and the XX at Chester was a good 100 miles south of the western end. Of course the reason for this was the intervening north-and-south obstacle of the Pennine Hills, to which we shall return in connection with communications. The fact that the II was held at Caerleon-on-Usk probably means that the Welsh hillmen would still stand watching—although it is also true that the II stayed there long after all fear from the Welshmen must have been at an end. Were we dealing with modern governments, this matter might be explained by the desire to continue to utilize the large military reservation at Caerleon. Rome, on the other hand, was as ungrudging in military expenditure as she was economical in man power. She was, moreover, practical and supremely direct in all her measures, so the anomaly of leaving the II far off to the southwest in Caerleon remains unexplained.

Considering the Empire as a whole, the obvious weak point of the defence was the same as that of the original establishment under Augustus, i. e., the lack of a central reserve. Such a state of things would have been intolerable had the system been intended to resist a severe strain. Even in the face of the slight pressure which was all that the northern barbarians could exercise, it was thought worth while to lessen the danger by spending great sums on improving the lateral communications not only between legion and legion along the border itself but also between province and province.

The extreme care given to communications may be illustrated by examples taken from the province of Britain. The obstacle of the Pennines running north and south through the area between the wall and the legionary camps at Chester and York, was crossed from east to west by at least three lateral roads suitable for troops. The main crossing, about 70 miles from the wall and therefore level with York, left the great eastern road at Tadcaster, went over the Ilkley-Skipton gap, descended the Ribble valley and met the western road at Ribchester. About 20 miles due north of the Ilkley-Skipton line was another crossing from the Tees Valley at Bowes to the headwaters of the Eden near Kirkby Stephen. Twenty-five miles, or one day's forced march, south of the Ilkley gap another metalled road ran east from Manchester across the hill country. And in addition to all this there seem to have been several ways east and west over the Peak district itself.

Britain can also show great Roman causeways. One carried the western road over the marshes of the Mersey to Manchester. Another carried the great eastern road between London and York over the marshes of the Ouse and the Welland at Stamford.

Finally Britain has, in the Stane Street, a remarkable instance of strategic road building far behind the frontier to facilitate the movement of troops from province to province—in this case between Gaul and Britain. I have said that London was the chief city in the island and the centre of its road system, also that the chief approach to it from the Continent was across the straits of Dover and through Kent, but that an alternative approach was later arranged from Southampton Water. This alternative approach originally reached London by way of Winchester, Silchester and Staines, about 72 miles from, say, Southampton to London. For the sake of cutting the distance by not much more than 16 miles, one long day's march for hardened troops, the Roman government was willing to build 56 miles of metalled road from Chichester through Dorking direct on London.[5]

Although the existence of such a road abundantly proves that its builders expected that there would be times when a day saved in moving troops from province to province would be highly important, still the calculation underlying the Imperial military policy was that such times would be rare. A man assigned to a legion would usually know that it had not changed station since his great-grandfather's time, and the great-grandchildren of that man might count on finding it there still. An auxiliary soldier would find himself even more strictly localized. Since his ala or cohort would constitute a link in the chain of front-line defence along the frontier he might expect to spend practically his entire military life—25 years—patrolling the four-mile intervals between his own and the next two auxiliary camps. Naturally each stationary unit built up for itself the strongest kind of local associations. For instance, married quarters (or what were virtually married quarters—for the auxiliary soldiers, denied the right of contracting legal marriages, formed permanent attachments recognized by custom and legalized upon discharge) grew up around every station. Besides married quarters there were baths, temples, shops, and the cottages of discharged veterans who wished to live near their old comrades.

Although efficient for its mission of frontier defence, such a system was obviously ill-adapted to the rare emergencies of an invasion in force, for the legions of his province constituted the only concentrated field army under the orders of the provincial commander. The only way of getting reinforcements was to borrow from the next province. Owing to the local associations formed by the troops, and to the fact that each unit called away left a gap in the frontier defence in its own province, the custom grew up of answering requests for aid by dispatching, not perma-

[5] For Roman military roads in England, see Belloc: "Warfare In England," and "The Stane Street."

nent units, but temporary commands formed by detachments from a number of such units. These detachments were called vexillations (from "vexilla," the Latin for a standard). One cavalry vexillation serving against the Parthians under Trajan was drawn from no less than 5 alæ and fourteen "mounted cohorts." [6] The practice was sometimes followed during the offensive phase—the vexilla is expressly mentioned by Tacitus as accompanying the detachment of the XX Legion taken by Suetonius Paulinus to help him fight Boadicea. During the second century it hardened into a set custom rarely departed from, if at all.

Any soldier, or even any man of common sense, will agree that such scratch formations are inferior to permanent units taking the field as such. They can have no *esprit de corps*. The fact that the system was workable at all is the strongest possible testimony not only to the skill of the Roman command but also to the high standard and especially the uniformity obtained in the training of units. And yet the fact remains that the system did its work well.

How it worked may be illustrated by an outline of the crisis surmounted under Marcus Aurelius. In the first place the Parthians invaded Cappadocia in 162 A. D., won a decisive general action in that province, and devastated Syria. A field army was organized by drawing heavily on the Danubian troops for vexillations and the tide of battle was turned against the enemy. All this was not outside the Roman experience. The shuttlecock of war had been batted to and fro across the Euphrates ever since Crassus' time. Meanwhile the Roman intelligence service gave warning of coming trouble from the tribes around what is now Bohemia. By this time the Parthian war was nearing its end. With tenacity which reminds us of Tiberius' conduct in 6 A. D., the government of Marcus Aurelius decided not to recall the vexillations which the Danubian troops had sent to the East until a decision had been obtained there. In so doing they deliberately ran risks on the upper Danube, where the storm broke in the year 165 A. D. It does not seem certain that these tribes knew of the Parthian war and most improbable that they should have intentionally synchronized their attack with it. That it was necessary to fight on two fronts was

[6] Cheesman, 113.

only an unhappy coincidence for the Empire. On the upper Danube, the local Roman commanders, weakened by the absence of their numerous vexillations in the East, were unable to hold the frontier. They therefore set themselves to delay the barbarians' advance and postpone the crisis of the campaign until their vexillations could return. In the course of the year 165 the Parthians made peace and the vexillations started westward. It would take at least two weeks to get a courier from Venetia to Antioch, assuming that the Emperor was at the headquarters of the troops covering Italy so that no time need be lost in consulting him. When the vexillations had left Antioch, it would be another two months, and probably nearer three months, before they would be ready to go into action in Bosnia. When at last they arrived, the Roman command would have been able to act vigorously had it not been for a second unhappy chance which upset all calculations. The vexillations from the East brought the plague with them. The mortality was heavy and the army was badly demoralized in consequence, so that the barbarians overran what is now Switzerland, together with the country between the Save and Danube. Still the Save seems never to have been crossed, nor was Italy ever invaded. In 168, three years after the original loss of the Danube line, the frontier was re-established. In 169, the war was renewed but its theatre was now the neighborhood of the Danube, and after three years the two chief barbarian tribes were decisively defeated, one of them being wiped out in an attempt to retreat across the river.

Certainly it seems that the whole trouble came from the deliberate economy of the government in men.

How far the Roman art of war and the fighting power of the army were affected during the period of frontier defence, if at all, is hard to say. It seems as if the restriction of its mission must have brought about some decline, as the service gradually forgot that it had ever been a field army, and more and more came to think of itself as a constabulary rooted to particular spots of ground. And yet we must not exaggerate, but remember that, after all, the Roman army of the defensive period did its job and remained superior to all opponents.

In the army list, mounted infantry appears. Strictly speaking, this is a separate arm, mounted for transport and dismounted for action. It is sometimes resorted to by services which must increase their proportion of mounted men, but are content with half measures in so doing, since it is easier to convert infantry into mounted infantry than into cavalry. Some auxiliary cohorts were partly horse and partly foot—an arrangement which shows clearly how far the army had become a mere frontier patrol, for such a body could never act as a true tactical unit. There was a camel corps in the East. The importance of cavalry was increasing, and toward the end of the century cavalry units with the riders and forward parts of their horses completely covered by scale mail began to appear.[7]

Marcus Aurelius (161-180 A. D.), increased the establishment by adding two new legions which he stationed, one in Rhætia (Switzerland) and the other in Noricum (upper Austria). Toward the end of the phase, Septimius Severus (192-211 A. D.) sick of the turbulence and inefficiency of the Prætorians, broke the entire corps and arranged for their future recruitment by promoting distinguished officers and men from the frontier legions. The same Emperor added three more new legions, two for Mesopotamia and one in central Italy in reserve.[8] Throughout the second century the numeri were constantly being increased until there were scores of them. The additions and the crews of the fleets must have raised the total number of men in the imperial service to more than 400,000 at the beginning of the third century.

Although the army organization as a whole remained unchanged, certain changes in recruitment, discipline and morale can be traced. I have already said that neither the masses of the civil population nor the rank and file of the army itself could be expected to feel any strong patriotism for so huge a state. The mere idea of civilization is too abstract to kindle the least devotion in the average man. This want of patriotism naturally became more and more glaring as the achievements of civlization came to be thought commonplace, and no serious peril appeared to threaten its life. Furthermore, the very success of the Roman professional army, by removing even the idea of war from the minds of the great civilian majority, increased the unwarlike character of the masses. The ever-increasing wealth and peace of the provinces continued to tell in the same direction. Thus the recruiting ground of the

---

[7] Cheesman, 28, 30, and 128.   [8] Dion Cassius: Bk. 55, sec. 24.

army tended still more to contract to the neighbourhood of the frontiers.

A certain decline in discipline and in professional spirit seems to be indicated by two new developments which appear early in the third century.

The first of them concerned that permanent problem of long-service professional armies—married quarters. Augustus had forbidden soldiers to marry. But with a term of service of over twenty years, not even Roman discipline at its best could enforce the spirit of such an order. Accordingly the custom had grown up for many of the men to enter into what a modern world would call "common-law marriages" which were fully legalized upon their discharge. Now Septimius Severus (193-211) gave the men leave to marry.

The same Emperor permitted or encouraged the special-duty men of each legion, i.e., the regimental clerks, artificers, ordnance personnel, musicians, etc., to form associations know as "colleges."[9] How far these colleges were autonomous, voluntary associations we cannot tell. The development coincided in time with the multiplication of colleges composed of men exercising similar economic functions in civil life. Certainly, if the military colleges were autonomous "soldier committees," the effect upon discipline must have been bad.

In any event, it is certain that about the time these innovations were introduced, civilization in general began to decline.

All sorts of explanations have been given for the internal decay of the ancient world. Even the ridiculous suggestions that sexual immorality was a chief cause has been seriously made! Perhaps the most reasonable guess, and the only one which has any bearing on the military phase of the subject (with which alone we are here directly concerned), is that in all life there is a rhythm, a flux and reflux of energy. According to this idea, the effort involved in the maintenance of a high civilization is too great to be indefinitely pursued. After it has gone on for a certain time there must be repose. The human mind must lie fallow in barbarism, or an approach to it, until its energy return.

But if the underlying cause of the slackening energy of the ancient world is obscure, the symptoms are clear enough. From

[9] Cagnat: Lambese, 36–47.

235 to 297 A. D. is a phase of confusion. A series of Roman civil wars gives the barbarians many temporary successes. The immediate cause of the decline of ancient civilization was this third-century epidemic of civil wars.

Inasmuch as the civil wars were fought between groups of the Roman army acting in the interest of generals seeking the Empire, it has been assumed that they were caused by some weakness or fault in the army itself. The fact is otherwise; these civil wars were the cause of a certain decline in the discipline and professional spirit of the army, but they themselves were due not to military but to political weakness in the structure of the Empire itself.

Certainly the Roman army cannot be blamed for conquering the known world and thereby making patriotism impossible for the mass of mankind. If Augustus (acting wisely enough according to his lights) set up a centralized monarchy which repressed local initiative both military and civil, pretending meanwhile to preserve the republic and therefore failing to provide an adequate legal method of succession to the Empire, none of these things were done by the army which Augustus commanded and to which he owed his throne.

If the reader thinks I dwell too long on these political matters, let him remember that they alone explain the character of war from the third to the ninth century, and that the difficulty as to succession explains the Roman civil wars which began the decline.

The Senate, which had the sole legal right to replace a dead emperor, could no longer command respect for its decisions.[10] Indeed the vastness of the political unit, the repression of local civic initiative, and the relegation of all military work to a small professional army, all combined to make the "consent of the governed" within the Empire, a more and more passive thing. Hence there was no moral authority competent to prevent the legions of the East, or of the Danubian, or the Rhenish command, from proclaiming their general Emperor and marching on Rome against the Emperor there.

The reader may object that it was the duty of the army to resist the outer barbarians. The Roman army would have answered

[10] Ferrero: The Ruin of the Ancient Civilization and the Triumph of Christianity.

that these barbarians were a nuisance rather than a peril. It was impossible to think that they could ever destroy civilization, and as a matter of fact the northern barbarians never did. To be sure, if in order to make your general emperor you withdrew any considerable number of troops from any one section of frontier, the barbarians might break in and ravage. But they were not good at taking walled cities, and as soon as the regrettable unpleasantness over the imperial succession was cleaned up, these same barbarians would have to run for their lives over the border to escape being cut to pieces, as they invariably were if they could not get away.

War is always and necessarily destructive, but the Roman civil wars of the imperial epoch did not involve widespread destruction of property or intentional interference with the population. It has been metaphorically said that they were fought "over the heads" of the citizens. Even the barbarian raids, although far more serious in this respect, were limited as to the harm they could do, because (1) their aim was plunder rather than systematic destruction, (2) they could seldom take a walled city, (3) like all the rest of the world before the invention of gunpowder, they possessed no means of demolition except fire and human muscle. Even so they were bad enough and the harm they did was exaggerated in the public mind by contrast with the centuries of unbroken peace the interior Roman world had enjoyed.

The obvious palliative for such conditions was fortification. Septimius Severus (192–211 A. D.) supplemented Hadrian's earthen wall across Britain by a continuous wall of stone. Most of the cities of the Empire walled themselves in. Aurelian (270–275) went so far as to fortify the city of Rome itself, which had seen no enemy for nearly 500 years and was to see none for over a century more.

The interesting passage already referred to in the last chapter, from the third-century author, Dion Cassius,[11] shows that the weakness of the professional army system without reserves was understood. Dion makes Mæcenas, a first-century statesman, remark: ". . . if we check all military activity on their part (the Provincials), we shall run the risk of finding nothing but raw and untrained troops when we need a contingent for our assistance."

[11] Bk. 53, sec. 27.

Nevertheless he makes Mæcenas go on to argue against universal training because such training would make sedition more formidable, and against hastily raised troops because of the great distances to be traversed.

Despite this passage, it is probable that during the third century the Imperial government could not possibly have found time (in the intervals between civil wars and the assassinations of emperors) to overhaul the military system as a whole. No emperor tried it, but all did what they could with the means at hand. The abler emperors, "sweeping together household troops and fragments of the broken frontier armies and enlisting thousands of barbarian mercenaries,[12] . . . strove to keep a concentrated force at their disposal which they moved constantly backwards and forwards across the empire as each internal or external crisis demanded. It was this field army which shared in the imperial triumphs and received such rewards as the exhausted finances could bestow. In comparison with it such units of the old frontier troops, legions and auxilia alike, as maintained their old positions (and many did so) sank steadily in prestige and importance." [13]

These same abler emperors, Claudius II, Aurelian, Probus and Carus, tried to keep up discipline by savage punishments. Carus affected an extreme soldierly simplicity of dress and personal habits. Such measures could not fully remedy the evils of continuous political instability and the standard of discipline and training unquestionably declined. Probus was assassinated in an unpremeditated mutiny of the troops enraged at the efforts he personally required of them in "land reclamation," i. e., draining a marsh.

Incidentally, it should be said that the civil wars within the empire are of little interest to the military student. Indeed, this is true of most civil wars, because the base and political backing of neither side is as firm and definite as in wars between regularly constituted political units. Therefore the political rather than the military factors in war tend to predominate, and thereby rob the operations of strategic interest. To this general rule the American Civil War is an exception, for it was a war between two

[12] In numeri, not in the old auxiliary cohorts and alæ.
[13] Cheesman, 136.

sections almost as definite, in a military sense, as two separate countries. But almost all civil wars, for instance, the Wars of the Roses in England, the 16th century Wars of Religion in France and the 17th century civil wars in England, help to prove the rule.

Two points of tactical interest drawn from the civil wars will be considered in connexion with Vegetius and the 4th century Roman army.

Finally, I would remind the reader that the period of confusion saw not one definite lodgment effected by force within the boundaries of the empire. The nearest thing to it was Aurelian's voluntary abandonment of Dacia and retreat to the line of the lower Danube.

Throughout the phase of confusion the Roman military system did not break down. It is true that Decius (249–251 A. D.) fell in battle against the Goths and that Valerian (253–260 A. D.) was taken prisoner by the Persians, but these unprecedented disasters to the person of the Emperor were balanced by corresponding victories. Claudius Gothicus (268–270 A. D.) massacred 50,000 Goths at Nish in modern Serbia, and Carus (282–284 A. D.) temporarily swept the upper and middle Tigris-Euphrates region as no Emperor since Trajan had done, driving the Persians before him and capturing their capitals of Seleucia and Ctesiphon.

But although the Roman army did not collapse under the strain of the phase of confusion, the units which composed it became hopelessly disjointed and mixed up. We have seen that these units had become localized during the preceding phase of successful frontier defence and that when large field armies were called for they were formed, not by the removal of permanent units as such but by temporary bodies known as vexillations, each vexillation being drawn from a number of units. Now, after more than half a century, the vicious system of vexillations had brought matters to such a point that fragments of the same legion were to be found serving all over the place.[14] The old legion, 6000 strong, had broken up as a tactical unit. Many of the old auxiliary cohorts and alæ had disappeared altogether, for (in spite of the two centuries of tradition which might be behind it) such a unit did not have the same prestige as a legion and detachments from it were much more apt to lose their identity. Prob-

[14] Oman, Vol. 1, 7, and Cheesman, 140–141.

ably any intelligent officer in the entire service whose position permitted him to appreciate the situation of the army as a whole, would have told you that the first sufficient interval of peace and political stability would be used to overhaul the entire organization of the Roman army.

Such a lull was provided by Diocletian, who became Emperor in 284 A. D. and had consolidated his position throughout the entire Roman world by 297 A. D. For our purposes we may neglect the customary spasm of civil war between Diocletian's abdication in 305 and the beginning of Constantine's universal power in 314, and may consider as a whole the army reforms bearing the names of both Diocletian and Constantine.

With Diocletian's establishment of absolutism and with his changes in the civil administration, we are not concerned. His division of the Empire into four groups reduced the distance which a messenger must travel to and from Imperial Headquarters. In general it may be said that from Diocletian's time to the final breakdown of centralized administration there were usually at least two legitimate Emperors at a time. On the other hand, this division was purely administrative. In civilization and in feeling, the Roman world remained one thing. Indeed it might even be said that uniformity was carried to excess.

Besides the attempt to divide the administration of the Empire itself, Diocletian completely changed the mechanism of the Roman higher command. Formerly the Prætorian Prefect had been, under the Emperor, Commander-in-Chief. Now each and every Emperor had under him two "Masters of Soldiery," one Master of the Infantry and the other of the Cavalry,[15] incidentally indicating the increased importance of the cavalry arm. The titles suggest those of the Chiefs of Arms existing in so many contemporary armies, Chief of Infantry, of Cavalry, etc. Of course the "Magister Equitum" of the fourth century and after has no connexion with the temporary Magister Equitum, or Lieutenant Dictator of the early Republic.

Perhaps the most revolutionary of the fourth-century army reforms was the reorganization of permanent field armies, composed of the best troops in the service. These field armies were

[15] "Magistri Militum," one "Magister Peditum," and the other "Magister Equitum."

composed of three categories—the Palatine, Comitatensian, and Pseudo-Comitatensian troops. The Palatines took their name directly from the Palatia (Palaces), which were the official seats of the Roman government in every province, and indirectly from the Palatine hill in Rome from which the first Emperors had governed. They were not the personal escort of the Prince— that duty was performed by smaller bodies known as the Domestic or Scholarian troops. The Palatines were the crack troops of the new field armies, and it was significant of the way things were going that there were both Palatine legions and Palatine auxiliaries. Next after the Palatines came the Comitatenses, whose name means comrades or household troops and is derived from the same root as that from which we get our word "comrade." After them came the Pseudo-Comitatenses who were ranked lower than the Comitatenses and much lower than the Palatines but higher than the surviving frontier troops to whom we shall come in a moment. All told, the total strength in legionary soldiers belonging to these three categories amounted to about 33% of the strength in legionaries of the entire establishment. The field armies were held concentrated well behind the frontier, near large cities which were also road centres.

Conservative people found fault with the arrangement because it exposed the troops to the corruptions of city life and exposed the city people to the rowdyism of the soldiers.[16] This situation is one that is familiar to us all; the troops and the people being distinct, each wants the other for its own purposes, and at the same time each knows its own good points and fears degeneration through the bad influence of the other.

Meanwhile the remaining 66% of legionaries, together with a proportion of auxiliaries difficult to determine, were held in their old stations as Riparian or Limitanian (frontier) troops, continuing to enjoy, or endure, the fixed local ties which almost all their units had had for two centuries and many of them for a century before that. Service in the frontier troops was now hereditary in law as well as in fact—the son of a soldier was bound to enlist.[17] Indeed such procedure was now commonplace outside the army, for ever since Septimius Severus (192–211 A. D.)

[16] Ammianus Marcellinus: Bk. 22, ch. 4.
[17] Codex Theodosianus, VII, 22, quoted Cheesman, 137.

the Emperors of the decline had tried to stiffen the crumbling civilization over which they ruled by a whole series of laws compelling the sons of free handicraftsmen and even small business men to be about their fathers' businesses.

Naturally, the sons of soldiers could not, by themselves, be expected to fill the gaps caused by active service. Accordingly, we find in the fourth century a system of conscription of a sort which foreshadows the feudal armies of all mediæval Europe, inasmuch as the unit called upon to furnish a man to the colours is not a unit of population but a landed property of a certain size.[18] For the purposes of conscription, landed properties not large enough to be compelled to furnish a recruit would be lumped together until the required acreage was made up. The owners would then be compelled to furnish recruits in rotation. By modern standards the conscription was very light, for the number of troops to be raised in proportion to population was small. Furthermore, men were not always held for the full legionary term of service. When the needs of the service permitted, they were discharged after 15, 10, or even 5 years. Nevertheless the service was unpopular, soldiering often is; for instance it is unpopular to-day in large sections of English and American opinion. The English army of the 18th century was sometimes filled from the jails. In the 4th century the unpopularity was so great that fraud and even self-mutilation were often used to avoid it. The soldiers were branded like criminals to prevent their deserting.

Service in the legions was even more unpopular than in the auxiliaries, for the equipment of a legionary was heavier, the work more exhausting, the discipline more severe and the promotion slower.[19] It is possible that the new conditions of mobile warfare, which may have made it necessary for the soldier to carry more on his person than the localized troops of former times had done, helped to make it hard to get the men to carry the heavy legionary arms and armour. We know that, in the 16th century it was chiefly the necessity for increased mobility which caused armour to be laid aside.[20] At all events, the 4th century dislike for legionary

[18] Boutaric, 21 et seq., quoting Codex Theodosianus, VII, 13, together with laws of Valentinian and Valens.
[19] Vegetius: Bk. 2, ch. 3, quoted in Boutaric, 25.
[20] Dean: Helmets and Body Armour in Modern Warfare, 45–52.

service made it easier to get good men for the auxiliaries, and correspondingly lowered the spirit and efficiency of the legions.

Another change, only less striking than the organization of the field armies, was the reduction of the legions serving in those armies to 1000 men. Most auxiliary cohorts and alæ had been 1000 strong ever since Trajan's time, so now to make the permanent legionary unit of the same strength assured a greater measure of tactical uniformity by having the units all of the same size. Another change was to give the name "vexillation" to permanent cavalry units. We find the old name "cuneus" (wedge) also applied to 4th-century cavalry squadrons.

To make the legions in the field armies consist of no more than 1000 men did not mean a reduction in the total number of legionary soldiers. On the contrary, it seems that the number was considerably increased. The numbers of the 4th-century Roman army may be estimated, partially and very roughly, as follows: [21]

```
 33 Limitary legions at 6000 each...........................198,000
132 Field Army (i. e., Palatine, Comitatensian and Pseudo-
       Comitatensian) legions at 1000 each.................132,000
                                                           ───────
       Total legionary soldiers ...........................330,000

108 Units of Palatine Auxiliaries at 1000 each...........108,000
 91 Units of Cavalry at 1000 each.........................  91,000
"Domestics," i. e., personal escort of the Emperor.......  15,000
                                                           ───────
                                                           214,000
                                                           ───────
                                                           544,000
```

In part this total is too high, for we know that some legions formerly stationed on the frontiers were assigned to the field armies and have therefore been twice counted in the foregoing figures. On the other hand, it is certain that the grand total of the entire Roman service was far above the figure of 544,000 since the above figures do not include any auxiliaries but the Palatines. Now we know that there were many non-Palatine auxiliaries. Probably 200,000 is a conservative estimate of their numbers. The Roman service also included great numbers of numeri together with a new kind of barbarian auxiliary known as Federati. It included

[21] Compare Hodgkin, Vol. 1 ,Part 2, 628–631; Gibbon, Vol. 2, 294; Young, Vol. 1, 404.

also the crews of the fleets which controlled the seas and the great boundary rivers. Pausing for a moment to ask the reader to remember the word "Federati" to which I shall return in connexion with Theodosius, I give it as my own opinion that the total number of men in the 4th-century service may have amounted to three quarters of a million, a larger disciplined force than afterwards existed down to the Wars of the French Revolution and the largest professional army the world has ever known.

In view of the various civil wars in the phase of confusion, it would not be surprising to find that the standard of training and discipline had been lowered. On the contrary we are surprised that so large a measure of discipline was still in force. There is a story which is told, with variations, of many of the mutinies with which civil wars would begin; of mutineers murdering centurions nicknamed "hand me the other" from the habit of calling for a second switch with which to beat a soldier for some military offence, when they had already broken the first one over his back! The surprising thing is not that such centurions were murdered in the frequent mutinies but rather that they existed at all. Evidently the Roman noncommissioned and company officer was often of such a temper that he was willing to risk his own life in his effort to keep up discipline in his own cohort.

As to equipment we find a vastly increased number of cavalry units with both man and horse so well protected by scale mail, that the barbarians at Strassburg (A. D., 357) thought the only way to bring down such monsters was to slip under the belly of the horse and stab him from below.[22] In the opposite direction there was the tendency on the part of an increasing number of the infantry to give up both helmet and body armour and to rely more and more upon archery and other forms of fire action. This tendency Vegetius condemns as part of the degeneracy of his contemporaries [23] although it was probably a natural development of the time. An army whose main business is chasing raiders must be able to move fast and to skirmish and, in the rarer case of an invasion in force, the usefulness of the new field armies must have depended a good deal on the speed they could make over long distances.

[22] Ammianus Marcellinus: Bk. 16.
[23] Vegetius: Bk. 1, sec. 20, quoted Oman, Vol. 1, 18.

In 312 A. D., Constantine, whose power was then based chiefly upon Gaul, was threatened by Maxentius, Emperor of Italy. Although Maxentius had 200,000 troops to Constantine's 80,000, Constantine determined to invade Italy. Crossing the Alps, he met near Turin a large part of Maxentius' army. Finding himself inferior in cavalry, he drew up his infantry in two lines with a considerable distance between them and wide intervals between the units of the front line. When Maxentius' cavalry charged they were permitted to pass through the intervals. The first line then wheeled about, attacking their rear, while they were engaged in front with Constantine's second line, and almost destroyed them. What happened to Maxentius' infantry we are not told, which makes it seem that they made no effort to retrieve the defeat of their cavalry.[24]

The manœuvre of Constantine's first line indicates a high degree of discipline, control, and tactical flexibility. This may have been due to the personal excellence of Constantine, but at any rate it indicates that tactical flexibility was not yet unknown to the Roman infantry.

[24] Young, Vol. 1, 375.

CHAPTER III

THE IMPERIAL ROMAN ARMY

(FROM THE DEATH OF CONSTANTINE TO THE DEATH OF JUSTINIAN—337-565 A. D.)

THE Roman Empire never fell and the tradition of civilization was never broken. It is true that with the civil wars of the third century there began a long period of decline in population, in wealth, and in the arts, including the art of war; but the decline was due to internal causes far more than to external ones. Its outstanding feature was not successful invasion from without but an internal change in the Roman army which stood sentinel over the civilized world. That army, while remaining (in general) faithful to its trust and successful in discharging that trust, became predominantly barbarian in blood. As the internal decline continued to weaken (and especially to impoverish) the central government, at last the reality of power in the West was taken over by the provincial commanders-in-chief, barbarian-born men friendly to the civilization they served but incapable of administering successfully a civilized state because of the limitations of their minds.

Throughout the period covered by this chapter, the Roman army remained a highly trained, professional force, and continued to conduct its operations according to a doctrine of war suitable to such a force. Many of the identical units raised by Augustus and his immediate successors can still be traced into the early fifth century. This professional army remained successful. Although the internal decline of civilization continued, nevertheless the military victories of its defenders outnumbered their defeats and in the second half of the sixth century the greater part of the Roman world was still directly administered by the Imperial government from its new capital, Constantinople.

In the second half of the fourth century, within the Roman service (and in spite of the intense conservatism and strong traditional

244

feeling of that service) a momentous tactical revolution took place. Cavalry replaced infantry as the chief arm.

The supremacy of cavalry determined tactics for over a thousand years. It resulted in part, but only in part, from the general internal slackening of the energy of the declining ancient world. Special military conditions also helped to bring it about.

The first point to consider in connexion with the decline of infantry is the relaxation of Roman discipline which began in the confusion of the third century. The second point concerns equipment. By the fourth century the heavy legionary javelin, the pilum, was no longer carried. It had been replaced by a pike. As far as we can tell, the pike was usually light enough so that it could be hurled as the pilum had been.

This change in equipment helped to cause a loss of flexibility and offensive power on the part of infantry. The sword, or for that matter, the modern bayonet, as the chief close-quarters weapon of infantry, tends to produce an attack in skirmish line, with intervals and distances sufficient to permit a degree of individual fencing. The large, dense columns of the later Napoleonic period are not a true exception to this rule since it is not clear that they ever did much serious hand-to-hand fighting but were expected to act chiefly through the moral effect of their massed approach. On the other hand, the use of the pike required close formations and strict alignment. Any serious break in alignment admits the enemy because the pike must be levelled in order to be used, and when levelled cannot be traversed without first being raised upright, thus leaving the pikeman defenceless. Accordingly a body of pikemen is formidable for passive defence, as a hedgehog or porcupine is formidable, but its attacking power is limited. It can attack only slowly, and the troops must be brought to a remarkably high state of drill and discipline in order to be able to do even that. They must have good ground to advance over. Dislocation in their ranks is fatal; they are then like the porcupine unrolled, with his naked belly opposed to the claws and teeth of his destroyer.

Very few armies of pikemen have ever been able to attack successfully. Much of the offensive power of Alexander's army was developed by the cavalry. The Swiss (after their original startling successes in their native mountains) are always found acting as a part of armies whose other parts supplemented their work. All mediæval warfare illustrates the truth that a body of pikemen, not disciplined and drilled to perfection, must stand rigidly on the defensive or be destroyed.

Indeed the difficulties of delivering an attack with pikemen are so great that the Romans seem never to have attempted it. In an attack the pike was hurled as the old pilum had been and the attackers then fell to with the sword. The pike was undoubtedly needed because the discipline and instruction of infantry could no longer be depended upon to get them to stand firm before charging cavalry unless they were packed in dense formation and furnished with a weapon capable of keeping the horseman at a distance.

In this matter discipline is all important. Belloc's "Poitiers" [1] has an admirable discussion of it as follows:

The strength of an armed body consists in its cohesion. When the whole body is in peril, each individual member of it wants to get away. To prevent him from getting away is the whole object of discipline and military training. Each standing firm (or falling where he stands) preserves the unity, and therefore the efficacy, of the whole. A few yielding at the critical point (and the critical point is usually also the point where men most desire to yield) destroy the efficacy of nine times their number. Now, one of the things that frighten an individual man on foot most is another man galloping at him upon a horse. If many men gallop upon him so bunched on many horses, the effect is, to say the least, striking. If any one doubts this, let him try. If the men upon the horses are armed with a weapon that can get at the men on foot some feet ahead (such as is the lance) the threat is more efficacious still, and no single man (save here and there a fellow full of some religion) will meet it. But against this truth there is another truth to be set, which the individual man would never guess, and which is none the less experimentally certain—which is this: that if a certain number of men on foot stand firm when horses are galloping at them, the horses will swerve or balk before contact; in general, the mounted line will not be efficacious against the dismounted. There is here a contrast between the nerves of horses and the intelligence of men, as also between the rider's desire that his horse shall go forward, and the horse's training, which teaches him that not only his rider, but men in general, are his masters. . . .

To teach infantry that they can thus withstand cavalry, instruction is the instrument. You must drill them and form them constantly, and hammer it into them by repeated statement that if they stand firm all will be well. This has been done in the case of men on foot armed only with staves.

[1] Belloc: Poitiers, 112–114.

Now from all the circumstances of the 3rd and 4th centuries, and especially from the fact that popularity with their troops was all-important to the candidates for Emperor in the innumerable civil wars, we know that it was harder to bring the discipline of infantry to a point which would enable them to withstand the anguish of being charged by cavalry. Dense formations and the replacement of the pilum by the pike which would hold the cavalryman at a greater distance were therefore the natural expedients with which to meet such a situation.

Let us now consider in their chronological order the important general actions of Mursa (351), Strassburg (357), and Adrianople (378), noting how each of the three seems to mark a stage in the process we are considering.

The Diocletian-Constantinian reforms failed to check the internal decline of ancient civilization, and soon after Constantine's death the recurrent plague of civil wars, palace conspiracies, and assassinations of Emperors broke out again.

One incident of these civil wars was the hotly contested battle of Mursa, the modern Essek on the Drave. In 351 A. D., the Roman army of the East was opposed to that of the West and especially that of Gaul. The Emperor of the East—Constantius—was superior in light and heavy cavalry and also in archers. He had stirred up the tribes beyond the Rhine to invade Gaul and so retain as much as possible of the Roman army in Gaul to defend that province. Nevertheless, the Western troops at Mursa seem to have been superior in legionary infantry and also included a large force of German and Frankish auxiliaries without body armour. Constantius' troops attacked in oblique order, left in front, and succeeded in overlapping and rolling up the right of the Westerners. Meanwhile the unarmoured Germans had suffered severely from the fire of the Eastern archers, so that when the invulnerable Eastern lancers finally succeeded in breaking into the formation of the Gallic legions the Eastern light horse were easily able to complete the victory.[2]

The conditions under which the battle of Strassburg was fought in 357 A. D. spring directly from the campaign of Mursa six years before. The German barbarians stirred up by Constantius had pushed back the Roman frontier from the Rhine to about the

[2] Gibbon, Vol. 2, 368–369.

Meuse.   In 355, Constantius appointed his cousin Julian to the office of Cæsar of the West to go into Gaul to handle the situation. At the same time Constantius treacherously and secretly ordered the Roman commander in Switzerland (who was his own appointee) not to support Julian properly.   Meanwhile a rebellion of the Roman army north of the Seine temporarily increased Julian's difficulties.   The local commander there, learning that he had been falsely accused of treason, set himself up as Emperor in the hope of saving his own life, which he lost a month later by assassination.

In the campaigning season of 356, Julian failed to accomplish much.   Moving eastward from Reims, he lost two legions, wiped out in a barbarian surprise attack, and although he was able to advance to Cologne he could not maintain himself there, but felt it necessary to retreat and winter at Sens.

The year 357 opened badly.   The Roman commander in Switzerland, who was supposed to co-operate with Julian's eastward movement by northward attack against modern Württemberg and Baden, intentionally failed to do so.   Indeed he was so slack that he failed to destroy a barbarian raiding force which crossed the gap of Belfort, pushed down the Doubs and Saône to the gate of Lyons and returned safely.   Nevertheless, Julian pushed forward to Saverne, or Zabern, established a fortified post there, and prepared to strike with his little army of 13,000 against the enemy 35,000 strong concentrated near Strassburg.

The barbarians had felled great trees across the hilly roads, but Julian was able to advance with his cavalry (including fully armoured lancers and also horse-archers) on either flank of the infantry marching column.   Since Saverne is nearly 25 miles as the crow flies from Strassburg, we may assume that it must have been on the second or even the third day out that (in the afternoon) contact with the enemy was established.   Then followed an incident that throws a vivid light on the 4th-century Roman army. Julian assembled most of his troops and made a speech to them saying that he meant to halt for the night and attack in the morning.   The troops in their eagerness gnashed their teeth and clashed their shields loudly to express dissatisfaction.   Whereat Julian consulted his generals, who told him that discipline might suffer if the opinion of the army was not consulted and an immediate attack was ordered!

Both sides drew up in dense formation. Julian put most of his cavalry on his right and the barbarians placed their own cavalry opposite them, mixed with light armed men who were to try to crawl under the Roman horses' bellies and stab them from below—that being almost the only part of either horse or man unprotected by armor. The Roman cavalry disgraced themselves by stampeding at the very beginning of the battle and would have swept away the infantry had these last not stood firmly in their dense formation. Julian rallied the flyers but we do not hear of their accomplishing anything until the pursuit. The decisive phase of the action was a long stand-up fight between the opposing infantry, the Roman troops apparently doing most of their fighting by thrusting with the sword. Once the barbarians, with their superior weight and strength, broke deeply into the close ranks of the Roman "testudo" formation. But reserves were brought up, especially the Batavian auxiliaries under their "Reges" or tribal chieftains, and the battle was renewed. Their high training made it possible for the Roman troops to fight on hand to hand until at last the barbarians could stand the losses no longer and broke. Six thousand of their dead were counted on the field and many thousands were drowned in trying to cross the Rhine which cut off their retreat. The Roman army lost only four officers and 243 soldiers.[3]

In this action we find the infantry still doing most of the work but doing it in dense formation, which can hardly have been flexible enough to permit manœuvring.

An interesting example of the conservatism of the Roman service and its intense desire to preserve tradition is furnished by the use of the word "testudo" to describe the new, dense, battle formation. Literally the word testudo meant a turtle. Ever since early republican times it had been used of the close siege or escalade formation, with shields interlocked overhead to keep off missiles from the walls and thus resembling the turtle's shell. We now find it carried over to describe the new close formation, apparently for the express purpose of giving that novelty a traditional flavour.

Two other points connected with the aftermath of the battle are worth noting. Julian sent certain Frankish prisoners to the court of Constantius far away in the East, and Constantius

[3] Ammianus Marcellinus, Bk. 16.

promptly enlisted them in his own personal bodyguard   Then, when Gaul had been cleared of barbarians, it was thought a great thing that Julian was able to persuade his auxiliaries to help his legionaries rebuild the ruined cities. Finally the names of Julian's general officers, Dagalaif, Rhœmetalces, Hormisdas, Fullofaudes, Vadomar, Merobaudes, Davitta, Immo, Agila and Malarich show how many barbarian-born men were to be found even in the highest ranks of the Roman service.

After Strassburg, the next important Roman campaign was that of Adrianople. It was serious from the very first because when it began the Visigoths were already inside the Danube barrier with its Roman river fleet and its line of fortified strong points garrisoned by Riparian troops. The Visigoths were a border tribe, attracted like most border tribes by Roman civilization and therefore essentially friendly to the Empire, whose "allies" they had been for a century. They were being converted to Christianity. Naturally when attacked from the northeast by the Mongol Huns in 376 A. D., they asked to be received inside the Roman border with their families. It was finally granted on the severe conditions that they should give hostages and be disarmed.

The local Roman officials oppressed the wretched Goths, grafted and profiteered on their food supplies, and failed to disarm them. They stood this for over a year but finally revolted, the revolt beginning at Marcianople, the modern Shumla in Bulgaria west from the port of Varna. From there they moved on Adrianople, failed to rush its walls and began pillaging the countryside. The Emperor Valens was in the East fighting the Persians. He sent some of his generals against the Goths, and Gratian the Western Emperor sent reinforcements from the Gallic command.   The imperial troops won several minor actions but failed to get a decision and the war swayed to and fro from Thrace to the Dobrudja where we hear of a Roman attack in the close testudo formation upon a Gothic wagon camp.

The campaign of 378 opened well enough with the destruction of a Gothic detachment in a surprise night attack delivered by a far smaller body of Roman troops. About midsummer, Valens was in Constantinople with a large army at his back, peace having been made with the Persians. Meanwhile Gratian, the Western

Emperor, had smashed his local barbarians at Colmar in Alsace and was moving eastward. The position of the miserable Goths now became highly critical. They had merely been drifting about, pillaging, and had failed to make any solid lodgment in Roman land because of their inability to take walled cities. At their back they had the strong line of the Danube with the garrisons of its fortified posts and its river fleet. Valens marched to Adrianople, whereupon the barbarians concentrated in the neighbourhood, entrenching themselves in one of their great circular or oval camps, ringed about with wagons like a Boer laager.

Valens might have waited for Gratian, of whom he is said to have been jealous, but instead he decided to force a battle at once. His intelligence service underestimated the number of the Goths, and even had they not done so he knew that Roman armies were usually able to beat vastly superior numbers of barbarians not under Roman discipline. Drawing up his troops, legions in the centre, light infantry in front, and cavalry on either flank, he prepared to attack the wagon camp. It was about two in the afternoon of August 9th. The troops had marched from Adrianople at dawn, they had not been properly rationed, and they were suffering from want of water under a blazing sun.

It seems that Valens' intelligence officers, besides estimating the total number of the barbarians far too low, had also failed to find out that a very large detachment of mounted men were out of camp, foraging in the neighbourhood. On top of this, Valens neglected to throw out proper security patrols and covering detachments, at least on his left. The barbarians played hard for delay, sending messengers offering to surrender and meanwhile setting fire to the grass to hinder the Roman deployment.

Valens did not have his troops in hand; while negotiations were still going on his light infantry, without orders, made a premature attack on the wagon camp and failed to push it home. Thereupon the Roman cavalry on the wings attacked, although the left wing was not well concentrated. It had come up fast but had left behind it many stragglers and even lost units on the roads over which it had advanced. About the time that such of its units as had come up were committed to the attack on the wagon camp, the great mass of barbarian horsemen who had been out foraging suddenly appeared and charged their exposed outer flank. Naturally the cavalry of the Roman left were driven off the field, and their flight exposed the left of the Roman infantry. Julian's legions at Strassburg thirty years before had been able to meet such a situation but Valens' troops could not. Men and units got so jammed together that no effective resistance could be made. The Batavian auxiliaries of the reserve took to their heels, the Emperor was killed, and only a third of the army escaped.[4]

Even after such a disaster the barbarians utterly failed to consolidate their position within the Roman border. They could not so much as take the city of Adrianople, but merely went on drifting to and fro, ravaging. Philippopolis and Sofia also held out. Gratian, who had by this time reached Belgrade, appointed an able general—Theodosius—as Emperor of the East. Theodosius made his headquarters at Salonika. Then the two Emperors went to work on the problem much as Tiberius had gone to work in Pannonia nearly 300 years before. While refusing battle, they forced the Goths to keep concentrated in order to be able to resist them; they worked steadily to lessen the area subject to loot and they were always rounding up or massacring Gothic detachments. One particularly successful surprise attack was delivered by a lieutenant of Theodosius named Modar, himself a Goth but an orthodox Christian. Theodosius had been crowned in January, 379. By the end of 380 there was not a Goth alive south of the Danube who had not been captured and sold as a slave or else had consented to enlist in the Imperial Army. Six years later, when another Gothic force tried to cross the river, Theodosius' generals tricked them, the Roman river fleet rammed their light canoes, and the miserable barbarians were drowned by thousands.

The importance of the campaign of Adrianople is not its immediate consequences, which as we have seen were local, temporary and slight. The point is that after that campaign the Roman army was reorganized in a form big with consequences for the future.

In the first place, the tactical revolution in the relations between cavalry and infantry was now complete. Cavalry was now the chief arm. Vegetius seems to have written shortly after Adrianople, and in Roman tactics as he describes them it is the cavalry who (in all normal cases) are called upon to deliver the decisive attack. The light infantry would prepare and support the attack

[4] Ammianus Marcellinus, Bk. 31.

by their fire. But the heavy infantry were expected merely to stand firm "like a wall" behind their great shields, not stirring from their place for fear of breaking their strict alignment. Their immovable mass was the pivot of a defensive action, and in such an action they still played the chief part, for the light infantry could not, unaided, withstand the hostile shock and could not stand on the defensive at all—they must charge, skirmish or flee. Obviously a decision can seldom, if ever, be obtained without taking the offensive, and on the offensive the rôle of the Roman heavy infantry was now virtually limited to standing in reserve ready to repel hostile counterattacks should the Roman cavalry be repulsed.[5]

It is impossible to exaggerate the importance of the tactical revolution which made cavalry the chief arm.

I repeat that normally, for the most part because of the fear of men in general felt by horses, infantry is and must be the chief arm. Well-disciplined, unshaken infantry can not only stand off a superior number of cavalry; they can advance despite the opposition of that cavalry. Sometimes they can even break its cohesion, as Cæsar's legionaries broke the Pompeian cavalry at Pharsalia. Besides their tactical superiority, they have the economic advantage of being far less expensive to maintain than an equal number of cavalry.

But although the importance of the fourth-century supremacy of cavalry cannot be exaggerated, and although that supremacy was, in part, due to a certain decline in the discipline of infantry, still the reader should remember that there was another powerful force at work.

Besides the enormous moral effect of its charge, cavalry has also this advantage compared with infantry, that it is far more mobile. Now we have seen that for four centuries the task of the Roman army had been chiefly the repulse of frontier raids. Ever since Trajan's time it had been almost exclusively that. For raiding and the repulse of raids, cavalry was obviously better than foot because of its mobility. Naturally, the cavalry arm became more important on both sides of the frontier. Cavalry would see more of active service and therefore energetic and ambitious men would prefer a career in this arm, which would still further increase its

[5] Delpech, Vol. 2, 130–134, copiously quoting Vegetius.

importance. This was a natural and, under the conditions, an inevitable process; our own regular army when dealing with the Indians of the Great Plains or with Philippine insurrectos found that much of the work had to be done by mounted troops. Therefore the supremacy of cavalry from 380 to, say, 1500, was not due to folly but was brought about by virtue of special military conditions and partly by a decline in the discipline and instruction of infantry.

The reader must not think of the tactical revolution and the new preponderance of barbarian personnel as abrupt breaks in the traditions of the Roman service. It was no more than the culmination of a long and gradual development. Afterwards there were still many important elements of permanence. For instance there was the general doctrine of war. After the tactical revolution the fourth-century Roman army continued to maintain its traditional doctrine adapted to the nature of a professional, long-service force without large organized reserves and without an abundant and rapid supply of replacements. We find in Vegetius such maxims as the following: "No man is to be employed in the field who is not trained and tested in discipline" and correspondingly, "It is better to beat the enemy through want, surprises, and care over difficult places (i. e., through manœuvres) than by a battle in the open field."

As far as possible the idea is to win without fighting! Such doctrine is that of almost all professional armies everywhere, especially when they are opposed, as the Roman army was usually opposed, by forces more numerous but far less highly organized than itself. We have seen it successfully used not only since Tiberius' time but ever since Marius' campaign against the Cimbri and Teutones in 102 B. C. Nevertheless it is dangerous to the state that practices it and particularly dangerous if the citizens of that state (like the fourth-century Roman empire) are unwarlike and lacking in patriotism.

Still we must not exaggerate, for a civilized force is always superior to an equal number of barbarians and usually superior to a far greater number. Adrianople is the one example of a great disaster inflicted at barbarian hands. The effects of that disaster were local and temporary and in any case it is counterbalanced by the splendid succession of victories.

Besides completing the tactical revolution, Theodosius' reorganization brought about another fundamental change. It made barbarian personnel predominate over native.

Ever since early Republican times the Roman army had had in it non-citizen elements. By Constantine's time these elements, originally subordinate, were about equal in importance with the citizen elements, as is proved by the existence of numerous Palatine auxiliaries among the crack troops of the service.

Such a development was natural enough. I repeat that in so vast a community there could be no patriotism except in the tiny minority immediately concerned with public affairs. Familiarity with the comforts of a high civilization disinclined men to military service then as now. Accordingly, recruitment from within the Empire became increasingly difficult in spite of the infinitesimally small proportion of troops to population. The Imperial Government was forced to meet the difficulty by the same expedient which we see to-day in the Colonial armies of England and France—that is, by the employment of barbarians. These barbarians were in no way hostile to the civilized society which they policed; as long as they were paid they were tractable enough, and under Roman commanders imbued with a long tradition of civilized warfare, they would cheerfully cut to pieces many times their number of hostile barbarians from outside the frontiers. Nevertheless, as time went on the disinclination of civilized Romans for military service increased until the officers as well as the men gradually became largely barbarian in blood. The easiest way to enlist men was to accept in block the personal following of barbaric chieftains willing to serve as officers.

After 380, it was in no way an innovation that Theodosius enlisted or pressed into the Roman service great numbers of barbarian horsemen. The ominous new thing was that he paid them higher than the regular Roman troops and showed them greater consideration.

Moreover, these new auxiliaries were given a new status, that of "Federati," different both from that of the original auxiliary units and from that of the numeri. It seems that the Federati were technically allies, not subjects of the Empire; therefore their legal status resembled that of the allied contingents which had served in the armies of the Republic and of the early Empire.

In practice they seem to have differed from auxiliaries and numeri not only in that the commander of a federate unit was usually the tribal chief of its original personnel, but also in that he seems to have had considerable liberty in appointing his subordinate officers. Of course this patronage increased the independence and potential political importance of these commanders. On the other hand, there is nothing to show that such a unit continued to be tribally recruited as it was moved about from province to province.

The predominance of barbarian over native personnel in the Roman army determined the manner of the loss of centralized government in the West in a different way from that in which the thing is presented by many popular historians of the recent past. It is true that after Theodosius' death in 395 A. D. no Emperor effectively ruled the entire Roman world, and that the centralized administration in the West soon afterwards showed signs of breaking up. But this change did not come through successful attack from' without. It was the result of the increasing decline of civilization from internal causes. In no battle did barbarians from the outer darkness defeat a Roman army and permanently appropriate to themselves Roman land. To this general statement, only two local exceptions appear. A narrow belt south of the upper Danube was overrun, and in Britain small heathen pirate settlements on the south and east coasts cut off the Romanized Britons from communion with Christendom.

With these two exceptions, the chieftains who set themselves up as local governors in the provinces of the West, although most of them were indeed barbarian in blood, obtained their power not bcause of that fact but because they were commanders of auxiliary units in the Roman army. Their units had come to feel loyalty for them as their immediate commanders rather than to the Roman state they nominally served, but the numbers of those units were tiny compared to the populations they policed. For instance, Clovis' less than 8000 "Franks" came into a Gaul of millions.[6] Moreover it is highly doubtful whether any of the auxiliary units which installed their commanders as local governors were still tribally recruited or retained any tribal consciousness whatsoever. Their tribal names seem to have become mere regimental desig-

[6] Gregory of Tours' "Historia Francorum," quoted in Fustel de Coulanges: L'Invasion germanique et la fin de l'empire, 480.

nations. Before establishing themselves as provincial governors their chiefs engaged in civil wars between claimants for the title of Emperor, but we never hear of such a chieftain seeking the Empire for himself. They sometimes fought one another for more territory from which to collect taxes, but their taxes were the Roman taxes and were collected by the traditional Roman civil service. With two exceptions, no commander of auxiliaries ever made war upon an Emperor. The exceptions were first, the Vandal chief who looted Africa and then set up a dynasty which lasted for a century there, and second, Alaric in his brief and somewhat pardonable mutiny when the impoverished Imperial government failed to pay him as it had contracted to do. In general, the new provincial governors acknowledged the authority of the Emperor of the day; and he on his side apparently made no effort to make them pay him taxes.

There were invaders from without but those invaders were either destroyed like Radagaisus or beaten back like the Mongol Attila. Radagaisus raided Italy in 406 with 200,000 men at his back. His great following was opposed by a far smaller Roman force under the command of a general of barbaric blood—Stilicho the Vandal. It was hemmed in by means of entrenchments (much as Cæsar had hemmed in Vercingetorix at Alesia) and was wiped out.

The troops at the command of the Visigothic chieftain in Spain, the Vandal in Africa, the Herul or Ostrogoth in Italy, continued to be organized as they had been when units in the armies of the centralized Empire. That is, they were heavy cavalry armed chiefly with the lance and light infantry who were mainly archers. They were recruited from the descendants of the original unit, plus such newcomers, either barbarian or native, as that body chose to admit. Such admissions were rare, for the warband constituted a rich and highly privileged body. With one great exception—to which we shall come in a moment—there seems to have been no recruitment of provincials on a large scale, not because the local governors would have been unwilling to have their help (could they have obtained it without breaking down the exclusiveness of the privileged body upon which they depended for support) but because the provincials themselves were unwilling to serve in armies commanded by men heretical in religion.

Where there was no racial difference (as in the case of the Huns) the politics of the Dark Ages turned not upon the distinction between provincial and barbarian as such, but upon points of religion. The reason why the local governors of 5th-century Africa, Italy, and Spain could not recruit provincials was that the provincials were Catholic and the Governors Arian. To this state of affairs the great exception was northern Gaul. The Frankish chieftains were Catholics and their auxiliary forces were supplemented by troops recruited from the Roman population, equipped (and presumably organized) in the traditional Roman manner.

In view of the fundamental religio-political difference between Gaul and the other states governed by barbarian chieftains, and in view of the survival of infantry as the chief force in the Frankish armies, it will be convenient to leave Gaul on one side to be considered in the next chapter. Meanwhile we should remember that the declining population of the entire Roman world continued to think of itself as Roman. The various new local governors preserved a theoretical allegiance to the Emperor at Constantinople and that Emperor directly administered the Eastern half of the Roman world.

In the 6th century we have the restoration of direct imperial government throughout Africa, Italy and Southern Spain. This restoration was brought about by arms. Its campaigns, together with the contemporary episodes of the perpetual border war on the Persian frontier constitute our only detailed knowledge of the warfare of the time.

Justinian (A. D. 527–565) on becoming Emperor, inherited an army in which a determined effort had been made by Leo I (A. D. 457–474) and Zeno the Isaurian (A. D. 474–491) to reduce the relative importance of barbarian as compared with native personnel. This had been done by enlisting large numbers of Isaurian mountaineers from southern Anatolia who were apparently granted pay and privileges equal to those of the barbarian federate auxiliaries.

In the century and a quarter preceding Justinian, the total numbers of the Roman army of the East had fallen heavily. In 527 he effectively ruled the Balkan peninsula, Anatolia, Syria and Egypt, and commanded from 150,000 to 200,000 soldiers, whereas, in, say, 400 A. D., these same provinces were garrisoned by about 350,000 men. The cause of this decline was the continuing decline of civilization itself, of which the symptoms were depopulation, financial decay, and corrupt administration. This last reached such a point in Justinian's old age that he is said to have had a paper strength of 645,000 men and only 150,000 in reality to police his original dominions plus Africa, Italy and part of Spain.[7]

The diminished Roman army of the East was still organized, as prescribed by Diocletian more than two centuries before, into "Palatine" (i. e., Field Army) and "Limitary" (i. e., localized frontier) troops.[8] The tactical unit is still known by the old name of "numerus" translated into Greek as "katalogos" but all the other old names for units, legion, cohort, ala, etc., seem to have disappeared. The independence and patronage of the generals which we have discussed in connexion with the Theodosian reorganization had continued to increase, so that now native-born Roman generals as well as barbarian chieftains had great military households of personal retainers. That of Belisarius at the climax of his career was nearly 7000 strong.[9] Units were no longer designated with a number or regimental title but only with the name of their commander.

In equipment and tactics, the tendencies of relying upon cavalry rather than infantry, and also the increasing importance of archery fire had worked themselves out to their logical conclusion. As has been previously shown, these tendencies were due in part to a decline in the discipline and instruction of infantry and in part to special military circumstances, especially the use of the army as a constabulary. They were also fostered by the fact that the Eastern provinces had always been great cavalry and archery countries. There was still heavy armed infantry in Justinian's armies, but in all the battles of his reign we hear of only one feat of arms which it performed. That was the stand in the testudo formation with interlocked shields (and doubtless with the spear butts resting against the ground and the right foot as prescribed by Vegetius) backed up against the river Euphrates and confronted by the whole Persian army after the defeat at Sura in 531. Even this, however brilliant, was only a negative success. The Isaurians

---

[7] For these figures, see Young, Vol. 2, 205 and 322. Also Bury, E. B., Vol. 23, 523.

[8] Bury, E. B., Vol. 23, 523. Also Aussaresses, 9.

[9] Young, Vol. 2, 246.

were mostly foot archers. The flower of the native army were the heavy cavalry, fully armoured in scale mail and equipped as archers, with a sword, a little shield strapped to the upper left arm, and usually a lance as well. There were also lightly equipped horse archers, many of them Mongols, and barbarian heavy cavalrymen from the north armed with the lance.

At first glance one would think that the East-Roman heavy cavalry, with their lances and bows as well, were not organized on sound lines. Since fire delivered mounted must necessarily be inferior to infantry fire with a similar weapon, it seems as if foot archers ought easily to have obtained fire superiority over them. If this was so, then why not concentrate on shock tactics instead of losing time from training with the lance in order to practise shooting? A similar case is that of the 16th-century German mounted pistoleers whose fire was inferior to that of dismounted musketeers while they were usually routed by a vigorous charge of mounted lancers.

I think that the answer in both cases is to be found in the characteristics of the infantry which the late Roman and the early modern cavalrymen had to meet. In both cases the infantry in question was instructed to resist cavalry by arraying itself in masses of pikemen so dense that it necessarily lacked mobility, was clumsy in its formations and could not develop effective fire power. Heavy cavalry equipped both for fire and shock could ride down light infantry armed with missile weapons or drive them behind the heavy infantry where their fire would be ineffective. Then the cavalry would circle around the heavy infantry and fire into the fine target offered by its dense masses. The fact that the ancient light infantry were archers or slingers, and the ancient cavalry were archers, whereas the early modern light infantry were musketeers and their cavalry pistoleers, merely illustrates the similarity of the principle involved in both cases.

On the other hand, armoured cavalry equipped for both fire and shock must not be confused with light cavalry relying upon fire alone, such as the horse archers who defeated Crassus and gave the Crusaders so much hard work. There the principle is different inasmuch as this last kind of cavalry cannot close while their opponents retain any cohesion whatsoever.

There were in Justinian's day men of an antiquarian school of military thought who still deprecated archery and kept praising the old type of hand-to-hand fighting legionary of whom they read in their books, but their contentions were without effect. The practical soldiers of the time despised them as pedants, and insisted upon the variety of weapons, and especially the complete armour, enjoyed by their heavy armed horse archers.[10]

East-Roman generals could afford to take great liberties with their opponents, because the hostile armies were never flexible and lacked the power to manœuvre on the battlefield. With armies of anything like equal manœuvring power, Napoleon's maxim—"Beware when trying to outflank your opponent that you are not outflanked yourself"—comes into play; and yet the three great victories of Justinian's reign were all won by variations on the device of defensive envelopment from a concave formation!

At Daras in upper Mesopotamia in 530, Belisarius had 25,000 men against 40,000 Persians. The Persian infantry of that day fought behind great cumbrous wicker shields like their ancestors of 1000 years before. The Persians put their cavalry, their only striking force, on the wings. Belisarius refused his infantry centre and advanced his cavalry wings, covering his whole front with a non-continuous trench. The Persians, being unwilling to advance into his trap, made contact only on the wings, and were defeated by Belisarius' ability in using the superior tactical flexibility of the Roman cavalry units. A turning movement by a small body of 300 men, culminating in a surprise charge launched from behind the cover of a hill against the Persian left, contributed to the success.[11]

At Taginæ in Italy in 552, Narses had the unusually large force of 60,000 men but seems to have had no Roman infantry of the line with him.[12] Therefore, in order to have a pivot or core for the defensive action which he proposed to fight, he dismounted his heavy armed barbarian cavalry armed with the lance, and threw forward obliquely his wings of Roman foot archers and cavalry. The Ostrogoths, who were mostly mounted lancers and foot archers, could not co-ordinate the work of their two categories of troops. Their horse charged, bull fashion, against the Roman

[10] Procopius: "De Bello Persico," Bk. 1, sec. 1, quoted by Oman, Vol. 1, 25–26.

[11] Oman, Vol. 1, 27–29.   [12] Young, Vol. 2, 297.

centre but failed to break it and suffered severely from the Roman arrows.   Meanwhile a detached body of cavalry on the extreme Roman left was threatening the Gothic archers and preventing them from co-operating with the attack.   Finally, the main body of the Roman horse charged the disordered Gothic cavalry, broke them, and decided the day, for the wretched Gothic foot failed to make any sort of stand.

The next year, in 553, Italy was invaded by a huge marauding band of Alemanni plus Frankish hotheads who had joined the expedition on their own account without authorization from their government, 75,000 or 80,000 in all.[13] This great force split in two columns one of which marched down each side of the peninsula. They lost heavily by disease and by sudden attacks of the imperial garrisons, but these last were too few to stop them, and the eastern column escaped northward over the Alps in the Autumn.   The other column wintered in the South.

In the Spring of 554, Narses concentrated 18,000 near Rome, moved south and met the marauders near Casilinum, the modern Capua.[14] The Alemanni were 30,000 strong, all infantry, armed solely for shock and protected only by shields without helmets or body armour.   East-Roman generals were accustomed to study their enemy.   On reaching Italy, Belisarius' first care had been to size up the Gothic equipment and tactics—so we are not surprised to find Narses familiar with the crude tactics of the Alemanni who were accustomed to ploy into a single deep column or wedge without manœuvring power.

Accordingly he prepared to fight a delaying action with his centre and envelop their mass with his wings of horse archers. Against these last the wretched Alemanni were helpless because of their fire inferiority and their lack of defensive armour.   They were able to push back the Roman heavy infantry in the centre but when enveloped by the horse archers they could do nothing and were wiped out.   It is said that only five escaped!

The small numbers of the armies which fought Justinian's wars illustrate not only the high standard obtained by the Imperial troops but also the flimsy character of the Arian local governments of the West.   The original Vandal chieftain, with his mixed horde at his back, had been originally invited into Africa over a century

[13] Bury: Later Roman Empire, Vol. 2, 414.   [14] Hodgkin, Vol. 5, 38.

before Belisarius landed in arms. The fertile territory governed by the descendants of this horde is over 115 miles broad and nearly 950 miles long. And yet, when invaded by an Imperial expeditionary force of only 15,000 men, we find the Vandal state bursting like a bubble; worse still, only 5000 of Belisarius' force were cavalry and both actions of the Vandal war were cavalry fights.[15]

Obviously such figures show that the numerous civil population in whose territory the war was fought, remained completely passive. Half a thousand years of unbroken reliance upon a professional army had firmly convinced the masses throughout the Empire that in no war could they be expected to play an active part. The same thing is shown by Justinian's campaigns in Italy and Spain. But before considering these campaigns I digress to record an African incident which throws light upon the conditions of the time.

After the collapse of the Vandal state, the survivors of the army which had formed a privileged class in that state were given the chance to enlist in the Imperial army. Since their alternatives were slavery or death the poor devils naturally accepted and were embarked for Constantinople *en route* for the Persian frontier. Those who arrived seem to have served obediently enough inasmuch as we hear of no mutiny. Indeed they had little choice as they had no chance of getting home. The prospect of deserting to the Persians cannot have appealed to them. But 400 of them turned their ship about at Lesbos and returned to Africa with a favouring wind. On landing they found that half the Imperial garrison was in mutiny for arrears in pay. Moreover, the mutineers had been joined by that permanent component of Roman anarchy —runaway slaves. The 400 Vandals joined them and the mutiny dragged on for some time before being finally put down.[16]

Justinian's conquest of Italy, although a longer business than that of Africa, was achieved by campaigns of the same sort. As in Africa, the population was friendly to the Imperialists but inert and passive in the war. The disproportionately small number of regular troops, when compared with the large area to be conquered, is even more striking. The flimsy Ostrogothic state (its dynasty was still Ostrogothic and its small, highly privileged military caste may still have contained traces of its far-off Ostro-

[15] Hodgkin, Vol. 3, 598.   [16] Hodgkin, Vol. 4, 27-37.

gothic origin) controlled not only Italy and Sicily but also south-eastern France to the Rhone together with Dalmatia, Croatia, Switzerland and lower Austria to the Danube. Belisarius success-fully attacked in 536 with less than 9000 regulars.[17] One is re-minded of the collapse of the Neapolitian Bourbons before Gari-baldi.

It is true that there was another Imperial army operating east of the Adriatic, but that force was even smaller—3000 or 4000 men—and it was Belisarius' attack from the south that was the main blow.[18]   The Goths were not much more numerous; they could muster only 15,000 to besiege Rome when it opened its gates to the East-Romans, not enough to surround and contain the place.[19] By this time the wastage of campaigning, plus the tiny garrisons left in Palermo and Naples, had reduced Belisarius' numbers to 7500, but by great diplomatic efforts he persuaded some of the citizens to do guard duty on the walls and tormented the besiegers so much with sudden sallies of his regulars that they raised the siege.

That the war dragged on for nearly twenty years was entirely Justinian's fault for insisting upon a divided command and for losing touch with military affairs altogether and absorbing himself in theological speculation.   In the first four years when Belisarius had a free hand he so reduced the Goths that they held only a few points and those north of the Po.   Most of the fighting was position warfare, i. e., sieges.   Italy was full of citadels, and whichever side had the upper hand would try to peg out a larger area of occupa-tion by throwing forward tiny garrisons, or by besieging the en-emy's advance strong points.   When in 552 Justinian for the first time raised a large army, Narses promptly broke the back of the Goths for him in the following year at Taginæ.

Of Justinian's conquest of southern Spain we know very little. It was undertaken by local troops from the province of Africa and the operations seem to have been like those in Africa and Italy.[20] Andalusia, the richest and most thickly populated part of the pen-insula, was garrisoned, and although we hear of no further expedi-

[17] Young, Vol. 2, 217.
[18] Hodgkin, Vol. 4, 2.
[19] Bury: Later Roman Empire, Vol. 1, 392. Hodgkin's high figures can-not be reconciled with the events of the siege.
[20] Bury: Later Roman Empire, Vol. 1, 415.

tionary forces being sent out, nevertheless some cities held out against the feeble Visigoths until about 623 A. D.

Up to Justinian's death in 565 the Roman armies had never fallen back before military pressure. We have seen that the original loss of centralized administration in the West (except for the east coast of Britain and perhaps the upper Danube country) had come about through political rearrangement and not through military defeat. Now Africa, Italy, Dalmatia and southern Spain, a good half of the western Provinces, had been returned by arms to the direct control of the Emperors. The army which had been the instrument of their recovery was still incomparably the finest in the world.

CHAPTER IV

THE EAST-ROMAN ARMY

(AFTER THE DEATH OF JUSTINIAN, 575–1079 A. D.)

AND THE DARK AGES IN THE WEST, 451–1000

In the last three chapters we have considered the transformation of the Roman professional army from Augustus to Justinian. I now propose to follow that army down to the loss of its corporate tradition, and to discuss the change of military system in the West from professional to feudal forces.

Soon after the death of Justinian in 565, the Roman Empire enters upon a period of shrinking frontiers. It is true that, until the beginning of the Mohammedan conquests in 634, the underlying cause of the shrinkage was financial rather than military weakness. If the loosely organized Visigothic state was able successfully to besiege the Andalusian cities one by one, it was because Constantinople could not afford to raise and transport armies to relieve them. If the Lombards were able to spread themselves over much of Italy, it was for the same reason. The same thing is true of the Slavic occupation of the interior Balkans except that the early Slavs were quite willing to do homage and pay tribute to the Empire. Moreover, both Lombards and Slavs entered depopulated provinces where there was land enough and to spare, so that newcomers were welcome. The population of the Empire had long been on the decline and in Justinian's time a severe epidemic of plague made matters worse. This depopulation had helped produce the financial shortage which was aggravated not only by Justinian's far-flung campaigns but also by his passion for building. Religious troubles had increased Justinian's military tasks. He had to keep large forces in Egypt, in order to hold down the heretical Monophysites of the turbulent city of Alexandria. Finally, there was increased pressure upon the Persian frontier, always the chief military liability of the Empire, and this pressure continued throughout the reigns of Justinian's successors, so that there was no chance to get together a surplus in the exhausted treasury.

There is need here to repeat the discussion as to whether the Romans would have done better had they relied upon larger, short-service, armies. I have already said that, given the whole nature of their state and their great distances (as measured in the time required for troop movements), a professional long-service army was necessary to them. Axiomatically, such an army is more efficient than an equal number of short-service troops, and is therefore a smaller drain on the man-power of the community. But it is equally axiomatic that it is far more expensive in money than an equal, or even a considerably larger, number of conscripts need be. In deciding for a professional long-service force, the Roman Emperors deliberately accepted the comparatively high expense per man that such an organization involves. Down to the seventh-century Mohammedan invasions, the Roman troops were still the best in the world. If Visigoths, Lombards and Slavs were winning land from the Empire it was not because they were equally good soldiers. It was because the Roman treasury was no longer able to pay, equip and transport armies to take the field against them.

Towards the end of the sixth century the Roman army, whose long and glorious history we have reviewed, took its final definite form.

It so happens that we have from this period a sort of Training and Field Service Manual, the Strategicon of the Emperor Maurice (582–602), probably written about 579 when he was still only a General.[1] The Strategicon shows that the Roman army was still, man for man, far superior to its opponents. From it we learn that the Imperial Government was working to lessen the quasi-feudal tendency of the soldiers to attach themselves to particular generals rather than to the state and to remedy that main weakness of all long-service armies—the lack of trained replacements.

The Strategicon is a complete military manual. Its name is derived from "strategos" the Greek for "general" and might be translated "Manual for General Officers"; or from "strategeia" which would mean a Manual of Troop Leading. It embodies the correct principle that military instruction should begin at the top

[1] For the date, see Oman, Vol. 1, 173. The account of the Strategicon is from Aussaresses.

and radiate downwards throughout the army, and that it is supremely important that the higher officers should know their job.
After beginning with intelligence studies of the usual enemies of
the East-Romans, it takes up the civil laws concerning military
service and recruitment, the different qualities of recruitment, the
organization of the army in its different subdivisions—administrative and tactical—and the various staff departments charged
with administration and supply. It next deals with cavalry and
infantry training, then with field service, including intelligence
service in the field, espionage, and counter-espionage, etc., and
finally with tactics including both the morale and the mechanics
of combat.

The author recommends that the conduct of war should be
adapted to the tactics and organization of the enemy against whom
it is waged. Thus against the Avars of the lower Danube, who were
Tartar horsebowmen, the Roman commander should force the
fighting, taking care meanwhile to protect his flanks and rear and
above all to prevent surprise. Against the Lombards and other
Western peoples he should do exactly the opposite and never willingly accept battle except under peculiarly favourable circumstances, for these peoples are fierce fighters. On the other hand
they are careless as to their flanks and against surprises; their supply departments are ill-organized so that if the campaign be spun
out they are likely to go home in disgust. Maurice describes the
Lombards as mounted lancers. The Slavs who are all infantry are
formidable only because of the difficult nature of their country.
They can easily be beaten if the Roman army be not ambuscaded
or surprised in a wooded defile. Against the Persians, the most
dangerous enemy of all, the Roman commander should put forth
all his skill. Whenever he can he should support his cavalry
with good infantry.

The section dealing with recruitment tells us that the old theoretical liability to universal military service was still maintained
as it had been ever since Augustus. The army was conscript
as it had been at least since the fourth century. The various
units are of unequal value and it seems almost certain that at
least some of the crack corps are still barbaric in recruitment.
However, the author bases no hard and fast distinction upon this,
but solely upon military value. In any case, the barbarian element

was less important than formerly. The crack units were privileged in many ways, particularly so with regard to the number of camp followers or armed personal servants allowed them. The Bucelaries, as the personal escort of the Generals were called, were allowed as many of these as they chose. The cavalry of the line had one follower for every seven soldiers. All told, an army of 20,000 cavalry would have between four and five thousand followers.

The chief administrative and tactical unit is the "tagma," that is the company or troop. This unit is evidently the successor of the "numerus" as it is sometimes called "arithmos," the Greek translation of "numerus." It is also sometimes called a "band." Each tagma is divided into platoons of 100 and squads of 10 men. The fact that Maurice makes it only 300 strong, whereas the old numeri numbered 1000 men, may perhaps be explained by the decline of the total numbers of the Roman army. By Maurice's time the actual tagma may well have remained far below its original paper strength for so long a time that it seemed best to him to reorganize on the smaller basis.

Whereas in Justinian's time we hear of no echelon of command intermediate between the numerus and the army commander, Maurice organized a system of higher echelons (brigades and divisions we should call them). Previously the numerus or regiment, 1000 strong, had been the highest organized unit. Now command in the field was to be facilitated by an organization of three or more troops or companies in brigade, and three brigades in division at the outbreak of war. Justinian's arrangement reminds us of the pre-Revolutionary eighteenth-century armies, indivisible tactically. It should be noted, however, that Maurice does not recommend permanent higher units but assumes that the general will organize them upon the outbreak of war. It is interesting to find that Maurice recommends a practice afterwards followed by Napoleon, i. e., making the higher units unequal in strength so as to make it harder for the enemy to calculate the numbers of the whole army.

Still more important were the reforms in personnel. Maurice saw clearly the danger of too high a proportion of barbarian auxiliaries and that of the undue independence of the higher officers with their large bands of personal retainers. Therefore, although he did not do away with the auxiliary or federate troops, he counterbalanced them by the encouragement of recruiting among hardy peoples within the Empire. He took away from the general officers their power of patronage by retaining in the hands of the Emperor himself the appointment of all officers above the rank of centurion—as we should say, of all field officers. Undoubtedly it was these measures which gave the East-Roman armies the cohesion necessary to preserve Anatolia by halting the Saracen on the line of the Taurus Mountains. Junior officers were appointed from a cadet corps, the Spatharies, of whom a contingent served in the field with the headquarters company of each general.

In equipment only one new thing is to be found, the use of stirrups. Before Augustus' time the ancients all seem to have ridden on a mere blanket and surcingle. The cavalry of the early Empire had a shaped saddle with a high pommel and cantle but before the loss of pictorial record in the fourth century we have no indication of the use of stirrups. At some time during the fifth or the first three quarters of the sixth century, stirrups began to come in, just when it is impossible to say.

The tactical importance of stirrups is self-evident. Without them the ancient horseman was always liable to be pulled off his horse by any infantryman who could seize him by the foot. With them cavalry were far more formidable.

The passages dealing with the administrative staff sections show that the East-Roman Army had highly organized supply departments, medical and ambulance service, chaplain's department and pay department. The lives of the soldiers were so highly prized that the mounted ambulance men received increased pay for every seriously wounded man whom they rescued. The sections on cavalry and infantry training are interesting and thorough. They begin with recruit training and the school of the soldier and go upwards through the school of the company, the battalion, and the regiment or brigade, to that of the army.

The Field Service Regulations outline a sound service of security both on the march and in camp, together with a system of espionage and counter-espionage, rules for the examination of prisoners and for estimating the enemy's numbers. Field works and the fortification of the nightly camp are also considered.

The section dealing with combat recommends careful attention to the supply services during action. The morale of the troops is to be encouraged by all possible means. For Maurice, the typical engagement is a cavalry fight. He particularly insists on the greater mobility of cavalry and remarks that if necessary they can dismount and fight well on foot. When infantry are present their action is usually subordinate to that of the horse. The reader should note, however, that it is particularly in dealing with the Empire's strongest enemy, the Persian, that he recommends infantry support for the cavalry. He insists upon the importance of supports and reserves, of attacks upon the enemy's flank, and of security for the Roman flanks and rear. Whenever possible he recommends that the decisive attack should be launched from behind cover such as that of a ridge of land. In fact all supports and reserves are best kept out of sight until wanted.

The infantry was definitely an auxiliary arm. Only in a country so difficult as to hinder the movements of cavalry were the footmen expected to play the leading rôle. Nevertheless their organization and tactics were as carefully thought out as those of the cavalry. Their discipline and cohesion must have been high, for we hear of their delivering night attacks.

The tactical and administrative unit was the band or tagma, the successor of the old numerus. Its strength was nearer four than three hundred. Each infantry band was divided between heavy and light troops, very much as the sixteenth-century battalion was divided between pikemen and musketeers. The East-Roman light infantry were archers and javelin men.

In a mixed force of infantry and cavalry, if the proportion of infantry was high they would usually stand in the centre with cavalry on the wings and in reserve. If the proportion of infantry was low they would be held back and would be expected merely to stand fast and repel the enemy's counterattack if the Byzantine cavalry charge failed.

The offensive tactics of the East-Roman heavy infantry seem to imply the same contradiction already noticed in connexion with Julian the Apostate's victory at Strassburg in 357—an attack with sword and axe and yet that attack delivered in close order. We are distinctly told that the formation was a line of close columns, sixteen deep, with the shields of the rear ranks raised overhead as in the old siege testudo. And in the same breath we are told that the lances were hurled just before contact, like the old legionary pilum, and that the actual close fighting was with sword and axe. This contradiction vanishes if we assume that, after hurling their spears, the front ranks then deployed as swordsmen with the necessary intervals and distances. This is much what the legionaries of the republic and the early empire did after hurling their pilum. On this assumption the tactics in question, although a much more cautious, defensively minded system, nevertheless appear as a normal development, or deformation of the earlier practice. Since neither Ammianus nor Maurice mention such a deployment it remains mere assumption but an interesting and possible one. The line of columns instead of a single heavy line is also interesting. In the general conduct of war we find Maurice following directly the age-long traditions of the Roman professional army. For him the ideal of generalship is to win campaigns without fighting battles. When the decision to attack has been made, it is better to make partial rather than general attacks, and above all, to use stratagem and try to effect surprise. During sieges, when the Romans are besieging they are not to be in a hurry to assault. When they are the besieged they should beware of wasting men in sorties. Obviously such procedure tends to postpone the decision. Still it must be remembered that against most of their enemies, if the Romans could gain time, their loosely organized opponents would either commit some folly which would permit of attacking them under favourable circumstances or else, (owing to their imperfect organization) would find themselves faced with the alternative of retreat or starvation. Whereas on the other hand, a bull-headed immediate attack might involve the destruction of the Roman army if the enemy were superior in number, which was usually the case.

Within thirty years of Maurice's death, the Roman army reorganized by him had to face the Mohammedans.

As a sort of curtain-raiser to this titanic struggle, the long Roman-Persian war entered its last and most extensive phase. During the centuries of war to and fro across the Euphrates, the Romans had three times, under Trajan (98–117), Carus (281–284) and Julian (361–364) occupied Mesopotamia, while the Persians had never gone beyond Antioch. Now, however, the political position in the Eastern provinces had gone against the Imperial government. That government was orthodox-Catholic and many Syrians and Egyptians had become heretical in religion. In Egypt, matters were so bad that there were said to be only 30,000 orthodox in the province opposed to a solid mass of five or six million heretics. Since the modern mind is unfamiliar with the idea, it can never be too often repeated that from the 4th to the 17th century, politics hinged on points of religion. That the Persians, in 608–618 were able to overrun Syria and Egypt, to cross Asia Minor (which was not heretical), and besiege Constantinople was partly due to the incompetence of the reigning Emperor Phocas (602–610) but was chiefly due to heresy (and consequent disaffection) in Syria and Egypt. Heraclius (610–641) ousted them in a series of brilliant campaigns (622–628) full of stratagem and hard fighting, too. Sailing from Constantinople he landed his army in Cilicia and worked his way further east than any Emperor before or after him, dictating peace on the Iranian plateau in 628. Unfortunately the details of his campaigns are unknown. The mere geography of them proves his great ability and energy. More unfortunately still, Heraclius' reign is memorable not so much for the victories of his middle life as for the defeats inflicted upon the Empire in his invalid old age when he could no longer take the field.

Mohammed, dying in 632, left behind him a united Arabia, and a people at a white heat of enthusiasm for the conquest of the "infidel" world. His successors, the Caliphs, found Rome and Persia exhausted by recent war. In the case of Rome, there was also long-standing financial weakness, plus heresy in Syria and Egypt, the provinces nearest Arabia.

The Mohammedans, being originally desert men, preferred fighting on horseback. It had been their custom to skirmish but they now learned to charge home with the same extraordinary fanaticism which, in modern times, has made them such formidable foes in the Soudan and Afghanistan. In the apostolic age of Mohammedanism its warriors fought with the deliberate intention of seeking death. It was this spirit, and not the shortcomings of the forces opposed to them, which gave them their unbroken series of victories. It is hard enough to oppose such men

with modern high-power weapons.   In pre-gunpowder warfare
it was even more difficult.

Besides their extraordinarily high morale, the early Mohammedans had in their favour high mobility and superior numbers.
Their desert breeding and the fewness of their wants helped
them to move rapidly.   The fact that they were volunteers serving from religious enthusiasm and not for pay, made it possible
for Arabia, in spite of its poverty, to outnumber the armies which
Rome was able to mobilize.   Furthermore, the early Mohammedans, like the Romans of the great conquering time, could persuade.
In heretical Syria and Egypt their enthusiasm was contagious and
they made converts right and left.   The nearest historical parallel
to the early Mohammedan conquests is the Revolutionary and
Napoleonic period in France.   Here again we find rapidly raised
armies defeating professional troops by means of the same three
factors of superior mobility, numbers, and enthusiasm.   However,
even the most sincere admirer of the French Revolutionary spirit
must admit that the democratic theory has never aroused in men
the same utter contempt for death found among the early Mohammedans and occasionally, though rarely, among their successors
to this day.

The details of the early Mohammedan conquests are not clear,
but the astonishing fact is that the Romans were unable to win
a single battle.   At the Yarmuk, the decisive action in Syria,
the Romans had the upper hand all day through the superior fire
power of their Armenian archers.   It was near evening, when the
Armenians' ammunition had run low, that at last the Moslems
were able to close and get a decision.[2]   Within nine years of Mohammed's death in 632, his followers had conquered the entire
Near East, north to the Taurus Mountains and west to include
Tripoli.   Persia was entirely subjugated.   It is greatly to the
credit of the East-Roman military system that (after the heretical
provinces of Syria and Egypt had been conquered) the rest of
the Empire was able to put up so good a fight.   It took the Mohammedans over fifty years to win North Africa.   They did not finish
the job until 709.   In Asia Minor they could never get a foothold.
They attacked Constantinople by sea in 672, and besieged the place
for five years before they were beaten off.   They besieged it again

[2] Young, Vol. 2, 443.

in 717. This time their fleet was supported by an army which was able to cross Asia Minor and the whole expedition was on a larger scale than before. Nevertheless they were forced to raise the siege in the following year, saving only a small remnant of their forces.

The two defeats before Constantinople were the real turning points of the defence of Christendom against Islam. From a military point of view, they are interesting because of the great part played in them by the new invention of Greek fire. This was either a sort of low-power explosive or else crude petroleum from Baku. It was so efficient a combustible that by its use the Christians succeeded in destroying the Saracen fleet. Tubes furnished with plungers were mounted on the forecastles of the Christian ships and from them the liquid fire was squirted upon the Saracen vessels. The fire may also have been used in catapult projectiles.

After the disastrous failure of the second Saracen siege of Constantinople in 717–718, the military position of the East-Roman Empire stabilized on the line of the Taurus Mountains. The pressure was still that of Mohammedan against Christian rather than vice versa. As late as 806 and 838 the Saracens made determined efforts to conquer Asia Minor. But with the decline of their original fanaticism, the better military system of the East-Romans became able to cope with the superior numbers and high mobility of their enemies. Each of the last two invasions, after taking an important city, found the Christian resistance so stubborn that no attempt to hold the isolated conquest was made. Saracen attacks, no matter how great the numbers of the attackers, tended to become mere raids, and two could play at that game. Nevertheless the diminished Empire maintained a force of about 120,000 men—only 30,000 less than Justinian's army.[3]

Meanwhile, the interior Balkans and most of the remaining Imperial possessions in Italy were lost. Indeed there was very little resistance there, for the entire available strength of the Empire was absorbed in the desperate effort to stand off the Mohammedans. In the Balkans the feeble Slavs were accordingly allowed to occupy all but the coast lines and to live half in vassalage to the Empire, half in independence or even in fitful hostility to it. The

[3] Bury: Eastern Roman Empire, 226.

city of Rome, and with it the greater part of Italy, were lost not through military defeat but through a political quarrel, based upon religion. The able Emperor, Leo the Isaurian, who had commanded the successful defence of Constantinople, tried to banish all statues and pictures from the churches. Opinion in Italy ran so high against any such Judeo-Mohammedan innovation that the Italian domain of the Emperors rapidly shrank to the extreme south plus the district of Venice. When later Emperors returned to the traditional use of images, the harm had been done. The Popes had tasted independence and had no intention of giving it up.

As in the case of the sixth-century conquests of the Lombards in Italy there was still another reason for the gains made by the sixth- and seventh-century Slavs in the Balkans—depopulation. In the Imperial provinces the number of the inhabitants had been going down hill for centuries. It is clearly impossible to expect stubborn resistance to invasion from districts in which, after all, there is land enough and to spare for invaders and invaded alike. The newcomers dispossess almost no one.

The foregoing paragraphs should reconcile the reader's mind to the paradoxical fact that the East-Roman Empire, confined as it was to Asia Minor and the coasts of the Balkan peninsula, together with scraps of land in Dalmatia, Venetia, and Southern Italy, possessed incomparably the best military system then existing in the world.

The question naturally suggested by this statement is why the Empire of the eighth, ninth and early tenth centuries did not use its unequalled military machine for purposes of conquest. The answer is to be found in the social and economic conditions within the Empire itself.

The level of East-Roman or, as it is now possible to call it, Byzantine civilization and of wealth was higher than anywhere else in the world. This in itself was enough to cause outside pressure upon the Byzantine state. The nature and sources of that wealth were such as to leave little reasonable motive for aggression. The great wealth which the Empire enjoyed through the Dark and early Middle Ages was not primarily agricultural but commercial and industrial. It came from superiority to the rest of the known world in arts and crafts, and also through possession of Constantinople, the world's centre of commercial exchange These economic factors determined the military policy pursued by East-Roman statesmen. Since so great a part of their enormous riches was industrial and commercial in origin, they were far less concerned than other contemporary princes with attempts to enlarge their boundaries. Constantinople must be strategically secure and a sufficient amount of agricultural land must be held to make the Empire independent of foreign and therefore doubtful foodstuffs. But when these two ends had been assured, it was enough to hold the most defensible natural frontier, and folly to borrow trouble by attacking one's poorer neighbours. Thus understood, the cautious and unenterprising Byzantine strategy, at which the historians of yesterday were accustomed to sneer, appears reasonable enough.

The army which was the instrument of the defensive Byzantine policy was almost unchanged from the days of Maurice. Barbarian recruitment, already lessening in importance towards the end of the sixth century, had now ceased altogether. The temporary higher units described by Maurice had now become permanent, localized bodies distributed in depth. But with these two exceptions no important change can be recorded.

The army was still a permanent, professional, highly trained force, as Roman armies had been since Augustus about the beginning of the Christian era, or ever since Marius a century before that. It was still recruited by the same light conscription [4] based upon property in land which had existed at least since the fourth century. Rich men were keener to serve as officers than they had been during the later centuries of the old, universal dominion. That was only natural as the Empire grew smaller and more homogeneous, and as the old sense of world-wide security disappeared.

Except for his stirrups (which were already in use in Maurice's time) the East-Roman cataphractos, or heavy cavalryman, had not changed from his predecessors in the Imperial Army as early as the end of the second century. Like them he was fully armoured in scale mail, and like theirs his mount was armoured on the head, chest and shoulders. Only in the gravest emergencies, when there was a serious shortage of equipment, the scales of the armour might

[4] Leo the Wise: Tactica, Bk. 4, sec. 1, quoted in Oman, Vol. 1, 189.

be made of horn instead of metal, or even heavy leather shirts might be worn.

Like his predecessors in the Imperial service ever since the fourth century, the mail-clad Byzantine horseman was the chief reliance of armies. His tactics were exactly what they had been at least as early as the second half of the sixth century under Maurice. In fact, given the conservatism of the Roman service and the high level of intelligence throughout the Empire, it seems probable that Maurice's tactical method was already old in his day. With its provision for successive shocks, combination of frontal and flank charges, general elasticity and suppleness, it could hardly have been improved. Ambuscades and concealed turning movements were especially cultivated. There was a regular service of security in camp, on the march and in combat. The administrative and staff sections were unchanged since Maurice's time; and the signal service introduced, or perfected, under Justinian, was now carried so far that a Saracen raid in the Taurus, 400 miles straight away, could be signalled almost at once to Constantinople by a series of beacon fires.[5] At the warm springs of Dorylæum there was a huge military bathing plant capable of accommodating 7000 soldiers at once.[6]

The high ability and careful attention to detail evident throughout the Byzantine army system is particularly found in their intelligence studies of their enemies. In the "Tactica" of the Emperor Leo the Wise, written about 900, it is most interesting to see how the strong and weak points of each opponent are appreciated and measures recommended to neutralize the first and strike at the second.

The proof of the pudding is in the eating; and the excellence of the Byzantine army is shown by its success in defending for centuries the richest and therefore the most attacked state of the known world. In particular the success of the East-Romans in turning back the fanatical Mohammedan, and holding against him not only Constantinople but also all Anatolia west of the Taurus, has been insufficiently admitted. Their temporary checks have been dwelt upon by Western historians, and their victories have been ignored, such as that of the year 863 when a great Saracen army

[5] Bury: Eastern Roman Empire, 247.
[6] Bury: Eastern Roman Empire, 229.

was surrounded and completely destroyed by the well-timed concentration of the forces of ten separate "Themes." Any practical soldier can testify to the high degree of skill required for so elaborate a concentration in the face of the enemy. In Italy they held Apulia and Calabria, the toe and long heel of the boot, against all comers until late in the eleventh century.

That the East-Roman military system was superior to its rivals is additionally proved by the tenth- and eleventh-century expansion of the Empire.

Towards the end of the ninth century, political disintegration began to split up the enormous Saracen State. Now it was Saracen pressure that for two hundred years had been the greatest military liability of the East-Romans. Once this pressure was removed, they began to advance on all fronts and their advance went on from about 950 to after 1050 A. D.

In the Mediterranean they recovered Crete, Cyprus, and part of Sicily. On the Eastern frontier, advancing by little steps in the immemorial Roman fashion, they took first Cilicia, then Antioch (the great metropolis of northern Syria). The Emirs of Aleppo and Tripoli were made vassals. Farther to the north, Edessa beyond the Euphrates, together with all of Armenia, was added to the Empire. In Europe the entire Balkan peninsula was conquered and held up to the line of the Danube.

However, about the year 1000, although the East Roman military expansion was still going on, the economic position of the Empire began to change for the worse. The enormous wealth of Constantinople had been derived in part from the superiority of her arts and handicrafts to those of Western Christendom, and in part from her seaborne carrying trade. Now the West, where the level of civilization had been sinking lower and lower ever since the beginning of the Dark Ages, suddenly began a rapid recovery. Improved local arts and manufactures began to lessen the demand for Byzantine goods. The commercial Republics of the Italian coast began to compete with Byzantine shipping. The decline was gradual. Her vast accumulations made Constantinople still the richest city in the world. Nevertheless a professional army is always expensive in money and therefore the shrinking of Byzantine profits was a serious thing for the Imperial army. At the same time it seems that the civilian element in the Imperial bureaucracy was jealous of the army and correspondingly anxious to cut down military expenditure. Furthermore, without the backing of a warlike population, a professional army is necessarily brittle.

In such a state of things, a single great disaster in battle at Manzikert in 1071, followed by ten years of civil war, was enough to lose Asia Minor and thereby to break the immemorial tradition of the Roman service.

About the middle of the eleventh century a new enemy, the Seljuk Turks, began to press the Roman eastern frontier. They were formidable from their numbers, their savagery, and their fanaticism, for they were recent converts to Islam. On the other hand, they were horse archers pure and simple, and the tactical method worked out by the Romans for dealing with such troops had always been particularly successful. Briefly, that method consisted: first, in supporting the cavalry by infantry and especially foot archers who could always gain a superiority of fire over the horse archers; second, in never going all out in pursuit of the elusive swarms of the enemy unless there was an obstacle against which he could be pinned; and third, in taking pains with the service of security at all times, including security on the flanks and rear during combat. The rash Emperor Romanus neglected the first two rules and the treachery of one of his chief subordinates laid open the Roman rear and brought disaster.

The action took place far to the east at Manzikert near Lake Van. Romanus had concentrated all available mounted troops in a single great field army of over sixty thousand. He seems to have had no infantry with him except perhaps a campguard. Having established contact with the Turks in an open plain, he drove them before him, but could do them no serious harm because of their greater mobility. When fatigue and the approach of night compelled a retreat towards camp, the Romans had suffered less than the enemy. During the retreat, the encircling Turkish tactics were favoured by the treachery of the commander of the reserve. When Romanus ordered a halt to beat off the pursuing Turks, the reserve kept on towards the camp. Thereupon, the higher units still in action were beset on all sides by the Turkish skirmishers and drifted further and further apart in the twilight, until at last disorganization set in. The Emperor was captured and the Roman army virtually destroyed.[7]

Given the brittleness of a professional army based upon an unwarlike population, such a terrific smash as that of Manzikert jeopardized the whole military position of the Empire. When to such a peril there was added ten years of constant civil war it is no wonder that 1081 saw the Turks established on the eastern shore of the Marmora. Antioch held out behind her great walls until 1084, but of Asia Minor the Romans retained nothing except a few scraps of coast. The districts which had been the heart of the Empire were permanently turned into deserts by the savage and barbarous Seljuks.

A bit of military statistics shows how sudden and appalling was the collapse. The contingents of the standing army formerly recruited from Asia Minor have been estimated at 120,000 men. In 1078, only seven years after Manzikert, their survivors who could be mustered for service numbered only 10,000.[8]

The corporate tradition of the Roman service was broken. The Emperors and their generals might still show flashes of the old tactical skill. For a century after Manzikert, they might even win brilliant victories. But they won them at the head of an army that was little more than a hodge-podge of ill-assorted bodies of foreign mercenaries.

In 1071 the Roman service had been chiefly a cavalry army ever since Theodosius—about seven hundred years. It had been a professional force ever since Augustus—eleven hundred years. Since there is no reason for rejecting the date of the foundation of Rome itself in 753 B. C., we may say that the army that marched to Manzikert was heir to a continuous military tradition of over eighteen centuries.

I now turn from Eastern to Western Europe, from the armies which took orders from the Emperor, to those forces maintained (from the fifth century on) in the autonomous provinces of the West. The reader must not imagine that the appearance in the West of local governments practically independent of Constantinople implied a break in the tradition of Roman civilization by which those provinces lived. Indeed the tradition of Europe

---

[7] Oman, Vol. 1, 219–221.
[8] Oman, Vol. 1, 223, quoting Nicephorus Bryennius, Bk. 4, sec. 4.

(of which we in America are a part) remains Roman to this day. The new local governors were, for the most part, Roman in education. The tiny auxiliary units which followed them were of mixed recruitment despite their far-off tribal names which had been fossilized as mere labels in the Roman army list.

Nevertheless, the assumption of local power in the West by barbarian-born men, who necessarily suffered from the mental limitations of the barbarian, was an important step in the decline of the fatigued Roman society. Whereas Constantinople remained the capital of a highly civilized State, in the West the level of civilization sank lower and lower.

On the military side, the mark of the decline in Western civilization is that armies ceased to be professional and became feudal. In other words, the soldier, instead of serving a government which paid him, followed into battle an overlord who had guaranteed his land titles in return for his promise of military service. This capital change, appearing in the ninth century, determined the composition of armies until the sixteenth.

However, before discussing feudalism it is necessary first to appreciate the long survival of heavy infantry as the chief arm in Gaul. In the last chapter we saw that as early as the battle of Mursa in 315 A. D. the Roman troops stationed in that province were better infantry, although worse cavalry, than those from the eastern part of the Empire. Even after Theodosius' reorganization of the Roman army in 380 the infantry seems to have retained a greater importance relative to cavalry in Gaul than elsewhere in the Roman world.

Britain may be left out of account as military conditions there at this time are hopelessly obscure.

In the last chapter we also saw that among the local governments set up in the West by Roman commanders of barbaric descent, the Frankish state in Northern Gaul was exceptional because the Frankish dynasty was not Arian but Catholic in religion. It was therefore in sympathy with the mass of the provincials; whereas the other local governments of the West were disliked by the provincials because their dynasties and privileged classes were Arian heretics. The Frankish dynasty had another advantage, in that its territory included a large section of the frontier between civilization and barbarism, to wit, the Rhine. Since the Imperial

Roman armies had been stationed chiefly along the frontiers, the Franks inherited, as it were, a far larger number of the old localized Roman units than did the barbarian local governors of Spain, Africa and even of Italy. Accordingly the armies of the Arian chieftains of Spain and Italy were organized as cavalry and light infantry just as they had been when they served as auxiliary units in the armies of the centralized Empire. In Gaul, on the other hand, the army commanded by the Frankish chieftain was organized on the traditional Roman plan stiffened by the presence of heavy legionary infantry. We are distinctly told by Procopius that the Roman frontier troops of the Rhine command took service under Clovis (481–507) and that in the middle of the sixth century they were still equipped in the traditional Roman fashion, including the heavy nailed military boots, and still carried the Roman standards.[9] Modern historians who consider the Frankish chroniclers mere pedants because they continue to write of "legions" and "cohorts" may be entirely mistaken. The terms may still have been entirely applicable, for we cannot tell how long true legions were still organized. Indeed our general knowledge of the Frankish state tells in favour of the idea of continuity. No Frankish king before Dagobert (629–639 A. D.) put his name on the coinage. The Roman road system was systematically kept up and may even have been enlarged up to the eighth century.

Unfortunately we know practically nothing of the details of all this; tactics, for instance, are a blank. We cannot exactly fix the site even of the most important actions, such as the defeat of Attila in 451, the victory of Clovis over the Visigoths in 507, and that of Charles Martel over the Mohammedans in 732. Only the chance phrase of a chronicler informs us that heavy infantry was present against Attila, who makes a speech to his troops telling them to despise the Roman "testudines," i. e., their legionary infantry formed in solid masses.[10] All the knowledge we have of Charles Martel's tactics is a chronicler's metaphor that at Tours, Poitiers, or wherever the battle was actually fought, the Christians "stood motionless as a wall; they were like a belt of ice frozen together and not to be dissolved as they slew the Arabs with the sword." [11]

[9] Procopius: De Bello Gothico, Bk. 1, sec. 12, quoted Oman, Vol. 1, 53.
[10] Jordanes Gothicus, quoted Hodgkin, Vol. 2, 130.
[11] Isidorus Pacensis, quoted Oman, Vol. 1, 58.

This unmistakably suggests an infantry engagement, although it is so vague as to permit the supposition that the Frankish nobles were already accustomed to fight on horseback and dismounted merely to stiffen' their infantry.

The strategics of the turning back of the Saracen tide in the West are simple enough. Compared with the great armaments which had attacked Constantinople, the considerable Mohammedan forces operating in Gaul must have been mere detachments. Their first check was experienced when Toulouse successfully stood a siege in 720. In 732 a considerable force crossed the western Pyrenees and again attacked Toulouse, just as Wellington did in 1814. Unlike Wellington, the Moslems were beaten off. Instead of retreating they started off on a huge plundering raid, sacked Bordeaux, and made for Tours, attracted by the riches of the Shrine of St. Martin there. With such an important centre of population and communication as Toulouse untaken in their rear, it is impossible to think of the move north as a regular campaign. It was no more than a raid in spite of its large scale. Somewhere between Tours and Poitiers they were met and defeated by Charles Martel The battle, fought just a century after Mohammed's death, mark; the turning of the tide in the West. Thenceforward the Saracer was no longer a mortal danger but rather a constant irritant.

After 732 the Saracens' ability to irritate sprang from sea power. They held all the Mediterranean islands, and, although they could generally be kept out of the Ægean and Ionian Seas, they were always harrying the Provençal and Italian coasts. They even fortified and held headlands in the western Riviera and the Latian coast, and bedevilled the Campagna up to the gates of Rome.

In the ninth century appeared the Viking pirate, who was even more dangerous than the Saracen. He was a bolder and better fighting man. He was particularly formidable in dealing with islands, like Ireland and Britain, or with a coast deeply cut by navigable rivers such as that of Gaul from the Rhine to the Garonne. Sometimes he would sail around Spain and raid up the Rhone. His seamanship was admirable, and when he temporarily cut loose from his ships he was always careful to leave them beached under the protection of a stockade and a garrison. On such occasions he would secure mobility by stealing horses from the countryside although he would always fight on foot. Although his object was plunder he had no objection to fighting when attacked, and he soon learned all the siegecraft of the time.

Success encouraged the Vikings until piracy became the chief Scandinavian industry. They became so bold that they would winter on islands or defensible promontories in hostile territory, and push their mounted raids deep into the country. They ruined Ireland. They came within an ace of ruining England in Alfred's time, and they besieged Paris. Towards the end of the ninth century they brought Christendom lower than we have ever been brought before or since. Such an achievement on the part of men who were, after all, only bandits on a large scale indicates exceptional military weakness on the part of the civilized society attacked. What were the conditions of that weakness we shall see in a moment, when we consider the means to correct them.

Besides the Saracens and the Vikings, the third scourge of Christendom during the Dark Ages was the Magyars. These were a tribe of Tartar horsebowmen, originally no doubt from the Steppes of Central Asia or Southern Russia. Late in the ninth century, just after the worst of the Viking raids had passed, they established themselves in what is now Hungary. They had no bases like the Viking ship camps, nor were they skilful besiegers of cities like the later Vikings, but depended altogether upon their extraordinary mobility. This was so great that even when in great force they could often outstrip the unsystematic news-bearing system of the time and surprise peaceful districts before their approach was known. In battle, their method was to avoid hand-to-hand fighting and circle around their enemy, pouring in arrows, to retreat when charged, still firing; and if possible to lure their opponents by feigned flights, into some trap of unfavourable ground. Their horsemanship may be judged by the extent of the last and worst of their great circular raids, that of 954 A. D. Starting from Hungary they devastated Bavaria and what is now Württemberg and Baden, crossed the Rhine near Worms and pillaged as far north as Maestricht and as far west as Laon. From Champagne they moved into Burgundy, where for the first time they met with resistance. Accordingly they crossed the Alps, hurried across Lombardy and Venetia, and got back again to Hungary, a circuit of nearly 2000 miles.

The reason for the extraordinary weakness of civilized Christendom in the face of the Saracens, Vikings and Magyars was the complete paralysis of initiative among populations accustomed for seven hundred years (from Augustus to the dynasty of Charlemagne) to Imperial bureaucratic government, supported by a professional army. Both government and military service had so long ceased to concern the average man that he had become sheeplike. Now that ever-increasing impoverishment and slackness had weakened the central government's power to defend him and every district must beat off the heathen robbers for itself, he put up a poor fight. Even where he was willing, the poverty of the time denied him proper equipment. He utterly lacked mobility and the habit of arms.

The remedy chosen was feudalism. In the high Imperial time there had appeared a very rich class which had administered local government. Wealth had remained highly concentrated although the rich had become countrymen instead of townsmen. In the second half of the ninth century, those local magnates were one by one given, or permitted to assume, hereditary lordship and especially military command over the countrysides which they dominated. The Counts and Dukes who administered whole provinces, each containing many local lords, achieved hereditary powers. All these "feudal" lords were expected to keep always on foot, at their own expense, a band of fully equipped troops who were their personal followers, exactly as the 5th- and 6th-century Roman commanders of auxiliaries had done. Even certain rich Roman landed proprietors in the countrysides of the lower Empire [12] had done the like. Earlier in this chapter we have seen that the Roman conscription ever since the 4th century had been based not upon population but upon the holding of property in land. Of course such localized troops could not be kept long away from home. As early as the reign of Charlemagne, about 800 A. D., we find the Imperial laws establishing limits of time beyond which men could not be forced to keep the field at their own expense outside their own district. [13] The Western world was beginning to return to the principle of short service.

Such a system solved the all-important 9th-century problem

[12] Lecrivain: Soldats privés du Bas Empire; in Mélanges de l'école de Rome, Vol. C, 1890.
[13] Boutaric, 73–80.

of local defence. For campaigns on a large scale it had obvious weaknesses, for even if the contingents of the great vassals were fairly uniform in equipment and training, still the loyalty of these contingents would be to their immediate superior rather than to the king or other commander-in-chief. Furthermore the service was short—usually only 40 days. Accordingly discipline was apt to be bad. Only under exceptional circumstances, to quote Belloc, "upon occasions at long distances from home, and after long companionship in the field, if there were also present a very leading character among the feudal superiors, and especially if that character were clothed with titular rank . . . could the typical feudal army achieve unity of command." [14]

I repeat, the idea of raising an army by summoning various lords each to bring his vassals, could not have arisen except in a time in which the problem of local defence was paramount. It is idle to enlarge upon the shortcomings of the feudal system. The men of the 9th century had to use the social forces ready to their hand. Just so, no statesman of to-day can long persuade our town-bred proletariat to behave like independent self-supporting citizens.

The formula of feudal law was that each great vassal "held his lands of the king," i. e., the king guaranteed his title to them and in return he owed the king so many "knights," i. e., fully armed and armoured cavalrymen, for a certain number of days in the year, exclusive of defence of his own locality for which he was fully liable at all times.

The new magnates were also expected to keep in repair at least one highly fortified point or "castle" for their own domicile and a refuge for their poorer neighbours. Town fortification was encouraged.

Fortification saved invaluable time and feudal cavalry were exactly the troops needed for the emergency. Even in small numbers they could enormously lessen the area subject to loot, by hanging on the flanks of the raiders, especially the Vikings who were the worst raiders of all, and cutting off stragglers. Being mounted, they could concentrate quickly. Being fully equipped and well practiced in arms, they could smash the bandits when they had caught them. Of course the new methods would have

[14] Belloc: Crécy, 84–85.

accomplished little had the morale of society continued to decline, but it did not. Christendom discovered just the necessary degree of vigour within itself to use the new methods successfully against the gravest of all her perils. By the end of the 9th century the tide was turned against Vikings and Saracens, and soon after the middle of the 10th the Magyars were broken. The crucial date is the successful resistance of Paris to a Viking siege in 886 A. D.

This siege of Paris (885–886) merits description not only because of the immense political importance of the successful defence but also because we know its details better than those of any other siege from Justinian's wars in the 6th century to the Crusading sieges in the 12th.[15]

Besides the importance of the place in itself, its position on an island in the longest navigable river in France, the Seine, made it a protection to the country further upstream. The city had a wooden bridge to each bank of the river. The bridge piers had stone foundations, and each bridge had a fortified stone bridge-head although the northern one was unfinished. The Danes sailed up the Seine in great force, carried a fortified bridge at Pontoise, and appeared before Paris, November 25, 885. They promised to leave the city alone if permitted to pass upstream under the bridges, which was refused. They then assaulted the northern bridge-head but failed, and next morning found that the defenders had doubled its height with a wooden superstructure. Until February 26, 886, they vainly attacked it with every device known to ancient siege-work at its best, except catapults. Of these the besieged had a number, and were therefore able to retain fire superiority until late in the siege. On February 5th a flood carried away a section of the northern bridge while the bridge-head was held by only 12 men whom the besiegers were able to smoke out. Curiously enough, since their aim was plunder and since the fall of the bridge opened to them the unprotected interior of the country, the pirates stayed on instead of moving upstream. In March a relieving force appeared. The place was reprovisioned, the northern bridge restored, and the bridge-head built up again.

After this, although the relieving troops retired, communication with the outside world was kept up after a fashion. In May

[15] Oman, Vol. 1, 141–148.

a surprise attack came near success but failed. In June a second attempt at relief was defeated. Soon afterwards the pirates delivered a last assault which proved to be the crisis of the siege. By this time they had built so many catapults that they had fire superiority. With this advantage they attacked the place on all sides but were again, and this time finally, repulsed. Whereupon, having learned that the feeble Emperor, Charles the Fat, had gathered a great army, they were glad to take a bribe from him to quit Paris, and ravaged for a while further to the south. This lame and impotent conclusion did not spoil the moral effect of the successful resistance. Afterwards Viking defeats were more numerous than victories. It was the turning point in the peril of all our civilization.

CHAPTER V

GENERAL DISCUSSION OF FEUDAL WARFARE, TOGETHER WITH THE CAMPAIGN OF HASTINGS, 1066 A. D.

FEUDALISM, through which ninth-century Christendom had been able to beat off the Vikings, endured as the framework of society for over half a thousand years. Its persistence enables us to treat as a whole the period extending from the ninth to the sixteenth century. I therefore begin this chapter with the general discussion of military conditions throughout the period.

It so happens that we have an outside description of the early feudal type of armies from the critical pen of an enemy, the East-Roman emperor Leo the Wise, who reigned at Constantinople about the year 900.

The Franks and Lombards are bold and daring to excess, although the latter are not all that they once were: they regard the smallest movement to the rear as a disgrace, and they will fight whenever you offer them battle. When their knights are hard put to it in a cavalry fight, they will turn their horses loose, dismount, and stand back to back against very superior numbers rather than fly. So formidable is the charge of the Frankish chivalry with their broadsword, lance, and shield, that it is best to decline a pitched battle with them till you have put all the chances on your own side. You should take advantage of their indiscipline and disorder; whether fighting on foot or on horseback, they charge in dense, unwieldy masses, which cannot manœuvre, because they have neither organization nor drill. Tribes and families stand together, or the sworn war-bands of chiefs, but there is nothing to compare to our own orderly division into battalions and brigades. Hence they readily fall into confusion if suddenly attacked in flank and rear—a thing easy to accomplish, as they are utterly careless and neglect the use of pickets and vedettes and the proper surveying of the countryside. They encamp, too, confusedly and without fortifying themselves, so that they can be easily cut up by a night attack. Nothing succeeds better against them than a feigned flight, which draws them into an ambush; for they follow hastily and invariably fall into the snare. But perhaps the best tactics of all are to protract the campaign, and lead them into hills and desolate tracts, for they take no care about their commissariat, and when their stores run low their vigour melts away. They are impatient of hunger and thirst, and after a few days of privation desert their standards and steal away home as best they can. For they are destitute of all respect for their commanders—one noble thinks himself as good as another—and they will deliberately disobey orders when they grow discontented. Nor are their chiefs above the temptation of taking bribes; a moderate sum of money will frustrate one of their expeditions. On the whole, therefore, it is easier and less costly to wear out a Frankish army by skirmishes, protracted operations in desolate districts, and the cutting off of its supplies, than to attempt to destroy it at a single blow.[1]

This passage is of the utmost interest. From it we see at once that we are dealing with a level of civilization lower than that of ancient Rome or mediæval' Constantinople. The Romanized provinces of the West no longer maintain highly organized, professional armies. For want of regular echelons of command, their troops manœuvre with difficulty. They are undisciplined. They have no service of security and no staff departments. On the other hand, they are full of fight, and of a sense of military honour.

Of course Leo's interest was the purely practical one of how best to oppose the Westerners. His account of them must therefore be supplemented by some consideration of the social conditions underlying the simple organization of feudal troops.

Throughout western Christendom in the early Middle Ages agriculture, rather than industry or commerce, was the chief source of wealth. Indeed this is true of all simple times. Feudalism was based upon a combination between agriculture and military service. The cultivator, who was in practice almost a free peasant, was not in legal theory the owner of his land. Theoretically his land was owned by a local lord to whom he must pay certain fixed dues in amounts fixed by custom. In return the lord with his household of armed retainers was bound to protect his dependents. The local lord in turn owed military service to some great lord who on his side guaranteed the local lord's land titles. Thus all vassals were required to fight in defence of the territory of their feudal superiors, and in return were entitled to protection.

Feudalism was not essentially an oppression. The fixed dues paid by the cultivator were but a small part of his total produce. They were more of a tax (payable to those who governed and fought) than a rent. These small dues once paid, no man could be dispossessed of his holding. He was secure in his tenure. Men

[1] Oman, Vol. 1, 204–205.

were proud of being good lords and loyal vassals. In the Song of Roland when a fighter has performed some conspicuously distinguished service the poet says of him that he has "done great vassalage." [2] There seems to have been no higher term of praise. To any disparagement of feudalism it is answer enough to ask whether the modern proletarian is cheerfully willing to die for his capitalist employer.

On the other hand, feudalism, which had solved the all-important problem of local defence, was weak and chaotic at the top. In a time without strong central governments it was one of the simplest and most natural ways of protecting a district, but for more extensive operations it was deficient. Indeed a lover of peace might call it an admirable device for minimizing aggressive war on a large scale at any distance from home.

The limitation of feudal troops was that they were at the disposal of their commanders only within severe limitations of place and time. Although the upper class spent much of their time in individual military exercises, there was no chance for drill and manœuvre of large bodies except on the rare occasion of an actual campaign. Not only was the time within which a man was bound to follow his lord in offensive operations, outside of the territory of that lord, strictly limited in time, generally to forty days, but also it was difficult for a king or great lord to get his vassals to serve for any great length of time in distant parts of his own territory. Finally, before a combination of local lords the overlord would be powerless. It is notable that between the fifth and the sixteenth centuries we hear nothing of disciplinary executions. Accordingly, a feudal superior planning large-scale operations had first of all to get around the limitations of the feudal obligation.

He might try to pay his vassals to keep the field beyond their stipulated obligatory term of service. The difficulty there was that it would usually be hard to pay them enough to offset their natural desire to go home. He might hire soldiers of fortune, cosmopolitan mercenaries: such troops would at least stay with the colours as long as they were paid. They would serve against anyone, except perhaps their own individual feudal superiors, and therefore they were the natural resource of an overlord who wished to subdue rebellious vassals. The trouble with them was that they

[2] A good verse translation, by C. Scott Moncrieff, publ. Dutton, 1920.

were indiscriminate plunderers and could rarely be expected to endure operations involving strain for the sake of a cause which interested them only financially. An even more important limitation on the paying of vassals and the hiring of mercenaries was that no mediæval state could raise money on any considerable scale. Taxation and credit were equally undeveloped. It was the shortage of cash which enfeebled all attempts to hire men.

The greatest mediæval operations were conducted by volunteer armies, willing for some exceptional reason to disregard the limitations of feudal service. Thus the army of 50,000 men which followed William the Conqueror to England were moved by his promise of lands when that country should be conquered. The most important volunteer armies of the Middle Ages were the Crusaders to the East. Local Crusades against the Moors in Spain or the heretics of Languedoc were partial exceptions; like that of the Crusades to Palestine, their motive was religious enthusiasm, but the shorter distance to be traversed was a temptation to shorten the term of service. It was no use starting for Jerusalem unless you were willing to stay out a long time.[3]

Furthermore, it should be noticed that even these exceptional volunteer expeditions were composed of men whose whole notion of the conduct of war was derived from the short local mobilizations characteristic of the time. All mediæval campaigns and battles were the work of men accustomed only to short-service, highly localized, troops. Even the germ of regularly paid national armies is not found before the fourteenth century.

The obvious strong point of short-service troops, at their best, is the enthusiasm common to amateurs in any occupation. Their obvious weak point is that, as compared with professional armies, the mechanism of operations is deficient. Thus the tactics of short-term troops always tend to approach those of a horde or mob, although under civilized conditions they seldom fall quite as low as that.

Now although the level of civilization had fallen low during the Dark Ages, nevertheless civilization of a sort was always maintained. Indeed the primary fact about the Dark Ages is the tenacity with which Christendom, impoverished and degraded though she was, clung to the forms which had been handed down to her

³ Boutaric, Bk. 3.

from the high Imperial time. Her titles, Emperor, King, Duke and Count, were those of the later Empire. She inherited and preserved intact the organization of the Church. Her learning was repetitive, her arts simple and sometimes even crude copies of traditional Roman forms.

So it was with the Art of War. One of the tests by which civilized man is known is his power to learn not only through observation and analysis of the present but also through records of the past. The soldiers of the Middle Ages meet this test by their study of Vegetius' book "De Re Militari." Vegetius came down from the fourth century to the Mediævals as a representative of the great past from which they had received their religion, the Latin language spoken by all their educated men, and, in general, the full tradition of their society.[4]

A more developed historic sense applied to the ancient documents (such as Cæsar) in the possession of the Mediævals, might have discovered that the Imperial Army of Vegetius' day was inferior to that of earlier times. On the other hand, we have seen that feudal social conditions tended to perpetuate a manner of conducting war which resembled Vegetius' practice and differed from Cæsar's, particularly in giving most of the offensive work to the cavalry. In many ways Cæsar's army, four hundred years before Vegetius, differed from the fourth-century Roman army far more than that army differed from those of a thousand years later, in the time of Edward III.

The direct influence of Vegetius upon mediæval warfare is proved not only by testimony that his book was the habitual reading of the educated soldiers of the time, but also by the many striking resemblances between his precepts and what they actually did.

Around 1000 A. D., he was the favourite author of Fulk the Black, the able and ferocious Count of Anjoy. Two hundred years later, the "De Re Militari" was carried everywhere in the campaigns of the Plantagenets, especially Fulk's great-great-great-grandson, Henry II of England, and Henry's son, Richard Cœur de Lion. The book was popularized for court and camp by a French translation made about 1300, under the title of "The Art of Knighthood," for the word "miles," a soldier, had come to mean "knight," i.e., the soldier par excellence. Towards the end of the 15th cen-

[4] For the influence of Vegetius see Delpech, especially Vol. 2, 125–146.

tury a half dozen editions of Vegetius were among the first books printed, one of them an English translation from the Caxton press.

The main point in which mediæval practice resembled Vegetian precept was in considering cavalry as the chief, infantry as the auxiliary arm. The foot are to assist charges of horse by means of missiles. When armed with spear and shield they may play the chief part in an immobile, defensive action, but Vegetius recommends that they should not attempt to advance, as this tended to break up their ranks. Being immobile they could almost never achieve a decision. Mediæval heavy infantry who disregarded this advice were invariably beaten, as were the English detachments at Hastings (1066), the Flemish and German townsmen at Bouvines (1214), and the Londoners at Lewes (1264).

In comparing ancient with mediæval war, I venture once more to remind the reader that ancient infantry never had to resist heavy cavalry equipped with stirrups. It is possible that the Greek and Macedonian phalanx could not have advanced against mediæval cavalry for fear of opening its ranks. How difficult it is to advance without breaking ranks can easily be proved by watching a contemporary war strength company trying to advance in close order under peace-time conditions across a parade ground or even on an armory floor. Even with everything in its favour it requires the highest discipline and training, and it is not surprising that in action the job was too much for all mediæval infantry except Swiss.

The European reputation achieved by the 15th-century Swiss is one of the chief indications that mediæval war was about to become modern war.

Even the Roman legions of the great time, armed with the pilum (a sort of heavy javelin) and the short stabbing sword, never had to face cavalry who could not be pulled off their horses at close quarters for want of stirrups.

But besides the main point as to cavalry *vs.* infantry there are a number of other striking points of likeness between Vegetius and the soldiers of the Middle Ages. They agree in considering the right as the post of honour—perhaps because of the desire to get at the enemy's weaponless left-hand side. In the mind of the Latin author, the circle, with pikes sloped forward, butts resting on the ground, is the strongest defensive formation for infantry;

we find it adopted over and over again in mediæval defensive battles. Vegetius considers a wedge-shaped formation useful for the rare occasion of an infantry offensive. We shall see it adopted by the infantry of the Flemish and Rhenish cities at Bouvines in 1214 and recommended in the manual, known as the "Siete Partidas," of Alfonso the Wise of Castile in 1260. As to equipment, Vegetius criticizes severely the abandonment of defensive armour by his contemporaries; it was among the strongest desires of the mediæval fighting man to make his armour as invulnerable as he could. Vegetius recommends the usual mediæval practice of carrying two swords of unequal length. There are other points of correspondence such as getting the sun at your back, the use of the dragon as a common emblem for the designation flags of units, and the name dragon-bearers for the men who carried them. There is the same method of firing the wooden props used to shore up mines in siegework. Finally there is the striking fact that Vegetius speaks of the crossbow, calling it a manubalista or arcubalista. Thereafter we have no mention of such a weapon earlier than that of William's crossbowmen at Hastings in 1066.[5]

Of course we cannot be certain how much of all this was due to a general survival of Roman tradition, irrespective of any particular manual such as that of Vegetius, or how much to the mother wit of the mediævals themselves acting independently of all tradition. In general we know that the Middle Ages were strongly traditional; they preferred to develop what they had rather than to innovate. Thus it is common knowledge that their marvellous creation of Gothic architecture crowned a regular process of development. It had roots in the recent past. On the other hand, what we know of the educated men of the early Middle Ages, with their revival of the Roman law and their enthusiasm for antique philosophy, would lead us to believe that in military things there may possibly have been a certain amount of deliberate revival due to the study of documents—in this case Vegetius. In the matter of the crossbow, those direct heirs of Rome, the Byzantines, certainly knew nothing of such a weapon. The Byzantine Princess-Historian Anna Comnena has recorded her surprise at seeing the crossbowmen of the First Crusade.[6]

[5] Delpech, Vol. 2, 266, quoting "Ex Gestis Guillelmi."
[6] Oman, Vol. I, 139.

The reader must not take the men of the Middle Ages for pedants. On the contrary, all that we know of the 11th, 12th and 13th centuries—considering not only their equipment and military architecture but also their arts and crafts together with their economic, social and political arrangements—shows their temper to have been exceptionally practical. However much such men might enlarge their knowledge by study, they were not likely to lose their simplicity of aim and directness of method. I have dwelt upon the matter of Vegetius because it was for a long time the fashion to regard the men of the Middle Ages as far more crude and limited than they really were.

At all events, the popularity of Vegetius in the Middle Ages emphasizes the continuity of ancient and mediæval military thought. It is astonishing to note how these short-service troops, with all their headlong lust for fighting and their simple tactics, imitated in every way they could the permanent professional army of the later Empire.

On the economic and social side, another important survival was open-field agriculture as opposed to fields enclosed by fences. This must have existed in the fourth century or cavalry could not have become dominant over infantry at that time. We know that it existed in the Middle Ages. Indeed had it not continued, we may be sure that cavalry could not have survived as the chief arm, for obviously any system of fences would have emboldened infantry to resist a mounted charge. The Bayeux tapestry represents a mediæval plough with a forward truck resting on two wheels and a man sitting upon it exactly as men sit on the forward carriage of ploughs in the large fields of the American West.[7] In smaller enclosed fields there would more often be the necessity to turn the furrow and under such conditions a single ploughman walking behind is better able to make the frequent adjustments required.

The men of the Middle Ages, although united as to the desirability of complete armour, were limited in their power of realizing this ideal by want of money. A complete armour cost the price of a small farm. Therefore in any large force only a minority would be fully armoured and many would not be armoured at all. Besides being expensive, complete armour was heavy. Even in the chain-mail period previous to the fourteenth-century introduction

[7] Belloc: Book of the Bayeux Tapestry, Fig. 12.

of plate armour, a complete suit weighed over thirty pounds.[8] Furthermore, the chain mail had to be backed with heavy quilting or wadding to cushion the shock of a heavy blow. To fight in complete armour, and even to march in it when near contact with the enemy, was so fatiguing that it seemed desirable to spare the armoured man all possible strain. Accordingly he was normally accompanied by one or more unarmoured or half-armoured attendants who helped him put on, take off and adjust his armour, cared for his horse and performed general fatigue duties. Such attendants would themselves be mounted in order to accompany their master. Below them again were the feudal infantry, the lees or residue of the army—men too poor to afford either armour or a horse.

The reader inclined to disparage the mediæval knight because of the crowd of attendants he dragged about with him should remember that the same line of reasoning would compel him to condemn the contemporary tank, aeroplane, railroad artillery and other specialized services because of their numerous mechanics and other non-combatant personnel. Obviously, any specialized category of troops is cumbrous compared to an all-around personnel. This accusation has some force against the mediæval knight, and against the late-Roman mailed cavalryman, who also required attendants, as we have seen. On the other hand, it is equally obvious that the lower categories of all specialized services have some combatant value in themselves. Indeed we shall see in a moment that this was even truer of mediæval conditions than it is to-day. Finally, it is clear that specialized troops, with all their defects, have corresponding virtues.

The different categories of mediæval troops roughly corresponded with differences of social rank, especially at the beginning of the Middle Ages. The mediæval chroniclers used the Latin word "miles"—a soldier—in the sense of the soldier par excellence, that is the fully armoured cavalryman. This word "miles" came to have our modern meaning of "knight" with the connotations of social rank and highly developed sense of honour which our word knight implies. As time went on, however, its social significance became more important and its military significance correspondingly less so, and by the fourteenth century the number of

[8] Dean, 45–50.

"knights" in an army bore no relation to the number of fully equipped men at arms.

Finally, in connection with the different categories of mediæval troops it should be remembered that the numerical proportion of unarmoured and ill-armoured men would be large in a force raised for local defence, smaller in one which was to operate at a distance from its base, and smaller still in one which was to go overseas, inasmuch as it would not pay to arrange for the transportation and subsistence of a greater number of low-grade troops than would suffice to attend the well armed and fully armoured men.

Having considered the social conditions underlying the feudal armies and the different categories into which their recruitment was divided, the reader is now able to appreciate their tactics.

Mediæval battles divide into two classes according to the presence or absence of solid heavy infantry or dismounted cavalry on the field.

If neither side possessed solid infantry or chose to dismount a part or all of its cavalry, then the action took the form of a rapid and shifting cavalry fight. Such actions were decided by dash and by the judicious handling of reserves. Of this sort were Muret (1213), Charles of Anjou's battles (1266–1271), the Marchfield (1278), and Patay (1429).

When one side had solid infantry (or dismounted cavalry) steady enough to serve as a core or pivot for the action, then the fight developed into a sort of siege of this body. Such an action may be considered as the typical mediæval battle for it was natural for the side which felt itself the weaker to dismount all or part of its armoured men, so as to be able to stand on the defensive, which cavalry cannot do. Such a policy enabled a commander to get some work out of the low-grade components of the force under him. Obviously low-grade troops would be of little use in an attack upon the enemy's armoured men. Therefore in an attack they would play little or no part. But in a defensive they could be formed up in solid masses behind a front rank or so of armoured comrades. Man for man their part in the fighting would be far less than that of the front ranks. Still it would not be negligible, for numerically they would form by far the greater part of the mass against which the attacking cavalry would surge. Examples of this typical kind of mediæval battle are numerous. Our one scrap of information as to Charles Martel's battle near Tours in 732 seems to put it in this class. Thereafter we have cavalry attacks against infantry or dismounted cavalry at Hastings (1066), Bremûle (1119), Legnano (1176), Steppes (1213), Falkirk (1298), Courtrai (1302), Crécy (1346), and most of the Spanish battles.

As long as the dismounted troops stood fast, sheltering themselves behind a solid hedge of pikes, they were hard to break. The butt of the pike would often be rested on the ground and steadied by the right foot as recommended by Vegetius. Such a pure defensive might win by itself as at Crécy, in case the enemy persisted in attacking until the cohesion of his own force was broken. Or the dismounted men might win by a short offensive return following the repulse of repeated attacks as at Courtrai and Bannockburn.

Since true infantry as the chief reliance of mediæval armies is to be found only in impoverished districts like Scotland, Ireland, Wales, Scandinavia and Switzerland, it is not surprising to find few cases in which troops on foot assume the offensive—as distinguished from the counter-offensives of Courtrai or Bannockburn. Moreover, infantry attacks always fail, as at Bouvines (1214), Majorca (1229),[9] and Lewes (1264) [10] and as did the dismounted cavalry attack at Poitiers (1356).

Poitiers and Tinchebrai (1106), if we except lesser fights like Cocherel and Auray (1364), are the only examples before the fifteenth century of battles fought between cavalry armies in which both sides dismounted all, or by far the greater part of their horsemen. It should be noted that at Tinchebrai the side won which kept some troops mounted against its entirely dismounted enemy. And at Poitiers the Black Prince's decisive counter-attack was a mounted charge.

In a purely cavalry action the fire of dismounted archers or crossbowmen was of little effect. They were easily brushed out of the way. On the other hand, when the action centred about an immobile mass of foot, then the question of fire superiority became important. The tactical principle here is the same as that which increases the importance of artillery in position warfare. Of course the mediæval cult of armour tended to reduce the importance of archery, but we have seen that complete armour was so expensive that it could never become universal. Furthermore

<hr>

[9] Delpech, Vol. 1, 318.   [10] Oman, Vol. 1, 421–431.

the armour of the horse was seldom as complete as that of his rider. Accordingly in typical mediæval cases of a mounted attack against dismounted pikemen, fire superiority was usually decisive. Indeed it was almost invariably so.

Outside of Spain, Hungary and the East, we find no use made of fire delivered mounted. This device, so important in later Roman times, was not entirely unknown. In the pursuit scene of the Bayeux tapestry a horse archer is represented. It probably went out of general use because the fierce combative spirit and the convention of knightly honour made men want to charge straight for their enemy and decide the issue by hard knocks.

When mounted fire is used we never find it delivered by mailed cavalry equally able to charge as in late Roman times. Mediæval fire power cavalry were invariably Hungarian or Turkish light horse, armed with the bow, or Spanish javelin men. In any case they were not expected to charge home.

Incidentally the persistence of the javelin from Hannibal's Numidians to the African Moors who invaded Spain, from them to the Spanish Christians of the Middle Ages, and from them to the Portuguese (not the Spanish) bullfighter of to-day, is a curious example of continuity over nearly two thousand five hundred years. To this day the Portuguese bullfighter avoids the shock of a charging bull by dexterously wheeling his horse, and at the same time tries to knock a coloured rosette from the bull's withers by means of a light javelin much like those which helped win Cannæ and put Cæsar in peril at the Ruspina.

Mediæval strategy was always simple and direct. Immediate battle was almost always its first consideration, especially on the part of the aggressor who had to get a decision quickly before his army melted away from him. If the defender were decidedly the weaker, and if he wished to spin out the campaign, he would usually stand behind walls. Once surrounded there, his troops could not get away from him except to the enemy. Usually he would fight, for it was a point of knightly honour to protect one's vassals from ravage, and the same sense of honour made it a questionable proceeding to refuse battle on anything like equal terms, On the other hand, this simple strategy was often very good. especially in the early Middle Ages. In the fourteenth century it fell off.

So much for the general discussion of mediæval military conditions.

We have seen that, from the third century on, civilization was steadily going downhill on its material side, and that its lowest point was reached during the ninth-century Viking raids. After the repulse, conversion and incorporation of the Vikings and Magyars, Western Christendom sank into a sort of lethargy until about the year 1000. Then matters began to improve. The long dormant energies of Europe began to revive in a sort of sudden springtime. The improvement was many-sided; a general historian of the period would chiefly consider it in the new strength of the Papacy, which I mention here only to remind the reader that the politics of the time tended to turn chiefly on points of religion. The seafaring Italian cities began to drive Saracen shipping from the Western Mediterranean. Volunteers streamed out to join the men of the Pyrenean valleys in their slow, constant, southward drives against the Moslems of Spain. But in military matters, and indeed in all secular affairs, the leaders in the springtime of Europe were the Normans.

Northmen or Normans was an alternative name for the Scandinavian Vikings. In Gaul, Christendom had incorporated a number of them into its body by assigning to their chiefs the government of a considerable district, still called Normandy, about the mouth of the Seine. The move was quite in the spirit of the fifth century. Unlike the fifth-century settlements, however, the slight infusion of Scandinavian blood into the governing class of this Gallic district produced a new thing, to wit, a breed of men of greater energy and precision of mind than had been seen in the West for centuries.

The Normans made armies worthy of the name once more possible because they introduced accuracy into the surveying of land, and method into the collection of taxes. Since mediæval taxation was based on land value, a fairly accurate survey was requisite to an efficient system of collection. The tax-gatherer is the ultimate foundation of an army, as our own Regulars have been reminded since the Armistice. The Norman forces remained feudal, but the occasional employment of mercenaries became possible; larger numbers of feudal troops could be mobilized and when mobilized could be maintained for a longer time. Mailed cavalry, as everywhere else in Europe, remained the chief arm, but its tactics were improved and made regular and it could be intelligently supported by infantry armed with the bow. Furthermore, the Normans were great fortifiers. Wherever they conquered, they closely dotted the country with works so solidly built of stone that they remain to this day. The details of their fortifications and siege-work we shall discuss presently. For the moment it will be enough to remind you that in a country so covered, operations tended to become either a war of raids or a war of sieges.

At this point it is convenient to consider briefly the chief articles of eleventh-century equipment. In hardly any particular did it materially differ from that of Vegetius' time. The sword was long, straight, and two-edged, exactly as the "spatha" of the auxiliaries had been ever since the first century. Even the word "spatha" has come down to our own time as the name for a sword in the Latin languages, "épée" in French and "espada" in Spanish. The lance was light enough to be held at arm's length or even used to thrust overhand.[11] Even in the eleventh century it was sometimes "laid in rest" by holding the hinder part of the shaft under the armpit so as to counterbalance the weight of the head.

As in ancient times, the chief missile weapon was the bow, in the immemorial short form drawn to the breast. The crossbow, which was at least as old as Vegetius, was also known, for William the Conquerer had crossbowmen with him at Hastings.[12] Arguing from what we know of the time in general, we are probably safe in believing that it had remained in use, at least in Gaul, throughout the Dark Ages. The effective point-blank range of archery fire is not certain. In Roman times it must have been over 70 yards, for that was the regulation Roman interval between towers on a wall. Of course, using high-angle fire against large targets such as a massed body of men, it would be much further—over 150 yards at least.

In the matter of defensive armour, the shield was sometimes narrow and kite-shaped with a rounded top, sometimes rounded or oval with a raised boss in the centre. The helmet was usually a conical steel cap; sometimes it had a nose guard hinged at the top so that it could be raised if desired. The mail shirt usually

---

[11] Belloc: Book of the Bayeux Tapestry, Figs. 22, 61, 63, 65, etc.
[12] Delpech, Vol. 2, 266, quoting "Ex Gestis Guillelmi."

took the form of metal rings sewed closely on a leather jerkin with elbow sleeves. This leather base of the mail shirt might take the form of a union suit with knee-length drawers.

The cavalryman used stirrups, as his Roman predecessors had done at least since Maurice's time. He sat upon a saddle with high pommel and cantle like a cowboy saddle to-day.

A curious fact is that the mace was often used by clergymen serving as soldiers. With this weapon these holy men escaped the text "he that taketh the sword shall perish by the sword," and also the maxim that the Church abhors bloodshed.

As a specimen of eleventh-century war, we cannot do better than take the Norman Conquest of England.

We have seen that Normandy differed from the rest of Latin Christendom in degree but by no means in kind. Her administration and military science were feudal but she applied them better than was done elsewhere. So England was feudal, although her feudal system seems to have been looser than that of the Continent. The one anomaly about her military methods was that, in a defensive, English armies made great play with a huge long-handled, two-handed pole-axe known as a "Danish axe." She was rich. In the generation before the conquest many Normans had emigrated to her, and individuals among them had obtained high position. No national feeling hindered this penetration, for the time had no such feeling, and lacked clear-cut national divisions. Its politics turned either upon points of religion or upon individual loyalty to an individual feudal superior.

William, Duke of Normandy, having a claim upon the English crown, declared war against Harold, who had gotten himself crowned. He built a numerous fleet and mobilized a great army, about fifty thousand strong, including volunteers from Italy and Spain. Some of his troops were serving for pay, others in the hope of securing English lands. I repeat that we shall misinterpret entirely the moral background of these wars if we imagine that there was any such thing as national patriotism involved, for there was not. Men were proud to serve as the sworn vassals of their "lord," or else (as in William's army) they would serve voluntarily as members of a sort of military stock company for the conquest and partition of certain territories in which the commander had been denied his rights. Nor must this moral claim be likened to the purely formal claims so often put forward as justification for modern wars of dynastic or national aggression. In such a time of united Christendom no mere marauding expedition directed against Christian men could have attracted so much support. It was the whole basis of William's action that he had been designated by Edward the Confessor, the last King of England, as next heir to the throne. Furthermore, Harold had been rescued from captivity by William, had become his brother in arms and received the honor of knighthood from his hands, and had solemnly sworn upon holy relics to support William's claim. Harold's conduct therefore involved gross personal ingratitude as well as perjury.

Harold, with the feudal forces of most of his kingdom, concentrated in the south of England. A strong detachment consisting of the vassals of the two northern earldoms remained near York to oppose an expected Scandinavian invasion in aid of Harold's exiled brother Tostig.

The early stages of the campaign are notable for two extraordinary pieces of marching by Harold and for the calculated self-restraint of William. The latter, after embarking from the Norman coast, was weather-bound by northerly winds in the Somme estuary. The same winds brought Tostig and the army of his Scandinavian friends to the mouth of the Humber. They must have been in considerable force, for they had 300 ships. In an action fought just south of York, on September 20th, they destroyed the forces of the two northern English earldoms and occupied the northern capital. Note carefully the time and distances involved in what followed. Harold had marched forth, leaving London on the 16th. On the 24th—nine days—he and his army had put nearly 200 miles of road behind them and reached Tadcaster, on the great North road of the Romans, ten miles southwest of York, a splendid piece of marching even if we assume that all his troops were mounted. They can hardly have been on foot, for they were in condition for a general action on the following day, the 25th.

Harold met the Norwegians at Stamford Bridge. They were on foot, and arrayed in solid masses. He attacked them with his mailed cavalry, delivering charge after charge until at last he broke and destroyed them.

He then moved to York and there rested his sorely tried troops.

Meanwhile, far to the south, William at last succeeded in crossing the Channel. He landed at Pevensey on the 28th, the third day after Harold's victory at Stamford Bridge. It is hard to imagine how Harold, at York, could have heard of that landing before the 1st. Nevertheless, he reached London in person on the 5th or 6th. More astonishing still, the greater part of his army duplicated its nine days' march and moved south out of London on the 11th. Most astonishing of all, Harold's troops did over 56 miles in the next 48 hours and established contact with the enemy late on the 13th. Such an achievement would have been possible only to troops in high training and possessed of the finest kind of march-discipline. There must have been a well-organized commissariat and the great Roman road between York and London must not only have been well kept up as a military highway but also efficiently cleared of civilian traffic.

On the other hand, Harold's impetuosity had caused him to run unnecessary risks. The northern levies, most of them certainly on foot and even their horse inferior in quality to his own striking force, could not keep up, and the local troops from the west had not had time to join. A few days' delay would have greatly increased his numbers. As it was, his strength was about equal to that of the Normans, i. e., around fifty thousand men. But in average quality Harold's force was inferior. His own large military household, the best of his troops, had just been through a severe strain fighting and marching at top speed steadily for nearly a month with only five days' rest. The greater part of his army was unarmoured, ill-armed levies hastily swept up from the country-sides.

William's conduct contrasts with Harold's inasmuch as the Norman's action was calculated and evidently followed a predetermined plan. He had not permitted Harold's absence in the north to tempt him into a dash at London less than 50 miles away, but had kept near the south coast, throwing up entrenchments at Hastings and Pevensey to protect his ships and stores and to cover a possible embarkation should he be defeated in the coming battle. William's chances of winning that battle would be bettered should Harold seek him out, because of the long distance separating Hastings from the north and west from which reinforcement for Harold might come. Meanwhile the Normans systematically

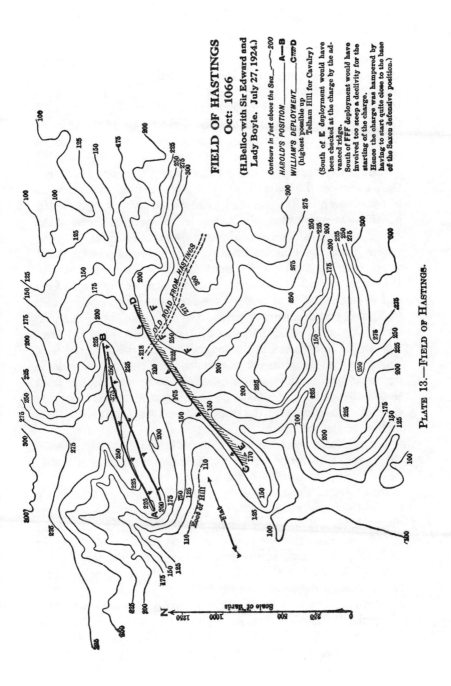

FIELD OF HASTINGS
Oct: 1066

(H.Belloc with Sir Edward and
Lady Boyle. July 27, 1924.)

Contours In feet above the Sea ____200
HAROLD'S POSITION ____A—B
WILLIAM'S DEPLOYMENT ____C////D
(highest possible up
Telham Hill for Cavalry)

(South of E deployment would have
been checked at the charge by the advanced ridge.
South of FFF deployment would have
involved too steep a declivity for the
starting of the charge.
Hence the charge was hampered by
having to start quite close to the base
of the Saxon defensive position.)

PLATE 13.—FIELD OF HASTINGS.

ravaged Kent and Sussex far and wide. William knew his man and judged—correctly as the event proved—that this might bring Harold to accept battle before all the northern and western contingents had joined. Over and above the strong feudal obligation to protect one's vassals, the Englishman had the additional motive that he himself was an usurper. The slightest sign of weakness on his part might bring his shaky political position down about his ears.[13]

Harold therefore advanced to the ridge which has ever since been known as Battle Hill, about five miles from William's entrenched camp at Hastings, and there waited to be attacked. His position was very strong. In his rear he had the great forest of the Weald, through which he could retreat in case of a check.

Seen from the north, a little east of south, the position itself was shaped like a "T" with a short upright which connected with the higher ground in rear and a long cross-bar nearly a mile from end to end. The front of the cross-bar was a long slope so steep that cavalrymen in armour must have had difficulty in charging up it. On the defenders' left, where it is gentlest, it is 1 in 15. Over most of the front it is 1 in 10, and on the right it is almost 1 in 8. Either end of the cross-bar is rounded, and between it and the higher ground to the north are gullies not so deep as the front slope but even steeper so as to be quite impracticable for charging cavalry. The summit of the cross-bar itself is not quite level; it is highest at the left centre.

There Harold posted himself with his large military household, the flower of his army. The rest, including his masses of hastily raised levies, stood on either side.

Incidentally, the length of the position enables us to estimate the depth of Harold's formation. I have said that the sharply defined ridge is just under a mile long, say 1500 yards. If Harold had 50,000 men his formation must have been just over 30 deep. In itself there is nothing surprising about such a depth, for Maurice dealing with the highly organized Roman army of the 6th century recommends a depth of thirty-two men when light troops intercalate themselves between the sixteen ranks of the heavy foot.

Despite the great natural strength of the position, William was bound to attack. The passage of time would increase Harold's

[13] For the strategy of 1066 see Belloc: "Warfare in England," 92–101.

numbers. Meanwhile the presence of the English army would limit foraging. Therefore, when contact was established late on the thirteenth of October the Duke prepared for an advance on the following day.

The Normans moved at dawn. After a march of about five miles they saw from Telham Hill the English army drawn up on the Hill of Battle opposite to them. They thereupon deployed for action in three lines; first, the lightly armed archers, then the pikemen (some if not all of whom wore armour), and last the armoured cavalry.

Like most engagements, the battle began with a fire fight. In spite of the steep slope of the hill against them, the Norman archers obtained an immediate fire superiority over the few bowmen in Harold's army. But when the Norman pikemen in their turn moved up and charged, the English received them with javelins, and with stones tied to the ends of sticks like the old-fashioned throwing-hammer familiar to athletes of a recent generation. The invaders were able to reach the English line but could make no impression whatsoever. The archers, although they had caused the English considerable loss, had not been able to shake them.

The Norman cavalry who were next to charge fared no better. Everywhere they were beaten back. Opposite the English right where the slope is steepest the repulse was so bloody that William's left fell into a panic. Now, however, came the turning-point of the action. It was vital to English success that they should stand fast on the summit of their ridge; in no other way could they meet the better armed and better disciplined Normans. Instead of standing fast, the ill-armed yokels of the English right lost their heads at the sight of the confusion among their recent assailants and rushed down the slope in pursuit. This gave William his opportunity. For a moment, indeed, the panic among his troops threatened to become general. A rumour ran down the line that he had been killed. In order to disprove it he had to raise the nose guard of his helmet and ride to and fro, showing his face to his men. But once the morale of his centre had been re-established it was easy to charge in on the left flank of the disorderly swarm of English who had tried to pursue the routed Norman left. In their disorder they were cut to pieces in a few moments. From this point on, Harold must have known that his chance was slim.

Nevertheless the next charge against the ridge, after some local and temporary success, was repulsed like the first. Thereupon part of the Norman horse either deliberately executed a feigned flight or else broke up in a second real panic. However their headlong retreat came about, it was enough to draw down another great body of the defenders, who were in their turn cut to pieces in the valley below.

This second piece of folly on the part of his own men made Harold's cause hopeless. Nevertheless his military household and the rest of his centre stood firm and rallied about them the remnants of the wings. By this time the battle had continued for several hours. Probably it was already afternoon. If by a miracle they could hold out until darkness came, they might get away.

The last stage of the action was a sort of siege of what was left of Harold's army, closely grouped upon the highest part of the ridge. Beset on all sides, the remnant of the English stood firm for hours and beat off every attack. For a time the Norman archers would shoot into the immovable target presented to them. Then their cavalry would charge, fail to break the ring, and draw off to allow the archers to shoot again. Finally, William ordered the archers to try high-angle fire. This proved effective. An arrow so shot wounded Harold in the eye. Not long afterwards a last charge got home, Harold was killed, and the English—what was left of them—broke and fled.

Even at this stage there was still some fight in the defeated army. In the twilight a number of Norman horse, plunging forward incautiously in pursuit, fell into one of the steep gullies between the cross-bar of the "T" and the higher ground farther to the north; whereupon some of the fleeing English turned upon them and inflicted considerable loss.

It is eloquent testimony to the "fog of war" and the severe strain of a day-long battle that at this point one of William's chief subordinates advised a retreat. Fortunately for the Duke, he himself was made of better stuff; he ordered the advance continued, or rather the pursuit of the beaten enemy.[14]

Completely victorious, William continued to act with method and restraint. Instead of dashing forward to London, he moved by

[14] Delpech, Vol. 2, 264–273. Oman, Vol. 1, 152–165, is still troubled by Wace's impossible palisades.

the right flank and secured Dover, the chief port of entry into the island. Then only did he march against the capital. When it was not surrendered to him at his approach, he wisely forbore to attack it. It should be noted that a first-class city was always, from its mere extent, too great to be contained by a mediæval army. The governmental finance of the time, even at its best, had not kept pace with the rapid growth of population and especially of towns. Simon de Montfort before Toulouse in 1218 and Joan of Arc's English opponents before Orleans in 1429 were unable, even with the aid of elaborate entrenchments, so much as to block-ade the circumference of the place attacked. Against London in 1066 the Conqueror contented himself with burning the southern suburb south of the Thames. He then circled westward, devastat-ing the country systematically, crossed the Thames at Wallingford, fifty miles up river, and moved northeast. By this time those in London saw that when he reached the coast northeast of the town they would be starved out, so wide and thorough had his devas-tation been. They therefore sent out a delegation which met him at Berkhampstead, some 30 miles northwest of London, and surrendered to him the city and the crown. This practically completed the conquest. Since the men of the time had no such thing as national patriotism, only isolated factional risings in distant districts remained to be suppressed; and in their suppression native levies willingly assisted William, now the legitimate king.[15]

William's rapid consolidation of his conquest was possible because England was then without any highly organized system of forti-fication. No sooner was he possesssed of his new kingdom than he began to secure himself therein by thickly studding it with perma-nent works of stone. The spirit of this enormous undertaking was altogether in the Roman tradition and the individual works were known as "castles" from the Latin "castellum," i. e., a fort. The complete difference between mediæval campaigns in theatres of war without castles and those conducted in theatres closely dotted with such works is obvious. To the strategic effect of the system, and to the strategic location of individual castles, I shall return in connexion with John Plantagenet's brilliant campaign of 1216, a campaign entirely dictated by the castle system. Mean-while I will describe the principle upon which they were sited, not

[15] Belloc: Warfare in England, 102–104.

with reference to the countryside as a whole but with regard to the actual location of their walls.

Unlike the Romans, the Normans (and with them all the other men of the Middle Ages) preferred inaccessible sites. The Romans of the high Imperial time, with their disciplined infantry, expected to hold their works easily and were always considering an active defence. Therefore, while they might prefer to build upon an elevation whose slopes would hinder assaults and give the defender's missile weapons a range greater than those of the besiegers, at the same time they would not site works upon a cliff or unduly steep hill or behind a river or marsh because such obstacles would prevent the garrison from sallying out. On the other hand, the mediævals preferred such sites to all others because, as we have seen, they normally lacked disciplined infantry altogether, and were concerned chiefly with passive defence. Therefore they were always trying to increase the number of obstacles opposed to a besieger, in order to make him win the fortress stone by stone—even if the accumulated obstacles hindered sorties. Up to 1300, they were even willing to hamper their own lateral communications in order to lengthen the besiegers' task although, as we shall see, this last policy was found to be mistaken and therefore given up.

Throughout Western Europe, no stone fortifications have come down to us from the Dark Ages. Apparently the men of those weak and troubled times used masonry chiefly in repairing some of the numerous and splendid ancient works about them. When they built on a new site, lack of money seems to have compelled them to content themselves with digging a ditch, heaping up the earth from the ditch into a mound, and crowning that mound with a palisade. Most of the forts that rendered such service against Vikings, Magyars and heathen Slavs must have been of this sort. The argument against the frequent use of stone-work in the Dark Ages is chiefly a negative one. No such stone-work has survived. However, many documents, even when not explicit, nevertheless imply that wood was the material normally used. We know that there was some stone construction—for instance in the two Paris bridge-heads which resisted the Vikings so well in 886. The analogy of contemporary church building would lead us to think that such works were exceedingly simple, heavy and squat.

The use of wood in fortification persisted into the 11th century in Western Europe, even into the early part of the 12th century. In one of the early scenes of the Bayeux tapestry, William the Conqueror's men are shown attacking with burning torches the defences of Dinant in Brittany [16]—which would of course, have been useless against masonry. Many of the Conqueror's own works with which he studded England seem to have been of wood. In Flanders, up to 1130, the local nobles were accustomed to build stockaded mound fortresses, with some sort of towers or turrets in the stockade and a citadel or keep to dominate the whole.[17] It is strange to find Flanders still so poor in the 12th century as not to be able to afford stone.

The Norman castle can easily be studied from the abundant remains still standing from Scotland to Sicily. Almost all its strength was concentrated in a single enormous tower known as a donjon or keep. There was an outer wall which enclosed a court-yard but the flankments upon it were only little turrets, not much more than sentry-boxes, and it was only a subordinate feature.[18]

The reason why the Norman military engineers preferred to put most of their money into a single tower was that it combined height and a maximum of space inside with only a narrow perimeter to be defended. Only men enough were needed to man the battlements and drop things down on anyone trying to sap the base of the wall. Increased height made it harder for the sappers to resist the fall of whatever was dropped. It also gave a more extensive view.

Sometimes the Norman keep was of the type known as a shell-keep—round with an open space in the centre. Such a work was more or less a natural development from the palisaded ring of the Dark Ages and might be used to replace it—especially as the artificial mounds might not be firm enough to stand the weight of a solid tower. The typical Norman keep was solid and square, with a square turret at each corner and often a flat strip buttress up the middle of each side. The entrance was usually one story above ground, up a stairway inside an oblong lower building resting against one side of the main structure. The masonry was rude, the stones small and separated by broad mortar joints. In the

[16] Belloc: Book of the Bayeux Tapestry, Fig. 25.
[17] Oman, Vol. 2, 12–13.
[18] Dieulafoy: Château Gaillard, 15–18, 22.

Conqueror's keep, the "White Tower" in the Tower of London, the joints are so broad that the wall contains more mortar than stone. The walls are no less than 15 feet thick at the ground level and 10 feet even at the top.[19]

In mediæval sieges we never hear of the Roman "agger," a huge mound high enough to command the defences which was established out of effective range and gradually extended towards the walls. Once it was complete the defenders had to resist storming columns advancing with a fairly broad front on a level, or even on a downward slope. No mediæval army could command the labor necessary to make such a thing.

But with the exception of the "agger," all the ancient siege devices were used throughout the Dark Ages and the 11th century. There seem to have been no new discoveries, except Greek fire, and undoubtedly the old machines were copied crudely and on a much smaller scale. Nevertheless it is surprising to find practically every one of the individual devices of ancient siege-work so continually in use.

Position warfare, as everybody realizes since the Great War, enormously increases the part played by the artillery. Up to 1100, the only known kinds of artillery were catapults worked by torsion and tension. A torsion catapult was made of a heavy timber frame with a mass of twisted rope strung across near the front. In this twisted rope was secured one end of a movable beam having a spoon-shaped hollow in its other end. This free end was pulled backwards and down by a sort of capstan or large winch at the rear of the frame, against the resistance of the twisted ropes, and the stone to be thrown was placed in the spoon-shaped cavity. The free end of the movable beam was then liberated by releasing a catch. The force of the twisted ropes then made the beam describe an upward and forward curve, moving fast enough to flip off the stone at a high angle of elevation. Such a catapult was known as a mangon, mangonel, or sling. Of course the projectiles would seldom be uniform in weight. Furthermore a wet or dry day would affect the ropes. Accordingly the shot group of such a machine was so large that it was generally used for bombarding large objectives.

A tension catapult, usually known as a ballista, was simply an

[19] Dict. de l'Arch., Articles "Donjon" and "Château."

exaggerated crossbow wound up by winches. It shot bolts or enormous arrows with great force, flat trajectory and considerable accuracy. Of course it could not penetrate walls; it was useful against small fairly distant objectives—such as men exposing themselves out of range of infantry weapons.

In making good their approach the besiegers would protect themselves against the plunging fire of the defenders behind mantlets, i. e., screens—strong but light enough to be moved as desired.

Unfortunately there is nothing to guide us in estimating the range of catapult artillery. To a man, the chroniclers are clergymen with the vaguest possible notions of military technique. Indeed their vagueness is such that they do not even name them uniformly but use all sorts of names interchangeably for the tension and torsion types.

Movable towers, as high as or higher than the defences, might be rolled up until drawbridges near their tops could be dropped upon the battlements. An assault might then be delivered up the towers and across the drawbridges. Meanwhile archers or crossbowmen posted on the tower tops would try to pick off the defenders who were resisting the storming party. It was by means of movable towers that the crusaders took Jerusalem in 1099.

The defects of the movable tower are obvious enough. It was not only heavy but top-heavy. Accordingly it could be moved forward only over ground that was smooth, level and particularly firm. Besides it needed protection against combustibles, generally by means of rawhides in front and to some extent upon its sides also. The defenders, like Red Indians besieging a frontier blockhouse, would shoot at it with arrows carrying balls of burning tow. Most effective of all would be the huge arrows from the tension type of catapult.

It was a little easier to move forward some sort of low shelter which would serve to protect an attack against the base of the defenders' walls. Such shelters were known as "cats," perhaps because their occupants were to claw their way into the wall. The Roman name for them had been "musculus," a rat, apparently because they gnawed their way in. They were fairly long, so that their occupants might come and go by the rear end (which must not be too close under the wall), and narrow and steep-roofed in proportion to their length so that they might be strong enough to resist stones and heavy weights dropped by the besieged from above. For greater strength, the roof would be steeply pointed, and protected against fire by means of rawhides.

Either the cat might be brought up within a few feet of the wall, which could then be attacked with ram or borer, or its head might be pushed up against a wall to give cover for pioneers attacking the masonry with pickaxe, hammer and crowbar. The ram and borer were both great beams, the largest that could be found, swung by chains from the ridgepole of the cat that sheltered them. They differed in that the ram had a broad solid head (like the forehead and horns of a true ram) with which it butted against the wall, whereas the borer had a pointed head intended to break down the opposing masonry stone by stone. If the wall were not too thick or too well built, the ram would crack and finally break it by repeated blows in the same spot. The action of the borer would, of course, be slower and more localized.

It is hard to see what any ram could have accomplished against a wall fifteen feet thick like those of the Conqueror's Tower of London. Nor can we estimate the time necessary for a borer (which was used less often than the ram) to make any sort of impression on such walls. Meanwhile the defenders, even if they failed to smash or burn the cat from above, might grip the head of the ram or borer with large pincers to prevent it from being pulled back for its forward stroke, or might try to deaden its blows by means of rope pads or sacks thickly stuffed with soft material with which they would cover the face of the wall at the point where the blows were falling. If pincers or padding succeeded, there was nothing for it but to advance the cat and sap the base of the wall with the pickaxe or with hammer and crowbar. As the mine gallery was driven into the wall, it was shored up with lumber. When it was judged that enough had been done, the lumber shoring would be burnt away and (if the hole had been made large enough) a section of the wall would come down, leaving a breach. This method of mining had been familiar to the ancients, like the ram and the movable tower, and is described by Vegetius.[20]

During this period, the defenders of a first-class stone fortress

[20] For mediæval siege machinery see Dict. de l'Arch., Article "Engin," and also Oman, Vol. 1, 131–138.

could usually content themselves with a passive defence of the most absolute kind, trusting in the height and thickness of the walls rather than in any effort of theirs to hinder the besiegers' operations. Of course such fortresses were costly to build. Once built, their enormous solidity enabled a handful of men inside one to resist an army for a long time. You will often see the statement that, under the military conditions of the time, such a fortress could not be taken except by famine. That is untrue, unless we enlarge the term military conditions to include political and economic conditions as well. It was because no one had the resources to keep a numerous army on foot and hard at work against such fortresses, that throughout the eleventh century they were almost never taken by regular siege. On the merits of the case in military engineering alone, they must have fallen in the end, even if provisions and water had held out. The military axiom still held good which makes the resistance of any fortress, however strong, calculable within limits of time, if besieged by numbers sufficient to blockade it and carry on an active regular siege at the same time. A garrison persistently attacked must decline in strength through casualties and through fatigue. Not even the Dark Ages and the eleventh century are exceptions to this invariable rule, although it must be admitted that they come near being the proverbial exception which proves it.

Such was the eleventh-century Art of War in Western Europe before the Crusades, those great campaigns which are a landmark in every department of mediæval civilization. I conclude this chapter with a discussion of their strategy.

The problem was the transport and subsistence of great and heterogeneous armies, based upon Latin Christendom centring about northern France, to the theatre of war in Palestine. Obviously the difficulties of such a problem, measured in terms of what we call staff work, were so great that it is hard to overstate them. It is true that the Magyars had been converted about the year 1000, so that the Danube Valley was now open to Christian armies as it had not been since the fifth century. Constantinople and part of the coasts of Anatolia, together with Cilicia, were also in friendly hands, although political difficulties with the Byzantines limited their co-operation with the Crusaders. To pay for passage by the sea at the hands of the Italian maritime republics was to avoid the risk of starvation by taking a heavy risk of being drowned. Moreover, the cost of such a passage was ruinous.

In the many books on the Crusades, none has yet attempted to study their staff work, with its financial and administrative ramifications. How well equipped and provisioned crusading armies sometimes were, can be judged from the achievement of the Provençals in 1096 bound for the First Crusade. Under Count Raymond IV of Toulouse, they most unwisely and unnecessarily tried to march down the rugged and inhospitable east coast of the Adriatic. The ignorance of geography which would permit such an attempt contrasts with the surprising measure of success. Instead of losing his entire command through starvation and exposure, Raymond actually came out at Durazzo with half his effective.

In Anatolia, the Byzantines had elaborate information of their lost provinces, including roads and distances, but this information was out of date because the Turks who had held the country for upwards of fifteen years had allowed many bridges and cisterns to become unserviceable and had ruined the country generally. In particular they had protected themselves by deliberately and minutely devastating a broad belt of country on their borders. As if this was not enough, the Turks, with admirable self-sacrifice, would devastate their own land about the line of march of a crusading army, as it approached. Furthermore, there was between the Byzantines and the Crusaders a divergence of political aim, the Byzantines desiring the recovery of Anatolia and the Crusaders the conquest of Palestine. Accordingly the Byzantines were always tempted to use the geographical ignorance of the Crusaders to make of them the unintentional servants of Constantinople.

The strategic successes and failures of the Crusades were as follows.

The penniless advance guard of the First Crusade (1096–99) reached Anatolia only to be promptly massacred by the Turks. The main body cleared the western coast of Asia Minor and captured Nicæa in return for refitment at Byzantine hands. They then took the southern of the two great routes across the interior, by way of Dorylæum (now Eski-Sher) and Iconium, and so to the chief pass over the Taurus, known as the Cilician Gates. They defeated the Turks at Dorylæum and again just before reaching the Taurus. Accordingly they won through safely although they suffered severely and lost many men from starvation.

Various detachments marched in 1102. One was destroyed by a mixture of folly and geographical ignorance which caused its leaders to entangle it in the mountains near Amasia east of Angora, contrary to advice given them in Constantinople. The other two, although their line of march was sensible enough, were ruined through lack of water and inability to cope with the perpetual skirmishing of the Turks.

The Second Crusade of 1148–49 marched in two detachments. The Germans moved from Nicæa via Dorylæum but ran out of food 70 or 80 miles short of Iconium and had to turn back, losing most of their effective by starvation and the Turkish arrows. The French, under their King Louis VII, kept within Byzantine territory by marching down the west coast as far as the mouth of the Mæander and then ascending the valley of that stream. Checked by the Turks east of Laodicea, they turned southeast to Adalia. This place they reached safely, although beginning to suffer from short rations. There the king, knights, and nobles embarked for Palestine, leaving the infantry to be destroyed in the impossible attempt to march along the impracticable sea-coast east of Adalia.

The Third Crusade of 1190 was led by three great soldiers, Richard Cœur de Lion, Philip Augustus, and the Emperor Frederic Barbarossa. Richard and Philip went by sea. Frederic and his Germans followed the route of Louis VII as far as Laodicea; thence they moved east on Iconium, which they took by assault. On the way they lost many horses by the Turkish arrows, but thanks to their crossbowmen they inflicted more harm than they received. As usual, they were beginning to suffer from starvation before reaching Iconium. After the capture of that place, the Sultan proposed a truce, so that they finished their march in peace.

After the successes of the First Crusade and of Barbarossa in crossing Asia Minor, it is surprising to read Oman's statement that they had "little or no organization." [21] Of course no large disorderly mass of men without discipline or organized transport could possibly have fought and marched successfully for six weeks through devastated country.

[21] Oman, Vol. 1, 251.

Once established in the Holy Land, the Crusaders failed because their Army of Occupation, aside from temporary reinforcements, was never sufficiently numerous to extend their holdings eastward to the desert. At the height of their power they were able to annoy but never wholly to interrupt communication between Egypt and Damascus. When the Mohammedans of Mesopotamia, Syria and Egypt became united under an able man like Saladin, the position of the Christians became one of deadly peril.

In their two invasions of Egypt, the Crusaders failed through ignorance, or insufficient appreciation, of geography. They should have landed at Alexandria, or better still at Pelusium near the modern Port Said, and then marched on Cairo along one side of the Nile Delta. Instead, they twice made the mistake of being tempted by the town of Damietta, on the coast of the Delta itself. Inasmuch as the Delta was a network of branches and canals, impassable under military conditions, both invasions failed completely.

CHAPTER VI

CRUSADING TACTICS AND MURET

1099–1213 A. D.

IN every department of civilization and in every phase of the military art, the returning Crusaders were the schoolmasters of Latin Christendom. The mind of the West, already alert and vigorous, was enlarged enormously by travel and by the energy generated through participation in a vast common effort.

First of all, the economic side of crusading warfare was altogether different from that of the sporadic struggles in Western Europe. In one form or another the Christians of Palestine were able to count on heavy subsidies from their home lands. This made possible not only the construction of complicated fortresses on a scale hitherto unknown; it also resulted in gains as to the permanence and specialization of personnel.

Let us consider for a moment some of the ways in which this increase in the permanency and specialization of personnel came about. The military orders of the Temple and the Hospital were able to give their number a continuous military education, often enough to fit them to act as chiefs of staffs to kings. Thus we see Gilbert the Templar successfully extricating the army of Louis VII of France from the Anatolian mountains east of Laodicea in 1147, and we shall see Garin the Hospitaller acting as an efficient chief of staff under Philip Augustus at Bouvines. On several occasions we seem to see an organized pioneer corps at work, in the army of Louis VII and again in that of Cœur de Lion in 1190. In each case this corps was recruited from the unarmed pilgrims to the Holy Land. Finally, something like an Intelligence Department was created in the shape of a highly paid espionage service. Even regular written studies of the forces of prospective opponents together with the topography of prospective theatres of war were made. Two of these reports dealing with the forces of the Sultan of Egypt and the topography of that country have been preserved. They

321

include a description of the roads and a schedule of road distances from Gaza to Cairo and Alexandria.[1]

In equipment, after 1100 the rapid progress of Christendom is reflected by a series of improvements in armour. Ring-mail sewed to a base becomes true chain-mail with each link engaged to the links adjoining. Mail breeches become common and the sleeves of the mail shirt are extended to the wrist. The helmet becomes the pot-helm furnished with slits through which to see and breathe. Anyone who has never tried it will be surprised to find how much he can see through even tiny slits when they are properly placed, as in some aviators' goggles, and in Eskimo wooden snow goggles. The trouble with the great pot-helm was first its weight, which might amount to 18 pounds. This produced fatigue and made it necessary to support it upon a great roll or lining of padding. Second, there was the fact that on account of its weight it consequently could not be made to fit the head closely and therefore its wearer risked his nose if his helmet were thrust violently back against his face. About the year 1200 this last defect was remedied by making the helmet pointed in front. With the improvement in chain-mail the shield became smaller and less pointed. The chain-mail, being flexible, hindered the wearer's movements very little. A full suit might weigh as little as 31 pounds; the shirt alone ranged from 14 to 32 lbs. Nevertheless chain-mail had one defect; however impenetrable, it could not protect its wearer from a bruise or even from having his bones broken. It offered no resistance to shock. Accordingly it had to be backed with a coat of leather or heavy padding called a gambeson or hacqueton. These gambesons were so strongly made that even by themselves they could keep out the arrows of the short bow. Sometimes they alone were worn by mounted men-at-arms engaged in some mission requiring even more than the usual high mobility of 12th- and 13th-century cavalry. Usually they were the sole armour of foot soldiers. One Moslem chronicler speaks of Cœur de Lion's crossbowmen at Arsouf (1191) with their gambesons stuck so full of Turkish arrows that they looked like hedgehogs, and still marching along quite unhurt.[2]

---

[1] For the military orders, see Delpech, Vol. 2, 222–223; for pioneers, Vol. 2, 225–226; for the intelligence service, Vol. 2, 226–237.

[2] Oman, Vol. 1, 309, quoting Boha-ed-din.

After 1200 helmets gradually began to be furnished with movable visors. At the same time appear the partial beginnings of plate armour. Even with a good gambeson no chain-mail could protect against the shock of the heaviest sort of blows—especially downward blows in which the weight of the weapons was added to the force of the striker. When cavalry was fighting cavalry, and infantry, infantry, a downward blow which missed the helmet was apt to strike the shoulder. Cavalry fighting infantry were apt to receive cuts on the knee or thigh. Accordingly during the 13th century we see first shoulder plates and then knee and thigh plates gradually coming into fashion. Such plates were worn over the usual chain-mail so that they added to the net weight to be carried. Commanders of the time were sensitive about the loss of mobility caused by this extra weight. One of many examples is Simon de Montfort at the siege of Toulouse in 1218, five years after his great victory at Muret. Since the besieged were more numerous than his own men, the striking force under his own hand intended to reinforce any point in the partial besieging lines needed the greatest possible mobility. De Montfort therefore was careful to have his men strip off their thigh pieces. Horse armour, in the form of housings or "bardings" of loose hanging cloth or felt is found in the 13th century. Occasionally toward the end of the century it is even reinforced with mail.[3]

In the matter of tactics, the crusading fights show a marked and fairly regular progress, divided into three definite phases.

The first phase of six years, from 1097 to 1102, may be called the phase of encounter. During this time neither side made any effort to adapt its tactics to those of the enemy, and the actions were decided chiefly through the chances of war and the errors of individual commanders. The Christians were usually, but not invariably, successful through their superiority in shock tactics and close combat.

In the second phase of fifty-four years, from 1102 to 1156, the Christians had learned their lesson, which was that their mailed horsemen must be supported by solid infantry armed both with pikes and with missile weapons. The Moslems were unable to work out any counter-move, so the Christians were successful in every

[3] For 12th-century armor and equipment see Dict. du Mob., Vols. 5 and 6. Also Oman, Vol. 2, 3-9; Delpech, Vol. 1, 423-426, and Dean.

action. That the victories won did not bring greater results was due to no circumstance connected with tactics, but solely to the want of permanent Christian numbers.

In the third phase of over a century, from 1156 to the end of the Crusades in 1271, the Mohammedans had come to see that their chance lay in attempting to separate the Christian cavalry from their infantry. When the attempt succeeded the Crusaders were usually beaten; when cavalry and infantry stuck together they usually won. Even so, the victories of the Christians outnumbered their defeats. It was unfortunate political circumstances, together with the old chronic shortage of permanent numbers, which finally resulted in their expulsion from Syria and Palestine.

At this point the reader should note that there were two distinct tactical methods among the Moslems. The Turks of Asia Minor, northern Syria, and northern Mesopotamia were skirmishing horse archers of the immemorial Eastern sort, such as the Parthians and the Magyars had been. Their immediate ancestors had been Nomads. The Egyptians, and in general the Moslems of the old Arabic tradition, resembled their own ancestors in that their armies were composed of cavalry acting by shock supported by hordes of rabble infantry of whom the least worthless element consisted of negroes. In other words, they were the same Saracens against whom the Byzantines had fought.

The first general action was against the Turks. It was fought at Dorylæum, recently prominent in communiqués of the Greco-Kemalist war under its modern name of Eski-Sher. For greater ease in foraging, the huge army of the Crusaders was marching in two parallel columns only about five miles apart but not in continuous close touch with one another. The Turkish horse archers, also in great force, attacked the left column, but committed the serious error of not keeping the Christian right under proper observation. The left column formed in the usual western order of battle which we have seen at Hastings, with the infantry in front. Although the crusading command had organized their whole army in companies of 100 and platoons of 50 under designated leaders,[4] this organization had not succeeded in solidifying the infantry enough to enable them to resist the novel Turkish skirmishing

[4] Delpech, Vol. 2, 150, quoting William of Tyre.

tactics. When the knights charged, their blow was spent in air. The Turks nimbly avoided the shock and then lapped around their flank units as these became exposed so that they were continually forced back on their infantry. These last attempted a defensive on true Vegetian lines but lacked the cohesion to make it good. Demoralization threatened, and fatigue on the part of the knights, who could neither close with the nimble enemy nor obtain repose because of the weakness of the Christian foot, would have brought disaster had it not been for the appearance of the cavalry of the right-hand column, which came suddenly over a ridge upon the Turkish left and rear. The Turks were thus trapped not by design on the part of the Crusaders but merely because the distance gained by the right (while the left was fighting) naturally brought it against the Turkish left rear. In such a position the heavier Western men and horses easily smashed their opponents.

At Antioch, where the next general action was fought, the crusading foot was stiffened by the presence of many knights who had by this time lost their horses during the long campaign. Secondly, the Turks foolishly engaged in a narrow plain only two miles wide, between an unfordable river and a range of hills too steep for cavalry. The Crusaders had only to extend from river to hills, meanwhile protecting their rear by a suitable detachment, in order to win.

Even when Jerusalem had been taken and the mass of the Crusaders had gone home, the handful who remained, as at the first battle of Ramleh in September, 1101, were still able to win victories by virtue of their superior military qualities—provided that horse and foot kept together. A great army of Egyptians was dispersed by less than 300 Christian knights supported by 900 infantry.

A few months later another action on the same field showed the lesson had not been thoroughly learned. In passing, it should be said that the importance of Ramleh was that it was a great road centre. In infidel hands it cut off Jerusalem from Jaffa and the coast.

Finding an Egyptian force in possession of this important crossroad, the King of Jerusalem, Baldwin I, correctly decided to attack, but committed the folly of doing so with only about 700 mailed cavalry and no infantry. It is true that he had beaten

a similar force on the same field with even fewer armoured horsemen, but on that occasion he had been supported by foot who
had borne themselves well. Now his knights were swallowed up
and massacred, Baldwin himself barely escaping. This time the
lesson was learned, for thereafter no crusading army marched
without infantry.

Shortly after his defeat Baldwin sallied out from Jaffa, where
he had taken refuge. This time his cavalry numbered less than
two hundred, but with the aid of a solid body of infantry (composed of the crews of a fleet newly come from the West) he beat off
great numbers of Egyptians and finally occupied their camp. In
square or, more probably, circular formation, the Christian pikemen and crossbowmen stood firm against the Mohammedans,
furnishing an asylum for the knights within which they could
rest safely between charges.

For half a century, the Christians were never beaten. After
Jaffa, Hab, Hazarth and Marj-es-Safar were equally glorious
victories against heavy odds. In the campaign of Bosra in 1146,
they marched for over a hundred miles through the desert east
of the Jordan and back again, always in the presence of a numerous
enemy whom they defeated in every combat. In this operation
they lost so few men that they were able to bring back all their
dead and so permit the infidels to believe that not one Christian
had fallen.

Not until after 1156 did the Moslem hit upon the idea of attacking the Christians only when their horse was separated from their
foot. The first break in the long series of Christian victories was
in this year at the Ford of Jacob over the Jordan. The infidels,
who had retreated before the crusading cavalry and infantry
combined, successfully attacked the cavalry when separated
from its infantry support. Sometimes they would bring this about
by simulating flight. When the Christian horse and foot could
be attacked separately Islam usually won. When the two arms
kept together the infidels were usually beaten.

The one conspicuous exception to this rule seems to prove not
the self-sufficiency of mailed cavalry, but under favourable circumstances, that of infantry. In 1124 the militia infantry of the
Commune of Jerusalem, acting absolutely without cavalry, showed
so bold a front against an Egyptian raiding force that these last

retired without daring to attack. We shall meet with municipal militia infantry again.

The endless war hung level with varying fortunes until 1183. Then the political situation shifted against the Christians because of the consolidation of Egypt, Mesopotamia and the Moslem parts of Syria under the rule of Saladin who virtually destroyed the Kingdom of Jerusalem at the great and disastrous battle of Hattin in 1187. His army on that occasion was, as usual, very large. It included 10,000 mailed cavalry intended for shock action together with numbers of horse archers. To relieve the town of Tiberias on the Sea of Galilee, which was besieged by Saladin, the Christians reduced the garrisons of all their fortresses dangerously low and took the field with practically their entire force. This amounted to five or six thousand mailed cavalry, 18,000 foot, and many light horse archers armed in the Turkish fashion and called Turcopoles. They concentrated at Saffaria, only 16 miles west of Tiberias, but separated from that town by waterless desert which was particularly hard to cross in the height of summer, for the month was July. Furthermore, Saladin had ravaged the country well. After much discussion, pro and con, the Christians resolved to advance, confident in their unusual numerical strength and tempted by Saladin's dangerous position with the lake at his back. On the first day they advanced ten miles. Meanwhile Saladin had refused to show his hand. He had contented himself with skirmishing and setting fire to the parched grass. In the afternoon the Christians were so fatigued that it was, most unwisely, decided to make a waterless camp. All night the Turks kept up a harassing fire of arrows. In the morning the march was resumed under distressing conditions. All were suffering so from thirst that when a stream of water was reached the infantry broke ranks to drink. Hitherto the watchful Saladin had seen no chance to attack as the two arms had covered one another admirably. Now when charged, the foot became demoralized. Refusing to obey orders to rally on the cavalry, they tried to make a separate stand by themselves on the hill of Hattin where they were soon destroyed. Saladin now surrounded the Christian cavalry. So many horses had been shot that the main body lost all momentum and huddled stupidly together at a standstill. Seeing this, the advance guard saved themselves by a sudden charge which broke through the

Saracens in their front. The main body finally surrendered from thirst and fatigue, for the armoured men had suffered little from the arrows, which had been effective only against their horses.

It is significant of the atmosphere of these wars that Saladin treated the captured King of Jerusalem with honour, but instantly massacred two hundred and thirty knights of the Military Orders. Reginald of Châtillon, a baron who had greatly harassed the Moslems, being offered the alternatives of Islam or death, proudly chose death. Saladin himself struck the first blow at him as he stood there defenceless, and he was then cut to pieces by the guards. Hattin is an example of bad leadership. Even at the last, the successful charge of the advance guard proves that more could have been done. It should be noted that the crisis of the action was the moment when the tired infantry misconducted themselves and became separated. It is interesting to learn that Saladin had organized his ammunition supply of arrows with particular care.[5]

Although Hattin ruined the Kingdom of Jerusalem, nevertheless that great soldier Cœur de Lion four years later at Arsouf (1191) was able to beat Saladin handsomely in a general action. Richard's force was very strong, perhaps as high as 100,000. The staff and medical services were carefully organized. Inasmuch as clean clothing reduced the danger from Oriental epidemics, there was even a corps of laundresses, strong enough to keep up with the column on foot and carefully recruited so as not to be a cause of scandal and disorder in the Christian army![6] Cœur de Lion was particularly famous for his success in espionage work, in which he spent money lavishly.

The line of operations lay along the coast southward from Acre in order to prepare a base for a subsequent advance eastward to Jerusalem. On the march the column was closely beset by Saladin, whose plan was especially to harass the rear so that it would have to halt and face about, thus making a gap into which the Moslems might be able to charge. So high was the Christian discipline and so great Richard's prudence that the opportunity never came. Richard's tactics were for the infantry to cover the marching column with their missiles. Only if the Moslems should so thoroughly commit themselves to the action as to have difficulty in

[5] Delpech, Vol. 1, 372, quoting Roudatain.
[6] Delpech, Vol. 1, 377, quoting the Itinerarium.

breaking it off, were the cavalry to charge.   Just before reaching Arsouf the opportunity came and the charge was delivered.   Saladin's army was so thoroughly defeated that only political dissension prevented an advance against Jerusalem.

Want of space prevents consideration of Mansourah, the last of the great crusading actions, where St. Louis was nearly destroyed through the indiscipline of his brother the Count of Artois, and through his own necessity of separating from his infantry in order to cross a deep ford.   The position was finally saved by the arrival of the footmen.

The ultimate failure of the Crusades was due to no inferiority in fighting power.   Man for man the Christians were better fighters and, for the most part, better generals.   They solved their tactical problem in five years (1097–1102) whereas it took the Moslems fifty years even to begin to match them.   It was geographical difficulties, the want of permanent numbers, and (after 1150) an unfavourable political situation which brought about the ruin of the Kingdom of Jerusalem by the single disaster of Hattin, and prevented the success of later efforts to re-establish the position.

In Spain, the chief theatre of war against Islam and one in which conditions were more equal than in Palestine, the Christians won.

In the Spanish wars we can trace only one distinctive tactical development, that of the light cavalry known as "Genetours." Mounted on the light Spanish horses known as "Jennets" and armed with long light lances or javelins, the Genetours were intended for skirmishing.   The survival of their method of combat among the Portuguese bullfighters of to-day was noted in the last chapter.

With the exception of the Genetours, tactical developments in Spain seem to have resembled contemporary developments in Palestine.   Our scanty knowledge of the 11th century and earlier battles, indicates that they were cavalry fights pure and simple. After 1150 we find solid infantry, pikemen and crossbowmen, on both sides; indeed they seem to have been more prominent among the infidels than among the Christians.[7]   Such infantry, however, were no more fit for the offensive than any other mediæval infantry.   A striking demonstration is the combat of Majorca in 1229. There the young king Jaime of Aragon, although he had only four

[7] Mangin: La Force Noire, 126–127 and 133–139.

hundred mailed cavalry with him, overruled his timid councillors and decided to attack some 2000 Moslem pikemen advancing against him. Noting that the advance had disordered their ranks and made gaps in the hedge of spear-points, he very truly remarked that under such conditions any troops could be beaten. He charged and destroyed them.[8]

After 1100 the increase of Christendom in energy, wealth and knowledge brought about rapid improvement in fortification. Much larger and more complicated works could now be built. On the other hand, siege machinery was improved and sieges grew more methodical, so that a more active defence became necessary. The result was that the typical first-class fortress completely changed its character. The Donjon became only the last refuge of the garrison. The outer walled enclosure now became the main line of resistance and was accordingly strengthened with towers whose size made them little fortresses in themselves, while their bold profile enabled their defenders to flank the adjoining towers together with the intervening curtain walls. Overhanging wooden galleries known as hoardings were provided at the crest of walls and towers so as to give the besieged a better command of the base of the defences—the point which the besiegers must attack. In deforested Syria these hoardings were replaced by permanent stone machicolations which served the same purpose and served it better.

The castle of Kerak-in-Moab, in Palestine east of the Dead Sea, may serve as an example of the new type of fortress with its accumulation of obstacles. It was probably built about 1140. In plan it is an irregular parallelogram, protected on three sides by natural escarpments. In front there is a dry ditch cut in the rock. Immediately behind this rises the front curtain wall, flanked by good-sized square towers at the corners. The gate is close to one of these towers. On entering one finds oneself not in the castle court but in a long narrow passage between the outer wall and an inner wall close to and parallel with it. This passage is closed by two portcullises which with that of the gate itself makes three in all. The main gate of Tientsin, familiar to the Chinese Expeditionary Force of 1900, had a somewhat similar arrangement. Inside, another inner wall divides the total enclosed space into an inner and an outer court or "ward." At the rear end of the inner ward

[8] Delpech, Vol. 1, 318–319, quoting Jaime of Aragon.

is the Donjon Keep. The entire rear end of the castle surmounts a steep escarpment running down to a large cistern.

This castle is a fine specimen of the mid-12th-century fortification. It was often attacked but never with success and it was taken by Saladin in 1188, the year after Hattin, only by starvation after months of close blockade. Obviously such a fortress marks a great advance over the isolated Norman keep with its outer ward of mere palisading, or at most of light stone-work with a plain flat trace and no powerful flankments.[9]

The finest fortress of the 12th century, at least in the West, is the Saucy Castle, "Château Gaillard" on a cliff over the Seine between Paris and Rouen. It was built in a single year, 1195, by Richard Cœur de Lion (whose talents as an organizer and tactician we have touched upon in considering the campaign of Arsouf) to be the citadel of a vast entrenched camp intended to cover Normandy against Philip Augustus of France. Unfortunately our space does not permit consideration of Richard's entrenched camp as a whole. The castle itself is too good to be typical of even the first-class fortresses of its time. It is a supreme example of what an exceptional genius could do about the year 1200 when that genius ruled from Scotland to the Pyrenees and controlled the finest treasury in Europe.

Château Gaillard is built upon a typical mediæval fortress site—backed up against sheer precipices, with a single narrow approach on the level, only about twenty yards wide at its narrowest point.

A besieger attacking by this single approach was confronted by the apex of a triangular outer ward flanked by five towers. At the base of the triangle was a ditch crossed by a movable bridge with a zigzag approach ⌐┐ so that a storming party would not be able to rush it at speed.[9] Behind the ditch was the second ward, also flanked by towers, and within the second ward is the third or inner ward—the most powerful of all. This inner ward was unique in mediæval fortification inasmuch as it had no towers but had its entire wall scalloped as if towers had been cut in slices and placed alongside one another. In the inner ward rose the Donjon, the culminating point of the entire scheme. Experience

[9] Oman, Vol. 2, 31.

had shown that the corners of the old square Donjons were weak points. Accordingly this huge tower (60 feet high and 50 feet broad at the base) was round with a pointed spur of solid masonry toward the side from which attack must come.

The ditches were cut in the solid rock upon which the walls rested. The walls themselves sloped forward at their bases to give the sapper a more difficult task and to make stones bound outward when dropped from the battlements against the base-slope. In his anxiety to avoid dead space, the designer increased the height of the slope in the re-entrants between the scallops of the inner walls so that the scalloped trace was far more pronounced at the top and flatter at the bottom. The Donjon was furnished with stone machicolation widely spaced and carried on pointed arches resting on projecting buttresses. The battlements of all the other works were provided with holes at the base of the crenelation just above the top of the curtain for the insertion of beams to carry projecting hoards.

A fortress like Château Gaillard was designed primarily to resist mining. Its masonry was too good to have been vulnerable to rams and borers. Movable towers for escalade could rarely be used in 12th-century sieges because of the improvement in combustibles. In 1190, just six years before building Château Gaillard, Cœur de Lion himself, at the siege of Acre, had found himself obliged to coat his movable towers with iron sheeting—a ruinously expensive business.

Besides the improvement in combustibles, there had been an improvement in artillery. To the tension and torsion types of catapult a third and still more powerful type was added, worked by a counterpoise. The counterpoise catapult was generally known as a trebuchet—although the chronic mediæval confusion in all military terms continued to complicate artillery nomenclature. Such a catapult had a high timber frame for base. To the upper part of this frame was pivoted a movable beam, with the pivot much nearer one end than the other. To the short end was attached a huge hanging timber bucket which was filled with stones to serve as a counterpoise. The long end had either a spoon-shaped rest for the projectiles (as in the mangonel) or else a sort of sling. It was drawn down and released like the mangonel and like the mangonel was generally used for high-angle bombardment of large objectives. During the siege of Acre a projectile probably from such a catapult surprised all who saw it by a carry of well over 800 yards.[10] What the ordinary maximum was we do not know.

Thirteenth-century artillery had the same fascination for its users as has the artillery of to-day. In 1210, at the siege of Termes during the Albigensian War, de Montfort's chief of artillery was a priest, the Archdeacon William of Paris, who during the Crusades in Palestine had conceived such a passion for his catapults that he refused the fat bishopric of Beziers—"loving better to follow the wars and handle the artillery." [11]

How the sieges of the time were conducted we can see by following step by step Philip Augustus' great siege of the unrivalled fortress of Château Gaillard in 1203–04. The fortress was particularly strong and only seven years old and Philip was one of the richest and most formidable rulers of his time.

The King of France sat down before Château Gaillard in August, 1203, beating off an attempt at relief. He easily took the extensive defences of the great entrenched camp of which the castle was the citadel, for the garrison which held the place against him numbered only 200. He spent the autumn in building lines of circumvallation and contravallation to hold off relieving forces and shut in the place. In February the regular siege was begun. The first step was to widen the high neck of land leading to the apex of the outer ward. The besiegers then built shelters like early modern parallels of approach and set up a number of catapults. They built movable towers which were still useful in obtaining fire superiority on account of their great height, although it was no longer thought safe to risk them right up against the walls. Apparently fire superiority was obtained, for when the ditch had been partly filled an escalade of the tower at the apex of the triangular advanced work by means of ladders was tried. The attempt failed because the ladders were too short, but the assailants were able to maintain their position at the base of the tower. Here they began to sap the defences. A mine-chamber was made, shored up with wood, and fired in the traditional Vegetian way. So large a breach then appeared that the small garrison did not try to defend it but

[10] Belloc in "Land and Water" for April 3, 1919.
[11] Rev. J. Astruc: "Conquête de la Vicompté de Carcassonne" (pamphlet, Carcassonne, 1912).

retreated to the second ward, setting fire to whatever would burn in the outer ward and raising the drawbridge behind them.

Surprisingly enough, the second ward was taken by surprise. One of its forward corners was occupied by the castle chapel whose basement was used for latrines. This basement had a window looking out over the cliff which was large enough to admit a man. One night a handful of daring Frenchmen managed to get into it. Apparently the besiegers had not thought it worth while to watch closely a side so difficult to approach. When the few French in the latrines set up a ferocious din to simulate the presence of a large force, the garrison became panic-stricken. Instead of destroying the gallant handful as they could easily have done, they took refuge in the inner ward. The assailants then were able to lower the drawbridge leading to the outer ward already in French possession. In defence of this timid decision it should be said that the defenders were now only 180 strong. Therefore they had reason to fear being cut off from the inner ward in case the French had been more numerous than they actually were.

The attack upon the scalloped inner ward was now begun. A particularly large catapult (which seems to have hurled stones pointblank or nearly so) was set to work. At the same time a mine gallery was driven under the base of the walls. The defenders succeeded in getting possession of the gallery by means of a counter-mine. However, all this digging had so weakened the foundations that a considerable part of the tottering wall was finally brought down by the catapult. By this time the garrison was reduced to twenty knights and 120 other ranks—140 in all. Although they concentrated to defend the breach they failed to hold it. They could not even make good their retreat to the Donjon which could be entered only by a steep and narrow flight of steps leading to a tiny door fifty feet above the inner court. The surrender took place on March 6th—only five weeks after the regular attack on the outer ward had been begun. It would be interesting to know the effective of the garrison on February 1st and also how many of the casualties which finally reduced it to 140 were due to famine and how many to the activities of the besiegers.[12]

[12] For the construction and siege of Château Gaillard see Dieulafoy: Château Gaillard et l'Architecture Militaire au XIIème Siècle; also Dict. de l'Arch., various articles, especially Vol. 3, 93–102.

Before we pass to the description of western campaigns, certain changed conditions of recruitment and strategy must be mentioned. By 1200 A. D. the knights were only a small part of a normal force of heavy cavalry. The majority of such troops were "sergeants"— a name originally given to feudal tenants whose incomes were too small to be considered a "knight's fee" and afterwards used of mounted men-at-arms not of noble blood serving for a fixed rate of pay. Usually in a 13th-century army there would be four or five sergeants per knight, although the proportion might fall as low as two to one, or rise as high as ten (or even twelve) to one in exceptional cases. Thus the numbers of a force can never be accurately established from the figures for knights alone.

Besides sergeants, a 13th-century knight would normally have with him a mounted and fully armed personal attendant known as a "squire," and at least one imperfectly armed mounted groom.

Besides sergeants, another new sort of troops was municipal troops—townsmen independently organized as such and serving as infantry. Mediæval towns were rapidly growing in numbers and prosperity. Moreover, the Guild system gave to the town populace a far greater measure of economic liberty and a correspondingly higher spirit than that of the town proletariat of to-day. It is therefore not surprising to learn that their militia were apt to be solid troops.

We have seen the brave stand of the Jerusalem municipal militia in 1126, and at Legnano in 1178 it was the obstinate resistance of the Lombard pikemen to the Emperor's knights which permitted the routed men-at-arms of their own side to rally unmolested, charge, and win the day.

At this point it is necessary to say a word as to the effect of fortification and in particular the castle system upon mediæval strategy. On the one hand, the enormous number of strong castles dotted thickly all over Christendom required an invader intending permanent occupation of a district to settle down to a long series of sieges. When the castles were strongly garrisoned it was dangerous to thrust an army deep into hostile territory. On the other hand, the low economic development of the time, which made it exceedingly difficult to keep on foot large permanent garrisons, tended to make the garrisons too weak numerically to cut the communications in rear of an invader. Not military incapacity but the smallness of the garrisons of the time caused so many mediæval armies to astonish modern students by leaving untaken fortresses in their rear. Philip Augustus could have marched past the 200 men in Château Gaillard with impunity had he so desired.

The campaign of Muret, which we shall now consider, is an example of just such marching past fortresses and also of the unequal morale of warfare within Christendom. It is not an example of raiding because Pedro of Aragon was marching toward a secondary base in Toulouse.

The Albigensian Crusade was almost entirely a war of positions; its twenty years of fighting can show only two general actions, Castelnaudary and Muret. The Crusade had been undertaken in 1209 against Raymond of Toulouse and certain other southern lords, notably the Counts of Foix and Comminges, who had been protecting the Manichean heretics known as Albigenses. A huge army took the field and captured Béziers and Carcassonne. After which almost all of them went home in the typical crusading fashion, leaving Simon de Montfort (the father of the Magna Charta Simon de Montfort) to carry on with very slender resources. This he did by means of his own genius, by the high strategical value of Carcassonne, and by the high morale of his troops. This high morale was kept up by the fact that the Albigensian heresy was of a nasty repulsive sort. Even the southern lords favoured it not from belief but because it was, in a sense, their ally in their perpetual attempt to get hold of church property.

The cowardly and slothful Count of Toulouse did not dare meet the Crusaders in the field. On the other hand, de Montfort was unable to do anything against Toulouse, because of its size. William the Conqueror had been equally unable to attack London. Furthermore, he was in a theatre amply covered by fortified towns and by the castle system. Since his army was much smaller than William's had been, it was his game to encircle Toulouse as closely as possible by holding strong points round about. The morale and fighting power of his numerous enemies was so low that by 1213 Raymond's large holdings were reduced to little more than Toulouse and Montauban. Pujols, only eight miles east of Toulouse, and Muret, twelve miles south of Raymond's capital, were held by Montfortist garrisons. The summer of 1213 saw the war transformed by the intervention against de Montfort of the King of Aragon.

So unmilitary are mediæval chroniclers that we are not certain of Pedro's route across the Pyrenees. He may have used the Somport pass, but his concentration point, Lerida, makes it probable that he moved by the Spanish part of the Cerdagne and then by the Puymorens pass. If he did so he would have found Foix friendly but would have been forced to circle around de Montfort's garrisons in Pamiers and Muret. That in Muret was weak, that in Pamiers probably so. Pedro was politically compelled to win quickly, before the Pope in distant Rome could take diplomatic action against him.

Even before his arrival the Toulousans had been so encouraged that they had taken Pujols and massacred its garrison. Their junction once made, Pedro and Raymond moved upon Muret together. Their strategy was as simple and logical as de Montfort's had been. The first stage of their task was evidently to disengage Toulouse from the neighbourhood of crusading garrisons. Pujols gone, Muret was their obvious next objective.

The position of Muret was strong—a narrow triangle with the unfordable Garonne on one side and the Louge (a brook with banks so high and steep as to make it a first-class military obstacle) on another. The castle, which stood at the apex of the triangle, was strong but the defences of the town were weak. The garrison numbered only thirty knights and seven hundred poorly armed infantry. The place, being ill provisioned, must soon have fallen if not relieved.

When de Montfort heard of the move against Muret he was even weaker than usual in numbers for he could muster only 870 mailed cavalry. On the other hand, this little force was of excellent quality and included the high proportion of 270 knights. With even more than his usual boldness, de Montfort threw himself into Muret. Starting from Fanjeaux he made the intervening 75 miles in two and a half days' marching—a creditable performance considering that some of his detachments had done an extra 17 miles between Carcassonne and Fanjeaux which made over 90 miles in all.

In spite of the great disparity in numbers (for Raymond's and Pedro's combined armies were probably at least as high as 4000 cavalry and thirty or forty thousand infantry) de Montfort was compelled to take the offensive because of political necessity. He and the Crusade were by this time so unpopular in the South, where his name is still hated to-day after 700 years, that he feared that the slightest sign of weakness (or even of caution) on his part would start a general insurrection in which his scattered garrisons would be nowhere. He must at all costs keep up the terror of his name which was his chief asset.

So thoroughly afraid of de Montfort were the southern lords that Raymond actually proposed to Pedro to strengthen the entrenchments of the camp and behind them to await the microscopic crusading army. Pedro merely laughed at the idea that de Montfort might attack.

The crusading leader's first move was a ruse intended to commit the besiegers to an assault on the town. This he did by throwing open the Toulouse Gate, at the northwest corner of the place, which opened upon a bridge over the Louge ravine. The first of the three "battles" of hostile cavalry, together with many of their infantry, promptly attacked. Most foolishly, the southerners charged through the gate, naturally found themselves helpless in narrow and crooked streets typical of a mediæval town, and were easily driven out by the crusading infantry. Nothing daunted, the attacking troops fell out of ranks not far from the town and began to eat and drink.

De Montfort now executed a second ruse by simulating flight with his cavalry. Between the walls and the Garonne was a roadway on a lower level than the town itself. Near its centre it communicated with the bridge over the river by which the Crusaders had come. At its northeast end it led to the narrow bridge over the mouth of the Louge by which the castle communicated with the open country. Its southwest approach was through a low outwork which covered the southern corner of the town and communicated with the "Sales Gate"—the one opening in the wall between the Garonne and the Louge.

Over the low walls of the outwork the besiegers saw the crusading cavalry file out of the Sales Gate and turn the corner. Very naturally under the circumstances, they assumed that de Montfort meant to retreat by the bridge over the Garonne and were thrown still further off their guard. Instead of retreating, the crusading column continued on, crossed the castle bridge out of sight of the southerners who had been attacking the Toulouse Gate, and (still unobserved) gained the north bank of the Louge.[13]

What must have been the southerners' consternation when the first of the "battles" of the Crusaders appeared on their flank,

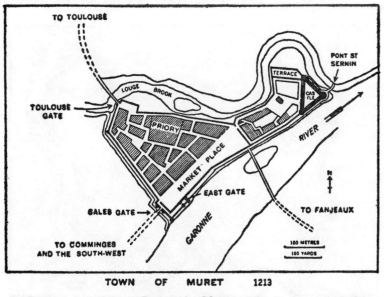

TOWN   OF   MURET   1213

PLATE 14.—MURET.

formed line to its left, and charged them. They were scattered in an instant; some of their knights had even taken off their mail shirts.

This operation, together with Simon's whole performance at Muret deserves to be dwelt upon as a perfect example of the rapidity and precision of manœuvre possible to 13th-century cavalry at their best. The time element can be computed with some accuracy as follows.

The full distance from the Sales Gate, past the town, over the bridge, and up the abrupt ramp leading to the plain is nearly seven hundred yards. From the numerous mediæval gates extant,

[13] For de Montfort's whole manœuvre see Dieulafoy, Muret. See Plates 14–17.

together with the extant brick remains of the northern abutment of the bridge in question, we may be certain that the formation was a column of twos. We may be almost equally certain that the gait was a walk, for (in the first place) it would have been nearly impossible to trot up the final steep ramp, (secondly) silence was desired, and (thirdly) to trot through such a long narrow space would

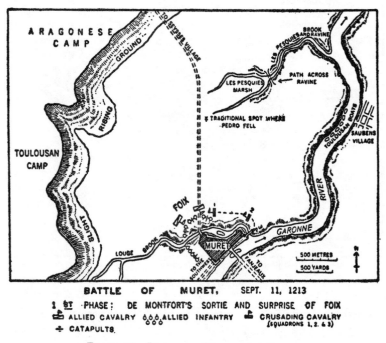

BATTLE   OF   MURET,   SEPT. 11, 1213

1 ST ·PHASE: DE MONTFORT'S SORTIE AND SURPRISE OF FOIX

ALLIED CAVALRY   ALLIED INFANTRY   CRUSADING CAVALRY (SQUADRONS 1, 2, & 3)

CATAPULTS.

PLATE 15.—BATTLE OF MURET: 1ST PHASE.

have exposed the cavalry to the risk of a serious snarl in case a single horse fell or behaved badly—in which case the whole operation would have been compromised. Assuming the gait to have been a walk, we are entitled to reduce the distance occupied by each horse to three yards, allowing a bare one foot between nose and crupper. The length of the entire column must therefore have been at least $450 \times 3 = 1350$ yards, nearly double the distance to be traversed, and the minimum length of each squadron must have been 450 yards. Before falling out to eat and drink, we may be sure that the Toulousans and Catalans must have retreated at least a hundred and fifty yards north of the Toulouse Gate in order that so large a target as they would present might be out of long bow-shot. Therefore the head of the crusading column would come into plain sight practically as soon as it topped the ramp and gained the plain. Historians who assume that the deployment could have been made out of sight of the Toulousans and Catalans have simply never troubled to walk over the battlefield. Assuming a walking gait to be four miles per hour, i. e., 117 yards per minute, the rear of the first crusading squadron would be in the plain al-most exactly four minutes after the van had come in sight of the enemy in front of the Toulouse Gate. The greater part of the 600 yards separating the Crusaders from the enemy would almost certainly be covered at a trot of, say, eight miles an hour, before breaking to a gallop for the final shock. Two minutes plus the time necessary for deployment, must therefore be added to the original four. In all, at least seven minutes must have elapsed between the first observation of the Crusaders by Foix's command and the delivery of the crusading charge.

Meanwhile the main body of the besiegers was getting to horse, crying "Aragon," "Foix," or "Comminges," according to their allegiance. The Spaniards formed, but the formation was ragged. In part this may have been due to haste, although they must have had over fifteen minutes in which to get in line, assuming a mini-mum of eight minutes from the disclosure of the operation to the deployment of the second crusading squadron plus an additional minimum of eight minutes for the second squadron to catch up with the first and for the two together to do the mile which sepa-rated them from Pedro's people. In part it certainly resulted from the folly and indiscipline of the Spanish knights; every important man among them (so Pedro's son, King Jaime, tells us) wanted to fight his own battle with the enemy, making strict alignment and combined action impossible. Furthermore, as we learn from other chroniclers, Pedro himself exercised no effective command but yielded to his chivalric enthusiasm by exchanging armour with one of his knights and posting himself in the front ranks—a piece of generous but unmilitary folly surprising in a soldier of his con-siderable experience since it lost him all control over his forces in reserve. The Aragonese were facing south astride the Seysses road about a mile out of Muret, with the Pesquies marsh covering their left.

Having broken Foix's command, the first crusading squadron had to wheel half right in order to strike Pedro. By spurring hard, the second, with a straighter course to follow, was able to catch up. Both together went at the Aragonese, sweeping before them some of Foix's routed horsemen. Count Simon's orders on no

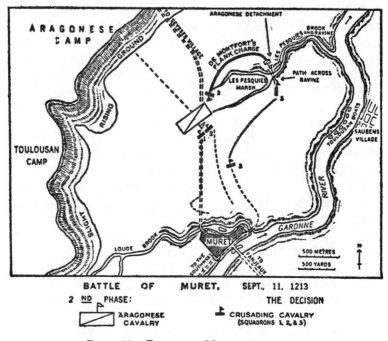

PLATE 16.—BATTLE OF MURET: 2ND PHASE.

account to engage in individual jousting but to charge boot to boot were so well obeyed that the shock was simultaneous all along their line. It was so violent that the Crusaders plunged into the horsemen opposed to them "like a stone into a pool." Pedro's people stood firm and closed around them, hiding them from the third "battle," and the mêlée swayed back and forth with a din "as of countless axemen hewing down a forest."

De Montfort, with the idea of charging in on Pedro's left,

worked rapidly north and east around the marsh until he found himself blocked by Pesquies ravine, which the chroniclers describe as a "fossatum" (i. e., a ditch or trench). Cut in the steep banks of this obstacle was a narrow path, blocked at the further end by a strong Aragonese combat patrol or covering detachment. Such covering detachments were familiar enough, as we learn from the "Siete Partidas" of Alfonso the Wise of Castile, written about 1260, in which they are called "Alas" or "Citaras."[14] If it be objected that Pedro was in no mood to think of such details as posting this detachment, we may fairly imagine some grizzled knight of Aragon who knew enough to take on the job by himself with his own immediate followers.

To go from line to column and try to force the narrow path in the face of opposition was a bad business, but de Montfort had no choice. Time was passing, he had the marsh on his left and the ravine stretching away at his right. At the head of his men he crossed the ravine and set his horse to scramble up the further bank. In this unfavourable position, as he struggled to protect himself from the blows he could not yet hope to return, he broke his left stirrup leather—the third time one part or other of his equipment had played him false that day—but with great dexterity he kept his seat. Reaching the summit of the bank, he unhorsed the nearest enemy with a blow of the fist to the jaw—the Spaniard must have been wearing not a closed pot-helm but an open-faced steel cap. This man seems to have been the detachment commander, for when his followers saw him fall they broke up and fled on the instant. The flight exposed to Count Simon the left flank of the Aragonese main body. He got his three hundred across, deployed them and charged.

All this time the first two crusading squadrons had been fighting hard. Although their close formation and the fury of their charge had carried them deep into the ranks of their enemies, still these last had not broken but closed in around them. Strict order and alignment had gone and the fighting was man to man. The knight who had taken the part of Pedro could not equal his master's prowess, and Pedro himself forgot caution and cried out "I am the King," whereupon those who had sworn to have his life closed around him and killed him despite his valour and his skill in arms.

[14] Quoted by Delpech, Vol. 1, 275.

Whether the king fell after or before de Montfort's charge is uncertain; those who killed him were with the second squadron. In either case, his fall and the flank charge decided the day and a general rout ensued. The five hundred knights of his household fell almost to a man around his body, unsupported by the rest of the leaderless mass of horsemen. The southerners paid a bitter price for Pedro's chivalrous folly in jamming himself into the fight-

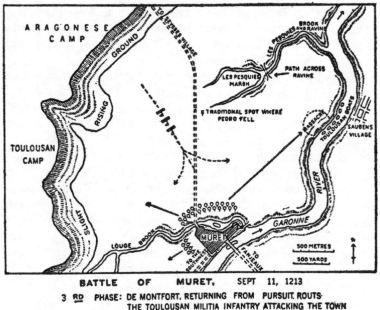

BATTLE OF MURET, SEPT 11, 1213

3 RD PHASE: DE MONTFORT, RETURNING FROM PURSUIT ROUTS THE TOULOUSAN MILITIA INFANTRY ATTACKING THE TOWN

ᵒₒᵒₒᵒₒ TOULOUSAN INFANTRY ⚔ CRUSADING CAVALRY

PLATE 17.—BATTLE OF MURET: 3RD PHASE.

ing and thereby giving up all attempt to direct operations. Raymond and the Count of Comminges seem never to have been engaged at all. We hear of them only as fleeing from the field.

Count Simon, on the other hand, was as wise in victory as he had been furious in attack. While directing, or (more probably) permitting the pursuit of the fugitives by his first two squadrons, he kept the third squadron (his own immediate command) well under his hand and followed the pursuit at a distance so as to intervene in case of a rally. After a short pursuit, he judged that the fleeing horsemen were making for Toulouse, incapable of renewing the battle. Recalling the pursuers, at the head of his three squadrons he returned towards Muret.

Meanwhile the Toulousan communal militia had altogether misconceived the result of the cavalry action. Only a part of these troops had taken part in Foix's unsuccessful attack and subsequent rout at the hands of the first crusading squadron. And of that part only those north of the Louge had actually endured the crusading charge and the rout, those between the Louge and the Garonne had merely retreated (hastily enough no doubt) in order to conform to the flight of those to the north. By far the greater part of them therefore were quite fresh. At first they barricaded themselves in their camp, fearing they would be attacked. But townsmen in mediæval warfare were apt to suffer from rashness; one of many examples is the behaviour of the Londoners at Lewes in 1264. It has been supposed that dust may have hidden the cavalry flight from the Toulousans or there may have been clumps of trees to block their view. Knowing de Montfort to be heavily outnumbered, they believed a rumour of his defeat, sallied out from their camp, and beset the town from all sides.

In Muret, Count Simon's victory was already known by messenger. Bishop Fulk of Toulouse, who was of Simon's party and had remained in the town, sent to tell his obstreperous flock of this and offered them mercy but they would not believe and wounded his parlementaire. Startled at the sight of the Crusaders returning victorious and about to fall upon the rear of their extended formation, they broke up in a panic and were slaughtered far and wide. Some fled to camp and were killed there, others made for the boats which had brought up their siege material and were now anchored about a mile north of the town. A few escaped so, but most were butchered on the high banks by de Montfort's people.

In 1875 a flood of the Garonne undercut and brought down much of the bank, revealing an immense mass of their bones, opposite Saubens and about seven hundred yards upstream from that village. Other skeletons are scattered about to the north of this spot; to this day they are turned up sometimes by the spade and the plough.

The total losses of the vanquished were enormous while the

victors lost only one knight and, at most, eight "sergeants"—a fully armed man in a position to defend himself was already in 1213 so completely protected by his chain-mail armour. Infantry normally accounted for most mediæval battle casualties. Furthermore the dismounted and wounded knights of the losing side could be massacred at leisure if the victors so chose, as they emphatically did on this occasion.

De Montfort's rashness in attacking with only a narrow bridge for retreat in case of a check is explained as Napoleon's putting in the guard at Waterloo is explained, by the political necessity for victory. The tower of the castle commanding the bridge could perhaps, by a plunging fire of missiles from its great height, have kept a little space clear should the Crusaders be driven back.

The rout of Pedro's infantry, most of whom were communal militia from Toulouse, may seem like an exception to the general conduct of such troops. However, it should be remembered that the men of southern France were richer and less warlike than most Christians of the time, that on this occasion they were completely surprised by the sudden arrival of the terrible de Montfort whom they had thought destroyed, and finally that flexibility and speed at getting into formation to stand off cavalry was never a strong point with mediæval foot.

It should be noted further that the victory of Muret did not cause the surrender of Toulouse, which continued impregnable to de Montfort and finally yielded through political action, not to capture.[15]

[15] For a fuller account of the Albigensian War, including Muret, see Chs. 4 and 5 of "The Inquisition: A Military and Political Study of Its Establishment," Hoffman Nickerson.

Anglade's "Muret" reprints in full all the original authorities.

CHAPTER VII

CULMINATION OF MEDIÆVAL WARFARE

1214–1302 A. D.

IN this chapter I shall consider first the campaign and battle of Bouvines, second, John Plantagenet's campaign of 1216, and, third, the culmination of mediæval cavalry tactics in the battles delivered by Charles of Anjou. I shall end the chapter with a discussion of the causes which, in the following century, were to bring about the decreasing efficiency and consequent decline of the mounted man at arms.

In regard to the number of troops engaged, the greatest battle of the European Middle Ages is Bouvines. Fought in 1214, the year after Muret, it was an action of a very different sort. Here it is the infantry of the communes who form the pivot upon which everything turns. Before taking up the battle itself, let us consider the strategy leading up to it and the political circumstances which determined its morale.

Again, as at Muret, we find religious enthusiasm on the part of the French as the cause of their high morale; their King Philip Augustus could truthfully represent himself as the Champion of the Church against the Coalition which menaced both the Papacy and himself. The soul of that coalition was John Plantagenet, King of England in succession to his brother Cœur de Lion. Like all the men of his family, John was a highly educated man and a great soldier. He had for allies his nephew Otto IV, Holy Roman Emperor, and also the Count of Flanders, one of Philip's chief vassals.

Although prevented by political circumstances from putting forth their full strength, both sides made great efforts to raise troops. The Pope had put up a candidate for Emperor against Otto and that candidate was alienating South Germany. Furthermore, John could not trust the English baronage. Philip Augustus, on his side, was somewhat weakened inasmuch as a number of

his barons would go off from time to time to fight under de Montfort against the Albigenses, but this drain on his resources diminished them less in proportion than did the difficulties of Otto and
John. On the other hand, John had the finest Treasury Department in Europe and hired mercenaries lavishly. His father, Henry
II of England, had been the first sovereign in Europe to commute
feudal military service by a system of money payments known as
"scutage"—an important step in the transition from personal services and dues in kind to so-called "money economics." Flanders, the most populous district in Latin Christendom, turned
out in great force.

John now conceived an extensive strategic scheme. Although
he had lost Normandy in 1204 after the fall of Château Gaillard,
he still held southwestern France. He himself, with part of his
mercenaries, would land at La Rochelle and advance into the
Loire districts taken from him by Philip ten years before, refusing
battle when the French attacked him and so manœuvring as
to draw them as far as possible to the south and west. Meanwhile
Otto was to march westward on the familiar line—Cologne—
Aix-la-Chapelle—Liége. In what is now Belgium the Germans
would be joined by the Count of Flanders, the contingents of the
minor allies, and the remainder of John's mercenaries. They would
then march unopposed on Paris.

This very reasonable plan failed through inaccurate timing
and through Philip's combination of good judgment and good
luck. John did his part admirably. Braving winter storms,
he crossed to La Rochelle in mid-February and began consolidating his political and military position in the counties of Poitou,
La Marche and Angoulême. When Philip hastened to meet him
he continued to move to and fro erratically so as not to be brought
to battle. Early in April he turned south through Limoges and
Périgueux to the county of Agenais on the Garonne. Wisely refusing to follow, Philip returned to Paris leaving a detachment in
John's front to contain him. Against this detachment John showed
great activity. In May he advanced northward, won an engagement under the walls of Nantes, and occupied Angers. He would
probably have destroyed Philip's detachment, which he outnumbered, had it not been for the last-minute defection of
a number of French barons serving in his ranks, which forced

him to refuse battle and retreat south of the Loire. It was now June.[1]

Meanwhile after beginning well by reaching Aix-la-Chapelle on March 23rd, Otto had lingered inexcusably there until July, getting himself married and consolidating his political position. At last he reached Nivelles on July 12th and was in Valenciennes on July 20th. By this time Philip, without too greatly weakening his detachment against John, had had time to raise a considerable army and concentrate it at Péronne.

In mailed cavalry both sides had about eleven thousand. The poorly armed feudal infantry may be disregarded. In solid municipal militia infantry the French had from twenty to thirty thousand whereas Otto had a huge multitude of perhaps seventy-odd thousand. Of course the French were a homogeneous force acting against a coalition.

Even yet, although his inexcusable slowness had prevented his marching unopposed upon Paris, Otto's game was a winning one. The theatre of war was more wooded and the river valleys far more marshy than to-day. As long as Otto stayed behind the marshes of the Scheldt his overwhelming numerical superiority in infantry made it impossible for the French to attack. At the same time they could not prevent him, in Valenciennes, from raiding far and wide—so many roads converged upon that town. Meanwhile, reinforcements for his army kept coming in.

In this difficult position Philip moved from Péronne on Tournai, by Douai, Seclin and Bouvines bridge. The semi-independent municipalities of Douai and Tournai (although in Flemish territory) sympathized with the French. The march took five days, beginning with a forced march of 45 miles and ending July 26th with an easy stage of 9. Between Bouvines and Tournai the country was open and suitable for cavalry. Philip therefore hoped to draw out Otto by devastating the countrysides of the German's Flemish allies.

The move failed; Otto merely moved some ten miles up the Scheldt to Mortagne. Here, being only about six miles from Tournai, he was able to observe Philip closely, while still well covered by terrain difficult for cavalry because of woods and inundations. Also he was almost due south of the French army and between it

[1] Norgate, 196–202. See Plates 18–19.

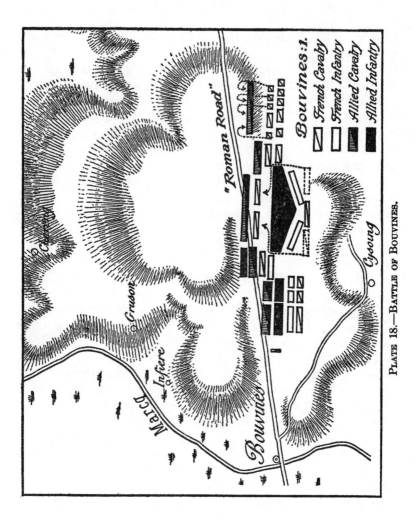

Bouvines :1.

French Cavalry
French Infantry
Allied Cavalry
Allied Infantry

"Roman Road"

Marcq Inf̃ere

Bouvines

Gruson

Cisoing

Cysoing

PLATE 18.—BATTLE OF BOUVINES.

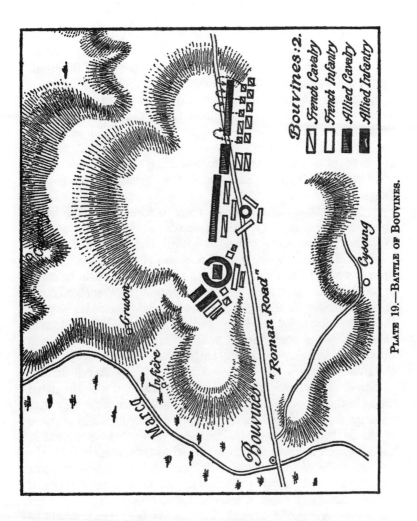

Bouvines :2.

◫ French Cavalry
▢ French Infantry
▨ Allied Cavalry
▰ Allied Infantry

Marcq

Infière

Grubon

Bouvines

"Roman Road"

Cysoing

PLATE 19.—BATTLE OF BOUVINES.

and Paris. The intelligence service of both armies was working well. Disaffected nobles on both sides systematically reported to each of the hostile commanders the proceedings even of the secret councils of war held in the other camp.

Philip saw that he must retreat. So far, in the earlier leisurely stages of the campaign in which there had been plenty of time to consider each decision, the French had had somewhat the worst of it. Philip's aim in moving on Tournai, that is his hope of tempting Otto into attacking him in open country, had not been realized, and the French position was dangerous.

On July 26th decision followed upon decision in the two head-quarters with a rapidity which reminds us of the Campaign of Waterloo. First Otto called a council and showed complete intelligence returns of the inferior numbers of the French. There-upon it was decided that some vigorous move should soon be made in order to take advantage of the rashness of the French advance upon Tournai. A disaffected noble hastily informed Philip of the entire discussion, and also reported on the difficult terrain about Mortagne over which it would be impossible for the French cavalry to attack. Philip instantly called his inner council, in the greatest secrecy. It was now afternoon. The French decided to retreat on Bouvines, slowly and well in hand but with simulated panic, in the hope of tempting Otto to attack them while they were crossing the bridge and causeway over the rivulets and marshes of the Marque. News of the intended retreat was given out in the afternoon and was promptly carried to Otto, magnified by the genuine panic of the citizens of Tournai at the prospect of being abandoned. On receiving this news, Otto called a second council in the evening, at which it was decided to attack the French next day at the bridge of Bouvines. A minority held that it would be imprudent to attack in such open country but the majority be-lieved the reports of panic in the French camp and were unwill-ing to miss the chance of attacking their enemy strung out while crossing the obstacle.

In the morning the French slowly retreated, moving first their transport, next their foot, and finally their cavalry. All combat troops were kept well closed up and prepared to form front to the rear. The bridge had been widened, in order to hasten a possible retreat. Otto followed so hastily that he could have been attacked as his advance guard cleared the marshes and this course was advised by Garin the Hospitaller whom we find acting as a sort of chief of staff to Philip. However, it was finally decided to draw him further out.

The stand was made about three miles east of the bridge. Otto lost a possible advantage by drawing up his front northwest to southeast instead of north to south. A north-south front would have backed the French up against the bridge, and assured his own retreat. The front he chose gave him only the advantage of a slight slope down which his centre could charge. The order of battle was the same on both sides—the municipal militia infantry of the communes in the centre, cavalry on each wing, and a cavalry reserve in rear of the centre under the commander-in-chief.

The numerous Rhenish and Flemish pikemen, apparently in a wedge-shaped formation, succeeded in splitting the centre of the French communal infantry. When Philip charged them he was unhorsed and for some moments in great personal danger. On the other hand, we have seen that the ranks of mediæval pikemen were always disordered by a forward movement, even when that movement (as in the present case) had been successful or even (as in the case of Moorish pikemen of Majorca in 1129) when it had been absolutely unopposed. Presently some units of French horse either cut through the mass or worked around its flanks, checked the Emperor and his cavalry reserve, and then charged the Imperial infantry in the rear. The Rhinelanders and Flemings were the best municipal infantry in Europe. Nevertheless, when struck on two fronts by the French knights and sergeants they were broken and massacred. Meanwhile the French right wing commanded by Garin the Hospitaller had broken the Imperial left. Otto fled.

The last act of the battle was to overcome the desperate resistance of part of the Imperial right. Here certain units of infantry and cavalry were closely combined, quite as in Palestine, the pikemen forming a circle and affording a refuge for their horsemen between charges. It should be remarked that to open the necessary gaps in the circle for the passage of retreating horsemen and then close them against pursuit implies cool, well-drilled troops. Only by an overwhelming concentration against them were these determined men finally beaten.[2]

The battle destroyed the anti-Papal coalition and ended John's hope of re-establishing his position on the continent.

In 1216, two years after Bouvines, we find John driven to bay in England by wealthy rebels aided by French troops. Against this combination he preserved the English Crown to the Plantagenets by winning a masterly campaign which shows us mediæval strategy at its best. It shows us also the strategic effect of the system of castles.

We have already seen how strong castles were under mediæval conditions. The point I now wish to emphasize is their great numbers. In England every port on the south coast was held by a castle. From Dover to Southampton—not much over a hundred miles—there were eleven and these eleven were backed by a double line further inland. The line of the Thames was held as in a vise by the Tower of London, Windsor, Reading, Wallingford and Oxford, five first-class fortresses within less than sixty miles as the crow flies. And so it was everywhere.

We are accustomed to think of castles as the private possession of rich men. But in all the good time of the early Middle Ages, including the thirteenth century, they were crown property and their commanders the revocable appointees of the King.

In part the castles which were to play so large a part in 1216 were of earlier construction. Many of them dated back to the generation after the conquest. Nevertheless before considering 1216 it will be convenient to consider thirteenth-century fortification and siege-work in general even if the order of time be somewhat violated thereby.

In the thirteenth-century castles, we find that the mistake made in putting the entrance to the Donjon of Château Gaillard so high, is never repeated. Thenceforward, Donjons were entered from the inner court level. The Donjon itself begins to lose in importance relative to the inner ward with its flanking towers. Instead of being the core of the defence (as it was before 1200), it is now often placed, as at Coucy, directly in the assailants'

---

[2] For the campaign and battle, see Delpech, Vol. 1, 4–175 and 456–457. Oman, Vol. 1, 467–490 is not so good, especially on the preliminaries of the action. Dieulafoy, "Muret," 5–6, has a note on tactics.

path in attacking the inner ward. Sometimes there is no Donjon at all, as at Krak-des-Chevaliers, Athlit, and Caerphilly.

The reason for the decreased importance of the Donjon in the general scheme of defence was that the military engineers of the time were so impressed with the importance of the flanking fire to be obtained from towers mutually supporting one another that when building new fortresses they did not care to spend money on a single great tower which, by itself, did not develop any flanking fire at all. They preferred to increase the size of the towers set in the curtain wall. They were concerned to rid themselves of dead space, for at Provins and in the addition made to Carcassonne about 1280 we find the towers no longer rounded in front but pointed like a Vauban bastion.

Besides the attention paid to flanking fire by the thirteenth-century builders, we find them providing for a more active defence. This was done by means of barbacans, a word supposedly derived from the Arabic Bab-Khaneh, meaning a gatehouse. A barbacan, as its name implies, was often placed just outside a gate. They were comparatively low works of considerable extent, built with a rounded trace, their purpose being to shelter bodies of men assembled for sorties.

It is surprising that stone machicolation gained ground so slowly, for wooden hoardings could be burned and were far more vulnerable to stones thrown by catapults. But although we have seen stone machicolation at Château Gaillard (1196), and although it was common in thirteenth-century crusading castles built in deforested Syria, it is not found again in the West before 1300. The Donjon of Coucy (1230) had masonry corbels or brackets for its hoardings, but the hoardings themselves seem to have been of wood. It is equally surprising to find the excessive subdivision and difficulty of communication between the various parts of the defence continued in the thirteenth-century work after they had proved disastrous at Château Gaillard. It is true that Coucy had only one main line of defence outside of its Donjon; the designer preferred to put his money in increased height and thickness of walls rather than into an accumulation of obstacles. But even Coucy was so cut up that Viollet le Duc estimated that at least 500 men would be needed to guard its circuit of 475 yards, of which only about 150 are approachable on level ground.

In siege-work, the twelfth century had refined upon the counterpoise catapult by making the counterpoise movable. This ensured greater ease in the adjustment of fire, for the range could be controlled by regulating the distance from counterpoise to pivot. An even more satisfactory arrangement was to have the main counterpoise fixed and to supplement it by a smaller secondary counterpoise which was movable. Unfortunately even with the movable counterpoise there was another variable which must have been next to impossible to control, i. e., the weight of the projectile. Before an accurate fire of any intensity could be directed against a given point, say the roof and battlements of a particular tower, a besieger had to have so strong a corps of artificers chipping stones down to a uniform weight that the game was not worth the candle.

Not improved catapults but improved mining was the chief study of thirteenth-century engineers. When the fortresses to be attacked were not founded upon bare rocks, they preferred to dig an underground tunnel or gallery. A "cat" could be attacked from above and had the further disadvantage of showing the besieged the precise point where the mine-chamber was to be dug.

In 1285, when the Mameluke Sultan of Egypt besieged Markab, a Syrian castle of the Knights of the Hospital, he first took the outer defences and then attacked the inner ward. By mining he then brought down part of a tower of the neighbouring curtain wall, making a breach from which he was repulsed with heavy casualties. He then mined again and in eight days established a mine chamber under the great tower. Preferring to capture the place intact for his own use, he forbore to fire the mine and instead he sent a flag of truce to the besieged, offering safe conduct to engineers whom they might send out to inspect his mine. The Christian engineers on their return reported that the great tower must fall when the mine was fired. Whereupon the knights—professional enemies of Islam though they were—surrendered on terms and retired unmolested with their horses, baggage and treasure.[3]

At John's siege of Rochester Castle in 1215 interesting details of the working of what we should call his ordnance department have been preserved. On the second day of the siege, we find him

[3] Oman, Vol. 2, 51–52.

ordering all the smiths of Canterbury, 30 miles away, to make as many pickaxes as they could and send them to him as fast as they could be made. A little later he writes to the Justiciar—as we should say, the Chief Justice of the Kingdom—to send him 40 bacon pigs of the fattest and least good for eating, the grease to be used in firing the timbers of the mine chamber by which he brought down one of the square angle turrets of the rectangular Norman keep. Even then the garrison defended the breach until weakened by famine, when they surrendered. The siege began Oct. 13 and lasted until November 30—48 days in all.[4]

John's campaign of 1216 is an example of a campaign won by strategy alone without a battle in the field—like Napoleon's campaign of Ulm in 1805. It differs from Ulm in that its success was less crushing, although quite as definite, and was achieved not by marching alone but by a combination of marching and siege-work.

In June, 1215, John had yielded to his gang of wealthy rebels and signed Magna Charta. Immediately after that surrender he began preparing to renew the struggle. As usual in the Middle Ages, we find the mass of the nation (including all the towns except London) in sympathy with the King, whose power was a sort of shield for them against the oligarchy of the nobles. On the other hand, London, the centre of wealth and (as in 1066) a military factor of the utmost importance, was for the rebels because London was controlled by the influence of rich merchants who sympathized with the feudal oligarchy. John hired mercenaries right and left on the continent and used many of them in garrisoning the castles. Although the sympathy of the nation with him was at first only passive, nevertheless his own skill as a soldier and diplomat was so high that by the end of 1215 he had reduced his opponents almost to despair. In their despair they proposed revolution and offered the crown of England to the son of Philip Augustus—Louis, afterwards Louis VII of France. French aid to the rebels began to come in during the winter of 1215–16.

The decisive summer campaign of 1216 opened with a series of reverses for John. He tried to prevent Louis's landing but late in May the French prince made good his crossing to the eastern

---

[4] Norgate, 249–251. For 13th-century fortification and siege-work see Dict. de l'Arch. See also Oman, Vol. 2, 38–53.

tip of Kent. John's next decision was to attack the French before the English rebels could join them. But when the moment came he dared not deliver battle for most of his mercenaries were vassals to the house of Capet. An action in the field against the son of their own overlord might strain their loyalty. Leaving a strong and trusty garrison in Dover Castle, John retreated on Winchester.

Considering only the military aspect of affairs, Louis should have laid siege to Dover at once. However, in a civil war political factors are even more important than in foreign wars. Either from political motives or from folly, Louis preferred to enter London in triumph and be fêted there. Even then he made no move against the untaken fortress in his rear but moved on Winchester, taking the castles of Reigate, Guilford, and Farnham, as he came. Again John dared not risk an action, and on June 14, Louis entered Winchester unopposed. Here he received homage from the chiefs of the minority of English nobles who had up to that time supported the legitimate king. Meanwhile detachments of rebels had swept the eastern counties and taken the town (although not the castle) of Lincoln.

From about the end of June to the middle of July there was a pause. John had retreated into the southwest, apparently lost. It was true that he still held a number of strong points throughout the kingdom. In particular there were the four great strongholds of Windsor, Reading, Wallingford, and Oxford which commanded the line of the Thames and split almost in two the rebel holdings north and south of that river. Dover Castle had not even been attacked. Moreover, the English municipalities (except London, the greatest of them all) were loyal throughout. On the other hand, London's support of the rebels, together with John's inability to deliver battle, made the position seem hopeless.

Now when the Plantagenet cause was lowest the nation began to move. For the first time in English history there appears a true national resistance to the foreigner and to the oligarchic revolutionaries allied to the foreigner. Of course the movement was not on the scale of similar modern movements. National patriotism was in its infancy. Still it was real enough to change the whole situation. In the districts held by the rebels the farmers began banding together much like American minute-men—except that the thirteenth-century minute-men took arms for the King instead of against him. Although such troops can effect nothing decisive, they have an infinite capacity for worrying an invader.

The national movement might not have enabled John to resist had it not been for Louis' error in failing to secure' Dover. From Paris, Philip Augustus taunted his son for trying to conquer England without first seizing its key. Nevertheless soon after taking Winchester Louis went back to London—to be again feasted and to do his best to reconcile the quarrels and jealousies between his French and English supporters. Not until July 25th did he move from London on Dover. It was too late. John was now strong enough to begin the operation which was to assure the continuance of his dynasty.

About July 27th a considerable body of French and rebels besieged Windsor to free London of its nearest hostile garrison, very much as Pedro and Raymond three years before had tried to disengage Toulouse.

Dover resisted so gallantly as to immobilize Louis himself and an important part of his force far from the decisive theatre of operations. The garrison of Windsor did so well that the siege there dwindled to a blockade. The garrison of Lincoln Castle likewise held out against a detachment of rebels.

In the worst of his defeat John had consolidated the southwest, strengthening and provisioning the royal castles there. Now, about the middle of July, before Louis and the rebels had started from London to besiege his garrisons in Dover and Windsor, he felt himself strong enough to move. From Dorset he marched north and recovered Worcester. Thereafter until the end of August he went up and down establishing the line of the Severn as a western limit to the rebellion.

As late as August 19th one of his letters shows that he still expected or pretended to expect an attack by Louis upon the west. In reality the forces of the invader and the rebels were fully occupied before Dover and Windsor. Neither siege was making rapid progress and Louis's Frenchmen, as was the exasperating custom of feudal armies serving far afield, were beginning to melt away homewards. At Dover where the rebels and the invaders were making their main effort the resistance was particularly stout. Louis himself in front of the place was entirely out of the game about to begin elsewhere. Thus the resistance of Dover had already made possible the recovery of Worcester and was to be the foundation of all that followed.

When informed of the true position of his enemies, John formed a plan which in conception and execution shows his high ability as a strategist. No first-class city of the Middle Ages could be directly attacked with success. They were too big and too populous for the armies of the time. Therefore he could not move on London. Weakened as he was by his numerous garrisons he did not yet desire battle. He had already established a westward limit for the rebellion by his chain of garrisoned strong points in Dorset and along the Severn. He would now establish a northward limit by throwing another chain of strong points eastward to the North Sea. His enemies would then be penned in the extreme southeast. With the national resistance already afoot, their surrender or destruction would be only a question of time. In an age without maps or any other of the mechanical aids to modern staff work, such a plan stamps its author as a great soldier.

John's execution was as clever as his conception was broad and sound. On September 2nd he moved east from Cirencester to Burford, then to Oxford, Wallingford, and Reading. His advance appeared to be aimed at Windsor, and in order to convince the besiegers of that point that he was about to attack them he sent a contingent of Welsh archers to shoot into their camp at night. The French and the rebels stood to arms to receive him and thus he achieved his object, which was to gain a start on them for his northward march. Instead he slipped away by Anglesbury and Bedford, making for Cambridge. As soon as this was known to the besiegers of Windsor they saw at once the strength of his move. The movements of their party had been cramped all along by the Thames castles. They were now limited on the west. To be limited on the north would bring them to the brink of defeat. They therefore raised the siege, burnt their siege machinery and hurried towards Cambridge. If they could reach that place ahead of John they could prevent him from getting control of the northern roads.

The situation was now the familiar one of two armies converging on the same point, in this case Cambridge. Perhaps the best known parallel is Moore's and Napoleon's race for Benavente in

1808, although Moore was not out to garrison road centres (as John undoubtedly was) but was merely trying to get away. John won the race with his well-trained mercenary army and in so doing won the campaign and saved his dynasty. He now had the opportunity of planting a garrison across every road north from London. With his army in being near by, the rebels were trapped unless they could achieve the difficult task of breaking his ring.

PLATE 20.—THE CAMPAIGN OF JOHN PLANTAGENET IN 1216.

After John's arrival in Cambridge on September 15th, the rest of the campaign followed by itself. As the enemy approached he refused battle and continued his eastward movement by Clare and Hedingham. Baffled, the recent besiegers of Windsor turned south to help Louis besiege Dover. The rebel siege of Lincoln Castle was easily raised. The Scotch king who had marched past John's northern garrisons right down to London now scuttled home again. Indeed he was almost caught by John as he did so. From Lincoln John moved to the east coast so that the ring about London was complete. It was just after mid-September, and in

the countrysides of the southern counties the national resistance
to the foreigners was continually growing.

The final surrender of Dover, and even John's death late in
October, came too late to affect the result. Now that he had
enclosed the rebellion, the loss of his splendid generalship was
balanced by the political gain to the royal cause through the
softening of the enmities his strong personality had aroused.
As Belloc truly says "John was in his grave, but he had won.
And he had won as a strategist." [5]

If the campaigns of John Plantagenet may be considered typical
of mediæval strategy at its best, the culmination of mediæval
tactics is found in the operations of Charles of Anjou. That wicked
but able brother of St. Louis could handle mailed cavalry with
a varied skill never before or afterwards attained.

His first major action was fought at Benevento in 1266 under
the following circumstances. Between the Papacy and the
Hohenstaufen family who were kings of Naples and Sicily there
had been a long and bitter feud. The Pope of the day offered their
Crown to Charles and gave him money to hire mercenaries. Like
William the Conqueror, Charles also promised lands in his new
kingdom to such nobles as would bring a contingent to help him
win it. He himself arrived in Rome in May, 1265, but the greater
part of the adventurers joined him only in January, 1266. By this
time money was running low so that he had to advance at once
despite the bad season, in order to reach hostile territory where
his army could live off the country. Charles therefore allowed the
late comers only eight days' rest in Rome and then led them
forward by the Latin Way.

King Manfred posted himself at Capua in great force, fortified the
bridge over the Volturno and prepared to hold the line of that river.
The weakness of his position was political, for many of his subjects
were disloyal. When an advanced detachment of his was beaten
on the Garigliano, the whole country between that river and the
Volturno went over to Charles. The Volturno position looked so
strong that Charles was willing to risk the Apennines in February
in order to turn it. The invading army suffered severely from

[5] Belloc: Warfare in England, 129–138. Norgate is useful for details here
and there but makes no pretence to analyze and understand military affairs.
See Plate 20.

cold and snow. All wheeled transport had to be abandoned; many horses died. Provisions began to run short. Finally, when approaching Benevento, Manfred and his army were found occupying that town. The Hohenstaufen had received prompt intelligence of Charles' move and with a good high road to march on had easily gained his front.[6]

Charles' position was now as bad as before Capua, plus a grave peril in the matter of supplies. The Calore was as impassable as the Volturno. Had Manfred merely refused battle the French must have dispersed or starved. On the other hand, Manfred's position was unsuitable for an advance as he had only a single bridge by which to cross.

Charles was inferior in numbers. Severe march casualties had reduced him to four thousand six hundred mailed cavalry. To support them he had a few good mercenary crossbowmen but most of his foot were mere feudal infantry. Manfred's army was larger but less homogeneous and in part disloyal. It included ten thousand Saracens, most of them foot archers with some light cavalry, all devoted to their protectors the Hohenstaufens. In mailed cavalry there were three thousand six hundred—fourteen hundred traitorous feudal men-at-arms from Manfred's subjects, nine hundred Italian mercenaries and twelve hundred German mercenaries equipped not with the usual chain-mail and gambeson but with a newfangled sort of armour of iron plates. These last were the most formidable of Manfred's troops.

On the morning of February 26th Manfred sent his Saracens across the Calore to skirmish. They easily drove in Charles' infantry who came out to oppose them, but were sent flying by a charge of a thousand mounted sergeants. Whereupon Manfred's German mercenaries, in their plate armour, advanced across the bridge and charged to prevent the massacre of the fleeing Saracens.

It is not clear whether the decision to advance the Germans was Manfred's or that of the unit commander carried away by seeing the defeat of the Saracens. If the king deliberately committed the folly of engaging, then he must have thought the French to be in even worse condition than they actually were, or else he must have feared that his own bad political position might grow still

[6] Oman, Vol. 1, 496–499.

more unfavourable should he temporize. At, all events, the Germans charged and battle was seriously joined.

The mailed horsemen of both armies were arranged in three "battles," one behind the other. Advancing at a slow trot with ranks well closed up, at first the Germans swept everything before them. Against chain-mail, even when backed by a heavy reinforcement of wadding, a blow might bruise even when it did not penetrate. But all strokes rebounded from the solid German plate. Seeing his first battle giving way, Charles put in his second. Against these too the Germans still held out, so that a charge by Manfred's rear battles would probably have won the day. Unfortunately for him, they were kept out of action until too late by the slow business of defiling over Benevento bridge. The day was saved for Charles by the discovery that the plate armour—not yet as perfect as it later became—left the Germans' armpits unprotected as they raised their swords to strike. The cry to thrust under the armpits was passed down the French line and by this device the Germans were broken.

The rest of the action was soon over. When the Italian mercenaries of Manfred's second battle finally arrived on the scene, Charles charged them at once in front and in flank and rear as well so that they were dispersed in a few moments. As the second battle had come up too late to support the Germans, so Manfred and his third battle were too late to support them. The numerous traitors in his ranks swerved off just before the shock, and Manfred himself was killed.

The victory was won by Charles' quickness and address in supporting one battle by another, together with the timely discovery of the way to beat the Germans.[7]

Having possessed the Kingdom of Naples for two years after Benevento, in 1268 Charles had to resist the invasion of Conradin, the fifteen-year-old nephew of Manfred and last of the Hohenstaufen.

Naturally, because of his extreme youth, Conradin was in the hands of advisers. He received some support from Alfonso the Wise of Castile, whose mother had been a Hohenstaufen princess, and he himself mortgaged his German duchy of Suabia to raise money, but in spite of all efforts his cause was weak on the

[7] Delpech, Vol. 2, 99–106.

financial side. His strength lay in the zeal with which the numerous imperialists throughout Italy supported him. Charles, on the other hand, had made himself hated, so that the Kingdom of Naples was as full of traitors as it had been under Manfred.

Conradin crossed the Alps in October, 1267, and was gladly received in Verona. Meanwhile his party gained control of Rome. Hoping to hold the line of the Apennines, Charles thrust himself forward past Rome into Tuscany. But hardly had he done so when widespread insurrections against him began in Sicily and among the Saracens of the mainland. When a detachment of his was repulsed from Rome he went back to besiege the Saracen stronghold of Lucera in Apulia. Conradin marched unopposed on Rome and in July, 1268, was enthusiastically welcomed to that city. Hurrying back from Apulia Charles concentrated on the Garigliano.

The situation was now much what it had been two years before with Charles as the defending instead of the attacking party. Again the invaders determined to turn the defenders' left. Here, however, the resemblance ends, for Conradin's advisers wanted to join hands with their friends the Saracens of Lucera. Accordingly they marched up the Anio valley by the Valerian Way, intending to cross the Apennines and then march down the eastern side of the peninsula until they could join hands with the Lucerans.

The season was favourable, the plan was sound, and its execution was vigorous. Conradin's troops were all mounted. Leaving Rome on the 18th, they did over sixty miles in four days, passed the town of Tagliacozzo, and came out in the upland plains east of that town. They undoubtedly knew that Charles had many secret partisans in Rome who would send him intelligence of their move. Nevertheless, granted their own speed over the steep passes, the chances of a successful turning movement were in their favour, for the news of their eastward march would have to travel sixty miles south to Charles at, say, Ceprano before that Prince could begin to move to intercept them. That Charles was able to do so was due to no fault in their plan but to his own rapid decision and extraordinary energy. Within twenty-four hours of Conradin's move from Rome, Charles knew it. Whereupon he dashed northward from Ceprano (moving undoubtedly by Sora) at top speed, sometimes even marching into the night. In three days, with a slightly shorter distance to cover, he managed to reach Conradin's front. Despite his terrific march, when Charles' vanguard met Conradin's just east of the upper Salto River, it was the invaders who gave ground, abandoning the obstacle of the Salto and its ravine to the tired French. Had Conradin's advisers known their enemy's extreme fatigue, they might have won by an immediate attack. It is reasonable to suppose that they did not know it, and that the reason why they made no move for the rest of the day was that they were so surprised to find Charles in their front.[8]

On the morning of August 23rd, the two armies drew up facing one another across the Salto ravine which was spanned by a single bridge. Conradin had about five thousand armoured horsemen, several hundred of whom were Spaniards and the rest about equally divided between Germans and Italians. The Spaniards and Germans wore plate armour but (unlike the Germans at Benevento) they wore it over their chain-mail.

Charles had only three thousand mailed cavalry, including a few Italians of his party. The rest were about half French mercenaries, half French knights and squires who had received feudal grants of land in his new kingdom and were consequently devoted to his cause. The rest of his force was foot—apparently not of first quality. In view of this grave numerical inferiority in horse, Charles determined upon a defensive action. On the previous day, the superior dash of his advance guard had given him an obstacle to cover his front—the Salto with its ravine. This he was firmly resolved not to cross. On the other hand, his infantry were not good enough to take up the usual immobile mediæval defensive. Even after their day of rest they must have been badly fatigued by the forced marches.

Charles had, as his chief military adviser, Alard of St. Valery, a veteran of the wars of Syria and a most skilful soldier. Between them they devised a solution of the difficulty not altogether unlike one of the stock tactical methods of Napoleon. Like the Revolutionary Emperor, they proposed to gain time and tire out the enemy by opposing to him a part of their force. Not until after this fraction was completely fought out was the remainder to enter the combat and attempt a decision.

[8] Oman, Vol. 1, 505–508.

Of course, the details of the tactics employed bore no relation to those later used by Napoleon. The reserve, which included eight hundred North-French knights, was kept out of sight just behind a crest. With it were Charles and Alard, who concealed themselves on the crest itself. As to the line of resistance and its supports, the difficulty was the weakness of the infantry. It was accordingly reinforced by the grooms and servants, and placed in close individual support to the cavalry of the forward divisions. These last were formed in successive open lines "as foragers," i. e., with wide intervals. Each horsemen was followed by two dismounted men with instructions to strike at the hostile horses. The necessity for sticking to the infantry would obviously prevent the cavalry from charging more then a few yards. On the other hand, their open order left them free to skirmish by fencing actively with their opponents from the saddle, while the pikes of the infantry would give them some protection against the shock of their enemies.

The device was risky, inasmuch as the skirmishing tactics of mixed forces of cavalry and infantry could not possibly defeat good hostile cavalry. Evidently Charles' infantry was not considered good enough to stand alone. Nevertheless the scheme worked. The mixed force put up so good a fight that Conradin's people took them for Charles' entire army. When at last it was brushed aside, the invaders thought the battle was over. This misunderstanding was aided by the general belief in their army that Charles had fallen early in the action because the commander of his delaying units, dressed in the royal armour, had been killed. Some of the enemy scattered to plunder. Those still with the colours were tired out by the weight and rigidity of their plate armour and the skirmishing tactics of Charles' delaying troops.

Charles now engaged his reserve in two sections. The first section simulated fear by swerving aside just before the shock, then wheeling off to the rear. Charles now charged with his second section, while the first section again wheeled and struck the hostile flank. The hostile ranks had, of course, been loosened by their first charge. Nevertheless the plate armour seemed impenetrable. Charles now hit upon another of his expedients. He passed the word down the line for his horsemen to close with the tired and overweighted enemy, wrestle with them, and throw them down from their saddles. By so doing they broke the enemy's last resistance.[9]

Charles' versatility is still further proved by his conduct of operations against the mobile Mohammedans in Tunisia. At the battle of Carthage in 1280, two years after Tagliacozzo, he executed successfully a movement which superlatively proved the manœuvring power of thirteenth-century cavalry. Charles was anxious to bring his nimble Moorish enemies to close action. He was facing east, they west. Both he and they rested their northern flank on the sea. Charles first advanced eastward, then wheeled about and simulated flight toward the west, followed by the Moors. He then made a left turn through three-quarters of a circle and drove his lighter opponents northward into the sea. To make such an evolution successfully implies the greatest possible suppleness and speed of manœuvre.[10]

I have already called the campaigns of Charles of Anjou the culmination of mediæval cavalry tactics. Their versatility results from a long development beginning in the ninth century and continuing unchecked until the second half of the thirteenth. I have now to describe the way in which mediæval cavalry declined. In its outline the affair is very simple. The plate armour worn by the defeated side at Benevento and Tagliacozzo was adopted throughout Christendom and its great weight destroyed the ability of its wearers to manœuvre.

The reader must distinguish clearly between the absolute decline of cavalry, compared to its own standard of achievement, and the relative decline of cavalry as compared with infantry. Had mediæval cavalry maintained its tactical standard, or had it developed it even further, nevertheless it seems as certain as any historical guesswork can be, that the general rise in civilization would have resulted in better disciplined armies. This, in turn, would almost inevitably have restored infantry to its normal place as the chief arm. At the same time, the fact is that the loss of tactical flexibility on the part of cavalry came about before there was any marked improvement in infantry. When the infantry improvements did come they found cavalry tactics already in decay. For the present we are concerned not

[9] Delpech, Vol. 2, 107–119.
[10] Delpech, Vol. 1, 440–441, and Vol. 2, 88–89.

with the later improvement in infantry but with the decline of cavalry.

The reader may well ask why the plate armour which implied such tactical degeneration was not discouraged by the abler commanders of the time, especially in view of the defeat of its wearers at Tagliacozzo and Benevento. A most varied combination of causes converged to bring about its adoption everywhere. First, despite the beginning of English and French nationalism, the framework of society remained feudal. A king or great lord could summon his vassals to take the field but could not prescribe the armour which they were to wear. Only the strongest disciplinary authority could have compelled men to put away so efficient a means of increasing their individual safety at the expense of the collective efficiency of the army as a whole. Now feudalism, while encouraging military honour, was almost the negation of strict discipline. Second, military men continued to learn military theory from Vegetius, who is never tired of recommending invulnerability and of cursing the soldiers of his day for laying aside their armour. At the same time missile weapons were being improved; the crossbow was now so strong that it had to be bent by means of a lever or even by a winch, and the power of the English longbow was to astonish fourteenth-century Europe. Finally the Crusades had ceased, and with them the importation of Arabian blooded stock which had made the European horses faster and more agile. It became necessary to cover the horse as well as his rider with the heavy iron plating, for a man weighted with the new armour could not rise to his feet unaided if his horse were killed under him. All these causes combined to make men forget the lesson of Benevento and Tagliacozzo.

Accordingly, in the course of the fourteenth century, all the heavy cavalry in Christendom adopted plate armour and went so far as to extend its use to their horses. To cope with such armour the cavalry lance was increased from nine to sixteen feet in length and correspondingly thickened. Encumbered with such a weapon and burdened with his horse with over 100 pounds of iron, the men-at-arms of the fourteenth and fifteenth centuries could no longer gallop, wheel, and deliver flank attacks. Charges in open order, like that of Charles' advanced units at Tagliacozzo, were completely beyond them. They became a sort of projectile capable only of charging heavily straight to their front, or at best a one-man tank. By 1410, Monstrelet tells us, the French knights and men-at-arms were amazed at the unheard-of sight of a body of cavalry able to "turn at the gallop."[11]

The decline in cavalry tactics towards the end of the thirteenth century was not an isolated fact. On the contrary it is interesting and curious to note in how many fields the generation of St. Louis saw the zenith of mediævalism. In art it saw the culmination of the Gothic, in philosophy Aquinas. In their political and social life men seem to have been happier than ever before or since. The death of St. Louis in 1271 marked the beginning of a general decline.

Naturally, art and philosophy had no direct influence on soldiership. On the other hand, the political and social decline immediately affected military affairs. As in the decline of every society, the heart of the business was moral. There was a tendency to abandon reality for illusion. In the next chapter we shall see even so great a man as Edward III of England making war not with common-sense strategy but in a fashion touched with theatrical unreality.

Another aspect of the political and social decline deeply affected the fourteenth-century armies of the French. That was the sharp new hostility of the feudal nobles towards the lower social strata from which infantry was recruited. The crusading victories, and also Bouvines, had been won by close and cordial co-operation between men-at-arms and footmen. Since then the townsmen serving as infantry had continued to increase both in absolute numbers and in relation to the community. Most of the fire power of the fourteenth-century French army was developed by hired Genoese crossbowmen. The hostility of the men-at-arms toward the infantry had no justification. It was entirely a product of class rivalry and class jealousy from which the earlier Middle Ages had been free.

Just after the turn of the century in 1302, the shocking and unnecessary disaster of Courtrai cast a lurid light upon the weakness of the French armies. A mixed French force comprising both cavalry and infantry was opposed by the infantry of the populous Flemish towns, chiefly Bruges. The Flemings stood in

[11] Monstrelet (Edition d'Arc), Vol. 2, 102, quoted by Delpech, Vol. 1, 443. See also Delpech, Vol. 2, 120–124.

a difficult, boggy terrain cut up by bridges and canals. The French command, very properly, opened the action by advancing its infantry. These last obtained fire superiority and began to inflict severe losses upon the enemy. Victory was in sight, whereupon the French nobles who were of course serving as men-at-arms, instead of rejoicing at the success of their plebeian comrades, flew into a rage for jealousy! A chronicler tells the story:

> Lords, see for yourselves,
> What our footmen are doing:
> The Flemings are all but discomfited.
> Forward great lords and little lords
> Look to it that we have the honour
> And the victory in this battle.
> Let us order the infantry to retreat,
> They have done their duty very well.[12]

To the honour of the French command, the Chancellor opposed the wanton folly of retiring the foot. His opposition, however, was overruled by the Commander-in-Chief, Artois the king's brother, who called him coward and stung him into sacrificing his life by rushing alone among the enemy. Naturally, the successful French foot could not understand the order to retreat. Most of them dispersed in discouragement and disgust. A considerable number were ridden down by their own cavalry. Under such conditions it is not surprising that the charge of the French men-at-arms failed. The heavily weighted horses stuck in the heavy ground and the Flemings massacred their riders.

For the first time since Adrianople nearly a thousand years before, infantry had defeated the proudest cavalry in Christendom. The fact that the defeat was due to special circumstances did not lessen the event, and the behaviour of the French command promised badly for the future.

---

[12] Rhymed Chronicle of Geoffrey of Paris, quoted in Boutaric, 211:
> "Seignors, regardez à vos elz
> Comment nos gens de pié le font:
> Flamens près de desconfis sont.
> Avant, seignors, grans et menors,
> Gardez que nos aions l'ennor
> Et le pris de ceste bataille.
> Faisons retraire la piétaille,
> Se ont très-bien fait leur devoir.

CHAPTER VIII

THE DECLINE OF MEDIÆVAL CAVALRY AND THE REAPPEARANCE OF INFANTRY

1302–1494 A. D.

In the last chapter I considered the thirteenth-century culmination of mediæval cavalry tactics and the causes of their decline. In this chapter I shall trace the working out of these causes and the rise of infantry. In spite of the importance of the longbow, together with the habit of dismounting the men-at-arms in battle, I shall consider the Hundred Years War as a step in the decline of cavalry, rather than the reappearance of infantry. True infantry, capable of playing the chief part in an offensive action, reappears with the Swiss pikemen. The account of the rise of the Swiss will be brief, as they will again appear in a later chapter dealing with the sixteenth century. I shall close with a word on late-mediæval fortification and the beginnings of gunpowder artillery.

While the unreasoning contempt of the French nobles for their own footmen (and indeed for all infantrymen) was growing up, the English were developing a new infantry weapon—the longbow—and testing it in their wars against the Scotch.

The longbow was the chief infantry missile weapon of its time. Simple development from the primitive shortbow as it was, it seems nevertheless to have been as powerful as the windlass-crossbow and was far superior to that weapon in range and in rapidity of fire. As to range, modern experiments prove that accurate shooting can be done at a range of 240 yards and a 9-foot target with an 18-inch bull's-eye. With high-angle distance shooting, a good archer ought to be able to carry 300 or even 350 yards. In 1795, a Turkish diplomat in England is reliably reported to have shot 482 yards.[1]

The longbow was the invention of the Welsh. As early as the

[1] E. B., Vol. 2, 365, article "Archery."

siege of Abergavenny in 1182, Welsh arrows penetrated an oak board 4 inches thick. In that campaign a knight was hit by an arrow which went through the skirts of his mail shirt, then through his mail breeches, then through his thigh, and finally into his horse's flank. Nevertheless it was slow to gain in general favour, for as late as 1281 we find crossbowmen in England still receiving double the wages of archers.

I have said that it was against the Scotch that the tactics of the longbow were worked out. The strength of a Scotch army was its pikemen, formed in deep masses. Poverty forbade the Scotch pikemen armour, and also forbade the growth of a numerous Scottish cavalry. What cavalry there was, was good. Scottish archers were few and not particularly efficient.

A series of fights, of which the chief was Falkirk (1298), repeated the lesson of Hastings by showing that (given the achievement of fire superiority by their auxiliary infantry) cavalry could destroy an army composed of infantry alone. The great disaster of Bannockburn (1314) showed that unless fire superiority was maintained, cavalry charges against the steady Scotch pikemen were more than useless.

Bannockburn was on a larger scale than Courtrai twelve years before and the losing command, although bad, was not so abominable as in the earlier fight. Therefore Bannockburn marks a more advanced stage of the rise of infantry and deserves description.

The Scotch were covering the siege of Stirling, the chief strategic point in Scotland. They took up a defensive position with their flanks covered by woods and marshy ground. In front they dug a line of small hidden pot-holes as traps for the English horse. The English cavalry, charging without proper archery preparation, were, of course, bloodily repulsed. Throughout the fight the archers were chiefly used for the risky business of overhead fire—with which they hit a few Scots in the breast and many of their own people in the back. The one try at opening fire from a flank was easily checked by a charge delivered by the few Scotch cavalry present and the entire English army finally broke up and fled.

After Bannockburn, another series of fights, from Dupplin Moor (1332) to Halidon Hill (1333), showed the English that they could successfully stand on the defensive against superior numbers of Scots by dismounting their men-at-arms and supporting them with their archers. As in the cases we have been studying, an infantry force in close formation, pike butts firmly grounded, could generally stand off a much larger force which had to open its ranks by advancing to the actual "push of pike." Meanwhile the archers would be able to inflict heavy casualties upon them. When the unsuccessful Scotch began to fall off to the rear, the men-at-arms could mount and destroy them as their heavy masses could not quickly reform.[2]

It was after a half-century of English experience with the long-bow against the Scotch that Edward III in 1345 invaded France and conducted the campaign of Crécy.

In the first place, Edward had a moral claim to the French crown. Throughout the Middle Ages—even in their decay—a barefaced land-grabbing expedition would have been unthinkable among Christian men. Edward's claim was not of the best, nor was it admitted by many Frenchmen except those inhabiting the southwestern corner of France which had been Plantagenet land for two hundred years. Still it had some force.

Edward's military problem was difficult. France was wealthier and more populous than England, so that even under equal conditions of transport the French could have put a larger force in the field. Moreover, the conditions were not equal inasmuch as the English army must be shipped overseas, i. e., across the Channel. There was no question of raising volunteers as in the Conqueror's day; times had changed and the men must be paid. It was financially impossible to transport and maintain an army which should be even approximately equal in numbers to the French forces it would have to face.

In this situation, it was clearly Edward's business to try to make up in quality what he lacked in quantity. Accordingly in 1346 he made use of a new method of recruiting, the indenture system. In the last chapter the reader will have noticed the increasing importance of mercenaries. Edward now sought to combine the advantages of paid volunteer troops with the spontaneous loyalty of feudal forces. This he did by contracting with a number of his subjects to raise troops for him—the contractor to command his

[2] For the development of the longbow and the Scotch wars see Oman, Vol. 2, 57–108.

unit, to keep it in the field for a fixed time, and for so doing to receive a stipulated sum from the royal treasury. In legal theory all this had no connexion with the feudal obligation. In practice the contractors would be found chiefly among the king's greater vassals, and their men (especially at this early stage of the indenture system) would be the more warlike and adventurous of their own feudal dependents.

By this system of indentures Edward collected a force of between six and seven thousand men-at-arms, about ten thousand archers, and between three and four thousand Welsh infantry. Adding to these numbers the squires and armed attendants of the men-at-arms, we get something like 35,000 for the grand total. The staff departments, i. e., smiths, artificers, etc., were carefully organized and there were five small cannon.

Obviously such a force was insufficient for the conquest of France. Granted the power of the longbow and the disorganization of the French as shown at Courtrai, still Edward had only the choice between attempting to consolidate a foothold on the French coast or making a great raid deep into the country. With the theatricalism of the mediæval decadence strong in him, Edward decided to raid. By landing on the Channel coast he could relieve French pressure on his lands in the southwest. Strategically that was something. He might pick up enough plunder and ransom money to make the expedition pay its way, and at any rate he would have had a chance to do chivalric deeds.

Even the trivial objective of raiding was neither actively nor judiciously pursued. Having landed almost unopposed near the tip of the Cotentin Peninsula on July 12th, Edward drifted eastward across rich Normandy, until on August 7th he was stopped by the Seine at Elbœuf about twelve miles up river from Rouen. It is an eloquent commentary on his claim to the French crown that as he went he sacked towns and ravaged right and left. Meanwhile the large forces of the French were slowly concentrating on Paris. In particular the French command desired to await the arrival of certain contingents which had been operating against Edward's possessions in the southwest. Accordingly, no field force opposed his slow eastward march and (by what seems mere sloth and folly) that march was not even closely observed. This much was done; the bridge over the Seine at Elbœuf was broken and thus the English were checked.

From the seventh to the twenty-fifth of August, Edward's aim was to escape. He must at all costs avoid battle with superior French numbers until he had a clear line of retreat. No point on the Norman coast would do, for he had sent home his fleet. Accordingly he must cross the Seine and get away, northward.

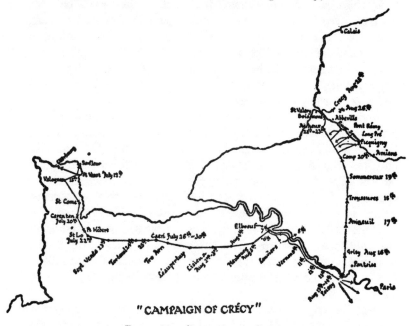

"CAMPAIGN OF CRÉCY"

PLATE 21.—CAMPAIGN OF CRÉCY.

The only bridge downstream from Elbœuf was at Rouen—a first-class city too formidable to be attacked. Therefore he was under the hard necessity of working upstream, looking for a chance to cross, and all the time drawing nearer to the gathering French army in Paris. It was a desperate game which might well have ended in disaster, for the bridges were all broken. Not before reaching Poissy, over 50 miles upstream from Elbœuf and only 13 miles as the crow flies below Paris, was an imperfectly destroyed bridge found which his artificers (his engineers as we should say) were able to repair. On August 15th he crossed.

While the English were crossing, a formal challenge came in from the French king inviting them to battle near Paris. Edward sent back word that he would fight far to the south, then hurried his command northward by forced marches, gaining a day and a half start by the trick.

Even so, the crossing of the Seine gave him no safety, for he would soon be pinned against the Somme with the great French army on his heels. Only a second and still more remarkable piece of luck got his command across near the river mouth on August 24th. At that he lost his train and his booty. Having at last a clear line of retreat toward the Straits of Dover, he turned on the 26th and waited to be attacked.

After such a haphazard campaign, it is a relief to consider the brilliant conduct of the action itself on the English side. In the first place, Edward's position was well chosen. The English front was about 1700 yards long, and therefore tenable by their force now reduced by the losses of the campaign to about 25 or 30 thousand men, of whom 10,000 lay in reserve under the King. The right was covered by the village of Crécy and by the marsh valley of the little river, Maye, the left by the village of Wadicourt and by a park of wagons. In front was a gently sloping valley. The precise formation of the troops, as in practically all mediæval fights, is unknown. The men-at-arms stood in three "battles," one in reserve in rear of centre and the other two separately near the flanks of the front line. On either side of the bodies of dismounted men-at-arms in the first line were 7000 archers in open order, in quincunx like the trees in an orchard, so that any five of them made a figure like a five-spot at cards in order to get the best fire effect. It is possible that archers even stood before the men-at-arms in the front line. They had dug many little holes, like the "pots" at Bannockburn, to make the French horses stumble, and they may have had pointed stakes driven into the ground before them. Edward's entire army was strictly disciplined, largely no doubt by his own forceful character.

The French were more than twice but less than thrice as numerous as the English. For missile infantry they had 6000 Genoese mercenaries armed with the crossbow. In men-at-arms they were very strong and they had a great rabble of ill-armed peasant infantry.

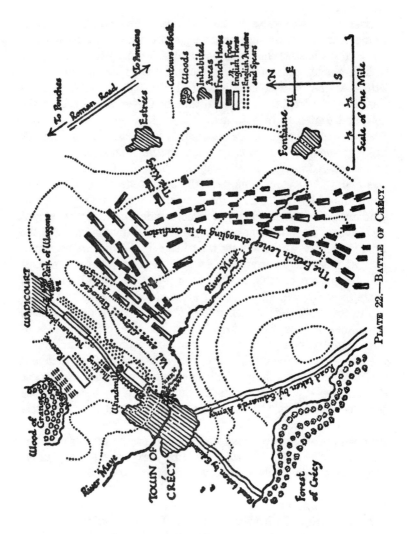

PLATE 22.—BATTLE OF CRÉCY.

Against Edward's disciplined force in their prepared position, the French came struggling up confusedly. The action began about five in the afternoon after a rainstorm which drenched the ground. It opened with a fire fight between the archers of the English front line and the only disciplined body opposed to them—the Genoese mercenary crossbowmen. These troops advanced slowly, pausing twice to rectify their alignment as is necessary for the full effect of short-range weapons. They had been 15,000 strong as the campaign opened but one chronicler reduces their battle effective to 6000. At any rate, they were overwhelmingly defeated in the first few seconds of the fire fight. The English longbow not only outranged them but could shoot three arrows while they were laboriously winding up their machines by means of their little winches.

Disgusted at what he saw, the Duke d'Alençon, who led the men-at-arms of the French van, spurred his command forward upon the Genoese, their own comrades, exactly as had been done at Courtrai forty-four years before and with the same result. The ground, although not marshy or broken by ditches as at Courtrai, was slippery from the severe summer shower. The front of the charge was irregular from the first, and riding over the wretched Genoese tangled it still more. Even at their best, the heavy fourteenth-century chargers burdened with 140 pounds of iron could not rapidly cross a beaten zone. Their twelfth- and thirteenth-century predecessors had been crossed with Arabian racing blood, and had carried men weighted only by wadded coats and light chainmail. Above all, no army on the Continent had ever faced such fire. Horses went down right and left, and men were sometimes hurt in the joints of their armour. Some may even have been hurt through the armour itself. Later in the action the French King himself was slightly wounded in the neck by an arrow. The little English cannon added to the confusion. The only moment of peril was early in the action upon the English right and there units from the reserve quickly re-established the position. The great charge failed utterly.

The rest of the battle was no more than a confused surging of French units, arriving haphazard upon the field, against the strict English line. We hear of no manœuvring whatsoever. At midnight the last attacks ceased. There was no pursuit.

Edward continued his interrupted retreat to Calais and for a full year besieged that city until he took it. It was the one permanent fruit of the campaign.[3]

In 1356, ten years after Crécy, the campaign of Poitiers repeated most of the features of the earlier operation. In each case there was the strategic motive of diversion; the purpose of the move might be said to be the removal of French pressure upon a friendly force at the other end of France. In each case this motive was slight and the expedition was really no more than a great raid, penetrating haphazard and at leisure deep into France, next retreating hastily before superior French numbers, then defeating those superior numbers in a brilliant defence action, and finally continuing its interrupted retreat.

The commander at Poitiers was Edward the Black Prince, son to Edward III. Like his father, he was a good tactician, but lacked ability in planning a campaign. Unlike Edward III, he was headstrong, sometimes wasting invaluable time by sitting still, sometimes demanding so long a march from his men as to lay them up for several days.

The Prince based himself on Gascony, the district between the Garonne and the Pyrenees which was devoted to the Plantagenets. His force was small, more than ten but probably less than thirteen thousand. He had from 3500 to 4000 men-at-arms, most of them Gascon, with whom we must reckon at least an equal number of armed attendants. He had also from 2500 to 3000 English archers, fighting on foot but mounted for transportation, and 1000 lightly armed infantry. Since the French troops later mobilized against him were also far fewer than their predecessors at Crécy, we may suppose that the Black Death (the horrible pestilence which had swept Europe since that campaign) had so strained the economics of the time as to make it difficult to raise large forces.

With his little force, Prince Edward set out from Bergerac. During August he worked northward through Limousin and Berry, plundering as he went. He maintained a speed of about ten miles a day, and this even rate of advance was the one piece of strict method in his movements. Reaching Vierzon on August 28th he turned westward. On that same day, unknown of course

[3] Belloc, Crécy. See Plates 21 and 22.

to the Prince, King John of France arrived in the town of Chartres and began to concentrate troops there.

Shortly after leaving Vierzon the Black Prince delivered his only attack against a fortified place during the campaign. This was at Romorantin—the "Romo" of our American aviators in France in 1918—where the castle was held by a French detachment. It held out five days, the donjon surrendering September 3rd. On the day of that surrender King John, his concentration made, was marching south out of Chartres.

The Anglo-Gascon force was now operating in unfriendly country 200 miles from its base. From the first its commander had expected sooner or later to be attacked by superior numbers. Nevertheless, instead of turning southward, the Black Prince deliberately chose to run unnecessary risks by going on to the west. He may have hoped to get across the Loire and join the Plantagenet force operating north of that river. But on the other hand it had been reported to him that the bridges were cut; since he had this information it seems probable that he knew the river to be flooded too deep to ford. What makes his conduct harder to understand is that the point he made for was Tours, too large and strong a town for him to think of attacking. Worst of all, when from Romorantin five of his regular ten-mile marches had brought him to Tours on September 8th, he merely encamped before the town and sat idle until the 11th.

Meanwhile, although he did not know it, every hour increased his danger. Even as he reached Tours John was across the Loire at Blois, another French detachment was crossing at Amboise, and a third was preparing to cross at Tours itself.

When at last, on the 11th, the Prince learned his peril, he at once started southward by forced marches. In the race which now began he had in his favour the smallness of his force. On the other hand, he had against him the fact that he chose to cling to a long wagon train loaded with the booty of his raid, and the further fact that it is comparatively easy to scout forward in an advance and difficult to scout to the rear in a retreat. The Anglo-Gascons marched well, but the French marched better. On the evening of September 13th the pursued reached LaHaye des Cartes as the pursuers entered Loches twenty miles away. On the 14th the Prince did 15 miles and reached Châtellerault but the King did 20 and slept in LaHaye.

At this point, when only 15 miles separated him from his enemies the Prince took it into his head that he had shaken off pursuit. Accordingly he sat still in Châtellerault for two whole days—the 15th and 16th! Meanwhile John was acting far more vigorously but quite as strangely. After straining every nerve to pursue the English he was now only 15 miles behind them. He decided not to follow them further but to try to reach the neighbourhood of Poitiers ahead of them by a long detour eastward. He may have known of the extreme fatigue of the Anglo-Gascons, and if he did know it then his move was wise. On the other hand, if he feared to engage before joining the reinforcement which he knew awaited him in the considerable town of Poitiers, why had he already chased the English so hard? Had the pursued been able and willing to continue their march, then John's detour would have lost him his prey.

Two days' good marching carried the French to Chauvigny. They had passed to the eastward of the Anglo-Gascons, still motionless in Châtellerault, and both parties were now about equally distant from Poitiers, the French east and the Anglo-Gascons northeast of the town. On the third day, the 17th, the two forces blundered into contact with one another.

John's game was simple enough. It was merely to reach Poitiers, join his contingent there, and after that find the Prince and fight him. The Prince had a more difficult hand to play. Poitiers, which lay across his line of retreat, was too big and strong for him to tackle even could he have spared the time. Therefore he must make at least a small detour in passing the place. Furthermore he must guard as best he could against the chance of being attacked on the march, burdened as he was with his great wagon train of booty. His decision was to leave the main Paris-Bordeaux road which runs along the left bank of the river Clain between Châtellerault and Poitiers. Instead he would cross the Clain near Châtellerault and follow an old Roman road towards Poitiers up the right bank of that stream; within a few miles of Poitiers he would detour to the east of it through bypaths and strike the great Bordeaux road again south of the town. The plan would have been excellent had John been coming down from

the north.   As matters really stood, with John marching westward from Chauvigny, the two armies were bound to pass close
together.   In the event, with both armies going blind, as it were,

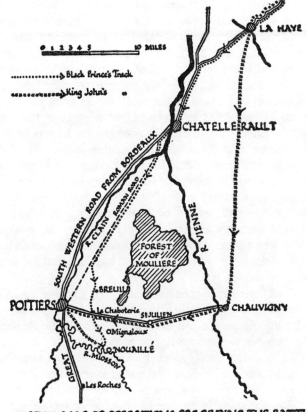

SKETCH MAP OF OPERATIONS PRECEDING THE BATTLE
OF POITIERS

PLATE 23.—OPERATIONS PRECEDING BATTLE OF POITIERS.

without distant reconnaissance, the Anglo-Gascon advance party
struck the French rear-guard when the latter was about 2½ miles
east of Poitiers.

The meeting, unexpected as it was to both sides, completely
upset the calculations of the Prince.   Although the French rear-

guard soon drew off to Poitiers, still he knew that his chance of getting away without fighting was gone. His force was already tired with 16 miles of going, nevertheless he dragged it forward another two miles in order to be sure of at least a little leisure on the following morning. A reconnaissance towards Poitiers assured him that it was indeed John and the main French army that he had in his front. With dawn of the 18th he scouted forward another two miles, found a defensive position to which he led his tired force, and there awaited attack.

Given John's situation, a modern commander might well have moved south out of Poitiers by the great Bordeaux road. By such a move the French could easily have gotten south of the Prince, even had the latter abandoned his wagons, for he was forced to move by narrow country roads and winding lanes. Once south of the invader, the French could then have compelled him to battle on ground chosen by themselves. On the other hand, such a course would have been contrary to the habit of immediate combat bred by the short term of service of feudal troops. It might have shocked contemporary ideas of knightly honour. It would certainly have seemed unnatural to the intensity of the French blood. Apparently John never even thought of anything but finding his enemy and attacking him.

One day was spent in negotiations, and it is typical of the Middle Ages even in their decline that the intermediary in these was a Cardinal. For the sake of an unmolested retreat, the Prince was ready to free his prisoners without ransom and to make other concessions, but the negotiations broke down when the French insisted that he and a hundred designated knights must surrender as hostages. Meanwhile the Anglo-Gascons who had done over twenty miles the day before, were undoubtedly too tired to slip away southward, and the French who had done fifteen miles a day for three days running were likewise too tired to attack. On the morning of September 19th the French moved out to attack the Prince's position.

That position had been chosen with the idea of fighting a rearguard action to cover a retreat southward. Behind it the little river Miosson was crossed by a ford and a bridge which could be blocked by small detachments in order to check pursuit. Under the conditions of the times, the position was long for the force which had to hold it—almost exactly 1000 yards—but it was nevertheless extremely strong against frontal attack.   In front it had a dip or draw about 30 feet deep, the southern slope of which was thickly covered by vineyards.   In this part of France the vine is cultivated upon strong stakes about four feet high, set just far enough apart for the cultivator to slip between them, but much too close for horses or even for a regularly formed body of men on foot. At the top of the slope the vineyards were bounded by a hedge, and for passage through them there were only two sunken country lanes, one near the centre and the other to the left of the defenders. The steep slopes of the Miosson valley, together with a patch of marsh at the lower end of the draw, protected the left flank. The one weakness of the position was that the right flank was in 'the air.

In his dispositions the Black Prince did his utmost to remedy this weakness by covering the open flank with a wagon-park. He lined the hedge and the sunken lanes with archers and posted other archers as skirmishers among the vines.   These formed an ideal cover for such troops, being just low enough to permit them to use their weapons while covering them against a charge. To support the archers he proposed to dismount his men-at-arms except for a small mounted reserve in rear of his exposed right flank.

I have said that the Prince had no mind to fight if he could help it.   Early in the morning when no signs of a French attack were seen, he sent some of the most valuable loot-wagons, under a strong escort, back over the Miosson by the ford in rear of his left flank.   He himself with his great banner rode down to superintend the crossing.   Evidently if he were left alone he intended to draw off the rest of his army.   If the French attack had been delayed until the whole Anglo-Gascon force was in column of route, it seems as if John would have had an easy victory.   As luck would have it, the attack developed when most of the Black Prince's men were still standing to in their chosen position and he himself was still near by.

John had about twice as many men-at-arms as the Prince, say 8000, with what proportion of armed attendants we cannot say. The number of these last may have been at least 8000 more.   To set against the 2500 English archers there were 2000 crossbowmen and 1000 mercenaries armed with the javelin.

The experience of Crécy had disposed the French to look for some new device with which to oppose the English. The dispositions finally adopted were suggested by a Scotchman long familiar with the Plantagenet tactics. John divided his army into four bodies formed in depth. The first was composed of all the missile infantry plus a small picked body of mounted knights. These last were to dash at the archers while the infantry engaged them in a fire fight. The main attack would then be delivered by the other three divisions composed—and here came in the striking innovation—of dismounted men-at-arms and other dismounted cavalry. The underlying idea here was that the horse was more vulnerable to arrow fire than the man. It was hard to armour him as thoroughly as his rider and if stung he became unmanageable. Why could not the man-at-arms attack on foot as he was accustomed to assault in siege warfare?

The idea was sound as far as it went, but it had the weak point of neglecting the factor of weight. Men too heavily armoured to skirmish and manœuvre freely on horseback could not march any distance on foot and then successfully engage fresh men who had been resting or standing still. Nor could they dismount close up to the hostile position for fear of a counter-stroke during the unfamiliar process of dismounting and forming up on foot.

When the French van came in sight of the Anglo-Gascon position they saw the Prince's great banner drawing off towards the Miosson and soon disappearing below the steep slope of the valley. From this the vanguard commanders correctly estimated that a retreat had begun. The sight was too much for their good judgment. One of them who objected that the hostile position was strong and that the first of their dismounted supporting divisions was still far behind was overruled by calling him coward. About nine o'clock, it has been estimated, the French van charged.

The mounted men could charge only four abreast up the two sunken lanes. They had to stand a terrible close fire from both flanks and in such a formation their charge was blocked by the first casualties. They were nearly all killed, but by concentrating upon themselves the English fire they gained for the French infantry a chance to close. Dodging forward through the grapestakes the crossbowmen and javelin men engaged the defenders of the position. At this point, however, the right of the assailants was enveloped and enfiladed at close quarters by the fire of a new body of defenders. These were the troops assigned as escorts to the advance party of wagons. The Prince had quickly ordered them back and they had naturally come into action in prolongation of the left of the original line at the hedge. Their unexpected appearance was decisive. All that was left of the French van—its infantry—broke.

Meanwhile the first of the French dismounted battalions had been struggling forward and was now ready to engage. It had been dismounted half a mile from the English position so that the effort of the mere approach march must have been a torture. Nevertheless its men managed to lumber forward up the slope through the vines and engaged the enemy at the hedge. Against them the arrow fire could do little. The Prince soon found it necessary to engage his reserve, keeping back only 400 men. The reinforcement made the defenders superior in number. Nevertheless the French fought so gallantly that only by the greatest effort was the position made good. It was about ten o'clock.

Now came the decisive phase of the action. The Anglo-Gascon line had been sorely tried and the second French dismounted division was now ready to engage. Had they shown the same spirit as their forerunners, victory must have been theirs. Instead, as the scanty remnants of the heroic first dismounted division dragged themselves back towards them they broke and fled without a blow struck!

It is right to call this piece of misconduct the decisive phase of the action for it prevented a decision in favour of the French, who seemed sure of winning. Except for their little reserve of 400, the Anglo-Gascons were badly fatigued. Some were carrying the wounded to the rear. Others were replacing broken swords or lances from the equipment of the fallen. The archers were looking everywhere for arrows, even pulling them out of the bodies of the dead and wounded. Still the fight was not yet over. Despite the failure of his leading units, the King of France was leading to the attack the last and largest of his three dismounted divisions. He had dismounted about a mile from the Prince's position and the fatigue of so long a march would somewhat compensate for the greater fatigue of the defenders. These last had now for the first time the advantage of numbers.

The Black Prince determined upon a general counter-attack. He mounted his men-at-arms—their horses were still quite fresh— and he put his reserve in the front rank. After shooting their last few arrows the archers were to engage hand to hand. A small

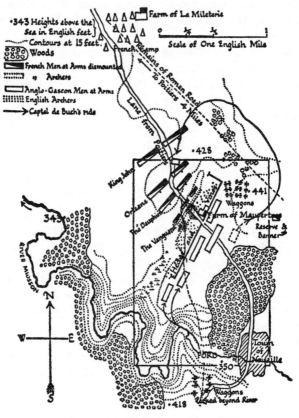

PLATE 24.—BATTLE OF POITIERS.

mounted detachment less than two hundred strong was to turn the French left, keeping well out of sight. They would then charge the hostile rear after the fighting in front had begun.

These dispositions made, the Prince advanced his main body. The French took the shock well and for a long time the combatants swayed to and fro. Then the flanking detachment engaged, launching its charge suddenly from behind cover and displaying a banner for the sake of the moral effect. The stratagem, for it was hardly more than that, succeeded. King John, after fighting with the greatest gallantry, was captured and the remnant of his army was destroyed.

Strategically the Prince made no use of his victory. He merely continued his interrupted retreat to Bordeaux, taking with him his prisoner. The treaty of Bretigny five years later, with its tripling of the Plantagenet holdings in France, was not the result of further military successes but of King John's dislike of captivity. He had been held all that time.[4]

After Poitiers, the rest of the Hundred Years War shows us no new developments of the art of war. From this time on commanders often dismounted their men-at-arms for an attack. In 1364 the combats of Cocherel and Auray show the practice followed, even when the defenders had so few archers that these last could not greatly have hindered a mounted charge. In 1367, at Navarette in Spain, the French auxiliaries of one Spanish faction dismounted their men-at-arms and so did the English supporters of the other faction. In 1385, at Aljubarotta in Portugal, the English contingent in the Portuguese army and the French serving with the Spanish invaders both did the same thing. In spite of so frequent a use of dismounted cavalry, true infantry never appears as the main reliance of armies during the Hundred Years War. Even the English archer was considered no more than an invaluable auxiliary to the men-at-arms.

Meanwhile if the long war failed to bring about the reappearance of infantry as the chief arm, it did make the professional mercenary soldier far more important than before, as compared with feudal troops. In all the engagements mentioned in the last paragraph, both the French and English forces were almost entirely mercenaries.

It should be noted that the increased importance of mercenaries was not due to a marked increase in the aggregate wealth of the time. On the contrary, after the terrible calamity of the Black Death the aggregate of wealth was not more but less than it had been for some generations. Hired men played a larger part because governmental centralization, especially on the financial side, was on the increase.

[4] Belloc, Poitiers. See Plates 23 and 24.

The fourteenth-century mercenaries treated their profession frankly as a means of raising money. They were called the "Free Companies" and they lived up to the name. Often they organized themselves democratically, like the Trade Gilds of the time, electing their officers for a certain term as Gild Magistrates were elected.[5] When unemployed they were a pest.

Before Aljubarotta was fought, the Hundred Years War had entered into a new phase. Between 1369 and 1374, without a single general action, the French Crown had narrowed down the Plantagenet holdings in France to the neighbourhood of Bordeaux and Bayonne. At bottom the reason for so much success was political. North of the Garonne the Plantagenets could inspire no loyalty.

On its military side, the recovery of so much territory by the French Crown was due to a new tactical method connected with the name of Du Guesclin. This man, who was Constable of France, and therefore Commander-in-Chief under the King, was free from the theatricalism of his time. To him victory was important and picturesque attitudes were not. Furthermore, he had grasped the fact that the strength of the Plantagenet tactics lay in the ability to defend a prepared position. Accordingly he took pains not to give them the kind of action in which they excelled.

Du Guesclin's resource was small war. He excelled in night attacks, ambuscades, and all sorts of stratagems. He was a skilful besieger, so much so that his assaults upon fortresses helped to give a new turn to fortification, as we shall see in the concluding paragraphs of this chapter dealing with military engineering. He loved to cut up convoys and to fall suddenly upon hostile detachments. To him, it was no shame whatsoever to retire without fighting when outnumbered. Joined with the favourable political factors, such methods achieved success after success.[6]

To follow the strict chronological order would now compel me to consider the achievements of the Swiss—that is, the reappearance of infantry as the chief arm. But for the sake of clearness I prefer first to describe the closing phases of the Hundred Years War.

Serious fighting began again in 1415, when Henry V of England

[5] Fortescue, Vol. 1, 51.   [6] Dict. du Mob., Vol. 6, 380–382.

landed an army of about 30,000 men at the mouth of the Seine and
laid siege to Harfleur. He bombarded the place with cannon and
took it after thirty-five days. Meanwhile dysentery, together
with the casualties of the siege, destroyed one-third of the English
effective, leaving him only 20,000 strong. As usual under the
Valois, the French were slow to mobilize and consequently failed to
relieve the place.

When at last Harfleur fell on September 18th, the season was
far advanced. Although he knew that a hostile army greatly
outnumbering his own would soon be in the field, a spirit of bravado
led Henry to march across country towards Calais—a folly which
invited the destruction of his entire force.

The campaign which followed shows us both sides tediously
repeating the mistakes of Crécy and Poitiers.

Deliberately following the precedent of the Crécy campaign
of seventy years before, Henry made for the ford of Blanchetaque
at the mouth of the Somme. It was strongly guarded so that he
was forced to work up the Somme looking for a chance to cross,
but everywhere finding the bridges broken and all passages held
by French detachments. Not until he reached Nesle was he able
to cross by an undefended ford. He then turned north toward
Calais, and at Agincourt on October 24th found his way blocked
by the great French army. For nineteen days his force had kept
up an average of over fourteen miles a day. Naturally so great
an effort had told heavily upon it. In spite of systematic plundering, supply had been very difficult. Furthermore, the plundering
had so angered the country people that they massacred all English
stragglers. Accordingly Henry's effectives were reduced to about
15,000. The one thing in his favour was that his troops were well
in hand.

The French, on their side, numbered about 60,000. They had
mobilized slowly. Still full of feudal pride, their commander,
Charles d'Albret, Constable of France, had refused to take with
him 6000 crossbowmen of the Parisian municipal militia who
volunteered for the expedition. "What need have we of these
shopkeepers? " said the nobles.[7]

Had the huge but clumsy French force been able to bring its
overwhelming numbers to bear, Henry must have been wiped

[7] Boutaric, 212.

out. He was ready to negotiate on any but the most humiliating terms. As it was, the Constable committed every possible fault. Finding himself across the English line of march, he failed to attack at once and put off the action until the following day, October 25th. He then engaged on a narrow front, scarcely over 1000 yards, flanked on both sides by thick woods through which it was impossible to take formed bodies of troops. These woods he failed to reconnoitre. Finally, he did not even try to use his archers and crossbowmen, but in each division of his army he masked them by forming them behind his men-at-arms. Naturally, on so narrow a front, his three divisions were arranged in depth. In the first two of them the greater part of the men-at-arms were dismounted, with mounted units covering the wings.

The different French units failed to support one another. Lack of reconnaissance permitted the English to push forward strong flanking parties of archers who fired upon both flanks from the cover of the woods. A heavy rain which had turned the ground into mud made the heavily weighted fifteenth-century men-at-arms, clumsy enough at best, almost helpless. The lightly armed English archers, on the other hand, were far better able to move about. Henry had ordered them to carry stakes which could be hastily driven into the ground to serve as a palisade. But when they had shot all their arrows they were able to close successfully with the lumbering French men-at-arms.

Although the victory greatly increased English prestige, it had no direct strategic result whatsoever. Henry's little force, exhausted by its own efforts, merely continued its retreat on Calais.[3]

After Agincourt (1415) the long succession of English victories (which lasted until 1429 and brought about the occupation of practically all France north of the Loire) resulted more from the political factions of the French than from any other cause. While the factions fought each other, the small well-disciplined English forces could do much as they pleased. Furthermore, the mercenary adventurers in the French service were willing enough to have the war drag on, because they feared to see their occupation gone at the peace.

At the siege of Orleans in 1428–29, the English were too few even

[3] Dict. du Mob., Vol. 6, 382–387; Fortescue, Vol. 1, 54–62.

to blockade the place properly. Like de Montfort before Toulouse in 1218, all they could do was to set up a partial blockade by establishing themselves in redoubts known as bastiles, opposite a part of the circumferences of the defences. Their one hope was to wear down the morale of the garrison and citizens. In this their great asset was the terror of their name and the corresponding discouragement of the French.

During the first phase of the siege of Orleans, the skirmish known as the battle of the Herrings shows no tactical advance on either side. A French force based upon Orleans was trying to intercept an English convoy approaching by the great Paris-Étampes road with lenten provisions of fish for the besiegers. The French had a chance to surprise the convoy, or at the very least to strike it while in column of route, but this chance was deliberately thrown away by a bad command which postponed the attack. When the attack was finally delivered, the escort was ready to meet it—deployed in the time-honoured English prepared defensive position with men-at-arms dismounted and archers protected by their sharp stakes. The French made their usual bull-headed frontal attack and were broken with heavy loss. After seventy years' experience of the English tactics it was a miserable showing.

When Joan of Arc appeared, the whole situation changed. As soon as the morale and activity of the French were restored under her inspiration, their superior numbers were bound to tell. In the fighting at the St. Loup redoubt the French were 1500 to 400. At Les Tourelles redoubt the odds were even greater, 5000 to 400 or 500. There was nothing for the English but retreat. Their prestige once broken, the operation became hopeless.

Joan's victory of Patay, which cleared the English out of the Loire valley, was won partly by the new French spirit of enterprise, partly by a piece of indiscipline on the part of the enemy. The strict discipline which had been such an asset throughout the long war was now weakening. At Patay the French knew that the English were advancing southward but did not know their exact position, which was covered by a wood. A stag blundered in among the English, and the loud sportsman's halloo which they raised told the French exactly where they were. Attacked unexpectedly with no time to prepare a position and before the archers had had time to plant their pointed stakes, the invaders were helpless. They were swept away by a vigorous cavalry charge.[9]

The new spirit with which Joan had inspired the French did not die with her death. It spread to the peasants, who kept up a steady guerrilla warfare against the English. Under such circumstances the invaders steadily lost ground. All the calculations of the soldiers of the time were upset by so new and unexpected a thing as a genuine popular resistance. There was no precedent for it except the English popular resistance under John two centuries before—an incident probably long forgotten. Along with the new spirit among the French peasantry there was a lull in the factional quarrels of the French nobles.

The final expulsion of the English from France (except Calais) came about in 1453. From this time on the English archer has no further lesson to teach us. Archers played a considerable part in the English civil wars known as the Wars of the Roses, but these wars have little interest for the military student. Their long survival in England—we find archers among the troops raised to resist a possible landing from the Spanish Armada in 1588—did not affect the art of war.

Important French military reforms helped to bring about the end of the long war. Chief among these was the establishment by the French Crown of a permanent, regularly paid, professional army. West of the Adriatic such a thing had not been seen in Christendom since the decline of Rome.

This momentous change was effected by two royal decrees of Charles VII (1422–1461), the first passed at the request of the States General (i. e., Parliament) in 1439, the second on initiative of the Crown in 1444. For our purposes the two decrees may be treated as one. The crying need for reform sprang from the disturbances caused by the "Free Companies" of mercenary adventurers. Accordingly the Crown took upon itself the appointment of all captains of companies, and expressly forbade the raising of troops by unauthorized persons. Fifteen "Compagnies des Ordonnances du Roi," i. e., "Of the King's Servants" or "For the King's Service," were raised. It is interesting to note that the legislator seems to fear that it may be difficult to keep the size of the companies within bounds. Each of them was strictly limited

[9] Anatole France, Joan of Arc.

to 100 "lances," the term lance being understood as a man-at-arms, his squire, his groom (who is to be armed with a cutlass), and three archers. The total enlisted strength was thus fixed at 18,000.[10]

These Ordonnance Companies were to serve as an example for Christendom. The type of army represented by them was to dominate European warfare until the French Revolution imagined the armed nation. To this day the United States Regular Army is a professional force nationally recruited, and so is the post-war army of the German Reich, while the British army is of the same sort plus a considerable barbarian element. Another provision in the same decree made for discipline and centralization under the Crown by providing that all nobles must be responsible to the King for the acts of their own vassals when on royal service, exactly as the King's hired captains had always been held responsible for their commands.

Besides the decree establishing the Ordonnance Companies, Charles VII's reign saw two other major innovations. A permanent artillery department was organized and in 1436 the first chief of the French artillery, with the title of "Master of the Artillery" was commissioned and took the oath.[11]

In 1448 the Crown tried to establish an organized militia force throughout the Kingdom. The officers of the King were to choose out of every parish a man to serve in the new body. They were called "Francs (i. e., free) Archers" because they were exempted from certain taxes, and because most of them were armed with the bow. Inspired by the patriotic desire to get rid of the English, they did some good service in the last battles of the Hundred Years War. But on the whole their record was decidedly spotty, as might have been expected from such a force. Their chief importance was that their establishment showed a desire to give some sort of organization to infantry and to carry forward the principle of centralization under the Crown.[12]

The natural opposition of the nobles to the new state of things was lessened by the fact that enlistment in the Ordonnance Companies offered a career to the more active and ambitious individuals among the nobility itself. Even the chance of becoming an archer in an Ordonnance Company was a stepping stone to greater things.

[10] Boutaric, 308–317.   [11] Dict. du Mob., 392.   [12] Boutaric, 317–335.

In France, the middle and end of the fifteenth century, which saw such notable reforms in military organization, saw no corresponding development in tactics. There was a reaction against the headstrong folly and blind belief in the man-at-arms which had lost so many battles, but that reaction produced no new thought-out system of its own. In tactical doctrine, especially as to the relation between infantry and cavalry, the period is one of confusion.

As instances of this confusion, I shall quote two passages from de Comines, for many years a councillor to Louis XI of France; together with a royal decree of Charles VIII, Louis' successor.

In the first passage, de Comines discusses the conduct of the Burgundians at the battle of Montlhéry in 1465:

> It was at first proposed that everyone without exception, should dismount; and afterwards this proposal was modified, for almost all the men-at-arms mounted. Several good knights and esquires were commanded to remain afoot . . . for among the Burgundians at that time those who dismounted with the archers were the most honoured (of all), and always a great number of men of good condition followed this custom, so that the people should be encouraged and should fight better. And this custom they learned from the English in whose company Duke Philip in his youth had made war in France. . . .[13]

This passage shows clearly that the connexion of the English habit of dismounting their men-at-arms with their inveterate preference for defensive tactics had not been grasped at all. Evidently neither the Burgundians nor any other French faction had reasoned the matter out. As late as 1465, in this same haphazard battle of Montlhéry, we find certain units of Burgundian men-at-arms riding down their own archers after the abominable fashion of Courtrai (1302) and Crécy (1346).[14]

---

[13] De Comines: Memoirs, Bk. I, Ch. III.
"De prime face fut advisé que tout se mettroit à pied, sans nul excepter; et depuis muerent propos, car presque tous ces hommes d'armes monterent à cheval. Plusieurs bons chevaliers et escuyers furent ordonnés a demourer à pied, . . . car entre les Bourguignons lors estoient les plus honorés ceux qui descendoient avec les archiers; et toujours s'y mettoit grande quantité de gens de bien, afin que le peuple en fust plus assuré et combatist mieux, et tenoient cela des Anglois, avec les quels le duc Phillipe avoit fait la guerre en France, durant sa jeunesse. . . ."
[14] Dict. du Mob., Vol. 6, 396, 399.

In the second passage from de Comines, that highly placed and experienced man quaintly expresses his own idea of tactics as follows:

> . . . my opinion is that the sovereign thing in the world for battles is to have archers; but they should number thousands, for in small numbers they are worth nothing, and they should be ill mounted, so that they may have no regret whatsoever at losing their horses, or else they should have no horses at all. . . .[15]

Before commenting on this opinion of de Comines, I prefer to contrast with it a decree of Charles VIII (1483–1498) issued in 1485. The purpose of the decree is to re-establish the Francs Archers, for it seems that that militia infantry had died out since its creation in 1448. The preamble runs as follows:

> Whereas it is necessary, together with . . . our ordonnance (sc. companies) who are all mounted, to have . . . a number of infantry . . . whereas mounted men cannot easily accomplish great exploits without infantry . . .[16]

On comparing this passage with de Comines' on archers, the confusion of late fifteenth-century tactical doctrine is clear. While de Comines rates archers above men-at-arms, Charles VIII makes them only a necessary auxiliary arm, a statement which might have been truly made at any time during the long supremacy of cavalry.

The source of such a confusion is to be found in the experience of the Hundred Years War. While fire superiority had always been important in supporting attacks against an immobile defensive and in helping to repel attacks against such a defensive, nevertheless the English longbow had made it more important still. Fur-

---

[15] De Comines: Memoirs, Bk. I, Ch. IV.

". . . mon advis est, que la souveraine chose du monde pour les batailles, sont les archiers mais qu'ils soient à milliers, car en petit nombre ne valent rien, et que ce soient gens mal montés, a ce qu'ils n'ayent point le regret de perdre leurs chevaux, ou du tout n'en ayent point; . . ."

[16] Ordonnance (i. e., decree) du 8 Decembre, 1485; Godefroy, Charles VIII, 502, quoted Boutaric, 329.

"Attendu qu'il serait necessaire, avec . . . nos ordonnances, qui sont tous à cheval, avoir . . . quelques nombres de gens de guerre à pied, . . . attendu que, gens de cheval ne peuvent aisément faire grand exploit sans gens de pied . . ."

thermore, the increasing weight and clumsiness of plate armour had deprived the armoured horseman of the rapidity and suppleness of movement which would have helped him to cope with the English tactics.

On the other hand, archers were not tactically self-sufficient. In an action between two mounted bodies they were not worth while. In the open they could not stand on the defensive without strong supports of dismounted men-at-arms to take the shock of the hostile charge. Whenever they could they covered themselves with stakes or some other form of entrenchment. Most important of all, they lacked offensive power because (under normal conditions) they could not close. It needed the heavy mud of Agincourt to enable them to do so—even in support of their own men-at-arms. All told then, the English archers never made infantry the chief arm. The Hundred Years War shows us the decadence of mediæval cavalry. Despite de Comines, it does not mark the beginning of the superiority of infantry.

The first nation to astonish Europe with an infantry of real offensive power were the Swiss. As with the Scotch, poverty forbade these mountaineers to develop a numerous and efficient cavalry. Moreover, the mountainous nature of the country, as in ancient Greece, tended to limit mounted action. Therefore the Swiss were footmen not by choice but by neccessity.

The same cause—poverty—forbade the Swiss complete armour, and this again suited their rough country since an unarmoured man can better scramble over difficult ground.

Military genius enabled the fourteenth- and fifteenth-century Swiss to get over the foregoing limitations—as the Scotch, for instance, never did. The problem was the same as that of the professional Roman army in the fourth century. Its general terms had remained unchanged for a thousand years. For a fuller discussion I refer my readers to my account of the fourth century and also to my general discussion of mediæval war. Suffice it here that once the cavalryman was provided with a shaped saddle and stirrups, together with armour both for himself and for his horse, the infantryman found it necessary to have a weapon long enough to keep him at a distance. Hence the pike. Whether, granted a higher standard of discipline plus individual initiative, the sword and buckler man (such as the old Roman legionary) would have survived and done better than the pikeman, we cannot tell. It seems possible. The offensive weakness of the pike was that to use it it had to be levelled, and once levelled it could not be traversed freely from side to side because of the close deep formations necessitated by its use. Hence pikemen can be used only in regular formations of the strictest sort and have great difficulty in making good any gap which may appear in their ranks. Once a bad gap does appear, they are at the mercy of cavalry or of resolute infantry armed with the sword.

Now anyone who has drilled or watched other men drilling knows how extraordinarily hard it is to advance in close order and still maintain a regular front. Take even so small a unit as a war-strength company. Put them on a level parade ground in the midst of profound peace and tell them to advance in company front for a hundred yards. Their line will ripple to and fro constantly as they try to correct the beginnings of little dislocations. It is astonishing how much practice the thing takes. Imagine then a body of several thousand pikemen advancing in action, and remember that the penetration of a single bad gap by the enemy may well mean disaster. Then you will have an idea of the extraordinary perfection of drill and discipline required for such a movement.

This necessary perfection the Swiss achieved; and to that achievement (not to the equipment, which was only the instrument with which the thing was done) they owed their unique position in fifteenth-century Europe. Even to-day, in the military exercise of rifle shooting their whole citizenry, in their spare time, show a continuous application unequalled in the world. They are always at it. Just so in the late mediæval period we are not surprised to learn that from childhood they were always practising the advance in close order. Boys too young to carry a man's-size pike received little pikes with which to drill. Military drills and reviews took place on holidays and Fair days. They were even used at the celebration of weddings.[17]

The Swiss perfection of drill and discipline was well served by a highly specialized equipment. They developed a pike with an

[17] For the intense Swiss application and for their march music, see Fortescue, Vol. 1, 83–84. For their equipment and formations see Dodge: Gustavus Adolphus, 11–13.

18-foot shaft and beyond that a 3-foot iron shank to keep the head from being cut off by a sword stroke. In all history such a monster can be compared only with the Macedonian sarissa, and even under Alexander we never hear of the Macedonian phalanx either repulsing or delivering flank attacks like the Swiss. It gave them no less than four rows of points protruding beyond the front. We know that they marched in cadence to music—apparently they were the first modern men to do so. Besides pikemen they had halberdiers, evidently to finish the job after the pikemen. The halberd was a battle-axe with a handle no less than eight feet long, and like the long pike must have taken great strength and endless practice to wield. In the hands of a powerful veteran it was probably more effective against the perfected plate armour of the day than any other infantry or cavalry weapon—it could even decapitate a horse. Besides pikemen and halberdiers the Swiss had a small proportion of missile troops used for skirmishing. These were at first crossbowmen, later arquebusiers, but were never of first-rate importance.

A Swiss army was usually formed in three masses. It might attempt to envelop a flank or to pierce the opposing centre by means of the time-honoured wedge formation. When threatened with envelopment they formed square, not the earlier mediæval circle. The missile troops, and apparently the halberdiers, were posted at the corners. The Swiss infantry could move rapidly without losing formation, an ominous fact for the increasingly cumbrous cavalry of the time.

The Swiss campaigns divide into two phases. In the first (1315–1476) we find them defending their independence first against the House of Austria and then against that of Burgundy. In the second phase, from 1476 on, war became the chief industry of the country and the Swiss hired themselves out as soldiers in a purely commercial spirit.

The first of the Swiss victories was at Morgarten in 1315. In it we find few of the characteristic features of later Swiss tactics. A large Austrian army from 15,000 to 20,000 strong, relying chiefly upon its men-at-arms, invaded the Swiss valleys and foolishly involved themselves in an icy mountain pass between a lake and a precipice. The Swiss numbered only 1300 to 1500 unarmoured foot but on such a terrain they had it all their own way. From above they riddled the Austrian formation by rolling down tree-trunks and boulders upon it. In the panic which ensued, the mountaineers attacked with the halberd and destroyed their opponents.

At Laupen in 1339, the first signs of offensive power on the part of the Swiss infantry appear. Here the Swiss drove the hostile infantry from the field, and then successfully stood off the charges of the men-at-arms.

The important victory of Sempach (1386) finally freed the Swiss from the Austrian House of Hapsburg. Here again the mountaineers were outnumbered, although not so heavily as at Morgarten. At Sempach they had between 1500 and 1600 men against 6000 Austrians. The terrain was sloping meadowland cut up by hedges and streams. I would remind the reader that open field agriculture had been from the beginning an important factor in the supremacy of cavalry. The Austrians therefore dismounted their men-at-arms and at the first shock they drove back the Swiss. Their success, however, was short-lived. We have already seen how impossible it was to advance for any distance on foot while wearing the heavy plate armour of the time, without extreme fatigue. In this case the difficulty of the ground and still more the sun of a hot July day made the task of the cumbrous Austrian men-at-arms still harder. Meanwhile the Swiss, unburdened by armour, charged again and again. At last the Hapsburg troops broke and their commander was killed.

Sempach taught the Swiss their strength. Two years later at Näfels a mere handful of them defeated another Austrian army.

Perhaps the most striking of all their feats of arms is the battle fought near Basle in 1444. At this time the Hundred Years War was drawing to a close, and consequently there were great numbers of unemployed mercenary adventurers known as Free-Lances—men ready to sell their swords to the highest bidder. With their aid the Hapsburgs made a last attempt to conquer the Swiss. The Free-Lances were from 30,000 to 50,000 strong. Either in bravado or (more probably) in desperation, a tiny Swiss force of from 1200 to 1600 men met them in the field. It is not surprising that so large a body of professional soldiers was able to destroy such a handful of opponents. The point is that the Swiss handful did so well and inflicted such heavy losses on the overwhelming force of freebooters that these last decided they had had enough. Instead of persisting in their invasion they were glad to retire.

The fame of the Swiss was raised to its highest point by their war against Charles the Rash, Duke of Burgundy—at the time one of the most powerful princes in Christendom. Hostilities began after a complicated series of intrigues between the French Crown, the Hapsburgs, the Duke and the Swiss.

The first battle was fought in March, 1476, near the town of Grandson whose castle Charles had just retaken from the Swiss. The Swiss were moving to relieve the place, but when they heard of its fall they nevertheless continued their advance. Their formation was in two separate bodies, one of which was to attack the Burgundian entrenched camp in front. Meanwhile the other was to make a turning movement out of sight behind some high hills and suddenly attack the camp in flank. Learning of the approach of the Swiss, Charles seems to have thought that the first of their two bodies was their entire army. At all events he pushed forward his cavalry over an unfavourable terrain, charged, and was sharply repulsed.

The mobility of the Swiss now came into play with decisive effect. Charles ordered his cavalry to retreat towards the camp, intending to renew the fight on better ground. Had he been opposed by mediæval infantry of the normal type he would have had ample time to make new dispositions. As it was, the Swiss pressed him so hotly that his retreating troops, in order to break contact, had to turn their retreat into a flight and arrived at the camp in confusion with the Swiss still close at their heels. Just at this point the sudden and unexpected appearance of the second body of Swiss (who had now completed their turning movement), threw the whole Burgundian army into a panic. Practically without resistance they abandoned their camp with its entrenchments and artillery and fled in disorder. Throughout the action the Burgundians had been so nonplussed by the hostile tactics that the losses of both sides were insignificant.

In June of the same year—1476—about three months after Grandson, the Swiss again defeated Charles at the far bloodier battle of Morat. After a considerable effort to raise troops the Duke had with him rather more than 20,000 men including 3000 English archers. With this force, supported by a formidable artillery, he laid siege to the little town of Morat. The Swiss moved to raise the siege with 35,000 men, of whom 4000 were cavalry—an unusually high proportion of this arm for a Swiss army. Of the infantry 11,000 were pikemen and 10,000 had halberds. Ten thousand carried the crude infantry firearms of the time.

The Swiss took position on some rising ground overlooking Charles' camp and there waited to be attacked. The Duke however had learned caution at Grandson. He drew up his troops on level ground below the Swiss position, held them there motionless for some hours under a heavy rain, and finally withdrew behind his entrenchments. The Swiss then determined to take the offensive. As at Grandson, they sent a good-sized detachment to make a turning movement behind cover. Their frontal attack was checked (indeed their long pikes were not suited to assaulting entrenchments) but at least it succeeded in concentrating the enemy's attention against itself. The flank attack together with a brisk sortie from the town succeeded in carrying the Burgundian palisades after heavy losses on both sides. The rain probably softened the bowstrings of the English archers and this may have prevented them from doing themselves justice.[18]

In 1477 the Swiss for the first time sent an army away from their native mountains. Acting in concert with certain lowland cities allied with them against Charles, they advanced to Nancy and there destroyed the Duke's last army. As at Grandson and Morat, it was their manœuvring power and mobility which obtained the decision by means of a combined front and flank attack.

Already, in 1474, the Swiss had begun the practice of hiring themselves out as soldiers to foreign governments; and for over a century they were so much in demand that war became the chief industry of the country.

The fortunes of the Swiss on the battlefields of the sixteenth century do not concern this chapter. Let it here suffice that having begun as brilliant and daring innovators in tactics, they were extremely slow to keep pace with later improvements introduced in the infantry of other nations. In particular they long persisted in the extremely broad and deep phalanx formation with which their first victories were won, and they never excelled in fire power.

[18] Dict. du Mob., Vol. 6, 400–402.

Nevertheless it remains their great achievement that they were the first since the Romans to develop a real attacking infantry.

At the close of the fifteenth century, Christendom had not yet learned the Swiss lesson. The age of cavalry was closing but had not yet completely closed. It was left for the infantry footmen of the sixteenth century to re-establish infantry as the chief arm.

I will close this chapter by considering briefly late-mediæval fortification and the influence of gunpowder.

The chief improvement introduced into fortification by the engineers of the fourteenth century was stone machicolation. We have seen that the chief problem of the mediæval military architect was defence against sapping or battering the base of his walls. We have seen also that the men of the twelfth and thirteenth centuries attempted a solution by means of overhanging wooden galleries known as "hoards" or "hoardings." However, it was the weakness of a hoarding that it might be burned. As the improvement in combustibles increased the seriousness of this danger, the fourteenth-century engineers replaced the hoarding with an overhang all of stone which permitted a direct command of the wall base.

It is true that long before the fourteenth century, stone machicolations were to be found in the crusading castles built in the treeless country of Syria. It is also true that exceptional instances of it are found in the West. Thus the Castle of Ghent, built as early as 1180, shows an imperfect and non-continuous form of it. The donjon of Château Gaillard (1198) has it in a very perfect form. Despite such exceptions, the use of stone machicolation did not become general before 1300. The thirteenth-century architect of Coucy compromised by having wooden hoardings carried on stone brackets.

In the fifteenth century, pre-gunpowder fortifications culminated in the establishment of easy lateral communication throughout the perimeter of the defence. At first glance this seems obvious enough. In the U. S. Army Field Service Regulations of 1914, Section 193, "good communications throughout the position" are laid down axiomatically as one of the requisites to be sought in a defensive position, and in permanent fortifications the same principle obtains. Therefore its late appearance in mediæval military engineering deserves explanation. The reason was that mediæval engineers so feared surprise that they were willing to sacrifice communication in order to delay a besieger by making each part of their fortresses as independent as possible. For instance, the fourteenth-century walls of Avignon have stone machicolation, but there the towers still interrupt the curtain walls. To pass through a tower from one curtain to another sometimes one had to cross little drawbridges, and always to pass through narrow doors and go up and down steps. This system was intended to compel the besiegers to take the castle stone by stone, each tower being an independent redoubt. But it had the disadvantage of demanding a numerous garrison and the exercise of the greatest vigilance at all points, for if the besiegers could get a foothold anywhere it was hard to concentrate the garrison against them because of the difficult lateral communications of the defence. If a tower could be surprised and suddenly rushed, the assailants could be dislodged only with difficulty. With the longbows and powerful crossbows of the second half of the fourteenth century, and with the increasing proportion of trained and disciplined mercenary troops in the armies of the time, an energetic leader like Du Guesclin could often rush twelfth- and thirteenth-century works. The curtains, which were lower than the towers, could frequently be escaladed with ladders. Accordingly we find that by 1400 a new system of defence was put in force.

The castle of Pierrefonds is perhaps the best example of the new system. First, there is a low outwork, without flankments. This runs close under three sides of the castle proper, which is a parallelogram a little over 100 yards on its long sides and about 75 yards on the ends. The curtains are over 100 feet high and the entire circuit of the defence can be made on the same level. Stone machicolations and two stages of battlements run all around. The better to resist mining, the lower walls have no loop-holes but are solid throughout, except for a small sally port on the side opposite to the main entrance. Viollet-le-Duc estimates that the ends could be defended with 40 men each and the sides with 60 men each, while to attack effectively on two sides at once would necessitate a besieging army of at least 2000 men and probably many more.[19]

At this point matters stood when the influence of gunpowder

[19] For machicolation and for fifteenth-century fortification, see Dict. de l'Arch.

began to be felt in sieges. The time and place of its invention, and whether or not it had anything to do with incendiary mixtures such as Greek fire, are equally unknown. That the Chinese or Mohammedans first used it has been alleged but never proved. Roger Bacon (1214–1294), the Oxford Franciscan, in his "De Mirabili Potestate Artis et Naturæ," written in 1242, gives a receipt for making gunpowder, says it was already known in his time, and treats of it solely as an explosive, not as a propellant. The first well-authenticated case of its use in war was in Edward III's Crécy campaign in 1346.

Fourteenth-century cannon were small and of no great power. Early in the following century they became larger and more serious affairs. In 1415 they played an important part in Henry V's siege of Harfleur. Here they seem to have been used principally in harassing fire; the inhabitants begged Henry to accept their surrender . . . "for the fire was to them intolerable."[20]

In the last of the great mediæval sieges, that of Constantinople by the Turks in 1453, the garrison numbered only 9000 men to defend a land front of about 9500 yards and a sea front of nearly 30,000. The defences were so strong that behind them this tiny force resisted for 55 days an enormous Turkish army equipped with the finest siege artillery hitherto known. In particular there were three enormous 25-inch cannon cast by a Christian renegade in the service of the Sultan. Their huge stone bullets, weighing from 1200 to 1500 pounds, when fired at a high angle could range a mile and then bury themselves six feet in the earth. Some of them are still to be seen. These guns had no carriages. They had to be laboriously wedged into position on the ground by means of rocks and lumber, and their rate of fire was only seven shots per day and one per night. Nevertheless they were powerful enough to keep the entire besieged population repairing the damage done, and they ended by making an enormous breach through which the Turks entered on the fifty-fifth day of the siege.[21]

Evidently, when the strongest city in the world could hold out less than two months, gunpowder had revolutionized military

[20] Fortescue: History of the British Army, Vol. I, 55. From the "Gesta Henrici Quinti" and Monstrelet.
[21] Schlumberger.

engineering. In general, from the middle of the century on, sieges tended to become shorter and shorter. By 1500 artillery had established a complete superiority over the fortification of the day, the reason being that mediæval fortresses had no provision for emplacements in which cannon of any size could be mounted for counter-battery work.

While the fifteenth-century cannon were revolutionizing siege-work and position warfare in general, firearms of all sorts were without effect upon open warfare. The early hand-firearms, in particular, were so crude that their effect upon tactics was negligible.

The reason for the impotence of early artillery in mobile warfare is to be found in the imperfection of the gun-carriages. Not until near the end of our period was a carriage devised which made possible a reasonably rapid adjustment of fire. The French artillerists seem to have been its inventors. In 1494 the army of Charles VIII of France astonished Italy with its field-guns unlimbering for action like modern pieces. These cannon had two wheels and a trail. They were even capable of a few degrees of elevation or depression obtained as follows: the trail was divided into an upper and a lower section, hinged together in front. The gun itself was solidly set in the upper section. At the rear end of the lower section was a stepped bracket for maintaining the upper section (and hence the gun) at the elevation desired. Since the weight of the gun bore heavily on the bracket and hinge, it was a slow, hard job to change elevation. Nevertheless the fact that it could be done at all marks a notable advance.[22]

Indeed the appearance of true field artillery in Charles VIII's Italian expedition in 1494 makes of that campaign a convenient point at which to end an account of the Mediæval Art of War.

In closing let us briefly run over the new factors about to put an end to the long supremacy of cavalry. First of all, cavalry itself had for two centuries been stiff and overburdened with the great weight of plate armour. Second, the French had now set up a permanent, disciplined, professional army. The Swiss had so perfected their drill as to develop a true attacking infantry. The French, again, had produced field artillery. These new things (together with the invention of efficient hand-firearms which was to come in the near future) were to revolutionize the Art of War.

[22] Dict. de l'Arch., Vol. 5, 246–260.

BIBLIOGRAPHY

PART II

AMMIANUS MARCELLINUS, *Roman History.*

Ammianus was born about 325–330 and lived until after 391. He was therefore a contemporary of Julian, Valens, and Theodosius. He was a professional soldier, saw much active service, and seems to have served on Julian's staff in that emperor's campaigns. Hence he was probably present at the battle of Strassburg.

ANGLADE, PROFESSEUR JOSEPH, *La Bataille de Muret.* Toulouse, 1913.

Valuable for voluminous quotations from the sources, the more important being given in full.

ASTRUC, REV. PROFESSEUR J., *La Conquête de la Vicomté de Carcassonne par Simon de Montfort.* Pamphlet, Carcassonne, 1912.

Incidental mention.

AUSSARESSES, F., *L'Armée byzantine à la fin du VIème siècle d'après le Strategicon de l'Empereur Maurice.* Paris, 1909.

BELLOC, HILAIRE, *Book of the Bayeux Tapestry.* New York, 1914.

Complete reproduction of the Tapestry which is our chief source of knowledge of the equipment of the time.

BELLOC, HILAIRE, *Crécy.* London, 1912.

Monograph on the campaign and battle, with an introduction on Mediæval Warfare in general and the difficulties of its study.

BELLOC, HILAIRE, *Poitiers.* London, 1913.

Monograph on the campaign and battle.

BELLOC, HILAIRE, *The Stane Street.* London, 1913.

Incidental reference.

BELLOC, HILAIRE, *Warfare in England.* London.

Small book, three-quarters of which covers the mediæval period. Concerned chiefly with strategy and the influence of geography thereon. Very little on tactics. The only good account of John's fine campaign of 1216.

BOUTARIC, EDGARD, *Institutions militaires de la France avant les armées permanentes.* Paris, 1863.

The classic on its subject. Needs correction on the Dark Ages because of its old-fashioned exaggeration of Teutonic influence.

BURY, PROFESSOR J. B., *History of the Later Roman Empire, 395–800 A. D.* 2 vol. London and New York, 1889.

Less full but more accurate and critical than Hodgkin.

BURY, PROFESSOR J. B., *History of the Eastern Roman Empire, 802–867 A. D.* London and New York, 1912.

Incidental reference.

408

CAGNAT, R., *Les Deux camps de la Légion IIIe Auguste à Lambese d'après les fouilles récentes.* Paris, 1918.

Monograph shedding considerable light on Roman garrison life, the legionary staff, and the various bodies of special duty men.

CAGNAT, R., *La Frontière militaire de la Tripolitaine à l'époque romaine.* Paris, 1912.

Monograph on the remains of Roman frontier posts along the edge of the desert.

CHEESMAN, G. L., *The Auxilia of the Roman Imperial Army.* Oxford, 1914.

Particularly good on recruitment and frontier defence. Unfortunately he ends about 300 A. D.

COULANGES, FUSTEL DE, *Histoire des institutions politiques de l'ancienne France: L'Invasion germanique et la fin de l'Empire.* Paris, 1891.

Concerns itself only incidentally with events outside Gaul, but is, nevertheless, the best account of the process by which centralized Roman government was originally lost in the West.

DEAN, BASHFORD, *Helmets and Body Armor in Modern Warfare.* New Haven, Conn., 1920.

The introduction (pp. 25–50) has a good outline of the use of armour in the mediæval and early modern period, giving weights, illustrations, etc.

DELPECH, HENRI, *La Tactique au 13me siècle.* 2 vol., Paris, 1886.

Still the best study of Mediæval Tactics. Gives the theoretical background on Vegetius, the increased skill and flexibility in cavalry tactics up to about 1270 A. D., and indicates the loss of manœuvring power through the excessive weight of plate armour. (See Dieulafoy for Muret.)

DIEULAFOY, MARCEL, *Le Bataille de Muret.* Paris, 1899.

Supersedes Delpech on Muret, gives a number of quotations of original sources, but is unduly contemptuous of the Middle Ages.

DIEULAFOY, MARCEL, *La Château Gaillard et l'architecture militaire au XIIIe siècle.* Paris, 1898.

Monograph containing detailed description and a number of valuable plates. Attempts the hopeless task of proving a Persian origin for mediæval military architecture.

DION CASSIUS, *Roman History.*

Dion Cassius lived about 150–235 A. D. A lawyer by profession, he rose to high political office, including the government of the provinces of Dalmatia, Africa, and Pannonia. As such he must have exercised military command. He was an intimate friend of the able and soldierly Emperor Septimius Severus (reigned 192–211).

DODGE, LT. COL. THEODORE AYRAULT, *Cæsar.* Boston, 1900.

The last chapter, XLVI, gives an outline of the Art of War of the Roman Empire.

DODGE, LT. COL. THEODORE AYRAULT, *Gustavus Adolphus.* Boston, 1896.

Chap. I, "The Era of Cavalry," outlines (roughly and most insufficiently) the Art of War, A. D. 378–1315. Chap. II, "The Reappearance of Infantry," attempts to outline the Art of War, A. D. 1315–1500. The best of this chapter is the discussion of the Swiss.

Encyclopædia Britannica (E. B.), 11th Edition.

FERRERO, GUGLIELMO, *Greatness and Decline of Rome*, Vol. 5, "The Republic of Augustus." New York, 1909.

Describes the strategy of the Pannonian revolt and the invasion of Germany.

FERRERO, GUGLIELMO, *Ruin of Ancient Civilization and Triumph of Christianity*. New York, 1921.

Analyzes the third-century decline, showing it to have been political, financial, social, and religious rather than military.

FORTESCUE, JOHN W., *History of the British Army*. 10 vol., London and New York, 1899.

The standard work on the subject. Occasionally suffers from undue nationalist partiality.

FRANCE, ANATOLE, *Joan of Arc*. London and New York, 1909.

Full account of the siege of Orleans and Joan's campaigns.

GIBBON, EDWARD, *History of the Decline and Fall of the Roman Empire* (Harper edition). 6 vol., New York, 1900.

Incidental reference.

HAVERFIELD, PROF. FRANCIS J., "Britain" and "Roman Army," articles in *Encyclopædia Britannica*, 11th Edition.

Incidental reference.

HODGKIN, THOMAS, *Italy and Her Invaders*. 8 vol., Oxford, 1892.

Old-fashioned but full account of Italian affairs, 363–814 A. D. Needs checking by more recent writers, but is still valuable on account of the mass of detail given.

JOSEPHUS, FLAVIUS, *Jewish War*.

Josephus held high command among the Jewish rebels at the beginning of the war. Later he went over to the Romans and accompanied Titus' army during the siege of Jerusalem.

MANGIN, LIEUTENANT COLONEL, *La Force Noire*. Paris.

General Mangin, as he now is, is virtually the founder of the French black army, and was among the French army commanders during the recent war. Chapters i and ii of Book 2 discuss the use of negro troops by the Moors in Spain and incidentally contain information as to this little known period.

MONCRIEFF, CHARLES SCOTT, *The Song of Roland*, verse translation. New York, 1920.

Incidental reference.

NICKERSON, HOFFMAN, *The Inquisition: A Political and Military History of Its Establishment*. Boston, 1923.

Contains an account of the Albigensian War.

NORGATE, KATE, *John Lackland*. London and New York, 1902.

Valuable for occasional detail, although no attempt to analyze military affairs is made, and the author entirely misses John's high strategic ability.

This book is dedicated to darling
MAISIE *with so much love*

*'HOW TO GET INTO THIS BOOK. Knock the Knocker on the
Door ... Then, if you are very quiet, you will hear a teeny tiny voice
say ... "Take down the key." ... Put the Key in the Keyhole, which
it fits exactly, unlock the door and WALK IN.'*
English Fairy Tales, Joseph Jacobs, 1890

HODDER CHILDREN'S BOOKS

First published in Great Britain in 2019 by Hodder and Stoughton

3 5 7 9 10 8 6 4 2

Text and illustrations copyright © Cressida Cowell, 2019

The moral rights of the author have been asserted.

A CIP catalogue record for this book
is available from the British Library.

HBK ISBN 978 1 444 94144 9
PBK ISBN 978 1 444 94147 0

Printed and bound in Great Britain by Clays Ltd, Elcograf S.p.A.

The paper and board used in this book are made from
wood from responsible sources.

MIX
Paper from
responsible sources
FSC® C104740

Hodder Children's Books
An imprint of
Hachette Children's Group
Part of Hodder and Stoughton
Carmelite House
50 Victoria Embankment
London EC4Y 0DZ

An Hachette UK Company
www.hachette.co.uk

www.hachettechildrens.co.uk

The Wizards of ONCE

Knock Three Times

written and illustrated by

CRESSIDA COWELL

Hodder Children's Books

This is a story with two heroes.

The girl, Wish, is a Warrior...
BUT underneath her eyepatch
she has an EXRAORDINARILY
POWERFUL Magic Eye.

The boy, Xar, is a WiZard...
and he means well, but he has
a Witchstain on his hand,
that is trying to control him.

CONQUERED
WARRIOR
TERRITORIES
This way to the Warrior Capital
Ghost Mountains
WARRIOR
EMPIRE
The Sweet Track
Iron Warrior Fort
The
QUEENDOM
OF
SYCHORAX
THE
BADWOODS
Sinister Clearing
Wizard Fort
LD
WOODS
ENCANZO's
KINGDOM
the
Lost
Ragged River

Note by Cressida Cowell
Lost Language EXPERT

A long time ago, a young girl exploring the back of a cave somewhere in the British Isles discovered these papers, known as the 'Wizard books', hidden behind a large stone. Nobody has ever been able to read them, for they were written so very far away in the distant past that they used a vocabulary and a script that has never been seen before.

I have spent many happy years translating the papers of Hiccup the Viking from Old Norse into English. So I was excited to accept this even greater challenge, for these Wizard books were written in such a dark age that the language they used has been completely lost to us over the years.

After many years of study I have finally cracked the code of this lost language. And in doing so, I have uncovered something TRULY extraordinary.

Believe the unbelievable.

Every fairy story you have ever read has its basis in some truth.

It was not only dragons living in the distant darkness. Dragons were only a very, very small part of it.

THIS was a time of MAGIC

Prologue

Once there were wildwoods.

The Wizards had lived in the wildwoods for as long as anyone could remember, and they were intending to live there forever, along with all the other Magic things.

Until the Warriors came. The Warriors invaded from across the seas, and although they had no Magic, they brought a new weapon that they called IRON . . . *and iron was the only thing that Magic would not work on.*

From that moment on, Wizards and Warriors were fighting each other to the death in the wildwoods.

Until one day . . .

A young Warrior queen called SYCHORAX fell in love with a young Wizard king called ENCANZO. Wizards and Warriors should NEVER fall in love. So Sychorax had taken the Spell of Love Denied to make her love die. And the love had died indeed . . . and Sychorax had married a Warrior, like she was supposed to.

And Encanzo had married a Wizard, just as a Wizard should.

So the danger of a curse ought to have been avoided. But . . .

Thirteen years ago, Sychorax had a daughter whose name was WISH.

And Wish had a terrible secret. The lingering true love kiss of the Wizard Encanzo had made Queen Sychorax's daughter Magic. And for the first time in human history, *Wish had a Magic-that-works-on-iron*.

And thirteen years ago, Encanzo had a son whose name was XAR.

And Xar had a terrible secret. Xar stole some Magic from a Witch, *and the stain of the Witch Magic was beginning to control him*.

This is the story of how Xar and Wish met, and how they made friends even though they had been brought up to hate each other like poison.

Wish and Xar have run away from their parents, searching for the ingredients for a spell to get rid of Witches. They are outcasts, hunted by Wizards and Warriors alike, and by something far, far worse.

WITCHES.

WITCHES MUST NEVER GET HOLD OF MAGIC-THAT-WORKS-ON-IRON . . .

But . . .

Twice, Wish and Xar have escaped the talons of the Witches. TWICE, they have cheated death.

1. Betrayal

Three thousand years ago, at the end of the era that would later be known as the Bronze Age, the whole of the British Isles were covered in wildwoods.

Good things lived in the wildwoods, animals and Magic creatures and humans who minded their own business, but bad things lived there at that time too, some very bad things.

Two of these bad things were flying above the forest even now. The bad things were presently invisible, but if human eyes could have seen them they would have noticed that they had soft black wings like the wings of crows, and fingers that ended in talons like a bird of prey, and noses a little like a beak. In fact, they were WITCHES, not good Witches, but very *bad* Witches indeed, and they were flying high, just below the clouds, and as they flew they were watching something down below.

Xar, Wish
and Bodkin

The *something* was
a door, but instead of
being where a door
really ought to be,
vertically opening and
shutting between rooms
that are safely on the ground
in an orderly kind of way,
this particular door was flying
through the air, flat on its front like
a carpet, just above the treetops.
It was the little moving speck of
the flying door that had first attracted the
Witches' attention as they flew, with lazy
wingbeats in the strong currents of air high above
the trees, on their way back to their nests in the
Lachrymose Mountains. But it wasn't the door *itself* that
was now holding their scrutiny.

There were three children lying on their stomachs
on top of the flying door.

The invisible Witches looked down at the children.

And the children looked down over the edge of the
flying door, looking for something in the forest.

The Witches were hungry, so hungry that long
dribbles of black saliva were dripping from their lips.
They hadn't seen anything so delicious as these children

in weeks, no, perhaps years (and that will give you an idea why people didn't really *like* Witches, either in the Bronze Age, or any other age that the Witches happened to turn up in).

But something was making those Witches pause before swooping on the tasty, unaware little morsels below and fastening their claws into them.

'Thaw si ti gniod tou ereh?' whined Breakneck, waggling her nose from side to side. 'Yhw si ydobon gnitcetorp ti? Od uoy kniht ti dluoc eb a part?'*

Ripgrizzle was pausing too, although the smell of the blood of the human children (which to a Witch is as delicious as that of a cake baking in the oven) was wafting up to him and making him drool like a dog. He was desperate to snatch the treats from under Breakneck's waggling nose and fly back to his nest to feed on the tender darlings all by himself.

But he too was cautious. Before the return of the Witches to the wildwoods, the air would have been full of flying things – birds and sprites and cockatrices, dragons, piskies, all manner of glorious Magical creatures. But now, this early in the morning, which was too close to the night hours of the Witching-time, the forest was as quiet as death, and the Warrior humans kept their

---

* Witches speak the same language as we do, but each individual word is back to front. This means 'What is it doing out here? Why is nobody protecting it? Do you think it could be a trap?'

babies locked up safe in their castles, and the Wizard humans kept their babies safe in their treehouse forts. So what were *these* human babies doing then, flying, cool as you like, on the back of a Magical flying door, miles and miles away from any human habitation? Perhaps Breakneck was right. Maybe it was a trap.

The children were talking to one another, and one of them was singing rather shakily, with false bravery: '*NO FEAR!* That's the Warriors' marching song! *NO FEAR!* We sing it as we march along!'

Ripgrizzle's gigantic ears curled up at the edges, swivelling and tilting towards the child in order to catch the sound. The eye in the middle of his forehead opened up sleepily. The two Witches flew, unseen, lower, lower, to listen to the children's conversation.

The first young person was a Wizard boy called Xar (his name was pronounced 'Zar' – I don't know why, spelling is *weird*). The Witches did not know it, but Xar was the son of Encanzo, King of Wizards, and Xar had a very dangerous secret, which was that he had stolen some Magic from a Witch and was having trouble controlling it. The Witch-Magic was hidden below a glove in a cut on his right hand, but the Witches could smell it nonetheless, and the smell confused them.

The second was a Warrior princess called Wish, daughter of Sychorax, Queen of the Warriors, and Wish, too, had a very dangerous secret, which was that beneath her eyepatch she had a Magic eye, and Warriors were not supposed to have any Magic at all.

The third was a Warrior boy called Bodkin. Bodkin was Wish's Assistant Bodyguard, and he was finding this position really rather testing because he didn't like fighting very much, he had an unfortunate tendency to fall asleep in situations of physical danger, and trying to control the uncontrollable little princess was an impossible task because she seemed to have absolutely no idea what rules were at all. Bodkin was the one singing that song, rather unconvincingly.

The three children were looking rather more ragged and sad than they had been two weeks earlier when they had run away from Wish's and Xar's parents. They had started out joyously, in the way that these journeys often begin. Running away had seemed like it would be an exciting adventure, but now they were hungry and tired and frightened, for they knew they were being hunted

No fear!! sang Bodkin, Wish's Assistant Bodyguard

by the Warriors and the Wizards and the Witches, and that they must never be caught. If the *Warriors* caught them, Sychorax would lock up Wish in iron Warrior fort where the Witches could not get hold of her. If the *Wizards* caught them, Encanzo would lock up Xar in the prison of Gormincrag where his Witchstain could be treated. And if the *Witches* caught them . . . well that was such a scary idea our heroes were trying their hardest not to think about it.

So for the past two days they had been looking for the house of the sister of Caliburn, Xar's talking raven, where they hoped to be able to hide.

'I KNOW my sister lives somewhere around here,' said Caliburn for the umpteenth time. 'She moved here a while ago, back when I was still a human . . .'

Caliburn was actually a Wizard who had lived many lifetimes, and in the previous one he had indeed been a human. And he hadn't been just *any* old human, either, he had been the great Wizard Pentaglion. Unfortunately Caliburn had come down in the world and returned to the wildwoods in this

Caliburn, Xar's talking raven

present lifetime in the form of a bird. (A rather untidy bird, for Caliburn was continually losing his feathers in his anxiety at the impossible task of trying to keep Xar out of trouble.)

'I know that my sister has one of the ingredients we need for the spell to get rid of Witches, the tears of the Drood, and maybe we can persuade her to give it to us,' said Caliburn. 'And she'll give us a bed for the night, and a good meal, and she'll protect us for a while . . .'

None of them were feeling very strong at all, and the idea of a bed for a night and a good meal was even more attractive than the idea that Caliburn's sister might give them one of the ingredients they needed for their quest. In fact, it brought tears to Bodkin's eyes.

'What does your sister's house look like, Caliburn?' asked Bodkin.

Caliburn looked a little shifty. 'Oh, you know, just like any other old human habitation. I haven't been there in years. I'll know it when I see it.'

'Your sister must have a very big house,' said Wish doubtfully. 'Look how many of us there are! Are you quite sure she'll want to have all of us to stay?'

Caliburn gave an airy wave of his wing. 'Oh, my sister has loads of room! Of course she'll have us all to stay . . .'

'Even though we're a bit, well . . . ODD?' said Wish,

wistfully. 'I can't believe that your sister won't mind about us being Wizards and Warriors working together, Caliburn – everyone else hates that. And some people even might say we were sort of . . . *cursed*.'

Wish *was* a little odd-looking – a funny little scrawny girl with hair so quivering with Magic that it vibrated and lifted with static electricity every time she moved. She had a pale little face that looked as if the tide had washed over it and taken away all the sharp bits, and a kind but determined expression.

That determination of hers was being severely tested. Her armour was dented, she hadn't eaten in three days, and her face and hands and legs were deeply scratched from a terrible battle they had a week ago when they were ambushed by wyverns (a type of dragon very common in the Bronze Age).

With all her heart Wish wanted to believe that Caliburn had a sister who would

Wish WAS a little odd-looking . . .

welcome them, even though they were outlaws, disobeying the laws of the wildwood universe … but deep down she had a hollow feeling that this was very unlikely.

'Let's face it, Caliburn,' said Wish, trying to be practical and not mind too much, 'we don't really fit in anywhere. No one is going to want us.'

'My sister isn't as prejudiced as everyone else,' said Caliburn. 'There are kind people in the world. You just have to find them.'

'You're quite sure your sister hasn't died and come back as a raven too, and the reason we can't find her house is that she's now living in some sort of NEST?' said Bodkin suspiciously.

'No, no,' said Caliburn. And then, less certainly,

No one is going to want us..

'Probably not . . .'

Bodkin didn't quite know how to say this without hurting Caliburn's feelings, but they had been searching for Caliburn's sister's house for quite a while now without finding any sign of it. 'Are you quite sure that you've got this right, Caliburn?' said Bodkin. 'You've only just remembered that you HAVE a sister.'

'Living many lifetimes is difficult,' said Caliburn, rather flustered. 'It takes a while to remember what happened in the previous ones. But now my memory has been jogged I know I have a sister and she's down in that forest somewhere . . .'

'Well, I think we should give up looking for your sister and march right into that Drood stronghold on the Lake of the Lost, and just take their tears from them,' said Xar, who was not a patient person.

'You don't understand!' said Caliburn. 'The Droods are unrelenting, unforgiving and the greatest Wizards in the wildwoods, and they really don't like having their tears taken! They'll kill us if they catch us . . . Much easier for my sister just to GIVE them to us . . .'

And then Wish spotted something that wasn't the welcoming fires of Caliburn's sister's house, but something much more sinister.

'Some people are following us down there in the forest,' whispered Wish, putting up her eyepatch a smidgeon because she could see better through her

Magic eye. Sure enough, down in the tangle of green woods below them, way in the distance, there were the little flickering lights of many, many torches coming through the trees in their direction.

'Do you think it could be your sister, Caliburn?' Xar whispered hopefully, his tummy giving the most gigantic rumble. Only Xar could mistake the ominous torches of what was clearly a hunting party for a welcoming greeting from Caliburn's sister. But then, Xar was an optimistic sort of person, who hoped for the best at all times.

He had a deep cut over his right temple from where a wyvern had earlier tried to take his eye out, and an old bit of shirt wrapped round his leg covering a wound from a boggart-bite that was going septic, but he wasn't going to let little things like these get him down. Xar was a happy-go-lucky sort of boy, with a wide-awake look in his eyes that suggested that he was determined to enjoy life despite unimportant details like infected boggart-bites

17

← Squeezjoos

and wyvern injuries.
As Xar was also a
boy of considerable
charm and charisma, he
had a lot of companions,
and flying with the door
were six of his sprites and three
hairy fairies. These tiny little insect-y
creatures, so paper-thin you could see their hearts, were
buzzing around in a state of such alarm that blue electric
sparks were coming out of their ears.

'Beware . . .' they hissed. 'Beware beware beware . . .'

'No, it's definitely not my sister,' said Caliburn,
shading a wing over one of his eyes and squinting so he
could see better. 'They're banging war drums. My sister
wouldn't bang war drums, unless she's changed a very
good deal in the last twenty years.'

'Don't worry, sprites,' said Xar soothingly, for
although Xar often led his companions into difficulty,
he did take his responsibilities as the leader of his band
very seriously. 'I'll look after you . . .'

'Of coursse you will, Masster!' squeaked Squeezjoos,
one of the smallest and most enthusiastic of the hairy
fairies. 'You iss the most brilliantastic leader in the whole
world ever and you woulds never leads us into any trouble!'

'But I don't understand it . . .' said Wish,

18

bewildered. 'Nobody knows which way we went – the sprites have dimmed their lights, we're flying so close to the tops of the trees that nobody can see us from below, so how can they be following us?'

'Maybe they picked up the scent of Crusher and the snowcats,' Bodkin suggested.

Xar had other companions too and they were down on the ground. A giant called Crusher, three beautiful snowcats, some wolves, a bear, and a werewolf called Lonesome were following on foot, way below on the forest floor.

'Impossible!' Xar whispered back. 'I'm unbeatable at running away and so are my companions! We're completely untrackable . . .'

As well as being just a *trifle* conceited, Xar was indeed very good at running away. He was the most disobedient boy in the Wizard kingdom, always getting into trouble for doing things like:

you woulds never leads us = into any trouble . . .

Getting his sprites to charm his older brother Looter's spelling staffs so that every time Looter tried to use them, they spanked him on the bottom . . . Painting spots on the Magic mirror in the main hall so everyone who looked in it thought they were coming down with something infectious . . . Pouring Animation Potion on the trousers of Ranter, his least favourite teacher, so whenever Ranter tried to put them on, the trousers skipped out of reach.

As a result, Xar had spent his entire short life running away from the wrath of his father, his teachers, and the other Wizards, so he had become something of a running away *expert*.

'Maybe someone'ssss betrayed us,' hissed Tiffinstorm, one of Xar's larger sprites, eyes narrowing jealously. 'Probably that werewolf. Never trust a werewolf who you met in a prison. That's good advice, kids.'

'Don't you dare accuse the werewolf just because he's a werewolf!' said Xar fierily.

Wish agreed with Xar.

'Nobody's betrayed us,' said Wish, soothingly, 'we're on the same side, now, Tiffinstorm. We're all outlaws together, remember?

'But who is chasing us down there in the forest?' worried Wish.

Caliburn began to list their enemies. 'Well, it could be the Droods . . . or Xar's father . . . or Wish's mother . . .

And what about the Witchsmeller? *He* hates you . . . Or the Warrior emperor? He'll want to get rid of Magic-that-works-on-iron at all costs . . .'

Squeezjoos bared his little teeth and squeaked, '*I'sll gets them for you, Master! I'sll bites great chunks out of their iron bottoms! I'sll makes their noses drip for a week and ties knots in their sandwiches! I'sll makes holes in theys socks so theys keep puttings theys big toes throughs it in a REALLY ANNOYING way! I'sll put itching powder in theys knickers and I'sll leave little fluffballs in theys tummy buttons and theys will NEVERS KNOW where the fluff is coming from!'*

As Squeezjoos was not a great deal bigger than a dormouse, and the threat of fluff-in-the-tummy-button was not exactly life-threatening, none of this was likely to be terribly worrying to a Drood or a heavily armed iron Warrior, but Xar thanked him solemnly and said, 'Yes of course you can, Squeezjoos, just as soon as I give the order.'

The one enemy that Caliburn did not mention was *Witches.* Which, given that there were two very large Witches hovering right above their heads at that very moment, was a tiny bit ironic. There was even rather a large clue that Witches were closer than they might realise. Around Xar's waist, attached to his belt, hung two Witch feathers, and when Witches were close these Witch feathers burned green with a strange unnatural

21

light. They were burning green *now*, my goodness they were, greener than emerald, brighter than starlight, but Xar and Wish and Bodkin had not noticed, so intent were they on staring down at what was going on in the forest below them.

The only person who HAD noticed the glowing of the Witch feathers was The Baby. The Baby was the smallest hairy fairy of all, and he was going wild with agitation.

But The Baby was still in his egg, and he could only say one word: 'Goo!'

And nobody listens to babies, even when they have something very important to say.

So although The Baby rolled around urgently in his egg, bumping into people and shouting 'Goo! Goo! Goo!' at the top of his Baby voice, none of the other sprites would listen and Xar just batted him away, saying, 'Not now, Baby, we can't play now.'

The Witches, sharpening their talons and hovering not more than ten feet above the door, grinned at each other – nasty grins, for Witches have nasty senses of humour. How amusing! These children were so busy worrying about the danger from *below*, they were completely ignoring the much more serious danger threatening them from *above*.

And they were running away from their parents!

That would explain why they were out at night, so far away from their Tribes and their kinsmen . . . it wasn't a trap at all . . .

The Witches prepared to swoop.

But then the Witches stiffened as something poked out of the back of Wish's waistcoat, swivelling, as if sniffing the air, and then hopping up on to the top of Wish's head to peer over the edge of the door with the others.

The something was a spoon, and it happened to be alive.

The Enchanted Spoon was followed by a key, and a fork and a number of little Enchanted Pins.

None of this was odd to the Witches. Enchanted objects were perfectly normal back in those days.

But these enchanted objects weren't normal at all, they were very odd indeed . . .

These enchanted objects . . .

. . . were made of iron.

The Witches' eyes blazed red and visible for one horrified moment.

'It'sssss herrrr . . .' hissed the Witches.

'It'ssss HERRRRRR . . .' The Witches growled like dogs. 'The girl with the Magic eye who has *Magic-that-works-on-iron* . . .'

In an unusual coincidence, Wish, peering

downwards,
also whispered
under her breath at the very
same time as the Witches: 'It's *HER* . . .'

'It's her . . . it's her . . . it's HER . . .!'

'It's my mother!' cried Wish. 'That's who's following us! Okay, nobody panic . . . Stay calm . . . Key! Could you hop into the keyhole for me?'

When Wish wanted to fly the door as quickly as possible she needed the key to be in the keyhole so that she could steer the door at speed.

'Of course,' boasted the key in a creaky little voice. 'You see, spoon? The fork is a mere food carrier, a pathetic little potato piercer . . . but *I* have a very important role.'

The key and the fork were both in love with the Enchanted Spoon, so the key never lost an opportunity to show off.

24

The fork waggled its prongs furiously at the key, and the key stuck out its little iron chest and hopped self-importantly into the keyhole.

'We'll just very quietly sneak away . . .' said Wish. 'Softly, everyone . . . make as little noise as you can . . .'

But before Wish could move the key and send the door skimming silently away across the treetops, she noticed something very odd was up with Squeezjoos.

He had been getting thoroughly over-excited, doing somersaults in the air, squeaking dire threats about making holes in people's socks, and protecting Xar, and accidentally biting his own tail, and at the sighting of

Wish's mother
he seemed to
completely
lose it. His
little bumbly
body shot
fizzily with
sparks, his
spotty eyes lit up
a luminous bright
green, and he shrieked at
the top of his voice:

'SOOJZEEKS TO THE RESCUE!!! *CHAAAAARGE!!!!*'

And the little sprite threw himself in a mad zooming dive downwards in a lunatic one-hairy-fairy attack on Queen Sychorax's entire advancing army.

'What . . . is . . . he . . . *doing???????*' gasped Xar.

And just as the goggle-eyed children on the back of the door were taking in this *first* incomprehensible disaster, a *second one* sprang up, bright, fierce, flaming, in front of their very eyes.

'My mother!' cried Wish. *'She's setting the forest alight!'*

SOOjeeks to the ReScUE!!
C-H-A-A-A-R-GE!!

Ariel

Bumbleboozle

Squeezjoos

The Baby

Hinkypunk

Xar's Sprites

Tiffinstorm

Mustardthought

Timeloss

the Once-Sprite

2. The Trees are Screaming

eanwhile, down on the ground, Crusher the giant, and Xar's snowcats, Kingcat, Nighteye and Forestheart, his werewolf, Lonesome, his bear and his wolves were making their way swiftly and quietly through the wildwoods. Wolves and giants are quite common, but I wish you could have seen the snowcats. Beautiful creatures they were, larger than lions, fur as deep as powder snow, padding through the ancient forest, whiskers twitching. Like the children on the flying door, they were looking skinnier and hungrier and a lot more bedraggled than they had been two weeks earlier. The snowcats had deep wounds from the talons of wyverns on their faces, the bear had torn his ear, and Lonesome was limping.

None would have known that they had passed that way, for as Xar said, they were untrackable, untraceable. Even giants know how to tread lightly on the world, so although Crusher was nearly as tall as the tallest of the trees around him, he did not make a footprint on the undergrowth below as he walked through the holloways, planting his great walking staff gently in the ground and humming happily to himself. Crusher was a Longstepper

High-Walker giant, and these giants are BIG, so they tend to have BIG thoughts. Wandering gets their giant brains working, so as Crusher walked, his head was smoking with inspiration, and he was thinking in time to each giant gentle step:

'I wonder if you could say that trees have brains? They certainly learn . . . and just because they learn in their roots, is that enough to say that they do not have brains like humans and giants do?'

And then he stopped suddenly. He put his ear to the nearest tree.

His face, with wandering lines like an ancient map, normally gently interested in the world about him, assumed a very concerned and grim expression indeed.

Slowly he bent down to his animal companions.

'Now, I do not want you to panic, creatures of the forest,' said Crusher. 'But the trees are screaming.'

There are people who think that just because trees do not have mouths, they cannot talk. Those people are wrong, and they are often the kind of people who think that other people have to be exactly like themselves to count as people at all. Trees speak to each other just as you and I do, but you have to have the right ears for listening. They send out messages on sound waves that

"Do not worry, dear trees . . ."
said Crusher

giant ears can hear, scent chemicals that giant noses can smell, and just because our tiny little human ears and noses are too small to hear or smell or detect them, this does not mean that those messages are not there.

As Crusher said, the trees were screaming.

And the message they were screaming, with the crackling of their roots and every electrical and chemical signal they could muster, was: 'FIRE! FIRE! FIRE! FIRE!'

It was very generous of the trees to scream that message, really. For it was not a message that their fellow trees could respond to. Trees live life in the slow lane. So although they can move their leaves in the direction of sunlight, and they can grow their roots in the direction of water, this all happens very slowly, and what they cannot do, in the face of the immediate, instant, quick destruction that is FIRE, is wrench up their mud-clogged roots from the ground they are growing in and run as fast as they can for their lives.

But the animals can. And maybe the trees are more intelligent than we are, and know that their species' lives are eventually dependent on the other species around them.

So the snowcats' ears pricked up, the werewolf's nose was set a-sniffing, sniff, sniff, sniff: they caught the smell, the sound of the messages the trees were screaming, before even the first whiff of burning wood, the first howl of a distant terrified fox.

And they panicked.

Snorting, howling, wild with fear, the animals and the Magic creatures ran as fast as they could, uncaring of the brambles that ripped, the branches that spiked, joining a deluge of other fleeing animals – hedgehogs, wolves, bears, deer, birds, insects, hobs, goblins, all careering madly through the forest to get away from the age-old enemy, fire.

35

The sprites and the birds and all things with wings were the lucky ones.

Crusher had to follow more slowly, for giants, like trees, do not move quickly, and tears were trickling down his wrinkled face as he moved through the forest, touching each precious ancient tree in sympathy as he walked.

The fire caught from tree to tree, faster than fairies, faster than Witches. Trees that had been growing for hundreds, sometimes thousands of years, burned bright and were destroyed in an instant. The roar of the flames as the wind carried the bright, destructive inferno faster, swifter, higher, bigger, brighter, bolder, quick as thought and more terrible than could be imagined.

Up above, the children on the door responded instantly.

Wish grabbed the Enchanted Key and pointed DOWN.

'We have to save Squeezjoos and Crusher and the animals!' shouted Xar, and with a great screech, the door shot downwards towards the burning forest, the sprites bravely following behind it, in a wild screeching trail of humming sprite dust, even though every sprite instinct was telling them to fly away.

It was unbelievably fortunate that the door and the sprites and the raven chose that blink of a second to plunge downwards.

For at precisely the moment that they swooped, the Witches attacked.

SSSSSCCCCRRIIIIIIITCH!!!!!!!!!

There was a tearing noise, as if the air itself was being ripped apart.

Just in case YOU have never been dive-bombed by a Witch, I will explain what happens. When Witches are invisible, they can do no harm. Their hands just pass right through you, like the hands of ghosts. So as Breakneck and Ripgrizzle screeched downward, they were turning themselves visible as they plunged. First two screaming heads appeared, liquefying at the edges into spitting sparks and foul vapour, and then the two Witches blasted down on Wish and Xar and Bodkin on their Enchanted Door like a couple of infinitely evil peregrine falcons.

When Witches attack, they assault all your senses at the same time. Their stink is unbearable, the most nauseating bad egg and rotten corpse smell you can possibly imagine, and they release it in a cloud of venom. Their scream is like the death agony of five hundred foxes, and it buries itself in your brain and reverberates around your head till you feel like you might go crazy.

Ripgrizzle had two fish-like eyes buried so deep on either side of his axe-sharp nose you could not see into the pitiless depths of them – not that you would want to.

The mouth, dripping that revolting black saliva from the fangs. A body like a human mixed with a panther, talons long as swords, and black feathery wings.

Breakneck was no prettier.

The Witches swooped, but they were a blink or two too late, for the children on their door had that very second gone into a dive downwards to help their friends, so the Witches' talons closed only on empty air, and they let out screeches of infuriated disappointment.

The sprites and the children and Caliburn the raven FINALLY looked over their shoulders and realised they were being attacked.

Pandemonium ensued,
as the rescuing-Squeezjoos-
and-Crusher-and-the-animals
mission turned abruptly into a desperate-flight-from-
the-attacking-Witches mission.

'AIEEEEEEEEEEEEE!!!!' screamed the Witches.

'Goo!' cried The Baby, which in Baby-language
means: 'I've been *trying* to tell you this for ages, but
nobody listens to babies, *oh* no . . .'

'FLYYYYYYYYYY!!!!!' yelled Xar, shooting
arrows at the Witches as Wish desperately hauled the key
back and forth in wild swivelling motions so that
the door slalomed this way and that in crazy swirls
to evade the mind-boggling horror of the
pursuing Witches, while still following

the little tiny spark of the charging Squeezjoos, who was continuing to shriek, 'SOOJZEEKS TO THE RESCUE! *CHAAAAAAARGE!!!!*' at the top of his voice.

'Don't worry, princess!' said Bodkin, trying to draw Wish's Enchanted Sword*, but unable to get it out of the scabbard, so he had to pull out his bow and arrows instead. '*I'll* save you!'

But Bodkin had a bit of a disadvantage as a bodyguard. He had a medical condition that caused him to fall asleep in conditions of extreme danger.

He had barely said these last brave words before he collapsed, snoring loudly, and began to slide downwards on the door.

Snore, snore.

'Bodkin! Wake up!' yelled Wish, and Xar had to give up shooting arrows at the Witches, while he and Wish took hold of Bodkin by both arms to prevent him from slipping off the door entirely.

---

* The Enchanted Sword was a special Witch-killing sword

Bodkin woke up with a start, mumbling, 'Who? What? Where?'

'Forest in Drood Territory . . .' panted the little princess. 'Being chased by the Witches . . . Squeezjoos attacking my mother's forces entirely on his own . . .'

'Oh! Yes!' said Bodkin, scrambling back on to the Enchanted Door. '*We can do this!* My iron arrows will work much better on Witches than Xar's bone ones!' Bodkin put away the Enchanted Sword, and instead fitted an arrow into his bow, took careful aim, and then fell asleep again, shooting himself in the foot and falling heavily on Wish. This jogged her hand, and the key that was controlling the steering shot out of the keyhole so violently that the door went into abrupt reverse, travelling backwards with such speed that it nearly shot into the open jaws of the pursuing Witches.

What with one thing and another, the young outlaws weren't really working together in the most brilliant fashion . . .

The key had got entangled in Wish's hair, so the fork came to the rescue, leaping into the keyhole, using its prongs as a key substitute. Wish took hold of the fork and got control of the door again, narrowly avoiding the swiping talons of the Witches.

The upside-down fork looked up smugly at the furious key, and that look meant: '*Look at me, spoon, look at me!!* . . . us forks can be important too!'

'Forks are mere *food carriers*, they're not qualified to operate keyholes!' squeaked the key. 'Come out of there right now or this flight will end in disaster!'

'SQUEEZJOOS! COME BACK!' roared Xar.

REEEEOOOOOOW! The flying door swooped and swirled and dodged through the treetops, shaving off leaves and nearly unseating its riders, who were hanging on for dear life. Bodkin reawoke, and this time didn't even attempt to shoot anything, shaking the arrow out of his foot and concentrating on not falling off the door.

Wish was trying not to lose sight of Squeezjoos, who was flying at full speed over the burning trees towards the approaching torches and flares of the Warriors. Goodness knows how the little hairy fairy thought he was going to attack an entire Warrior army all on his own, but that appeared to be his plan.

Down below on the forest floor, Queen Sychorax and her iron Warriors were at full gallop as they raced through the trees on horseback.

Queen Sychorax didn't look a bit like Wish.

It was most out of character for Queen Sychorax to have a daughter so unlike herself, but even great queens cannot *entirely* control what their offspring are going to look like.

Queen Sychorax was dressed for war, with an iron

breastplate, iron helmet, and so many weapons she looked like a statue to some alien god of war. She was also loaded with jewels, furs, and clothes of the finest materials the early Iron Age could supply, for Queen Sychorax felt that if she was going to be forced to travel into the wilderness of the godforsaken forest in pursuit of a disobedient daughter, she should jolly well do it in *style*, for mistletoe's sake.

She was in a bit of a mood.

'Witches,' breathed Queen Sychorax, looking upwards from the back of her galloping horse. 'I knew it! I KNEW they'd be after her! *SHOOT DOWN THE WITCHES!*'

ZING! ZING! ZING!

Arrows shot upwards from the forest floor, narrowly missing both the door and the Witches.

'Your mother's shooting at us!' said Bodkin in amazement. 'As if we haven't got enough problems . . .'

'She's not shooting at *us*, she's shooting at the Witches,' said Wish, grim with determination as she flew that door – really rather *well*, actually, considering that she was having to use a fork in the keyhole instead of a key, if anybody had had the time or been in the mood to appreciate her growing door-flying skills – at astonishing speed just above the smoke and the chaos of the burning forest.

Arrows rained upwards, narrowly missing their targets.

'Oh for goodness' sake!' snapped Queen Sychorax to her Warriors. 'Can't you even hit a couple of great gawping Witches at close distance?'

She sighed.

'I don't know, if you want something doing, you have to do it yourself . . .' Queen Sychorax pulled up her horse, got out her bow and arrow, and took careful aim.

REOOOOW!

Wish made another desperate turn of the door through the billowing smoke, but this time it was just a smidgeon too late, and one of Ripgrizzle's talons got hold of the door, and sent it revolving in circles, shooting into the talons of Breakneck. Breakneck got a good hold of the spinning door, kept it steady, and Ripgrizzle gave an evil grin as he prepared to swoop.

They couldn't get away now.

But one final ZING! from below, and Ripgrizzle's grin of gloating triumph turned to an expression of acute surprise.

And then Ripgrizzle fell from the air, dead as a stone, with one of Queen Sychorax's arrows in his heart.

BOOM! He landed on the forest floor, Warriors scattering in all directions from the ensuing Witch crater and a whole load of billowing green smoke.

With a whine of horror and fright, Breakneck let go

of the Enchanted Door and fled for her life in a whirr of black feathers.

Sychorax's arrow also stopped the charging Squeezjoos.

On the arrow's path to Ripgrizzle, it had skimmed so close to Squeezjoos that it had removed the tip of one of Squeezjoos's antennae, giving the little hairy fairy such a shock that he stopped mid-charge. He blinked twice and the green faded from his little spotty eyes, as if he was just waking up from a sleep, like Bodkin, and—

'Where am I?' squeaked Squeezjoos, giving a violent start as he took in Sychorax's Warrior army gathered in horrifying masses below him.

'Save meeeeeeeeeeeeeee!' He panicked, and turned around, flying as fast as his little humming wings could carry him back to what he thought was the safety of Wish and Xar and Bodkin on the back of the door, and hiding himself in Wish's hair beside the spoon and the key.

'Good shot, Queen Sychorax!' said Bodkin in relief, looking down over the side of the door and trying to see Wish's mother through the smoke of the Witch's landing way below. 'Yes, you were right, she was shooting at the Witches. Thank goodness she's such a good shot . . .'

Xar hated Queen Sychorax, but even *he* was impressed. 'Maybe she's not as bad as I thou— Hang on a second! What is she doing?'

Sychorax had got back on her horse. 'Now shoot down the door,' she ordered her deputy. 'I'm presuming you can at least hit something as large as *that*?'

'But your Majesty!' spluttered the deputy. 'Your own daughter is on the back of that door!'

'My own daughter,' spat Queen Sychorax, grinding her pretty little teeth, 'has more than one life.* And if she didn't want her door shot down, she shouldn't have got born with this Magic-that-works-on-iron in that abnormal and eccentric fashion. SHOOT DOWN THE DOOR!'

---

* LONG story.

Arrows rained upwards once more.

'Put the door in reverse!' yelled Xar. 'I take it back, she IS as bad as I thought!'

'But what on earth is Queen Sychorax doing? Why is she shooting at us?' said Bodkin, thoroughly bewildered. 'Has she gone totally mad?'

'Well, she's never been exactly a HUGGY sort of mother,' said Wish. 'But I'm sure there's some sort of perfectly reasonable explanation . . .'

And they were about to get that explanation.

BAM!

A direct hit on the Enchanted Door by a carefully aimed spear pierced the Magic that was delicately holding the jigsaw pieces of the door together.

'Keep it together, Wish!' shouted Caliburn.
'Think of the door as a complete door!'
But Wish was not yet sufficiently in
control of her Magic powers when taken
by surprise like this. The door shattered
into a thousand pieces, and the
three children plummeted towards
the ground.

3. Queen Sychorax is not a Huggy Sort of Mother

They were extremely fortunate that their door was shot down right above Crusher and the running animals.

'LOOK OUT, ABOVE!' cried Crusher, coming to a crashing halt as bits of door rained down. The animals, mad with terror though they were at the following fire, came to a trembling halt, for they loved their humans, and they ran back to see if they could help.

Xar and Bodkin fell into the branches of a tree, and Wish was saved by all six sprites catching bits of her clothes and breaking her fall before she finally fell into the cupped palms of Crusher.

Little Squeezjoos nearly came to an untimely end. He fell out of Wish's hair, and was too late to duck a flying fragment of the shattered door that hit him momentarily unconscious, and he would have fallen down into the blazing undergrowth if Xar had not risked his life by reaching out way too far from the tree and saving him.

Crusher then gently extracted Xar and Bodkin from the tree and put them and Wish on the ground, telling them to climb aboard the snowcats who would carry them quicker than the giant could run.

'RUN SWIFT,' said the giant.

Bodkin and Wish and Xar leapt aboard the snowcats. 'FLY!' cried Xar, and with great, terrified bounds, their soft fur blackened and raised in petrified quills, Kingcat, Nighteye, Forestheart and the wolves and the bear leapt through the dark dusty rain that was now falling, bits of soft grey ash, and ROOOOARR! The hot roar of the fire pursued them, mixed with the noise of the Warrior hunt, the scream of the dogs, the screech of the Warrior horns, the iron sound of the beating hooves as they pounded through the burning forest.

That was the sound of the new Iron Age, that Warrior hunt.

The forest was being burnt down, so that the Warriors could build their forts and their fields and their new modern world. For the Warriors argued that the modern way was the right way, surely? Time cannot run backwards, could it? That would be nonsense, and Warriors do not believe in nonsense. The forest had to come down so the Warriors could move humanity forward in a civilised and forward-looking manner. The giants had to leave because they took up way too much room. The sprites had to die because their habitats were needed to make all the THINGS that Warriors need. It was regrettable, but there it was. It was all in the name of progress.

So all over the wildwoods, these hunts were being carried out, with the mad barking of dogs and the shrill crying of horns, and Warriors on horseback hunting down the giants, or the shining elves, or the long-haired ogres, or the lumpen boggarts.

This time it was slightly different of course, for Queen Sychorax was hunting down her own daughter.

There she was, right at the front of the stampeding Warrior force, for Queen Sychorax always had to be the fastest, ram-rod straight on the back of her hunting horse, crying out orders, entirely oblivious to the roar of the fire behind her.

They caught up with Crusher first.

Even with his great giant strides, he moved slower than the snowcats because he kept on stopping to reassure the trees. Calm in the chaos, he laid his giant hands on oak, on elm, on ash, on alder, on blackthorn, on beech, on hawthorn, hazel, holly, on lime and maple, on yew and poplar and willow, all the dear, soon-to-be-torchlight trees, saying, 'Do not be afraid, dear trees. The forest will grow again, I promise. I will cherish your descendants . . . This too will pass . . .'

BAAAAAM! The Warrior hunt was upon him.

Queen Sychorax launched her spear first. Crusher looked down with a bemused expression, picking it out of his leg as if it were an irritating thorn or needle. The Warriors surrounded the giant, confusing him with the

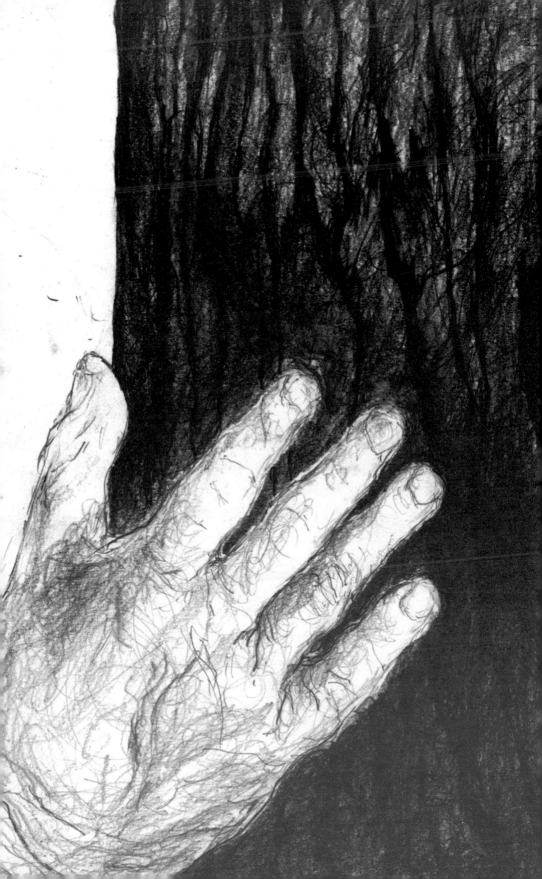

clamour of their horns, for giants have very sensitive hearing, and the loudness and the pitch befuddled his ears so much that he lost his balance and fell to the ground as suddenly as a great oak struck by lightning.

The Warriors scattered in all directions as he dropped, and then regathered again around the fallen giant, winding strands of his hair and the edges of his clothes around their weapons and then driving those weapons into the ground so that when he opened his eyes, blinking, he was stuck to the earth by a pincushion of spears, axes and arrows.

One of the Warriors then rode her horse right up the chest of the giant, rearing it up into the air and punching up her spear in a victory salute, shouting, 'GOT HIM, YOUR MAJESTY!'

'Very good,' cried Sychorax. 'Stern-and-True Justice! Vengeance! Tenacity! Unrelenting! Drama! Unforgiving!'

These were the names of Wish's six elder stepsisters, tall, good-looking, blonde young women with bulging biceps and golden torcs around their necks, heavily armed with spears and axes and every kind of helpful weapon. 'Hunt down your sister and the other two!' ordered Queen Sychorax, adding, 'Be careful not to hurt her, mind . . .'

Wish's stepsisters nodded, and with great whooping cries, they kicked their heels on the leopard-spotted

56

flanks of their hunting horses, and galloped off after the retreating snowcats.

The stepsisters were excellent Warriors, strong of arm, fast of throw, with any softness of heart well drilled out of them, so they very quickly ran down the snowcats. They brought down the sprites with sprite nets so exquisitely thrown that it brought tears to the eyes of their teacher, Madam Dreadlock, who was galloping on a sturdy horse beside them, crying with pride at the brilliance with which her pupils knocked Wish and Bodkin and Xar off their snowcats in single blows around the midriff, and then entwined them in iron nets.

'Call off your beastly animals!' snarled Stern-and-True Justice. 'Or I will KILL your disgusting sprites!'

'She means it,' said Wish, who knew her eldest stepsister well. Justice was perfectly capable of killing a sprite in cold blood. Wish herself had automatically curled up into a defensive little ball like a hedgehog.

Wish's Enchanted Pins, Spoon, Fork and Key were all attacking the stepsisters, the pins pushing themselves into any soft fleshy bits they could find, but Wish called them off, shouting, 'Enchanted things! Snowcats! Wolves! Bear! Keep your distance . . .'

Reluctantly, the iron enchanted objects backed away, but not before Justice grabbed the Enchanted Spoon and all of Xar's animals dropped to the ground, growling.

Xar started to curse the sisters but Justice stopped him with a gentle tap of her mace that knocked him out. And then the pleasant young Warrior women dragged the three children in the nets behind them, back to where Queen Sychorax was waiting with her Warriors beside the fallen giant. The victorious stepsisters gave poor little Wish some good healthy whacks with their mace and spear-sticks along the way, just to punish her for getting them all out on this horrible journey into the middle of nowhere.

Queen Sychorax's Warriors were getting a little restive, looking over their shoulders somewhat anxiously at the howl of the fiery furnace getting louder and louder, hoping that the mother-and-daughter chat wasn't going to go on too long, for mistletoe's sake. But Queen Sychorax herself was sitting bolt upright on her horse, apparently unaware of the advancing danger.

Her stepdaughters dragged the three nets in front of her.

'Here she is, the weird little rat,' said Stern-and-True Justice, 'looking even more odd and weak than ever. She really is a dreadful, dirty little beast. Do you want us to kick her for you some more, Mother?'

'Not now, Justice,' said Queen Sychorax, getting off her horse and opening up the net containing Wish with the end of her sceptre.

Wish uncurled herself and stood up.

Queen Sychorax took off her helmet and her face underneath the helmet was rather colder and sterner than the helmet itself. As I said before, Queen Sychorax was in a bit of a mood.

'You broke your promise,' said Queen Sychorax grimly, with that awful edge of disappointment in her golden pear drop of a voice. 'You said you would return with me to iron Warrior fort, and instead you ran away.'

'I told you, Mother, Xar and Bodkin and I are searching for the ingredients for a spell to get rid of Witches,' said Wish, very white. 'And what are you doing setting fire to the forest? I think you should calm down and stop over-reacting.'

'Calm down?' raged Queen Sychorax. 'Over-reacting?'

'Look, Wish!' said Sychorax. She got hold of Wish's shoulder, turned her round and pointed her finger at a huge mushrooming cloud that was rising above the trees where the dead Witch had landed. The cloud was at least a hundred feet wide, a nasty sulphurous green, and pulsating with a poison that made the Spell of Love Denied look like lemonade.

'That crater with the dead Witch in it will still be poisonous in another twenty years,' said Sychorax. 'These are *Witches*, not mischievous little curse sprites. There

59

is no such thing as a spell to defeat them – that is pure fantasy and wish-fulfillment on your part. Return to the iron Warrior castle, behind my wall, and I will keep you safe . . .'

Sychorax's tone had changed and become coaxing, pleasant.

'. . . and Dreadlock here, your beloved teacher, will teach you how to be a proper Warrior, won't you, Dreadlock? And then you'll forget about all this silly Magic business . . .'

Madam Dreadlock, sitting like a judgemental walrus on horseback beside Wish's older stepsisters, bowed obediently but shot Wish a look of the purest dislike. Wish was the most unsatisfactory pupil she had ever taught, with absolutely not the foggiest idea of whether the angles of the hypotenuse added up to x or y, and she couldn't do spelling HOWEVER loudly Madam Dreadlock shouted at her.*

---

* Editor's note: Wish was dyslexic. Of course, they didn't CALL it dyslexia back in the Bronze Age, but she was, and teachers like Madam Dreadlock weren't very understanding about this to say the least.

You have disgraced
your Warrior Tribe AGAIN!!

'Your trigonometry homework was due last Tuesday,' barked Madam Dreadlock automatically. 'And I need the door of my Punishment Cupboard* returned in tip-top mint condition—'

'Yes, not now, Dreadlock,' said Queen Sychorax hurriedly. 'I'm sure you can make allowances under the circumstances . . .'

But Wish had had quite enough experience of Madam Dreadlock and her mother's iron Warrior fort. She backed away from her mother.

'No,' said Wish defiantly. 'Xar and I are going to show you how Wizards and Warriors CAN work together to fight the Witches!'

'HA! HA! HA!' Wish's stepsisters laughed so hard at this that they nearly fell over.

Queen Sychorax's eyes hardened into stones.

'*Now* she's in for it,' said Drama, Wish's sixth stepsister, with satisfaction.

'YOU, a leader?' spat Queen Sychorax in a voice like an adder strike. 'A worm with the *flu* would make a better leader than you! I have met *jellyfish* with greater leadership potential! Look at what trouble you've already led your wicked and foolish companions into! Covered in wounds, even weaker than you normally are, you haven't eaten for days, you have NO FRIENDS and

* The door the children had been travelling on was originally the door to Madam Dreadlock's Punishment Cupboard and it would now need rather a lot of work to return to tip-top mint condition.

nowhere to hide . . . and I only just saved you from
falling into the talons of the Witches! You call this
leadership?'

Wish flinched. Every single poison arrow of a word
her mother said was something Wish had already been
worrying was true. But Queen Sychorax hadn't finished
yet.

'Consorting with Wizards and werewolves and other
low lifes! Riding beasts! Performing Magic! I cannot
believe that my *own daughter* is so miserably unworthy
compared to my stepdaughters!' said Queen Sychorax.

The stepsisters giggled smugly.

'YOU, Wish,' finished Queen Sychorax, with
magnificent scorn, 'are an embarrassment and a traitor
and a disgrace to your tribe!'

Six months ago a speech like this would have
crushed Wish. But that was before she met Xar, and
Xar had given her courage, and she found that she was
no longer afraid of a mother who set fire to forests and
imprisoned her beloved vegetarian giant with spears, and
called her horrible names.

'I am not an embarrassment or a traitor or a disgrace
to my tribe,' said Wish coldly. 'Release my giant, release
my friends Xar and Bodkin, my sprites, my animals, my
enchanted objects, and stop the fire!'

Queen Sychorax stared in astonishment. But she

recovered quickly.

'It is a great deal easier to *start* a fire, than stop it,' said Queen Sychorax.

She reached out and grabbed Wish's arms so that she could not put up her eyepatch.

'You are coming back home whether you like it or not!' said Queen Sychorax grimly. 'This so-called spell of yours to get rid of Witches isn't a proper spell. You have to understand that your best hope of survival is to be locked up safe forever. You need to face real life and grow up sharpish!

'*And to help you do that, when we get back home I will put your evil bandit friends in the deepest darkest dungeon I can find, and I will melt down that ridiculous Enchanted Spoon of yours, and turn him into hairpins!*'

Now Queen Sychorax probably didn't *mean* that – she had just lost her temper – but with that last, bitterly snapped out comment I think you can safely say that the mother-and-daughter negotiations pretty much broke down for the moment.

'Oh dear oh dear oh dear . . .' moaned Caliburn, for with Wish's arms imprisoned so firmly by the grim hands of Queen Sychorax, there was absolutely nothing Wish could do – she couldn't reach her eyepatch to use the Magic eye . . .

Xar was out like a light, Crusher was entirely

incapacitated, the sprites and
Bodkin were all tangled up in iron-
clad nets, Justice was looking delightedly at
the Enchanted Spoon hoping that she was going to be
able to melt it *personally*, the snowcats, wolves and bear
were too scared of something happening to Wish or the
sprites to move, fire was now reaching the edges of the
clearing and was heating up the bottoms of the Warriors
at the back of the crowd so fiercely that only the most
iron-strict of Warrior training was preventing them from
leaping from their saddles shouting YARROOOOO or
something similar . . .

Yes, I think you could definitely say that this was a
crisis, and we're only at the end of CHAPTER THREE,
for mistletoe's sake.

And quite a lot had happened *already* – what with
the Witch attack, and the capture by Warriors, it had
been a very busy half an hour, what with one thing
and another. You have to feel for poor Caliburn in this
situation. He was the oldest creature in that clearing by
far, and this really wasn't good for his old bird heart.

'What's going to happen now????' panicked
Caliburn. 'I mean, I'm only a bird. I could peck
someone, but I'm not sure it would help . . .'

4. Exit, Rescued By a Bear

ROOOOOOOOOAW!

Into this scene in which Queen Sychorax appeared to have regained control of the situation – apart from the FIRE of course, for as Queen Sychorax said herself, fires are easier to *start* than they are to stop, and once started they are difficult to keep in check – there leapt a gigantic brown bear.

The bear was unimaginably enormous, three times the size of a normal bear. Its ragged fur, upraised either in fury or fright, made it seem even bigger than it actually was.

It leapt into the clearing, reared on to its hind legs, and beat its gigantic chest with its enormous paws. On its entrance, Warriors scattered in all directions in shock. Behind the bear came the thunder and shaking of colossal feet pounding into the ground like mini earthquakes, and one, two, three, four, five Thunderdell giants stormed into the clearing, followed by a little owl with spotted brown wings.

Whatever Caliburn or anyone else was expecting to happen next, they weren't expecting *this*.

Queen Sychorax was so surprised she relaxed her iron grip on Wish's arms.

66

Wish leapt away from Queen Sychorax and hauled up the edge of her eyepatch with shaking hands.

One of the many advantages of having a Magic eye is that you can make things happen extremely quickly. Wish had been taught by Caliburn how to make iron things move just by looking at them.

So she looked across at Crusher and then at Bodkin, Xar and the sprites, and . . .

PING! PING! PING! PING! PING! The spears, daggers, axes and maces that were pinning the edges of Crusher's clothes and his hair to the ground rocketed into the air, releasing him. The iron nets entangling the sprites and Bodkin and Xar fell open.

Then Wish looked across at Justice holding the Enchanted Spoon tight in her hands and . . . the spoon plunged forward with extraordinary strength towards Wish. For some strange reason, Justice's hands were now magnetically attached to it, as if by supernatural glue. Justice was dragged, still holding on to the spoon, off her horse and did a swallow dive into the mud of the forest floor with phenomenal velocity. And boing! Boing! Boing! As the Enchanted Spoon jumped towards its beloved Wish with an attraction that was really quite touching to see, boing, boing, boing, Justice was dragged behind it, her nose and tummy and entire front being slammed into the mud at each bounce. The fork jabbed into her bottom to make her let go, and the key rammed her knuckles, and although it was all rather undignified, I'm afraid I'm not a bit sorry for her.

ROOOOOOOOOOOAAW! The bear continued to roar on its hind legs.

The noise woke Xar, who came to, sitting upright abruptly. Bodkin had already scrambled out of the net entangling him and got to his feet.

REOOOOOOOOOAW!! The bear crashed back to the ground on all four legs.

'Get on my back,' said the bear to Wish. And the bear slumped right down on the forest floor on its tummy so that they could climb on to it.

'Quick, quick!' snapped the bear. 'We haven't got much time!'

'Bears can't talk,' said Wish stupidly, because that was the first thing that came into her head.

'I'm not really a bear,' said the bear.

'Of course not,' said Wish. 'How silly of me.'

'But I *am* a friend,' said the bear.

Now, even in a situation as grim and disastrous as this one, I am not recommending that you climb on the back of a bear who is a *total stranger*.

But Caliburn swooped downwards, shrieking, 'The bear is my sister! She's definitely my sister! I'd recognise her anywhere!'

Six months ago, Wish would have found this extremely disconcerting.

But after spending some considerable time in the world of Magic, the idea of Caliburn having a bear for a sister suddenly seemed reasonably normal.

So, shaking with nerves, Wish hauled herself on to the back of the bear, taking hold of her long brown fur as she climbed it like a hillock. The bear generously barely even flinched even though Wish must have been pulling her hair, and Xar and Bodkin climbed up behind her.

'Hold tight,' said the bear, getting to her feet.

'Don't forget the door!' Caliburn reminded Wish.

'Oh! Yes! Quite right – we can't leave the door behind!' said Wish. She turned round, lifted up her eyepatch a smidgeon and focussed on the fragments of the door lying all about the clearing in thousands of tiny little pieces, and they rose, whizzing and humming into the air, delighted that they hadn't been forgotten. There wasn't time to put all the fragments back in the right places, so they just jammed together any old how, forming a very eccentric impression of a door.

And then the bear charged straight at the most fiery part of the forest.

'What is the bear doing? It's going to burn us all to death!' shouted Bodkin, terrified.

'Stay close to the bear, sprites!' said Caliburn,
landing on Bodkin's shoulder and gripping so tight with
his claws that Bodkin cried out. The sprites landed on
the bear and the bear ran right through the flames and
they did not burn. 'Illusions . . .' explained the owl,
crouched down on the bear's back just in front of Wish.
'Some of these flames are illusions.' Behind the bear ran
the snowcats, wolves, and Xar's much smaller, more-
normal-sized bear, followed by the Thunderdell
giants, who tore up the burning trees on either
side and threw them down behind them, and the
flames leapt up and the Warriors could
not follow.

Queen Sychorax was left, mouth
open, unable to stop them. One

second the children were there, and in her power. The next they were gone.

5. The Tunnel of Fire

The bear ran through the fire, followed by the Thunderdell giants.

One of the bear's eyes was gleaming with a bright white star of light, and this starlight seemed to be able to see which of the flames were real and which were illusions.

Wish's heart was beating so hard she thought it might jump right out of her chest. *What are we doing, trusting this bear that we've only just met, and where is she taking us?* But somehow she knew she *could* trust this bear, that this was a bear who was on her side, and she held on to the bear's long shaggy fur with all of her might, and although the brown fur might be gleaming just a little spookily with a blue supernatural light, there was a solidity and power in the bear's body beneath her that was comfortingly real as it powered through the forest.

For a couple of terrifying minutes they ran through the inferno, the bear knowing the path to take.

The heat was so strong that the top of Bodkin's helmet started to melt. Fire, fire all around.

And then they were out of the fire and into the quiet forest.

At least we're out of the flames . . . thought Wish slightly hysterically to herself, trying to stay on TOP of the bear, because she wasn't very good at riding things without falling off.

The bear kept running, the Thunderdell giants and Crusher and the now-set-alight door following behind them, the wolves in a crazy pack all around, the snowcats with hair all-on-end with fright.

'This is the place,' said the bear, stopping a moment. The Thunderdell giants halted and with great heaves they pulled up the nearest trees by the roots. Then they turned and carefully put the trees down some distance away, whispering words of thanks to the trees as they did so.

'Oh! The poor trees!' said Wish. 'What are they doing?'

'They're creating a firebreak,' said Caliburn. 'If there's a gap in the forest, the fire won't be able to cross it.'

The Thunderdell giants were joined by more Thunderdells, and more and more and more, and the giants worked together to pull up the trees and make a gap in the forest that the fire could not cross.

76

Meanwhile Crusher knelt by the fallen trees, laying his hands on them and reassuring them that their sacrifice will have been worth it.

'Man-made fires are never a good idea,' said Crusher, 'but the forest will return, trust me, dear trees . . .'

'As long as that dreadful Sychorax woman doesn't try and plant her fields here,' sniffed the bear disapprovingly.

'Sprite-who-looks-like-a-bright-blue-twig, can you help me?' said the bear to Ariel.

'My name isss Ariel,' hissed Ariel.

'Nice name,' said the bear. 'Sprite-whose-name-is-Ariel, can you carry a flame of the fire for me?'

'Of courssse,' said Ariel, flying down to a flaming twig lying on the forest floor, and putting a little bit of it in the fire-box he carried around his waist. (Warriors carried tinder-boxes, but Wizards and sprites carried fire-boxes, which had little flames like lighted candles, kept alight by the power of Magic in a tiny box.)

'I'm a fire-collector,' explained the bear, looking over her shoulder at Wish, and Wish thought, *Aren't all fires exactly the same?* But she nodded, as if fire-collecting was a perfectly normal hobby, like collecting books or jewels or money or different coloured spell-bags.

Then the bear looked up at the sky and lightning

77

flashed from her starlight eye, and there were gigantic rolls of thunder and the lightning criss-crossed and zig-zagged across the sky, and the clouds opened, and the rain poured down on the forest fire. The flaming Enchanted Door following them was instantly quenched by the water with a damp protesting hiss.

'Weather spelling . . .' said Xar, impressed, for controlling the weather was very advanced Magic indeed, and even his own father, the great King Wizard Encanzo, had trouble with it.

'The rain and the firebreak will stop the fire from spreading,' said the bear.

They left the Thunderdell giants tending to the firebreak and making sure the fire did not leap across it.

The bear and the animals and Crusher ran on, leaving the fire behind, and the rain ran into Wish's eyes so that she could barely see. Eventually the animals came to a part of the forest where the ancient yews had grown so gnarled and bulging over the last three thousand years or so that they seemed to have faces, and their roots had twisted and turned into things that looked like feet, and the sprites had their wands out, for when you are in the presence of the Old Magic it makes you feel just . . . a little bit . . . *uneasy*.

A mist had descended, and the night was full of noises, of will-o'-the-wisps whooping out of nowhere and coo-ing '*Come this way*' in a spooky kind of way, and although even a five-year-old knows not to follow a will-o'-the-wisp however longingly they may coo (wisps are harmless, until you follow them, and then they can lead you to Very Dangerous Things indeed) it is still a little unnerving.

'Oh dear, I think we may be lost!' said the bear, not sounding unhappy at all, but if anything, really rather delighted. The strange blue light that had lit up the bear's fur as they ran through the fire, and had made it seem like she was from another world, had dimmed, along with the white light of her eye, and she was now just an ordinary (if unfeasibly large) wet brown bear. 'Does anyone know the way?'

'You're supposed to be taking US somewhere!' Bodkin pointed out. 'Caliburn said you had some sort of house?'

'We're definitely somewhere near the Lake of the Lost,' said Caliburn with a shiver.

'Oh good,' said the bear, 'because as it happens, I'm looking for a large mound which is currently situated somewhere near the Lake of the Lost. A mound with a great chalk horse drawn on the side of it . . . I think it's a horse, or it could be a dragon, I'm never quite sure. Keep your eyes peeled, everyone.'

On they searched, through territory where the trees

seemed to be getting older and older, until eventually they came upon the large mound the bear had described, or rather the mound seemed to come upon *them*, for it rose suddenly and enormously out of the mist like a gigantic creature creeping up on them.

The mound was as round as a wheel and as big as a hill. It was far too large to be man-made, but also far too perfectly circular to be a natural formation, so it was a contradiction of itself even at first sight. A colossal leaping animal was drawn on one side of it, just to their right, made out of paths of chalk

Pook's Hill

in the grass. They were
too close up to see whether
or not the tremendous chalk picture
looked more like a horse or a dragon.

    By now everyone was as
thoroughly drenched as if they had
been swimming in the ocean. Wish was

wet through and starting to shiver, and dying to get to anywhere that might offer some warmth and food and protection from the rain.

'What is this? We can't shelter here. It seems to be just a hill without any trees on it!' objected Xar.

'That's why we go INSIDE the hill,' said the bear. 'The main entrance is around the other side, but we can get in here too. I just have to remember the password to let us in ...'

But the bear had unfortunately forgotten the password that would let them into the hill. She tried all sorts of words: 'Magic ... Tuesday ... Arctic ... tangerine ... honeydew ...' Loads and loads of lovely words, but none of them seemed to be the right ones.

'I don't know WHY they keep on changing the password!' said the bear irritably.

'You're the one who *sets* the password!' the little owl reminded her.

'Well I don't know why I keep on changing it!' said the bear. 'But how

silly of me! We can
use the door . . .
whose door is this?'
They had all forgotten
about the Enchanted Door that
was following them, but they
now turned round and took a
good look at it.

The door was looking
thoroughly dejected. It was
burnt through, still steaming
and bursting into the odd
flame, and jumbled up in all the
wrong places.

'It's mine,' admitted Wish.

'You're not a very
considerate door owner,' said
the little owl severely. 'This door
needs some serious love and

THE
PUNISHMENT
CUPBOARD.
Magic
is
BANNED

Whose door
is this?

attention. But still . . . use the door to let us in.'

'But I don't know how to do that,' said Wish.

'What on earth are you carrying a door around with you for then?' asked the owl, fixing Wish with its beady eye.

'We've been flying on the back of it,' said Wish, and even to her own ears this sounded a little ridiculous.

The owl tut-tutted like anything.

'*Rugs* are for flying on, *carpets* are for flying on, *doors* are for opening and shutting . . .' snapped the owl. 'Who is in charge of the education of this child?'

'I am,' admitted Caliburn. 'But I haven't had very long to teach her, and—'

'Well, *I* think,' said the bear thoughtfully, 'that a flying door is a wonderfully *creative* idea. What is your name, wonderful child?'

Wish wasn't feeling very wonderful, all dripping wet sitting on the back of the bear, but nonetheless she replied shyly, 'Wish.'

WATCH me, Spoon! Watch me deal with this unlocking emergency!

'You see, a wonderful name for a wonderful child,' said the bear encouragingly. 'What you should do now, Wish, is THINK the door on to the side of the mound. Imagine it is happening with the whole of your mind ...'

'Maybe put your eyepatch up just a smidgeon,' Caliburn whispered in her ear.

Wish put her eyepatch up a smidgeon and imagined the door fitting on to the side of the mound, and the door obligingly shuffled across to the hill and shrugged itself dejectedly into the side of it, dripping with water.

'Brilliant!' said the bear admiringly.

'It's not brilliant, it's very basic telekinesis,' humphed the grumpy little owl. 'I presume you have a key?'

'She does indeed!' whooped the key, hopping delightedly out of Wish's hair and down to the ground, and plugging itself into the keyhole.

'The key unlocks the
door, once, twice . . . And then
you step forward, Wish . . . and
knock three times,' explained the
bear.
'I suppose you did all right, fork,
for a steering job in an emergency,
although it did, as I predicted, end in
disaster,' said Wish's Enchanted
Key chattily in its little creaky
voice, and showing off like
anything as it made a great
display of swivelling around
in the keyhole. 'But you see,
nobody unlocks a door like a
proper KEY . . .'
And then Wish
stepped forward, and
knocked three
times.

Knock!

Knock!

knock!

RAT!

TAT!

TAT!

And slowly, slowly, the poor battered door opened –
C-R-E-A-K!

– to reveal, behind it, wonder of wonders, a great
open hall – or was it a gigantic corridor? To the left and
right of them it carried on without stopping, until it
curved away, and you could not see the end of it.

The hall was lit with candles and there was a much
larger open door on the other side. Through that door
they could hear a faint whispering of welcoming sprites
and in the distance the sound of chattering voices, the
howl of wolves and the clunk of giants' boots, all warm
and cosy and homey as anything.

'That's impossible!' breathed Bodkin with an open
mouth. 'That was a hill . . . a solid hillside! How can the
door make a doorway suddenly appear into some kind
of *hall?*'

The door felt like it had always been there, cut into
the mound. One side, the rain, the forest. Step over the
threshold and on the other side, the warmth of the hall.

'I'm so confused,' said Bodkin. 'Is this a house, or is
this a hill? Where are we?'

'Humph,' said the little owl. 'Have you never seen
Magic performed before, child?'

The hall appeared to be made out of gigantic stones, all fitting together perfectly, and any cracks between them made watertight with burnt soil. Wish had seen buildings similar in places of worship, or passage tombs, but nothing of this extraordinary size before. Many of the stones were covered in deep patterns cut into the rock – diamond shapes, swirls and, more interestingly, suns drawn in many different types of ways, crescent moons, whole moons, slivers of moons, and long wavy lines that looked like winding rivers but which Wish knew were in fact calendars, ways of telling the time. Wish's heart lifted with excitement. Wherever they were must be a very important place indeed.

They all stepped over the threshold and into the hall. (When I say ALL, of course I mean the children, Caliburn, the sprites, Lonesome and the wolves and the snowcats – the bear and Crusher were too big to fit through the door.)

'Make the door bigger so that we can all come through,' the little owl ordered Wish.

'I really can't do that,' said Wish. 'I've learnt about telekinesis, but I haven't done making things bigger.'

'Tut tut!' said the owl. 'Here's a child who really needs to work on her positive thinking. Just because you've never done something before doesn't mean it can't be done. All you have to do is—'

But the owl didn't need to explain.

On the other side of the door the bear had *finally* remembered the password.

'Oh! Don't worry! I've remembered the password now!' said the bear. 'It's my mother's maiden name! ARDEN!!!'

As soon as the bear spoke the word ARDEN there was a loud

BOOOOOM!

And the entire side of the hill exploded, leaving an enormous gap for Crusher and the bear to get through.

Coughing and spluttering, Crusher and the bear stepped through into the hall beside the children, both of them so covered with chalk dust that they looked like they had been caught out in a sudden snowstorm.

'There!' said the bear with satisfaction, showering them all with chalk dust as she gave herself a good old shake. 'I knew I'd remember the password in the end! But we mustn't get distracted . . . We need to get you to the study area as soon as we can before the house piskies detect us!'

'Pissssskiessss???' hissed the sprites in horror. 'There are *piskies* in this house? We's HATE piskies.' They drew all their weapons and hissed with fury, because sprites do indeed absolutely *loathe* piskies for reasons that everyone has forgotten because they go way back in fairy lore, but the hatred still shines as bright as if whatever-the-original-crime-was had happened only yesterday.

'Yes, of course there are piskies,' snapped the owl. 'All the best houses are infested with piskies. They're a pain in the neck, but put away your weapons, sprites! I will have no fighting in our house, and the first one who casts a spell will be thrown out into the rain.'

Grumbling, the sprites put their sharpened thorns and bows and arrows away.

'Remember,' said the owl, 'we may have rescued you, but YOU ARE NOT STAYING HERE. This is just an overnight visit and I think that it would be best if we kept it a secret between ourselves, and piskies absolutely cannot keep a secret, so everyone needs to be as quiet as possible until we reach the safety of the study. Close the door, Wish! And bring it with us!'

Wish closed the door with her mind and – Cre-e-

Piskies

e-eak! – the door closed, shutting out the view into the raining forest. And when the door detached itself from the inside wall of the hill, there was nothing to say that a door had ever been there.

'*How are you doing that?*' said Bodkin, and even Xar was impressed.

Meanwhile the bear said the password backwards: 'NEDRA!' and the entire side of the hill jammed itself back into the gap with another BOOOOOM! that made the whole mound shake and covered them all in yet another shower of chalk dust.

'*Messy,*' said the owl reprovingly.

'Sorry,' said the bear apologetically, wiping her nose with her paw and getting it all chalky.

'Come along! Come along!' said the owl, spitting chalk dust out of its beak and shooing the dripping party through the hall, and they tiptoed across the flagstones, leaving great puddles of watery footsteps. 'As quiet as you can . . .'

It was too late. The sound of the bear's entrance had already attracted the piskies' attention. There was a hissssss of excitement and a glowing band of bright warm piskies burst into the hall just as they were crossing it . . .

'*Piskies!*' hissed Xar's sprites in horror.

Now, piskies look quite a lot like sprites, but woe

93

betide you if you confuse the two, for they get very offended if you do. They are a bit like hairy fairies who have never grown up, but furrier and fuzzier, with weird exploding hairstyles that the sprites think they only grow that way to show off. They tend to be brown when they are inside, but as soon as they are outside they can turn any colour they want, for piskies are chameleons. They are very small and a lot of them were riding on the backs of wasps, which they keep as pets.

'Hello! Hello! Hello! Welcome, welcome, welcome!' The piskies beamed, buzzing around the visitors in great warm swarms. 'What have we here? New people?'

'Nothing to see here, piskies!' said the little owl. 'Nobody's staying! Just some hospital cases that we rescued from the fire. They're not staying long because there's an awful lot of them. They'll just be here for ONE DAY while we treat their door and feed them up. Don't tell anyone, piskies! SHOO!'

'We won't tell we won't tell . . .' buzzed the piskies. 'One bear one giant three drowned humans three wolves three snowcats eight USELESS sprites . . . one peregrine falcon and a Baby . . . all very WET . . . But we won't tell we won't tell . . . we won't tell NO ONE, will we, piskies?' replied the piskies, delighted to get a reaction from the sprites, who were hissing with annoyance.

'NONONO!' sang the piskies, answering themselves

as some of their party buzzed off to tell everyone. 'We won't tell we won't tell, your secret's safe with US . . .'

The owl shooed them all through the hall, and instead of the door on the other side leading into another room, it led into a courtyard which was more like an enormous clearing where many, many trees were growing. The clearing was too large to see the other side, and it was ringed with the grassy hill, which on the inside appeared to be supported by more sacred rocks, carved again with spirals and diamonds and waves.

'Wow,' said Wish admiringly, looking up at the sky. 'How does that work? The mound looks like a normal hill on the outside, but inside it has a hollow centre.'

'Magical spaces work very differently from normal spaces,' said Caliburn.

They certainly did.

What appeared to be a normal-sized hillside on the outside was a far bigger space on the inside. This clearing was HUGE, and smoke coming out of all the trees from firesides deep underground meant that many,

many chambers and great halls for all the habitations must be hollowed out in the tree roots. It was just as Wish and Bodkin had seen once before when they visited Xar's

95

Wizard fort on the edge of the Badwoods. There were the shadowy shapes of giants in the distance among the trees, the lights of sprites, and the outlines of crowds of chattering Wizards.

'Keep in the shadows!' ordered the little owl. 'We're nearly there! No one needs to know we're here ...'

Tell that to the piskies, gathering in greater and greater numbers, who had now organised an entire flying band of musical instruments to follow them as well (for piskies love music and dancing) – fiddles and drums and flute-type thingummies playing themselves to a tune that went something like this:

'It's sweet to go travelling ... in lakes and forests and on foam ... butits*so*muchsweeter ... yesits*so*muchsweeter ... tocomeHOME!'

'Nobody's HOME!' said the owl. 'This is just a flying visit, FOR ONE NIGHT ONLY ... *THESE PEOPLE ARE NOT BEING ADMITTED PERMANENTLY!*'

'Here they are!' sang the fiddles.

'LOOK OVER HERE!' boomed the drums.

'Welcome, welcome, secret visitors!' trilled the flute-type thingummies ...

'Onebearonegiantthreedrownedhumans ... threewolvesthreesnowcats ... NINEuselesssprites*one*peregrinefalconandaBaby ... *WELCOME ALL!*' sang the piskies.

'Oh for goodness' sake,' said the owl.

'You're HOME, you're HOME, welcome to your HOME!' sang everyone all together at full blast. 'Your Magical, marv-e-llous, magnifi-cent . . . new HO-O-O-OME!!!!'

'For absolutely the last time!' spluttered the owl. 'This is NOT THESE PEOPLE'S NEW HOME! There's absolutely loads of them, we haven't got room and so whoever they are, they're just passing through.'

'I told you your sister wouldn't want us,' whispered Wish sadly to Caliburn. 'It's just like I said . . . we're a bit odd, and we don't really fit in anywhere . . .'

'No, no,' Caliburn whispered back, 'I'm sure she wants us really . . . It's just that this owl of hers needs a little time to get used to us.'

'Thank goodness!' said the bear in relief. 'We've reached my study! Or as some people call it, the Lair of the Bear.'

The Lair of the Bear, or the study, was a great oak liberally festooned with countless balls of mistletoe. They managed to get there with Xar's sprites only getting into *one* wrestling match with the piskies, and Squeezjoos only biting off *one* shoe of a piskie who was trying to pick Xar's pocket, and it was in the nick of time, for the utter commotion was beginning to draw the attention of the other inhabitants of the hillside.

'Now ... what was the password again?' the bear wondered to herself, coming to a gentle lumbering halt and accidentally sitting on a snowcat, who let out a protesting howl. 'Sorry ...' said the bear, hurriedly getting to her feet.

'ARDEN! The password is ARDEN!' shrieked the little owl.

And as the owl spoke, the roots of the oak rustled and moved to reveal a hollow space. The roots took in the size of the various bears and snowcats, and moved wider, wider, revealing an enormous hollow that led on to a gigantic winding staircase down into the Lair of the Bear,

'Down into the tree!' ordered the little owl, all of a fluster, sending a couple of piskies scattering away with one urgent sweep of its claw, and everyone apart from Crusher went down the winding staircase. 'Wait here,' the owl said to Crusher, 'and inform anyone who asks that We Are Not to be Disturbed and It is None of Their Business ...'

'NEDRA!' snapped the owl, and the tree roots shuffled and closed, and the little party were now in the Lair of the Bear.

This way to the Lair of the Bear →

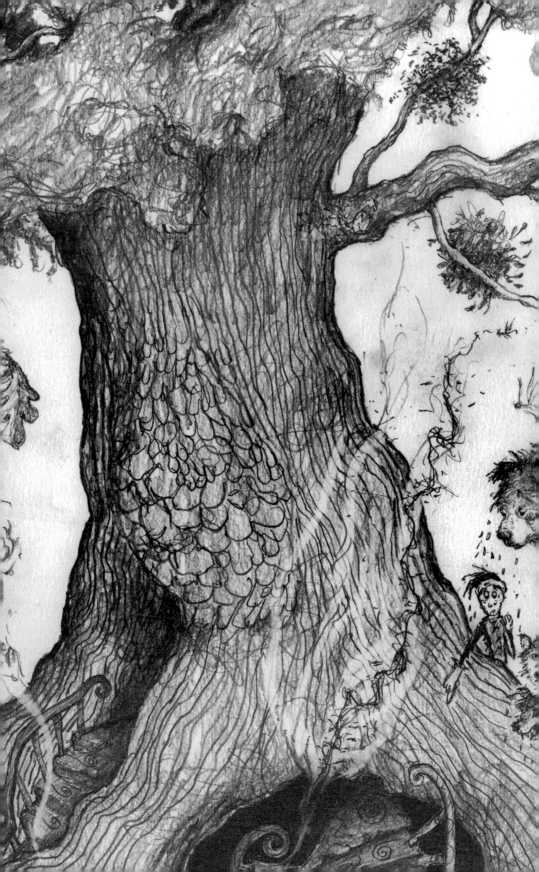

6. In the Lair of the Bear

The Lair of the Bear was exceptionally messy. There was a fire in the centre of it and there were books everywhere, on bookcases that were higgledy-piggledy and wandered all over the place with the tree roots. Then there were birds perching on the books, and the visitors had to be careful not to step on the droppings, and not to knock over smaller fires with little cauldrons on them everywhere you looked.

Even as they came in, one of the cauldrons was boiling over. Great violet-coloured smoke bubbles came out of it and landed on some papers on the floor, that promptly burst into the flames. The bear broke into a gentle run and extinguished the flames by sitting on them. Hsss.

'Whoops,' said the bear guiltily. 'I forgot I left that on.'

'Wow!' said Wish, looking around the room. The birds whirled into the air, trilling and clucking and twittering, then flew off to fetch blankets, holding them by the edges in their beaks, and draping them round the shivering children, and the wolves and the snowcats. 'What a wonderful room! And thank you so much for saving us in the forest back there. I cannot tell you how grateful we are ...'

'Hmmm,' said the bear. 'One of them has manners,

at least. That's a start.'

Getting to her feet, the bear continued. 'Before we go any further, can I just say, brother, what a joy it is to see you again! What an unexpected, accidental, magnificent DELIGHT!'

The bear hugged the raven.

And the bear and the raven began to dance, which was very sweet really, and although it was fine for the raven to dance in the air, the bear was too big for all the mess in the room. As she whirled around in galumphing circles, her bottom knocked over piles of books and her nose knocked over cauldrons, and snowcats had to scatter out of the way, and everyone had to pick everything up as it fell over.

'Will someone please tell me what is going on?' asked Bodkin, speaking for everyone. 'Where are we? And why is your sister a bear?'

Caliburn the raven landed on the bear's head.

'This bear is not only my sister, she is my twin,' said Caliburn proudly. 'Meet Perdita.'

There was a big silence.

'Okay . . .' said Bodkin, looking to Xar for guidance. 'This is weird.'

'Don't look at me,' said Xar, shrugging his shoulders. 'I'm a Wizard, but even for the Wizarding world, this is weird.'

Wish blinked. She looked from the bear to the bird. 'For twins, you really are not very alike,' said Wish eventually.

'Yes, I think I did mention that I wasn't really a bear, didn't I?' explained the bear. 'It's just a transformation. You see? Watch while I transform back again. Transformation is one of my favourites of the Wizarding skills.'

And in front of Wish's eyes, the bear transformed. It was a spectacular moment.

One moment the bear was a great, magnificent bear-like beast. The next, the outline of the bear melted and shrivelled and became, smaller, smaller . . . until it turned into a small, very untidy-looking woman of goodness-knows-WHAT-age, rather eccentrically dressed, but with very smiley eyes.

'You're still not very alike,' said Bodkin, looking from one to the other and shaking his head. 'One of you is small and black and feathery. And the other one is a human. Not much of a family resemblance, I'd say . . .'

'*You* transform back into a human now, brother,' urged Perdita, looking up at Caliburn, who was still sitting on her head.

The raven tipped his head down and looked sadly into her eyes. 'Unfortunately, I can't,' said Caliburn. 'At the moment this is a sort of temporarily permanent transformation, for this lifetime, at least.'

'Oh, I'm so sorry,' said Perdita.

'It could have been worse,' said Caliburn gloomily.

'I could have been a cockroach.'

Perdita (Caliburn's sister)

'That is so true,' said Perdita. 'It is always important to look on the bright side . . . And, brother, even in bird form, it's so wonderful to see you again!' Perdita held out her arms and danced, as Caliburn took flight and fluttered in and out of them. 'Oh sister, me too!' said Caliburn joyfully.

'The question is, though,' said Perdita, stopping dancing and coming to a halt again. 'Who on earth are all these people and animals and Magical creatures travelling with you?'

'Well, the humans are Xar, Bodkin, and Wish,' explained Caliburn. 'The sprites are Tiffinstorm, Timeloss, Mustardthought, Hinkypunk, Ariel, Bumbleboozle, Squeezjoos, Once-sprite, The Baby. The snowcats are Nighteye, Kingcat, Forestheart. Lonesome is the werewolf. And then there're the wolves, peregrine falcon, bears who don't like to be named because they prefer to be wild—'

'Most understandable,' said Perdita, nodding her head.

'And finally,' finished Caliburn, 'last but of course not least, the giant upstairs is Crusher.'

'This little owl here is Hoola ...' said Perdita. Hoola, now perched on Perdita's shoulder, gave them a stiff little bow and ruffled her feathers at them. 'And it's marvellous to meet you all ... Any friends of my brother's are friends of mine ... but what, for mistletoe's sake, are you doing in this sacred part of the forest? And why were you being chased by that appalling Queen Sychorax, who has clearly now taken total leave of her senses

Hoola the huffy little owl,

by setting fire to our beautiful wildwoods?'

'Ah yes,' said Caliburn, looking very shifty indeed. 'We have a few little problems that we were hoping you were going to help us with, Perdita ... You remember the tears of the Drood that you gave me twenty years ago? I was hoping you might give me a few more ...'

'Whaaaatttt??' cried Perdita. And then she looked wildly around the room, leaned forward and hissed. 'Sssshhhhhhhhhhhh! What if the piskies were to hear? We're right next door to the Lake of the Lost here. If the Droods were ever to find out that I had got hold of any of their tears I would not only be out of my job but they would absolutely KILL me! They're awfully touchy about their tears.'

'Yes, I know,' said Caliburn, gloomily. 'The Droods found out I'd been using their tears in a spell when I was the Wizard Pentaglion, and that's why they turned me into a raven.'

'The Droods found out you had their tears?' gasped Perdita. 'Oh my goodness, brother, you really *are* lucky that you didn't end up as a cockroach!'

'So if you DO happen to have any more of the Droods' tears, Perdita, somewhere in this study of yours,' said Caliburn in a wheedling sort of voice, 'you'd be much better off giving them to US ... We can take them off your hands ...'

'I may still have a few left – I need them for some of my trickier spelling – but I absolutely can't put a dangerous ingredient like Droods' tears into your hands again,' sniffed Perdita. 'I'm already regretting giving them to you *once* . . . I'm certainly not going to make the same mistake *twice*.'

'I thought you might say that,' said Caliburn, sadly. 'And what about the scales of a Nuckalavee? Do you happen to have any of those?'

'*The scales of a Nuckalavee????*' gasped Perdita, even more horrified than she had been when Caliburn talked about Droods' tears. 'No, I don't have any scales of a Nuckalavee, brother! Worse and worse . . . Nuckalavee scales are deeply powerful Magic and only a MAD PERSON would go on a quest to get the scales of a Nuckalavee! It's almost certain death . . . What on earth have you got yourselves into? Why do you need these terrible ingredients anyway?'

'We're trying to make a spell to get rid of Witches,' explained Caliburn.

'There is *no* spell strong enough to get rid of Witches,' said Perdita.

'We think we've found one,' said Caliburn. 'If you can't *give* the Droods' tears to us, will you let us stay here and train ourselves up so we can go on a quest to get them ourselves?'

'Hang on a second,' said Xar suspiciously. 'What do you mean, "train us up"? What is this place, anyway?'

'This is Pook's Hill, the Learning Place for Spectacularly Gifted Wizards,' said Perdita.

'A learning place is just a fancy name for a *school*!!!!' said Xar in horror. He punched the air in panic. 'I've been tricked! Let me out of here! I HATE SCHOOLS! THEY SHOULD BE BANNED! *DOWN WITH SCHOOLS!!!!!*'

'Don't worry,' said Hoola firmly. 'We will let you out of Pook's Hill with pleasure. There's no question of you staying. I am in charge of admissions, and you do not fill any of the admission criteria. You are *not* spectacularly gifted Wizards. The Wish-girl had trouble with anything more complicated than the most basic of telekinesis. And the Xar-boy looks completely out of control.'

'Yes but we're not really a learning place *only* for spectacularly gifted Wizards, are we, Hoola?' said Perdita persuasively. 'You just keep calling it that.'

'It means we get sent more children,' explained Hoola. 'Every parent seems to think they have a spectacularly gifted offspring, even though it's completely obvious that not *everyone's* offspring can be spectacularly gifted.'

'ALL children are spectacularly gifted and learning should be for everyone!' said Perdita enthusiastically.

'But the second boy is an actual *Warrior!*' objected Hoola. 'You have to draw the line somewhere!'

'The boy's ancestors are not the boy's fault,' said Perdita. 'And he will have gifts – we just have to find them. I love a challenge . . .'

'I'm so glad you said that,' said Caliburn, for he had been wondering how he was going to introduce the *exact* nature of Xar and Wish's spectacular gifts. 'Because the girl and the boy here are more gifted than they may look. Underneath her eyepatch, Wish, for instance, has a Magic eye . . .'

Even Hoola was impressed by that, and let out a HOOO! of admiration. Magic eyes were very rare indeed. Only one or two Wizards every generation have a Magic eye.

'I can't take my eyepatch off,' explained Wish, 'because the eye goes a bit crazy when I do.'

'Don't worry,' said Perdita. 'I can see through eyepatches.'

Perdita knelt down in front of Wish. Wish tried to look at the kindly face in front of her, even though it made her eyes water to do so.

Powerful Wizards are always hard to look at, and Perdita was a good deal more powerful than most. So her face was constantly changing, the outline blurring and moving and hazing, like smoke coming off the sea,

110

and sometimes it looked like she had a lot of wrinkles wandering over her face like the lines on an old map, and sometimes it looked like she was only a little older than Wish herself.

Only Perdita's eyes stayed steady, so Wish concentrated on those, and it was a moment before Wish realised that the eyes that twinkled at her were ever so slightly different colours . . . and as Wish carried on staring at the left eye, little spots began to appear on it, like raindrops landing on a lake, and slowly the eye changed to a colour that Wish had never seen before, apart from in her own eye when she was looking in a mirror . . .

'Oh!' said Wish in delight. '*You* have a Magic eye too! But I would never have even noticed if you hadn't pointed it out to me . . .'

'That's because it's under control,' said Perdita, and swiftly the eye changed colour again, back to something more ordinary.

And then Perdita stiffened. All the joyful kind delight at recognising one of her own kind went out of her face in a blink.

And it was because the Enchanted Spoon had hopped up out of Wish's hair to say hello.

Now that they weren't in the hurry and scurry of running away, Perdita could get a good look at that

111

spoon and, up close, it was quite clear that it was made of iron.

Perdita turned absolutely white. And then she straightened, and for one second she stood before them as a bear again, roaring, before turning once more into a human. A very grim-looking human. Even her eyes had stopped twinkling.

'*She has Magic-that-works-on-iron* . . .' whispered Perdita.

Turning to Caliburn she said, 'Oh brother, what is going on here, and brother, what have you done?'

7. Are They IN the Learning Place for Spectacularly Gifted Wizards or Are They NOT?

aliburn had to give quite a *long* explanation about what was going on, about Sychorax and Encanzo being in love once long ago, and the Spell of Love Denied and everything – I won't go into it all again, because you, dear reader, know it already.

Perdita was furious. 'You mean that's what you wanted my Droods' tears for???'

'Yes, but I'd looked into the future, you see, and I saw that a curse would fall on the wildwoods and disaster and calamity would follow if I didn't stop the love from happening . . .' explained Caliburn.

'The curse fell on the wildwoods anyway!' stormed Perdita. 'And I think what we have here is disaster and calamity in spades. When will you ever learn, Caliburn, to be very, very careful about looking into the future? It can so easily end in tears, and you can't change it anyway!'

'I know, I know,' said Caliburn, hanging his head. 'I really have learnt my lesson this time . . .'

However, Caliburn ended, rather craftily he felt, with: '. . . but the children's ancestors are not the children's fault, and you have to admit the girl's enchanted objects are *charming* . . .'

Realising that it was its moment, the Enchanted Spoon gave a happy little somersault on Wish's head, and the fork and the key came hopping out enthusiastically, followed by the pins, and they put on a lively little gymnastic display, trying to look cute in order to win over Perdita. The little owl, Hoola, put a wing to her forehead and groaned.

'They're delightful, you see!' said Caliburn. 'Very well-intentioned little enchanted objects . . . reflecting the character of the girl . . .'

'*But they're made out of iron!*' objected Perdita. '*Everyone's* going to be after that kind of Magic! The emperor of Warriors, Sychorax, the Droods and, oh my goodness . . . the KINGWITCH . . .'

'And . . . *hang on a second.*' Hoola's head swivelled round three hundred and sixty degrees, in that disconcerting way that owls are so fond of, to get a good look at Xar. 'We've heard about the *girl's* disastrous, dangerous gift . . . what's wrong with the *boy?*'

'I beg your pardon?' said Caliburn innocently.

'You heard,' said Hoola. 'What's wrong with *him?* You said he had some sort of gift too . . .'

'The boy just had this *teeny* accident with a Witchstain . . .' said Caliburn, and again, he went into a long, complicated explanation about what had happened, trying to play it all down, but ending with,

114

'He is, admittedly, finding it a little difficult to control . . .'

'That's not true!' objected Xar. 'I have it perfectly under control!'

Xar took his glove off to show Perdita how brilliantly he could control the Witchstain, and a green bolt of lightning shot randomly off it and incinerated her chair. Hurriedly, Xar put his glove back on again.

There was a horrified silence.

'Maybe not *perfectly*,' admitted Xar.

'The spell that gets rid of Witches will get rid of Xar's Witchstain as well, though,' explained Wish.

'If it really is a true spell,' said Hoola. 'It could be just make-believe . . . Wish wants so much to find a cure for Witches that she has made up this spell of yours.'

'However the spell was written with MY feather,' said Caliburn. 'So it might be a memory of a spell written by MYSELF in a former life, when I was the great Wizard Pentaglion.'

Perdita was impressed. 'Yes,' admitted Perdita, 'that does mean the spell is worth a closer look.'

'Spelling Book!' commanded Wish, putting up her eyepatch a little. The Spelling Book jumped out of Wish's pocket and eagerly turned its own pages to the spell to get rid of Witches.

Perdita snapped her fingers. The desk that she had sent flying with her bottom when she was a bear was currently upended, the top against one of the walls, legs stretched out stiffly in the air. The little wooden desk legs softened and waggled as the desk struggled to turn itself upright. With a final heave the desk tipped itself the right way up, all four legs landing on the floor, and then it scuttled sideways like a crab towards Perdita, coming to a halt in front of her. Everyone had to duck as papers, feather pens, books and boxes flew through the air and landed higgledy-piggledy all over the desk. A chair scuttled into place just in time to catch Perdita as she sat down.

Perdita knocked once, twice, thrice on the top of one of the boxes sitting on the desk. The box opened, and five pairs of eyeglasses waved their legs in the air and grappled with each other in a tangled and untidy mess.

'Oh!' exclaimed Wish in delight, 'living spectacles!'

The spoon, the key, the fork and the pins hopped

forward curiously, unsure of what to make of these new enchanted cousins. None of them had ever met anyone else who had enchanted objects before, so this was a fresh and fascinating experience.

The spectacles were horrified at this attention, firmly snapping down the lid of their box.

'They're a bit shy,' warned Perdita, and in response to a quiet word from Wish, the spoon and its companions retreated back into Wish's pockets and hair so as not to alarm the eyeglasses further.

Slo-o-owly the box opened and the eyeglasses blinked through the crack of the lid, like the huge bug eyes of jungle creatures that had just woken up.

Blink, blink.

Wish held her breath with the effort of trying not to laugh.

Gra-a-adually the eyeglasses climbed over the edge of the box like cautious spiders. Haltingly, they stalked gently forward on their long unsteady limbs, still clearly a bit sleepy, and circled in front of Perdita with tentative daddy-long-legs strides so that she could choose one of them to look through.

'Choose the one with the limp,' whispered Wish. She had already decided that her favourite was a pair of glasses that had clearly been through a difficult time, and had one smashed glass and a stem that had been broken and mended again several times.

'Yes, I love that pair,' said Perdita, 'but this time I think I'll go for ... the rose-coloured ones.'

'Oh noooooooo ...' said Hoola, furiously putting her wings in front of her eyes. 'Mistress! Not the ROSE-COLOURED ones! When will you ever learn?'

But the four other pairs of spectacles scrambled back into the box, clearly delighted to be able to go back to sleep, and the pair with the pink glass and twig-like stems stalked up Perdita's untidy clothes on to her face and settled themselves on her nose.

'Let me see now ...' said Perdita, adjusting them more firmly and opening up the Spelling Book.

The Spelling Book

A Complete Guide to the Entire Magical World

The spelling Book
Invisibility

Wish making
her own hand
invisible with her
Magic eye

Invisibility is a Magical power to be used with
caution, because if you stay invisible too long, it
can start to affect your mind in dangerous and
unpredictable ways. Here, Wish is using her Magic
eye to turn her own hand invisible.

page 4,310,690

Fire-Collecting

For Perdita, fire represents a source of light and wisdom. The fire that she burns in the grate at Pook's hill, (or in her own fire-box, if she has to travel), is part of a fire that has been burning for many, many years, back into deep and distant time, and therefore she must never let it go out.

page 4,310,691

Dragons

Dragons had long ago retreated to the freezing cold of the northern polar regions, but ever since the end of the Ice Age, they had been moving south, and many dragons were now making their homes in the jungles of the wildwoods.

Fluffbuttles

Fluffbuttles have a slight problem with CAMOUFLAGE...

Fluffbuttles are creatures whose innocence and lack of defence methods puts them in peril in the dangerous wildwoods. This is not helped by the fact that they have a large and distinctive target mark on the end of their fluffy tails. Werefoxes are their main predators.

happy little Fluffbuttles bouncing through the grasses

A Spell to Get Rid of WITCHES

Ingredients:

1. Giant's Last Breath from Castle Death.

2. Feathers from a Witch

3. Tears from a Frozen Queen,

4. Scales of the Nuckalavee

5. Tears of the Drood from the Lake of the Lost.

'Yes, this is clearly one of our real Wizard spells and it's an exceptionally powerful lovespell.'

'I knew it!' said Caliburn in delight.

'There are five ingredients,' continued Perdita, 'and the number five is very important in Wizard beliefs because there are five elements: air, fire, water, earth and aether. There are five seasons: spring, summer, autumn, winter and eternity. And there are five directions: north, south, west, east and centre.'

'Why would a lovespell work to get rid of Witches?' asked Xar.

'Because Witches are the opposite of love, so love may be the only thing that will work against them,' said Perdita. 'The five ingredients here are all the ingredients you need for a long and lasting love. Giant's Last Breath is forgiveness. Feathers from a Witch is desire. Tears from a Frozen Queen is tenderness. Scales of a Nuckalavee is courage. And Tears of the Drood from the Lake of the Lost is endurance.'

'The good news is that we already have the first three ingredients . . .' said Caliburn.

'And the bad news,' said Hoola, determined to look on the gloomy side, 'is that the last two ingredients are impossible to get.'

'But you can help us, Perdita, because you're the best . . .' Caliburn reminded her, landing on her shoulder and nibbling on her ear.

It appeared that Perdita had a tiny flaw.

'No, mistress, no! Don't fall for it!' begged Hoola. 'Don't let your brother sweet-talk you again!'

But a small smile had already appeared on Perdita's face, and her eyes behind the rose-coloured glasses began to twinkle. 'I AM the best,' admitted Perdita.

'You're the best! You're the best! You're just the most marvellous, magnificent best!' said Caliburn. 'And see how you love an impossible quest!'

The human and the raven began to sing together, some old tune that they both knew from childhood. And Perdita's glasses rushed to join in the dancing.

And Perdita's glasses RUSHED to join in the dancing

We're the best! We're the best!

We're the best! We're the best!
We're just the most marvellous magnificent best!
See how we LOVE an impossible quest…
Make butters that fly! Make sticks that can walk!
Unfeasible mirrors that see and can talk
Lift curses that shrivel and dry up the rain
Wake love that has died and will not grow again
Impossible things, nonsensical things, let me live my life
With impossible things!
I'm a bear! You're a bird! This ridiculous premise is
clearly absurd
But for ludicrous Magic we are the last word,
Because…
We're the best! We're the best!
We're just the most marvellous magnificent best!
And…

See how we LOVE
an impossible quest!

'Oh I LOVE it here!' said Wish. 'Please please *please* let me in . . .'

'You can stay!' said Perdita, excitedly opening wide her arms. 'This is the challenge I've been waiting for!'

It was so wonderful, after weeks of wandering, friendless and alone, horribly aware that they were cursed and outlaws, to have someone actually WANTING them to stay.

'Hurrah!' said Caliburn, and Wish's heart leapt, only to fall again as Hoola the little owl landed on the desk and waddled to the centre of it, her wings on her hips.

'HANG ON A SECOND,' fumed Hoola. 'Don't forget *I* have to say yes too! What if the other children in

"HANG ON
A
SECOND!"
said
Hoola

this school write home to their parents to say that we're hiding these outlaws? The Droods will shut the whole school down! Not to mention sending us all off on some deathly shadow quest . . .'

'You're right,' said Perdita. 'Thank you, Hoola! We'll have to disguise Wish's enchanted objects. Bring them out, Wish . . .'

The spoon jumped briskly from the top of Wish's head, followed by the key, fork and pins, and they trotted out on to the desk in front of Perdita. Perdita blinked, twice, three times, and slowly the little objects changed colour, from grey to gold. The enchanted things were absolutely thrilled with the transformation. They stuck out what-would-be-their-chests-if-they-were-human, and paraded around the desk, busting with pride at their new look.

'They're still made of iron,' explained Perdita. 'But now they look like they're gold.'

'And what are we doing to do about the *Warrior*?' said Hoola, pointing at Bodkin.

'Yes, he's a bit trickier,' admitted Perdita, thoughtfully. 'We could disguise him as a hob – they're not very good at Magic.'

'What's a hob?' asked Bodkin, knowing he wasn't going to like the answer.

Perdita blinked, once, twice, three times.

'Oh . . .' said Bodkin, as he looked down at the soft brown fur that had suddenly appeared all over his body. 'My father would be so ashamed if he could see me now . . . And a *tail*! Was that really necessary?'

'Yes, sorry about that,' said Perdita. 'You can't be a hob without a tail.'

'It's brilliant, Perdita, brilliant!' said Caliburn admiringly.

'It IS rather brilliant, isn't it?' said Perdita with satisfaction.

Perdita disguised Xar's green arm by turning the rest of him green as well, and did the same for all of Xar's companions, including the snowcats, the sprites, Lonesome the werewolf, and Wish herself. Even the Once-sprite's peregrine falcon and Caliburn himself were turned a very bright, unnatural green, which Caliburn thought made them look ridiculous.

'If anyone asks, say you are bog Wizards from the east,' said Perdita.

Finally, she lent Wish her pair of broken glasses to wear over her eyepatch. 'Maybe you could not mention about the Magic eye,' said Perdita thoughtfully. 'And just try and give the impression that the Magic is coming from somewhere else . . .'

'I can do that!' said Wish.

'But I haven't said yes, yet!' warned Hoola.

HA   HA   HA
HA
HA

Bodkin
as a
Hob.

'Oh *please* say yes,' said
Caliburn, sensing weakness.
'We've answered all your
questions. The disguises are wonderful. Won't you give
us a chance?'

'After all, they ARE family,' said Perdita.

'Everyone is chasing us . . .' said Caliburn.

'We're wet, we're cold, we're hungry,' said Bodkin,
his tummy rumbling.

Wish laid a hand on Hoola's wing. She looked
into the little owl's eyes.

'And we're scared, and
we have nowhere else to
go,' said Wish.

There was a long silence.

Hoola looked at them all. Bedraggled, covered in scratches, the Bodkin-turned-into-a-hob was limping, the Xar-boy had a really nasty wound on his leg that looked like it was going septic.

It would take a harder owl than Hoola to turn down such a plea.

'Oh, bother,' sighed Hoola. 'Bother bother bother bother BOTHER. All right then, you're in. But that boy with the cursed hand better not start misbehaving, or you'll all be out again . . .'

'We're IN!' shouted Caliburn.

And way, way up at the entrance to Perdita's study, the piskies, who had been trying to eavesdrop but hadn't been able to hear anything, heard the loudness of this cry and reacted jubilantly, shouting, 'They're IN they're IN they're IN! Hurrah hurrah hurrah!'

'The longer you stay here the better,' said Perdita's warm, hypnotic voice. 'It will give you time to heal, and you have so much to learn. Stay here for as long as you can . . .'

'All right then,' said Xar, grumpily. 'We'll stay . . . not for TOO long though . . .'

It would take a harder owl than Hoola to turn down such a plea.

And in his head he thought: *Just until I can burgle some of those Droods' tears . . .*

Perdita nodded, and then turned to Ariel.

'You can add the piece of flame that we took from the forest fire to the fire on my hearth-stone, Sprite-whose-name-is-Ariel,' said Perdita, 'it will be happy there . . .'

So Ariel opened his fire-box, and when he added the little piece of flame to Perdita's fire, the flames there burnt bright and high as if they were welcoming it.

'But why would you want to keep a piece of fire from such an unhappy experience?' asked Wish curiously.

'You're *already* asking questions, how wonderful!' said Perdita, which was interesting, because Wish was normally told off for asking too many questions. 'Life is made up of so many things, happy, sad, indifferent and you cannot ignore the sad things, or even the indifferent. That drop of fire will only make my own fire the stronger . . .'

Now that Hoola had finally agreed to let them into the learning place, she became very practical. 'Okay, I'm going to show you all to your sleeping quarters,' said Hoola, 'and you can get warm and dry. The snowcats and Magical creatures can stay with you, but there's a special area for giants. This bear needs to go urgently to a sleeping cave – it's *way* past its bed time for the winter.'

The sleepy bear agreed with a great bear yawn.

'You're just in time for supper at the dining hall,' finished Hoola, 'so I'll take you to that, and then I'll drop the door and the boys off at the infirmary – they all need urgent medical attention.'

And then they trooped up the stairs to be greeted with rapturous delight by the piskies. Perdita turned Crusher green and then she hurried off, saying she had work to do making good the hole they had made in the Magic protecting the school by bringing iron in with them, and Hoola would look after them in the meantime.

'Onebearonegianttwodrownedhumansthreewolves threesnowcatsNINEuselesspritesoneperegrinefalcon andaBabyALLTHECOLOURGREEN . . . *and a hob*! *WELCOME ALL*!' sang the piskies as they trooped off towards the sleeping quarters.

'Oh for goodness' sake,' said Hoola.

'You're HOME, you're HOME, welcome to your HOME!' sang everyone all together at full blast.

'Your Magical,
marv–e–llous,
magnifi–cent . . .
. . . new HO-O-O-OME!!!!'

8. The Nuckalavee

I have to say, I am deeply relieved that for the moment Wish and Xar have found themselves a new home, a bed for the night, and many nights to come, and a nice warm meal to fill their empty tummies. They will be there for a long while, now, thank goodness, for it was not only poor old Caliburn and the sleepy bear who needed a little peaceful time to rest, and to heal. Caliburn was so ragged he had lost all of the feathers around his neck, poor bird, and you could see the pink of his skin there and on the top of his head. And they all had burns from the fire, and had lost weight from their days on the run, so Wish and Xar and Bodkin were as bony as twigs and needed to put on strength.

I wish I could describe the food that was prepared that midwinter's evening and the careless way that they enjoyed it, for it truly was delicious. Perdita made it all, and she was the most excellent cook, for until you have tasted nettle soup mixed with Magic, you really have not tasted heaven. But, sadly, I can't entirely concentrate on how scrumptious it all is.

Unfortunately I am the narrator, so I can see *beyond* Pook's Hill, the cosy dome of chalk horse and green grass that is protecting our heroes at the moment, and what I see makes me nervous.

I can see the Nuckalavee.

The Nuckalavee is a quiet presence in the ocean, but he's a bad one.

He contains more nightmares than a Quagmire's head could hold. There're sour things in the Nuckalavee . . . disappointed hopes and the end of dreams and staffs of power too longing with evil to be left in the hands of women or men. So he is not a monster to visit lightly. In fact, no one approaches the Nuckalavee but if they are on a shadow quest, and those on a shadow quest no longer care if they live or die, which is why they are known as 'shadows'.

No one that I have heard of yet has taken the scales of a Nuckalavee and lived.

So the Nuckalavee is out there, and the Nuckalavee is waiting.

I can see Queen Sychorax too.

She is nice and cosy camping out in her richly embroidered royal tent, in the smoking remains of the forest she has burnt around her, and she has just received a visitor. The visitor is a soldier wearing the colours of the emperor, and the emperor is supposed to be her leader, so unfortunately she has to meet his Warrior, midnight or no midnight, whether she wants to or not.

'Why are you here?' snaps Queen Sychorax. 'One

'My name is Thunderous Thighs HIMSELF and I will be your husband and king.'

OH for goodness sake...

might almost say I was being *stalked* . . .'

'I am here,' announces the visitor, 'in the name of LOVE.'

'LOVE?' says Queen Sychorax in a voice of snow and raising one eyebrow.

'My name is Thunderous Thighs Himself,' announces this Warrior soldier, puffing out his chest. 'I have been sent here urgently by the emperor of Warriors because the emperor is concerned that these territories are being run by a defenceless female. So I am here to offer you my hand in marriage, to be your husband and king.'

Queen Sychorax's eyes narrow. '*Really?*' purrs Queen Sychorax.

'I am a giant-killer extraordinaire,' boasts Thunderous Thighs Himself. 'I have strangled many an elf with my bare hands. I am very good looking. My axe work is magnificent, but I am also a Warrior in LOVE.'

Queen Sychorax walks around Thunderous Thighs Himself. She sniffs.

Thunderous Thighs Himself feels a slight stirring of unease. He reaches into his waistcoat for his love poetry but Queen Sychorax accidentally clonks him in the midriff with one of her sceptres.

He doubles over in pain.

'Let me tell you,' says Queen Sychorax, smiling, 'what I think of LOVE.'

Gracefully she reaches out a hand to help Thunderous Thighs Himself to his feet again.

The moment he touches her ice-cold hand, however, there is a loud explosion, a great deal of nauseous smoke, and Thunderous Thighs Himself completely disappears.

His clothes are there, in a slightly singed pile. His love poetry rains softly through the room, blackened and blasted. But of Thunderous Thighs Himself, no sign at all.

However there *is* a small round bead, circling on the

"That," says Queen Sychorax, "is what I think of LOVE"

floor at Queen Sychorax's feet, that hadn't been there before.

Delicately, smoothly, Queen Sychorax bends down and picks up the small round bead.

Gently, tenderly, Queen Sychorax attaches the bead next to the many other beads hanging on the necklace around her throat.

The bead she attaches is, by coincidence, *exactly* the same pattern as that on the helmet of Thunderous Thighs Himself . . .

'*That*,' says Queen Sychorax, 'is what I think of LOVE.'

Oh, she's a cold one, that Queen Sychorax.

And she will not rest till she has got hold of Wish and put her back in iron Warrior fort, locked her up as tightly as if she were trapped in the bead

DEFENCELESS female!

How DARE he!

sniff!

of a necklace.

Queen Sychorax is very confident that she will find out EXACTLY where the children are, and EXACTLY how to find them. For as the narrator, I know something you do not know.

Xar was right. It was not a coincidence that Queen Sychorax had discovered them in that forest.

SOMEONE had betrayed them.

There was a traitor in their party.

Who could it be? Was Tiffinstorm right? Can you REALLY not trust a werewolf you met in a prison?

They had better WATCH OUT, for the traitor is still there with them . . .

And even if the traitor did not carry on betraying them, it was already too late.

Queen Sychorax had one of Wish's pins.

In the confusion of running away through the fire, it had stuck itself particularly firmly into a bit of Queen Sychorax's armour, and it could not work its way out in time.

Queen Sychorax had that pin, and all she had to do was set it free and follow it, and it would lead her back to Wish.

Encanzo's out there, somewhere, too, brooding on Queen Sychorax.

Further away than that, I can see through the

145

ball of iron where Wish has imprisoned the great bad
Kingwitch himself. He is all curled up in his bed of iron,
scratching, scratching, pecking his way out, like a chick
from an egg. If you think that the two Witches that you
have seen already are bad enough, well the Kingwitch
is badder by far, and makes the pair of them look like a
couple of dusty old scarecrows. The Kingwitch has the
salt-ditch, rotten-egg, corpse-breath, arsenic-wicked
stench of the truly evil, and he has a tiny speck of blue
dust that belongs to Wish, and he will use it when he
gets the chance.

The Kingwitch will take his time.

But the Kingwitch will find a way.

So Perdita and Caliburn and Hoola and Crusher
are going to have to hide our heroes, teach them, guide
them well, if they're going to have any sort of chance
against the future that is waiting for them.

Look inside the ball of iron
where Wish has imprisoned the
great bad Kingwitch himself

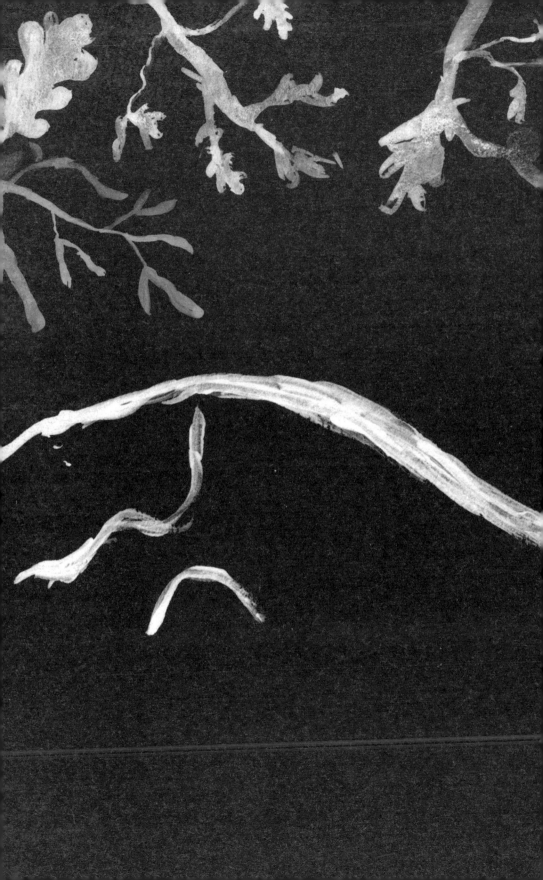

PART

Two

Refuge

There are
Kind people in
the world...
You just have
to find them.

9. The Learning Place for Spectacularly Gifted Wizards

hat marked the beginning of the happiest, most peaceful time in Wish's small, short life. It wasn't anything like being taught by Madam Dreadlock. For the first time, Wish could practise all the powers that she had spent so many years covering up and smothering. She could never imagine that such a wonderful timetable could exist in the world. There were whole *terms* on trees. The different kinds, how to recognise them from their leaves, talking to them, tending them, what different woods did what different things.

And then there was starcraft, and invisibility, and transforming-into-animals, and bringing-things-to-life, not to mention flying-without-wings . . .

There was also word-learning and number-learning, of course, but they were a very small part of the timetable, and the teacher who taught them, Madam Mellows, was much more understanding than Madam Dreadlock. She had an entire set of letters and numbers that were all alive, and she kept them in boxes, a bit like Perdita's spectacle boxes.

Wish found it far easier to remember the lesson of the day when it was demonstrated by small furry or spiky or twiggy number animals and letter animals performing cartwheels and handsprings in front of her eyes.

The other Wizard and Magical creature children were very friendly and welcoming. As Perdita had said, they completely accepted that Xar and his companions were green because of coming from the east. So Wish and Bodkin found themselves, for the first time in their lives, making actual *friends*, with a Drood girl, who came from the Lake of the Lost, and had enchanted objects just like Wish (but not made out of *iron*, of course) and a boggart boy who came from under the ooze in the north.

At first, Bodkin thought that the long brown fur covering him all over in his disguise as a hob was horribly itchy and undignified, but after a while he realised how practical it was, warm and cosy, and really rather beautiful, particularly when you brushed it till it shone. He became proud of it, and the lovely important swooshing noise it made when he walked. And the tail! Don't get him started on the tail. Bodkin wondered how he'd ever lived life before without a tail. It was so *expressive*.

A tail was so expressive.

droopy when you were sad...

Perky when you were happy, droopy when you were sad, and extremely useful in the tree-climbing lessons. Bodkin could be up in the top of the tree canopy in three, four swings with that helpful addition of the tail, while the others were still climbing up the lower branches.

Bodkin had learnt to read and write from overhearing things while he swept the corners in classrooms. Now, for the first time, somebody was actually *teaching* him as though he was a real person, and not just somebody to give orders to. Bodkin was a fast learner, and he was very quickly shooting ahead in a lot of the classes – the ones that involved not actually doing Magic of course – and there were a surprising amount of them.*

He was at a disadvantage in the classes where Magic had to be performed, but Perdita had given him a do-it-yourself Magic staff that did a simple spell, which was 'sticking things to other things', in order to hide that he couldn't do any Magic at all.

---

* History of Magic, tree-climbing, wort-cunning, leechdom and starcraft (the three last being study of herbs and plants, medical remedies, and the art of interpreting and reading the stars, those sorts of things).

and extremely useful in the tree-climbing lessons

Everyone looked forward to
Perdita's lessons. That spring, Perdita
was teaching spell-making and tree studies and
transformation.

'Wonderful!' she said, when somebody performed a
spell correctly. 'Marvellous!'

And a strange thing happened. Whoever she said
this to really did begin to think that they were quite
marvellous after all. It was particularly effective with
Xar. Xar had never had a mother – she died when he
was born – so he was quite surprised when Perdita took
out her rose-tinted spectacles and said things like, 'How
fascinatingly creative!' when told the story about how he

had accidentally melted one of the chairs. It made Xar behave better because he wanted to impress her.

At first, Xar was constantly in trouble.

Some of this wasn't entirely Xar's fault. His hand with the Witchstain on it seemed to have a mind of its own and often did the absolute opposite of what he wanted, in a spectacular way. So, for instance, the class would be practising shrinking spells and Xar would try and copy what everyone else was doing, and find himself *growing* instead of shrinking. On that occasion he grew even larger than Crusher, and the teacher assumed he did it on purpose to be cheeky and sent him to Perdita for insolence.

Xar was never quite sure how Perdita was going to react when he was sent to the Lair of the Bear.

Sometimes she was understanding, but other times she seemed very stern and bear-like, and punished him if he deserved it. Or it might be she was in the middle of some spell of her own, so she would be distracted and entirely uninterested in why Xar had been sent to her, and get Xar to hold the cooking pot steady while Hoola stirred it.

On the shrinking-but-accidentally-growing-instead occasion, she wasn't in the Lair of the Bear. The study was deserted, so he searched it very thoroughly, to see if he could find the Droods' tears, which he was sure she must have hidden somewhere. But Hoola came in and interrupted him, so he had to wander round the learning place until he found Perdita, eventually, in one of the side clearings. She was in the middle of a conference with a whole load of philosopher giants on the unexpected consequences and logistical possibilities of TIME TRAVEL, which was one of the very few things that the Magic people had not worked out how to do yet.

So although *terribly* sympathetic, Perdita waved him away, recommending Xar work out a way to get smaller again himself. He had to spend two days as a giant, before he got back to the right size again.

It was all a little difficult to predict.

But as time went on, Xar worked out a way of tricking the hand with the Witchstain by performing the exact opposite of whatever spell they were supposed to be doing. This didn't work *every* time, but enough so that he was in trouble a little less often.

So even Xar ended up liking the learning place more than he expected. He was very popular and had crowds of friends.

And after a while, they were all so busy that they nearly forgot that there was a world outside the charmed chalk circle of Pook's Hill. Three months passed. The bear came out of his sleeping cave. Their wounds from

the fights with the wyverns and the Witches healed, and
it all felt like they had arrived only yesterday.

Not that everything always went well.

Wish, of course, had a very powerful Magic indeed.
More powerful, Perdita thought, than the Magic of
most of the other Wizards in the whole of Pook's Hill
put together, and maybe even more than that. Time
would tell.

But Wish had *terrible* trouble with the spellfighting.

In spellfighting you were supposed to turn yourself
into different animals, and fight as those animals. Wish
started off well, transforming into snowcat, lion, drearer,
ghoulfeast in impressively rapid progression . . . but her
default position was always a fluffbuttle.

She did not know why this happened. She just
panicked, mid-fight . . .

Her Magic eye blinked, before she could stop it . . .

. . . and there she was, a fluffbuttle again.

A fluffbuttle was, as the name suggests, not a
particularly scary creature. Slightly smaller than a bunny
rabbit, the fluffbuttle had so many natural predators in
the wildwoods that Perdita had had to set up a special
fluffbuttle animal sanctuary, because she was genuinely
worried that the fluffbuttles might be in danger of being
hunted into extinction. The sanctuary was located just
beside the infirmary and Bodkin spent hours leaning

dreamingly over the fence watching them, for it really was a great pleasure to see the little fluffbuttles scampering about, squeaking at each other.

Once Wish had transformed into fluffbuttle form during the spellfighting, she didn't seem to be able to transform out of it. So, unless the opponent had accidentally transformed into a *carrot* – which was unlikely but not impossible because ghoulfeasts were as allergic to carrots as vampires were to garlic, so if spellfighters were trying to be clever, sometimes they did go for the vegetable option – Wish automatically forfeited the fight.

And Perdita and Hoola and Caliburn exchanged significant glances with each other. Bodkin knew what those glances meant. They meant, 'Wish is no more ready to fight the Kingwitch in single combat than a fluffbuttle.'

But on the whole, everything was moving in a positive direction.

Xar was trying his hardest and he had improved greatly, in behaviour and thoughtfulness. Wish was struggling with the spellfighting, but she was learning so many other useful skills and had never been so content in her life. Even Bodkin had settled into being a hob.

Until Madam Clairvoy came to the school.

She was a new teacher, and from the moment she arrived, things went downhill.

Madam Clairvoy taught starcraft and she was every
bit as mean as Madam Dreadlock, just horrible in a
different way. Madam Clairvoy never shouted, but she
was sarcastic, and she provoked Xar's pride. Xar wasn't
very good at starcraft, and it was one of the lessons in
which Bodkin shone, so Madam Clairvoy spent a lot of
time comparing Xar to Bodkin. 'Even a *hob* can do this,
Xar!' said Madam Clairvoy. 'So why, then, cannot you?'

This caused trouble between Xar and Bodkin,
and Xar then acted up in the lesson, showing off, and
getting into trouble, and he was sent to Perdita for
being disruptive, and Madam Perdita was only halfway
understanding.

'Madam Clairvoy is so *mean!*' stormed Xar.

'The world is full of people who
are mean, Xar,' said Perdita.

Madam Clairvoy

'You have to learn how to deal with them without losing your temper.'

The meaner Madam Clairvoy was, the worse Xar behaved, even in other lessons as well.

So Wish was increasingly worried about Xar, who was being sent to Madam Perdita so much of the time that she thought he might be expelled. And Xar was beginning to draw away from them. Now he wouldn't be seen with Bodkin, because Bodkin was a hob, and hobs were a little embarrassing.

'Sometimes I feel like the spoon in the middle of the key and the fork,' Wish confessed to Caliburn one evening.

And even the spoon, the key and the fork were quarrelling again in a way they had stopped doing for a while. The fork would ambush the spoon and pin it down on every occasion it could, and the spoon started hiding from both of them. Tiffinstorm and Hinkypunk fell out over something and weren't speaking to each other.

And worse than that . . .

Oh much worse than that . . .

WITCHES were appearing, to the north, to the south, to the west, to the east, surrounding the school. The Witches didn't dare get too close, for Pook's Hill was protected by very powerful Magic. They were just roosting, high up in the treetops, like a gathering cloud of crows. They hadn't attacked anyone yet.

But they made everyone feel nervous.

And then two much more alarming incidents happened, that meant they were not going to be able to stay in Pook's Hill forever.

10. Two Alarming Incidents

The first alarming incident concerned Squeezjoos.

They had never really got to the bottom of why Squeezjoos had gone a little crazy and attacked Queen Sychorax's army all on his own. He seemed fine again once he got to Pook's Hill, so they didn't worry too much about it.

But then one day, Squeezjoos came to them all and said, in a slightly wobbly voice:

'I iss feelings a little bit funny . . .'

'Is it my imagination,' said Caliburn, 'or is Squeezjoos looking a little more green than the rest of us?'

"I iss
feelings
a little
bit funny . . ."

'And he's behaving very oddly – he keeps gobbling up my spellsss!' said Tiffinstorm.

'I doesss not!' said Squeezjoos. 'Is liess, all liess . . . ooh, is that a piskie over there?'

Tiffinstorm jumped and drew her wand, a sharpened thorn, and whirled around in the air to face the imaginary piskie. And while she was distracted, Squeezjoos reached out, bit one of the spells off her belt, and zipped off again.

'Don't eat that, it's a fire-spell!' hissed Tiffinstorm. But it was too late. Squeezjoos had already swallowed the spell. 'I'ss hassn't eaten anything,' said Squeezjoos, blinking with huge innocent bug eyes and shaking his little head so vigorously that smoke came out of his ears. But then – Oh! He went cross-eyed and, 'hIC!' he accidentally hiccuped, and a great spout of flame came out of his mouth and set fire to one of the leaves of Tiffinstorm's dress. She hastily put it out.

'Ooh!' said Squeezjoos putting a little hairy hand over his mouth in surprise. '*Peppery!*'

'Squeezjoos, stay still for a second, we need to have a look at you,' said Xar.

'I isss fine! I iss fine! I iss fine!' chanted Squeezjoos, nipping out of the way, but Xar eventually caught him in his cupped hands. And when Xar opened his hands a smidgeon, they got a good look at Squeezjoos, and his fur was definitely tinged with a deep hint of emerald that was darker than it ought to be, and you could even see a slight lime tint to his little spotty eyeballs.

'I isss FINE, let me go!' said Squeezjoos crossly, letting out little tongues of flame every single time he opened his mouth, and then when Xar didn't let him go immediately, his little eyeballs suddenly flashed a very bright pure green and he leant down and bit Xar.

'OW!' yelled Xar, dropping the little hairy fairy.

The green disappeared as quickly as it had flared, like sheet lightning, and Squeezjoos was mortified, for he hero-worshipped Xar. 'I isss so sorry!' whimpered Squeezjoos with huge horrified eyes. 'Forgives me Masster . . . I don't knowsss whatss came over me. It was an accident.' He went cross-eyed. 'Hic! . . .' said Squeezjoos, in surprise, shooting

164

out a flame, and then putting his hand over his mouth
again. 'OOOh! . . . *Spicy*!' And then he shot this way
and that, with a 'Hic! Ooh! *Scorchy* . . .' and a 'Hic! Ooh
. . . *Sweltry*!' and 'Hic! Ooh! . . . *Zesty*!' Until finally he
collapsed on his back on Wish's shoulder, moaning,
'Squeezjoos feeling *so sick* . . .'

And then he threw up, so violently,
and fierily that
they had to
rush him to
Perdita's tree
office to give
him urgent
medical
attention,
wrapping him
up in one of Xar's
flameproof handkerchiefs
to get him there.

You would never have
thought that one little sprite
could have eaten so many
spells, but Squeezjoos threw up
lovespells, invisibility spells, stink
spells, curse spells, every kind of
spell you could think of. When he

165

was throwing up the invisibility spells he disappeared for a moment, but they still knew where he was from the 'Hic! Ooh! . . . *Gassy!*' noises. Eventually he got to the water spells, and that was good because they seemed to quench everything else, and by that time the little sprite was so exhausted he fell asleep, snoring loudly. Every now and then little mustard-coloured snot balloons drifted out of his nose, up into the air, where they burst, spraying the remains of stink spells all over everybody.

Wish explained to Perdita that Squeezjoos had been stained with the Witchblood trying to save Xar long ago in the forest, and how they had put him on the Stone-That-Takes-Away-Magic, but that Xar may have taken him off a little too quickly.

Perdita gave the little sleeping sprite a thorough examination, and when she finished she looked very grave. Even looking at Squeezjoos through her rose-coloured spectacles wasn't really helping.

'Is he going to die?' whispered Xar.

'No, no,' said Perdita hastily, 'he's just sleeping. Look, he's waking up!'

Squeezjoos sat up, shaking his head, and a few little mustard bubbles fell out of his ears, and a great big bubble of a stink spell burped out of his mouth.

'Yes . . .' said Perdita, 'if the little hairy fairy put his hand on the Stone-That-Takes-Away-Magic, that will

166

have got rid of most of the bad Magic, so he won't die
... but the Witchblood is giving him a craving for
power which is why he is eating all these spells, and
there is this remote possibility that he *may*—'

'Fly off to join the Witches at some point,' Caliburn
finished the sentence for her.

'NO!' gasped Xar. 'Squeezjoos would never leave me
and fly away, would you Squeezjoos?'

'I's bets he wouldn'ts. You isss lovely, Master, best
Masster in the world. Who iss he, this Squeezjooossss?
Who are we talking about?' asked Squeezjoos in an
interested sort of way, hovering in front of Xar.

'What do you mean who is *he*? He is *you*! *You're*
Squeezjoos!' said Xar in alarm.

'I isss not!' sang Squeezjoos happily, kissing Xar on
the nose. 'I iss *SOOJZEEKS!*'

'I believe "Soojzeeks" may be Witch-speak for
Squeezjoos, spelt backwards,' said Perdita, looking very
worried indeed, 'which is not a good sign, but I will
start administering my most potent antidotes, and we
shall just have to hope for the best. On the plus side, he
does seem awfully fond of you all ...'

The remains of one of the lovespells were still
fizzing around Squeezjoos's little hairy fairy bloodstream
and so he was buzzing around trying to kiss everybody,
squealing, 'Soojzeeks lovesssss YOU ... and YOU ...

and YOU . . . and *YOU!*'

'Oh dear,' sighed Perdita. 'This explains why there have been so many Witch sightings near the school recently . . .'

'*What?*' said Wish, sharply.

'They can't get into this school,' said Perdita soothingly. 'My Magic is invulnerable, but they may sense you are here and that Squeezjoos is turning towards them.'

It was all very well to say 'don't worry', but it was a horrible feeling to think that the Witches were gathering, hissing invisibly in the darkness, sharpening their talons, whether they could actually get in or not. And even worse to think that adorable little Squeezjoos might end up going over to the dark side.

So that was the FIRST incident that gave Wish and Xar an anxious feeling that they were no longer safe in the school, and that they really should be leaving and getting on with the quest to find the Nuckalavee so they could get rid of the Witches forever, and save Xar and Squeezjoos at the same time.

The next incident was, if anything, even more alarming.

One morning, Perdita was giving Xar, Wish and Bodkin a 'catch-up' lesson on trees, in her study, because they were a bit behind the other pupils in this subject.

Xar found these
kinds of lessons boring.
He much preferred the
ones where they turned
into birds, or deer, or
different kinds of fish.
Fidgeting wildly, his eye
landed on a bottle marked
'Interesting Transformation
Potion, Treat With Extreme
Caution', poking out of one of
Perdita's many pockets. Perdita was
distracted, excited about telling them
how trees secretly talked to one another
by sending each other chemical messages.
Xar winked at Squeezjoos, who giggled,
and picked the pocket of Perdita,
giving the bottle to Xar, who put it
in his waistcoat. Only Bodkin saw
him do it.

When they left the room, Xar
showed Wish and Bodkin the
bottle, and said he was going to
taste it.

'Xar, don't be stupid,' said
Wish.

Interestin
Transf
Poti

Effects wear
twelve hour

'We should give that back to Madam Perdita,' said
Bodkin.

'Oh, are you going to tell on me?' said Xar
jeeringly.

'We're not going to tell on you. We're trying all the
time not to get you expelled!' said Wish in exasperation.
'Didn't you learn anything from the whole Witchstain
disaster?'

'But this isn't Witchblood, it's just some old
transformation potion. Aren't you interested in what the

Interesting Transformation Medicine might be?' said Xar. 'I dare you, Bodkin, to taste it with me . . . Go on, don't be a stick-in-the-mud old hob for once!'

To do Xar justice, he said this quite affectionately – he just thought he was teasing Bodkin, but Bodkin was in a sensitive mood.

Underneath his green fur, Bodkin was turning very red. 'I am not a stick-in-the-mud old hob,' said Bodkin.

'Of course you're not!' said Wish. 'Don't listen to him, Bodkin, you don't have to prove anything.'

'Does anyone have a spoon they can lend me?' teased Xar, uncorking the bottle. The Enchanted Spoon buried itself very firmly in Wish's waistcoat.

'No way!' said Wish.

'Okay, I'll just swig it straight from the bottle, very cautiously of course,' said Xar. 'And then Bodkin, you can have a taste afterwards . . . or are you Warriors too *scared*?'

'I am not scared!' said Bodkin furiously, absolutely purple under the fur, if anyone could have seen it. 'And I am NOT a stick-in-the-mud old hob!'

Wish closed her eyes and held her head in her hands as Xar tipped back his head and drank very incautiously indeed from the bottle, then handed it to Bodkin, who defiantly took a good swig himself. There was a loud

BOOM!

BOOM!!

But when Wish
opened her eyes again,
expecting to find two
graxerturgleburkins in front of
her, or worse, there was only one
Bodkin and one Xar, looking entirely
unchanged, if a tiny bit traumatised.
'Phew!' said Wish. 'It hasn't worked
...you probably have to boil it up or

172

PART TWO: REFUGE

something. But you were both still incredibly stupid to try it, and I'm getting fed up with you squabbling all the time. And have you forgotten that we're all on a quest together? I thought I could rely on you, at least, Bodkin, to be a bit sensible, and—'

But she was interrupted by Bodkin.

'Oh, it's worked all right,' said Bodkin.

'And it's certainly *interesting*,' said Xar.

'This is a disaster!' said Bodkin, who looked like he was panicking somewhat. 'This is a total, bronze-bottomed, fire-breathing, howling hairy disaster!'

'What on earth do you mean?' said Wish. 'Nothing's happened . . . you look exactly the same.'

'Except that Bodkin's turned into *me*, and *I've* turned into the stick-in-the-mud old hob!' said the boy who looked like he was Bodkin, but who was in fact Xar. '*We've switched places!*'

'Ah,' said Wish.

'Now that IS interesting,' said Caliburn.

'We have to tell Madam Perdita immediately so she can get us the antidote!' said Xar.

But Wish wouldn't hear of that, particularly once she had read the small print on the other side of the bottle that Xar hadn't bothered to read. 'No way,' said Wish. 'You've been in such trouble already, Xar. At any other school they'd have expelled you ages ago . . . And

173

it says here that it's perfectly
safe as long as you don't drink
the whole bottle, and the
effects will wear off after
twelve hours or so.'

'A whole DAY being
Bodkin!' said Xar in
horror.

'A whole DAY being
Xar!' echoed Bodkin,
equally appalled.

Unfortunately, once
Wish had established
that they were perfectly
safe, she wasn't a bit
sympathetic. 'Maybe
it'll be good for
you,' she said.
And the sprites
thought it was
hysterical.

So . . .

Bodkin and
Xar had to go
through the day being each
other.

11. The Surprising Things You Learn When You Spend a Day as Someone Else

Xar was surprised at how lonely it was to be Bodkin. Of course the sprites and the animals couldn't hang out with him as much, because that would have attracted attention, so they just suddenly weren't there any more, and it gave him a very odd feeling to be totally . . . alone.

Did Bodkin always feel this alone?

It wasn't that anyone was positively *mean* to him. They just tended to ignore him when he said things. Their eyes passed over him as if he wasn't really there.

Apart from Wish.

Xar could see why Bodkin liked Wish so much. She was the only person who seemed interested when he said something. *When I get back to being Xar again, I'm going to be a lot nicer to old Bodkin,* thought Xar.

And Bodkin found he learnt a great deal from a day being Xar as well.

At first it was nice to have everyone laughing when he made a joke, everyone looking to him for guidance, all the attention from the other Wizards and the sprites. But then it began to feel like quite a lot of pressure to be funny, to be naughty, to amuse everyone. And being told off all the time turned out to be extremely wearing.

As for the hand with the Witchstain, Bodkin didn't

see how Xar could stand it. He couldn't remember Xar
ever mentioning this (maybe Xar was too proud), but it
hurt all the time, a burning, itching, yearning ache. And
worse than that, he could feel it trying to control him,
lead him in the wrong direction, confusing his thoughts
and turning them upside-down and inside out. It was
most unpleasant.

Oh dear oh dear oh dear . . . thought Bodkin. *I'm
worried that time is running out for poor old Xar. I had no idea
that the Witchstain was such a burden.*

Last lesson was with Madam Clairvoy.

After a whole day of being told off by teacher after
teacher, Bodkin was thoroughly fed up and he found
himself answering back and being nearly as cheeky as
Xar would have been himself. Madam Clairvoy was in a
really mean mood and she gave Bodkin two detentions
for 'rudeness and insubordination', and Bodkin felt
a little guilty about that until he realised that Xar
wouldn't turn up for the detentions anyway.

At the end of the class, Bodkin headed with relief to
the door, for there were only a couple more hours to go
and then he could go back to being himself again. Xar
followed, equally keen to get to the end of this stupid
day as quickly as possible.

But Madam Clairvoy called Xar back.

'Stay behind, Bodkin,' said Madam Clairvoy. Xar

couldn't quite get used to being Bodkin, so he looked
around him for a second, before he realised that Madam
Clairvoy was talking to *him*. Why did she want Bodkin
to stay behind?

Bodkin was wondering that too. And as he looked
over at Madam Clairvoy, he had a sudden, shocking
realisation. A memory of something that he had seen
once, long ago, in the dungeons of Warrior fort . . .

He knew why Madam Clairvoy wanted to see
Bodkin, and he had to prevent that at all costs.

'Bodkin can't stay behind, Madam Clairvoy,'
said Bodkin with real urgency in his voice.
'Madam Perdita wants to see him and
Wish and me in the Lair of the Bear
right now.'

'I'm sure Madam Perdita can
wait a few moments,' snapped
Madam Clairvoy. 'Off with
you, now, Xar! I've had
quite enough of YOU for
one day!'

And she shooed Bodkin
out of the room.

Madam Clairvoy carefully shut
the door behind him.

Bodkin knelt down so that he could hear what was
going on in the room. He put his eye to the keyhole of
the door.

Madam Clairvoy glided to a cupboard in the corner
of the room, and opened it. There was something
inside. And what she did next, Xar, and Bodkin,
watching through the keyhole, could not really believe.

She took off her head, as if she was taking off a hat.

The now headless woman gave a quick, satisfied
pat of Madam Clairvoy's hair, and placed the head of
Madam Clairvoy on a stand inside the cupboard. And
peering, goggle-eyed, into the cupboard, Xar realised
there was ANOTHER head in there. The arms of
Madam Clairvoy reached inside the cupboard, picked
up this other head and put it on her shoulders, gently
pushing it down as if to make it secure.

And then she turned round.

And it wasn't Madam Clairvoy standing in front of Xar.

It was Queen Sychorax.

12. The Story Takes Another Unexpected Turn

ell, well, well.

Unsurprisingly, Xar just stood there, with his mouth open. Xar was never that glad to meet Queen Sychorax, who he would have described, if asked, as very scary indeed. Super scary. Scarier than a whole load of vampires feeling a little peckish because their blood sugar was running a little low. But how much scarier than ever was she when you met her swapping heads and pretending to be someone other than she was?

You're not supposed to BE here!!! thought Xar, rather hysterically to himself. *You're a Warrior! We should at least be safe from you in a learning place for gifted Wizards!*

But he didn't say that. He was much too flabbergasted.

All he said instead, in a bewildered sort of way, was, 'Queen Sychorax! What on earth are *you* doing here? Why did Madam Perdita let YOU in?'

'Madam Perdita thinks I am Madam Clairvoy,' snapped Queen Sychorax. 'Madam Perdita may think of herself as a great leader, but she's a fool, and like so many other fools, she is not clever enough to look past appearances . . . She interviewed me a couple of weeks ago as a new teacher for the starcraft lessons, and she didn't even guess that I was a Warrior.

'Now, I know perfectly well that it is *you*, Bodkin, who is hiding underneath that really rather pathetic hob disguise, so don't waste my time trying to deny it,' said Queen Sychorax.

(For Queen Sychorax, of course, was not quite as clever as she thought she was, and she was under the impression that she was talking to Bodkin.)

'I have a task for you, Bodkin. I want you to get me the spoon and the Enchanted Sword and Wish's Spelling Book,' ordered Queen Sychorax. 'I've been trying to get hold of them, but Wish never lets them out of her sight. But Wish trusts you, Bodkin. She will give them to you if you ask to borrow them for a moment. I'm sure you can think of a reason why you need to borrow them.'

Xar kept quiet, thinking, *What is going on???*

Why is the ridiculous Bodkin boy staring at me with his mouth open? thought Queen Sychorax irritably.

She then spoke very slowly, as if she thought Bodkin was a little slow on the uptake.

'Wish will not give herself up to me unless I have the spoon and the sword and the Spelling Book,' explained Queen Sychorax. 'As soon as I have those things I can take you and Wish back to the safety of iron Warrior fort. You know in your heart of hearts that

183

the fort is the only place where she will be safe from the Kingwitch. If *I* can get in to this learning place, you can be sure that the Kingwitch can too . . . and it is your duty as her bodyguard to protect her.'

Xar said nothing.

Queen Sychorax smiled, one of her lovely golden ones, sweeter than honey. 'If you do as I want, I will reward you, Bodkin,' cooed Queen Sychorax. 'Do you want to be an Assistant Bodyguard all your life? If you bring me the spoon, the Spelling Book and the sword, I will never tell her you did it willingly. I will say that I took them off you by force . . . and finally you will be worthy of her, for I will make you a knight Warrior and a Hero of my Queendom. Think how sad your father would be to see you dressed like this, as a ridiculous hob, and how PROUD he would be if his only son was made a knight Warrior!'

No, you won't make Bodkin a knight Warrior, thought Xar. *Don't believe her, Bodkin! She's a lying, cheating queen who doesn't keep her promises!*

Queen Sychorax's honey smile faded as she revealed the sting behind the sweetness.

'But if you do not do as I want, there will be penalties,' said Queen Sychorax grimly. 'I will tell Wish that YOU are the one who betrayed her . . . YOU are the one who sent word to me about where you were in the wood . . .'

Bodkin betrayed us!!! thought Xar. *It was Bodkin's fault that Queen Sychorax ambushed us in the forest all along!*

'. . . and Wish will never trust you again, Bodkin,' said Queen Sychorax, sorrowfully. 'Never love you again . . . There was never any chance of her loving you of course, as a mere Assistant Bodyguard of no birth or consequence at all, while Wish is a royal personage, but there was still *hope* . . . You could still have held her sword, polished her armour and done all those Assistant-Bodyguardy-type things . . .' Queen Sychorax was a little vague at this point because she really hadn't a clue what an Assistant Bodyguard's duties were – they were way below her notice. 'But if you go the way you are choosing, all hope will be gone, not to mention Wish falling into the grip of the Kingwitch.'

There was a long, long silence.

Outside the room, kneeling by the keyhole of the door, Bodkin was crying. He wiped away his tears with the back of his sleeve, got up, and ran away.

Inside the room, Queen Sychorax was waiting for an answer from the boy she thought was Bodkin.

'I can see you are beginning to come back to your senses,' said Queen Sychorax with satisfaction. 'You are beginning to realise that your recent defiance has been a mistake.'

At last Xar answered.

'It is *you*, Queen Sychorax, who has made a mistake,' said Xar, almost too cross to get the words out.

It was Queen Sychorax's turn to be surprised.

'*I beg your pardon?*' said Queen Sychorax.

And then, when Xar whipped out Bodkin's do-it-yourself Magic staff, and pointed it at her, she was more surprised still.

What does this stupid staff do, again? thought Xar. *Oh yes . . . it 'sticks-things-to-other-things'. Well, I can work with that.*

PEEEOOW!!! He pointed the staff and it stuck Queen Sychorax's hands to the table.

'Have you gone completely mad?' said Queen Sychorax, staring at her hands, trying to pull them off the table and getting increasingly irritated as she realised that wasn't possible. 'Pointing a Magical weapon at a teacher? USING a Magical weapon on a teacher! I'll report you . . . You'll be expelled! Put that staff down, you disobedient Bodkin-boy!'

'You're not the only one who can look like someone

else!' raged Xar. 'I'm not Bodkin, you stupid Queen!'

'Oh, don't be ridiculous!' snapped Queen Sychorax. 'Of course you're Bodkin! I saw through your ridiculous disguises in about two seconds – a little green colouring and some fur isn't going to trick *me*. Release me, or I will tell Wish all about your betrayal.'

'Tell away!' yelled Xar. 'I don't care! Because I may be looking like Bodkin at the moment, but I'm not really Bodkin! I'm *Xar* . . .'

Now it was Queen Sychorax's turn for her jaw to drop and to stare at Xar with a goggle-eyed expression of amazement.

'No . . .' whispered Queen Sychorax, 'it's not possible . . .'

'We took the Interesting Transformation Potion and changed places,' said Xar.

'Oh dear,' whispered Queen Sychorax. 'It *is* possible . . .'

'I'M Xar, And YOU,' shouted Xar, 'are the WICKEDEST most TREACHEROUS most LYING Warrior Queen I have met in my ENTIRE LIFE!!! I have met ADDERS more straightforward than you are! YOU'RE TRICKIER THAN A TRICK LOAD OF WEREFOXES! YOU'RE MORE CROOKED THAN THE BACK OF A CROOKED-BACK SNAIL!

Only Xar could be that rude.

187

Queen Sychorax turned as white as a sheet.

'Okay,' said Queen Sychorax, her lips pursing sourly. 'You're definitely Xar-son-of-Encanzo.'

Xar was the rudest boy that Queen Sychorax had ever met and a real thorn in Queen Sychorax's side. Queen Sychorax was used to people being terrified of her, or at least respectful. But in this particular thirteen-year-old boy she always seemed to have met her match, and that was why she had been so mean to him when she was looking like Madam Clairvoy. But Xar was even trickier than she was. And he was a lot ruder.

'I OUGHT TO HAVE KNOWN THAT HORRIBLE MADAM CLAIRVOY WAS YOU ALL ALONG!' roared Xar. 'YOU MAY HAVE THE MOST BEAUTIFUL NOSE IN THE WILDWOODS BUT EVERY SINGLE TIME YOU TELL A LIE IT GETS JUST A LITTLE BIT POINTIER!'

Queen Sychorax sniffed thoughtfully. It was nonsense, of course, but Queen Sychorax was very proud of her nose, which was, indeed the most beautiful nose in the wildwoods, and the thought of it getting pointier, or being any other shape than the perfect shape it was, was *most* disagreeable. The beastly boy!

Queen Sychorax was nothing if not adaptable. She was thinking. Fast.

'Even if you *are* Xar-son-of-Encanzo, you're in

big trouble,' said Queen Sychorax. 'I have sent word, anonymously, to your father that you are hiding here, and my spies tell me that Encanzo is about to turn up to claim his son, and take you back to the prison of Gormincrag where you belong.'

Xar had calmed down. Now he was less angry, but very sad.

'Well, he won't find me here,' said Xar. 'We're running away again – and we were happy here,' said Xar longingly. 'Wish was happy. Bodkin was happy. I was happy, and you've made us run away . . .'

'The happiness was just an illusion, wasn't it?' said Queen Sychorax. 'This is real life, and in real life Wizards and Warriors can never be friends. Who are you going to run away *with*? The Bodkin boy who has already betrayed you? He can't come with you, surely . . . and if Wish can't even trust *Bodkin*, why would she trust you?'

'I would think about your own problems, if I were you, Queen Sychorax,' Xar advised her. 'You're stuck to that table. You can't reach the cupboard to put your Madam Clairvoy head on. So Madam Perdita and everyone are going to find you here, a queen of Warriors in a learning place for Wizards.'

'For all her roaring, Madam Perdita is soft,' said Queen Sychorax scornfully. 'She will let me go.'

Xar walked towards the door, and just as he reached

it, he turned round.

'You were never going to make Bodkin into a knight Warrior and a Hero of your Queendom, were you, Queen Sychorax?' said Xar.

'Of course not!' said Queen Sychorax. 'We Warriors have very strict rules about that sort of thing. Once a servant always a servant. I just said that because lies sometimes have to be told—'

'. . . in pursuit of the higher good,' Xar finished her own saying for her.

'And Bodkin believed me because he *wanted* to believe me,' said Queen Sychorax. 'Love is weakness, Xar-son-of-Encanzo – you need to remember that if you want to be a leader one day. But who am I talking to? You, of all people, should know that. The boy who wanted power so much that he took Magic from a Witch . . .'

'I was young, and I made a mistake, but maybe I am not what you see. You may think of yourself as a great leader, Queen Sychorax,' said Xar, 'but like so many other fools, perhaps you are not clever enough to see past appearances.'

Only Xar would have had the cheek to quote Queen Sychorax back at Queen Sychorax.

'I don't yet know what I want to become,' said Xar. 'But I do know, whatever it is, I don't want it to be what

YOU seem to have become.'

He shut the door very quietly.

And that last comment made Queen Sychorax think a good deal more than any of the insults.

I do not want to
become what YOU
have become...

191

13 . Bodkin's Letter

Xar was expecting Bodkin to be outside the door of Queen Sychorax's room, but Bodkin was not there.

It took Xar a bit of time to find Wish, but eventually he found her running through one of the courtyards, surrounded by all the sprites and animals. *She* was looking for *him*. She was carrying a letter, folded in half, and Xar's waistcoat.

'Bodkin gave me this letter, but he said I couldn't look at it until I was with you,' said Wish. 'And then he ran off. He wouldn't let any of us go with him except Nighteye, and he looked so upset . . . What's happened? You *are* still Xar, aren't you? You haven't switched back again yet?'

'That's not the problem,' said Xar grimly. He explained about Queen Sychorax, and Bodkin betraying them both, and Wish could not believe it.

They looked at the letter together. It was written in scribbled, hasty handwriting and it said:

Dear Wish and Xar,

By the time you read this, you will know I have betrayed you.

I don't know how to say how sorry I am. I wanted to keep Wish safe, and I did not realise how bad Queen Sychorax had become until she burnt down the forest, and then it was too late.

I should have told you, but I could not bear to see the look on your faces when you found out.

I found a page in the Spelling Book that told me where to find the Nuckalavee, and I ~~will~~ am going away on a Shadow Quest, to get the scales, to prove that I have courage, and that I can be a hero too.

Please do not follow me, it is too dangerous. Stay safe here with Madam Perdita, and learn how to be heroes and Wizards.

If I don't come back, I will have got what I deserved.

Very best wishes,

Bodkin
would be -
Your bodyguard and -
betrayer

P.S. I have taken Nighteye with me. I won't let her come to any harm

'This is partly your fault, Xar!' said Wish, turning on Xar fiercely.

'Hang on a second, *Bodkin's* the traitor, not *me*!' protested Xar. 'Don't blame this on *me*!'

'You're not very TACTFUL!' said Wish in a rage because she was worried about Bodkin. 'You kept going on and on about how he was a hob and everything . . .'

Xar opened up his mouth to protest . . . and then shut it again. Maybe he hadn't been quite as tactful as he might have been.

'Poor Bodkin . . . He only did it because he was jealous,' said Wish. 'I wish he'd told me . . .'

'Poor Bodkin . . .' agreed the key in a little creaky voice, drooping on the letter. 'Jealousy makes you do stupid things, doesn't it, fork? Luckily *I've* never been the jealous type . . .'

And then suddenly, in the distance, out in the woods, there was an unforeseen, dreadful noise.

Wish turned white.

The Witches that were out there waiting had been quiet, so quiet, up until now. Eerily quiet.

But Wish knew that new, fresh sound. It was the dreadful, heart-stopping noise of attacking Witches.

'*Bodkin!*' gasped Wish. 'They must be ambushing him! We have to help . . . Thank goodness he's taken the sword with him.'

'Maybe *not* "thank goodness",' said Xar, even whiter than Wish. 'Because if Bodkin took the sword with him, the iron will have created a hole in the Magic protecting Pook's Hill . . .'

Xar was right.

When Bodkin took the sword out of the school, the iron had indeed tunnelled a hole in the Magic, and even now, a gigantic feathered nightmare was crawling rat-like through that hole.

For the first time in hundreds of years, the sacred space of the learning place was invaded by a WITCH.

Much nearer than those distant dreadful noises, there was a confused screeching, and a great cry of 'WITCH ATTACK!' and the sound of swarms and swarms of piskies from inside the school hissing, 'witcheswitcheswi tcheswitcheswitcheswitches . . .'

The Witch feathers in Xar's waistcoat glowed with a strange unnatural light.

And little Squeezjoos's eyes lit up with a similar, unearthly green, as he crept forward in the air, hissing, 'sehctiw . . . sehctiw . . . sehctiw . . .'

Instinctively, Xar grabbed the little sprite, and put him in one of his pockets, buttoning it tight, and sticking it fast with the do-it-yourself Magic staff.

'Lets me *out!!!*' squeaked Squeezjoos, peering through a little tear in the material.

'No, Squeezjoos,' said Xar, 'I think you're safer in there for the moment.'

Wish and Xar ran towards the noise, the animals running beside them, their huge sympathetic bodies giving them courage, and the sprites flying above in a twitter of speculation.

It is sometimes only when we sense we are about to lose something that we really see it and appreciate it. The electric shock of the attack had woken Xar into a state of bright awakeness, so that every one of his senses was highly alert, and as he ran through the beloved, friendly, messy world of Pook's Hill in his bare hob feet, vaulting over the twisting tree trunks, gaining speed with every comforting familiar piece of ground that his feet touched, he had the oddest and dreadest sensation that he was seeing it for the very first and also the very last time.

He hadn't wanted to come here. But now he didn't want to leave.

They burst into the eastern clearing to find Perdita, great streams of Magic coming out of her fingers, fighting a swooping, diving shock of a Witch.

They were too late to help her.

Wish had her eyepatch up, ready, as they ran forward.

Perdita swelled. The energy force wracking her got more and more intense, and a great heat came off her so that Xar and Wish had to throw up their arms in front of their faces to protect themselves . . . and they were blown right off their feet by some sort of combined explosion from Perdita and the Witch.

There was a terrible tearing shrieking, and the ghastly vision of the swooping Witch turned invisible again . . . and patterings of green blood fell like rain as the Witch retreated, back towards the hole in the Magic at the eastern entrance of the school.

The animals gave howls of victory all around Xar.

The Witch has gone, thought Xar.

But at what dreadful cost?

'Madam Elfrida! Mister Yewtree! Chase the creature from the school. Close up the Magic there. Don't step in the Witchblood,' screamed Hoola.

Madam Elfrida and Mister Yewtree ran after the invisible, retreating Witch, carefully avoiding the drips of green.

The terrible form of Perdita, in the shape of a great unmoving bear, lay on the ground.

Oh no . . . please let her be all right, begged Wish to herself.

Xar and Wish crawled forward to Perdita's side. She was still steaming hot, too hot to touch.

'Is she going to be all right?' whispered Wish.

'I don't know,' hooted Hoola, anxiously fluttering

above Perdita's heart.

For a few dreadful seconds the bear remained unmoving.

And then an eyelid flickered, and weakly the bear opened an eye.

'Oh, by the great green gods that protect us,' breathed Hoola, 'I think she didn't have to use a life . . . I think she will survive. No thanks to *you*,' snapped Hoola fiercely, her head swivelling round to look furiously at Wish. 'It's all very well for you young people . . . *You* may have many lives, Wish, but Madam Perdita may only have one left.'

The relief of Perdita being alive was almost as if Wish's own heart had stopped for a second, only to start beating again.

A little troop of piskies came buzzing up in a state of high excitement, for nothing as sensational as this had happened in many a long while. 'Madam Elfrida says she has made good the hole in the Magic, and she thinks it was just the one Witch who got in,' one of the piskies gabbled before they all flew off back to where the action was.

Thank goodness – so at least that was *one* problem solved.

'I'm so sorry, Perdita,' said Wish. 'But Bodkin is in trouble. We have to leave in a hurry. Thank you for everything.'

At this the bear lifted her head weakly. 'No!'
growled Perdita-as-a-bear, and she staggered to her
feet, shook her shaggy fur, and in front of their eyes the
outline of the bear faded. She stood before them, much
smaller than normal, and terribly old and weak. Her face
was blasted with Witch-lightning. 'You should not leave
. . . it is too dangerous . . .'

'You know they must leave, Madam!' snapped
Hoola. 'It is only your weakness that has let them stay
here this long. I don't like to say, "I told you so," but
for the first time in centuries, a WITCH has entered this
sacred learning place. And these cursed children have let
it in. I TOLD you that the boy was unsaveable, and that
we'd have to expel him in the end.'

Xar's face darkened, and he looked furious.

'I TOLD you that the girl's Magic could not be
controlled, and that she would bring bad luck on all of
us,' said Hoola. 'What am I supposed to do with all this
Witchblood?'

Hoola pointed an angry wing at the steaming spots
of green that the teachers were now surrounding with
forcefields so that nobody accidentally stepped on them.

'It'll be years before we get those stains out.
Maybe even decades! And listen to those hell creatures
clamouring outside . . . Look at the calamities these
children have brought on us! Burning forests . . . Witch

attacks . . . And now Pook's Hill itself is in danger . . .'

'We're sorry about everything . . . but we have to go to the Nuckalavee to save Bodkin!' said Wish in a wretched state of anxiety. 'Xar and Bodkin changed places, and— It's too long to explain. Please let us out!'

'I said it myself,' said Perdita sadly, 'you were always just passing through. You can't run away forever . . . But when I said that,' she continued, bursting into tears, 'I never knew I was going to *like* you all so much . . .'

Caliburn patted her on the shoulder with one wing.

'Love is weakness,' warned Hoola, still huffy.

'Maybe it is,' said Perdita, smiling, 'but what a very nice weakness, it is indeed.'

'Can you come too, Perdita?' asked Wish, wistfully, for she knew what the answer was already.

Perdita looked affectionately into Wish's eye. 'I cannot,' said Perdita. 'Spells must be tended, suppers must be made, trees must be looked after, even when the world is burning. This is *your* quest . . . And my brother will look after you, won't you, brother?'

Caliburn sighed. 'I'll do my best. Thank you, sister, for hiding us for so long. We leave Pook's Hill a lot more prepared than we were when we arrived.'

'Until we meet again!' replied Perdita. 'And if you need me, all you have to do is . . . *Knock three times . . .*'

Right on cue, just as Perdita finished speaking,

there was a very loud knocking at the eastern entrance.
KNOCK! KNOCK! KNOCK!

Hoola's head swivelled round one hundred and
eighty degrees. 'Whoooo could that be?'

'Oh! Maybe it's Bodkin!' said Wish in horror.
'Trying to get back in because the Witches are attacking
him! Let him in! Let him in!'

Perdita tipped her head to one side, listening. 'That's
not Bodkin,' she said. 'The Nuckalavee is to the west.
Summon your door, and Hoola, take them all to the
western entrance very secretly and quietly, and then I'll
go and see who's at the *eastern* entrance. Whoever they
are, they may be in trouble.'

'But Madam, are you well enough?' asked Hoola.

Perdita drew herself up to her full height. She
looked quite *wild*, for she had been in the middle of
looking after a spell when the Witch attack happened,
and she had been so distracted that as well as everything
else the spell had exploded on her. So she had bits of
slimy seaweed tangled in her scorched hair, and other
unidentifiable but revolting-looking ingredients smeared
all over her clothes, and her hands were wrist deep
in some sort of goo that had a sulphurous and most
appalling stink of rotten eggs.

And on top of that, she could hardly stand up
because she was so bruised and battered by fighting off

the Witch. She clearly wasn't well at all. But . . .

'I'm *fine*, Hoola, stop fussing!' snapped Perdita. 'I'm only four hundred and eighty-five years old, after all, the prime of middle age. I don't know why you keep treating me as if I'm on the brink of death. OFF YOU GO!'

As soon as she had said these words a great humming, bee-cloud of piskies appeared out of nowhere, several of them so wildly over-excited that they actually threw up.

'Nothing to see here, piskies . . .' said Hoola uneasily, but she might as well have been hooting at the wind.

'They're OFF! They're OFF! On a VERY SECRET QUEST! One bear one giant TWO humans three wolves three snowcats eight USELESS sprites one peregrine falcon and a Baby noneofthemgreenanymore . . . *OFF* . . . on a very, very secret . . . absolutelycrazy . . . madlysuicidal . . . absolutelySecret . . . terrifyingStupyfyingIdioticLuniotic*LOSEYOUR BREFFDIOTIC*deathdefyingIMPOSSIBLE newQUEST!' sang the piskies.

Perdita transformed into a bear larger than Wish had ever seen before and ROARED at the piskies, who stopped buzzing a moment in shock.

'That's better,' said Perdita, changing back into herself again. 'Now, piskies. I have somebody arriving at the eastern entrance . . .'

'OOOOOOOOOO,' said the piskies.

'. . . and you absolutely must NOT tell anyone they are here. Not a word, piskies. I mean it . . . NOT A WORD.'

'OOOOOOOOO, wewonttellwewonttell . . .' sang the piskies, in a positive swarm of delight, and they buzzed off in vast bee-swarm numbers, a hum of creative curiosity to see what was going on in the eastern entrance.

Only one or two very tiny ones were left to squeak about what Xar and Wish were doing.

'I have faith in you, Xar,' said Perdita. 'Never forget that. And I have a parting gift for you . . .' She pressed something into Xar's hand. He shoved it in the pocket of his waistcoat, trying not to cry and pretending he did not care, and then they all hurried off after Hoola towards the west.

Perdita watched them go a moment. And then she turned

"No No No! We won't tell, your secret's safe with US..."

and limped to the east, where the knocking was getting
more and more urgent.

'You'd better use invisibility spells now,' Hoola
warned Xar and Wish as they reached the western
perimeter of the learning place. 'From the moment
you leave this place, the Witches will be watching.
Remember, *don't stay invisible too long*, just until you get
out of range of the Witches who are surrounding us.
Invisibility is very bad for you.'

The sprites took out their wands, and Xar and Wish
used their spelling staffs to turn everyone invisible. As
she looked down at her disappearing legs, Wish felt a
familiar queasy lurch of the stomach. Turning invisible
was almost like parts of you were going to sleep, or as if
you had become a ghost.

Hoola led them to the wall at the edge of the
mound, and Wish put the door up against it and
knocked three times with her now-invisible fist.

Knock!

Knock!

Knock!

The door swung open.

Outside, the cold night air was full of shrieks and the
screams of Witches, so loud and eerie Wish's blood ran
cold to hear them. It went against every instinct to leave
the warmth and safety of the learning place.

But they had to do this.

The invisible Wish and Xar walked through, leaving Hoola and two little piskies hovering on the other side.

Wish made it bigger for a second, so Crusher the giant could walk through the door too.

And then smaller again.

And then slowly, sadly, Wish closed the door.

'HOOOOOOOOO . . . ' Hoola hooted through the keyhole.

'One giant one bear TWO humans three wolves three snowcats eight USELESS sprites one peregrine falcon and a Baby noneofthemgreenanymore... OFF . . . on a very, very secret . . . absolutely crazy . . . madlysuicidal . . . absolutelySecret . . . terrifyingstupyfyingidiotic new QUEST,' chanted the two little piskies from the other side of the door. 'Leaving their wond-er-ful . . . marv-ellous . . . magnif-icent new Ho-o-ome . . . probably never to see it again . . . but to die miles away from anywhere in the ravenous jaws of the Nuckalavee . . . instead of staying cosycomfyhappy . . . and I think it's galiciousstarcurlers for supper again . . .'

'We'll be back, I promise,' Wish whispered back through the keyhole.

She let her hand rest on the door a second. And then, firmly, she stepped away.

'Follow Bodkin and Nighteye,' Xar whispered into the invisible ears of the snowcats.

Then they climbed on the invisible door and Wish
whispered a word to make it fly, moved the key, and they
flew very low over the ground – for up above was the
terrifying sight of the Witches attacking the school. Wish
could see the dark outlines of their feathers, swarms
of them, Magic screaming out of their mouths like
lightning, and her palms began to sweat.

*Love is weakness...
But what a very
nice weakness it is indeed.*

14. Encanzo and Sychorax Have a Little Explaining to Do

Wish and Xar only just left in time, for:

Knock!

Knock!

Knock!

KNOCK *knock* KNOCK *knock* KNOCK!!!!!

The person knocking frantically at the eastern door was Xar's father Encanzo.

The eastern door was the official entrance, so it was enormous and had a stone with big curly sprite writing on it saying 'Pook's Hill, the Learning Place for Spectacularly Gifted Wizards', just in case anybody had any doubt where they were.

Encanzo wasn't just knocking with both fists, he was drumming on the door with his feet, shouting, 'COME ON! COME ON! FOR MISTLETOE'S SAKE, *LET US IN!!!*' for he was in a terrible state.

Riding through the forest on their snowcats, Encanzo and Looter, Xar's elder brother, had been ambushed by Witches. Encanzo had begun by fighting them off with Magic, but there were too many of the creatures, so in desperation Encanzo had to set up a forcefield over the two of them, and they had only just reached the learning place in time. Now they had their backs against the door and Witches were attacking the forcefield with terrible cries.

Looter was tall, handsome, good-looking and extremely pleased with himself. He had just spent three months changed into a graxerturgleburkin,* but he seemed to have recovered from the experience. In fact, it may even have improved him somewhat. He was *ever so slightly* less self-satisfied than he had been three months earlier.

But right at this very moment he was looking absolutely petrified. Looter had never come this close to a Witch before, and he was cowering at the back of the forcefield, scrabbling at the door as the terrifying creatures swooped and struck. It was so dark that you could not really see them, but you could hear the appalling noise as they dived, and see the red of their eyes.

Knock!

---

* Long story. You can read about it in 'Wizards of Once, Twice Magic' if you like.

Knock!

Knock!

KNOCK! KNOCK! KNOCK! KNOCK!!!!!!!!

And then, to Looter and Encanzo's intense relief . . .

'All right, all *right!*' came a rather harassed voice
from a long way away. 'I'm coming! I've just forgotten
the password. What is it again? Oh, I remember now . . .
ARDEN!'

C-R-e-e-e-akkkkk! The door opened. The light
was so dazzling that Encanzo and Looter couldn't quite
see what they were stepping into, but they and their
snowcats FELL in through the door, Encanzo exploding
the forcefield simultaneously so that the attacking
Witches fell back with terrible screams of pain.

SLAM! The door closed behind them with the
sound of a rain of talons landing as it shut.

'Thank the green gods . . . ' gasped Encanzo, and
Looter was so out of his mind with fear that he could
only just gulp slightly. Even Encanzo's very dignified
ancient snowcat had his fur standing up like the quills
on a hedgehog, and his equally distinguished sprite was
a mess of anxiety.

But when Encanzo and Looter's eyes adjusted,
to their surprise they were not standing in the large
impressive entrance hall that the appearance of the
eastern entrance for the Learning Place for Spectacularly

211

Gifted Wizards might suggest.

No, they were standing in a small, very tidy study. There was only one person in the room and that person was Queen Sychorax, sitting down with her hands on the desk.

Looter and Encanzo could not have been more surprised than Queen Sychorax.

For from *Queen Sychorax's* point of view, the knocking had come from the other side of her cupboard door.

Imagine how alarming it must have been to have the door of a cupboard in which you have very tidily left the head of Madam Clairvoy, suddenly start knocking at you, and behind that door hear the dreadful scream of attacking Witches.

That would be truly terrifying, particularly when you can't run away, because your hands are stuck to the desk. She hadn't been behaving very well recently, but you have to feel sorry for Queen Sychorax in this situation. A lesser person than Queen Sychorax would have passed out with the shock of it.

Encanzo and Looter ought to have been less amazed, because space and time can work in a mysterious and unexpected way in the Wizarding world, particularly where doors are concerned. But the truth is, you never quite get used to it when it takes you by surprise like this.

And it is impossible to explain quite how this worked in human physical terms, but Madam Perdita was in a hurry, and she just wanted to get these two people together as quickly as possible, so the old door trick was the quickest way to do it.

Neither Encanzo nor Sychorax were even remotely pleased to see each other.

'*You* . . .' hissed Queen Sychorax.

'You!!!' spat King Encanzo.

There was always a little hiss or a frizzle in the atmosphere when these two met, a sort of jarring in the universe more noticeable on the outside than on the in, but if it were possible for the air to suddenly darken as if internal thunderclouds were gathering, then it did, and a couple of the candles blew out, just like that. *Pffft*.

Encanzo was particularly irritated to find himself confronted by his old enemy when he was in such an undignified condition, shirt raked to ribbons by Witches' talons, one side of his face blasted by Witch lightning. He adjusted the ruins of his waistcoat, as if that was going to make any difference, and straightened up to his most majestic and magnificent height.

BAM!

To both the monarchs' surprise, the actual door to Queen Sychorax's room now opened on the other side of the room, and in ran the owner of the harassed voice Encanzo had heard a couple of minutes earlier. Perdita was looking, if anything, even more ragged and frazzled than Encanzo, with five pairs of spectacles crawling all over her, several bits of clothing on back to front, Witch burns on her face and what appeared to be bits of food in her hair.

'Yes, yes, yes, we're going to have to be quick here. This isn't a good time for visitors!' snapped Madam Perdita. 'I'm containing a Witch attack, and then I have to get back to rather a complicated recipe for the young people's supper . . .'

'Who ARE you?' demanded Encanzo. 'If you're supposed to be containing a Witch attack you're not doing a very good job of it! You are facing a sustained assault by the forces of dark Magic and I need to speak to the head of the learning place, not the cook!'

'I just told you, the Witch attack is completely under control, and I AM the head of the learning place! The head of the learning place should *always* be the cook, it's the most important job,' explained Perdita.

'Well, I am King Encanzo, King of Wizards,' said Encanzo fiercely, 'and—'

'Yes, yes,' interrupted Madam Perdita impatiently. 'I know who you are, and you are bringing your son Looter to be a pupil here, because you think he's spectacularly gifted. Run along through that door there, Looter, dear, you're admitted . . .'

Looter goggled at her.

He was used to being the most important person in his father's and everyone else's life, not swept out of the way as if he were nothing.

'Do you not realise who you are speaking to?' said Encanzo sharply. 'This is my eldest son, who will be the next King of Wizards, so you are incredibly lucky to have the honour of schooling him.'

'Quick, quick,' said Madam Perdita, not obviously impressed, 'you're a bit in the way at the moment, Looter, but I'm sure you'll make a *lovely* spectacularly gifted Wizard. Just step through the door and ask the piskies to take you to the sanitorium, to have a look at those Witch burns you have on your arm, and then to the head of Year Ivy*, she'll look after you.'

Almost as if hypnotised, Looter moved towards the door of the room, opened it, stepped through, and the door shut after him.

A little chorus of excitable piskie voices came floating through the door. The little voices sounded somewhat dubious.

'WELCOME largeverypleasedwithyourselfboy whothinkshe'ssocleverandusedtobeagraxerturgle burkinandwhoisusedtotellingeveryonewhattodo! WELCOME to your marvellous . . . magnificent . . . magical new ho-o-ome!'

'Mff,' sniffed Madam Perdita thoughtfully. 'Looter's spectacular gifts aren't *immediately* apparent, but I'm

---

*Year 12

217

sure we will find them, we always do . . . Now,' she
said briskly, 'I understand, Encanzo, you are also here
to collect your *other* son, the one who is spectacularly
cursed?'

'You knew about that?' said Encanzo, trying to
regain control of the situation.

'You're too late,' said Madam Perdita.

With a wink of Madam Perdita's eye, she released
Queen Sychorax's hand from the desk. Queen Sychorax
leapt to her feet.

'Do sit down,' said Madam Perdita.

'I prefer to stand,' said Queen Sychorax.

'As do I,' said King Encanzo.

'As you wish,' said Madam Perdita.

She snapped her fingers. A chair ran towards her. She
sat down.

Both Encanzo and Sychorax regretted saying they
would stand because suddenly it felt like Perdita was the
royalty, sitting on her throne, even with bits of food in
her hair, and *they* were the naughty children who had
been sent to the head.

'You don't mind if I knit? It helps me to
concentrate,' said Madam Perdita. One knitting needle
pushed its way through the keyhole of the cupboard and
flew into Madam Perdita's left hand. The other knitting
needle pushed its way through the keyhole of the door,

and flew into Madam Perdita's right hand.

Madam Perdita began to knit, unravelling her own scarf as she went and using it as the wool.

'*You*, Sychorax and Encanzo, have a little explaining to do,' said Madam Perdita, and now she sounded very grim indeed. 'You are too late to catch your children. They and their bodyguard have gone to see the Nuckalavee.'

Both Sychorax and Encanzo whitened in horror.

'And you let them?' gasped Sychorax.

'But that's like sending them to their deaths!' said Encanzo. 'Why did you not keep them here?'

'This is a learning place, not a prison,' said Perdita, knitting away merrily. 'Although both you and Sychorax seem very fond of locking your children up.'

Now Sychorax and Encanzo went from white to red with embarrassment.

'I had no choice!' said Encanzo. 'You said so yourself! Xar is spectacularly cursed!'

'As is Wish!' said Sychorax.

'Then *uncurse* them,' said Perdita.

'There's no such thing as *uncursing*,' said Encanzo.

'The young people seem to think so,' said Perdita. 'Which is why they are off to find the ingredients of the spell to get rid of Witches.'

'Wish fulfillment,' said Sychorax.

'Child's play,' said Encanzo.

'And *dangerous* child's play, at that,' said Sychorax. 'Listen to the sound of those creatures out there! You've exposed our children to the Witches who are hunting them . . .'

'Perhaps,' said Perdita. 'But the young people are in grave danger already, and you do not seem to be helping them with that so far.'

Both Encanzo and Sychorax turned red.

'I've very much enjoyed getting to know your children over the past few months,' said Perdita, continuing to knit. 'It seems to me that the reason that Xar got the Witchstain in the first place is that he was so desperate not to let his father down by having no Magic at all, that he was prepared to go to extreme lengths to get just a little approval.'

'You can't blame ME for this!' growled Encanzo.

'Have you noticed,' said Perdita, 'that the more you tell Xar off, the more disobedient he becomes?'

Encanzo was silent.

'And as for Wish, I have never met a child with Magic as powerful as she has, but she seems to think, Queen Sychorax, that *you*, her own mother, are ashamed of her,' said Perdita.

'Am I supposed to be PROUD of a daughter with such cursed Magical skills?' stormed Queen Sychorax.

'She's an embarrassment. How dare you tell us what to do? We know best, for we are the children's parents!'

'And how do you think your parenting is going so far?' asked Perdita sweetly.

There was an uncomfortable silence inside the study.

Outside, the screaming of the Witches seemed to be underlining that the answer to that question was: *Not very WELL, actually, since you mention it.*

'We're doing our best!' protested Encanzo. 'Being a parent is not as easy as it looks!'

'That, at least, is true,' admitted Perdita. 'Very well then, if you want to stop them, you're going to have to catch them. Which is why I brought you together. That, and showing you, Sychorax, what a *real* learning place ought to be like.' Perdita seemed amused about something. 'Did you think I did not see through the Madam Clairvoy disguise? Of course I did . . . I just thought you might learn something from being in Pook's Hill.'

'This is a ridiculous place!' raged Sychorax. 'Children being taught by birds! Lessons in tree climbing! I am the only person in this entire establishment teaching anything sensible . . . '

'But the children are happy,' said Madam Perdita. 'What should they be learning, Sychorax? How to burn down a forest? However, if *you* haven't learnt anything,

221

never mind. I could be wrong, of course, there's always that possibility.'

Madam Perdita considered that improbable possibility for one interested moment, and then rejected it.

'No,' said Perdita briskly, 'no, I'm not wrong.'

As Madam Perdita was talking, Sychorax suddenly realised that along with a bit of rug from the floor, the edges of Sychorax's *own cloak* were unravelling themselves and being knitted into Perdita's knitting, along with little pieces of Encanzo's shirt. 'What on earth are you doing?' snapped Sychorax, trying to wrench her cloak away, but it held surprisingly fast.

Encanzo looked amused, but said, 'Stop that, Madam Perdita.'

'Oh, I do apologise,' said Madam Perdita, 'this is a very bad habit of mine . . .'

A little pair of bronze scissors hopped out of her pocket, danced up to the pieces of thread and snipped them apart, snip, snip.

'Now I brought you together, for you both want the same thing, do you not? You want to catch your children, so catch them if you can. They have gone to find the Nuckalavee, so you can follow them and find them, the two of you, alone . . . For neither of you want anyone to know the secrets of your past, do you? You'd rather that the Wizards and the Warriors did not find out that you were once in love and that that is the reason that Wish has been born with Magic-mixed-with-iron?'

'It *is* best if we keep this to ourselves,' admitted Sychorax.

'Just one other reason that the predicament the young people find themselves in may be more YOUR fault than their own . . .' Perdita reminded them.

Sychorax's hands were in fists. Normally nobody tells the truth to queens, and she wasn't enjoying the experience. But what could she do? This was Madam Perdita's territory. She had to bide her time and wait for revenge.

'Encanzo knows where the Nuckalavee can be found, don't you, Encanzo?' said Madam Perdita.

'I do,' said Encanzo. 'The Nuckalavee was part of my shadow quest, after you abandoned me, Sychorax,' said Encanzo. 'I nearly never came back.'

'A quest where you gave the Nuckalavee your heart,' said Perdita, in her cosiest voice.

'You gave the Nuckalavee your heart?' said Sychorax, forgetting her fury at Perdita for a moment and raising one eyebrow at Encanzo.

'Well, what was I supposed to do with it after you had stomped all over it?' said Encanzo bitterly. 'I couldn't go on living with a broken heart. It was very

223

inconvenient – the edges of it were all uncomfortable in my chest. I had to get on with my life, live and love again . . .'

'So the two of you can go together,' said Perdita, getting up. 'With absolutely no chance of either of you catching any of that nasty love disease again. One without a heart. The other having drunk the Spell of Love Denied. No risk whatsoever, I would say.'

'We're free to go?' said Encanzo.

'*Of course* you're free to go!' said Perdita, extremely exasperated. 'I don't know WHY everyone keeps saying that! This is a learning place, not a prison. I may not agree with your methods of child rearing, but they are, after all, your children. It sounds like the Witch attack is now under control.'

The sound of the screaming outside had indeed died down somewhat.

'But I would recommend invisibility, nonetheless,' Perdita advised, 'and suggest you leave by the cupboard door, thereby avoiding the piskies. Or better still, the trapdoor. I have Witchblood to clean up and a recipe to finish. Off you go!'

15. The Chase

eanwhile, Bodkin had left Pook's Hill by the western entrance. It was lucky that he was still in the body of Xar, for it meant that he could use Xar's powers and make himself invisible. He had a piece of map torn from the Spelling Book, and it said the Isle of the Nuckalavee was opposite somewhere called the Beach of Shoes, and that was to the west.

Bodkin had a slight setback when he saw the huge dark outlines of the Witches roosting in the treetops above him, like gigantic crows. Even though he knew they couldn't see him, he passed out on the back of Nighteye. When he woke up again a few seconds later, he was so rigid with fear, his hands clutching Nighteye's fur hadn't even unclenched. Looking back over his shoulder as Nighteye ran on, he could see that the Witches were still unmoving.

After a while, when it seemed clear that he wasn't being followed, he stopped Nighteye and turned himself visible again, for he didn't know how long he would continue to inhabit the body of Xar, and when he was back in his own body, he wouldn't have any Magical powers at all. Even the staff that Perdita had given him was with Xar now, so he couldn't use that. Not that 'sticking things to other things' was likely to be *all* that useful when you were facing what must be the terrible nightmare of a Nuckalavee . . .

I have the sword, though! I can use the sword, thought Bodkin with excitement. As he rode on, he was still elated at leaving the school without being discovered.

I'll show Wish what a Hero I can be . . . I've betrayed her, but now I will prove myself.

But then there was a dreadful scream behind him, which was the sound of the triumphant Witches discovering the hole in the Magic that Bodkin had made when he took the iron Enchanted Sword out of Pook's Hill. In terror, Bodkin thought it might be the Witches coming after him. He urged Nighteye on, on. He had entered a bit of the forest that had been scorched to the ground by Sychorax's wildfire, so the burnt landscape was depressing. And by the time he found a place to sleep for the night, the enormity of what he had done was beginning to creep over him.

He shivered under brambles, trying to get to sleep on a cold, cold night, hugging as close as he could to Nighteye in the hope of getting some warmth. The snowcat's fur was soaked through. Her tail was in a puddle. Bodkin cried himself to sleep.

Xar and Wish left from the western entrance about an hour after Bodkin. They, too, escaped without

apparently being detected by the Witches, who were
now attacking Encanzo and Looter on the other side
of Pook's Hill. On and away they flew on the back
of the Enchanted Door, just above the level of the
undergrowth, following the very faint noise of the
running snowcats and wolves, who were panting with
fear as they ran through the burnt forest. Wish and Xar
looked over their shoulders every two or three minutes
to check that they were not being pursued by Witches.

To Wish's intense relief, the snowcats following the
traces of Bodkin's path were heading further and further
west. *So Bodkin must have got away without the Witches
seeing him*, thought Wish jubilantly.

After a while, they felt confident that they were far
enough away to turn themselves visible again. And Xar
let Squeezjoos out of his pocket. The little sprite was
recovered from the odd attacks that seemed to beset him
when he was too close to Witches, but he was terribly
upset. 'Why dids you shut me up?' asked Squeezjoos.

'It was for your own good, Squeezjoos,' said Xar.
'You have to trust me, I know best.'

Squeezjoos could not stay cross with Xar for long.
He looked into Xar's eyes, and licked him on the face.
'It's true!' said Squeezjoos. 'You DOESSS know best!'

Eventually they were too tired to go any further.

Squeezjoos was so exhausted that he actually crawled

back into Xar's pocket and did up the buttons himself. Lonesome had a thorn in his paw and was limping.

'We need to sleep,' said Xar. 'Daytime is a better time for travelling anyway – less chance of Witches. We'll catch up with Bodkin and Nighteye tomorrow.' Xar was in a belligerent mood, exhilarated to be back on their quest again, but still oddly cross with Perdita for letting them go. 'Nobody wants us, even *her*, but we can do this on our own.'

Talking about Perdita made him look in his pocket for the thing that she had given him just before he left. It was one of her handkerchiefs, wrapped tightly round something in a little bottle, and when he unwound it, out fell . . .

'*The Droods' tears!*' gasped Caliburn. 'The fifth ingredient in the spell to get rid of Witches!'

Sure enough, there were five shining tears of the Droods from the Lake of the Lost, gleaming like dark diamonds in the centre of the bottle.

'My sister trusts me again!' said Caliburn. 'Even though I made a mistake last time!'

'She trusts me too!' said Xar, all his ill humour disappearing. 'Even though I have the Witchstain.'

'There's a note,' said Wish, picking up a piece of paper that had been wrapped around the bottle along with the handkerchief.

The note was in Perdita's handwriting and read:

Dear All,

You have truly earned these Drood's Tears. Life is made up of sorrow as well as joy, and there is a reason why tears are such an important ingredient in so many spells. You may try as hard as you can, and yet still fail...

BUT being a Wizard is about making impossible things happen, and happy endings have to be fought for.

Good luck!

Love Perdita

'Maybe we *did* belong in Pook's Hill, after all,' said Xar. He tied Perdita's handkerchief around his arm with the Witchstain. 'If I ever wanted a mother – and I *don't*,' he added hurriedly, 'I would choose a mother like Perdita.'

Perdita's present made them all feel more cheerful. They were progressing in their quest. If they had been successful in getting four of the ingredients, surely they could win the last one, and save Bodkin at the same time?

It was raining, so Tiffinstorm set up a weather spell to protect them while they slept.

'Whyissitalwaysmewhohastodoeverything?' complained Tiffinstorm, getting out a number four wand and taking a weather spell out of her spell bag. She batted the spell up in the air with her wand, and a nice little umbrella of wind sprang out of the end of the spell, hovering some three or four feet above them, and the rain poured over the edges in a waterfall.

So Wish and Xar slept far better than poor Bodkin that night.

They slept wrapped up in the middle of the comforting heat of a tangle of animals – the shaggy fur of the snowcats, the werewolf and the wolves, and the bear, keeping them warm. And curled around them all, in a protective way, was the great sleeping form of Crusher the giant. Longstepper High-Walker giants

don't need weather spells. They are waterproof. Their
great bodies give off such warmth that the rain just
bounces off them, turning into steam.

In the middle of the night, Xar could feel his
appearance changing back from Bodkin-as-a-hob into
Xar again. It was the same strange, unsettling feeling as
it had been last time – very sick-making – and when
he looked at his arms, he could see the fur gradually
dissolving, leaving his own Xar-like skin beneath. He
rolled over and went back to sleep again.

When Wish woke up every now and then, she
could see that the snowcats were taking turns to keep
awake. One time it was Kingcat keeping lookout,
watching the skies above through the glass of the rain-
washed spell. The next it was Forestheart. So she would
fall asleep with the comforting drumming of the rain
on the spell above, the desolation of leaving Pook's Hill
alleviated by the closeness of her friends.

Bodkin, don't be afraid . . . thought Wish dreamily.
We're coming to find you.

About half an hour after Wish and Xar left Pook's Hill,
Encanzo and Sychorax set out in pursuit.

They had to share a ride on Encanzo's snowcat and
there was a big argument about who should ride at the
front and who should ride at the back.

231

They began the
trip invisible, but by the
time they set out, Perdita and
her Wizards had made good
the Magic protecting Pook's
Hill and the Witch attack was
over. In their invisible
state, they had to weave
their way past several
Witch corpses, which
explained why the
Witches had stopped
their invasion. The
Witches had now retreated
to the treetops where they
were chanting dreadful curses,
like vengeful monkeys.
Sychorax and Encanzo rode
without talking to each other, both
of them grimly angry. Once they
reached the scorched part of the forest,
Encanzo turned them visible again. The
broken stumps of trees were quiet, so quiet.
As Sychorax rode through the forest that she herself

had burnt to the ground, steadily growing in her mind's eye with each leap of the snowcat were the remembered ghosts of trees that were heavy with the numberless leaves of the summer time. The memory of a much younger Encanzo riding by her side, and they were hunting deer perhaps, flocks of birds shocked up into the air as they raced past, out of control with youth, and the wind making them giddy by blowing straight into their brains, and the seemingly endless forest stretching out in front of them.

And then she blinked, and here in the present there were no trees. Which was a shame, because when she stopped to think about it, Sychorax *liked* trees. The ashy remains of the tree stumps were making her feel uncomfortable and, irritably, she stared straight ahead so she didn't have to look at them.

They rode until they were so tired they were in danger of falling off the snowcat.

I did thi

And they
made camp in the
open air.

'Once you were a wild thing,
just like me, Queen Sychorax,' said
Encanzo bitterly, staring into the fire of
many colours he had conjured up with
his staff as they settled down for a few
hours of sleep on the forest floor. 'But
it will be many years since your Majesty
camped out without your toothpick.'

'I am a Warrior,' said Sychorax, tossing
her head. 'We camp out all the time.'

This was a lie. It had indeed been a very
long time since Sychorax had camped out in
the woods without a richly embroidered tent,
a feather bed, a tiptoeing lady to turn down
the warm, dry covers and wish her a good
night's sleep.

But she was too proud to show that she
minded.

'I am sorry I cannot offer you trees
for shelter,' said Encanzo, pointing
upwards at the empty darkness. The
bleak, cold rain was coming down
very heavily now.

'Once, there would have been branches above us where birds used to sing,' continued Encanzo, 'homes where the forest creatures lived . . . But they are burnt, all burnt, so that you Warriors can build your forts and your fields and all the THINGS you need to have – the nick-nacks, that golden bracelet around your wrist . . .

'But I ask you, Sychorax, is it worth the freedom you have had to give up? The moon, the stars, the wind, you sold them for?'

Sychorax did not answer.

She WAS getting awfully wet.

Her bottom was definitely soggy. She thought she may have sat on a damp patch.

'Let me tell you a story,' said Encanzo, 'of how twenty years ago my heart turned into stone.'

No! I do not want to hear it!

The Story of
How Encanzo's heart
turned into a
Stone   you have
          to look
          inside the
          hut of
          the
          Wizard
          Who
          Waits

How the boy, Tor, Became the Wizard, Encanzo

'Once upon a time, long, long ago, there was a young Wizard known as Tor, who fell in love with a young Warrior princess. Wizards and Warriors should NEVER fall in love, but the young Warrior princess declared she did not care for silly rules such as this one. The young Warrior princess promised she would marry Tor. She promised on her heart that they would run away together, and find themselves a world where it did not matter where they came from, where Wizards and Warriors could love and live in peace.

TOR'S SONG Never and Forever – Part 2

They told me careful where you love
But I did not listen

My heart was born when I met you, I got my second chance
Flying side by side together in a never-ending dance
Why should I listen?

But now I'm
Waiting
For the knock on the door
When SHE will come
Forever waiting
And waiting …
And waiting.

Closing
My eyes until SHE comes back
Longing
For the knock on the door
When SHE will come …
Forever waiting
And waiting …
And waiting.

But the princess did not keep her promise . . .'

'I had responsibilities, duties!' interrupted
Sychorax. Encanzo carried on as if she had not spoken.

'She took the Spell of Love Denied and the
love died in her heart . . . She wrote a letter to the
Wizard boy saying she did not love him and she never
had. Meanwhile, Tor waited many long weeks in the
appointed waiting place. He got the letter. He read it,
refused to believe it. A hut grew around him and the
sprites in the forest felt so sorry for him, they brought
him food and water. They called him "the Wizard-who-
waits".

'I will take you inside that hut now. Look at
him, the poor young Wizard-who-waits,' said Encanzo
bitterly.

'Two long years he waited, said Encanzo. Until he
realised . . . she was never coming back. And THAT,' said
Encanzo, 'was when the young Wizard turned his heart
into stone, and become the Wizard sitting before you
now. The Wizard Encanzo.'

And Encanzo turned
his heart into a stone.

No longer... WAITING
for the knock on the door.
No longer longing.
For there is no song...
there is no heart
there is no knock

And the true love never comes.

Listen. Be careful where you love.
I will make a new start.
Without a heart.

There was a short pause as Encanzo came to the end of his story. Queen Sychorax swallowed hard . . .

and then Encanzo thrust his staff into the ground and he muttered a few words, and a weather spell rushed out of the end of the staff forming a protective canopy over where Encanzo was intending to sleep.

'I can extend the spell to cover *you* as well, if you like,' says Encanzo.

Queen Sychorax put her pretty little nose up in the air.

'Humph,' said Queen Sychorax. 'I do not need your spell. We Warriors are not afraid of a little rain. We are made of tougher material than that.'

'Suit yourself,' said Encanzo, shrugging, wrapping himself in his cloak and falling asleep under the protection of the spell.

Queen Sychorax settled underneath a little tangle of burnt and broken brambles. It took a while for her to fall asleep in the pouring rain. It was going to be a miserable night for Queen Sychorax.

And it may be uncharitable of me as a narrator, and I really shouldn't comment . . .

BUT

I think . . .

I think . . .

I feel sorry for her even though she has brought this all on herself.

I feel sorry for her, even though she has brought this on herself.

Follow me,
if you DARE...

NOW . . . I do not want to alarm you, dear reader, of
course I do not.

But I have to tell you, it would be truly remarkable if three
children, a flying door, four snowcats, various wolves, a werewolf,
a bear, two adults, numerous sprites, and a humungous
Longstepper High-Walker giant were able to leave Pook's Hill
without even ONE Witch noticing, even if they were invisible
at the time.

The fact is, although Perdita and Hoola and Elfrida and
the other teachers were able to fight off the Witches and make
the learning place safe by sealing up the hole in the Magic
made by the Enchanted Sword, there were other Witches who
had noticed the exit of these three separate parties while the
fight was going on.

And they were following.

They did not want anyone to notice, so the Witches were
pursuing, not in the air, but on foot, or rather using their
folded-up wings as if they were legs, scuttling in between the
burnt trees of the broken forest.

They had used the opportunity of the hole made by
Bodkin to attack Pook's Hill, because there were things in the
learning place that they wanted.

But why were they now choosing NOT to attack the
various parties on the quest to find the Nuckalavee?

We are about to find out why . . .

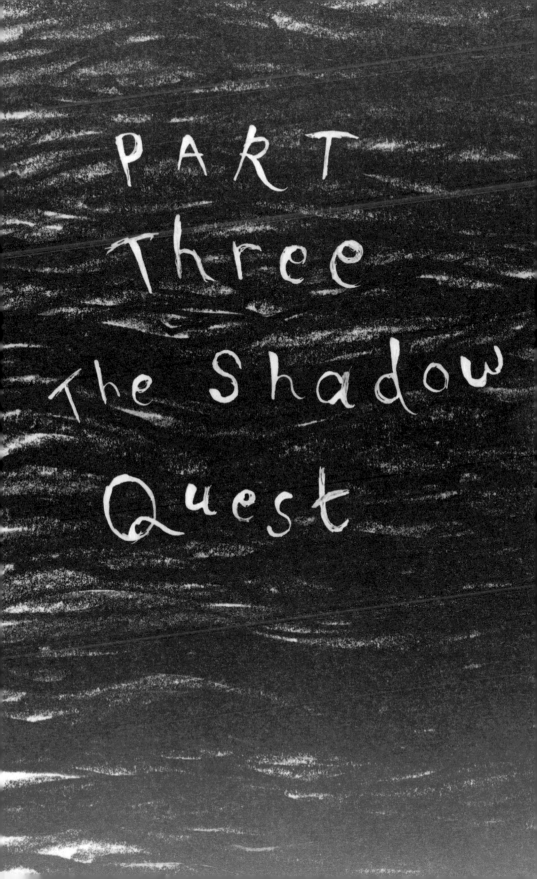

PART
Three

The Shadow

Quest

16. The Beach of Shoes

When Bodkin woke up, cold, shivering, the transformation medicine that turned him into Xar had worn off, as had any residual excitement. Maybe there was some bit of Xar that was still left in there when he had briefly taken over Xar's body. But whatever mad impulse had taken him over, it was now gone.

He looked down at his arms, skinny as weeds.

He wasn't even a hob any more. He was just *Bodkin* ... an extremely ordinary Assistant Bodyguard who had betrayed the trust of his princess.

Bodkin was used to being alone, even when he was in company.

But for the first time in his life he really was completely ...

ALONE.

With shaking hands he took out the map that he had torn from the Spelling Book that showed him the way to the Nuckalavee. The path that led through the burnt forest was shining bright on the map, which meant that he was heading in the right direction. The path ended somewhere called the Beach of Shoes, and opposite this beach was an island called the Isle of the Nuckalavee.

There was a warning on the bottom of the map, saying in big dark letters:

DON'T FORGET TO
TAKE OFF YOUR SHOES.

But there was no time to wonder what that might mean.

Bodkin drank a glug of water from his water bottle. He was sick with hunger, but the burnt forest contained no food and he couldn't return now. He had to go on, riding on Nighteye's back, all the while taking terrified glances up at the sky above, scared that at any moment he might see a Witch, even though Witches weren't all that keen on flying during the daytime. The broken trees didn't provide much camouflage.

Bodkin arrived at the Beach of Shoes very late in the evening, hungry and thirsty, and so terrified by the sight of the distant island of the Nuckalavee, crouching like a dark predatory creature on the horizon, he fell asleep on Nighteye's back and Nighteye had to carry him on, in a dead faint, to the edge of the water.

He woke up again at the brink of the ocean, waves breaking on the shore, looking out at the island. Bodkin shivered and thought, 'I have to do this, for HER . . . I have to prove that *I* can be a hero too, even if I will only be a dead hero . . . Maybe if I'm a dead hero, she'll at least forgive me.'

Nighteye swam out to the island, with Bodkin, who could not swim, holding on to her tail.

What am I doing? thought Bodkin. *Some hero I am. I can't even swim.*

Bodkin and Nighteye landed on the Isle of the Nuckalavee, and Nighteye shook off the water like a cat. Bodkin felt rising determination as he put a hand on the hilt of the Enchanted Sword and pulled down his visor.

Before him were the sands of the beach, and the waters of the ocean were running into a dark and dreadful cave, open like the jaws of a monster. The Cave of the Nuckalavee. Bodkin felt his heart shrivel within him as he looked at it.

But I got here on my own! I can do this! thought Bodkin. *I'm stronger than they think I am!*

He tried to pull out the Enchanted Sword, but for some reason it would not budge from its scabbard. It was stuck fast, as if it were glued there.

By the whiskers of werewolves! thought Bodkin. *I'm not even strong enough to draw the sword!*

But Bodkin made himself put one foot in front of the other, even though it felt like each foot was made out of lead.

Bodkin stopped suddenly.

Feeling he'd forgotten something.

What was it?

What on earth could it be?

He looked down.

I've forgotten to take off my shoes!!!

Bodkin's eyes closed and his head slumped gently to one side.

Snore!

He tipped forward, face down in the sand.

There was a terrible high-screeching noise from behind and above, like the sound of swooping furies. The sound of many, many scrabbling feet on the sand, panting furiously, running towards the intruders.

Nighteye gave a terrified yowl, her fur all on end. She picked up the fallen Bodkin and ran into the Cave of the Nuckalavee, the unconscious Bodkin dangling from her mouth, like a cat carrying a kitten.

And goodness knows what awaited them in there.

No, I don't think Bodkin was *quite* ready to perform a quest all on his own.

Wish and Xar and their companions arrived at the Beach of Shoes the next morning, so early that the sun was not yet up.

They had lost track of Bodkin for a bit, and it took the snowcats a while to pick up his scent again. When they finally reached the Beach of Shoes, Wish and Xar found a small log boat hidden in a reed bank which

they would be able to use to cross the sea to the island
of the Nuckalavee. They hid the Enchanted Door under
branches and leaves.*

Many of the rocks on the beach had sprite writing that
gleamed in the light of the moon scrawled all over them.

The sprite writing said, quite politely,

PLEASE TAKE OFF YOUR SHOES ...

And then added, more ominously,

... OR *ELSE* ...

'You have to take your shoes off,' explained Caliburn,
'out of respect for the sea, and the impossible quest.
Then you become the shadow men and women, the
shoeless ones, and only when you return are you allowed
to put them back on again.'

Obediently, Wish and Crusher took off their shoes.
Xar wasn't wearing any shoes anyway because he had left
the Learning Place for Gifted Wizards dressed as a hob.

Crusher walked ahead a few steps and carefully laid
down his shoes in the grass at the edge of the beach.

And for the first time the children noticed that all
along the outer permimeter of the shore, higher than
the tide could reach, was a line of shoes patiently waiting
for their owners to come back. Some of them had been
waiting a long, long time. Their leather was wind-battered,
storm-eaten, half-broken and buried in the sand. Others

---

* For complicated Magical reasons, doors have difficulty flying over oceans.
They get seasick, and capsize.

looked perkier and more hopeful, as if their owners had only just taken them off and were about to return.

'Not very many people come back to collect their ssshooessssss . . .' squeaked Bumbleboozle in nervous alarm.

Ariel's eyes gleamed green and then red. 'Particularly when you consssssider these are the shoes of some of the greatest Wizards in the wildwoods . . .'

They couldn't find Bodkin's shoes, so they weren't sure if he had got there before them or not.

Crusher picked up the small boat, carefully carried it across the beach and put it gently in the water. The others followed in his giant footsteps.

There were will-o'-the-wisps flying right out of the bogs and on to the beach in a glorious firework display, singing and taunting and pulling the hair of the sprites.

Will-o'-the-wisps are mean little faeries that sprites hate even more than piskies. At least piskies are only mischievous. Will-o'-the-wisps wilfully lead unwary travellers to their doom.

'Don't you DARE go after the will-o'-the-wisps, sprites!' shouted Xar, shaking his fist. 'I'm warning you all! Pay no attention!'

But it was very hard to ignore the impudent little creatures, and their eerie song sent a chill into Wish's soul and made her swallow hard. Whatever was over on that island must be very, very scary indeed.

'The Nuckalavee!' sang the will-o'-the-wisps. 'The fools on their way to the Nuckalavee ...'

The Fools on Their Way to the Nuckalavee

Care-less, love-less, heart-worn, soul-blast?
Come this way ...
Thought-less ... shoe-less ... hope-less?
Come this way ...
Love is weakness ...
Love is kindness ...
Love is childish ...
Love is thoughtless ...
No more second chances
No more silly dances
LOVE is weakness ... so
Come this Way ...

'Take no notice. Don't look back until we've got in the boat,' said Caliburn, all of a fluster.

Crusher tied a rope to the front of the boat and they all jumped in. The giant waded out thigh-deep, and then he gave a great shiver of 'it's cold!' before holding his nose and launching himself into the sea in a great breaststroke, sending backward waves that nearly overturned their boat.

When the sky turned dark, the moon shone and
the swimming giant pulled the boat after him along
the path of the moon, heading out to the island of the
Nuckalavee with the sprites singing overhead.

The wolves and the snowcats put their heads over
the side of the boat, wind waggling their ears, as they
looked back at the beach. They could still see the shoes.

The shoes were waiting.

They would wait forever if they had to.

*And little did they know it, but there were eyes OTHER
than the eyes of will-o'-the-wisps watching them leave the
Beach of Shoes . . .*

The eyes of *WITCHES*.

Witches were crouching like great dark spiders in
the reed beds, muttering to each other, 'Sehs gnimoc . . .
sehs gnimoc . . .' which means, 'She's coming . . . she's
coming . . .'

But oddly, they did not yet attack. They were
waiting too.

What were *they* waiting for?

Crusher swam through the quiet black water, so
far out that they could no longer see the shore and the
beach with the waiting shoes behind them, and then
Wish began to feel not-so-brave.

As they drew closer to the island of the Nuckalavee,
the shadowy outline coming nearer and nearer, bottles

253

began to appear in the ocean – at first only a few passing the log boat every now and then, but then there were more of them, and more, and more and more.

Xar leant over the side of the log boat and picked one out of the water. It was a perfectly ordinary bottle with a blank piece of paper on it, and a bit of hair, and a fingernail, and some other things he couldn't quite identify.

'Why are all these bottles here?' asked Wish.

'They're curse bottles,' said Xar, putting the bottle back in the water. 'Somebody on that island must be putting them in the water and pushing them out to sea. Whoever it is really doesn't like someone else, but I don't know who. Normally you write the name of the person you are cursing on that piece of paper, but there's nothing written on the paper.'

Wish shivered. There were so many bottles bobbing past in the sea around them. That was an awful lot of cursing, and she didn't really want to meet whoever was behind it.

Mists suddenly descended out of nowhere, great choking sea mists, treacherous, shifting, there one minute

Curse bottles →

gone the next, sometimes so thick that they could barely see the comforting head of Crusher swimming out in front of them.

But they knew they were still going the right way, for they were following the bottles.

Ariel tasted the mist. 'This fog is not natural – it is Magic, summoned by the Droods,' whispered Ariel, his eyes gleaming red for danger in the swirling, confusing fog all around them. 'The Droods are concealing something.'

The mists cleared and there it was, finally, close-up.

The Isle of the Nuckalavee.

'Oh my goodnesssss!' squeaked Bumbleboozle, turning multiple somersaults in panic. 'It's not an island, it's a MONSTER! Look at how big its JAWS are . . . Pleassse let's go back . . .'

But Wish screwed up her eyes and flicked up her eyepatch a smidgeon because her Magic eye was good at seeing through magic-made mist.

'That isn't a mouth,' she said at last. 'It's a CAVE . . .'

A dark island, shrouded in fog, with a gigantic dark sea cave like the open mouth of a monster.

17. In the Sea Cave of the Nuckalavee

The sea and the bobbing bottles went right inside the cave, but it was very dark in there and they did not dare take the log boat in, in case the cave narrowed further down and the boat got stuck. They wanted to get off the Isle of the Nuckalavee as quickly as they could once they'd completed their quest.

If they completed their quest, that is.

So Crusher the giant dragged the boat up the beach and left it there, beside forty or fifty other log boats hauled up high above the sands. A bit like the shoes, these boats were a melancholy presence, because whoever had crossed the sea in them had made a one-way trip and never returned.

They made themselves slo-o-o-owly enter the sea cave, trying to ignore every nerve in their bodies screaming 'DON'T GO IN! DON'T GO IN!', not to mention Bumbleboozle buzzing around in such a state of anxiety that she had blown up like a pufferfish.

Poor little Squeezjoos had not left Xar's pocket since they had travelled further and further away from Perdita's healing influence. He was trembling and going rigid again, the Witchblood poison affecting him as it had done once before. Now he put one green eye to a hole in Xar's pocket and peered out fearfully.

It was not surprising that they needed COURAGE to go into that cave. For there were extraordinary rock formations that looked uncannily like TEETH, and gave the impression that you might indeed be entering the mouth of a monster, as Bumbleboozle had suggested. And this cave contained some of the Droods' greatest secrets, so all around them in the cavern's hush there came a wicked whisper of '*Beware* . . . ' that sent the hairs at the back of everyone's necks quivering electrically upward, along with strange scuttling noises, that might have been the pattering feet of rats or mice, or were they just the fearful scurry of Wish's frantically beating heart?

'Beware . . . Beware . . . beware . . .' sang the unknown voices, and they could be ghosts or they might be will-o'-the-wisps that were appearing out of nowhere, laughing and cackling, and then adding more eerily, '*Come here only if you dare* . . .' as they dived and swooped and vanished back into the darkness, leaving haunting echo whispers of 'Beware . . .' in sound and in sprite writing fading into the dark air in front of them. And then they heard louder scraping noises, this time made by larger and more malevolent creatures with paws that had talons.

'I bet those are nixes,' said Caliburn, shivering. 'I HATE nixes . . . horrible animals. Everyone, watch out, for they'll strangle you if they catch you.'

'Isss ssppooky down here,' whispered poor little
Squeezjoos from Xar's pocket. 'I'sss really don't like it . . .
can't we go home to Pook's Hill? Pleeeeeasssee??'

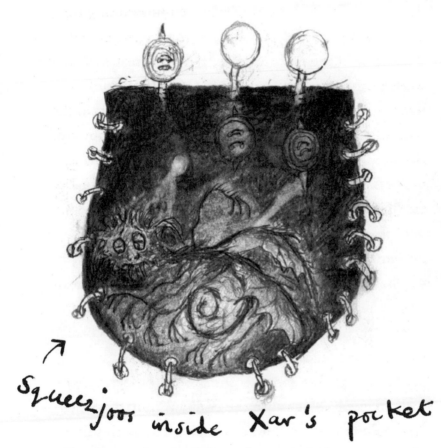

Squeezjoos inside Xar's pocket

But Squeezjoos's plight only reminded everyone of
the urgency of their quest.

'We have to go on,' said Wish. 'We must find Bodkin
and get the scales of the Nuckalavee so we can make
that spell as quickly as possible.'

259

Now this was where Xar was extremely helpful as a companion. When things were really dangerous Xar's eyes would light up, and he would stick out his chest and whistle, out of tune, as if he didn't care about any of it. 'Bit damp and smelly in here,' sniffed Xar, and even if he was more scared than he looked, his cheerful defiance was useful in fooling them all that this was a lot less dangerous than it seemed.

So on, on, they went. Sometimes the cave narrowed and the beach disappeared entirely, and Crusher had to carry them across the water to the next bit of shore. Xar had explored many a sea cave in his short life, but this was the largest he had ever seen, and it was a long time before they reached what surely must have been the heart of the island, where the cave opened up to reveal a great underwater lake.

All around was darkness and a smell of secrets that made them all shiver with the coldness of it, the air so chokingly foul it was hard to breathe. The sprites lit up as high and bright as they could so that they could see, and the weird green light of little cave slugs gave off a gentle, queasy glow.

On the edge of the lake was a great heaped-up mound of treasure in the form of

Magical objects the Droods deemed too powerful to be in the world. Harps that played themselves, arrows made of moon, hats with wings and seven-league boots and talking heads and speaking stones and singing swords, all bewitched items of such threatening strength that the air around the heap of treasure gave off a sickly shimmering stench of muffled, ghastly power.

The sprites hissed like hornets.

'That treasure is *cursed*,' hissed Ariel uneasily. 'Lettsss go back . . .'

In front of them, the lake was smooth and serene as a sheet of black glass.

And deathly still, sitting upright in the lake like rows and rows of soldiers, were thousands and thousands and *thousands* of bottles.

'Uh-oh,' gulped Caliburn. 'I think we may have found what we are looking for . . .'

They certainly had.

For high up on a ledge on those very cavern walls, Bodkin was lying, having cried himself to sleep. He was beyond hope, poor Bodkin. He knew he was going to die here in the darkness.

A little higher up still perched Nighteye the snowcat, clinging to the walls, his head drooping, poor cat, for he too was in despair.

But now Nighteye lifted his head eagerly, his

Bodkin knew he was going to die there, alone in that darkness.

whiskers twitched, he
swivelled his black-tipped
ears. He let out a happy
yowly miaow of excitement as
he caught the sound of approaching
sprites and humans and a giant that
he recognised.

'Don't worry, Nighteye, we'll be fine,'
lied Bodkin, waking and trying to give
the snowcat the reassurance that he did not
believe himself, and he closed his weary eyes
again.

And then Bodkin heard the voices of Wish
and Xar.

For a second he thought he was
hallucinating, for he hadn't eaten anything for a
while now, and all he had had to drink was the

drops of water that he could
lick from the cavern walls.
He lifted up his poor
exhausted head . . .
And to his total delight, *there they
were*!
Wonderful Wish, her hair all a mess
with electric anxiety, and staunch, proud
Xar, cheek to the backbone, whistling
to pretend he wasn't scared as he looked
around at the terrifying cavern.
His friends.
He thought he'd never see them again.
'I'm up here, Wish and Xar!' he whispered in
a shaky voice from way, way up in the heights of
the cavern. They looked up.
'Bodkin!' cried Xar.
'You're alive!' shouted Wish, waving madly back.
But the moment of delight passed in an instant,
as Bodkin remembered why they were all there.
They mustn't risk their lives to save him, he
wasn't worth it.
'You shouldn't have come!' cried
Bodkin in a terrified whisper. 'Go back!

Leave me here! I betrayed you to Queen Sychorax . . .' said Bodkin.

'We forgive you, Bodkin. You thought it was for the best and you made a mistake,' said Wish. 'We all make mistakes. We all need second chances.'

'And I'm useless . . .' said Bodkin.

'You're not useless. Xar should never have said that!' Wish shouted. 'Should you, Xar?'

'No, no, I shouldn't!' Xar cried. 'You're not useless! Why are you up there?'

'I kept my shoes on,' said Bodkin.

There was a silence.

'Well you have to admit, that is a BIT useless,' muttered Xar.

'Shut up, Xar,' hissed Wish,

'Oh!' Xar hurriedly remembered that he was supposed to be being tactful and boosting Bodkin's confidence. 'I'm sure you had a very good reason, Bodkin, but why did you keep your shoes on? There were all those signs up and everything . . .'

'I fainted on the beach . . . and then when I came to, I forgot to take my shoes off . . . The only thing I'm supposed to be good at is following rules and I can't even do *that*!' said Bodkin. 'Go away! I'm not worth it!'

'You ARE worth it, Bodkin!' Xar shouted up in response to agonised tugs on his jacket, reminders from Wish that he was supposed to be Being Nice. Xar tried to think of something nice to say. 'You've got a . . . you've got a . . . you've got a . . . very nice smile!'

Oh, for mistletoe's sake, thought Xar to himself. *Can't I think of anything better than that?*

But there was a short silence from above.

Bodkin appeared to quite like that.

'Have I?' said Bodkin in a quavery, quite-pleased voice.

A glimmer of light was returning to Bodkin's dark world. Whatever happened next, at least they both forgave him.

'Don't worry, Bodkin,' said Wish. 'We're going to save you. Come down from there!'

'You don't understand,' said Bodkin, 'I kept my shoes on, and I was so scared that I didn't even realise until I was standing right in front of that ruddy great THING . . . It gave me the shock of my life I can tell you . . . and that THING really didn't like it . . . It was going to kill me, if I hadn't climbed up here . . . It didn't even let me get to the bit where you bargain with it, but I suggest you don't even try that. I really don't think that THING is going to be reasoned with. Go back to Perdita! There has to be a better way than this— OH!'

Bodkin broke off, and pointed down towards the lake.
'*IT'S COMING BACK!* RUN AWAY, GUYS,
RUN AWAY!!!'

What was that, surfacing in the distant waters of the
lake, like the back of a humpback whale, sending the
curse bottles dancing and bobbing in the water?

It was not a whale.

It was an eyelid that slowly opened to reveal a
gigantic yellow eye. And then slowly two, three, four, five
. . . countless more giant eyes opened in the lake. And
the dripping head of the most enormous monster they
had ever seen, rose, slowly, slowly, out of the lake, like
the rearing of a mountain, and fixed them with its many
yellow eyes.

'I don't seem to be able to draw the Enchanted
Sword, it's stuck in the scabbard and the scabbard is
stuck in my belt!' cried Bodkin.

'Don't worry, Bodkin! We have our staffs and I
brought your own staff too!' yelled Xar, throwing
Bodkin the do-it-yourself Magic staff. Bodkin caught it
in one shaking hand.

'GET READY TO DEFEND US, SPRITES!' cried
Xar, as Wish and he pointed their own shaking staffs at
the emerging monster.

'*How?????*' squeaked Bumbleboozle, looking up as
the creature coming out of the water revealed itself to be

larger and larger and larger.

The monster opened its mouth and its breath was cold as corpses.

'WHO,' said the monster, 'are you?'

'Who,' said the monster, 'are you?'

18. Dead Boys Can't Make Bargains

The Nuckalavee was in darkness so they could not really see him properly. But whatever he was, he was BIG. He loomed over them like a great gloomy precipice, only his thirteen yellow eyes visible, staring down at them. His voice bellowed and echoed most eerily round that cavern. Every now and then he gulped, as if there was something stuck in his throat and it was bothering him. It was most disconcerting.

'WHOOOOOO ARE YOUOUUUUUUUU?' repeated the Nuckalavee. '*Gulp.*'

Both Wish and Xar knew better than to answer that question correctly. You start telling your real name to a beast that ghastly in a cave that eerie, and you're deader than doornails before you've even started.

They tried to keep their Magic staffs steady, pointing them straight at the gigantic horror in front of them, but my goodness, even the staff in Xar's hand was slipping and sliding in his panicky sweating palm.

'We are humans,' said Wish.

'Very, very powerful humans,' said Xar, hoping to impress the mammoth opponent in front of him. 'We may look unimpressive but we have Magic swords, and Magic eyes, and the girl here has more than one life and everything . . . and we're here on a very important shadow quest.'

'Your Magic will not work in here,' said the Nuckalavee.

Oh dear.

Xar tried to cast a spell with his staff, and sure enough, nothing happened.

Wish put her eyepatch up a smidgeon, and her Magic wasn't working either.

Oh dear oh dear oh DEAR. This already wasn't going well.

'Why were you talking to the dead Wizard?' said the Nuckalavee.

'Dead Wizard? What dead Wizard?' said Xar.

All thirteen of the Nuckalavee's eyes turned towards Bodkin, crouched, shaking, on his ledge.

'*That* dead Wizard,' said the Nuckalavee. 'The boy-who-didn't-take-his-shoes-off.'

'He's not a dead Wizard, he's a Warrior and he's alive,' said Wish.

Unbeknownst to Wish and Xar, this was good news for the Nuckalavee. The Nuckalavee had an aura about him that dampened and digested the Magic of Wizards, but it worked better when they had their shoes off. The Nuckalavee's Magic-quenching properties travelled up through their bare feet and smothered the Magic inside them most effectively.

When they kept their shoes on, the Nuckalavee had to fight them before he killed them, which took a lot of energy. Even though Wizard *Magic* didn't work well against him, Wizards were very clever and tricksy at using Magical objects.

However if the boy-who-didn't-take-his-shoes-off wasn't a Wizard after all, he wasn't going to be a problem.

The Nuckalavee relaxed.

'He won't be alive for long,' said the Nuckalavee. 'He can't stay up there forever. He will starve and if he comes down, I will kill him. Normally I offer visitors to my island the chance to make a bargain with me. But they have to take their shoes off before they come here. This boy was dead the moment he stepped on my island ... *in shoes,*' said the Nuckalavee. 'Dead boys can't make bargains.'

It wasn't a great start to a conversation, on the whole.

'*You*, however, are both shoeless,' said the Nuckalavee. 'And therefore you are welcome to try to make a bargain with me ... *if you wish.* What are you bringing me?' asked the Nuckalavee.

'We're not bringing you anything,' said Xar. 'We didn't know we were supposed to bring you something.'

'Don't you know the rules of this particular shadow quest?' asked the Nuckalavee.

The eyes, from their various different perches on the Nuckalavee's great barnacled head, swivelled in to look down. Six of them looked at Xar. And seven of them at Wish.

The eyes were old, and it was very difficult to see their expression.

'Foolish,' said the Nuckalavee, 'to come on a quest without knowing the rules yet.'

'But the rules are a secret!' Wish pointed out. 'Apart from the bit about taking off your shoes!'

'Taking off your shoes is polite,' said the Nuckalavee, 'and shows me that you can follow the rules.'

'Now let me tell you the rules of this particular shadow quest,' continued the Nuckalavee. 'You don't have to accept the bargain I offer, because at least you have taken your shoes off. You can walk away from this cavern free and alive. But if you take the bargain, then you must keep to the rules and pay the price I ask. Is that understood?'

'Yes,' said Wish.

'I am a sin-collector . . .' said the Nuckalavee, 'a secret-keeper . . . a guardian of power . . . I am a prisoner of the Droods, and the shadow men and women come to me and I look after objects for them that are too dangerous to be in the world.'

That would explain the extraordinary amount of treasure in that cavern.

This was the secret of the Nuckalavee. It was all treasure that the Droods and the Wizards considered needed guarding.

'And in return . . .' said the Nuckalavee.

'Yes,' said Xar. 'In return?'

'You answer a riddle that I ask you,' said the Nuckalavee. 'If you win, you walk out of here, free and alive.'

'And if we lose?' asked Xar.

'The shadow men and women who lose stay here on this island to look after me,' said the Nuckalavee. 'I turn them into nixes and they become my slaves forever . . .'

Oh dear.

A nasty clammy cold feeling stole over Wish and Xar.

'The clever and the lucky know the answer to my riddle,' said the Nuckalavee. 'They are the ones who escape. Accepting my bargain takes courage.

'Now, what is the treasure that you have brought me?' said the Nuckalavee. 'Is it that staff you are carrying? It looks a very powerful one . . .'

'We already said, we have nothing to bring you,' said

Wish, her voice trembling with fear. 'And in fact, we are wanting to change the rules slightly . . .'

The Nuckalavee's eyes narrowed. His yellow eyes blazed orange for a second. 'I hate it when people want to change the rules,' said the Nuckalavee. 'It's like people who come here without removing their shoes. Very rude.'

'It's just a *small* change . . .' said Wish. 'We don't want to BRING you something, we want to TAKE something from you. Two things, actually. If we lose, we will stay here as your slaves. But if we win, you must give back the life of my bodyguard, and . . . you must also give us four of your scales,' stammered Wish. Suddenly the request did seem a little, well, *cheeky*. 'I hope you won't miss them. You have an awful lot of scales, after all.'

All thirteen of the Nuckalavee's eyes swivelled to look at Wish.

'Really?' said the Nuckalavee. 'You want me to give you four of my scales?' said the Nuckalavee, repeating Wish's request thoughtfully. 'Now, that IS an interesting suggestion. My scales are very precious, of course . . . they're powerful, powerful Magic, and they make the bearer a mighty Wizard indeed. But Magic as potent as this must be handled very carefully.'

'It's for a good cause,' said Wish. 'The

scales are ingredients in a spell to get rid of Witches.'

The Nuckalavee thought for a very long time, all of his yellow eyes looking this way and that over Wish and Xar and their companions. Wish could feel her stomach going liquid with fear.

'If you want to change the rules,' said the Nuckalavee, at last, 'in all fairness, *I* must be allowed to change the rules too. You have asked for two things, so if you guess the answer to my riddle, I will want two things back. You must not only answer my riddle correctly, you must also perform a task for me. If you do both of those things, you can walk out of this cavern free as birds, and take the boy-who-didn't-take-his-shoes-off with you. Otherwise, you stay here as my slaves just like the others.'

'What is this task we have to perform?' said Xar.

'I have something in my throat that has been bothering me for twenty years,' said the Nuckalavee, and he gulped again. They could hear from his voice that there was indeed something that had lodged in there. 'You must walk into my mouth, and remove it for me.'

'But if we walk into your mouth, you might just swallow us!' said Xar.

'I promise not to swallow you,' said the Nuckalavee. 'That is part of the bargain. I want this thing removed, and you can remove it. And I think that you are both lucky and clever, and that you will know the answer to my riddle. Do you take my offer?'

'You swear that if we walk into your mouth, you will not shut your mouth and swallow us?' said Wish suspiciously.

'You drive a hard bargain, small girl. But I swear by mistletoe and all things Magic, I will not shut my mouth and swallow you,' said the Nuckalavee. 'My life shall be the forfeit, if I break this promise. That is our contract, if you care to take it. But if you do *not* take it . . . the boy-who-did-not-take-his-shoes-off is dead indeed.'

How could they turn this deal down when Bodkin's life would be the forfeit?

The idea of climbing into the Nuckalavee's mouth and removing something from it, trusting that he would not close it, was very unpleasant indeed. But what do you expect from a shadow quest? Of course it was going to be gruesome, and challenging, and terrifying. If the ingredient you are searching for represents courage, well, it seems logical that your bravery should be properly tested in order to find it.

Wish and Xar had a short, whispered conversation.

'I think the Nuckalavee wants us to win the bargain. His voice sounds terrible. I know how I feel if I even have a sore throat for a week. Imagine having one for *twenty years*!' said Wish. 'The Nuckalavee will feel better if we take whatever it is out, and a promise made on mistletoe and all things Magic is an unbreakable promise.'

'We've come all this way,' said Xar. 'And we need those scales. The Nuckalavee says we are lucky and clever, and we are . . . He thinks we might know the answer to his question. We need to have courage . . .'

'Don't take the bargain, Wish and Xar!' Bodkin shouted down. 'Seriously, Wish, as your bodyguard I have to urge you not to do this!'

But Xar and Wish took the Nuckalavee's bargain.

They swore the oath of the shadow quest.

And the Nuckalavee asked his riddle.

19. The Riddle of the Nuckalavee

'Before I ask my riddle I need to tell you a story,' said the Nuckalavee. 'Listen well . . .

'By extraordinary coincidence,' said the Nuckalavee, 'you are not the first people to have asked to change the rules. Twenty years ago, someone *else* asked to change the rules, and by very strange coincidence, that person asked for the very same thing you have asked . . .'

'Oh dear,' groaned Caliburn. 'I HATE coincidences, I really, really do . . .'

'About twenty years ago,' said the Nuckalavee, 'I was visited in this very cavern by a young man. The young man was carrying many wonderful Magical objects. I hoped he wanted to leave them for me to guard, but instead he offered me a different bargain. I would give him four of my scales, and then if I asked him a riddle to which he knew the answer, he would walk out of the cavern, free and alive. If, on the other hand, I asked him a riddle he could not answer, he would give me his heart. For the young man was heart sick – ever so heart sick. He did not care, this boy, if he was risking his heart, apparently, for he was in love with a young lady who was not in love with him.

'Well, I thought, what a stupid boy! Even if I gave

him some of my beautiful shining scales, he would not be able to take them anywhere because if I had his heart, I would have ALL of him, and the wonderful Magical objects into the bargain. Doesn't that make logical sense?'

'It's a bit gruesome,' said Wish, grimacing. 'But I guess it makes sense.'

'So, even though it was a little unorthodox, and a breaking of the rules, because it looked like such an easy win for me, I took the boy's bargain.

'The boy thought he was lucky, and he knew he was clever. But *I* was cleverer, and I asked him a riddle, and I made it a hard one, so he would not know the answer . . .

'So far, so good.

'The boy lost. So the boy was supposed to give me his heart, and therefore all of him. He was supposed to walk into my mouth, with his heart safe inside of him. But the boy' – now the Nuckalavee gnashed his teeth at the memory of it – 'but the boy was tricksy, ever so *tricksy* . . .

'*He had made his heart into a stone!*' said the indignant Nuckalavee.

'He threw the stone into my mouth, it lodged in my throat . . . and he ran out of this very cavern with my scales still warm in his hand. He took with him the Magical Cup of Second Chances that ought to have been mine, and he escaped out of here, quite lickety-split! That thieving MAGPIE of a trickery spick of a boy! And oh . . .' groaned the Nuckalavee, 'that stone that was his heart got lodged in my throat, and it has *ached* me ever since . . .' (That must be the strange gulping noise the Nuckalavee made every now and then.)

'I think a nix did bite him, at least, on the finger,' said the Nuckalavee. 'And so he carries a little memory of us with him, for the bite of a nix has a sting. But if I ever get my hands on that trickster of a boy I will swallow the rest of him whole, no questions asked!

'And every day I get the nixes to send out curse-bottles, with curses in them, and I have been waiting to know the Boy-who-Tricked-Me's name, so that it can be written on that curse . . . One day the curse will reach him,' said the Nuckalavee, 'and then he'll be sorry.

'So my question is . . .' said the Nuckalavee, eyes narrowing.

'*What is the name of the wicked licketty-split of a trickery spick of a boy?*

'That's the question. Tell me the answer and, if the answer is true, it will Magically appear in every one of the curse bottles floating in this lake around me, and that's how you'll know you've won the first part of our bargain,' said the Nuckalavee.

'You trickster!' fumed Wish. 'You said it was a

question we might know the answer to! If it was twenty years ago it could have been ANYBODY!'

How could they possibly guess the name of this unknown boy?

It could be any name at all. There were as many names in the world as there were trees in the wildwoods, or curse bottles in a lake.

The children began discussing random names: Tinker, Jack-in-irons, Torremalay, Rumbelsomething, and so on, any name at all that popped into their heads.

'Think,' said the Nuckalavee, bringing his great head with those glowing yellow eyes on it, closer and closer to the children standing on the beach. '*Think*, as hard as you can . . .'

'Hang on a second, it wasn't just anybody,' said Xar, slowly, remembering another story. 'That's why it's not a coincidence!'

The bite on the finger . . . Wasn't *his father* once long ago meant to have gone on a shadow quest, after Sychorax had abandoned him? Didn't *his father* have one finger that had a melancholy mark on it like a dark purple bruise? Was that the bite of a nix?

'I know who it was!' shouted Xar.

'Oh I know, too,' moaned Caliburn. 'Don't say, Xar, don't say!'

But it was too late.

'The boy's name was Tor,' said Xar
excitedly. 'But he's now called . . .
ENCANZO!!!'

ENCANZO! ENCANZO!
ENCANZO! called the echoes
in the cavern. ENCANZO!
ENCANZO! ENCANZO!

20. Did you think a Quest for Courage was going to be easy?

'Oh dear oh dear oh dear oh dear,' said Caliburn.

As Xar spoke the name, the Nuckalavee sighed, a sigh of satisfaction.

Blink! Blink! Blink!

With a flash of Magic, every single curse bottle bobbing in the lake lit up with light. And in every single curse bottle there blazed the word:

Encanzo!

with a bright, vengeful orange light.

'You're right!' whispered the Nuckalavee, eyes agleam with hatred of the boy called Tor. 'I feel it in my heart that you are RIGHT. The treasure-hunting, staff-stealing, trickery spick of a burglar of a boy WAS called Tor . . . and he used MY treasures, MY staff, MY cup, MY scales, MY adderstone, MY treasures to become the greatest Wizard in the wildwoods. So the boy called Tor has become the noble *Encanzo*, the great *Encanzo*, the oh-so-clever *Encanzo* . . . I've heard that name, even down here in my dark and terrible dungeon, and I should have guessed it was him.'

The Nuckalavee spat out every 'Encanzo' with as much disgust as if the word had been made out of burnt-and-bitter mustardseed mixed with the pus-like ooze of putrid-green-bad-eggs.

'I've been cursing him ever since,' spat the Nuckalavee. 'Every night I get the nixes to build a little bonfire down here in my dungeon and scramble the wrong way around it, wishing ill on the boy who stole my treasures and all of his descendants.'

'Oh dear . . .' said Caliburn. 'Oh dear oh dear oh dear . . .'

It was clearly going to be quite important for the Nuckalavee NEVER to find out that one of Encanzo's descendants was standing right in front of him.

Unless he already knew . . .

'I thought that you might know the answer,' said the Nuckalavee, all thirteen yellow eyes now burning orange in fury, 'because in *another* extraordinary coincidence, YOU, boy, are carrying the very staff that Encanzo was carrying when he tricked me twenty years ago. Where did you get that staff, boy?'

'I stole it,' said Xar, looking the Nuckalavee straight in all his eyes, one by one. 'We have answered your question correctly. Now give us those scales!'

'Oh, I've been tricked before, so I don't make the same mistake twice,' said the Nuckalavee. 'You will climb into my throat and remove the stone that is lodged there. Bring the stone out of my throat, where it has been burning, itching, torturing me – take it out of here and up to me and THEN I'll give you four of my scales. And then you and your companions can leave this cavern with your hearts intact, and with your bodyguard and your selves free and alive.'

Suddenly the second part of the bargain they had made with the Nuckalavee seemed very, very foolish indeed.

'But you might close your mouth and swallow us,' said Wish, in a very small voice indeed.

'I've already promised not to,' said the Nuckalavee. 'By Magic and mistletoe, and giving my life as forfeit. Complete the bargain and remove the stone, on your honour.'

The monster put his head down and they saw him clearly for the first time.

Ah, it was a scary one, that Nuckalavee, now that they saw him right up close.

Great dark tentacles swung from his ancient, barnacled chin, and these tentacles were slimy with secrets, besmeared with curses, encrusted with hates and petty spites and mean little thoughts, and every kind of thing you might want to dispose of, and they were clinging like glue to the hairs on those tentacles.

The monster rested his chin on the ground before them, and opened his great mouth like a gigantic cavern.

A smell in that mouth of disappointed hopes, and deep despair, and power bad and power strong, secrets

that the Droods wanted to get rid of, Magical objects
too wild for the hearts of men, lies so bitter they would
turn your lips green to speak them. There right in front
of them were the giant daggers of his great green teeth,
and even more spookily, and horribly, down right at
the bottom of his throat, you could see *another* mouth,
further down, *another* set of jaws, closed tight shut, so
that nothing that went down there would ever get out.

'We do have to keep our promise,' said Wish,
shivering, trying to concentrate, even though the stink
of the monster's breath was confusing her, as she peered
inside the great grim depths. 'Just as the Nuckalavee
must keep his. We said that this was a test of our
courage, didn't we?'

They *had* said that, but they hadn't quite realised
exactly how courageous they were going to have to be.

The sprites and Caliburn offered to fly in first and
see where the stone was lodged. Which was brave of
them, not only for the obvious reasons, but because
sprites have a very strong sense of smell, and so for them
this stink was even worse than it was for the humans.
They buzzed into the mouth of the great beast, wands
drawn, prickling with anxiety, and quivering with
revulsion, and they were gone for so long that Wish and
Xar began to get nervous.

When they eventually emerged, they all looked

green with nausea, and Bumbleboozle actually threw up. 'Isss YUCKY in there,' said Bumbleboozle. 'But we found the ssstone,' said Ariel. 'A small grey stone, stuck tight as anything. We couldn't budge it . . .'

'It looksss very ssssorre in there, very sore,' said Bumbleboozle.

There was no point in trying to transform into birds, or fish, or anything Perdita had been teaching them at school, because when they got down there, they wouldn't have hands to remove the stone with.

'Didn't I TELL you that education wasn't important?' fumed Xar. 'Perdita said we were learning all that stuff for a reason, that we might need it in the fight against the Nuckalavee.'

They did a quick mental review of the things they had learnt at Pook's Hill over the last six months:

Transformation, telepathy, speaking to animals, illusions, wort-cunning, starcraft, leechdom.

And it did seem that none of these skills would come in handy right now.

'But that doesn't mean they're useless on EVERY occasion, Xar,' said Wish. 'There are some quests where speaking to animals might be terribly important.'

'Well, not right now it isn't,' grumbled Xar.

Sometimes there are problems that even *Magic* can't help you with. You have to do it the good old-fashioned way.

'You're going to have to let me down on a rope, and I'll try and dislodge it,' said Xar. 'I should have spent the last three months practising my rope work – that would have been a lot more helpful.'

Crusher had a long rope twisted round his waist and he tied one end round a stalactite, and the other end round Xar. The giant braced himself against one of the Nuckalavee's gigantic green teeth. And then slowly, slowly he let Xar down the throat of the Nuckalavee, the sprites buzzing in with him, to give out some light from their glowing bodies and offer helpful advice.

'Stop!' yelled Xar, when he spotted the stone, half way down the creature's gullet. It was much smaller than Xar expected, so Encanzo must have shrunk down his broken heart to fit into the confines of the pebble. Crusher held the rope steady and with a shiver of revulsion, Xar reached out to try and work the stone free.

You, dear reader, I hope will never have been in the position of being lowered down the throat of a Nuckalavee, trying to remove a stone that has been stuck in it for twenty years, while being dripped on by the disgusting goo that is sludging down the sides of the monster's throat walls.

However, it is likely that you have been in the situation of trying to do something tricky, like take the top off a bottle, or mend something that is stuck, or turn a handle that WILL NOT BUDGE, so you will probably sympathise with Xar, who was trying to do something rather like this under very trying, frightening (and disgusting) circumstances, while being given useful suggestions by the sprites, such as:

'What happensss if you wigglesss it the other way?'

'Try pulling it . . .'

'Try squiggling it . . .'

'Have you tried wiggling it?'

But absolutely nothing worked.

'Okay, Wish!' Xar

shouted up. 'I'm going to need your help! Even if I get this beastly thing out, I don't want to drop it, so we need two pairs of hands!'

So Wish attached herself to another rope, and Crusher lowered her down to help Xar.

Together they squiggled, and they wiggled, and their two pairs of hands worked the stone out of the sore burning spot where it had been bothering the Nuckalavee for the past twenty years.

'We've got it!' cried Wish in relief. 'Haul us up, Crusher!'

Up where he was balancing on the rim of the Nuckalavee's mouth, Crusher began to haul in both of them at once with all the strength that a Longstepper High-Walker giant can gather.

Meanwhile, all the

time that they had been so intent on getting the stone out of the throat, Bodkin had been perching high on the ridge in the cavern walls, watching the Nuckalavee.

And what Bodkin had seen made his heart beat ever so quick.

Slowly,

Slowly,

Ever so slowly,

As Crusher and Wish and Xar and the sprites and Caliburn were all concentrating on getting the stone out of the Nuckalavee's throat . . . the Nuckalavee was very gently lowering his top jaw.

Slowly,

Slowly,

Ever so slowly,

The Nuckalavee was shutting his mouth.

Bodkin opened his own mouth to shout out a warning but he was so scared, no sound came out.

What on earth could he do?

Wait a second . . . The Nuckalavee had said that the Magic of *Wizards* did not work in here. The Enchanted Sword was stuck in the scabbard. But how about the do-it-yourself Magic staff? That wasn't the Magic of Wizards, that worked on its own.

Do something, Bodkin!

Maybe the staff would work in here . . .

He pointed the do-it-yourself staff at his forehead.

Squelch! The staff stuck firmly to his right temple.

Great.

Now he had a staff stuck to his head.

This sort of thing never seemed to happen to proper heroes in stories.

Great.

Now he had a staff stuck to his head.

It took a few moments for Bodkin to remember the right words to get the staff to un-stick. Which it did, with another protesting squelch!

Okay, so he had a weapon that at least *worked*, although it was a little difficult to see how sticking things to other things was going to be helpful in this kind of emergency. He gathered all his courage together. Wish and Xar were dangling down inside the throat of that monster. They were his friends. And even though Bodkin was ABSOLUTELY PETRIFIED of the Nuckalavee,

Slowly,

Slowly,

Ever so slowly,

Bodkin climbed down from his hiding place.

It was like a very sinister game of grandmother's footsteps, with no grandmothers involved.

When one of the Nuckalavee's eyes flicked in his direction, Bodkin froze. But he kept on moving, slowly, slowly. Because he had a very bad feeling about what the Nuckalavee was going to do next.

And Bodkin was right.

The moment that Wish shouted, 'We've got it!' and Crusher began to haul on the ropes to bring Wish and Xar up, the Nuckalavee's eyes blazed

297

orange and he shut his mouth very, very quickly indeed.

WHIRRRAMMMMM!

The Nuckalavee's jaws slammed shut, with Wish and Xar and the sprites and Caliburn and Crusher all inside.

Crusher's rope was still tied to the rock on the beach. The Nuckalavee jerked his head to work the rope free. The rope held, because the rope of a Longstepper High-Walker giant is made of strong stuff.

And Bodkin ran, as fast as he could towards the rock and the rope.

He didn't have a plan.

He just ran towards the rock and the rope.

The Nuckalavee's eyes blazed orange at him.

You're putting your filthy shoes on my beach!!! is what the Nuckalavee would have said if he didn't have his mouth full at the time.

The Nuckalavee jerked his head a second time, and this time

SNAP!

Bodkin only just got hold of the rope before it snapped from the rock and he was hauled high up into the air, dangling from one end of it.

GO, Bodkin, go!

21. Will the Parents Be Too Late?

eanwhile, Encanzo and Sychorax had reached the beach opposite the Isle of the Nuckalavee and were following on a boat, in a sea of curse bottles, and every curse bottle now had a name in it. Encanzo reached down and picked out a curse bottle. He smeared away the seawater, and there, gleaming bright in the sunlight, was a name picked out in sprite writing, and the name was 'Encanzo'.

Sychorax looked out at the sea of bobbing bottles, the name 'Encanzo' trapped in the heart of them, gleaming, an o here, a z there, as the sunlight caught the letters. 'Someone out there *really* doesn't like you,' said Sychorax.

Encanzo turned white as snow when he saw his name in the bottles.

'What did you do to deserve this hatred?' said Sychorax.

'I came here to get rid of my heart,' said Encanzo bitterly. 'What use did I have of it? You betrayed me, and I was in a state of despair. This was my shadow man quest . . . '

Sychorax was now seeing with her own eyes the consequences of her actions on another heart, another soul, and that is always a difficult moment. It is one thing to know something vaguely. It is quite another to plant your feet in the exact footsteps of where another has gone. Sychorax was planting her pretty little feet in the hopeless footprints of the young Wizard she had once loved, the boy named Tor whose heart she had broken twenty weary years ago, and it was a most uncomfortable feeling, for with each step she could feel the lost boy's despair.

'But you endured, as I did,' said Sychorax, making herself feel better. 'There are very few who come away from a shadow man quest and live, and those who do are stronger than ever.'

'I have endured without a heart,' said Encanzo. 'And in the course of stealing myself a second chance I tricked the Nuckalavee most royally.'

'Ah . . .' said Sychorax. That explained all the curse bottles. The Nuckalavee was looking for revenge.

'Now that the Nuckalavee knows my name, Wish and Xar are in terrible trouble,' said Encanzo grimly. 'We must be quick now, Sychorax. If you want to come with me, you'll have to transform. Don't pretend you don't remember how to do it . . . it was I who taught you, long ago, don't you remember?'

Sychorax did remember.

'I only use Magic for a purpose,' said Queen Sychorax.

'Ah . . .' taunted Encanzo, 'so you never enjoy it?'
Sychorax blushed.

'What better purpose are you waiting for?' said
Encanzo. 'We will have to transform into swifts, for
they are the fastest—'

'Oh not *swifts* . . .' said Sychorax, for swifts were
symbolic of an uncomfortable memory for her. 'What's
this obsession with *swifts*, with you? Why not eagles?
Peregrine falcons? Sparrowhawks? They're all fast flyers,
particularly when they're hunting . . . And eagles are royal
birds, Encanzo – don't forget our pedigree, we need to
maintain our dignity, we should at least be birds of prey.'

'Oh for goodness' sake,' snapped Encanzo. 'There
isn't a snowflake in a bonfire's chance of me ever falling
in love with a she-wolf like you again, Sychorax! I have
no heart. I'M going as a swift, because swifts are the
fastest and most agile flyers, but *you* can be whatever you
like! TRANSFORM!'

Encanzo thrust his arm with his staff up into the air,
shouting out the word, and, sighing, Sychorax closed
her own fist around the staff as well. Sychorax was
highly competitive, so if swifts were the most agile flyers,
Sychorax was going to have to be one too. She wasn't
going to have Encanzo shooting off into the distance
leaving her behind, however royal the wings of an eagle
might be.

There was a great chemical explosion, and there, where there had been Sychorax and Encanzo, were two small brown swifts, wings beating the air.

Sychorax had forgotten how wonderful it was to live life as a bird. All the weary gold that weighed her down, the thick furs, the heavy flesh, lightened to paper-thinness before vanishing. She could feel her heart, so dull, so leaden, lightening with it, feel the air rushing into the quick of her bones with such a heady haste that she launched herself into the air the instant her flagging arms turned into joyous wings.

Encanzo hovered before her, crying with a bright pure call.

They ought to have been eagles. With eagle wings she might have remembered she was hunting. With eagle eyes she might have only focussed on the prey.

But swifts can stay in the air for six, ten months at a time. In a single lifetime a swift spends such a time flying that they could have flown seven times to the moon and back.

It was impossible not to be distracted by the pure joy of flying when you had wings so reactive to the breeze that it was almost like they were part of the wind itself, the sky above calling her to stay up there forever and never to go down.

With every beat of those curved bright wings she

was going back in time to when the young Wizard Tor first taught her to transform, a time when she was a careless young princess, as wild and fast and free as the swift itself.

The will-o'-the-wisps called after them their haunting cry:

> Love is weakness . . .
> Love is kindness . . .
> Love is childish . . .
> Love is thoughtless . . .
>
> Care-not, love-less, heart-worn, soul-blast?
> *Come this way . . .*
> Thought-less . . . care-less . . . hope-less?
> *Come this way . . .*
> No more second chances
> No more silly dances
> LOVE is weakness . . . so
> *Come this way. . .*

Will the parents-transformed-into-swifts be able

to reach their children in time to be able to save the situation?

Swifts fly swiftly, as their name suggests.

But unfortunately, even the wings of swifts will be too slow for this task. Even Magic has to obey logic and the laws of physics. I am the narrator, and even MY Magic will not get them there in time.

The children are on their own, and the situation is dire.

Love is weakness ...
Come this way ...

22. Inside the Mouth of the Nuckalavee

There was chaos inside the mouth of the Nuckalavee. Darkness and a terrible rushing noise, like a roaring, churning, bellowing tide.

'THE NUCKALAVEE IS TRYING TO SWALLOW US! HANG ON AS TIGHT AS YOU CAN!' shouted Wish. She and Xar were using all their energy to cling on as hard as they could to Crusher's rope while they swung wildly this way, that way, this way, that way, turning somersaults, doing back flips, losing all sense of what was up and what was down. The sprites had lost their lights in the confusion as they rattled all around.

Down below them, the Nuckalavee's *second* set of jaws had opened, the ones hidden down at the bottom of his throat, and if they dropped through those, they would never get out again.

Crusher, the great Longstepper High-Walker giant, hung on grimly, one great arm clasping the ropes Wish and Xar were holding, the other one gripping the inside of the Nuckalavee's mouth. He was desperately trying to keep a hold on both as the Nuckalavee shook his head this way and that, and the gigantic muscles of his great gullet tried again and again to swallow them.

I . . . can't . . . hold . . . on . . . any more . . . thought Xar as the rope shuddered and swung chaotically.

Don't
fall
asleep,
Bodkin!

And just as Wish began losing
her grip, and was about to be
jolted off the rope entirely . . .
. . . the Nuckalavee stopped
shaking his head.

Because while Xar and Wish and Crusher
were being jangled about like stones in a bucket, on
the OUTSIDE of the Nuckalavee's mouth, Bodkin was
being thrown about this way and that just as violently
as they were on the other end of Crusher's rope. He
had a brief moment of panic as he looked down and
remembered, *Oh yes, I'm dangling a hundred feet up, from
the jaws of a Nuckalavee, and my friends are actually INSIDE
the Nuckalavee, and it's my job to save them* . . .

The rope had stopped shaking, and was now swaying
gently from side to side in a way that was really quite
drowsy making . . . Oh no! It was happening again!

'Don't fall asleep, Bodkin!' cried Caliburn, flapping

around in frantic circles because there wasn't a lot he could do himself while he was in bird form. 'The one thing you mustn't do is fall asleep!'

Caliburn was right.

Bodkin was *never* going to be a hero if he kept falling asleep in a crisis situation.

He *had* to stay awake.

So even though the familiar woozy feeling was coming over Bodkin, *this time* he fought it with EVERY FIBRE OF HIS HEART AND SOUL.

Wake up! Bodkin said to himself sharply, as his eyelids drooped. *Wake up now!* THIS IS YOUR CHANCE TO BE A HERO!

THINK!

Wake up!
This is my
chance to
be a
HERO!

The reason that the rope had suddenly stopped shaking was because the Nuckalavee had lost sight of Bodkin.

The last the monster had seen of the-boy-who-didn't-take-his-shoes-off was down on the beach, running towards him. But the boy had disappeared. Was he really a Wizard and not a Warrior, as the girl had claimed? Had he used some Magical object to turn himself invisible? Maybe he was a scarier opponent than he had looked.

The Nuckalavee's thirteen eyes swivelled in all directions, looking for the boy. No sign.

The Nuckalavee hated getting out of the water, his bulk was too much for that. But this was an emergency. He dragged the front half of his enormous body out on to the beach to get a closer look at the crevices high up in the cavern. No boy. Where had he gone?

Bodkin, meanwhile, had thought of a plan.

Bodkin swung the rope back, forth, back, forth, as though he was on a rope swing, until he hit the side of the cavern wall. He hung there a second, before kicking off with such force that he and the rope swung all the way round the Nuckalavee's chin, past the creature's ears on the other side, and he landed on the Nuckalavee's snout.

The Nuckalavee suddenly remembered the rope

dangling from the outside of his mouth. He tried to look down, but his thirteen eyes were perched right on top of his head, and he couldn't see under his own chin. Which is why he missed seeing Bodkin, who was now standing on top of the Nuckalavee's nose.

The staff that Bodkin was holding only did one thing. It was a staff-that-stuck-things-to-other-things.

You might have thought that this was quite a limited spell. It certainly wasn't one of the flashier, more spectacular ones, like mind control or invisibility or transformation or shapeshifting.

But sometimes it isn't the spells *themselves* that are important.

It is the clever ways you use them.

Bodkin used that spell intelligently now. He touched the staff on one of the Nuckalavee's nostrils and, SQUERRRRCHHHHHHH!

The nostril closed in on itself, as one side of the nostril stuck itself to the other side.

The Nuckalavee tried to snort through it, and SQUERRRRCHHHHHH! Bodkin touched the staff on the other nostril, and it closed up too.

Still holding the rope, Bodkin launched himself off the Nuckalavee's nose with as much careless recklessness as if he had been Xar himself.

Round the other side of the Nuckalavee, Bodkin fell

so that the rope had wound itself in a circle all the way round the Nuckalavee's head. And when Bodkin swung back down to the bottom of the circle, he touched the staff to the rope and it stuck tight.

The Nuckalavee tried to breathe through his nostrils, but they would not unblock.

The Nuckalavee tried to open his mouth that he had been keeping closed so firmly.

But his mouth would not open.

The Nuckalavee was part of a crocodilian family of monsters that have great strength in the muscles that grasp prey, so they exert extraordinary force when they are keeping their jaws shut. But the muscles that OPEN the jaws are far

SQUERCH!

weaker, so weak, even, that they cannot break through the rope of a Longstepper High-Walker giant.

And then there was chaos in the cavern of the Nuckalavee.

The Nuckalavee's thirteen eyes bulged and blazed with absolute incandescent fury.

He thrashed about in the underground lake, with Bodkin desperately hanging on to the madly jerking rope.

Lightning bolts shot off the Nuckalavee's tentacles as his enormous body swung this way and that in the jangling mass of curse bottles . . .

But however hard he thrashed, the Nuckalavee could not catch his breath.

The Nuckalavee knew when he was beaten.

The jerking of the great monster's body became weaker and weaker.

And now that he knew he was vanquished, the Nuckalavee was dignified in defeat. He lay his head down quietly on the beach, and closed all thirteen of his eyes, and resigned himself to death.

After all, he had broken a promise to Xar and Wish that he would not close his jaws while they were taking out the stone, and he had promised by mistletoe and Magic, may his own life be forfeit. That is a very solemn promise, and you break it at your peril, so the Nuckalavee must have known he was risking the wrath of Fate.

Bodkin dropped on to the beach when the Nuckalavee laid down his head. He unstuck the rope that was tied under the monster's chin, and the Nuckalavee's jaws relaxed and his mouth opened.

Inside the throat of the Nuckalavee, the world

stopped rocking for Wish and Xar. Crusher pulled them up and they slipped and slid out of the open mouth of the Nuckalavee, the stone held tight in the palm of Xar's hand.

'You were brilliant, Bodkin!' said Caliburn admiringly. 'You're a hero! You should have seen him, Xar and Wish!'

'You saved our lives! I KNEW you'd be a hero when the time came!' said Wish. 'Didn't I say it?'

Xar shook Bodkin's hand. 'Yes, Wish was right all along, you *are* a hero, Bodkin.'

You're a HERO, Bodkin!

It was a magnificent moment for Bodkin.

Xar bowed to Bodkin and then clapped him on the back. 'Here, you take the stone and complete the bargain, because if it wasn't for you we would never have got it.'

Bodkin thought he was going to burst with pride.

Wish, proud of him, Bodkin!

Xar, bowing to him, Bodkin!

He had overcome his fear. He hadn't fainted or fallen asleep. He had acted like a hero. And most importantly of all, he hadn't been an idiot for coming here, the jealousy of the betrayal was forgotten and forgiven, the quest had been a success in the end, all because of *him*.

It was a magnificent moment for Bodkin.

He stepped forward importantly towards their fallen opponent.

He bowed, because that is the polite and gracious thing to do to a defeated adversary.

Bodkin held up the stone. 'Nuckalavee, I am so sorry that I offended you by forgetting to remove my shoes when I landed on your island. We have answered your question. We have completed the task you set us. Here is the stone that has been worrying you for the last twenty years. Now you must complete the bargain and give us four of your scales.'

The Nuckalavee opened his thirteen eyes, wearily, slowly.

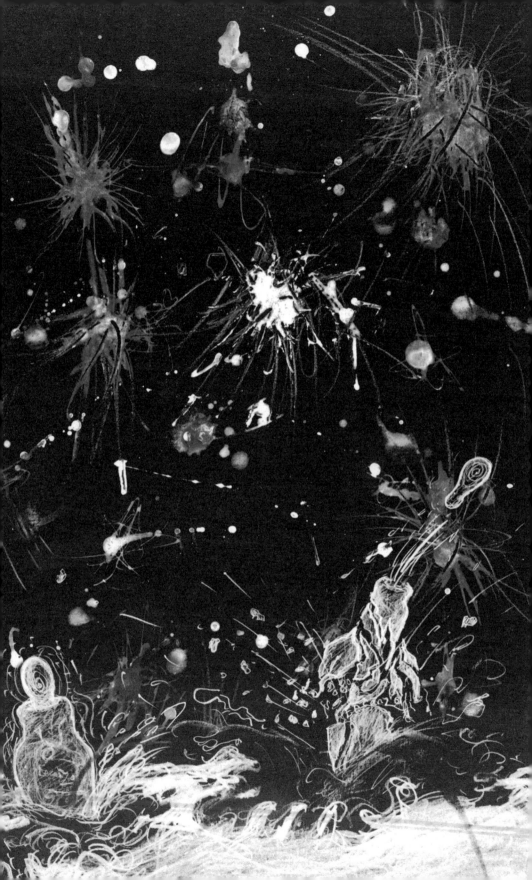

'You have the scales already,' said the Nuckalavee.

'What do you mean, we have the scales already?' said Xar, bewildered. 'No we don't! You can't try and trick us AGAIN!'

Xar reached out to take four of the Nuckalavee's shining scales—

But all at once, the curse bottles with the name 'Encanzo' exploded into little pieces. They ducked so as not to be hit by the flying glass.

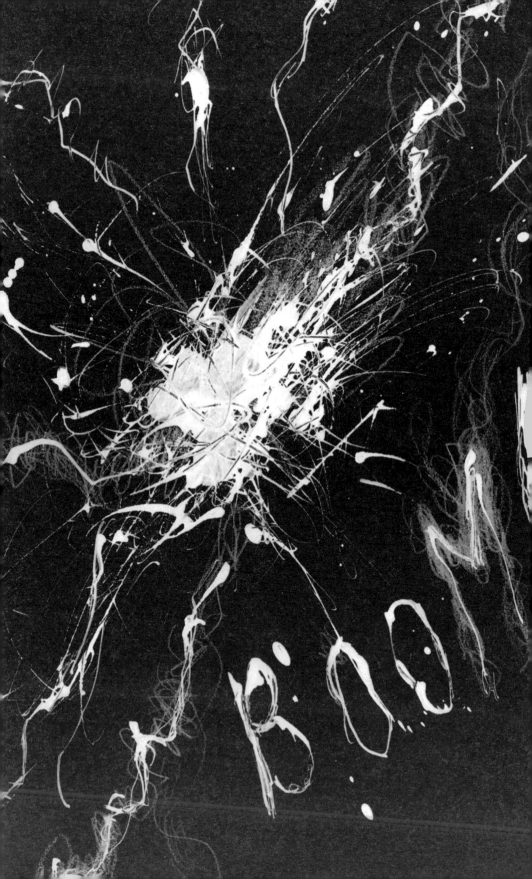

And the scales exploded off the outline of the Nuckalavee. They tried to catch the scales raining all around them, but the scales slipped through their fingers, burning bright silver for a moment, before they faded and seemed to melt into the beach.

But the Nuckalavee seemed somehow . . . *happier* without his scales.

Younger, even. He shone like a star in the cavern, glowing white as coral.

It was as if a spell had been lifted, and the beast had awoken from a trance that bound him.

A moment earlier he had seemed like he was on the edge of death, barely breathing. Now he seemed re-born.

'Thank you for breaking the Riddle and the Curse of the Nuckalavee,' said the scale-less creature before them, still weak, but gathering strength in front of their eyes.

A great sweep of the Nuckalavee's tail toppled the treasure heap, as if he no longer cared about the treasure any more.

Magic boots and caps with wings and singing swords went bouncing around the cavern in lunatic directions. Xar and Wish and Bodkin had to throw themselves on the ground to get out of the way as arrows made of moon, and horns of plenty spewing out food, and harps playing themselves in a cacophony of noise, flew around the cavern in mad eccentric circles.

'Oh dear . . .' moaned Caliburn, 'oh dear oh dear oh dear . . . all the Magical objects are escaping . . .'

Sure enough, the seven league boots were marching up the cavern walls and then right out of the cave itself, running away as fast as they could, followed by Magic staffs of indescribable power, and golden shields of destiny, and all manner of other dangerous objects that ought to be kept safe and guarded, and out of human reach.

But worse than this, much worse than this . . .

The Nuckalavee turned, and dived into the darkness of the water.

And then the Nuckalavee swam away, and out into the open sea.

Shielding their faces with their arms, Xar and Wish and Bodkin watched him go with open mouths.

'Um . . . what just happened?' said Xar.

'He's GONE! The Nuckalavee has gone! But more importantly, where are the scales?' panicked Wish.

They dropped to their knees on the beach, but the last remains of the Nuckalavee's scales slipped through their fingers like mist.

The Nuckalavee had vanished as completely as if he had never existed.

Scales of the Nuckalavee melting into the beach

And after all that work, after Xar and Wish rescuing Bodkin, and Bodkin rescuing Wish and Xar, they had failed nonetheless.

NO SCALES.

The last ingredient in the spell to get rid of Witches had gone forever.

It had all been for nothing.

NO SCALES,

And, believe it or not, there was worse to come.

With a magnificent, sweeping flourish, the Enchanted Sword *finally* drew itself out of its own scabbard, and placed itself into Bodkin's trembling hand.

Behind them, in a dark corner of the cavern, there came a horrible creaking hiss of a whisper.

'Foolish,' croaked the voice, 'to go on a quest without knowing the rules yet.'

They whirled around.

Out of the darkness, out of the heap of dark treasure the Nuckalavee had been guarding, there rolled, trapped in a ball of iron . . .

The Kingwitch.

UH - OH . .

23. We Are All on a Quest Without Knowing the Rules Yet

Yes, it is so, so tricky to know the rules of the quest you are going on until you reach the end of it.

This was why the Witches had wanted them to get to the Isle of the Nuckalavee.

The Kingwitch was there.

The Kingwitch was trapped inside a great ball of iron.

And only Wish could get him out.

The Kingwitch was encased in a ball of iron that Wish's Magic had melted all around him in a huge misshapen mass of spears and arrows and shields. He was clutching a tiny piece of blue dust in one claw, and he had been rubbing that piece of dust against the walls of his iron prison with such ferocity that he had turned a small patch of it invisible. Wish could just see one dreadful Witch eye glaring out at her from inside the iron ball.

The Kingwitch had been captured by the Droods and their giants with terrible difficulty, and was rolled painstakingly carefully by giant hands out of the sea and hidden in this cavern. The Droods and the giants had wedged the ball of iron tight under a crevice and heaped it up with treasure, but the newly freed Nuckalavee had accidentally knocked it free with one swipe of his joyful tail.

So, like the rest of the treasure in that cavern, the ball of iron with the Kingwitch inside it was no longer guarded but free to move of its own accord, and it rolled slowly but steadily towards them like a dark and dreadful fate.

'Wissssshhhhhh . . .' whispered the Kingwitch inside the ball of iron. 'Wisssshhhhh . . . *I* have a bargain to offer you too . . . Come closer . . .'

'Don't listen, Wish!' shrieked Caliburn, putting his wings over Wish's ears, as they all backed away from the iron ball. 'Don't listen!'

'Bring me the sprite and Xar and I will take away the Witch-Magic that is poisoning them once and for all . . .' said the Kingwitch.

'And in return,' continued the Kingwitch, 'you will releasssse me from this iron prison . . . And then you and I, Wish, will settle this once and for all in a single spellfight . . .'

It was always going to come down to this. The Kingwitch led the Witches, and while he was safe inside the ball of iron, he couldn't lead them to victory. But if he could persuade Wish to release him, and challenge Wish to a spellfight, why, then he might get his talons on the Magic-that-works-on-iron . . .

Because they had all seen, back in Pook's Hill, how bad Wish was at spellfights.

But it was almost as if Wish and Xar were hypnotised by the voice of the Kingwitch as he rolled towards them . . . *And then Xar began to walk towards the Kingwitch of his own accord.*

Little Squeezjoos, who had been tucked, worryingly rigid and still in Xar's pocket since they had left the healing comfort of Perdita, now lifted his head and began to move. He bit off the buttons that secured the pocket and he flew out towards the Kingwitch.

'I iss feelings a little funny again . . .' said poor little Squeezjoos uncertainly, flying towards the Kingwitch upside down. 'Oh! It's the Chiwgink! Hello Chiwgink!'

'Come back, Xar!' cried Bodkin, grabbing hold of the edge of Xar's waistcoat, and dragging him back. 'Xar! What are you doing?'

But Xar was half eaten by the Witch-Magic already, and he did not seem to hear what Bodkin was saying.

'Xar, come to me . . . and Wissssh . . .' whispered the Kingwitch. '*Wisssssshhhhhhhhhhhhhhhhhhhh* . . . Give me your Magic . . . Give me your Magic . . . GIVE ME YOUR MAGIC . . .'

Louder still chanted the Kingwitch in the ball of iron, louder and louder, until the chant became an unbearable screech and the ball of iron was moving faster, faster.

'GIVE ME YOUR MAGIC!!!!'

'DON'T LISTEN!' bellowed Bodkin, leaping in front of Xar and Wish, and he held up the Enchanted Sword, which blazed for one moment with a light so blindingly bright that Xar's hypnotised eyes refocussed, and he came to his senses.

'RUUUUUUUNNNNNNNNN!' shouted Bodkin.

OUT of the cavern the children ran, terrified, as the ball of iron rolled after them.

UP the tunnels of the Nuckalavee's cave.

ON TO the beach, where the log boat was waiting for them.

But above their heads, as they ran across the sand,

there was a whirr of soft wings, and two swifts flew round and round.

'My father!' yelled Xar.

The swifts circled once more and then hovered in front of the children for a second before their wings turned into the long trails of sleeves, and Sychorax and Encanzo landed lightly on the beach in front of them.

They looked absolutely hopping mad.

Great thunderclouds were rolling off the top of Encanzo's head. Sychorax was white with fury.

'Oh dear, my mother as well . . .' sighed Wish.

24. Two Angry Parents

Hurriedly, Bodkin hid the stone-that-was-Encanzo's-heart in his pocket.

'QUICK! The Witches are coming!' cried Sychorax. 'Encanzo can take all of you in the boat to safety! And— Oh, by mistletoe and all things dark, *THE KINGWITCH!* . . . As I thought, the Droods must have captured him!'

Sure enough, the ball of iron containing the Kingwitch came rolling out of the mouth of the cavern, and halted as if waiting for something.

Hovering over the ball of iron was Squeezjoos.

In the terror of the moment of running away, they had forgotten about the little sprite, and this time he was too far away for Xar to grab him and put him in his pocket.

'Come here, Squeezjoos!' shouted Xar. But Squeezjoos did not seem to hear

And worst of all...
What was happening to
Squeezjoos?

"I iss with the Chiwgink..."

his old friend Xar. He had turned a very bright green indeed, and his eyes were a little feverish. 'I iss with the *Chiwgink* ...' chanted Squeezjoos. 'I iss with the *Chiwgink*!'

'Squeezjoos is saying he's with the Kingwitch,' said Caliburn, sadly. 'Chiwgink is 'Kingwitch' spelt backwards ... *sort of* ...'

'Come with us, Squeezjooos!' cried Xar. '*Please* come with us!'

But Squeezjoos slipped between Xar's fingers.

'I'sss can't ...' said Squeezjoos sadly, a desperate look in his eye, before he started shaking again, and flying back and forth like a poor little upside-down trapped bumblebee.

Squeezjoos!

Come here!

'We can't leave without Squeezjoos!' said Xar.

'Don't be ridiculous! You can't fight the Kingwitch,' shouted Encanzo. 'LOOK UP THERE!'

Wish and Xar and Bodkin looked up, and in the distance the sky was dark with Witches. They were flying

in from all directions, screaming wildly, heading towards the island of the Nuckalavee.

'Quick! Wish! Make a forcefield!' yelled Xar.

Wish took off her eyepatch. She thought of fires, and fires leapt up, forming a protective circle around the children and turning into a great humming forcefield.

We can still fight him. The Kingwitch can't get out of the ball of iron . . . thought Wish. *Don't think of what he's like . . .*

Horrible images of the times she had met the Kingwitch before had leapt into her brain and were making her sweat with fear. The Kingwitch, curled up like a great dark grasshopper inside the stone she had released him from in the first place . . . The Kingwitch springing in the air, great dark feathers spread wide, talons like swords, terrifying Magic blasting out of his mouth . . .

Don't be scared or that will make the forcefield weaken . . . He's trapped and he can't do any harm to us from in there . . . Wish's thoughts chased around inside her skull like panicking rabbits.

Only I can let him out, and until then we are perfectly safe . . .
WHAM!

The first Witch lunged down from above and rammed into Wish's forcefield with such violence that Wish fell over, gasping, as if someone had punched her in the stomach, and—

WHAM!

Another Witch punched into the forcefield again.

Sychorax drew her bow and arrows and shot at the departing Witch, and the creature let out a dreadful screech as it escaped upwards into the air.

But the sky was full of Witches, flying closer, closer.

'We'll go back for Squeezjoos later when we've got all the ingredients of the spell!' shouted Xar, trying to keep his balance inside the rocking, shaking forcefield.

'It won't do Squeezjoos any good if we stay here to get killed by Witches . . .'

WHAM! Another great ram of the Kingwitch in the ball of iron and the entire side of Wish's forcefield caved in.

'We need to go NOW!' shouted Sychorax. 'And get to the safety of the Beach of Shoes . . . THE WITCHES WON'T DARE ATTACK WITH MY IRON WARRIORS THERE!'

Sychorax had sent word to her Warriors to make haste to the Beach of Shoes. She did not know whether they had got there yet . . . but crafty war leader that she was, she wanted the Witches to *think* they were there.

'INTO THE BOAT!' roared Encanzo. Scrambling, tumbling across the beach inside Wish's dented forcefield, Wish, Xar and Bodkin ran after Sychorax and Encanzo towards the sea. The Kingwitch in the ball of iron followed them, gaining momentum as it went

downhill on
the gentle slope
of the beach.

'Only a little
further . . .' panted
Xar.

They got to
the log boat in the
absolute nick of
time. For as they
scrambled in, and
Encanzo pushed
the boat off the
shore, another great
Witch swooped to get
them.

'DUUUUCCKKKK!'
screamed Bodkin, and they
had a nightmare vision of the
talons of the Witch.

But Encanzo's staff sent
the boat shooting off the
sand with such Magical
speed that they all fell flat
on their backs –

SPPPLLLASSSHHHHHHHHHHH!

The great ball of iron slammed into the shallow water of the beach with such ferocity that a huge spray of water still reached them as they sped away.

Trembling, shaking, water in her hair and in her eyes, some of it sea and some of it tears, Wish looked back. The ball of iron with the Kingwitch inside it was stopped dead for the moment, half buried in the sludge and sand, surrounded by great whirlpool ripples. Wish half-expected it to be following after them, but even the Kingwitch seemed to have accepted that a ball of iron cannot roll on water.

Crusher came panting up and tried to catch Squeezjoos, but the little sprite dodged out of the way, screeching 'I iss with the Chiwgink!' Crusher tried again, but Squeezjoos was too quick for him and Crusher had to leave too, diving after them all.

Squeezjoos watched them go, buzzing upside down forlornly. Sometimes he seemed to get up a manic energy, fizzing with bright green sparks, and then he calmed down and

I iss with the chiwgink

Wish could not bear to look at him, so alone and so desolate. She thought she heard him shout something . . . she wasn't sure whether it was, 'Don't leave me!'

or 'Please save me!'

Whatever it was, it was unbearable.

'We *will* save you, Squeezjoos, I promise!' shouted Wish, tears running down her face, and then she turned to Caliburn. 'They won't hurt him, will they, Caliburn?'

'No, they won't hurt him,' said Caliburn sadly. 'He is the Witches' creature now, so they won't hurt him . . .'

'TRUST ME, SQUEEZJOOS, WE'LL BE BACK TO RESCUE YOU!' hollered Xar, who was also crying. 'I ALWAYS LOOK AFTER MY SPRITES!'

Squeezjoos shouted something back, but again he was too far away to be sure of what he said, but I think it was something like: 'Don't worry, Masster! I trusts you! And I iss FINE! I iss upside-down and with the Chiwgink . . . but I iss FINE!'

And then he was too far away for them to see him any more.

They had only just got away in time.

Most of the Witches had reached the island now and although the ball of iron could not follow them on water, the Witches had wings and they were after that boat like eagles pursuing a mouse.

Encanzo shot back at them
with great blasts of Magic from
his spelling staff.

Sychorax took down a few
with her iron arrows. But there
were too many of them.

And Wish set up another
forcefield, this time over
the entire boat, as the
screaming, screeching,
yelling nightmares of
Witches dived again
and again, talons out,
trying to rip open the
forcefield and get at
them.

My goodness, that boat went fast when Encanzo was spelling it. The boat skimmed across the open water of the sea. Encanzo muttered a few words and the front end of the boat reared up, and then they fairly *flew* across the water, humming on the top of the waves, sending three horrible Witches who had landed on top of the forcefield spiralling away.

The onslaught of the Witches was relentless. Again and again they attacked. The boat was in imminent danger of being capsized, and Wish was struggling to maintain the forcefield. Just when she was thinking once again, *I can't hold on much longer* . . . the attacks abruptly ceased.

They were getting near the Beach of Shoes, and from the sky the Witches could see something that Encanzo and Sychorax could not yet see.

The approach of Sychorax's army.

Sychorax had sent word for them to follow her, and the Witches could see the torches of many, many Warriors moving through the trees in the distance. The Witches were scared of the iron-tipped arrows, the spears, the swords. They let out snarls and screams of disappointment. But they would get another chance, they knew that. Screeching like banshees, the Witches whirled around, back towards the Isle of the Nuckalavee.

'Oh, thank goodness,' sighed Wish in trembling relief. 'But what are they doing now?'

'They're going to collect the treasures that the Nuckalavee has been guarding for all these years,' said Encanzo grimly. 'The Witches will now get hold of staffs of power so old and so evil that they were put there out of harm's way centuries ago. This has been the Droods' hiding place for hundreds and hundreds of years, and you have just allowed all these terrible weapons to fall into the hands of the Witches!'

Oh, those parents were so, so cross.

'Why can't you be more like Drama, or Unforgiving? Why is my own daughter so much less obedient than my stepdaughters!' stormed Sychorax.

'When will you children learn that *we* know best, and *you* shouldn't break the rules?' raged Encanzo.

'But *you* broke the rules!' Xar pointed out. 'All those years ago, you came to the Nuckalavee on a shadow quest! You stole some of his treasure yourself . . .'

'I tricked the Nuckalavee,' said Encanzo. 'I stole *a few little bits of treasure* . . . I didn't blow up the ENTIRE WHOLE SPELL that bound him!'

The force of Encanzo's anger carried that boat with such alarming speed that when it finally landed on the Beach of Shoes it just carried right up on the sand for a good thirty feet or so, before coming to a sludgy halt.

Encanzo helped Sychorax out of the boat, and guiltily, the children climbed out after them.

The two royal parents stood in front of their children, hands on their hips.

'Every single thing that you two do makes things WORSE!' roared Encanzo. 'We are TRYING to help you, but you just get deeper and deeper into more and more serious trouble . . . What if the Droods find out that *you* were the ones who released the Kingwitch, on top of everything else?'

'And what if the Kingwitch were to break out of that iron prison that holds him?' cried Sychorax. 'You have just armed his Witch army with forces that will be impossible to contain!'

Everything you do makes things WORSE!

You are BAD!

'What's more, on top of everything else, because
of *your* wilful disobedience, *your* selfishness, that silly
woman Perdita has lost Pook's Hill! The Droods
removed her when they found out she had been
harbouring you two outlaws . . .' said Encanzo.

Oh no!

That made Caliburn cry too. 'My poor sister! How
she loved that learning place. I should never have taken
you there . . .'

Wish and Xar bowed their heads in front of their
furious parents.

'You two just have to face facts. Wizards and Warriors
are enemies and they should never be together,' said
Sychorax. 'Encanzo and I learnt that years ago . . .'

'But you're working together *now*,' Wish pointed out
miserably.

'Only to try and contain the DISASTERS that you
are bringing on the wildwoods by persisting in this
catastrophic friendship of yours!' said Sychorax.

'Xar will come back with me to the prison of
Gormincrag, and we will do what we can to try and
find a cure for that Witchstain,' said Encanzo.

'And Wish will come back with *me*, to my iron fort,
and I will keep you safe from the Witches forever,' said
Sychorax. 'You must never see each other again, and we
will remove all these unsuitable companions from you

because they are clearly unable to control you or offer you good advice . . .'

'But Ariel and I are bound to look after Xar until he grows into a wise and thoughtful adult!' protested Caliburn.

'I release you from that duty!' said Encanzo from between gritted teeth. 'From this moment you are FREE!'

'But we do not wish to be free,' said Caliburn. 'It is not yet time . . .'

The quest had failed.

What had Perdita said in her note, wrapped around the bottle with the Droods' tears in it?

There's a reason that tears are such an important ingredient in so many spells. Life is made up of sorrow as well as joy, and so you may fight as hard as you can, and yet still fail . . .

They had indeed fought as hard as they could . . . but they had still failed. There was no way they could get hold of the scales of a Nuckalavee *now*, for the Nuckalavee could be anywhere in the vast and lonely wastes of the great green ocean.

So they had no scales, Perdita had lost her learning place, they had released the Kingwitch from the Nuckalavee's safekeeping, and lost Squeezjoos.

Surely Fate was trying to tell them something. They were on the wrong track, Wish's idea about the spell was nonsense. Every single thing they had done really *had* made things worse.

Xar could feel his arm with the Witchstain on it burning him like fire. He could feel the desire to grow black wings, and join the Witches now raiding the undefended island of the Nuckalavee. There was no hope for him.

Wish and Xar were feeling so deflated and confused and depressed by the outcome of the adventure that they nearly forgot to fight back.

Until . . .

'Excuse me,' said a quiet voice behind all of them.

'Who is this?' snapped Encanzo.

Everyone had forgotten Bodkin.

'Oh, it is just Wish's bodyguard . . .' said Queen Sychorax, waving a contemptuous hand. 'A person of no importance. He betrayed Wish to me, but he should never have let her go astray in the first place. Assistant Bodyguard, you are dismissed from your position.'

'I am *Wish's* bodyguard, not *yours*, Majesty,' said Bodkin. 'And I wanted to talk to you about Encanzo's heart.'

There was a short pause while everyone tried to think what this might mean.

'My heart?' said Encanzo. 'What about my heart?'

'We took your heart out of the Nuckalavee,' said Bodkin.

'*On top of everything else you took my heart out of the Nuckalavee?*' gasped Encanzo. 'But it was safe there . . . *What have you done with it?*'

'I've hidden it,' said Bodkin.

"I've hidden it." Said Bodkin.

25. 'X' Marks the Spot

Sychorax sniffed. 'Very foolish of you to hide it in the Nuckalavee in the first place, Encanzo.'

'How was I to know that anyone would be totally idiotic enough to go in there and remove it!' stormed Encanzo. 'How could I have predicted the absolute madness of these ridiculous children? It's absolutely nonsensical of them.'

'Well, if you will be so careless with your heart, accidents are going to happen,' said Queen Sychorax.

'There's a bit of YOUR heart in there, too, Sychorax,' snapped Encanzo.

Ah, yes. When you have exchanged a true love kiss, a little mixing up of hearts is unfortunately inevitable, even if the kiss is later regretted.

Sychorax blushed. She tapped her pretty little foot on the beach.

'Yes, all right, all right,' admitted Sychorax irritably. 'I, too, may have been a little careless with my heart in the past . . . But it's all under control now. Where have you hidden this heart, you beastly bodyguard?'

'I'm afraid I can't say,' said Bodkin. 'I'll tell you where I've hidden it after King Encanzo gives me the four scales that he stole from the Nuckalavee twenty years ago. I expect you keep them in one of those handy pockets you have hanging from your belt, sir.'

There was a stunned silence.

Wish and Xar's heads lifted. Wish could feel her spirits lifting as well.

'Oh, very clever, Bodkin!' said Wish. '*Of course!* That's why the Nuckalavee said we had the scales already . . . *We WERE meant to find the last ingredient in the spell to get rid of Witches after all!*'

'WHAAAAT!' cried Queen Sychorax. 'I keep on telling you! There is no such thing as a spell to get rid of Witches!!!'

But Xar and Wish were not listening.

For them, this changed everything. Fate meant them to get the ingredients, and *that* meant they had a chance.

'Hand the scales over, Father,' said Xar.

What could Encanzo do? You can't leave your heart lying around for just *anyone* to find it.

Absolutely and completely and totally raging, Encanzo reached into his pocket, pulled out the four scales of the Nuckalavee and gave them to Bodkin.

'Okay, we'll be off now,' said Bodkin briskly.

'Where have you hidden my heart?' yelled Encanzo.

'I'll tell you once we're on our way,' said Bodkin.

'Where are you going, you foolish children?' asked Sychorax.

'Well, we have all of the ingredients now, don't we,

guys?' said Bodkin. 'So I expect we'll go off and put them together and make that spell . . .'

Wish put up her eyepatch a smidgeon and conjured up an image of the Enchanted Door of the Punishment Cupboard in her mind, and the door that they had hidden under some old bits of wood on the edge of the beach shook off the undergrowth covering it and flew over the sand, hovering helpfully in front of them.

And then Wish thought of shoes, and Wish and Crusher's shoes walked out from the line of shoes on the edge of the beach, and Wish and Crusher put them on. Xar and Wish and Bodkin climbed on the back of the hovering door.

Wish moved the key to UP, and as the door moved up and into the air, Bodkin shouted down to the parents while they were still in earshot:

'I buried your heart under the sand about fifty feet behind you. X marks the spot . . .'

marks
the
spot...
where the
♥ is buried...

Sure enough, while Encanzo and Sychorax were busy telling Wish and Xar off, Bodkin had crept away and buried the stone, putting two crossed twigs on top of it because it's surprisingly difficult to remember where you've put something when you bury it on a beach.

Encanzo and Sychorax ran across the sand and dug underneath the crossed twigs, and to their great relief, Encanzo's heart-that-had-turned-into-a-stone was just where Bodkin said it was.

'They've done well, really, haven't they? All on their own and everything,' said the voice of Madam Perdita. 'X marks the spot was a clever touch of Bodkin's . . .'

Queen Sychorax jumped. Standing at her elbow was Madam Perdita, laughing quietly to herself, with Hoola on her head. 'I wish you wouldn't do that,' snapped Queen Sychorax. 'It's very rude to materialise out of nothing without first announcing your presence . . .'

'Oh, hello, Madam Perdita! Hello, Hoola,' Wish shouted down, so guilty that she nearly fell off the door. 'We're so sorry about you losing your job at Pook's Hill . . .'

'Don't worry, it wasn't your fault!' Madam Perdita called up to Wish. 'And we needed a break from that learning place anyway, didn't we, Hoola? You just carry on with what you're doing, you're doing really well . . .

we're very proud of you.'

'What on earth are you talking about?' said Queen Sychorax.

Queen Sychorax shook her fist up at the door hovering just above the adults.

'Come back, Wish!' said Queen Sychorax. 'There is no hope! Life is complicated! Here in the real world, your bodyguard has already betrayed you!'

'I know that,' said Wish. 'But he's sorry, aren't you, Bodkin?'

'I'm very sorry,' said Bodkin. 'Couldn't be sorrier, but Xar and Wish have forgiven me, and I won't do it again.'

'Is that IT?' raged Queen Sychorax. 'He just says he's sorry, and you FORGIVE him? How can you ever trust him again, you fool?'

'I don't know,' explained Wish. 'I just can . . .'

Isn't it strange that the only conversations that mother and daughter seemed to have were shouted ones from the backs of doors?

'The thing is, Queen Sychorax,' Bodkin shouted down over the edge of the door, 'in *your* Warrior world, there's these immoveable class distinctions and everything – once a servant, always a servant . . . Whereas in *Wish's* world, a bodyguard can still be a hero.'

'Wish's world has never existed and it never will!' Queen Sychorax yelled.

'Come back down here, or I will arrest your
snowcats and your giant! I'M GOING TO LOCK UP
THAT GIANT AS AN ENEMY OF THE PEOPLE!'

Crusher was lumbering out of the sea. He looked
mildly surprised and anxious to find that Queen
Sychorax had drawn her bow and arrow and was
pointing it at him.

'UH-OH . . .' said Crusher.

In front of Queen Sychorax and Encanzo's eyes, the
mountain of a giant disappeared, faded into the wind as
if there were no giant there at all.

The snowcats and wolves were also there one
minute, and gone the next.

And when an extremely frustrated Sychorax pointed
her arrow upwards at the door, it, too, had vanished,
melted into air.

'It is incredibly ill-considered of you to teach them
invisibility, Madam Perdita,' said Encanzo. 'They are way
too young to be able to deal with such a dangerous
power.'

'I told them how risky it was,' said Perdita. 'I warned
them not to stay invisible too long. I trust them to cope.'

'You have taught Wish too much,' said Encanzo,
grimly, looking up at where the door once was. 'Beware,
Madam Perdita, for you may have signed her death
warrant. Once Wish is too powerful to be contained, she

can only be destroyed.'

'Tut, tut, tut,' tutted Perdita. 'Such violent talk is unnecessary. You and Sychorax still have so much to learn.'

'Children have a way of growing, even if you try and stop them,' said Perdita. 'Catch them if you can ...'

'Well, real life has caught up with *you*, hasn't it, Madam Perdita?' snapped Queen Sychorax. 'You've lost your precious learning place. See what happens if you meddle? You should never have taken the child in.'

'I know,' said Perdita sadly, eyes already welling with tears, for Perdita cried easily. 'But they are worth it, the young people. And they are more grateful than they sometimes look.'

'HOO!' hooted Hoola rudely, as if she did not agree with Perdita. 'Twenty-five years! Twenty-five years of building that Pook's Hill up from nothing!' she mourned. 'In the face of all those dreadful Droods saying a woman could never be the head.'

'Did they say that?' said Sychorax, outraged. 'How dare they?'

'I'm sorry, Madam Perdita, I know you will miss the teaching and all your experiments, not to mention your beautiful garden,' said Encanzo, with genuine concern.

'I'm even missing those pesky piskies,' admitted Perdita, tears running down her face with such regularity that her rose-coloured glasses were misting up. She clicked her fingers, and one of Sychorax's handkerchiefs wormed its way out of one of Sychorax's pockets and danced up to Perdita's nose, and Perdita blew her nose on it with a great trumpeting blast.

'I'm sorry too, even if it *was* all your own fault,' said Sychorax, sympathetic despite herself. She could appreciate the struggles of fellow women trying to run things. 'Keep the handkerchief,' (for Perdita was offering it back to her).

'Oh! Thank you, how kind,' Perdita said, smiling and recovering her composure. 'Never mind. If you ever need any help with your children in the future, all you need to do is . . . knock three times.'

'If we need any help??' said Sychorax, recovering from her moment of sympathy and remembering what a danger Perdita was to the future of the wildwoods. 'We're never going to need any assistance from *you*! You're a total liability! You're completely irresponsible!'

'And in the meantime, well, you're never too old to start again.' The sparkle had come back into Perdita's eyes. 'I've always wanted to see what went on in the northern territories . . . to find out what happens if you follow the Giants' Footsteps to the utter bitter end. So I've got out my favourite walking staff, and the old trusty walking books.'

She looked down at her feet. The boots really were *old*, decaying at the edges and falling to bits, and, frankly, even a bit smelly. Perdita stamped them a bit and one of the heels fell off, with, yes, a definite stinky whiff. 'A little brisk walking will work off the pong,' said Perdita enthusiastically. 'You *could* see this as a bit of a godsend . . . Wandering free, once again, with the wind in our hair and a song in our hearts, just as a Wizard ought to do. Isn't it wonderful to be given a chance to go a-wandering once again, eh, Hoola?'

Hoola ruffled her feathers indignantly. 'We're way too old to wander, Madam. Personally, I prefer a roof over my head.'

'That can be arranged,' said Sychorax, with grim promptness. 'I'm going to put out a warrant for the arrest of you and your owl, Madam Perdita, throughout my Warrior kingdom. You'd better get used to being invisible . . .'

Sychorax had drawn her bow and arrow once more.

But Perdita hadn't worked with teenagers for twenty-five years without learning to be prepared for unexpected changes of emotion. One minute she stood in front of them as a human in very old walking boots. The next she was a bear – a great roaring bear. And then she vanished. And all about the beach around them, bear prints appeared, one line going this way, another that way, wandering round in scatterbrained circles, myriad illusions of multiple bear prints appearing, disappearing, here one second, gone the next, lost and found all at the same time, in a way that thoroughly confused Sychorax, for she didn't know where to shoot.

Hoola hovered before them for a moment longer, hooting: 'HOOO! HOOO!' (which meant, 'How ruuuuuude! How ruuuuuude!') before disappearing like mist into the sea.

And King Encanzo and Queen Sychorax were left alone upon the beach.

The Witches up in the sky had disappeared. It was just the two of them, and Encanzo's very ancient sprite, his old snowcat, and the wind.

'Being a parent is very, very hard,' said Encanzo after a while.

'It most certainly is,' agreed Sychorax.

'They are extraordinarily annoying, those children,' said Encanzo. 'But I have to admit, I miss Xar when he is not there. And at heart, I know the silly little boy does mean well. I wish I could help him . . .'

Sychorax said nothing.

'You don't think,' said Encanzo, slowly, 'we might possibly be wrong about the choices that we made in the past?'

'Of course not!' snapped Queen Sychorax. 'We had

responsibilities! Duties to our people! Not to mention TRADITION.'

'Ah yes,' said Encanzo. 'Tradition . . . of course . . .'

There was another long silence.

'So . . . what do we do now then?' said Encanzo meditatively, as he watched Queen Sychorax's little irritated foot going tap, tap, tap in annoyance on a rock on the beach, and her pretty little nostrils flaring in and out with temper.

She really does have an extremely pretty nose, thought Encanzo.

I wish . . .

But then he stopped himself. For the world cannot be lost for the sake of pretty noses.

'We will have a temporary truce,' said Queen Sychorax. 'Not just for one night, but for however long it will take to catch those children. This is a state of emergency, and in a state of emergency, normal rules do not apply.'

'So, you will stop setting fire to the wildwoods?' said King Encanzo. 'And stop capturing my giants, and my elves, and generally making a menace of yourself?'

'*Temporarily,*' said Queen Sychorax. 'And in the meantime, I will take care of the Kingwitch and put him where he can never get out of that iron casing. You will get your Droods and Wizards to try and retrieve all these undesirable objects released from the guardianship of the Nuckalavee. And we will both strain every nerve ... every sinew ... every breath in our lungs, every itch in our fingers to CATCH those children.'

(Alongside the bearprints, an invisible hand was writing something on the beach, in letters so large they could only be read from above.)

'We will both lose our thrones, Encanzo, if we do not catch them,' warned Queen Sychorax. 'The Emperor of Warriors is watching me, the Droods are watching you ...'

'I have always admired your fighting spirit, Sychorax!' smiled Encanzo in admiration. 'You never know when you're beaten. What a magnificent woman you are, indeed! You're the only person even trickier than I am!'

'Well, I'm so glad you said that,' said Sychorax, her usual wintry smile warming up a bit, 'because most people see my strength as a bit of a downside, but when you're being a monarch you have to take difficult decisions and— *Hang on a second!*'

'Hang on a second, indeed ...' repeated Encanzo, as both monarchs' smiles faded. 'Are you thinking what I'm thinking? Is Perdita tricking the both of us? A TRUCE ... working together, side by side ... is that sensible, Sychorax? Do we trust ourselves?'

'Working together, *from a distance*,' said Sychorax

firmly. 'No turning into swifts or any such nonsense. I'm going to go right back behind my Wall and make it even *bigger*. And if Perdita can trick us, why, I think we can out-trick Perdita.'

Sychorax reached into a pocket hanging from her waist. 'This is something I carry around with me always, as a sort of promise to myself.'

She drew out a small glass phial from the pocket.

'It is the last drops of the Spell of Love Denied,' said Sychorax.

'You didn't drink it all!' said Encanzo in surprise.

'I could not quite bear to at the time,' admitted Sychorax. 'I wanted to save a smidgeon of the love, a memory of it, so that it was not entirely forgotten.'

Encanzo's face, so stern, so sad, turned young and eager for a second, like clouds lifting on a darkened hillside. It was as if, after all these years, the distant ghost of a young Warrior princess had arrived at the hut of his younger self, the poor Wizard-who-waits, and he lifted up his head, and there in the doorway ... there she was.

'You *did* love me, after all!' cried Encanzo.

'But that was my weakness,' said Sychorax. 'If I had drunk the whole

361

spell, Wish would never have been born with this curse, and none of this would have happened. So now we have to drink the last drops of the spell together, so that we can be strong enough to make this right again.'

Encanzo's sprite, a very ancient one that age had turned so twig-like in nature it very rarely spoke, now felt an urgent need to express its opinion. 'I must urge you, Majesties, not to drink this liquid . . .' And the sprite was so exasperated that it slapped its little stick-like hand on its forehead in its incredulity at the idiocy of these humans. It had to be said, the mixture in the bottom of the phial Queen Sychorax was holding up looked very evil indeed. As soon as she uncorked the bottle, there was a small explosion and queasy wisps of greasy green smoke curled up from the wicked liquid remains sloshing around in

Love is weakness!

the bottom of it. It was even crackling
a little, as if infested by a mini volcano
and little drops spat over the rim of
the bottle, landing on the grass, which
promptly turned black and died.

Short of a large sign saying 'DO
NOT DRINK ME. I AM RATHER
MORE DANGEROUS THAN A
DEADLY DEATH CAP MUSHROOM
SOAKED IN ARSENIC', this was a
potion that couldn't be making itself
any more clear that it would be
thoroughly disagreeable to digest.

'Excellent idea,' said Encanzo,
producing a cup from beneath his
cloak.

'I cannot stress more strongly that
YOU SHOULD NOT DRINK this
spell!' said Encanzo's sprite, panicking
on Encanzo's shoulder.

'Nonsense!' snapped Queen Sychorax.
'I've drunk this before! It's a little spicy but
perfectly safe . . . Cheers! *Love is weakness!*'

And Queen Sychorax threw back
her head and took a good swig of the
spell. 'It *has* got a little spicier over

the last twenty years,' Queen Sychorax admitted, as her lips turned yellow-black and parched as lemons, and she handed the cup to Encanzo. King Encanzo took the cup, drained the last drops, and then he threw the empty cup at a nearby stone so that it smashed.

Every piece of grass around the stone promptly burst into wicked yellow-green flames.

King Encanzo turned to Queen Sychorax. He swept her a magnificent bow.

Encanzo had been wondering what he should do with his heart now that it was turned into stone. Where could he keep it so it stayed as safely lost as it had been in the throat of the Nuckalavee?

And now he knew.

The safest place for this stone was around the neck of Queen Sychorax, the coldest woman in the wildwoods.

'Sychorax, Queen of the Warriors,' said King Encanzo. 'Will you do me the honour of keeping this stone on your necklace for me? For safekeeping? I know it will never turn back into a heart when it is around your cold neck.'

Queen Sychorax looked at

364

King Encanzo. Without speaking, she put the small grey pebble around her neck, next to the other, much more splendid beads.

Queen Sychorax nodded. And then she turned away.

If she hadn't been such a magnificent queen . . . if she hadn't just drunk the last drops of the Spell of Love Denied . . . you might have thought she was thinking about crying.

But . . .

'LOVE IS WEAKNESS!' cried Queen Sychorax.

'LOVE IS WEAKNESS!' replied King Encanzo.

And then they both climbed on the back of Encanzo's snowcat.

'I will escort you to your troops,' said Encanzo.

'I will allow you to escort me,' said Queen Sychorax.

They had a short swift exchange about who was going to be driving the snowcat. (Queen Sychorax won.)

And then they had a conversation that I am at a loss to understand, given the terrible nature of the spell they had just drunk.

These human beings make the same mistakes again and again and AGAIN . . .

'Will you also allow me to lend you my cloak?' said Encanzo. 'You look a little chilly.'

'Warrior queens never get cold – we are far too tough,' said Sychorax, shivering. 'But *you* look a little warm yourself. So I will carry your coat for you as a favour just this once, to prevent you from overheating . . .'

Encanzo gave his cloak to Queen Sychorax, and Queen Sychorax kicked her heels imperiously, and Encanzo's snowcat set off in the direction of Queen Sychorax's army.

Inexplicable.

And then the beach was empty.

Looking down over the edge of the door, high up in the air, Wish and Xar and their companions could finally see what Perdita had written in enormous letters in the sand of the empty beach.

26. Catch Them IF You Can

Up above, the invisible door flew much higher than Wish and Xar had ever flown before, as high as Wish dared fly it without them all passing out from lack of oxygen.

They didn't stay invisible long because Perdita had told them that it was dangerous.

Flying the door at that height was very hard work, so Wish could only take them as far as would be out of reach of Queen Sychorax's troops and Encanzo's Wizards and Droods. Xar knew a good hiding place (of course he did – Xar had good hiding places hidden all over the wildwoods). The hiding place was high on a mountaintop, in a great cave hidden behind a waterfall.

They were outlaws, on the run again.

They built the fire in the entrance to the cave, behind the waterfall so it wouldn't be seen by anyone who might be searching for them, but where they could still get a good view of the surrounding landscape. 'We'll take it in turns to keep watch through the night,' said Xar.

It was a cave that had been inhabited for many thousands of years before their own time, and they knew this because it was decorated with drawings of animals, bears and wolves and snowcats just like their own, and deeper in the cave still, with the bright red human handprints of their ancestors. This immediately made them feel at home, as if the hands of their forebears were waving them hello, helping them along in their quest with a handshake from the past.

Tiffinstorm had brought along a piece of fire from Perdita's grate in the Lair of the Bear, and somehow that made the cave feel more homely and as if Perdita was there with them. The sprites made the fire burn all different colours, and as the water of the sea steamed out of the shaggy fur of the animals and up into the night, they all felt the coldness of the Nuckalavee adventure being warmed out of them.

They were all tired, *so* tired, and happy and grateful and sad all at the same time. Happy and grateful to be back in the adventure of it all once more, sad because they were worried about Squeezjoos and were missing Perdita and Pook's Hill already. Happy and grateful because they had defeated the Nuckalavee, sad because they had temporarily lost Squeezjoos and knew that greater confrontation was still to come. Xar was unusually quiet.

'We've lost Squeezjoos,' said Xar. 'He is somewhere back there, with the Kingwitch, and it is all my fault, and the fault of this Witchstain.'

So it was Wish and Bodkin who had to cheer Xar up this time.

'Don't worry, Xar,' said Wish. 'We'll rescue Squeezjoos, I promise you we will, and we'll get rid of your Witchstain, too.'

Bodkin could feel his heart beating quick at the thought of it. *Courage!* thought Bodkin to himself. *I have fought the Nuckalavee and lived, so I am as brave as the others after all.*

'So,' said Bodkin. 'What do we do now?'

'I'm afraid you're not going to like the plan, Bodkin,' warned Wish.

Bodkin swallowed. He KNEW he wasn't going to like the plan. 'Tell me anyway,' said Bodkin. 'What IS the plan?'

'The good news is, we've got the ingredients for the spell to get rid of Witches,' said Wish.

'Here they are!' said the Once-sprite, getting them out of Xar's waistcoat and proudly displaying them. 'One giant's last breath from Castle Death (forgiveness). Two feathers from a Witch (desire). Three tears of a frozen queen (tenderness). Four scales of a Nuckalavee (courage). And five tears of the Drood from the Lake of the Lost (endurance).'

'Okay,' said Bodkin, 'we've got the ingredients . . . What's the bad news?'

'We make the spell, and then we go in search of the Kingwitch,' said Wish.

'*That's a terrible plan!*' said Bodkin.

'I said you wouldn't like it. But we promised Squeezjoos we would rescue him,' said Wish, 'and just as Perdita said, you can't run away forever. And when we find the Kingwitch, I'll make a bargain with him.'

'Bargaining with Witches isn't a good idea, Wish,' said Bodkin. 'Look how the bargaining with the Nuckalavee went! Not well, let's face it.'

'We didn't get rid of the Magic completely last time,' said Wish. 'But we have a second chance, and *this time* it's going to be different. I will say to the Kingwitch, if he takes away the last bit of Witchblood from Squeezjoos and Xar, I will use my Magic to let him out of his iron prison.'

'Brilliant plan!' said Xar admiringly. 'There's no other way for the Kingwitch to get out of that iron ball, so I bet he goes for it. And I promise I won't take my hand away too early this time.' *

'*You're going to let the Kingwitch out of his iron prison?*' squeaked Bodkin. '*DELIBERATELY? And THEN what are you going to do???*'

'We're going to FIGHT him,' said Wish. 'Using the spell to get rid of Witches, and the Enchanted Sword, and all our might and main . . .'

---

* In the first book of Wizards of Once, Xar puts his hand on the Stone-That-Takes-Away-Magic in order to get rid of the Witchstain, but he takes his hand off too early so some of the bad Magic remains.

'But you're absolutely *terrible* at spellfights, Wish!
Remember, back at the learning place, you kept losing
and turning into a fluffbuttle! And even Perdita said
you weren't ready to face the Kingwitch yet!' panicked
Bodkin.

'We haven't got time to be ready, Bodkin,' said Wish.
'Xar is getting worse every day, aren't you, Xar?'

'I have to admit I'm not feeling great,' admitted Xar.

'Anyway, there's a good chance we'll never be ready,'
said Wish.

'But if the Kingwitch wins the spellfight, he's going to
get his claws on Magic-that-works-on-iron!' said Bodkin.

'However, if we *don't* do this, Squeezjoos and Xar
are going to be lost forever,' said Wish. 'Squeezjoos will
be frightened and alone, and he's going to be relying on
US, Bodkin. Remember how *you* felt when you were in
the cavern of the Nuckalavee? What kept you going was
knowing that we were going to rescue you.'

Bodkin knew this was right.

'COURAGE!' said Xar. 'COURAGE and dancing
was what we do now ...'

So as night fell, the little party of outlaws danced
defiantly round their fire.

We never know what tomorrow might bring.

So tonight ... we must dance.

First they danced wildy, recklessly, to a song they

just made up on the spur of the moment, called

One More Second Chance

ONE more second chance
ONE more silly dance
I shall grow up and my heart will turn
As cold as a stone
As hard as a rock
I'll walk stiff and talk grave and only sleep in the
night-time

But till that time . . .

Dance, sprite, dance!
Dance by the light of the moon!
You've got to dance till the sun comes up
For tomorrow will come too soon

Howl, wolves, howl!
Yell to the wind in the trees
You have to make your voices heard
Above the roaring din of the breeze

We left our home a lifetime ago and we are wandering still
We don't know where we're going or what's behind that hill
But Wizards were built to wander and I never want to stop

So dance! Snowcats, dance! Make your old bones hop!

We cannot stop our dancing for this night-time is too cold
If we keep up this whirling, we never may grow old
So jiggle your antennae, sprites! Wolves move your
frosty bones!
If we cease the capering, our hearts will turn to stones!

And then Xar made his flute play that old favourite, 'Once We Wizards, Wandering Free'. And Caliburn sang 'We're the best! We're the best! We're just the most marvellous, magnificent best!' but it made him cry to sing it without Perdita, so they moved on to Crusher's song.

Let me lead a GIANT'S life
NO LITTLE steps, no holding back!
A GIANT way, a GIANT'S track!

We will leave them dancing, because that is always a good place to leave people. And as they danced, putting on their biggest, loudest GIANT voices, Crusher himself was wandering down in the valley, talking to the ruins of the trees in the forest that Sychorax had burnt.

'Fear not, dear trees, you shall rise again. I see you in my mind's eye, taller than I am ...stretching up your limbs to the watching moon...carrying the dreams of birds and the hopes of the world in your bright and spreading branches...

'You will grow again, dear trees, *that* I promise.

'For tomorrow is another day ...'

XAR will
save me...

Epilogue

by the Unknown Narrator

Looking into the past is like looking down into a deep, deep well. Imagine that deep, deep well, where the water at the bottom of it represents the time that a person first walked on the earth. People have been on this earth for so long that if you threw a stone down that well it would be at least five minutes before you heard the splash of the stone hitting the water.

Even down at the bottom of the well, people were telling stories, whispered in the night from adult to child and handed down like jewels from generation to generation, though the well is so deep and so dark, and they are so far away, that the stories can get lost to us.

But just recently, people have begun to write down their experiences, so that their voices are trapped in the paper of the trees they are writing on. We call these things 'books', and they will be a clever way of shedding a little light in the darkness . . .

This is one of those stories.

Notice how the crucible of the story changes those who listen to it, those who are within it, and the person who is telling it, all at the same time.

This thought it was a story with two heroes. It said that, confidently, right from the beginning, and on a number of occasions.

But lo! Stories, like queens and Wizards, are tricksy, *tricksy* things. The story changed Bodkin and Bodkin changed the story.

He wouldn't stay where he was supposed to, and somehow it ended up being a story with *three* heroes, which was as much a surprise to *me* as to anyone else.

The final reckoning with the Kingwitch is very, very close now. I know it, and the Kingwitch knows it, and he is ready for the final battle, clutching his piece of blue dust within his iron prison. He has Squeezjoos, and Wish and Xar will never abandon Squeezjoos, and they need to get to him *fast*.

'They will come to me,' whispers the Kingwitch to himself, sharpening his talons like a blacksmith sharpening a sword. 'Because love is weakness . . .'

So the end approaches quick now.

And with the end, I shall tell you who I am, at last.

However I warn you, this is a true story, and *true* stories, unlike fairy stories, do not always end happily. As Perdita said, there's a reason why tears are such an important ingredient in so many spells. Hopefully all will end well, but if not, please do not blame *me*, for as we have just seen, I am not as in control of where a true story goes as I would like to be. I have to tell what really happened.

But I am wishing with all my heart that all will end well.

Wish with me . . .

WISH that Wish and Xar and Bodkin can break out of the sad circles of the history of the wildwoods.

They are young, they are hopeful.

WISH that they can write their own story . . .

WISH . . .

And in the meantime . . .

Keep hoping . . .

Keep guessing . . .

Keep dreaming . . .

And keep telling your own stories.

Stories are very helpful if you get lost in the wildwoods.

Signed: *The Unknown Narrator*

ACKNOWLEDGEMENTS
(thankyous)

A whole team of people have
helped me write this book.

Thank you to my wonderful editor,
Anne McNeil, and my
magnificent agent, Caroline Walsh.

A special big thanks to Samuel Perrett,
Polly Lyall Grant, Lizz Skelly, and Camilla Leask.

And to everyone else at Hachette Children's Group,
Hilary Murray Hill, Andrew Sharp,
Valentina Fazio, Naomi Berwin, Katy Cattell,
Georgi Russell, Nicola Goode, Katherine Fox,
Alison Padley, Rebecca Livingstone.

'Squeezjoos is
helping too...'

Making — the

Thanks to all at Little Brown,
Megan Tingley, Jackie Engel,
Lisa Yoskowitz, Kristina Pisciotta.

And most important of all,
Maisie, Clemmie, Xanny.

And SIMON for his excellent
advice on absolutely everything.

I couldn't do it without you.

Magic happen

"Once we have accepted the story, we cannot escape the story's fate."

P.L. Travers, author of Mary Poppins

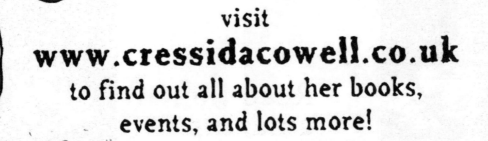

Read the amazing
HOW TO TRAIN YOUR
DRAGON
series

Love is...
a girl and her
Enchanted Spoon.